RACE IN SOCIETY

THE ENDURING AMERICAN DILEMMA

Second Edition

Margaret L. Andersen

University of Delaware

ROWMAN & LITTLEFIELD

Lanham • Boulder • New York • London

Acquisitions Editor: Mark Kerr
Assistant Editor: Courtney Packard
Sales and Marketing Inquiries: textbooks@rowman.com

Published by Rowman & Littlefield
An imprint of The Rowman & Littlefield Publishing Group, Inc.
4501 Forbes Boulevard, Suite 200, Lanham, Maryland 20706
www.rowman.com

6 Tinworth Street, London SE11 5AL, United Kingdom

British Library Cataloguing in Publication Information Available

Library of Congress Cataloging-in-Publication Data

Names: Andersen, Margaret L., author.
Title: Race in society : the enduring American dilemma / Margaret L.
    Andersen, University of Delaware.
Other titles: Enduring American dilemma
Description: Second edition. | Lanham : Rowman & Littlefield Publishing
    Group, [2021] | Includes bibliographical references and index. |
Summary: "'Race in Society' is a comprehensive book about the sociology
    of race in America. The purpose of this book is to introduce readers to
    current research scholarship on race, emphasizing the socially
    constructed basis of race and the persistence of racial inequality in
    American institutions"— Provided by publisher.
Identifiers: LCCN 2020045288 (print) | LCCN 2020045289 (ebook) |
    ISBN 9781538149454 (cloth) | ISBN 9781538129838 (paperback) |
    ISBN 9781538129845 (epub)
Subjects: LCSH: United States—Race relations. | Racism—United States. |
    Minorities—United States—Social conditions. | Race.
Classification: LCC E184.A1 A6195 2021 (print) | LCC E184.A1 (ebook) |
    DDC 305.800973—dc23
LC record available at https://lccn.loc.gov/2020045288
LC ebook record available at https://lccn.loc.gov/2020045289

Brief Contents

Detailed Contents

CHAPTER 11 Justice and Injustice: Race, Crime, and the Criminal Justice System   271

PART IV Race and Social Change

CHAPTER 12 The Long Search for Racial Justice: Learning from the Past and Moving Forward   299

Preface

Dilemma or Dream? The Quagmire of Race in America

As this book goes to press, the Black Lives Matter movement has awakened people in the United States—indeed, around the world—to the reality of racial injustice in the United States. The killing of George Floyd at the hands of the police in 2020, along with countless killings of other Black and Latino men and women, has sparked antiracism protests in every state and in places large and small where people of different racial-ethnic backgrounds, generations, and genders marched in the streets, demanding a commitment to antiracist action. Further, this antiracist movement has come about in the midst of a global pandemic that has disproportionately sickened and killed Black, Latino, Native, and Asian American people in the United States.

Only time will tell what changes this awakening of antiracist activism will bring, but we know that there is a long history to the movement for racial justice and that change will not come overnight or without additional struggle. Will the United States realize Dr. Martin Luther King Jr.'s (1963) dream to live in a world where people will "not be judged by the color of their skin but by the content of their character"? Will we maintain the momentum to face our racist history and transform institutions to overcome the systemic racism on which they have been built?

Calls for a reckoning with the United States' racial past have come from many voices—past and present. Among them is Swedish economist and Nobel Prize winner Karl Gunnar Myrdal, who in 1944 published *An American Dilemma*. *An American Dilemma*, a book that influenced the momentous 1954 Supreme Court decision *Brown v. Board of Education* and that continues to be known for its conclusion that the problem of race in the United States lies in the "hearts and minds" of Americans. Myrdal professed that there was a fundamental moral contradiction between the American values of "liberty, equality, justice, and fair opportunity" (1944:xlvii) and the persistence of racial discrimination. To Myrdal, the dilemma lay in reconciling these two conflicting realities.

Now, more than seventy-five years since Myrdal's book was published, the American promise of liberty and equality for all remains sadly unrealized. Racial inequality in the United States is certainly nothing like it was in Myrdal's time, nor does it look like it did as recently as 2008 when the nation elected its first Black president, Barack Obama. Yet many still think of racism as primarily residing in the hearts and minds of White Americans, as if race were primarily a problem of people's attitudes and beliefs. The recent rise of highly visible White supremacist actions also makes it seem as if racism is primarily a problem of highly bigoted people.

But today's dilemma about racial inequality is far more complex than Myrdal could have imagined. It would be great if changing race relations in the United States were just a matter of changing individual hearts and minds, as Myrdal implied. As difficult as it is to change attitudes and feelings, it is even harder to change social institutions. No doubt, racial attitudes are a manifestation of the racism that is built into the very foundation of society. Myrdal understood this. He wrote that America's race problem was an "integral part of the whole complex of problems in [the United States]" and could not be treated in isolation from those problems. He wrote further that the problem of race "exists and changes because of conditions and forces operating in the larger American society" (1944:liii). Race in US society may live in people's hearts and minds, but it is entrenched in the structure of society.

Haunting the American Dream is the horrid disparity in sickness and death for people of color that the COVID-19 pandemic revealed, as well as the persistence of racial segregation in neighborhoods and schools, high rates of poverty among people of color, and strong racial resentment by many who think people of color are somehow now getting an unfair advantage. People of color are routinely accused of having only themselves to blame if they cannot make it. Further, the professed American Dream that there is an open door for all who want to better themselves, their families, and their communities is discredited when children are held in cages at the border and refugees are barred from asylum in the United States when they are facing violence and potential death in their home nation.

At times, the American Dream seems more like a nightmare, such as when we saw the shooting and murder of innocent churchgoers in Charleston, South Carolina; a mass shooting of predominantly Latinos/as in a gay nightclub in Orlando, Florida; and the slaughter of mostly Latinos/as at a Walmart in El Paso, Texas, because the shooter (Patrick Crusius) thought Latinos were "taking over America." These and possibly other horrific acts of violence likely to occur before this book is published reveal a deep vein of bigotry and hatred in the United States. Acts of hatred targeted at different groups also reveal a link between racism, homophobia, xenophobia, and gender-based violence. Following the Orlando mass shooting, the editors of the *New York Times* wrote, "Hate crimes don't happen in a vacuum. They occur where bigotry is allowed to fester, where minorities are vilified and where people are scapegoated for political gain" (*New York Times* editorial board 2016). In other words, systemic racism breeds violence and creates a society where people are not safe.

Many people think that the racism of the past is long gone. The removal of many symbols from our nation's racist past (flags, product images, names of sports teams, and so forth) has produced a sense of hope that we are, at long last, moving toward a more just and inclusive world. In fact, it is surprising how quickly many of these symbols have been taken away, but people have been decrying their harm for years. Will symbolic change truly lead to substantial change? Reducing racial inequality requires more than removing racist iconography, although that is an important step.

Thoroughgoing change will probably take decades, and there is likely to be significant resistance from people trying to protect their own interests. There are signs that the United States is moving in a more racially just direction. The election of Kamala Harris, a Black, multiracial woman, as the nation's vice president is a historic first and should be celebrated. But even with this momentous change, there is much to be done, as the evidence in this book will show. Contradictions in how well we are doing in addressing racial inequality abound. As the ongoing struggle for racial justice unfolds, more than ever we need more education and understanding about race and racism. That is the purpose of this book.

Gunnar Myrdal could not have foreseen the greater complexity of race that we see today. More people than ever (although still a relatively small number) self-identify as "multiracial." Large numbers of diverse immigrant groups populate the United States. The Black-White model of understanding race in America is being eroded, as Latinos have surpassed African Americans as a proportion of the population. Moreover, this model of understanding race relations never acknowledged the long-standing presence of Asians and Native Americans in this country. Understanding race in this more multiracial, multicultural society is thus more challenging than ever before. Racism in the United States is sometimes quite overt and obvious, but it also takes more covert forms—forms that may not be so publicly witnessed but are daily felt by those who bear the brunt of racism's pain.

Merriam-Webster defines *quagmire* as "soft . . . land that shakes or yields under the foot." The quagmire of race in America is just that—a muddy mess that shifts and changes with each historic event that reshapes its meaning and nature. Race is a quagmire indeed, made murky by the many strong feelings and oft-held misconceptions about what race is and how people experience it. The good news is that more people seem to want to understand race, at least as indicated by the frequency with which race now comes up in public and private conversation.

Race in Society introduces readers to the rich research that now anchors sociological thinking about race. This scholarship is presented in the hope that it can better inform public understanding of the changing nature of racial inequality. The book is anchored in contemporary sociological scholarship (and some classic works) and is written in a narrative style to engage reader interest and make it accessible to a wide audience.

Several assumptions underlie this book:

- Most of us want to live in a society where everyone has a fair chance to be safe and secure and has opportunities for well-being.
- Many, if not most, people are misinformed about race, which leads not just to misunderstanding but also to mistrust, fear, anger, and hurt—emotions that stifle positive cross-group relationships.
- It is difficult, if not impossible, to avoid racial stereotyping because of the pervasiveness of pejorative images in popular culture.
- Racism exists despite the fact that so many people deny that it is still with us.
- Racism is not always overt; it may be invisible to those who do not experience its force, yet it can be made visible through education and careful study.
- People can benefit from racism even when they do not think of themselves as racists.
- Changing racial inequality necessitates change in our social institutions and social policies.

You may not agree with these underlying assumptions, but I hope they will guide your reading of this book. I ask you to consider how we might understand race differently from a perspective anchored in the rich scholarship of social science rather than in the popular perspective that generally blames people for their own shortcomings.

A Note on Language

Language is fraught with racial connotations, and words can hurt. Any book on race in the United States must be attentive to the words it uses. What we call people, how we express ideas, whose voice is active, whose passive—all of these practices can suggest racial meaning. While writing this book, I became keenly aware of how word choice conveys particular meanings about race—some intended, others not. In a society where race carries such weight, I want to make my choices involving words and labels clear and provide my reasons for using the words I do.

First, race itself is a social construct, as the early chapters of this book will show. Therefore the language we use to describe and define different racial-ethnic groups is loaded with social meaning. Simply naming major racial-ethnic groups in the United States inevitably oversimplifies the groups, as if our so-called racial population is easily divided five ways: White, Black (or African American), Latino/a (or Hispanic), Asian American, and Native American. We know that each of these groups is highly diverse, complex in its identities, and not fixed or immutable over the course of time and history.

I have capitalized *White* and *Black* throughout the book primarily when they are used as proper nouns or to modify people. For some this may appear jarring; for others, it is now common practice. Capitalizing *Black* is a practice long advocated by African American people because they see it as a proper noun—that is, an identity no different from calling someone a European person or an Asian American. The term *White* itself is fraught with political meaning, as new studies of Whiteness are also finding. Certainly not all Whites share the same advantages as the White population writ large. You will note, for reasons elaborated in chapter 1, that I never use the term *Caucasian* because of its racist origins—even though it is widespread as a label in American culture. Some will object to capitalizing White because it has been the practice of White supremacist groups. I realize that capitalizing these racial identities has the risk of reifying race as if race were a fixed thing. As you will learn in this book, it is not. Race is a social construction, but the capital letter is meant to respect the strong identities that race creates.

I also realize that some groups object to the labels in which they are generally included. The label *Latino*, for example, is an aggregated term that is meant to convey common experiences and linked interests, but it also hides people's specific identities as Chicano/a, Mexican, Puerto Rican, Guatemalan, and so forth. General labels cloak specific identities, but there is no other way to generalize about group experiences than to use aggregated terms. I have not adopted the term *Latinx*, now used by many as a way of eradicating the gender binary that the terms *Latino* and *Latina* connote. I have made this choice because of the lively debate among Latinos/as about whether the term *Latinx* disrespects traditional cultural values—including, among other things, that there is no *x* in the Spanish language. Even as using Latinx has become more common, a mere 3 percent of Latinos use the term, and the vast majority of Latinos prefer using other terms to describe themselves (Noe-Bustamante, Mora, and Lopez 2020).

The language used to describe indigenous people in the United States is also politically charged. Some now use the general term *indigenous people* to refer to all groups both within the mainland United States and in Hawaii and Alaska. Some prefer the term *Native* (capitalized to reflect it as a primary identity). Others use *American Indian*. There is no one perfect choice. In the end, I just had to live with these complexities but with a desire to be respectful of what people want to call themselves and to be sociological in analyzing group experiences.

In reporting data from federal agencies or others' research, I have used the terms found in the original source. In the census, for example, those terms are typically *non-Hispanic White*, *Black* (or *African American*), *Hispanic*, *Asian American*, and, sometimes, *multiracial*. There is maddeningly little data on Native Americans collected as part of routine surveys in many of these sources, so Native Americans are often omitted in some of the empirical data here, especially as presented in charts, figures, and tables.

I have found it impossible to avoid the term *minority* when referring to racial and ethnic groups who experience discrimination in US society. Many now object to this term because people of color are becoming a numerical majority in the United States. In many places, they already are in the majority. When used here, however, *minority* is used in the sociological sense of the term—that is, to refer to groups that share common historical and cultural experiences of prejudice and discrimination. In other words, *minority* refers to an experience, not numerical representation.

In sum, language often reflects the political and social status of groups, and I have tried to avoid using any language that unintentionally insults or belittles people. We also know that language shapes people's perceptions of reality. Being attentive to the language of race can help reduce racism. The language here may not always be perfect, and, as has happened before, language regarding race is likely to change in the future. I only ask that readers be attentive to the language they use, understanding that this is an important part of the path to greater racial equality.

Organization of the Book

Thinking in the sociology of race has changed dramatically in recent years, moving from a "racial and ethnic minorities" perspective to one that is more concept centered. It is no longer adequate to teach about race as a laundry list of different racial-ethnic "minority" group experiences. Rather, new scholarship examines how various group experiences are linked in a racialized social structure. The smorgasbord approach of comparing the experiences of different so-called "minority" groups no longer reflects the state of research on race and ethnicity. Such comparisons have been displaced by scholarship on the social construction of race and its different manifestations within the increasingly diverse racial-ethnic population of the United States.

This book is organized around several major conceptual themes. In part I ("The Social Construction of Race"), chapter 1 examines the social construction of race and ethnicity as they evolve within systems of power and privilege. Chapter 2 looks at the social dynamics of prejudice, bias, and racism, including color-blind racism. Chapter 3 reviews the enormous influence of the media on how people imagine race. And chapter 4 presents racial identities in their many evolving forms.

Part II ("Understanding Racial Stratification") includes two important chapters. First, chapter 5 briefly details the diverse histories of US racial-ethnic groups. Although a single chapter cannot possibly do justice to the rich past of so many groups, it is important to have some background in the history of race and ethnicity to understand the present. Chapter 6 details a theoretical framework for the empirical evidence that this book examines.

Part III ("Race and Social Institutions") focuses on institutional racism. Racial inequality continues to be a part of society's major institutions, shaping the opportunities (or lack thereof) available to various groups. Chapter 7 looks at work and the economy, including the connection between race and poverty. Chapter 8 discusses families and communities. Chapters 9, 10, and 11 focus on housing and educational segregation, health and environmental racism, and the criminal justice system, respectively.

Part IV ("Race and Social Change"), consisting only of chapter 12, provides an overview of the roots of racial protest. It concludes with sections that consider different frameworks for social change and how change is likely to be affected by the increasing diversity of the US population.

Pedagogical Features of *Race in Society*

This volume includes several features that will help readers think further about the issues raised within. Throughout the book, *textboxes* enhance core material. The box series titled "Living with Racism" provides first-person narratives about the experience of racism. A second box series, "Learning Our Past," provides glimpses into parts of US history that are often unknown or forgotten. Recognizing and understanding some of the harms of the past put the present into perspective and can help debunk some of the myths about racism that abound in the absence of a longer view.

Especially relevant in the context of renewed racial protest is the feature at the end of every chapter: "Taking Action against Racism." While learning more about race and racism, students often ask, "What can I do?" Although no one person can transform the vast racial inequality characteristic of our society, people can make a difference. This feature is intended to guide students to actions they can take, even if small ones, to make this a more just society. In some cases, this box includes individual actions in which students might want to engage; in other cases, the box features a project or organization that students will find inspiring.

Student exercises are included at the end of each chapter. These are intended to encourage readers to engage actively with the book's content and see for themselves some of the patterns and processes that mark racial and ethnic inequality. For instructors, these exercises can be the basis for class discussions and/or assignments. Each chapter also includes *critical-thinking questions* that enable readers to explore the subject matter more deeply.

The second edition of *Race in Society* includes *framing questions* for each major chapter head—intended to help students see the major thrust of this section of the chapter. The framing questions could also be used for classroom discussion and/or examinations.

Another feature, "Challenging Questions/Open to Debate," appears at the end of each chapter. It poses scenarios or questions on hotly debated current issues, such as the tension brought on by hate speech in the context of the right to free speech, immigration policy, the influence of race versus class, school choice, and affirmative action. The purpose is to explore diverse viewpoints on these hot-button issues.

Key terms are listed at the end of each chapter and are included in a *glossary* at the end of the book.

New to the Second Edition

I wrote the second edition of *Race in Society* in the midst of the COVID-19 pandemic and the revitalized protests against racism that have dramatically marked our nation's history in the summer of 2020. It was simply impossible to keep up with the many events, studies, commentaries, and data reports that were emerging as I wrote. But the national context has also made this book more important than ever, as so many people are clamoring for more information and education about race and racism. People are paying attention to race and racism in new and dramatic ways, making a new edition of this book especially timely.

Throughout the book I have updated and revised, where possible, to account for these emerging developments. For example, the COVID pandemic has highlighted racial disparities in health care in dramatic and tragic ways, and the most recent data available opens chapter 10 on health and the environment. The Black Lives Matter movement has inspired the public to new action to fight racial inequality; this movement, including its origins, is included in the chapter on social change (chapter 12). Changes because of the COVID pandemic and the new movement for racial justice inform much of the new material in this second edition, but so has the ongoing and unfolding research on racial inequality. And, in the ongoing attempt to move beyond the old "Black/White" model of thinking about race and ethnicity, this book continues to be as inclusive as possible of the many racial-ethnic groups that comprise our diverse society. Especially in the face of recognizing the value and dignity of Black American lives, we cannot forget the other groups who have been subjugated by our nation's racial past and present. These ideas guided the revision of this book.

Chapter-by-Chapter Changes

First, in chapter 1 there is a revised introduction intended to emphasize the different groups who are part of US racial inequality. There is more material throughout this chapter (indeed, throughout the book) on Latinos. This chapter introduces the concept of colonialism and its impact in defining Latinos/as in racial terms. The chapter also introduces the concept of colorism, in the context of discussion of skin tone and biological racism. At the request of reviewers, the chapter also brings the theme of intersectionality (that is, the interconnection between race and other forms of inequality, such as gender and class) to the forefront. And, because of its timeliness, there is new material on the 2020 census.

Chapter 2 has been updated throughout, especially to reflect new data on racial attitudes. There is new research included on the significance of racial resentment, as well as discussion of racial backlash and White rage. The chapter continues to focus on distinction between prejudice and racism, emphasizing the systemic basis of racism.

Chapter 3 is especially timely given current movements to remove racial representations that are harmful and represent a racist past. Still, the chapter points out how racial stereotypes permeate popular culture. There are new and current examples throughout this chapter, as well as current data on the inclusion of people of color in media organization and media usage by diverse groups. As in other chapters, new charts and graphs reflect these new data.

Even with the significance of the Black Lives Matter movement, multiracial and multiethnic identity remains an important topic, especially to younger generations. There is new material in chapter 4 on multiracial identities and multiracial relationships. The chapter also includes a discussion of the concept of *White fragility*, an idea that has captured the public's attention. New research on multiracial relationships is also highlighted in this chapter.

Chapter 5 provides much-needed historic background on immigration, and national immigration policy (or lack thereof) has become increasingly important in analyzing racial and ethnic inequality. Chapter 5 updates information on immigration, including a discussion of new and pathbreaking research on Chinese railroad workers. This chapter includes current attitudinal data on immigration, all of which reflect evolving US politics about immigration, the border wall, and national borders.

At the suggestion of reviewers of the first edition, chapter 6 has been reorganized to better emphasize different theoretical perspectives on racial inequality. Indeed, the chapter title has also been changed to reflect the theoretical focus of this chapter. There is a new section on colonialism and postcolonial theory, as well as an extended discussion of intersectional theory.

When the first edition of *Race in Society* was published, the US economy was strong, even with its persistent racial disparities. But the arrival of the COVID-19 pandemic changed everything. Although it is impossible to keep abreast of such rapidly evolving economic changes, chapter 7 has been updated throughout both to reflect the ongoing economic and work disparities based on race and also to note the disparate impact of economic change brought by the pandemic on Latino and African American workers—especially those in the service economy. Structural unemployment is still with us but complicated by the devastating impact of the COVID-19 pandemic on workers at all levels, most especially workers who do not have the resources to work at home—that is, people of color in low wage service jobs. There is new research reported here on wealth inequality, including student debt. And, as the nation now sees such a great need for an expanded social safety net, there is new research included here on federal assistance—and the lack thereof.

Chapter 8 on families and community specifically discusses US immigration policy as it affects families. There is updated data throughout on household and family structure, interracial marriage, and the impact of COVID-19 on care workers. Chapter 9 includes updated information on residential and educational segregation. There is also new material on the racial achievement gap and how that is likely to be affected by school closures during the pandemic.

Over the life of the first edition of this book, we could not have imagined the devastating impact of a viral pandemic on anyone—much less people of color. Chapter 10 now opens with evidence of the huge racial disparities that have been sadly, but vividly, unveiled by the COVID-19 pandemic. Likewise, chapter 11 has been updated to reflect current national discussions on policing and police violence. There is also more material on Latinos and criminal justice in this chapter now, as well as new material on hate crimes directed against Asian Americans given the racist labeling of the coronavirus. This chapter also now includes more framing in the context of historic acts of vigilante justice against people of color.

Finally, chapter 12 includes more history about the Chicano movement. The chapter continues to place contemporary racial protests in the context of the long history of struggle for racial justice with new focus on the impact of the Black Lives Matter movements and antiracist activism. And given the significance of electing Kamala Harris as vice president of the United States, I have included data detailing the unprecedented voter turnout for the 2020 US presidential election.

Instructor and Student Resources

- *Instructor's manual* and *test bank*. For each chapter in the text, the instructor's manual provides student learning objectives, key terms with definitions, discussion questions, and Web resources. The test bank includes a variety of multiple choice, true/false, and short answer questions and is available in either Word or Respondus format. In either format, the test bank can be fully edited and customized to best meet your needs. The instructor's manual and test bank are available to adopters for download on the text's catalog page at https://rowman .com/ISBN/9781442258020.
- *PowerPoint slides*. These provide the tables and figures from the text. The presentation is available for adopters to download on the text's catalog page at https://rowman.com/ISBN/9781442258020.
- *Companion website*. Accompanying the text is an open-access website designed to reinforce the main topics and help students master key vocabulary and concepts through flashcards and self-graded quizzes. Students can access the companion website from their computers or mobile devices at http://textbooks .rowman.com/andersen.

Acknowledgments

Writing a book is never a solo project, despite the long hours of sitting alone at one's desk. There are many people to thank for the many ways they have supported me as the book developed.

I am privileged to work amid a network of brilliant colleagues and friends with whom I have had many conversations about race over the years. Those conversations have shaped my thinking and are, no doubt, embedded in this book. As a White woman I have had to learn to listen, respect, question, and always empathize with those whose experiences are so very different from my own. Although I cannot claim to have lived racism in the ways many of my friends have, I have learned tremendously from each of them. These close friendships are at the heart of this book. I especially thank Maxine Baca Zinn, Elizabeth Higginbotham, Howard Taylor, Valerie Hans, Peggy Nelson, Karen Hansen, and Patricia Hill Collins for the many years of friendship, collaboration, and discussion of new research. I also thank all those scholars, many of them cited here, who are doing such excellent work on the subjects covered in this book. One text could not possibly do justice to all the nuances in your work, but I am profoundly grateful for what I have learned from you and how your work has guided my writing.

I give deep thanks to the many dear friends who have kept me on an even keel through the daily challenges of writing this book: Jack and Carolyn Batty; Mariette Buchman and David Altenhofen; Claudia and Richard Fischer; Angela March; Amber, Mark, Clara, and Luke Petry; Amy, Max, and Tony Stein-Miksitz; Nancy Roberts; Randall and JoAnn Stokes; Scott and Suzanne Supplee; Nancy and Tim Targett; and Debbie Watkins. I hope you all know how much your friendship and support mean to me. I am also deeply grateful to be part of the Social Inequality Writing Group. Our deep conversations and examination of feminist scholarship have enriched my thinking and this work. And to Kerry Ann Rockquemore, Julie Artis, Eric Johnson, and the National Center for Faculty Development and Diversity: the structure you provide for us has become a critical part of my daily writing practice. I also thank the many students who have taken my Racial Inequality course. I thank them for their willingness to explore openly the subject of race in a very diverse, open, and trusting environment.

Thanks also go to the reviewers who read all or part of the initial manuscript: Shelly Brown-Jeffy, University of North Carolina at Greensboro; Erica Chito Childs, Hunter College/CUNY Graduate Center; Amanda Lewis, University of Illinois at Chicago; Enid Logan, University of Minnesota; ConSandra McNeil, Jackson State University; Mary Romero, Arizona State University; and Amanda Roth, State University of New York–Geneseo.

A huge thanks goes to the team at Rowman & Littlefield! Mark Kerr, my editor, has been encouraging and excited about taking on this book, even when the pandemic kept us from talking about it for a while. He is a magnificent editor/publisher and a dear friend. Thanks as well to the entire R&L team: Jon Sisk, who has been a champion for my trade book on race, *Getting Smart about Race: An American Conversation*; Patricia Stevenson, for so carefully overseeing the final production process; Deborah F. Justice, for the extraordinary care in copyediting; and Courtney Packard for staying on top of all the details. It is a pleasure working with each one of you!

Critically important is the support and love I receive from my family. Our family proves that love is stronger than any differences we have based on race, gender, sexual orientation, age, faith, and religion. Thank you to Arlene Hanerfeld; Norman Andersen; Jessica Hanerfeld; Sarah

Hanerfeld; Kimball Johnson; Mary Brittain; and Debbie and Jim Lanier. And to Aubrey Hanerfeld and Aden Jonathan Carcopo—may you grow up in a world free of the virus and more racially just! To my husband, Richard Rosenfeld—I can't find new words to thank you again for supporting my writing, but each time I recognize you in a preface like this, it is just as heartfelt as the first time. I can only say thank you and promise to try to create more time away from my desk.

I dedicated the first edition of this book to William Julius Wilson and Lewis M. Killian, and I do so again because of the enormous significance they have had in shaping my thinking about racial inequality. As I said in the first edition, I began my sociological career as clueless as any White person living in the time and space from which I came. Bill Wilson's early and ongoing guidance and the depth of his ideas opened a new way of thinking for me. Bill also helped me to get my first book contract; his steadfast support over the years reverberates in how I now think about race. As I wrote the first edition and now the second and watched antiracist protests erupt across the nation, I could not help but think of Lewis Killian's extraordinary lessons. His book *The Impossible Revolution? Black Power and the American Dream* (1968), which greatly influenced me many years ago, continues to hold important lessons about our current situation. My path has gone in different directions from what I imagined early on, but I still feel the strong influence of these two people. I am solely responsible for any errors, omissions, and oversimplification.

About the Author

Margaret L. Andersen (PhD, MA, University of Massachusetts–Amherst; BA, Georgia State University) is the Edward F. and Elizabeth Goodman Rosenberg Professor Emerita of Sociology at the University of Delaware. She is author of several books, including *Getting Smart about Race: An American Conversation* (2020); *Thinking about Women*, published in its eleventh edition (2020); the best-selling anthology *Race, Class, and Gender* (coedited with Patricia Hill Collins; 10th ed., 2020); *Race and Ethnicity in Society: The Changing Landscape* (coedited with Elizabeth Higginbotham; 4th ed., 2016); *Sociology: The Essentials* (coauthored with Howard F. Taylor; 10th ed., 2020); *Living Art: The Life of Paul R. Jones, African American Art Collector* (2009); and *On Land and On Sea: A Century of Women in the Rosenfeld Collection* (2007).

She is an emeritus member and former chair of the national advisory board for Stanford University's Center for Comparative Studies in Race and Ethnicity, past vice president of the American Sociological Association, and past president of the Eastern Sociological Society. She has received two teaching awards from the University of Delaware and two prestigious awards from her professional organizations: the Eastern Sociological Society Merit Award for career contributions, and the American Sociological Association's Jessie Bernard Award, an award given for expanding the boundaries of sociology to include women. At the University of Delaware, she has served in several senior administrative positions, including vice provost for Faculty Affairs and Diversity, interim deputy provost, dean of the College of Arts and Sciences, and founder of the President's Diversity Initiative. She was granted an honorary degree from the University of Delaware in recognition of her teaching, scholarship, and service.

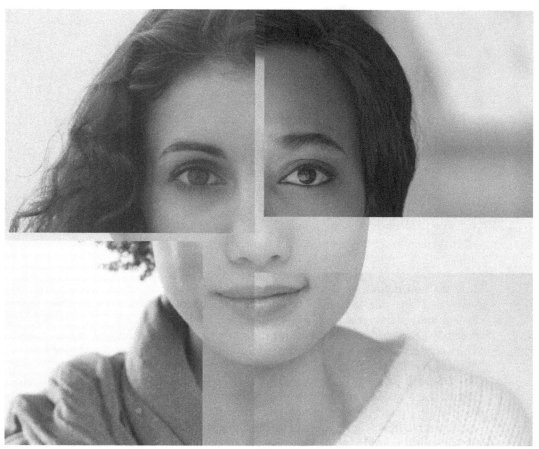

CHAPTER 1

Race

A Thoroughly Social Idea

Race is a pigment of the imagination.
—Rubén Rumbaut (2009:15)

OBJECTIVES

- Explain the historical origins of the one-drop rule
- Be able to criticize the idea of race as biologically or genetically based
- Connect the emergence of racial thinking to its historical origins
- Situate racial classification systems in their historical and social contexts

- Understand the difference between race and ethnicity
- Explain the process of racial formation and racialization
- Identify the multiple ways of defining race
- Understand race as a social construction

How do you define your racial identity? In other words, what "race"[1] are you? Answering this question may be easy for some, more difficult for others. Some readers might have very clear racial identities, identities that are linked to a strong sense of history and community. Some might not think of themselves in racial terms. White readers are especially unlikely to think of themselves in terms of race because "White" has been taken to be the racial norm in US society. That is, being "White" is not marked as a racial identity as it is for groups who experience racial discrimination. Some readers will have a multiracial identity, an identity that is increasingly common, especially among young people.

Some readers might think of themselves in ethnic, not racial, terms—that is, specific cultural, national, or religious backgrounds that are significant to who you are. For example, if you are Latino, do you think of yourself as having a race? What if you are Asian American or Muslim? Are Native Americans a race? If you were born outside of the United States, you may even think that all these designations are strange. The meaning that race carries in the United States seems quite odd to people from different cultures. Traditionally race in the United States has been perceived through a "Black/White" division, but that binary distinction is breaking down as the meaning of race has evolved and as the nation has become more diverse. At the heart of trying to define race is the reality of racial inequality—the persistent, though changeable, unequal distribution of economic, social, and cultural resources, as well as political power, along lines of race.

In this introduction, you will see how complicated the meaning of race is in the United States. The labels that people use to define people, as well as how you define yourself, are multifaceted, complex, and historically changeable. They are also highly politicized. Single labels associated with race do not capture the unique experiences of diverse people within the United States. The term *Latino*,[2] for example, refers to a whole array of different experiences. Some have now developed the term *Latinx* to replace *Latino* in an effort to avoid using *Latino* and *Latina* as gendered markers of identity. The usage of *Latinx* is, though, controversial within Latino

---

[1] This chapter will later explain why race is put in quotation marks here. For now, the answer is that race is a social phenomenon, not a fixed thing.

[2] For further discussion of the significance of language, see the "Note on Language" in the introduction to this book.

communities, with many arguing that *Latinx* erases the unique cultural heritage of Latin American people. Any label obscures the very different cultural and historical experiences of particular groups of Latin or Spanish descent. Some Chicanos, for example, do not want to be called *Latino* at all, thinking that the label erases the unique experiences of Chicanos, Puerto Ricans, Central Americans, and others in the United States and the Americas. Even *American* can be a charged term, because, although it is usually used to refer to the United States, seen in a more global perspective, the Americas include Central and South America and the Caribbean, where experiences of race and racism directly link the United States to the history of slavery throughout the Americas.

Thinking about Muslims further complicates our notions of race and ethnic identity. Muslims are not usually considered a race, but history shows us that race can be imposed on groups, as happened with Jewish people during the Holocaust. In addition, Native Americans have not typically been defined in terms of race, and, from their own perspective, it is their tribal identity that is salient, even though many will identify with other Native groups because of their common experiences of oppression. Groups can also become "racialized"—a concept we will further explore later in this chapter. For now, note that the very idea of race is changing, even while it remains highly significant in shaping people's experiences in all of society.

Even while the meaning of race is evolving and becoming more nuanced, discussion of race has become quite prominent in the public discourse. Overt displays of White supremacy have brought renewed attention to racism in the United States, and the racial disparities unveiled during the COVID-19 pandemic have revealed the vast inequality that concepts of race have produced throughout US history. Moreover, the increasingly visible diversity of the US population has showcased the significance of race and ethnicity in shaping public policies that will work for the good of the whole, as well as for the particular situations of diverse groups. The public attention to these facts has shattered any illusion that we are a "postracial society."

We are thus witnessing that the idea of race is not static. As this chapter will show, how race is perceived, defined, and felt is deeply connected to social institutions and to the political, economic, and cultural context of the time. As we will see, racial identity is about how individuals see themselves and each other, but notions of race and the racism that produces the idea of race are fundamentally rooted in the structure of society, not just in individual experiences. It is within individual experiences, however, that the societal basis of race is lived.

A Simple Experiment: Changing Your Race

Framing Question: Is race a fixed identity, or can it be changed?

Let's explore the idea of race further. Suppose that one day a stranger came to your door and told you she discovered a huge bureaucratic mistake made when you were born. She tells you that someone made an error when recording your birth certificate, and your birth certification records you as being of a different race than what you have thought all of your life. You now have the opportunity to change your race, but you must decide by the end of the day whether you will do so.

You are not the only person in this scenario. A very wealthy gentleman is willing to give a huge sum of money to anyone who agrees to change their race to match the state records. Nothing else about you would change. Your ideas, thoughts, level of education, job—everything would remain the same, but you would from now on be known and recognized as a member of your "new" race. You would live the rest of your life as a person of a different race.

This hypothetical situation assumes, of course, that a person's race can be changed. But what if you could change your race? *How much money would you want to change your race?*

A scenario like this has actually been studied by researchers who were interested in White people's perceptions of the "cost of being Black" (Mazzocco et al. 2006). The researchers were interested in White people's perceptions, so they only included White people in their research study. They presented to research subjects a hypothetical situation similar to the one above. In the study, the authors found that White Americans did not want very much money to become Black. On average, Whites wanted about $1,500 a year to change their race—far less than the $1 million subjects wanted to never watch television again! The researchers concluded that White Americans vastly underestimate the cost of being Black in the United States.

If you could change someone's race, how much do you think a White person would want to become Black? A Latino to become Asian? A Black person to become White? In a class this book's author taught, many Black students said they would not take any amount of money to be White. White students wanted large sums of money to become Black. All students agreed that you couldn't pay them enough to give up television!

Aside from the monetary award, what would it mean to change your race? Would you only change your appearance? Would your attitudes change? Your neighbors? Your friends? Your job? In other words, how would your life be lived differently if you were of a race other than the one you've assumed all your life? Such questions help you start to think about the significance and consequences of race in society.

The One-Drop Rule

Framing Question: In what ways does the one-drop rule influence how we think about race?

In some ways, changing race is not as far-fetched as you might think. Consider the actual case of Susie Guillory Phipps. Born in Louisiana in 1934, Susie Guillory grew up White, never thinking of herself in any other way. She married a White man, Andy Phipps. In 1977, she applied for a passport so that she and her husband could travel to South America. When she went to the Division of Vital Records in New Orleans to do so, she was told that her birth certificate recorded both her parents as "col"—that is, "colored," or Black (Trillin 1986; Wright 1994). Oddly enough, her children's birth certificates listed her and her two children as "White." Imagine her surprise on learning that the state considered her "Black."

Susie Phipps tried to get her birth certificate changed to reflect what she believed to be her true identity—"White"—but the state clerks would not budge. As it turns out, Susie Guillory Phipps's great-great-great-grandmother, Marguerite, had been a Black slave—five generations back.[3] A 1970 state law in Louisiana defined anyone with a trace of Black ancestry as "Black." Susie Phipps sued the state of Louisiana to have her birth certificate changed. She lost her case in 1983. The law was not overturned until years later.

At the time Phipps sued the state of Louisiana, people believed that each race had its own blood type. Blood type was also thought to be correlated with other physical and social features—an idea that we now know to be ludicrous but that nonetheless governed the laws of Southern states for years.

Louisiana was not unique among Southern states in defining a person's race by the **one-drop rule** (more formally known as **hypodescent**). The one-drop rule refers to the notion that a certain amount of so-called Black blood legally defines someone as Black. States varied in the particulars. Mississippi's 1800 constitution classified individuals as Black if they had "any appreciable amount of Negro blood" (section 263). North Carolina, Florida, and Texas defined *Black* as anyone having one-eighth Black ancestry.

Oddly enough, you might be considered a given race in one state and not in another. In Virginia, even as late as 1963, you were considered Indian if you lived on a reservation and had at least one Indian grandparent. Off the reservation, you would be considered Black (Cumminos 1963). Your official identity could even change over time within a given state. In 1785 Virginia, any person with "one-fourth part or more Negro blood" was deemed a "colored" person, but in 1910 the proportion was changed to one-sixteenth. In 1924, Virginia's Racial Integrity Act decreed that having *any trace* of African ancestry meant you were Black (Adelman 2003).

You might be surprised to learn that many of the state laws defining people in one race or another were not enacted until the early twentieth century—1911 in Texas and Arkansas, 1923 in North Carolina, 1924 in Virginia, 1927 in Georgia and Alabama (Murray 1997). Why then?

Known sardonically as the "Golden Age of Racism," the period spanning the late nineteenth and early twentieth centuries saw dramatic change in the racial social order of the United States. Slavery had ended with the close of the Civil War and the passage of the Thirteenth Amendment to the US Constitution in 1865. The period of Reconstruction in the South (1865–1877) had given newly emancipated Black Americans hope for full rights of citizenship, but, following Reconstruction, the nation remodeled a system of racial inequality that disenfranchised Black Americans in every aspect of life (Foner 1988).

---

[3] Marguerite was the slave of Marie Jeanne LaCasse, wife of French planter Joseph Gregory Guillory. After LaCasse's death, Joseph Guillory fathered four children with Marguerite, but she was still listed as Marie Jeanne LaCasse's property. LaCasse's White sons sued Joseph Gregory Guillory for all of LaCasse's property, including Marguerite, and Marguerite was turned over to the eldest son, Jean Baptiste Guillory. Joseph went to his son's home and kidnapped Marguerite at knifepoint. He then freed Marguerite (through what is known as *manumission*), on the condition that she stay with him until his death, which she did. When the sons attempted to have Marguerite returned to them, Marguerite sued in court and won, ensuring both her freedom and that of her four children. For more on Susie Phipps's case, see Jaynes 1982.

Retrenchment to greater racial subordination was cemented with the 1898 Supreme Court decision in *Plessy v. Ferguson*, which legally sanctioned strict racial segregation. Jim Crow segregation[4]—that is, the separate and fully unequal treatment of Black and White Americans—would govern the American South for years to come. That enactment of racial classification laws is an example of how extreme forms of racism tend to emerge during periods of rapid social change in the preexisting racial order, such as in the one that characterized the late nineteenth and early twentieth centuries in the United States. *Racial backlash* occurs when there is a movement to reestablish a social order defined along lines of race even when social trends have begun to dismantle the prior racial system (Roberts 2012).

Looking at Jim Crow segregation from today's vantage point, the laws and practices seem capricious, but they were taken for granted, at least by dominant groups. They were a mechanism that maintained and protected a racial order, assuring White supremacy in all aspects of life. We are now familiar with how Jim Crow mandated separate schools, separate restrooms, and separate seating on public buses, but the extremes to which the laws went to are sometimes stunning. For example, a 1935 North Carolina law decreed, "Books shall not be interchangeable between the white and colored schools, but shall continued [*sic*] by the race first using them" (1935, c. 422, s.2; cited in Murray 1997:331). Another example can be found in the state of Delaware, where law mandated not only separate schools for Whites and Blacks but also schools for those identified as Moors or Indians (Murray 1997). The degree to which these Jim Crow laws governed daily life is hard to overemphasize.

Why were laws defining race so important? For several reasons. They defined citizenship, and, for African Americans, they had defined ownership under slavery. Such laws were also designed to prevent intermarriage. Racial intermarriage was illegal in all Southern states until 1967, when the Supreme Court ruled in a case poignantly named *Loving v. Virginia* that laws prohibiting racial intermarriage were unconstitutional. These laws and the one-drop rule may seem antiquated to you now, but think about how much we still tend to define people in terms of "color."

The point is to see how the definition of race emerges for very specific *societal* reasons. The particular historical circumstances that define people in racial terms may change, but the notion of race persists. You might note that now race is defined in terms of "Black," "Brown," and "White." Who decides these labels? How they do emerge? Why do people think the tone of a person's skin defines race? The fact is that notions of race are deeply tied to systems of racial inequality—that is, social systems where dominant groups control, exploit, and define subordinate groups (Higginbotham and Andersen 2016). One of the most important lessons of this book is that *race is a social construction*. This means that race is not some fixed thing; rather, it is related to shifting, though enduring, social, cultural, economic, and political inequalities and human oppression (Gómez 2018). The remainder of this chapter explores what it means that race is a social construction.

---

[4] The term *Jim Crow* is said to originate from a White minstrel-show performer who in the mid-eighteen hundreds appeared in blackface as a character "Jim Crow" and who danced a ridiculously stereotypical jig. This insulting performance became a standard part of minstrel shows in the mid-nineteenth century in the United States.

The Myth of Biological Race

Framing Question: What does current science tell us about a biological basis for race?

When you encounter a person, most likely one of the first things you notice about them is their race—at least, this is so in the United States. On what do you base this judgment? Is it physical appearance? Skin tone? Facial features? Hair? Most people think they can "see" race because physical features are what make race "visible" to others. Scratch the surface, though, and you will discover that race is not as simple as it may seem.

Even now, with years of research telling us the contrary, many think that race is rooted in biological or genetic differences. The popularity of DNA test kits also makes it seem as if you can determine your true identity through your genes. Is this true? Using the technique of DNA sequencing, scientists working on the human genome project have mapped the more than twenty thousand extant human genes and have soundly concluded that *there is no such thing as a race gene.*

Of course, there are identifiable physical differences among human populations, and some of those physical characteristics are produced through genetic expression. DNA test kits can screen for genetically linked disease and can tell you something about your regional ancestral background, but they do not reveal some underlying essence of racial identity. A brief lesson in genetics helps us understand that genetic traits are not as simply determined as we might think (Feldman 2010; Mukherjee 2017).

The **genotype** of any organism, including humans, is the full set of genes found in that organism, including in the human body. An organism's **phenotype** refers to its *observable* characteristics. The genotype influences the phenotype, but the phenotype is also influenced by an organism's environment or *culture*. Some genotypic traits are discrete and fixed; that is, they are directly expressed, producing a particular outcome. Blood type is an example: a person has blood type A, B, AB, or O. Most observable characteristics in people—that is, their phenotype—fall along a continuum, influenced by inherited characteristics *and* the environment. Height is a good example. You might inherit the tendency to be tall or short, but your environment—your nutrition, for example—will significantly affect your actual height.

Skin color is a phenotypic trait. That is, although it is partially based on inherited genes, in any human grouping it is also influenced by environmental factors. Scientists now understand that skin color is likely determined by as many as six different genes. Genes also interact with each other. Even if skin color alone defined race, race would still not be comprised of discrete categories, as is true for blood type.

Most people do not understand the complexity that geneticists are now discovering. The mass media generally oversimplify research studies about genetics, leading the public to think there is a direct causal relationship between particular genes and a given condition. This direct causal relationship is generally not true. For example, there can be correlations between genes and particular diseases, but this does not necessarily mean that genes are causal determinants of disease (Brooks and King 2008). Health and disease are influenced by all kinds of social factors, including lifestyle, access to quality health care, and diet—all social and environmental factors, not genetically determined ones.

What about so-called race-based diseases, such as sickle cell anemia? Sickle cell occurs in offspring where both parents carry the sickle cell genetic trait. In the United States, sickle cell anemia is a disease that is most common among African and African American populations. But the genetic trait that produces sickle cell anemia has developed over time as a resistance to malaria. Thus, sickle cell anemia was first found in populations where malaria was most common, in such places as the Middle East, India, Greece, southern Italy, southern Turkey, and West Africa. Certain African populations actually have a very low rate of sickle cell disease. Again, even when a condition like sickle cell anemia is more common in a given population, the trait for it developed earlier in response to environmental conditions. Note that we do not call sickle cell an Italian or Turkish disease. Sickle cell, then, should not now be considered an African American disease either.

Likewise, Tay-Sachs is a disease that is associated with Ashkenazic Jewish people. It is a recessive genetic disorder, but it is not exclusive to Jewish populations. Tay-Sachs is also found among French Canadians, Louisiana Cajuns, and the Pennsylvania Dutch. As in the case of sickle cell anemia, a combination of a population's ancestry and geographic location will condition the likelihood of manifesting Tay-Sachs (Brooks and King 2008; Villarosa 2002).

Simply put, although there may be some genetic influence on what we call race traits, none of the characteristics we have used to define race (such as skin color, hair texture, or body form) corresponds to any true genetic difference between human populations. You simply cannot look at genes and then separate people into discrete, supposedly "racial" categories based on their genetic makeup. Biologists define a race as "a population that has significant genetic differences from other populations such that it can be considered a subspecies" (Graves, cited in Villarosa 2002). In the animal kingdom, animals are separated into distinct species: there is no subgroup to the human species.

At the level of genetic composition, scientists now know that there are far more similarities among people than there are differences. If you take any two people (including two people from supposedly different races) and analyze their genetic compositions, you will find that they are far more alike than different. This is a very important point for anyone who thinks of race as a biological given. So-called racial traits do not exist in discrete categories—a necessary condition to dividing any species into so-called race groups. The fact is that genetic variation among human beings is indeed very small (Mukherjee 2017). *There is only one human race.*

This truth has not stopped people over the years from trying to categorize people into so-called race groups. Over time people have created many different schemes for dividing human beings into races. At one time, some even thought that earwax could be used as a "marker" of race (Snipp 2010)! The schemes that have been developed throughout history reflect the racial politics and social systems of the time far more than they represent scientific fact.

Notions about how many races there are and what race means have also changed dramatically over time. This is because the meanings that humans have given to race reflect social, not biological, conditions. Contemporary scientists conclude that the "lay concept of race does not correspond to the variation that exists in nature" (Graves 2001:5).

The idea that human beings can be separated into races corresponds closely with the development of social institutions that have exploited people for the profit of others, such as slavery (Graves 2004; Jones 2013). The idea that humans can be divided into so-called races only makes sense within the context of a system of racial inequality. Such exploitation could only be justified (at least by the dominant group) if the group being oppressed is defined as something less than fully human (Fredrickson 2002). To understand the meaning of race, then, you must understand the social context from which the idea stems.

If race is false as a biological notion, then is there no such thing as race? Yes and no. There is no biological reality that divides people into separate races, but race is very real in its vast and significant human impact. As summed up by sociologist Ann Morning, who has extensively studied scientific constructions of race, there is a "longstanding belief that race is etched on the human body," and, as she continues to say, this "has far-reaching physical, social, economic, and political consequences" (Morning 2011:7). You will see the consequences of the social construction of race throughout this book, but for now, understand that the consequences of race reach into every dimension of our society. In other words, *race is real, but it is real because of its social origins and consequences.* The power that the idea of race has comes not from genetics but from the treatment of groups that notions of race have produced.

Race: A Modern Idea

Framing Question: What does it mean to say that racial inequality produces race, not the other way around?

It might surprise you to learn that race is a relatively modern idea. Over the ages, people in society have held negative ideas about those perceived as the "other." The term **xenophobia** ("fear of foreigners"), for example, stems from ancient Greece, where Greeks thought that all non-Greeks were barbarians (Graves 2004). In the Western world, there is ample evidence that some of the earliest cultures had definitions of groups that were ranked by descent and seeming physical differences (Bethencourt 2014). There is a big difference, though, between seeing strangers as outsiders or others and establishing a social system in which people perceived as being different are defined as less than human and believed to be innately inferior. Although the ancient Greeks did have slaves and disliked outsiders, whom they defined as somehow different, possibly even innately different, slaves were not treated like property in a formal, state-sanctioned system of slavery (Fredrickson 2002).

It seems that the term *race* was first used in the Middle Ages, but it only referred to animal breeds. With the advent of the scientific revolution, though, early scientists became obsessed with observing and classifying what they saw in nature. It did not take long before they tried to differentiate human groups based on presumed differences in their physical characteristics (Ferber 1998). An uneasy alliance was then forged between budding scientific thinking and the emergence of modern racism.

Historian Winthrop Jordan locates the origins of the idea of race in the early European conquest of African people. Jordan meticulously shows that when European explorers encountered Africans, the Europeans thought of Africans as primitive and savage. This belief was then used to rationalize what became the development of slavery in the New World, including the United States, the Caribbean, and Latin America (Jordan 1968).

Swedish botanist and physician Carl Linnaeus (1707–1778) was the first to develop elaborate taxonomies of plants and other parts of nature. He organized the plant and animal kingdoms into different species, according to the shared characteristics of these living organisms. Linnaeus identified human beings (*Homo sapiens*) and primates as part of the genus *Homo*. He further differentiated *Homo sapiens* into four groups: Europeans, American Indians, Asians, and Africans. Although he did not explicitly rank them, he did color-code them white, red, yellow, and black. Further, he described each group in what we would now see as a highly value-laden, Eurocentric perspective (Fredrickson 2002; Roberts 2012), describing Europeans as "gentle, acute, inventive . . . governed by customs" and Africans as "crafty, indolent, negligent . . . governed by caprice" (West 1982:56, cited in Ferber 1998:28–29).

Incredibly, the color scheme that Linnaeus invented persists to this day as people continue to describe human groups in terms of presumed color. Following Linnaeus, various other Europeans developed different schemes for classifying human beings as if they were of different biological types. While the Atlantic slave trade was flourishing, pseudoscientific thinkers developed various racial schemes to give supposed legitimacy to a highly unequal and oppressive system of human life.

In the early eighteenth century, French naturalist Georges-Louis Leclerc, Comte de Buffon (1707–1788), introduced the term *race* into the scientific lexicon to categorize human beings. Buffon thought that human variation was the result of differences in the climate where groups lived. He elevated people with white skin to the top of the hierarchy he'd created, writing that they were the essence of humanity. Absurdly enough, he thought that white was the "natural" color of human beings and that African people were dark because of their greater exposure to the sun. He even thought that if Africans would only move to Europe, their skin would lighten over time (Ferber 1998).

The idea that human beings could be divided into races culminated with the work of Johann Friedrich Blumenbach (1752–1840), German physician and naturalist. Like other naturalists of his time, Blumenbach believed humans could be classified into a taxonomy in which some human groups were superior to others. He thought there were five separate "varieties" of human beings: Caucasian, Mongolian, Ethiopian, American, and Malay. Blumenbach was particularly smitten by the people of the Russian Caucasus, who were mostly blond and light-skinned. He believed them to be the most beautiful people in the world. He placed them at the "top" of his alleged racial hierarchy of human beings.

Most people now have never heard of Johann Blumenbach, but his racist ideas persist. Have you ever referred to White people as "Caucasian" or checked a box marked "Caucasian" to indicate your race? Now that you know the origin of this label, perhaps you will cringe the next time you hear it. Would you ever have imagined that this term came from one man over two hundred years ago whose ideas about people from the Russian Caucasus seem so outlandish to us now? This shows how intractable some of the racist thinking of the past is in influencing our thinking today.

Where would such menacing ideas have come from? Remember that at the time Blumenbach was formulating his ideas, the Atlantic slave trade was flourishing. The Dutch, Spanish, and British empires had colonized much of the world—primarily for purposes of trade and the acquisition of wealth and profit. Human trafficking was pivotal to this system. Within such an economic system, the world was ripe for the scourge of racism. It is no coincidence that ideas about innate human differences were developed as part of the Atlantic slave trade and the development of an institutionalized system of slavery in North and South America. Slavery was a system that *depended on* classifying some groups as innately inferior to White European Americans. Only if some people could be considered something less than fully human could a system of racial subordination emerge.

The racism that was developing in the eighteenth century emerged alongside Western movements for democracy—namely, the French and American revolutions. It may seem inconceivable now that proclamations of equality, at least for men, could exist side by side with a flourishing system of racism. As historian George Fredrickson (2002) argues, aspirations for equality went hand in hand with racism. How? As people were rejecting old notions of the traditional order, they had to somehow rationalize the exploitation and mistreatment of others. The idea of race filled that need. If differences between two groups who are unequal were defined as "natural," then there was no need to question the social order.

Antiquated as early thinking about race seems now, its legacy lives on. Many people continue to think of race as somehow reflecting meaningful differences

The social construction of race is reproduced through various forms of everyday behavior. Race, for example, gets defined as "color" as people use different emojis on social media platforms.

Source: Alamy/Lauren Hurley.

between people, differences that get socially coded by "color." Skin tone continues to impact how people are perceived and treated. Lighter-skinned people are often more favored. **Colorism** refers to the prejudice and discrimination directed against darker-skin-toned people. (See more about colorism in chapter 4 of this book.) Lighter-skinned African Americans and Latinos may experience preferred treatment, perhaps even by members of their own group. Further, colorism occurs not only in the United States but also in other nations, where lighter skin brings more privileged status. At the same time, people with darker skin tone may be perceived by their own group members as somehow "more authentically ethnic" (Hunter 2007). In all of these ways, people continue to be ranked and evaluated based on long-standing ideas about color and race.

The social construction of race is reproduced through various forms of everyday behavior. Think of the emojis that people use on the Internet and their smartphones. Developed in Japan, the icon was originally a nonhuman-looking character depicted only in yellow, but it was soon expanded to show people in five different colors, ranging from a pink tone to very dark brown (see photo). Not until very recently did developers change the technology so users could shade the human icon, choosing from 151 different options. What is interesting, however, is how color has become the standard for defining human diversity (Phillip 2014). You might examine your own assumptions about how "color" continues to influence how you perceive people and how you are perceived in society.

Who Counts? Racial Classification Systems

Framing Question: How have racial categories been developed through different administrative practices, especially those of the government or other systems of official power?

Even though there is no such thing as a distinct human race, over time, people have put a lot of effort into classifying people into racial categories. The many different ways they have done so are intricately connected to the racial politics and interests of powerful groups in society. This fact reveals how deeply social the concept of race is.

Your birth certificate, for example, may or may not indicate your race, depending on the state where you were born. Not all states use the same criteria for assigning race on birth certificates. Only about half of the states now allow multiracial designation for newborns (Guarneri and Dick 2012; Mason, Nam, and Kim 2014). Typically the person recording the birth certificate will use the race of the mother to record a newborn's race, perhaps without even asking! Inconsistency often occurs between what is reported on a birth certificate and how parents define their own child. Why should we even care about a newborn's race? You might think that we should ignore the race designation altogether, but we would then have no way of reporting various vital statistics, such as the life expectancy of different groups, population rates, and so forth. "Counting" race has become a very politicized phenomenon.

The first attempt to count different populations in the United States came in 1787 with the writing of the US Constitution. Article I, Section 2 of the Constitution mandates that the population be counted every ten years in order to determine taxation and representation in the government. Who was counted and how was critical in establishing the political structure of the nation. To this day the decennial census determines state representation in the US Congress, along with other things.

As written in 1787, Article I of the US Constitution decreed that apportionment of the states in the national government would be "determined by adding to the whole Number of free Persons, including those bound to Service for a Term of Years, and excluding Indians not taxed, three fifths of all other Persons" (Anderson 1988:9, cited in Rodríguez 2000:66; and see the original text at US Constitution 1787). With this mandate, Black slaves were constitutionally defined as three-fifths of a person. Indentured servants, who were White, were to be counted as free persons. Most Indians were not counted at all. So-called taxed Indians—that is, those living in European settlements and likely including Indian women married to White men—were few (Rodríguez 2000:66). From the start, race was inscribed into the US Constitution as a category of citizenship (Snipp 2010)—or, in the case of African Americans and Indians, noncitizenship.

Although the first census in the United States in 1790 did not mention "race" per se, it classified people into four groups: free White males, free White females, slaves, and all other free persons, including indentured White servants, free Blacks, and taxed Indians. As the nation developed, census categories evolved to reflect changes in the population and White people's reactions to the growing immigrant population. The 1820 census was thus the first to categorize the "foreign-born" population, reflecting concerns about the so-called stock of new immigrant groups (Snipp 2010). This designation still appears in the census today. The 1820 census was also the first to categorize people by color: you were White, Black, or American Indian. Which category you fell into was the work of census enumerators who were instructed to note a person's "color"—presumably based solely on appearance.

In 1850, the national census added the category "mulatto," the first official acknowledgment of racial intermarriage between Blacks and Whites and between Blacks and American Indians. Thus the child of a Black-Indian relationship would be counted in a different "race" box than either parent.

"Chinese" and "Asian Indian" were added to the census of 1860, the result of the large-scale immigration of Chinese and other Asian workers who provided so much of the labor for an expanding nation. In 1870, "Japanese" was added as a racial-ethnic category, following the group's widespread immigration, often as contract labor.

Near the turn of the twentieth century, White anxieties about racial purity fueled many of the changes made in census classifications. Even though "race mixing" has been common throughout US history—through both involuntary and voluntary relationships—dominant ideologies have extolled "racial purity." Concerns about racial purity peaked by the 1890 census, when yet other categories denoting race were added. If you were counted in the 1890 census, you would have been considered White, Black, Chinese, Japanese, or American Indian (taxed or nontaxed). If you were mixed race, you would have been tallied as mulatto, "quadroon," or "octoroon." Reflecting the one-drop rule, these categories used "blood" as the marker of race. A mixed person was one-half Black; a quadroon, one-quarter; an octoroon, one-eighth.

Racial categories in the census changed again in 1900. Then you would be classified in one of five race groups (White, Black, Indian, Japanese, or Chinese). Mulatto and "other" reappeared in 1910. How was your race determined? You didn't check a box, as you would now. Instead, census counters simply looked at you and were told that "a person of mixed White and Negro blood was to be returned as Negro, no matter how small the percentage of Negro blood; someone part Indian and part Negro was also to be listed as Negro unless the Indian blood predominated" (Bennett 2000:169–70, cited in Snipp 2003).

Change came again in 1930 with new categories labeled "Mexican," "Hindu," "Korean," and "Filipino." Such fluctuating categories seem odd to us now, but they followed a racial logic that made sense at the time because of the social definitions imposed on various groups (Lee 1993). These shifting census categories show that one way in which race has been constructed is through the apparatus of the government—what sociologist C. Matthew Snipp calls "administrative definitions of race" (2010:110).

After the 1960 census, the federal government started collecting more detailed information about race, largely the result of the civil rights movement and subsequent efforts to monitor racial discrimination. The proliferation of federal agencies that collected data on race fostered great inconsistency in how race was counted. Because of this confusion, in 1977 the federal Office of Management and Budget adopted a policy requiring federal agencies to tabulate race using five groups: (1) American Indians and Alaska Natives, (2) Asians and Pacific Islanders, (3) non-Hispanic Blacks, (4) non-Hispanic Whites, and (5) Hispanics of any race.

Consistent with this directive, in 1980 the census included a designation for Hispanic origin for the first time. Advocacy groups, however, argued that some groups were being omitted from the census categories. Arab Americans, for example, fell into none of the census categories. Others, such as native Hawaiians, argued that they should not be lumped together with Asians and Pacific Islanders. How the census classified people into groups was quite a political matter.

As a result of political pressure, in 2000 the federal government once again modified its racial designations, developing designations that are still in place today, as you can see on the 2020 census form in figure 1.1. The first question on the 2020 census form asks whether the census taker is of Hispanic, Latino, or Spanish origin, and these categories are not considered a race. Latinos can, however, also identify in any racial group. The racial groups include White, Black or African American, American Indian and Alaska Native, with various options for Asian Americans, and a category for "others."

Doesn't it seem odd to you that Native Hawaiians, American Indians, and Chinese are considered "races" but Hispanics are not? If you think this is confusing, it is! But it shows the complexity of racial identities in a population as diverse as the United States and in a country where your race has so much to do with your life opportunities.

Why is it important to designate race at all? Perhaps you will conclude that we just shouldn't count people by race and ethnicity at all. But how would we then monitor discrimination or study such things as patterns of disease, school enrollment, voting rights, and the countless other matters that depend on some racial and ethnic designation? No doubt, the diversity in human identities gets disguised

> ➔ NOTE: Please answer BOTH Question 6 about Hispanic origin and Question 7 about race. For this census, Hispanic origins are not races.

6. Is this person of Hispanic, Latino, or Spanish origin?

☐ No, not of Hispanic, Latino, or Spanish origin

☐ Yes, Mexican, Mexican AM., Chicano

☐ Yes, Puerto Rican

☐ Yes, Cuban

☐ Yes, another Hispanic, Latino, or Spanish origin – *Print, for example, Salvadoran, Dominican, Colombian, Guatemalan, Spaniard, Ecuadorian, etc.* ↙

7. What is this person's race?
Mark ☒ *one or more boxes AND print origins.*

☐ White – *Print, for example, German, Irish, English, Italian, Lebanese, Egyptian, etc.* ↙

☐ Black or African Am. – *Print, for example, African American, Jamaican, Haitian, Nigerian, Ethiopian, Somali, etc.* ↙

☐ American Indian or Alaska Native – *Print name of enrolled or principal tribe(s), for example, Navajo Nation, Blackfeet Tribe, Mayan, Aztec, Native Village of Barrow Inupiat Traditional Government, Nome Eskimo Community, etc.* ↙

☐ Chinese	☐ Vietnamese	☐ Native Hawaiian
☐ Filipino	☐ Korean	☐ Samoan
☐ Asian Indian	☐ Japanese	☐ Chamorro
☐ Other Asian – *Print, for example, Pakistani, Cambodian, Hmong, etc.* ↙		☐ Other Pacific Islander – *Print, for example, Tongan, Fijian, Marshallese, etc.* ↙

☐ Some other race – *Print race or origin.* ↙

FIG. 1.1 Questions on Hispanic Origin and Race in the 2020 Census

Source: US Census Bureau 2019e.

by the generation of race and ethnic labels, but without census and other administrative data we would have little way of monitoring the life experiences of different groups.

Defining Race and Ethnicity: Intersecting Ideas

Framing Question: What is the difference between the concepts of race and ethnicity, and how do they intersect?

The distinction between race and ethnicity is complex and blurry—and is also quite specific to a given culture. What race means in the United States, for example, would not hold up in other parts of the world. In fact, people from outside the United States typically find the US conception of race quite strange.

Sociologists have long defined race and ethnicity as different concepts. The usual definition of an **ethnic group** is an identifiable group of people who share a common culture, language, regional origin, and/or religion. Ethnic groups also have a definition of themselves as a collective or "we." Jewish Americans constitute an ethnic group, as do Irish Americans, Italian Americans, and Arab Americans. You can see right away, though, that groups considered racial groups in the United States also share a common culture. African Americans, as an example, include Afro-Caribbeans, Cape Verdeans, descendants of US slaves, and even some Latinos. African Americans are certainly considered a racial group in the United States, but the label includes groups of diverse cultural origins even though African Americans on the whole also share common histories and cultural characteristics. Latinos are typically defined as an ethnic group descended from people with Latin backgrounds. But ethnic diversity among Latinos is rich and varied, and some might not speak Spanish at all. Although race and ethnicity are treated as separate concepts, the line between the two is not always firm.

Race is also constructed in relationship to ethnicity, meaning that race and ethnicity can reinforce each other. To explain, immigrants to the United States have historically faced a Black/White division. Outsiders themselves, immigrants have had to navigate this complex terrain. Some have had their racial-ethnic identity imposed on them by others, such as Vietnamese immigrants coming to the United States following the Vietnam War: they become "Asian," even though they may never before have defined themselves in this way (Kibria, Bowman, and O'Leary 2014). Immigrants from different Central American countries (El Salvador, Honduras, and Guatemala, for example) may all be perceived as "Mexican." The social construction of race can be based as much on contemporary political realities as on people's actual ethnic identity.

The meaning of Whiteness has also emerged in the context of the nation's history of immigration and race. Some immigrant groups might eventually become defined as White even though they may have been defined in other terms before. The Irish were once perceived as "Black," although they are now considered White (Roediger 2002). Both race and ethnicity have been created in the United States in the context of each group's placement within the nation's system of inequality. People have been sorted into categories that correspond with their placement in the labor market. For example, some Latinos may now be perceived as White if they hold high-status professional jobs, while those in the most menial occupations are perceived as "colored"—that is, brown. Also, Whiteness is always "constructed" in opposition to "Blackness." The constant tension between "White" and "Black" can only be understood in the context of the power differences that are part of the nation's system of racial inequality (Cottom 2019).

Even with a soft distinction between race and ethnicity, ethnicity can be just as damaging as race. Ethnicity can turn into **ethnocentrism**, the belief that one's group is superior to all other groups (also see chapter 2). When taken to extremes, ethnocentrism can have murderous consequences. Tragically, examples of such ethnic hatred abound: the Jewish Holocaust, the Turkish massacre of Armenians in World War I, the genocide of American Indians, the persistent persecution of the majority Sunni Muslims living in Syria under the rule of the Assad family, the suggestion that Muslims should be banned from entry into the United States, and many more.

Ethnicity can, at times, be somewhat less pronounced than race. **Symbolic ethnicity**, for example, is allegiance to an ethnic group that is felt without incorporating ethnicity into one's daily behavior (Gans 1979). Everyone can feel Irish on Saint Patrick's Day or Creole during Mardi Gras, but this kind of identification with ethnic celebration or pride comes without cost or consequence.

Both ethnicity and race must be understood in the context of how groups are treated in society. The distinction between race and ethnicity underscores yet again that both are social constructions (Kibria, Bowman, and O'Leary 2014). That is, groups may share a common culture, history, and heritage, *but how they come to be defined in society is a social process.* Moreover, as we will see, there are times when an ethnic group may become defined as a racial group, depending on social and historical circumstances.

Race and ethnicity also exist alongside and in interaction with other social factors—including gender, social class, sexuality, nationality, religion, and even age. **Intersectional theory** is a perspective underscoring that no one of these social factors exists in isolation from the others. Race, class, gender, sexuality, and other social factors intertwine to produce the particular experiences of all people in society. We will see how intersectionality operates throughout this book (see especially chapter 6), even while the book's primary focus is on racial inequality.

In this book, **race** is defined as a group treated as distinct in society based on presumed group characteristics that have been interpreted as signifying inferiority and superiority. The designation of a group as a race is then used to produce a social order of domination, power, and exploitation (Higginbotham and Andersen 2016, adapted from Wilson 1973).

Several ideas are included in this definition of race:

- It is the treatment of groups, not their individual attributes, that defines race and makes it meaningful in society.
- Race in the United States has been constructed through a history of conquest and exploitation.
- Understandings and definitions of race, both formal and informal, are fluid and change over time.
- Race is contextual; that is, you must understand the circumstances in which definitions of race arise to fully understand the idea of race.

- Race is both an individual identity and a collective process (Omi and Winant 1986 and 2015).
- The meaning of race is unstable and can be transformed through political struggle (Omi and Winant 1986).

To further understand the complexity of race and ethnicity, let's go back to the opening scenario of this chapter. How would you describe your race and your ethnicity? People regularly note their race on various official forms—not just in the census but also on credit applications, college admissions forms, driver's licenses, opinion polls and surveys, and any number of other places. Each may reflect a different scheme for counting and defining race and ethnicity.

If you were checking your racial identity on the census form shown in figure 1.1, what would you mark? For some, this may be a simple exercise; for others, not so much. What if you have a White parent and a Black parent? Would you check Black or White? What if one parent is Asian and the other Hispanic? What race and ethnicity are you?

As you answer these questions, you may see that the one-drop rule is still flourishing, even many years after its elimination from the law. Is your understanding of your race based on your appearance? Socialization in your family? Your ancestral past? Your attitudes and behaviors? If you are White, do you regularly think of yourself as even having a racial identity? Certainly African American and Latino people think of you that way, but White Americans generally do not have to think about their race, as Whiteness is a taken-for-granted racial identity. Are there places, other than standard forms, where a White person's race becomes more apparent? What does this suggest to you about race as a *contextual identity*?

The Many Meanings of Race

Framing Question: What does it mean to say that you can define race in multiple ways?

No single definition can capture the complex social reality of race in the United States. Race is multidimensional, and it is useful to identify the different ways that race is defined (Taylor 2008), as in the following:

- *Some understandings of race are biologically based.* Although you have learned that biological definitions of race are questionable, most people think of race as a fixed attribute of a person—something that cannot be changed. As you have seen, assumptions about the biological basis of race have been challenged by what we now know from science. Although certainly there are some physical characteristics that differentiate some people, biology does not determine one's racial experiences. Society does.
- *Some definitions of race are administrative or state-based rules and categories* (Rodríguez 2000; Snipp 2010). You have seen that racial categories can be produced by the government or other institutional agencies (such as the census, your birth certificate, school admissions processes, and countless other bureaucratic agencies). Another good example of how official racial-ethnic identities are produced is the federal acknowledgment process that determines whether a person formally "counts" as an American Indian. Managed through the US

Department of the Interior's Bureau of Indian Affairs, this elaborate process requires that you extensively document your membership in one of 574 recognized Indian tribes. Whether you ultimately count administratively as "Indian" may be inconsistent with how you actually define yourself. This shows how official agencies can "define" race, even if such designations are inconsistent with your own racial identity.

• *Race can be defined by how you define yourself.* Racial identity, examined in more detail in chapter 4, is a powerful part of people's self-concept. People can take great pride in their racial identity, placing a high value on being Chicana or Puertorriqueño or being part of a long legacy of African American heritage. In fact, people actually "perform race" as part of their daily expression of self, such as by displaying certain symbols or behaviors that signify race to others. "Doing race" (Markus and Moya 2010) can proclaim your membership as part of a racial group. You may even be judged by others as "not being Black enough" or as not "authentically Latino" if you do not exhibit certain attitudes and behaviors. In the past, an African American who was very light-skinned might decide to "pass" for White to escape the oppression of slavery or, later, of Jim Crow segregation. Interestingly, passing also required some effort by those around you who were willing to keep your secret (Hobbs 2014). This shows again that the definition of race, including how one presents oneself, is a highly social process. Simply put, "how individuals publicly identify is powerfully shaped by the norms of the time and place in which they live" (Saperstein and Penner 2014:188).

• *Race may be defined by how others define you.* People's stereotypes about race may actually influence how they see and define race. This idea has been shown in a clever set of research studies by sociologists Aliya Saperstein and Andrew Penner (Penner and Saperstein 2008 and 2013; Saperstein and Penner 2014). Saperstein and Penner have studied how interviewers classify a person's race based on certain social statuses. They have conclusively found that a person is much more likely to be classified as Black if they are unemployed, on welfare, poor, or incarcerated—all stereotypes associated with being Black. People who are married or living in the suburbs are more likely to be classified as White. This research shows that one's social status can actually define race, at least in the eyes of others.

• *The definition of race can be influenced by social class.* There is a high correlation between skin tone and social class status, most notably in Brazil and Mexico, where, as the saying goes, "Money whitens" (Schwartzman 2007). Lighter-skinned people in these complex systems of racial definition may be more likely to be perceived as White or possibly to perceive themselves as White. At the same time, shifts in racial politics, such as movements that emphasize racial pride, may lessen this tendency.

• *Finally, politics and social movements shape the definition of race.* The Black Power, Chicano, and Pan-Asian movements, as examples, encouraged people to embrace pride in their racial-ethnic group membership. Even the language used to describe race changed as a result. Terms such as *people of color* and even the change from *Negro* to (eventually) *African American* reflect the collective political identity that social movements for racial justice can inspire.

As you think about these multiple ways of defining race, you will see that race is not as simple as you might have initially thought. One thing becomes especially clear as we work through a definition of race: "The actual meaning of race lies not in people's physical characteristics but in the historical treatment of different groups and the significance that society gives to what is believed to differentiate so-called racial groups" (Higginbotham and Andersen 2016:1). In other words, what is important about race is not biological difference but how groups are treated.

A multidimensional definition of race emphasizes **racialization**, the social process by which a group comes to be defined as a race (Omi and Winant 1986). Some groups become "racialized"; others do not.

The classic example of racialization is Nazi Germany. During his dictatorship, Adolf Hitler racialized Jewish people. He simply made up the idea that so-called Aryan (White, blue-eyed, and blond) people constituted a superior race; he defined Jewish people as inherently inferior. Nazi Germany's extreme **anti-Semitism**—that is, the hatred of Jewish people—was based on racializing both groups. Racialization was an explicit racial policy of the Nazi state and had murderous consequences. Some six million Jewish people were exterminated, as were millions of gays, lesbians, disabled people, gypsies, and others perceived as unfit or inferior. If you ever doubted that race is a social construction, the Nazi Holocaust is strong evidence of the horrid human acts that can stem from racialization.

Race Is a Process, Not a Thing: Racial Formation

Framing Question: What does it mean to say that race is a social construction?

By now you should see that race is not a "thing" or some fixed attribute of individual people. Race is a social construction, created through the actions and beliefs of people, most often those with a vested interest in devising and maintaining a system of racial inequality. This idea has been well formulated in the concept of **racial formation** developed by sociologists Michael Omi and Howard Winant (1986 and 2015).

Omi and Winant define racial formation as the "process by which racial categories are created, inhabited, transformed, and/or destroyed" (Omi and Winant 1986:64). What they mean is that race is created through the actions of people, especially those with the power to shape race within social institutions. In this sense, race is not an objective thing but a subjective construction. As Omi and Winant put it, "racial categories and the meaning of race are given concrete expression by the specific social relations and historical context in which they are embedded" (1986:60). We have seen that the meaning of race changes at different points in time, although for most of US history race has been defined in fairly rigid Black/White terms.

The framework of racial formation emphasizes several important sociological points:

- *Racial formation is a process.* That is, race is not a fixed attribute of particular people or groups; rather, it develops in the context of how groups are treated and perceived by others.

- *Race is an emergent concept.* It is an idea that develops through the course of history.
- *The formation of "race" happens at the macro level of society through powerful social institutions.* Although race is reinforced at the *micro* level of society—that is, in everyday interactions—it is structured into social institutions.
- *Race is contested.* That is, groups can challenge dominant definitions of race such that ideas about race can change—for example, through the political efforts of social movements and social protest.

The process of racial formation helps us understand how a given group comes to be defined as a race. Asian Americans, for example, have been racialized at various points throughout American history. *Asian American* is a term, like *Latino*, that lumps together people who come from very different societies and cultures—indeed, societies that have at times even been at war with each other. Moreover, each group's history in the United States differs. Asian Americans are not a monolithic group: Chinese Americans, Japanese Americans, Filipinos, Korean Americans, and, more recently, Asian immigrants from Southeast Asia (Vietnam, Laos, and Cambodia, among other places) are much more ethnic groups than they are racial groups, but how they are regarded in American society shows the power of racial formation.

Omi and Winant's concept of racial formation shows that race is not fixed; rather, it changes over time. Think about how different racial-ethnic groups are defined. Would you say that Latinos are a race? Latinos are typically identified as an ethnic group, based on shared cultural characteristics of language and national origin. Included in the category of Latinos, however, are very different groups who may not share the same histories or current experiences. Some groups even disagree about what they want their group to be called. Latinos are as diverse as the peoples who figure in this designation—Chicanas/os, Mexican Americans, Puerto Ricans, Cubans, and others who have some kind of Spanish origin and/or indigenous origin.

With such different origins and histories, should Latinos even be considered a single group? Latinos have some but not all cultural characteristics in common. Chicanos, for example, are native to US soil and are only defined as *Chicano* because of their lands having been confiscated by the US government following the Mexican-American War (1846–1848). Puerto Ricans both on the US mainland and on the island of Puerto Rico hold US citizenship as the result of the 1917 Jones-Shafroth Act (US Congress 1917). Movement back and forth between the US mainland and the island of Puerto Rico has marked Puerto Ricans' history in the United States.

As different as Latinos are who fall under this label, they share histories of **colonialism**—that is, the practice by which dominant White groups acquired political and economic control over different Latino populations. Various Latino groups have thus been constructed as racial groups because of the context of racial inequality in US institutions. Further, this has happened even though substantial proportions of Latinos identify themselves as White (Gómez 2018).

In short, groups become racialized not because of inherent characteristics but because of their position in the US racial hierarchy. Groups can become racialized because of their low status in the social and economic structure of US society, as some would say is happening to many Latinos (Bonilla-Silva 2004).

From the perspective of racial formation theory, race can be deconstructed as well as constructed. That is, some groups previously designated as people of color may be perceived as "Whitened" by gains in social and economic status. European immigrant groups in the nineteenth and early twentieth centuries were sometimes initially defined as something other than White, but their ultimate success in America led to a perception of them as White. Asian Americans may also come to be considered White by their social and economic success. Sociologist Min Zhou cautions, however, that perceiving Asian Americans as White—the "model minority" stereotype—overlooks the persistent discrimination and racism that Asian Americans experience. As Zhou says, "Speaking perfect English, adopting mainstream cultural values, and even intermarrying members of the dominant group may help reduce this 'otherness' for particular individuals, but it has little effect on the group as a whole" (2004:35).

When you understand race as a process as opposed to an individual attribute, you can see that races are created, changed, and potentially destroyed through the actions of human beings. This framework also helps you understand that the construction of race is now changing, especially as different groups shape the American racial landscape. No longer is race just about a Black/White divide; even though this divide is still significant, race in the United States—along with ethnicity—is becoming increasingly complicated, as we will see throughout this book.

Conclusion

When you understand that race is a social construction, how does your thinking about race change? This is a question that you can answer as this volume unfolds. Race and the racism that accompanies it are embedded in social practices that are a part of society.

To some people, race appears to have lost its significance. Additionally, the increasingly complex and diverse character of US society leads many to think that race will become less important over time. People may think that the significance of race in the United States has dissipated, but the reality is quite different, as we have seen all too vividly with a recent resurgence in White supremacist movements and other troubling developments.

Race continues to shape all matters of human life, including opportunities, income, health, housing, education, and criminal justice—as well as interpersonal relationships and group identity.

We have seen in this chapter that race is manufactured by human beings as they construct powerful institutions. Race is a social construction and thus is in some ways a false construct. Still, its effects remain very real, as we will see in the chapters to come. The culprit in the problems of race and racism is a combination of human beliefs, attitudes, and actions, not something inherent in different groups or individuals. The formation of race and ethnicity is so dangerous precisely because these two concepts are so deeply enmeshed in the formation of prejudice and racism—subjects to which we turn in the next chapter.

Key Terms

anti-Semitism 20

colonialism 21

colorism 12

ethnic group 16

ethnocentrism 17

genotype 7

hypodescent 5

intersectional theory 17

one-drop rule 5

phenotype 7

race 17

racial formation 20

racialization 20

symbolic ethnicity 17

xenophobia 9

Critical-Thinking Questions

1. Having read this chapter, what would you say to someone who declares, "We're all just human beings; race doesn't matter anymore"?
2. What is colorism, and how has it influenced the idea of race?
3. What are the key points in understanding that race is a social construction?

Student Exercises

1.1. As described in the opening scenario in this chapter, ask yourself how much money you would want to change your race. How much would you want to give up your smartphone or to quit watching television? If you can, ask students or friends of different races how they would answer these questions. What do their responses and your own tell you about the value people place on their racial (or ethnic) identity?

1.2. Go to the Public Broadcasting Service (PBS) website for the film *Race: The Power of an Illusion*, and complete the "Sorting People" exercise, at http://www.pbs.org/race/002_SortingPeople/002_00-home.htm. Then answer the following questions:

1. How many did you get right?
2. What did you look for in order to identify people?
3. When you first meet someone, do you immediately note the person's race? If so, what do you look for in order to do so?
4. What have you learned about the definition of *race* from this exercise?

Challenging Questions/Open to Debate

Should we "count" race? Some think that people should not be asked to indicate their race on the many and various forms where this question is asked. Do you agree or disagree? Explain your answer in detail.

TAKING ACTION AGAINST RACISM

An Individual Inquiry

As you learn more about race and racism, you're likely to ask, "What can I do?" Your answer to this question will likely depend on your own racial and ethnic identity, but you can start by taking stock of your own resources. That is, what are your personal strengths? For example, are you a good leader or speaker? Is writing one of your strengths, or are you better at locating and organizing information? What areas for change are most important to you? What do you need to learn in order to be an effective change agent?

It is important to recognize that you may need to learn more before you can be an effective change agent. The "Taking Action against Racism" boxes that appear at the end of each chapter of this book are intended to help you do just that. You should also recognize that not everyone works for change in the same way. Being aware of your personal strengths and weaknesses will help you make decisions about how you can best contribute to any movement for change. Also recognize that racism affects every level of society: our consciousness; our interpersonal interactions; our families, schools, and communities; and the organizations we are part of, including those we participate in regularly, such as churches and workplaces, but also including state and federal government.

Effective change needs to happen at every level, but you can start with your own awareness by asking yourself, "What do I need to learn to be an effective ally in the cause for greater racial justice?"

Resource: Racial Equality Tools, https://www.racialequitytools.org

CHAPTER 2

What Do You Think?

Prejudice, Racism, and Color Blindness

Build bridges instead of walls.
—Justice Sonia Sotomayor (2013:164)

OBJECTIVES

- Learn the difference between prejudice and racism
- Define some of the consequences of prejudice and stereotypes
- Assess the causal connection between prejudice and discrimination
- Interpret changes in public attitudes about race
- Compare and contrast the different forms of racism
- Understand the concept of color-blind racism

No one wants to be called a racist, and yet **racism** is pervasive in society. The appellation is widely used but widely misunderstood. Some will insist they are not racist—such as by saying, "I don't see race; people are just people." Perhaps you think this yourself. Sometimes you might hear, "Well, people of color can be racist too." Can they? Is it possible for someone to be racist who is usually on the receiving end of racism? Or maybe you think that racists are people who chant about White supremacy, make overtly racist statements, or engage in openly hostile behavior toward people of color. In any one of these examples, there is some misunderstanding of what racism is.

You might remember that several years ago a video went viral in which a busload of fraternity members at the University of Oklahoma was filmed chanting an extremely racist song. In the video, the fraternity brothers, using the N-word, were singing about lynching Black people, as if this were a joke. In the days following, some described the men's behavior as a "horrible cancer." Others defended the young men, saying their behavior was an aberration and that the young men were "good boys" and certainly "not racist." One of the young men even described himself by saying, "I never thought of myself as a racist. I never considered it a possibility" (ABC News 2015; Crockett 2015; Linshi 2015).

How can someone engage in such obviously racist behavior and yet continue to believe they are not a racist? You might even recall Donald Trump tweeting, "I don't have a Racist bone in my body!"—which he'd posted only shortly after saying that four women of color should "go back and help fix the totally broken and crime infested places from which they came."[1] All four of the women were elected members of the US House of Representatives. Three were natural-born US citizens and the fourth a naturalized citizen and refugee from Somalia. How can someone think they are not racist when their words and actions clearly indicate otherwise?

Clearly calling someone a *racist* is a highly charged accusation in the United States. Many people think of racism mostly as bigotry—that is, overt expressions of group hatred. We will learn otherwise in this chapter. Although racism can be (and often is) manifested in overt group hatred, that is not the only form it takes. You might hear it said that "Prejudiced people are not the only racists in America" (Wellman 1977). What does that mean? And, more recently, you might have heard the phrase *systemic racism*—a new way to think about racism in society. What do

---

[1] @realDonaldTrump, accessed October 14, 2020, https://twitter.com/realDonaldTrump/status/1151129 281134768128 and https://twitter.com/realDonaldTrump/status/1150381395078000643.

people mean when they talk about systemic racism? Maybe they're not being clear, or perhaps they only mean that there is a lot of racism in society. In this chapter you will learn what systemic racism does mean and how racism is actually different from individual statements of prejudice.

When you see White supremacist actions or hear horrible statements reflecting racism, you might conclude that racism is located mostly in the minds of "sick" individuals. Many people think of racism in terms of overt bigotry and prejudice, but prejudice and racism are not the same thing. *Prejudice* is about individual attitudes. *Racism*, by contrast, is built into society. Sometimes you can see racism through observing individual attitudes and actions, but racism can be present even when prejudice is not, as we will see. One way to understand this distinction is to ask yourself, *If prejudice were eliminated, would racism go away?* The answer is no. Racism is pervasive in society, and it is more than prejudice or bigoted attitudes, disturbing as those are. Understanding racism requires looking beyond individual attitudes and behaviors. Understanding the difference between prejudice and racism requires careful analysis of each. We start with prejudice.

The Social Dynamics of Prejudice

Framing Question: What is prejudice, and is it the same thing as racism?

The term *prejudice* stems from the ancient Latin term *praejudicium*, meaning "prejudgment."[2] Social psychologist Gordon Allport, whose research on prejudice is examined further below, defines **prejudice** as "an avertive or hostile attitude toward a person who belongs to a group simply because he belongs to that group and is therefore presumed to have the objectionable qualities ascribed to the group" (1954:7).

Prejudgment is central to the concept of prejudice. *Prejudice is an attitude*, and people who display this attitude prejudge others based on some presumed characteristic, such as race, ethnicity, gender, age, disability, or any other of a myriad of characteristics that can become the basis of prejudice. Prejudice is also presumably linked to discriminatory behavior, to be examined later. For now, keep in mind that prejudice is an attitude or way of thinking. Discrimination is behavior.

Defining Prejudice

There are several ideas about prejudice embedded in its definition:

- Prejudice is generally a *negative* or hostile attitude. People can express prejudice in a positive way, as in "Women are more nurturing than men," but most of the time, and in its most harmful form, prejudice disparages people based on their presumed group membership, such as saying, "All jocks are stupid."
- Prejudice rests on *generalizations*. That is, prejudice is directed at all members of a group just because they are perceived as belonging to that group. Seeing all Muslims as potential terrorists is an example.

---

[2] Note that *prejudice* is a noun and should be used accordingly. People often misstate the word, using its adjectival form (*prejudiced*) when the noun is appropriate. To illustrate, a person may have a *prejudiced* attitude but is exhibiting *prejudice*.

- Prejudice is about *perception*. That is, it concerns how people see other people. Perception, not reality, forms prejudiced attitudes. Because prejudice is about perception, it can also lead you to *not* see unique features of individuals. For example, the perception, based on prejudice, that Asian Americans are all "good at math" might lead you to overlook the artistic or literary contributions that Asian Americans make.
- Prejudice rests on *group stereotypes*. Stereotypes especially flourish when people have little information about the targets of prejudice. Little or minimal contact between different groups (such as in racially segregated schools) is known to exacerbate prejudice; however, contact between groups can also reduce prejudice (Maunder, Day, and White 2020).
- Prejudice is *false* and *ill informed*. The perceptions prejudice fosters are generally based on incorrect ideas or, at the very least, limited true information about people. Thinking all Latino immigrants are "Mexican" when they, in fact, come from many different nations is an example. Educating oneself about other group experiences is thus key to reducing prejudice.
- Prejudice is *learned*. Prejudice is not something that just "comes naturally." It is commonly learned in the family but can also be learned within peer groups and through the media. Researchers have found, as one example, that medical students who hear supervising physicians make racist jokes or other negative racial comments are later more likely to exhibit racial bias themselves (Burke et al. 2017). Because prejudice is learned, antiracist advocates also argue that it can be "unlearned."
- Prejudice is both *affective* (about emotion) and *cognitive* (about thinking). This means that prejudice is not only about misjudgments. It also triggers intense feelings (Forman 2004).

Prejudice emerges from how groups are positioned relative to one another in society (Blumer 1958). Racial and ethnic groups in the United States are positioned by economic and social inequality, as well as by differences in group power. In a context of racial inequality, some groups have more power than others. This can help you understand why some things that some people see as "just for fun" are actually quite offensive to others. Think of racially themed parties on college campuses or of White people appearing in blackface. Why isn't it as offensive if campus parties stereotype Italian mobsters or White businessmen? The answer is that ridiculing a racial group is especially insulting because there are not equivalencies in how different racial and ethnic groups are perceived and treated in society. There is simply not an equal playing field when it comes to racial inequality. Prejudice can target various groups, but it is particularly harmful when directed against those with less power relative to a dominant group. In other words, prejudice is more than a state of mind. It is deeply tied to a group's status in society (Bobo 1999 and 2006).

Studying Prejudice: Its Origins

The social scientific study of prejudice originated with social psychologist Theodor Adorno. Son of a German Jewish father and an Italian Catholic mother, Adorno left

Germany in the 1930s, fleeing persecution by the Nazis. He first went to Britain and then, in 1938, to the United States, returning to Germany following World War II. Adorno questioned how the human mind could allow people to commit atrocities such as the mass execution of Jewish people during the Holocaust. He found his answer in the study of prejudice.

Adorno thought prejudice originated in feelings of insecurity and threat, identifying what he called the **authoritarian personality** (Adorno et al. 1950). Adorno analyzed people with such personalities as having little tolerance for difference, holding rigid judgments about others, and being strict and highly obedient to authority. Adorno reached these conclusions after witnessing how many German people succumbed to Hitler's influence. Adorno concluded that people with authoritarian personalities are particularly prone to prejudice. His analysis of prejudice helps explain the personality characteristics of many highly bigoted people even today.

Social psychologist Gordon Allport took the study of prejudice in a slightly different direction. Unlike Adorno, who rooted prejudice in the workings of individual personalities, Allport emphasized the social context in which prejudice emerges. Allport's book *The Nature of Prejudice* (1954) remains an important analysis of the social dynamics of prejudice.

Allport developed the "lens model" to explain how prejudice targets particular individuals but emerges within a broad social and historical context. In Allport's model, prejudice starts from group conflict and progresses through various "lenses." As you can see in figure 2.1, prejudice originates in a historical and cultural context and then proceeds to the situational context. Prejudice is then conditioned by the personality of the observer and then targets someone in an immediate situation. The lens model shows that prejudice occurs in immediate situations but stems from broad historical forces that influence how groups and people see each other. Without understanding the broader context, we cannot understand the full social psychology of prejudice.

Allport also identified a continuum of prejudice, ranging from its most mild forms to its most extreme. At the mild extreme of this continuum is *speaking poorly of others*, what Allport called "antilocution." Antilocution is a relatively mild form of prejudice, according to Allport, although such things as racist jokes or insults

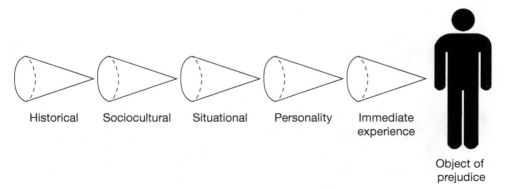

Historical   Sociocultural   Situational   Personality   Immediate experience

Object of prejudice

FIG. 2.1 Allport's Lens Model of Prejudice

Source: Adapted from Jones, Dovidio, and Vietze 2014.

toward people of color, even while seeming relatively mild, are nonetheless harmful to members of the targeted group.

The next point on Allport's continuum of prejudice is the *avoidance of other*, or what is now called **aversive racism**. Aversive racism occurs when someone, knowingly or not, avoids social contact with other racial-ethnic groups. There are countless examples, such as when a White person subtly—but surely—steps back when interacting with an Arab American or when White students do not select the one Latino or African American student in a class to join a study group. The tendency to avoid interracial contact is exacerbated by the segregation present in society, illustrating Allport's point that the broader social and historical context frames individual instances of prejudice.

Next along Allport's continuum of prejudice is **discrimination**—that is, treating people differently because of some presumed difference. Being slow to serve someone in a restaurant or not hiring someone for a job based on their race are both examples of discrimination. As we will see later, prejudice does not always result in discrimination, but, as this book will document, discrimination against racial-ethnic groups is pervasive in society.

Physical attack and *extermination* are at the extreme end of Allport's continuum of prejudice. Physical attack includes bodily attack as well as the destruction of property, such as lynchings, cross burnings, and the desecration of Jewish cemeteries. These forms of physical attack constitute **hate crime**, defined in law as criminal action taken against a person or property with the added element of bias

Many people associate segregation only with Black and White Americans, but the ugliness of racial segregation affects other groups too.

Source: Clark Brennan / Alamy Stock Photo.

(also see chapter 11). Under laws concerning hate crime, bias can be based on race, religion, disability, ethnic origin, or sexual orientation. Sadly, there are many recent examples of physical attack against people of color. Dylann Roof, a twenty-one-year-old White male, slaughtered nine Black parishioners at the Emanuel African Methodist Episcopal Church in Charleston, South Carolina, in 2015. Patrick Crusius, another avowed White supremacist, slaughtered twenty-three people, most of them Latinos, after marching into a Walmart in El Paso, Texas, in 2019. Crusius, a twenty-one-year-old White man, had posted an anti-immigrant manifesto referring to a "Hispanic invasion of Texas" and fearing "cultural and ethnic replacement" (Kennedy 2020). Dylann Roof was subsequently convicted of hate crime and sentenced to death; Patrick Crusius was indicted for several counts of capital murder and awaits trial.

Genocide is the most extreme form of prejudice along Allport's continuum. There are far too many tragic examples of genocide in the world, including in the United States: the mass execution of Jewish people and other minority groups during the Nazi Holocaust; the slaughter by ISIS extremists of Yazidis, a religious minority in Syria and Iraq; the mass murder of civilians in Aleppo, Syria, by Syrian troops loyal to President Bashar al-Assad; the extermination of so many Native Americans by European and White settlers in the United States. Genocide is an international crime, defined by the United Nations in the aftermath of World War II as the "intent to destroy, in whole or part, a national, ethnical [*sic*], racial or religious group" (United Nations 1948:174). There is no shortage of examples of genocide grounded in prejudice, whether that prejudice is based on race, religion, gender, homophobia, or other forms of group hatred.

The Correlates and Consequences of Prejudice

Framing Question: What are some of the ways prejudice is expressed, and what can be done to reduce it?

You can probably think of dozens, if not hundreds, of examples of prejudice and the various groups that experience the pain of prejudice. Gay men, lesbians, racial and ethnic minority groups, women, religious minorities, disabled people, older people, and countless other groups are all subjected to the harms of prejudice. Anti-Semitism is one form of prejudice that defines Jewish people as inferior and has been used to discriminate against them.

Is prejudice an inevitable feature of social life? Perhaps **ethnocentrism**—that is, the belief that one's group is superior to all others—is inevitable because people typically see others through the eyes of their own group experience. Ethnocentrism does not always produce prejudice, however. For example, you might favor your own family traditions over those of your in-laws. But when ethnocentrism involves negative judgments about others, prejudice occurs.

No one is free of prejudice, but certain social facts predict the likelihood someone will be prejudiced. People with more education are far less likely to openly express prejudiced attitudes than are those with less education (Kuppens and Spears 2014). Those who hold fundamentalist religious beliefs are also more likely to be racially prejudiced (Brandt and Reyna 2014). Older people are more likely than younger people to express prejudice (Franssen, Dhont, and Van Hiel 2013). Prejudice emerges in a social context, so it is not surprising that it is more common in some groups than in others.

Racial prejudice is also associated with a variety of other attitudes. Scholars have found that racial prejudice is, for example, strongly associated with support for the display of Confederate symbols (Strother, Piston, and Ogorzalek 2017). Does this mean that anyone who has Southern pride is a racist or holds prejudiced ideas? No; that would itself be a prejudiced idea. Still, the association between support for Confederate symbols and racial prejudice shows how prejudice influences attitudes not only toward other people but on a variety of current social issues as well.

Despite its tenacious hold, prejudice can be reduced. Years of research have shown that contact between groups can reduce racial prejudice (Pettigrew et al. 2011). This is particularly the case when young children interact in noncompetitive environments (Irizarry 2013). Having a romantic relationship with someone outside your own group also tends to reduce prejudice (Orta 2013). And studies have found that prejudice against African Americans is reduced when people have biracial friends (Levy et al. 2019). When people know more about each other, they are less likely to believe the misinformation about others on which prejudice relies.

The Harm of Stereotypes

The power of prejudice relies on stereotypes. It seems almost inevitable that people will categorize others: You meet someone for the first time and almost instantaneously categorize them, probably based at first on race and gender and possibly also on age and social class. These are some of the first salient features that people notice (Andersen and Taylor 2020).

A **stereotype** is an oversimplified set of beliefs about the members of a social group. Stereotypes assign characteristics to people who are presumed to be a part of a group. Numerous examples of stereotypes came to light during Donald Trump's presidency, such as his reference to Mexican immigrants as criminals and rapists, a gross stereotype that completely contradicts the well-documented fact that Mexican immigrants are actually *less likely* to commit crimes than are native-born citizens (see chapter 11).

Stereotypes are not always blatant, harmful, or accusatory. Stereotypes can be positive or possibly even neutral, such as the stereotype that all Norwegians are blond. Negative stereotypes are the ones that are quite harmful, regardless of the group they target. Virtually every racial and ethnic minority group throughout US history has been subject to demeaning and insulting stereotypes. The Irish have been stereotyped as hotheaded drunks, Italians as Mafia members, Mexican American women as hypersexual. African Americans are stereotyped as lazy, aggressive, and dependent on welfare. White working-class people are stereotyped as ignorant and as the most prejudiced people in America. Name a group, and you can probably immediately imagine some of the stereotypes that have been negatively associated with it.

Stereotypes permeate everyday life, especially in popular culture and the media (see chapter 3). Although some people believe that stereotypes are harmless, stereotypes actually have damaging consequences. An Asian student who possesses only average math skills may feel extra pressure to do well; the blonde who is very smart

LIVING WITH RACISM

From the moment my comrades in the military discovered I was an Indian, I was treated differently. My name disappeared. I was no longer Suina, Joseph, or Joe. Suddenly I was Chief, Indian, or Tonto. Occasionally I was referred to as Geronimo, Crazy Horse, or some other well-known warrior from the past. It was almost always with an affection that develops in a family, but clearly I was seen in the light of stereotypes that my fellow Marines from around the country had about Native Americans.

Sources: Suina 1992:20–21, in Strom 2013:16.

may be overly sensitive to how others view her, regardless of her academic ability; African Americans may take extra effort to be neat in public spaces because of the stereotype that they are dirty. Each of these examples shows how stereotypes negatively impact a person's self-confidence, levels of stress, academic performance, and general well-being. Above, the "Living with Racism" feature offers another example of what it's like to live with the burden of stereotypes.

Recent studies show the invisible yet consequential results of group stereotyping. Research by psychologist Claude Steele shows that people are very attuned to stereotypes about their own group. Stereotypes in a given situation can pose threats to a person's identity, leading them to distrust their surroundings. A number of social responses can result—perhaps withdrawal, anger, or depression. People know the stereotypes associated with their group identities and respond accordingly (Purdie-Vaughns et al. 2008).

Steele and his colleagues have identified **stereotype threat** as a situation in which a person feels the risk that their own behavior will confirm stereotypes others have about them. Steele's research on stereotype threat, done in laboratory settings, shows that invoking a racial stereotype can actually cause a test taker to perform more poorly than if no stereotype is present (Steele 2010; Steele and Aronson 1995).

Here is how Steele discovered this. Research subjects (Black and White) were told in a series of laboratory experiments that they were about to undergo a genuine test of their verbal abilities and limitations, thus invoking a stereotype for Black research subjects that they are less intelligent. In another set of tests, research subjects were told they should try hard but that the test would not evaluate their ability. Members of a third group were told they should take the challenge seriously even though the examiners were not going to evaluate their ability (Steele 2010; Steele and Aronson 1995). Only in the first case was a stereotype present for the Black test takers; that is, they experienced stereotype threat.

Steele and his colleagues consistently found that Black and White test scores differed, and significantly so, *only* when the threat of the stereotype existed—that Black students are less intelligent. Black test takers, aware they are perceived as less smart than White students, actually performed less well when the stereotype was invoked. Without the presence of stereotype threat, as in the second two conditions, Black and White test takers performed equally well.

This result has been tested in other experiments with similar results: feeling stereotype threat actually *lessens* African American student performance. Furthermore, this finding has been shown to occur for other groups, such as when women are aware of the stereotype that they are supposedly not as good at math as men (Casad, Petzel, and Ingalls 2019). Likewise, Mexican American students, whether immigrant or not, do less well when faced with the stereotype that Mexican immigrants have little command of English (Guyll et al. 2010). Researchers have also found stereotype threat to influence health care disparities for LGBTQ people (Fingerhut and Abdou 2017).

Most research on stereotype threat has been done in controlled experiments in a laboratory setting. You can probably imagine other real-life scenarios where stereotype threat produces apprehension and thus inhibits a person's behavior. Imagine a Latina student whose professor makes a comment in class that stereotypes Latinas. Might her test performance be affected? Flipping this example, if students communicate that Asian faculty members do not speak English clearly or that African American faculty members are not as authoritative as White male faculty (Gutiérrez y Muhs et al. 2012), might the mere presence of this stereotype shape how well a faculty member performs in class? Even seemingly innocuous comments and subtle expressions of stereotypes, sometimes made through no particular ill will, affect the behavior of people who are keenly aware of stereotypes about their group. Research finds, for example, that Latino students with a strong sense of their heritage believe that other students see them through the lens of stereotypes; this threat makes Latinos likely to change their behavior in the presence of non-Latinos (Erba 2018).

Implicit Bias

Research shows that social behavior is deeply affected by prejudice and stereotyping, even when not consciously intended. **Implicit bias** is the preference people may have for particular groups and the negative associations they hold, *even when they may not be aware of them* (Eberhardt 2019; Jones, Dovidio, and Vietze 2014). Implicit bias is guided by unconscious yet erroneous beliefs about particular racial-ethnic groups.

Implicit bias has been demonstrated through the Implicit Association Test (Greenwald, McGhee, and Schwartz 1998). The test, to be taken by individuals on a computer, has people quickly associate positive and negative qualities with rapidly shown images of different people who are presumably identifiable by their race. Bias is shown by the frequency with which people associate negative characteristics with people of color. This cleverly designed experimental test can reveal the implicit (or unconscious) biases that people may hold. The purpose of the test is not only to discover the underlying bias but also to make people more aware of their biases so that they can work harder to overcome them—or to at least make them less salient in interactions with others. Implicit bias, for example, has been used to train police to not so quickly associate Black men with criminality (Eberhardt 2019).

There is now a large body of research documenting the implicit biases that people hold against various groups: racial minorities, immigrants, LGBTQ people, disabled people, and even older people (Archambault et al. 2008; Blinder and Lundgren 2019; Harder, Keller, and Chopik 2019; Melamed et al. 2019). Implicit bias has been shown to influence how people view even very young children: Black children tend to be seen as both older and less innocent than White children; young

Black children are even seen as less "childlike" than are young White children (Goff et al. 2014).

It is through implicit bias that our culture leaves an invisible imprint in our minds. Although prejudice is usually assessed in attitudinal surveys that measure expressed beliefs, research on implicit bias shows that just beneath the surface lie judgments and associations that are triggered even when we might not realize it.

Everyone holds implicit biases. Regardless of our own racial, ethnic, or gender backgrounds, studies find that implicit bias continues to influence how we perceive one another. Implicit bias has also been linked to critical behaviors: It can cause physicians to minimize the seriousness of disease found in people of color or keep medical practitioners from referring critically ill Black patients to specialists (Stepanikova 2012). Implicit bias is also triggered when police officers encounter Black men with, all too often, deadly results (Eberhardt 2019).

The Prejudice-Discrimination Link

Framing Question: Does prejudice cause discrimination?

Most people assume that prejudice causes discrimination. Does it? Obviously the two are interconnected. Recall that prejudice is an attitude, while discrimination is a behavior. Early work by sociologist Robert Merton (1949) shows there is not necessarily a causal relationship between prejudice and discrimination. Important as prejudice is to shaping our behavior, it is not the only way to explain racial discrimination.

To demonstrate this concept, Merton developed a typology—a simple of way of showing different possible combinations of the presence or absence of prejudice and discrimination. He showed four possible outcomes (see table 2.1):

1. Both prejudice and discrimination are present (case 1).
2. Prejudice is present, but discrimination is not (case 2).
3. Prejudice is not present, but discrimination occurs (case 3).
4. Neither prejudice nor discrimination occurs (case 4).

TABLE 2.1 Prejudice and Discrimination: How Are They Related?

	Prejudice	
	+	**−**
Discrimination +	Case 1. + + bigot	Case 3. − + nonprejudiced, discriminator
−	Case 2. + − prejudiced, nondiscriminator	Case 4. − − "all-weather liberal"

What situations result for each of these scenarios? In case 1, someone is prejudiced and engages in discriminatory behavior. This is the classic bigot, someone whose views are overtly expressed and whose actions reflect prejudiced attitudes. In this case, prejudice and the resulting discriminatory behaviors are overt, intentional, and hostile—and directly linked.

Cases 2 and 3, however, show us that prejudice and discrimination are not necessarily directly linked. In case 2, someone who is prejudiced does not discriminate—perhaps because laws prohibit discrimination. Imagine a bigoted employer whose company rewards bosses who employ a diverse workforce. The boss may dislike Asian and Latino workers but will hire them anyway—and may even reap a reward in pay. In such a case, prejudice is present, but discrimination does not occur—unless, of course, the boss pays Asian and Latino workers less or treats them less well than other employees.

In case 3, one may not be prejudiced but still discriminate. Think of parents who seemingly hold no racial prejudice but who send their children to all-White private schools to "get the best education." Even with the best of intentions, in making such a choice parents reproduce the discrimination that produces educational segregation (see chapter 9).

Case 4 represents the person Merton called the "all-weather liberal." This person may not hold overtly prejudiced views and may not overtly discriminate. This is someone we would now call a *color-blind racist*. A color-blind racist can benefit from racial inequality but be largely unaware of this advantage and hold no overtly prejudicial attitudes. Such a person may hold no overt prejudice and does not consciously discriminate against others, yet does little to challenge racism in society. *Color-blind racism*, explored further later in this chapter, shows that even without overt prejudice and discrimination, racial inequality can—and does—persist (Burke 2019).

Polling for Prejudice: Have Attitudes Changed?

Framing Question: How have racial attitudes changed, and how do they vary among different groups?

Not that long ago, people believed that the overt expression of racial prejudice was declining and that the United States was becoming more racially tolerant. Recent history has shown those assumptions to be wrong. White supremacist actions have captured public attention, and the disparagement of immigrants and people of color has been heard from even the highest office in the land.

Still, most people now consider it inappropriate to express prejudice openly (Picca and Feagin 2007). Racial attitudes have changed, and, as a result, survey researchers no longer ask the same questions they used earlier to measure racial prejudice. For example, in 1942, survey researchers asked the public if they supported racially segregated schools. Fully 68 percent of White Americans said yes, compared with only 7 percent who said so by 1985. Researchers no longer ask the same question today. Instead, they ask whether the public sees racial segregation in US public schools as a serious problem. Now only half of White Americans say yes, compared to 68 percent of Black Americans and 65 percent of Hispanics (McCarthy 2019b).

Likewise, so many Americans now support the ideal of equal treatment that pollsters no longer ask whether people support the principle of equal opportunity.

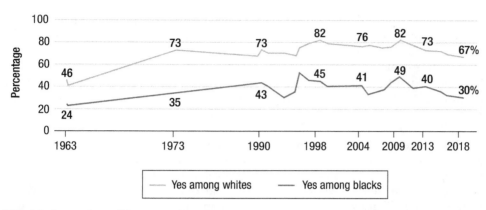

FIG. 2.2 Perceptions of Equal Job Opportunities

Source: Saad 2019.

Instead, they ask about people's perceptions of discrimination—whether race relations have improved and how satisfied people are with the treatment of different groups. Both Black and White Americans now have a less optimistic view of equal opportunity compared to just a few years ago (see figure 2.2.). Black Americans are far less likely, however, than White Americans to perceive equal job opportunities. This survey did not include Hispanics or Asians in the research sample, nor did it ask about their opportunities. Overall, perceptions that there is racial equality have, in 2020, reached an all-time low (Brenan 2020).

Although people seem, in general, to have accepted racial equality as an ideal, there are huge gaps in the extent to which White, Black, Hispanic, and Asian people perceive the persistence of racial discrimination. As figure 2.3 shows, White

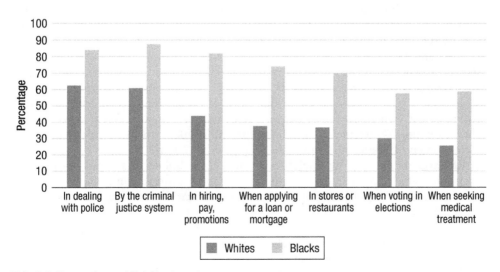

FIG. 2.3 Perceptions of Fair Treatment

Source: Horowitz, Brown, and Cox 2019.

Americans are far less likely than other groups to think that Black Americans are treated unfairly in their dealings with police; in hiring, pay, and promotions; when voting; and in other aspects of day-to-day life.

Change is also apparent, to some extent, in young people's racial attitudes. A huge majority of young people (72 percent) now say there is a lot of discrimination against Black people, Muslims, women, and transgender, gay, and lesbian people. Further, young people perceive these forms of discrimination as rising (Vandermaas-Peeler et al. 2018).

Like adults, however, young people's views on race relations vary by race, ethnicity, and gender. Eight in ten young Black Americans see race as an issue that affects them personally, compared to 55 percent of young Asian and Pacific Islanders, 53 percent of young Hispanics, and only 37 percent of young White people. Young White women (46 percent) are much more likely than young White men (29 percent) to say that race relations are a critical concern to them personally (Vandermaas-Peeler et al. 2018).

All told, it's clear that racial attitudes change over time but not always for the better. Also, large differences remain in how different groups see and understand race relations in America. We cannot assume that attitudinal change is always for the better. There is not necessarily positive change in racial attitudes. Quite the contrary—racial attitudes shift with the political and social developments of the time. Over half of White Americans and nearly three-quarters of Black Americans now say that race relations in the United States are generally bad, even after people had been more upbeat about this from about 2000 through 2013. Since about 2014, though, public opinion about the state of race relations has fallen to new lows, spurred most likely by the high-profile killings of Black citizens by police officers. Similar numbers of Americans believe that Donald Trump has made race relations worse (Horowitz et al. 2019; Saad 2020).

Public opinion polls also show a rise in what is called **racial resentment**—the belief among White people that people of color are somehow getting something for nothing or receiving special benefits based on race. Racial resentment includes the idea that White people, not people of color, are the aggrieved group (see figure 2.4). This sentiment is reflected in the attitude expressed by over half of White Americans who think we pay too much attention to race. Hispanic, Black, and Asian Americans are far less likely to believe this (see figure 2.5). Young people are not immune to these feelings; about one-third of young White people say discrimination against White people is as serious as discrimination against minority groups, although young White men (43 percent) are more likely to think this than young White women (29 percent; Vandermaas-Peeler et al. 2018).

Researchers have shown racial resentment to be linked to a variety of political beliefs and behaviors, including support for harsh anti-immigrant policies and punitive criminal justice policies; political party identification; and support for Donald Trump (Bobo 2018).

Ironically, racial resentment is rising even as White people on the whole continue to have higher incomes, higher levels of educational attainment, greater wealth, and lower unemployment than other groups—evidence of which you will see throughout this book. Racial resentment helps us, though, explain the *racial backlash* of recent years. Historian Carol Anderson has also documented that White hostility—*White rage*, as she calls it—typically follows periods of time when there

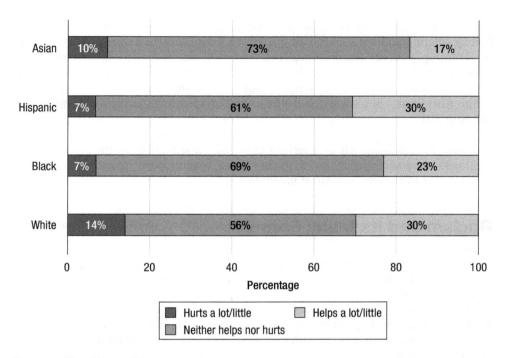

FIG. 2.4 How Different Groups See White Advantage

Source: Horowitz et al. 2019.

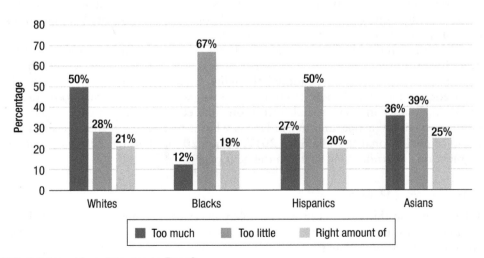

FIG. 2.5 How Much Attention to Race?

Source: Horowitz et al. 2019.

has actually been some Black advancement, such as following the presidency of Barack Obama and the subsequent growth of White supremacist movement during the Trump presidency (Anderson 2016). Anderson shows that we have seen similar responses to Black achievement before, such as during the Reconstruction period following the Civil War. Other scholars have also found that racial hostility among White Americans rises when the White unemployment rate increases (Jayadev and Johnson 2017).

Findings such as these indicate that racial perceptions are not mere attitudes, somehow free-floating without serious cause or consequence. To the contrary, perceptions—even when contrary to facts—are a potent force in society, especially when linked to the nation's racial inequalities.

Racism and Its Many Forms

Framing Question: What is systemic racism, and what different forms does it take?

The rise of overt racism in recent years in the United States has surprised many who thought the nation was becoming less racially hostile. Overt racist expression is, however, not the only form of racism. In fact, focusing solely on overtly racist behavior misses other ways racism is present in society. **Systemic racism** refers to the broad sweep of ideology, attitudes, emotions, habits, and behaviors situated within social institutions that support **White supremacy**—that is, the domination of White people over others (Feagin 2006). Systemic racism is more about power, income and wealth inequality, and other institutionally based injustices than it is about attitudes and ideas. The concept of systemic racism tells us that racism is built into the very structure of US social institutions.

Systemic racism is, then, far more than individual attitudes. Systemic racism is deeply rooted in society, not just in people's minds. Further, systemic racism has structured the foundation of US institutions. Systemic racism is not always obvious, especially to dominant groups, but it is present.

Racism seen in this light is a more collective or institutional phenomenon than prejudice. Certainly racism is manifested in people's thoughts and actions, but it need not be motivated by irrational thoughts. Systemic racism may not even be apparent to those who benefit from it. As we will see throughout this book, racism shapes inequality in every social institution—the economy, health care, education, families, criminal justice, and more. This is what it means to say that racism is systemic or institutional (Bonilla-Silva 2017; Feagin 2010a; Forman 2004; also see the segment on "Learning Our Past" on the next page).

Racism and Power

When you stop thinking about racism solely in terms of prejudice and start thinking about it as an institutional phenomenon, your view of racism changes. Racism emerges not out of people's attitudes but from what noted historian George Fredrickson calls "overtly racist regimes" (Fredrickson 2002:100). Fredrickson's observation points to an important element of racism—namely, that racism emerges only in societies where there is a racialized system of power. As Fredrickson points out, however, racism is structured into society's institutions, making it more difficult to identify and more difficult to change.

LEARNING OUR PAST

You can learn a lot about how ideas about race have shaped US history by looking at what some of our revered national leaders have said:

I am not, nor ever have been, in favor of bringing about in any way the social and political equality of the white and black races. . . . I will say in addition to this that there is a physical difference between the white and black races which I believe will forever forbid the two races living together on terms of social and political equality. And inasmuch as they cannot so live, while they do remain together there must be a position of superior and inferior, and I as much as any other man am in favor of having the superior position assigned to the white race.

—Abraham Lincoln (1858)

The Number of purely white People in the World is proportionately very small. All Africa is black or tawny. Asia chiefly tawny. America (exclusive of the new Comers) wholly so. And in Europe, the Spaniards, Italians, French, Russians and Swedes, are generally of what we call a swarthy Complexion; as are the Germans also, the Saxons only excepted, who with the English, make the principle Body of White People in the Face of the Earth. I could wish their Numbers were increased. . . . Why increase the Sons of Africa, by Planting them in America, where we have so fair an Opportunity, by excluding all Blacks and Tawneys, of increasing the lovely White and Red? But perhaps I am partial to the Complexion of my Country, for such Kind of Partiality is natural to Mankind.

—Benjamin Franklin (1751)

Racism is both a belief system and a social structure. As an ideology, it rests on the idea that a group is inferior because of some presumed cultural, biological, or other differences. As a social structure, **racism** means that groups defined as races are oppressed, controlled, and exploited socially, economically, politically, culturally, and psychologically by a dominant group (adapted from Wilson 1973:32). Racism is expressed in the "practices, institutions, and structures that a sense of deep difference justifies or validates" (Fredrickson 2002:4). In other words, the ideology of racism wrongly attempts to justify structured inequality that is based on presumed racial difference.

This definition of racism includes the following elements:

* Racism is *located in social institutions*, not just individual minds or attitudes.
* Racism is *not just fixed in people's minds*, although it may be manifested there. Restricting awareness of racism to individual bigotry misses the many ways racism works.
* Racism emerges because of relationships of *domination and subordination*. This means that racism is about exploitation, not just people's beliefs, although surely those beliefs buttress any system of racial inequality.
* Racism is *a principle of oppression that defends the advantages Whites have* because of the subordination of racial minorities (Wellman 1977). In the United States, this makes *White privilege* central to any discussion of racism.

- Racism is not just a holdover from the past. The past matters, but racism is *dynamic, and it changes with changes in society*. Our understanding of racism, therefore, has to change with the times.
- Racism continues to be *sanctioned through dominant cultural beliefs*. The United States has been founded on principles of individualism and equality, but those same ideals, when coupled with racism, produce beliefs that when people fail it is somehow their own fault. Such beliefs fall especially hard on poor people of color.
- Because racism is a *system of domination and subordination*, social, economic, political, and cultural opportunities are differentially distributed in society.
- *Racism intersects with other forms of inequality*, including gender, social class, age, nationality, sexuality, and other social identities. This means that not all people of color are equally disadvantaged. Highly successful Latinas and African Americans, for example, may even exceed the class status of some White Americans—a fact that can ignite racial resentment. Because of the intersectionality of multiple social factors, racial experiences are manifested differently.
- Racism develops in a *global context* (Chang 2010). The hierarchy of power from which racism has developed is a worldwide system of economic exploitation. The United States has a unique system of racism, but it is part of a system of global inequality.

Some say that racism is prejudice plus power, but this is too simple a formulation. Racism is not just the summation of many attitudes with power thrown in. Racism is a system of power, but saying racism is power plus prejudice makes racism seem like a system of attitudes when it is more than that. Racism is a principle of social domination that has been the very foundation for social institutions in the United States—ever since chattel slavery came to the nation's shores (see chapter 5). Although first established to justify the exploitation of Black labor and then used to justify formalized racial segregation, racism persists in the patterns of racial inequality that remain with us today. If we restrict our understanding of racism to prejudice, even with power thrown in, we miss the institutional forces that continue to influence racial inequality.

When we conceptualize racism as an institutional, not an attitudinal, phenomenon, we understand it as an **ideology**—that is, a whole constellation of beliefs developed to support a particular set of social, economic, political, and cultural relationships. Racial ideologies purport to justify the status quo, thereby enabling White supremacy. Racial ideology can change over time, but its purpose is always to justify and defend the status quo. The form and shape of racism as an ideology can change as the particulars of racial domination change. This is because racism is deeply linked to social institutions and institutional power.

Institutional racism refers to patterns of racial advantage and disadvantage. Eliminating racism is not just a matter of finding individuals who harbor racist views and changing their minds. Rather, changing institutional racism means transforming social practices and policies to address underlying institutional patterns that perpetuate racial inequality. The difference in thinking about racial inequality from a prejudice versus a racism framework is summarized in table 2.2.

TABLE 2.2 **Prejudice versus Racism Framework**

	Prejudice Framework	**Racism Framework**
Level of manifestation:	Individual	Institutional
How it is manifested:	Overtly, explicitly	Sometimes overtly, but also covertly
Where it is located:	Within people's minds (conscious)	Endemic in society, culturally sanctioned, embedded in social practices and policies
Cause of the problem:	Misinformation, individual attitudes	Legitimacy in social institutions, defense of White privilege and advantage
Solution to the problem:	Change attitudes, isolate bad people, eliminate bias, build tolerance	Transform social policies and social institutions

Laissez-Faire Racism

Racism is not always overt and obvious—at least, not to those who benefit most from it. New forms of racism emerge as social conditions change. One such change, as we have seen, is the fact that many White people no longer believe that race matters much, even though race shapes just about every aspect of people's lives in the United States. Half of White Americans now think we pay too much attention to race, as you saw in figure 2.4—strong evidence of laissez-faire racism.

Laissez faire, loosely translated from French, means, quite simply, "hands-off." **Laissez-faire racism** thus refers to the tendency of White people to "downplay, ignore, and minimize" the effects of racism (Bobo 2004:17). Laissez-faire racism is only minimally overt, but it is based on the idea that antiracist policies are no longer needed (thus "hands-off").

Laissez-faire racism has three key components:

1. persistent negative stereotyping of people of color
2. blaming people of color, especially African Americans, for the racial gap in socioeconomic status
3. resisting race-specific policies to ameliorate racial differences in status (Bobo 2004)

Laissez-faire racism is apparent when you hear someone say, "I don't dislike Black people (or Latinos or immigrants or any number of other groups), but I think we should get over this obsession with race." Or perhaps "I just think people should work hard if they want to make it." Such commonly expressed sentiments presume that anyone who works hard enough in America can succeed and that people who fail just did not work hard enough. This attitude, indeed, lies at the core of the American Dream: that with hard work and the right values, anyone can move from rags to riches. Laissez-faire racism creates a strong tendency to blame the existence of racial inequalities on the cultural values of less fortunate people.

Laissez-faire racism is anchored in several beliefs, including the belief that

- the United States is a **meritocracy**, where people rise according to their efforts
- people should not notice race
- any patterns of racial inequality persisting today are the result of cultural deficiencies or poor values held by the disadvantaged
- nothing systemic needs to be done to ameliorate the problem—also referred to as *racial apathy* (Forman 2004:45)

Laissez-faire racism has become a dominant lens through which many people, especially White people, view the state of race relations today. When more obvious forms of overt racism fade, it can be more difficult for those not disadvantaged by race to see the continuing significance of race. Further, in a society that values the idea of a color blindness, it is easy for people to not want race to matter even when it does. Color blindness is thus a new form of racial thinking.

"Gee, I Never Think of You as . . .": Color-Blind Racism

The waning of Jim Crow segregation and the increased visibility of people of color in positions of power and influence have led some to think the United States is becoming a "postracial" society (Pettigrew 2009). A greater acceptance of mixed-race couples, dramatic changes in the racial and ethnic populations of the nation, the removal of overt barriers to the advancement of people of color, and other significant social changes might make you think we have somehow moved "beyond race." Color-blind racism, then, might make you think that whatever racial inequities still exist must be the result of something besides racism.

Color-blind racism is the idea that it is best to just ignore race and to look at people as if they are all alike. According to this view, if people would only overlook race and not see "difference," then the effects of racism would just vanish (Andersen and Taylor 2020). Color-blind racism might be manifested by someone saying, "I don't think it's about race anymore; it's all about class." While well intended, such a statement deflects attention from how race actually intersects with social class in shaping people's life chances. Class matters, but race continues to matter as well, and ignoring that fact reproduces color-blind racism.

Color-blind racism, even when anchored in a desire for a more racially just society, is problematic for many reasons. To start with, if you are a woman, how would you feel if someone said to you, "Gee, I never think of you as a woman"? If you are a man, would you be insulted if someone said, "Gee, I never think of you as a man"? This is precisely what happens to people of color on a routine basis.

Denying that race matters—or saying that racism is about something else—vanishes the significance of race in people's experiences and also their identities. Among other things, despite the importance of class and its entanglement with race, race still matters, and it matters a lot in shaping people's life chances (West 1994). When White people speak from a position of racial privilege and deny how race still matters, they are rebuffing the very real, lived experience of those who do not experience racial privilege. This can make the experiences of people of color seem irrelevant or insignificant.

Color-blind racism is the denial, usually by people in the dominant group, that racism exists. Color-blind racism minimizes the significance of racism in both the lives of people of color *and* how society continues to be organized around racial inequality (Burke 2019). Through the lens of color-blind racism, someone might say, "People are all alike," leading to another conclusion—sometimes implicit, sometimes explicit—that if racial inequality is still present, it must be the result of some character flaw that people fail.

Unlike prejudice, color-blind racism is seldom overt. In fact, people who express color-blind racism are likely to think of themselves as well-meaning people, and they may be. Color-blind racism appears not to be about race when, in fact, it is actually all about race. Eduardo Bonilla-Silva calls it "racism without racists," because no one appears to be outwardly racist. Color-blind racism instead is "subtle, institutional, and apparently non-racial" (Bonilla-Silva 2017:3). Color-blind racism is also manifested in behavior, not just attitudes. Covert behaviors, such as ignoring when a person of color speaks in a meeting or classroom, reflect color-blind racism. Uprooting racism is then less about ferreting out racists than about transforming commonplace behaviors as well as social policies.

Color-blind racism is also particularly slippery because White people might think they are being nonracist by participating in Black culture. Charles Gallagher (2003) argues that, while White people might seem to be accepting the culture of people of color when they engage in hip-hop, wear fashion that emerges from the culture of people of color, or speak the lingo of various minority cultures, in actuality these behaviors do not challenge racism. This commodification of culture disregards the racial hierarchies from which the cultures emerged and bestows further privilege on the White people who consume them. Thus one can appear trendy by consuming Black culture even while never challenging the racial status quo.

The problem with color-blind racism is that it very easily slips into blaming people of color for their own predicament. If racial inequality is not about race, what do people think it is about? By ignoring race, color-blind racism shifts responsibility for racial inequality onto those most likely to suffer from it—those who have the least power and privilege in society.

Color-blind racism is powerful in part because it rests on an important value in US society: that all people are created equal. Of course, as prophetically spoken by the Reverend Martin Luther King Jr., we want to live in a society where people are not judged by the color of their skin but instead by the content of their character (1963). That value, however, does not have to mean disregarding race. The United States is most decidedly not a color-blind society. Even a glance at contemporary events—the resurgence of White supremacist actions; racist incidents on college campuses; persistent poverty among Latinos, Native, and African Americans; the racial achievement gap in education; and more—indicates that race still matters. As long as we blame people of color for their own predicament, we will not be able to understand why racial inequality persists. Of course, there are highly visible and successful people of color and their achievements are noteworthy, but is their success the product of a truly color-blind society? The evidence screams no, as subsequent chapters of this book will document.

"We're a colourblind company here, Johnson.
To us you are black and invisible."

Source: CartoonStock Ltd. / Joseph Rank.

Conclusion

The many forms that racism takes in the United States show how much we have yet to learn about how and why race matters. The good news is that, as this chapter shows, racism is not a fixed thing. As it has evolved along with changes in the racial social structure, people's minds have changed too. But social institutions are obstinate, and changing institutions requires more than changing people's minds. Scholar Ibram X. Kendi reminds us that overcoming racism does not mean being "nonracist"; it means becoming antiracist (2019:9). Change can come as more people challenge old ways of thinking about racism and confront the new ways racism appears today. In the following chapter, we examine how popular culture and the media shape how we think about race.

Key Terms

authoritarian personality 29

aversive racism 30

color-blind racism 44

discrimination 30

ethnocentrism 31

genocide 31

hate crime 30

ideology 42

implicit bias 34

institutional racism 42

laissez-faire racism 43

meritocracy 44

prejudice 27

racial resentment 38

racism 26

stereotype 32

stereotype threat 33

systemic racism 40

White supremacy 40

Critical-Thinking Questions

1. Based on your reading of this chapter, explain this statement: "Prejudiced people are not the only racists in America" (Wellman 1977:1).
2. What has influenced the attitudes of African American and White people over time? What explains the differences you see between the two groups?

Student Exercises

2.1. Do a small research study in which you ask different people the same question that was asked in the national poll shown on page 39 (figure 2.5): "Do you think there is too much, too little, or the right amount of attention paid to race and racial issues in our country these days?" Be sure to ask the question in these exact words in order to compare your results to the national sample represented in the chart. If you can, include people from the different groups found in the national sample. What are your results? How do your results compare to the national results? What explanations would you give for what you found?

2.2. Take the Implicit Association Test at https://implicit.harvard.edu/implicit/takea test.html. What results did you get, and what does this teach you about any implicit biases you may have toward a particular group? Do you think this test is an accurate assessment of your attitudes? If so, why? If not, why not?

Challenging Questions/Open to Debate

Hate speech is "speech that offends, threatens, or insults groups, based on race, color, religion, national origin, sexual orientation, disability, or other traits" (American Bar Association 2000). Imagine a scenario where an overtly racist speaker is scheduled to speak on a college campus.

- What would you do if you were the college president?
- Should the speaker be allowed to speak, given the constitutional right to free speech, or should the speech not be allowed, given penalties under law for hate crimes?

TAKING ACTION AGAINST RACISM

Responding to Racism

When you hear a prejudiced or racist comment, what should you do? We've all experienced this situation but are often uncertain how best to respond. If you say nothing, you may be colluding with racist thinking. Letting such comments go unchallenged is one way that prejudice and racism are perpetuated. Yet calling someone a racist, especially to their face, is not likely to be an effective strategy to reducing racism. What can you do?

It can be very awkward to respond—possibly even dangerous, depending on the situation and who you are. But there are ways to make a difference when confronted with hate speech. Sometimes, but depending on the context, saying something right away is the best thing to do, difficult as it may be. In public settings or if your tone is highly accusatory, it might make the person who made the comment only become defensive—in which case no good will come of the confrontation. Perhaps you could instead talk with the person later, in a more private setting, saying something like this: "When we were [in place], you said [racist comment]. I found this to be a very prejudiced [or racist] statement. Have you thought about how it would make [the person about whom the comment was made] feel to hear that? It made me feel [fill in the blank], and I would like you to not make such statements."

The purpose of this type of confrontation of racist comments is to help the person using such speech to develop greater empathy. Your intervention might not stop them from making racist comments in the future, but perhaps they will not make them in your presence anymore. You could also intervene by saying, "I understand why you might think that; we're all influenced by racism in society. But have you ever considered where these ideas come from and how they might make someone of that race feel?"

Resources:

- Australian Human Rights Commission, https://itstopswithme.humanrights.gov.au/learn-about-racism/respond-racism
- Ibram X. Kendi, *How to be an Antiracist* (New York: One World, 2019)

Source: Richard Levine / Alamy Stock Photo; Newscast Online Limited / Alamy Stock Photo

CHAPTER 3

Representing Race

Popular Culture and the Media

The esteem with which we regard the multiple cultures offered in our country enhances our possibilities for healthy survival and continued social development.
—Attributed to Maya Angelou

OBJECTIVES

- Describe how the media produces stereotypes and controlling images about diverse racial groups
- Relate the history and origin of racial representations
- Analyze the demographics of media audiences and the racial-ethnic content of media images
- Explain the themes that typically represent people of color in the media
- Assess the impact of media images on people of color
- Compare and contrast theories about the production of media images
- Identify how people can resist and change representations of race and ethnicity

You might not expect when you run your errands and go to the grocery store that you would be confronted with an array of racial and ethnic stereotypes. Until very recently, when it was removed because of national protests against systemic racism, one brand of pancake mix had a smiling image of Aunt Jemima—who was lighter skinned than she had been in the past but still based on a long-standing racial stereotype of Black women as servile and smiling.

Even with Aunt Jemima and other racist symbols gone, racial and gender stereotypes fill the market aisles. Try this: The next time you go to a market to shop, walk through every aisle and take note of the images of people you see on various products. Are you looking for drink mix? Margarita mix has a stereotyped Latina on its label—long, flowing hair, big red lips, and an alluring smile. Native American Indian chiefs in full headdress and feathers are on cornmeal labels. If you want some salsa, there's Paul Newman, dressed as a stereotyped Mexican bandit, adorned with mustache and sombrero. If food labels are any indication, Asian Americans don't even exist. White men don't get off easily either: Check out the paper towels with big, brawny, muscular men looking like they've spent their lives working out at the gym.

A few products present different racial-ethnic group images for different versions of the same product: Black women's faces appear on some packaging, while White women's faces appear on the very same product but with different packaging. Deodorants depict a variety of faces on the same product. Does this mean that your hair and underarms are the only places where a token acknowledgment of diversity is allowed?

If you are looking for racial integration, the only place you will likely find it is in the cereal and diaper aisles. Is the message that it's safe for children of different racial-ethnic groups to be together but not for adults?

You may never have paid particular attention to these everyday images, but they are pervasive. Racial and ethnic images are packaged and sold through a variety of products, media forms, and other avenues where social stereotypes are produced and consumed (see the section on "Living with Racism" on the next page). You might think they have no impact on you or anyone else, but research shows otherwise, as we will see in this chapter.

The images that represent race and ethnicity in popular culture and the media are massively important in shaping our views of each other and ourselves. What are these images? How did they originate, and how have they changed? Are they harmless? What purpose do they serve, and how do people understand and, at times, challenge them? These are the questions that guide this chapter.

The Power of Culture: Cultural Racism, Stereotypes, and Controlling Images

Framing Question: How do representations of race perpetuate perceptions of people of color in society?

The **culture** of any society provides a meaning system that enables its members to understand their world. As cultural analyst Stuart Hall (1997) puts it, culture provides shared meanings that orient people to their environment. Cultural representations are crucial in shaping people's understanding of themselves and others, including how race and ethnicity are constructed in society.

As we have already seen, race is not a fixed thing. It is constantly being changed, transformed, and even contested—a process that plays out through social institutions but is heavily shaped by cultural representations (Grzanka 2014; hooks 1992). Representations of race and ethnicity provide the meanings that we associate with different groups, even when we may be completely unaware of how such images affect us and others. Sociologists Danielle Dirks and Jennifer Mueller put it this way: "The power of popular culture lies in its ability to distort, shape, and produce reality, distorting [how] we think, feel, and operate in the social world" (2010:116).

In today's world, culture is largely shaped through the enormous power of the mass media and popular culture. The **mass media** refers to all those channels of communication that transmit information to a wide segment of the population (Andersen and Taylor 2020). The mass media now take many forms, including print media (books, newspapers, magazines), television, video, film, and social media (Facebook, Instagram, Twitter, Snapchat, and, perhaps soon, new forms yet unimagined). Part of contemporary mass media is **popular culture**—the beliefs, ideas, images, and objects that are part of everyday life. Popular culture may differ within different segments of the population, but it is widely influential in shaping our national values and beliefs. Furthermore, because of their immersion in popular culture, young people, children included, are particularly susceptible to its influence.

Popular culture is by its very nature ephemeral—that is, it is ever-changing, making it difficult to describe in a lasting way. Especially if you have no other way to "know" other people, popular culture can have a profound and lasting impact on how people think about racial-ethnic groups other than their own. The cartoon, television, and film characters you love, the music you listen to, the video games you play, the books you read, even the news you watch—all of these forms of culture shape your perception of others and yourself. You cannot help but be influenced by these appearances. When the media or our nation's leaders describe African American protestors as "thugs" but describe White supremacist protestors as "really fine people," how can this not affect our perception of each event? Ask yourself what images are shaping people's thinking now.

It is difficult to underestimate the power that the media have to shape ideas and beliefs. Can you imagine life without the media? Probably not. Try ignoring them in all their forms (print and electronic) for just one day, and you'll see how pervasive the media are in your life. How could the media not be influencing our understanding of race and ethnicity?

Culture is, of course, not monolithic. Diversity within culture means that groups do not necessarily share the exact same values or beliefs. The **dominant culture** is the culture associated with the most powerful group in society. It is the culture that is most pervasive throughout society and that tends to bind people together as "one." The dominant culture has the greatest hold on cultural values and ideas and is transmitted through images, texts, and other media throughout society. The dominant culture is what analysts call *hegemonic*. **Cultural hegemony** (pronounced "heh-JEM-o-nee") refers to the pervasive and excessive influence of one culture throughout society (Andersen and Taylor 2020).

As we will see, despite some positive changes in how the media represents race and ethnicity, the dominant culture still views people of color through a narrow lens that diminishes, distorts, and misrepresents reality. People of color are, of course, not the only groups so distorted. Media images misrepresent many groups, including women, people with disabilities, old people, and lesbian, gay, bisexual, and transgender people. Although all groups can be distorted through the media, people of color get distorted in particular ways, by means of depictions that make them seem inferior—or "other."

Here are just a few examples of these media distortions: Latinos, if visible in TV shows and movies at all, are typically cast in stereotypical roles as cheap labor, criminals, hypersexual characters, or law enforcers (Negrón-Muntaner 2015). Native Americans appear as sports mascots—caricatures that make American Indians seem warlike while also cartoonish and childlike; consider the Cleveland Indians mascot. In other venues, American Indians are rarely even present—a negligible percentage of television characters (Hunt, Ramón, and Tran 2019). African American women athletes, such as tennis's fabulously successful Williams sisters, are routinely described in terms that emphasize their sexuality. Asian Americans are sometimes depicted disparagingly; mostly they're just ignored. When depicted, Asian Americans are stereotyped as the "model minority," as if all Asian Americans are hardworking, compliant, and self-sufficient, values that have become defined as "Asian," not just American (Wang 2010).

In these and countless other ways, not only studied through research but also visible to a watchful eye, popular culture and the media create **racial frames**—that is, particular racial constructs that are fictitious but nonetheless mediate how we see ourselves and others. As explained by sociologists Adia Harvey Wingfield and Joe Feagin, racial framing refers to "the racial perceptions, stereotypes, images, ideologies, narratives, and emotive reactions used to make sense of a given situation, experience, or issue involving racial matters" (Wingfield and Feagin 2012:144; also see Feagin 2010b).

Cultural racism refers to the images and other messages that "affirm the assumed superiority of Whites and the assumed inferiority of people of color." These images and messages are so pervasive in society that, as educational expert and former college president Beverly Tatum says, they are like "smog in the air" (Tatum 1997:6). You may not even be aware of these images and messages—unless, of course, you are highly offended by them. Even when not obvious, though, racial images construct an understanding of race and ethnicity that lingers in the imagination.

By their very nature, media images are manufactured illusions that serve particular purposes, whether to sell products, market entertainment, or inform the public about national and world affairs. In a racially stratified society like the United States, cultural representations buttress a system of White supremacy—that is, cultural representations trivialize, ignore, and/or disparage people of color. By stereotyping people of color, popular culture and the media make the dominance of White people seem "natural." As we will see, even if you think "it's all in good fun," media images have a tremendous influence on our self-concepts, our understandings of each other, and our knowledge and information about race in society.

Surrounded by Stereotypes

In the previous chapter, a *stereotype* was defined as an oversimplified set of beliefs used to categorize members of a social group. Stereotypes are simplistic constructions, have little nuance, and overlook the complexity of real people, reducing people instead to one-dimensional characters.

The media are a particularly effective vehicle for communicating stereotypes because of their oversimplification. The mass media gauge their success by their ability to appeal to the largest possible audience, and they do this by and large by taking little risk and relying on stock characterizations and commonly held values. The mass media also build their power through repetition, recurring themes, and familiar images (Alsultany 2012), thus facilitating the presentation and perpetuation of stereotypes.

When people have little actual contact with each other, such as in a racially segregated society, stereotypes wield even greater power. Where there is no other basis for knowing one another, stereotypes fill the open space created by segregation.

Stereotypes are replete throughout the media. Select any group, and you likely can quickly imagine a stereotype about that group. Arab Americans, for example, are commonly presented as terrorists, belly dancers, oppressed women, or sheiks (Alsultany 2012; Shaheen 2014). This leaves little room for non-Arabs to imagine

Arab Americans as accomplished scholars, loving family members, working professionals, or other positive role models. Some groups are stereotyped in the media by not being visible at all, such as Asian Americans and American Indians, who are rarely portrayed in television dramas or, when present, appear as "sidekicks" or shadowy figures in the background.

Racial-ethnic stereotypes also overlap with gender stereotypes. Women of color are routinely stereotyped in suggestive and sexualized ways, often found in a jungle-like setting. If you doubt this statement, notice how common it is in women's magazines or fashion layouts to see women of color in animal prints, posed in a background dense with foliage. In fact, people of color are often portrayed as somehow closer to nature, a stereotype suggesting that people of color are somehow less than human, more like animals. At certain times in history, such stereotypes have been horribly overt. Now they are usually more covert but present nonetheless, such as when, during the presidential campaign of 2020, then-president Donald Trump referred to vice presidential candidate Kamala Harris as a monster (Summers 2020). As you look at the media and popular culture more critically, you may be surprised at how pervasive these stereotyped images are. See figure 3.1 as an illustration of how common the sexualization of women—and women of color in particular—is in some of the most popular films.

Objectifying "Others" through Controlling Images

The concept of a stereotype is important, but even more powerful is the idea of controlling images. A **controlling image** is a reference to stereotypes but with the added recognition that the image restricts and manipulates people (Collins 1990). Different from stereotypes, a controlling image is not a free-floating idea. As the founder of this concept, Patricia Hill Collins argues that controlling images are "major instruments of power" (1990:68). Controlling images are part of a system of domination—that is, part of the ideological justification for race, class, and gender oppression.

Collins teaches us that there have been four major controlling images specifically associated with African American women: (1) the mammy, (2) the matriarch, (3) the welfare mother, and (4) the Jezebel or the whore (Collins 1990). The "mammy" controlling image depicts Black women as servile, and happy to be so, content to care for others' children, even if they have to leave their own to do so (White 1999). Similar images falsely represent other women of color, such as when Latinas and immigrant women are depicted as "loving others' children like their own," a common description for Latina domestics.

Collins describes the second controlling image of Black women, the matriarch, as bossy, overly aggressive, and quick to emasculate Black men—the antithesis of the "mammy" image. The image distorts the historic strength Black women have shown in providing for their families under the most adverse conditions (Collins 1990). You see this controlling image now in the frequent depiction of Black women in films as the "angry Black woman." It can also be found in caricatures of Asian American women as aggressive and domineering "tiger moms" or "dragon ladies." Each of these controlling images distorts the actual lived experiences of women of color, reducing them instead to pejorative and unidimensional caricatures.

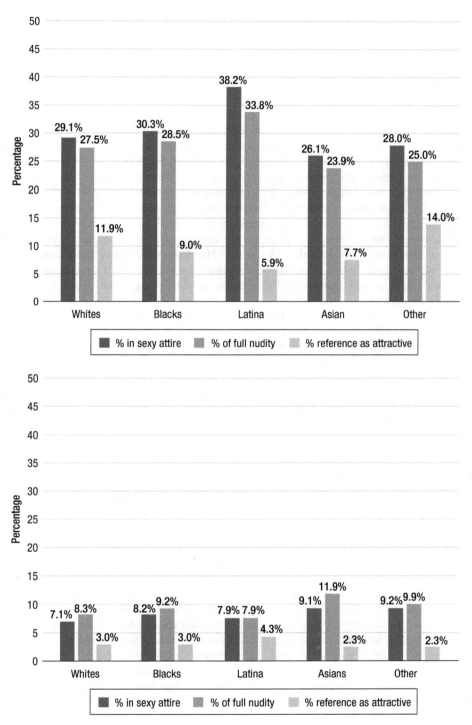

FIG. 3.1 Sexualization in the Top 100 Films of 2018, by Race/Ethnicity and Gender

Source: Smith et al. 2019.

The third controlling image of Black women is that of welfare cheats. Commonly targeting other women of color as well, this image depicts poor women of color as having children just to increase the size of their welfare check. This is a tenacious, though false, accusation directed at the most disadvantaged women, sometimes including poor White women. The controlling images distorts the fact that very few poor women actually receive so-called welfare anymore. Financial support in the form of TANF[1]—the federal "welfare" program for needy families—has fallen drastically since new welfare legislation was passed by Congress in 1996. Now only 23 percent of poor families receive TANF. In no state do TANF payments raise a family above the poverty line (Safawi and Floyd 2020).

The final controlling image of Black women Collins describes is the "Jezebel" or whore. This controlling image depicts Black women, and other women of color, as sexually loose and as objects for other's sexual pleasure. For Black women, the image obscures the historical and painful sexual abuse of Black women by White slave owners. For Latinas, the image translates into "the Madonna," on the one hand, or the whore, on the other (Vargas 2010). Likewise, Asian American women are constructed as either sexually exotic (the "lotus blossom") or aggressive and domineering. Through this controlling image Muslim women are also objectified as sexually exotic.

Controlling images of all women of color engage racial, sexual, and gendered imagery. Controlling images deny women of color *human agency*—that is, the right to define their own human identity (Vargas 2010). Controlling images both rely on and perpetuate **objectification**—the process of making a human being an object or thing. Objectification dehumanizes people. When you objectify someone, you see them as somehow less than human, which allows you to create a rationale for controlling and manipulating them. Making someone an "other," as has been the common historic plight of people of color, is a prerequisite for the exploitation of other human beings.

Echoes of the Past

Framing Question: How do images from the past linger today?

Many of the racist ideas and images we encounter today are permutations of racist ideas and images of the past. Not that long ago, you might have seen statues of Black jockeys as lawn ornaments on the properties of wealthy White people. During the late nineteenth century when Chinese people were immigrating to the United States as laborers, "yellow peril" was bemoaned, meant to portray the Chinese as a threat to Whites. The term was later extended to lament Japanese immigration as well. Up until 1971, when protests by the National Mexican-American Anti-Defamation Committee forced its elimination, the racist Frito Bandito cartoon mascot was used to sell corn chips. Frito Bandito spoke in an exaggerated quasi-Spanish accent, wore a huge sombrero, had a gold tooth and bulging stomach, and robbed people of their chips. The character was depicted as a devious villain. Imagine the young person who, knowing no Hispanic people, might grow up thinking of Latinos through this iconic and insulting invention.

---

[1] In 1996, the original federal welfare program, Aid to Families with Dependent Children, was replaced with a new program, Temporary Assistance for Needy Families (TANF), discussed further in chapter 7.

People hold a vigil in front of the statue of Albert Pike, a Confederate general, at Judiciary Square on Sunday, August 13, 2017, in Washington, DC, a day after the violence in Charlottesville, Virginia.

Source: Salwan Georges, *Washington Post* / Getty Images.

We can see how racist ideas and images in popular culture have a dirty history in the presentation of Black, Latino, Asian, and Native American people. And these racist ideas and images continue to transform into today's racist ideas and images—such as in the false belief that immigrants are somehow taking over the United States. You may recall Donald Trump, when he was president, repeatedly insisting that "we need to take our country back"—a notion that reflects this anti-immigrant controlling image.

Many of the images of the past continue to influence dominant understandings of race and ethnicity. Historically, racist images have been gross and explicitly demeaning. Black Sambo, Aunt Jemima, Uncle Ben, Speedy Gonzales—these and other racial-ethnic stereotypes have been widely distributed and consumed through popular culture (see "Learning Our Past," below). Historically, anti-Black images have also been used as a "yardstick" against which other groups have been either devalued or elevated (Dirks and Mueller 2010:116).

Over the years, for example, Disney films have been full of negative and stereotyped images of marginalized racial groups, affecting whole generations of children who grew up enamored of these films and other Disney products. The 1941 classic Disney film *Dumbo* shows a group of black crows whose dialect reflects stereotyped American Black speech patterns. The crows are shown happily singing, "Can't wait to spend our pay away" (Markus and Conner 2013). The same film shows a group of Black workers, supervised by a White man, who sing, "We work all day,

The Real Aunt Jemima

Who was Aunt Jemima? Was she only a stereotyped icon on boxes of pancakes? Yes and no. Certainly the stereotype of Aunt Jemima persisted over the years—until the image was removed from pancake mix in 2020. The image changed since its original inception, moving from a more dark-skinned, mammy-like image to a light-skinned Black woman with pearls and curls. Few people know that there was a real Black woman embedded in this iconic image.

The real "Aunt Jemima" was a Black woman named Nancy Green, born in 1834 as a slave in Montgomery County, Kentucky. Nancy Green was a gifted storyteller and skilled cook who became one of America's first Black corporate models. In the late nineteenth century, the owners of the Pearl Milling Company wanted to sell a ready-mix, self-rising pancake flour but needed an image for their product. Inspired by a blackface performer in a vaudeville show who had performed a tune called "Aunt Jemima," company owner R. T. Davis employed Nancy Green in 1890 to be a living trademark. Nancy Green was fifty-six years old.

The R. T. Davis Milling Company promoted the product at the World's Columbian Exposition in Chicago in 1893 with Green serving thousands of pancakes and demonstrating the product. Because of her storytelling and cooking skills, Green was a tremendous hit. The exhibition booth was so popular that special police were hired to keep the crowds moving. Nancy Green signed a lifetime contract and traveled extensively around the country promoting the pancake mix, no doubt earning huge profits for the company. She was tragically killed in a car accident in 1923.

In 2014, two of Nancy Green's descendants (her great-grandsons) filed suit in Chicago for $2 billion, claiming that Green was a key formulator of the recipe for pancake mix. A judge dismissed the case, arguing that the two men could not unequivocally prove they were descendants of Nancy Green.

What other legacies do you imagine might lie behind some of the common icons that you still see today?

Sources: Hine 1993; Manning 1998; Roberts 1994.

we work all night, we have no life to read and write, we're happy . . . we don't know when we get our pay, and when we do, we throw our money away" (Towbin et al. 2004). In the film *The Jungle Book*, at the head of a society of apes obviously meant to demean Black people is King Louie, an orangutan, who pleads for help to "be more human."

Disney is not the only company that reproduced such racist images. Looney Tunes cartoon mouse Speedy Gonzales was shelved in the late 1990s after protests that the character was racially stereotyped. Speedy Gonzales spoke in an exaggerated Mexican accent and, just as in other Hispanic stereotypes, wore an oversized sombrero and guarded the border against other "mice" coming into the country and getting all the cheese (Basset 2013; Markus and Conner 2013).

You don't have to watch movies and cartoons, though, to encounter harmful stereotypes. Everyday objects have used stereotypical images of Black Americans to do everything from holding cooking spices to covering toasters. Now called "Black collectibles," these daily-use objects exaggerated the presumed features of

African Americans, making Black Americans appear stupid, lovable, servile, and nonthreatening—and certainly inferior.

Black collectibles such as salt-and-pepper shakers, dolls, lawn jockeys, postcards, and other everyday items were popular from the 1880s through the 1950s. These everyday goods depicted Black people as dark-skinned, servile, and childlike. The "mammy" was typically overweight and smiling, appearing as if she aimed to please. Now prized among some collectors, these goods presented images of Black people that, in many ways, remain with us today. Black collectibles, however, were part of the racial ideology that cemented the inferiority of Black people in the White imagination. Such seemingly trivial, everyday objects were part of the ruling apparatus of society (Goings 1994; Mueller, Williams, and Dirks 2018).

Likewise, first introduced in the 1940s, Chiquita Banana was an advertising mascot designed to promote the nutritious value of bananas. Represented as a stereotypical Central American woman, Chiquita Banana originally appeared as having just come off a boat from "near the equator." The actual figure was a banana but designed as a hip-swirling woman who appealed to men with her flirtatious winking and suggestive dancing. At the time the image was introduced, the men, women, and children who worked on US–owned banana plantations in Central America were subjected to grueling work conditions and serious illness from pesticide poisoning (Gallagher and McWhirter 1998[2]). Wildly popular, the mocking image of Chiquita Banana became the basis for numerous live performances, including some by celebrity actress Carmen Miranda. To this day Chiquita Banana advertises bananas. The contemporary image is a Latina dressed in stereotypical Latin clothing and carrying fruit on her head. This stereotyped outfit can be seen all over Pinterest and can be purchased in costume form at Halloween outlets.

The iconography of the past provides a window through which we can now understand contemporary representations. Even the exaggerated way that some people now mock Spanish may have its origins in old presentations where characters spoke Spanish in an exaggerated and comical way. Viewed from today's perspective, past stereotypes seem exaggerated and offensive, but at the time they were taken for granted—at least by dominant groups. As you look at current racial and ethnic stereotypes, you can see how some of the old ones have been recycled for a new day (Mueller et al. 2018). All the more reason to become more critically attuned to current representations.

Who Sees What?

Framing Questions: Have media images of people of color changed in recent years? Why or why not?

With the growth of social media and an increasing array of media forms and networks, the US public is now exposed to a huge array of images and ideas that

---

[2] Following the publication of these reporters' story in the *Cincinnati Enquirer* in 1998, Chiquita sued the newspaper, and the reporters—who had received their information from an internal "leak"—were convicted of stealing internal e-mails. The newspaper had to retract the story and pay over $10 million to Chiquita because of the means by which the reporters had gained access to inside-company information. The facts of the story have not, however, been refuted and do not change what is written here (Zuckerman 1998).

communicate notions of race and ethnicity. Television, film, video, social media—these are only a few of the places where the public views racial and ethnic representations. Through advertisements alone, the typical person is exposed to hundreds, perhaps thousands, of images every day. You probably think you don't notice them, but ads have an impact—otherwise corporations would not spend the huge sums of money that they do to produce them. Ads are only one way that images are dispersed. Our exposure to manufactured images is so vast that it is almost impossible to measure.

Media images convey norms, values, and ideas to a public whose thinking and identities are then shaped by the images presented. This is true of all people, but it is especially true of children. Stereotypes learned at an early age, unless challenged, become a strong part of children's identity development. Scholars estimate that children spend a huge amount of time on various media, which has only increased in recent years. Black and Latino youth also consume more media than White children do. Teens spend an average of eight to nine hours per day on their phones. Even young infants are increasingly exposed to images on the screen. One report finds that infants spend about two hours per day in front of a screen (Ravichandran, De Bravo, and Beauport 2016). Little wonder that television is sometimes called the nation's babysitter!

When children watch, what do they see? Children of color are now 22 percent of the youth population (ages zero to seventeen years), but images of them do not account for anywhere near that proportion in the media forms that they watch, read, and hear. This can lead to feelings of being less important and less valued than others. Among Latino high school and college students, for example, greater exposure to mainstream media is associated with a more negative body image (Rivadeneyra, Ward, and Gordon 2007).

Children's media is also a place where White children learn racial stereotypes. As early as age three, the racial and ethnic images that White children see in the media teach them to exclude other children from play (Van Ausdale and Feagin 2000). Children's books and films also reflect the racism of color blindness, largely ignoring the realities of racism and the history and struggles of people of color (Winograd 2011). There are exceptions, of course, but you have to look to alternative sources other than the mainstream to find them—an ongoing challenge for parents who want to raise their children with a vision of a more racially inclusive society.

Social scientists use content analysis to document the images seen in the media. **Content analysis** is a method of research that systematically documents the images in various cultural artifacts. It is a way of recording what images appear and assessing changes over time. Because content analysis only details what appears in the media, it cannot tell you how people react to these images. For that, other methods of research are needed. Still, content analysis documents the systematic content of media images, even when those images may be barely noticed in any critical way by casual observers.

What does content analysis tell us about race and representation? The images of people of color have improved in recent years, especially as advertisers have tuned in to the increased diversity of the US population. The expansion of civil rights and

Race and Representation in the Media

- Racial-ethnic minorities are 39 percent of the US population but in 2018 played only 20 percent of leads in top theatrical films; this is an increase from 11 percent in 2011.
- Ninety-three percent of senior executives in the top Hollywood studios are White.
- Cast diversity in film has increased since 2011, but Latinos and Asians are each only 5 percent of film roles; Native Americans are less than 1 percent.
- By 2018, Black Americans comprised 11 percent of film directors, Asians 4 percent, and Latinos less than 1 percent.
- Only 1.5 percent of film writers are people of color.
- Eighty percent of video game characters are White; most are men.
- Stories about Latinos are less than 1 percent of news media coverage.

Sources: Hunt and Ramón 2020; Negrón-Muntaner 2015; Smith et al. 2019.

resulting job opportunities for people of color in the media have also produced a somewhat more diverse workforce, meaning gross stereotypes are less likely to be produced. But what do you see in the media?

Television

Even with the rise of social media and the ability to stream film and video, television remains the most popular medium for viewers, although it is giving way to streaming video. Ninety-seven percent of homes in the United States have at least one TV; most have more. On average, people watch some form of media about ten hours per day, four of which are watching live TV. African Americans watch more television than any other group. The US population also watches more television by far than people in other nations (Wambugu 2018).

As producers have become more aware of population diversity, they have tried to capture a wider market by projecting more diverse images. Yet underrepresentation endures. As only one example, American Indians are almost invisible on television, comprising a tiny percentage of those shown (see figure 3.2). Native Americans are actually more rarely portrayed now than they were in the 1950s and 1960s, when Westerns were very popular. Then, however, American Indians were crudely stereotyped and typically shown as sidekicks, background figures, or villains. Current portrayals of American Indians, rare as they are, either place them in earlier centuries or portray them as spiritual figures or as beleaguered by social problems (Leavitt et al. 2015).

Because the vast majority of TV shows are now set in urban locations, you might expect to see more diverse people on television and in a variety of roles, but television presents a narrow range of characters. African Americans are most commonly seen as entertainers, athletes, criminals, or sidekicks, and they are disproportionately shown in sitcoms and crime dramas. African American representation on television increased significantly in the 1980s, when they were about 22 percent of prime-time characters, but their representation has dropped since to about 17 percent of characters now (Hunt et al. 2019).

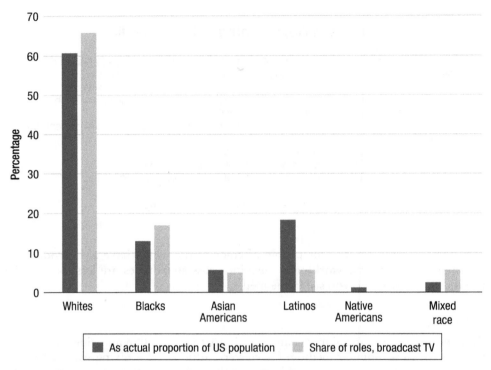

FIG. 3.2 What Does America Look Like? Reality versus TV

Sources: Hunt et al. 2019; US Census Bureau 2019d.

Latinos are also vastly underrepresented on television, except on Spanish-language television, which is rarely watched by White audiences. When Latinos appear on mainstream television, they are most often portrayed as hypersexual, subservient, or just plain stupid. Scholars who have studied changes in the representation of Latinos over the years find that Latinos are more negatively cast now than in earlier years, such as the 1950s and 1960s (Hunt et al. 2019; Mastro 2015).

Asian Americans, when seen at all, are often stereotyped as cab drivers; Southeast Asians, as convenience store clerks. Other Asian Americans are typically depicted as linked to technology (Thakore 2014). You can see in figure 3.2 (above) how underrepresented Asian Americans are in broadcast TV, especially relative to their proportion in the US population. The same is true for Latinos.

Research finds many consequences for exposure to racist stereotypes. Seeing African Americans in stereotypical roles on television, for example, influences how audiences understand the occupational roles of Black people (Mastro 2008; Punyanunt-Carter 2008). Frequent television viewing is also associated with greater endorsement of negative stereotypes by White people. On a more positive note, even brief exposure to positive and likable images in the media leads to better racial attitudes among White people (Oliver et al. 2015; Schmader, Block, and Lickel 2015).

The invisibility and stereotyping of people of color on television results in what cultural critics call **symbolic annihilation** (Gerbner 1972). Symbolic annihilation

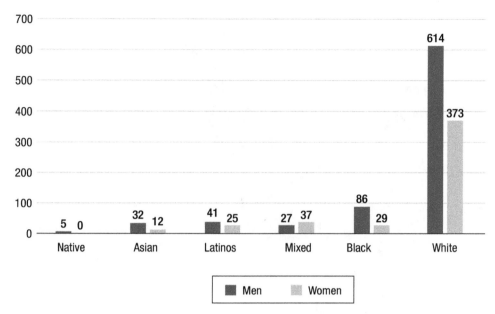

FIG. 3.3 Film Actor Counts

Source: Hunt et al. 2019.

refers to the under- and misrepresentation of certain groups of people in the media. When people of color are "symbolically annihilated," stereotypes fill the void.

Film

Film audiences are, in fact, a highly diverse population. As you can see in figures 3.3 and 3.4, even with some improvement in recent years, people of color are vastly underrepresented as actors in top-grossing films. Nonetheless, despite their under-representation, Latinos, Asians, and African Americans have higher movie-going rates than do White Americans (McNary 2018).

Stereotypes also remain. In film, African Americans are all too frequently portrayed as victims saved by White people (Hughey 2014; Vera and Gordon 2003). People of color are also more likely to appear in comedies, while White leads are more prominent in dramas.

Asian Americans in the movies are stereotyped in particular ways. Asian women are heavily sexualized as "exotic" but submissive beauties. Asian men are routinely shown in martial arts where White men usually beat them. Rarely are Asian men seen with White women, whereas Asian women are usually paired with non-Asian men (Hunt et al. 2019).

Progress is being made, especially as more people of color enter employment in the filmmaking industry. Even here, however, people of color are underrepresented as directors, writers, and producers (Hunt et al. 2019). Public social movements, such as the #MeToo movement and #OscarsSoWhite, have called attention to the absence of representation of women and people of color in the entertainment industry. By identifying barriers to the representation and employment of people of color,

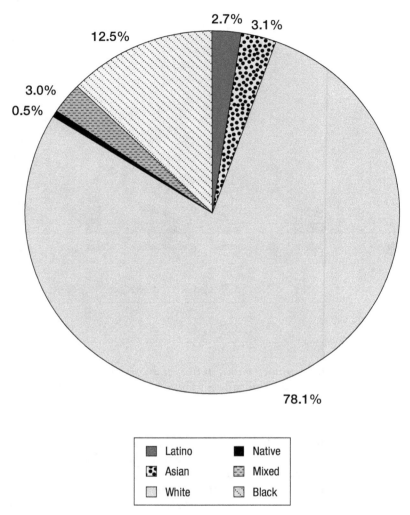

2.7% 3.1%

12.5%

3.0%

0.5%

78.1%

	Latino		Native
	Asian		Mixed
	White		Black

FIG. 3.4 Share of All Film Roles by Race/Ethnicity

Source: Hunt et al. 2019.

including women, such movements can foster a more diverse entertainment world, one where images not only better represent the population but also convey more positive and affirming images.

Video Games

Although few people probably think of it as a place where racial-ethnic images are created, video gaming is another site of **cultural production**—or the process by which cultural images are made. For many, playing video games now surpasses time spent watching television. As with other media, these games can have a significant impact on the formation of identity and beliefs about race and ethnicity.

The latest estimates are that more than half of Americans play video games regularly, although only about 10 percent call themselves "gamers." Asian Americans, Latinos, and African Americans are more likely to play video games than are White Americans. Asian Americans and Whites, though, are overrepresented as characters in video games, at least relative to their proportion in the US population (Embrick, Wright, and Lukács 2012).

In video games with characters, nearly all the heroes are White (87 percent). African Americans and Latinos are most often portrayed as athletes, and Asians and Pacific Islanders as wrestlers or fighters. Especially interesting is that, when African American characters in video games are victims of violence, they are likely to be shown as unharmed (Glaubke et al. 2001). Research shows that video game play has a significant effect on White players' views of Blacks and Asian Americans: the more time Whites spend playing video games, the less likely they are to have egalitarian views of Black and Asian people (Behm-Morawitz and Ta 2014).

News

The one place where you might expect greater accuracy in the representation and portrayal of race and ethnicity is in the news. Given its mission to report national and world events, we count on news for facts and accuracy. Yet even here people of color are under- and misrepresented. Think of the protests in the summer of 2020 after an unarmed Black man, George Floyd, was killed by a White police officer (Derek Chauvin) who kept his knee on Floyd's neck while Floyd called out, "I can't breathe" (Opel and Barker 2020). As people erupted in anger and frustration at yet another police killing of an unarmed Black person and demonstrated in cities throughout the nation, the protestors were typically referred to as "radical extremists" and "thugs," labels never similarly applied to White supremacist demonstrators. You may be able to find your own examples by paying attention to different incidents of terror, but here's one: After Dylann Roof fatally shot nine African American worshippers at Emanuel AME Church in Charleston, South Carolina, in 2015, he (just like Aurora movie shooter James Eagan Holmes, also White) was routinely referred to in media coverage as "mentally ill," "sick," or "just a whacked-out kid" (Butler 2015).

In part, racial misrepresentation in the news reflects the limited roles of people of color as news writers, editors, broadcasters, and producers. Of the top editors at the most widely circulated newspapers, 90 percent are White. Turn on any Sunday morning news program and see who hosts. Although White women have made some inroads, as of 2020 none of the major Sunday morning hosts were people of color. White men also dominate as experts on news issues, even when talking about racial issues (Hunt et al. 2019).

Careful analyses of news coverage have found that major newspapers feature seven times more quotes from men than from women. Even with somewhat greater inclusion of people of color as reporters and commentators now, there are few people of color as primary anchors on national evening news (Boguhn 2015; Women's Media Center 2019).

How people appear in the news also matters. As we will see next, people of color are overreported as criminals relative to the amount of crime they commit.

Of the Latinos who appear in the news, two-thirds are shown as either criminals or illegal immigrants. A slim 4 percent of guests on talk shows are Latino (Negrón-Muntaner 2015; Torres and López 2015). With such limited and misrepresentative imagery on the news, is it any wonder that viewers end up with such a limited understanding of the issues facing people of color in today's world?

The Internet

Finally, cyberspace is an increasingly important site for the production of culture. Facebook, Twitter, Snapchat, Instagram, and other social media play an increasingly important role in the cultural life of all Americans. The development and use of social media give people the opportunity to share information and entertainment in a highly democratic way, in that people can be less dependent on mainstream media for sharing information. At the same time, however, analyses of social media indicate the presence of rampant racism (Daniels 2013), raising new ethical issues about how much free speech should be tolerated in these new forms of communication.

Social media are also an increasingly important source of how people get the news. Information networks are now less dependent on the dominant media outlets. But people tend to be in social media feeds that provide information they already agree with, making it less likely that the media are a source for alternative and possibly opposing views. Moreover, the ease of posting on social media means that people are easily susceptible to so-called fake news—news that is completely untrue and yet easily shared and widely dispersed through social media. Social media can be used, however, to construct alternative narratives that are important in political activism, as has been shown in how organizers in movements such as Black Lives Matter have used social media for mobilizing support (Jackson, Bailey, and Welles 2020).

Race and Representation

Framing Question: What are the typical narrative themes in media representations of people of color, and how do they engage the intersections of race, gender, and sexuality?

Taken together, stereotypes presented on television, film, the news, the Internet, and other cultural sites distort the reality of life for people of color. Certain themes recur:

* associating race and criminality
* representing people of color as hypersexual
* constructing people of color as alien or "other"

In the absence of other images, these recurring themes leave a stamp on people's consciousness. Representations of groups that are pervasive in society generate how people see underrepresented groups.

Race and Criminalization

The media vastly overrepresent African Americans as criminals, but other men of color are not immune to this stereotype. Latino immigrants, in particular, have lately been portrayed as violent rapists and drug dealers, no matter the particular circumstances from which they come. Muslims, too, have been racialized and portrayed in criminal terms. At the same time, White people are underrepresented as criminals relative to the proportion of crimes White people actually commit.

The expansion of local news coverage has contributed to this characterization. As news coverage has moved to a twenty-four-hour cycle, local news affiliates need to fill the time allotted and do so inexpensively. Images of violent crime provide visual drama, more than would nonviolent crimes such as tax evasion, embezzlement, or government kickbacks. Similarly, images of looting or burning buildings during antiracist demonstrations provide more dramatic visual footage than do images of peaceful protests. The result is a distorted public image of the actual extent of crime by people of color (Iyengar 2010; Kaufman 2019; Peterson, Krivo, and Russell-Brown 2018).

With more exposure to criminalized images, White people are then more likely to support punitive criminal justice policies (Cervantes, Alvord, and Menjívar 2018). Criminalized racial stereotypes in the media also increase people's fear of crime. Now, even as the actual crime rate has declined, people believe there is more crime than in the previous year. As a result, the majority of the public think crime is a very or extremely serious problem (McCarthy 2019a).

Sexualizing Women of Color

A second recurring theme in media portrayals of people of color is hypersexualization. The body is one of the places where "the prevailing rules of a culture are written" (Gimlin 2002:3). For people of color, the body is a site for scripting racism and, for women, for scripting sexism. Women of color are depicted as oversexed and sexually loose, feeding some of the controlling images that we have already discussed. The sexualization of women of color is especially played out in music, where Black women with large breasts and big hips are cast in music videos and where Latinas are portrayed as "hot," seductive, and overly emotional and are dressed in loud colors (Vargas 2010).

Sports are also a place where Black American bodies are on display. Narrations by sports announcers tend to stereotype Black male athletes as naturally athletic, quick, and powerful. However, White male athletes are touted for their hard work, effort, and mental skill. Black and other minority athletes are depicted as more emotional (Arth and Billings 2019; Eastman and Billings 2001; McKay and Johnson 2008).

Making People Other: The Alien Narrative

A third recurring theme in racial representations is the "alien" or "other." This is especially now true for Latino immigrants. Think of how the image conjured up by the term "illegal alien" differs from that of the "undocumented worker." The language used to describe immigrants communicates otherness, thus influencing how immigrants are understood as well as shaping social policies around immigration.

Over the years, various immigrant groups, including Latinos and Asians, have been described as a "contagion," "pollutants," and "perils" and in other terms that imply immigrants threaten the fabric of American life—much the way that Chinese and Japanese immigrants were constructed in the earlier part of the twentieth century. Mexican and Central American immigrants have been nastily stereotyped as a threat, unlike earlier European immigrants, who are seen as positively contributing to the fabric of the nation (L. Chavez 2013; Cisneros 2008).

Images of immigrants as "invaders" generate support for punitive immigration policies, such as Donald Trump's calls to build a wall along the US–Mexican border and create a massive deportation force. Such policies rest on a stereotype of Latino immigrants as dangerous criminals. Likewise, closing borders to people from predominantly Muslim countries rests on a narrow stereotype of Muslim people as all potential terrorists. The inflammatory language of othering thwarts any chance for empathy or understanding the hard work of either immigrants or the dangers for refugees fleeing war-torn nations.

Isn't All in Good Fun?

Framing Question: What harm comes from racial images in popular culture?

Perhaps you're thinking that none of these images really affects you. After all, most of them come from the world of entertainment, so surely they're meant in good fun and don't actually influence you or others, right? Research shows otherwise.

Take the case of Native American sports mascots. You go to the stadium, root for your team, perhaps even perform the "tomahawk chop" as you sit on the edge of your seat, maybe wearing a T-shirt with an image of an Indian as your team's logo. What possible harm could come from this?

Picture the typical Native American mascot. It's likely a man wearing feathers, who has big teeth and a grin on his face and appears comical or fearsome. This image seriously distorts our perceptions of Native people. For one thing, why are the mascots always shown as men? Where are Native American women in this representation? The suggestion that Native people are fierce and warlike also miscasts the actual history of European aggression against American Indians. The stereotyped yet iconic image of American Indians offends people who see these misrepresentations as degrading and insulting to the complexity and richness of Native American nations.

Social psychologist Stephanie Fryberg has asked whether Native American mascots are just for fun or whether they cause harm (Fryberg and Watts 2010). Fryberg devised a series of carefully designed experiments to test the effect of Native American mascots on young Native American children, asking how exposure to these mascots affects Native children's self-image and academic achievement. She conducted her experiments at three Native American schools and one Native American college.

After being exposed to the typical mascot image, the students wrote down the first five thoughts that came to mind. Using social psychological instruments to measure various outcomes, Fryberg found that students who had been exposed to the mascot image reported lower self-esteem and a lower sense of community worth than did students who had not been exposed to the mascot. This consequence emerged regardless of whether the mascot image was more positive or more negative. In a second experiment, Fryberg also found that students reported lower goals for their future after exposure to the mascot image. She then tested a sample of European American students, using the exact same research protocol. She found that, following exposure to the mascots, European American students actually reported that their self-esteem went up!

Fryberg's research shows us that mascot images not only have a deleterious effect on young Native Americans but also elevate how White people think of themselves. These mascots have become so commonplace that few White people ever think about the harm they do to others. Imagine, though, how you might feel if your town had a team named the Pittsburgh Polacks or the Detroit Dykes or the Wisconsin Wetbacks (Churchill 1993). Are White people so accustomed to ridiculing Native people that they no longer empathize or understand why these images are so hurtful? What does it tell you about our culture that people can so blithely participate in stereotypes that mock Native American people? Are there any other racial-ethnic stereotypes so commonplace that you hardly even notice them anymore—unless, of course, they are applied to you?

Consider how some people celebrate Halloween. Holidays are occasions that confirm group identities; that is, they involve rituals that socialize people into a sense of community and help shape the collective consciousness (Durkheim [1895] 1964). In the case of Halloween, costumes that portray racial and ethnic stereotypes reinforce identity for White people. This has been illustrated by a study of college students who wrote diaries about their Halloween experiences. Students recorded how racial images were portrayed in Halloween costumes. The researchers concluded from the students' observations that Halloween costumes became "vehicles for transmitting racial judgments about people of color" (Mueller, Dirks, and Picca 2007:324), at the same time, therefore, confirming Whiteness as a "normal" identity.

Ghetto theme parties, common on many campuses, also insult Mexican Americans, Arab Americans, Native Americans, and just about any other racial or ethnic group you can imagine. Examples are plentiful, such as one "South of the Border" party on a New Jersey campus where White women students dressed as pregnant Latina maids (Georgevich 2007). How you would feel if you were a Mexican American or African American student on a campus where people ridiculed you by performing such a stereotype? What some White students think is "just for fun" has deeply harmful consequences for others.

Racially themed parties in fraternities and sororities can be especially vicious, because these environments are racially homogenous—that is, almost entirely White.[3] The parties also tend to happen behind closed doors. In these exclusionary environments, researchers have found that White male college students tend to perceive themselves, not people of color, as the real victims of racism. These students see racism in individualistic terms; they minimize the experience of race and say that people of color are overly sensitive to it. White male students also believe that people of color exploit race to make excuses for their behavior. Moreover, what they learn in college does not change these views (Cabrera 2014). All told, despite the cavalier attitude held by some that stereotypes do not matter that much, the fact is that they matter quite a lot.

---

[3] Black Greek fraternities, though generally all Black, do not engage in this kind of racist behavior. For analysis of the history and sociology of Black Greek organizations, see Hughey and Parks 2011.

Markets, Makers, and Money: The Media Constructs Race

Framing Question: How can we explain the continued construction of racialized images in the media and popular culture?

Popular culture and the media provide a basis for a shared experience in society, even though different groups use and experience the media in diverse ways. What we see in popular culture and the media is, of course, manipulated; that is, it consists of images that have been produced by people for a specific purpose, most often a commercial one. Why are the images what they are?

There are three ways we can explain racial and ethnic representations in popular culture and the media:

1. demographic changes in the population
2. the status of people of color in media organizations
3. critical race theory

First, *demographic changes in the population* mean that media audiences are more diverse than ever before. Because the majority of media outlets are commercially owned, the advertiser—not the customer—is king. To continually attract high viewership, the broadcaster knows that it is crucial to appeal to the widest possible audience. Advertisers and producers have recognized the importance of appealing to a diverse population and thus have increased the representation of diverse groups in their advertising and programming, compared to in the past. Particularly given the growth of Latino and Asian populations, you can expect that advertisers will want to promote content that capitalizes on these growing markets. Changes in media images can be heavily attributed to these market forces.

Second, change in racial representations has also come with *greater inclusion of people of color in the media workforce*. The images we see in popular culture and the media are manufactured. Like other products, media images are produced and distributed by those employed in media organizations. Without diversity in the workforce, workers might project only a limited view, one filled with group stereotypes. People of color have made many inroads into the media as employees; African American, Latino, Native American, and Asian American people are increasingly among film directors, reporters, and other media employees, but there is room for improvement (see figure 3.5). With greater inclusion, especially in top positions, it seems likely though that the representation and depiction of people of color in the media will change.

A third perspective, **critical race theory**, takes the viewpoint that the media and popular culture reflect and re-create hierarchical systems of race, class, and gender in society (Brooks and Hébert 2006; Dines and Humez 2014; Dirks and Mueller 2010). This interdisciplinary perspective emphasizes the role of power in constructing the meaning of race and its intersection with other social factors, such as gender and social class. Critical race theory situates the representations of race and ethnicity in the fact that the United States is a capitalist society. **Capitalism** is an economic system based on the pursuit of profit and private ownership. The mass media include a vast number of media forms and outlets, which you would think would produce a vigorous, enlightening competition of ideas, but, in truth, the majority of

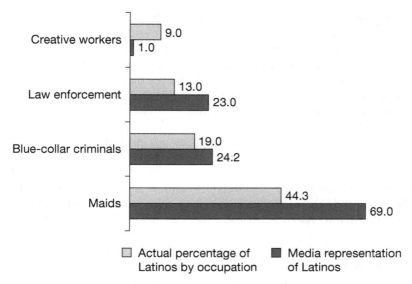

FIG. 3.5 Latino Roles in the Media and in the Actual Labor Force

Source: Negrón-Muntaner 2015.

news and media outlets are owned by only a few media groups, which can stifle the viewpoints offered. As just one example, ViacomCBS Inc. owns the CBS television network, Showtime, countless television and radio stations, book publishers, and various online properties. ViacomCBS also owns several cable networks, including BET, MTV, Nickelodeon, Comedy Central, and others, plus Paramount Pictures and more (Zacks 2017).

With so much of the media in the hands of so few, you cannot help but ask whose interests are served by the racial representations that appear. From the perspective of critical race theory, misleading representations in the media and popular culture are essential for maintaining particular systems of control and power. The presence of racist representations, whether intentional or not, thus serve the interests of powerful groups in society.

Race, Resistance, and Alternative Visions

Framing Question: How can people resist and transform racist images in the dominant culture?

We have seen how images of race and ethnicity in society are fundamental to how people think about race. At the same time, culture can be a vehicle for change. Although dominant representations reflect and reproduce racial inequality, it is also possible for culture to liberate us from the negativity and misrepresentation that is all too common in popular culture and the media. In other words, although the media and popular culture produce and reflect racial perceptions, they can also subvert them (Grzanka 2014). In one example, demonstrated though controlled laboratory research, social scientists found that exposure to educational TV sitcoms that portrayed diverse and likeable images of Arab and Muslim people resulted in a reduction of prejudice against Muslims (Sohad and Brauer 2018).

Throughout history, including recently, people have organized to resist racist images and to insist that there be better representation of people of color in the media. Many of the changes we see now have resulted from the mobilization of people of color insisting on more affirming and positive images in the dominant culture.

A **culture of resistance** refers to the cultural forms that people create explicitly to challenge the stereotypes and controlling images that appear in the dominant culture. There are numerous examples of cultures of resistance throughout American history and today.

Sometimes cultures of resistance appear as protests against corporations that produce racist images in their products. In 2003, for example, when retailer Abercrombie & Fitch marketed a T-shirt featuring the slogan "Wong Brothers Laundry Service: Two Wongs Can Make It White," a massive national outcry was raised. Students and others led a petition campaign to have the shirt removed because it was so offensive to Asian Americans and their allies. Abercrombie & Fitch initially responded by saying that their company did not single Asian Americans out—that, in fact, they had run campaigns that offended everybody! In the end, given the public outcry, Abercrombie & Fitch pulled the shirt from its shelves. A year and a half later, the company had to pay $40 million in a settlement for widespread ethnic and gender discrimination in hiring (Dirks and Mueller 2010; Greenhouse 2004).

Hip-hop music has also emerged as a culture of resistance. As a musical style, hip-hop has become mainstream, but young, urban Black men created hip-hop in the 1970s to fight against mainstream cultural messages depicting Black men as dangerous (Morgan and Fischer 2010:510). Hip-hop was a direct critique of the US system of justice. By deploying the vernacular of the streets, young Black teens reclaimed the cultural space to define themselves. Hip-hop thus became a tool to defy racism. In a similar vein, Muslim youth have now developed a style of punk music known as Taqwacore that challenges anti-Muslim racism and celebrates young Muslim's positive identity as "brown kids" (McDowell 2017). Other contemporary art forms, such as slam poetry, stem from the hip-hop movement and show how culture can be a source of affirmation, not just degradation, for those excluded from dominant cultural institutions.

A culture of resistance can also be a **culture of affirmation**. That is, culture can be the medium through which groups develop and assert a strongly positive identity for themselves. As with cultures of resistance, a culture of affirmation shows the creativity of people who produce new cultural forms with the specific purpose of showcasing the talents and strong identities of people of color (or other minorities).

There are numerous examples throughout American history of cultures of affirmation; among the best is the Harlem Renaissance (Huggins 2007; Lewis 1981; Marks 1999). The Harlem Renaissance spanned the period from the end of World War I until about the beginning of the Great Depression, in the early 1930s. It was a period a tremendous cultural expression by Black artists focused in Harlem in the areas of music, literature, dance, intellectual works, and the arts. Many of those artists are recognized today as among the greats of American culture: Romare Bearden, Langston Hughes, "Dizzy" Gillespie, Nella Larsen, Ella Fitzgerald, Bessie Smith, Billie Holiday, Louis Armstrong, and many others too numerous to mention.

Cultures of resistance and cultures of affirmation teach us that as people construct and see positive images of themselves and others they can transform our understanding of race and ethnicity. Such alternative cultures can be the basis for movements for social justice. This requires looking at the dominant culture with a critical eye but doing so without appropriating the culture of others (Gallagher 2003).

In today's world, Black and Latino culture has become especially popular among White youth. People can now "consume" Black culture through participation in a mainstream popular culture that has been very much influenced by African American culture—especially African American urban culture (Pitcher 2014). How that culture was made to flow into the mainstream has to do with the phenomenon of **cultural appropriation,** which occurs when privileged groups consume and "claim" the culture of an oppressed or colonized group. White people can now participate in "Blackness" without incurring any of the costs of being Black. Movie star Amandla Stenberg puts it well: "What would America be like if it loved Black people as much as it loves Black culture?" (Stenberg 2015).

Any person can work to produce more affirming and positive views of race and ethnicity. One example is found in the cartoon character Dora the Explorer. When Dora was developed in 2000, the creators hired sociologist Clara Rodriguez, an expert in media representations of Latinas/os, as a consultant to be sure that Dora would be a positive influence for young children. As Dora was developed, everything was "carefully crafted to make sure that Dora accurately portrayed Latinos" (Havrilla 2010). Dora, a seven-year-old Latina, is goal oriented and adventurous—a

Challenging racial stereotypes is an important step in reducing prejudice in its various forms.

Source: https://www.vichealth.vic.gov.au/programs-and-projects/see-beyond-race#

very different portrayal from the typical Latina image in the media. By introducing Dora and, later, her companion Diego as positive Latina/o role models, Rodriguez and the cartoon's producers have influenced how White children see Latinas/os and boosted the self-respect of Latina/o children.

Racial boundaries, hierarchies, and definitions are challenged by those who produce new visions for what is possible. The fact that race is fluid makes change possible. Culture is a major medium through which this can happen. As one small example, research finds that those who view inspiring videos about people of color develop stronger feelings of connectedness with diverse racial-ethnic groups (Oliver et al. 2015). Seeing more positive images also reduces stereotypes (Ramasubramanian 2015). Especially if you are a member of the dominant group, developing positive ideas about those who are "othered" requires looking with a critical eye and changing your way of thinking.

Conclusion

The mass media and popular culture have increasing influence on how people see each other and how they understand the society in which they live. Put simply, the media constructs reality but does not reflect it. Sometimes images in the media promotes color-blind racism—that is, the idea that race no longer matters and that everyone has the same chance to succeed, which we examined in the previous chapter.

Racial images in the media also have become something that White Americans can consume and enjoy but without any consequence for their status in society (Gallagher 2003). Race, then, becomes a style, not a matter of social inequality. As we have seen throughout this chapter, though, popular culture and the media continue to reproduce images that distort and undermine people of color. Although improvements have been made in the representation of people of color, much needs to be done if we are to project a more inclusive and realistic portrait of race and ethnicity in the United States. Because race and ethnicity are social constructions, transforming these images in the media is an important part of the movement for racial justice.

Key Terms

capitalism 70

content analysis 60

controlling image 54

critical race theory 70

cultural appropriation 73

cultural hegemony 52

cultural production 64

cultural racism 53

culture 51

culture of affirmation 72

culture of resistance 72

dominant culture 52

mass media 51

objectification 56

popular culture 51

racial frames 53

symbolic annihilation 62

Critical-Thinking Questions

1. Go back to the quotation by Maya Angelou that opened this chapter. How can popular culture and the media help build the esteem for multiple cultures in the United States that Angelou writes about?
2. How have you been influenced by some of the controlling images found in the types of media that you are most likely to use on a regular basis? How does the answer to this question likely differ if you are a person of color or a White person?

Student Exercises

3.1. Take a visit to your local grocery store. Walk through every aisle, making note of any stereotypes that you see. What does this exercise tell you about the presence of stereotypes in everyday life?
3.2. With the goal of doing a content analysis of some form of media or popular culture, first identify a very specific genre (sitcoms, police "reality" shows, advertisements in a particular theme magazine, or something quite focused so you can be systematic in your research). Then develop a careful plan by which you can do a content analysis of the images in this particular form of media. Describe your results in terms of the images that you find and what they portray. What do you conclude from this exercise? Does it change how you see the media and popular culture?

Challenging Questions/Open to Debate

Suppose that a student government has arranged a campus event featuring a standup comedian for a night of student entertainment. The contracts are signed, publicity is out, and the student organization has committed a lot of its budget to this event. As it turns out, the performer uses a lot of racial stereotypes in the stand-up act, and certain student groups on campus are protesting the event. Should the event be canceled, given the student demonstrations against it?

Would your answer change depending on which groups were being offended by the comedian?

If the performance is not canceled, are there other courses of action you could take?

TAKING ACTION AGAINST RACISM

Creating Cultural Competence

Our vast immersion in the dominant culture means that few of us know very much about the cultures of diverse people of color. You can change this situation in a number of ways—for example, by taking a course that introduces you to the culture of a group other than your own. This could be a course on Chicano/a or African American literature, the cultures of Native people, Asian American art and film, and so forth. Even without taking such a course, immersing yourself in alternative media that show-case the voices of people of color—from their own perspective—is a powerful way to challenge the hegemony of the dominant media.

Find out where there are local museums and other exhibits focusing on the accomplishments of people of color and make a point of visiting. Visit (in person or virtually) some of the significant national museums dedicated to preserving and documenting the history and culture of people of color.

Resources:

- National Museum of the American Indian: https://americanindian.si.edu
- National Museum of African American History and Culture: https://africa.si.edu
- Friends of the Proposed National Museum of the American Latino: https://americanlatinomuseum.org/press/
- Smithsonian Asian Pacific American Center: https://smithsonianapa.org

Source: Getty Images

CHAPTER 4

Who Do You Think You Are?

Racial Identities and Relationships

It is a peculiar sensation, this double-consciousness, this sense of always looking at one's self through the eyes of others, of measuring one's soul by the tape of a world that looks on in amused contempt and pity.

—W. E. B. Du Bois ([1903] 1996:5)

OBJECTIVES

- Understand the social-structural basis for racial identities
- Explain how multiracial identities challenge the traditional "Black/White" binary
- Identify and explain White privilege
- Detail the significance of racial microaggressions
- Discuss the factors that influence the development of interracial relationships

What is your ancestral heritage? Are you descended from immigrants? Unless you are Native American or descended from slaves who were forced to come to the Americas, your answer is yes. How do you define your identity in terms of race and ethnicity? Do you have a quick and straightforward answer, such as "African American," "Chicana," or "White"? Or is your answer one of multiple identities, such as that of US Representative Alexandria Ocasio-Cortez, who describes herself as Nuyorican, a person of Puerto Rican descent born and raised in New York? Like many people, Ocasio-Cortez describes her identity as from many different identities. She says, "I am the descendant of African slaves. I am the descendant of indigenous people. I am the descendant of Spanish colonizers, . . . I am a descendant of all sorts of folks. That doesn't mean I'm Black, that doesn't mean I'm Native, but I can tell the story of my ancestors" (Araujo 2019).

Like the identity of many people from mixed backgrounds, Ocasio-Cortez's identity shows us how complicated matters of racial and ethnic identity have become in such a diverse society. In a society structured around racial and ethnic inequalities, such as the United States—but also other nations—how we define ourselves and how others define us is a deeply sociological phenomenon. What it means to be "Black" and what it means to be "White" emerge from very specific social and historical circumstances—some of which are in our immediate experience, others of which stem from histories and events that long precede our individual lives. Our identities are fundamentally the result of social processes. You can see this by recalling a national controversy that emerged in the summer of 2015 involving Rachel Dolezal, then the president of the NAACP's chapter in Spokane, Washington.[1]

Rachel Dolezal resigned as president of this chapter of the NAACP when her parents (from whom she was estranged) announced to the national media that their daughter was White, not Black, as she had claimed. A national uproar ensued. As the news unfolded, we learned that Dolezal had changed her appearance over the years by darkening her skin, wearing an Afro-like hairstyle, and changing other things about her demeanor. As far as most people could tell, she looked like a light-skinned African American person. Her ex-husband is African American. Dolezal had been a passionate advocate for civil rights, had taught in an Africana studies program, and had served as a campus advisor to Black students. Few had questioned her commitment to racial justice.

As this controversy ensued, people on all sides of the political spectrum weighed in on Dolezal's racial identity. Some called her an impostor, but she insisted she was "not White." Her estranged parents wanted her to have a DNA test to prove that she was their White offspring. What if she was? Could she reasonably claim to be biracial, transracial, or Black—all terms she used at various times to describe herself? Did Dolezal have the right to call herself Black? Had she lived in a society with very different racial understandings, such as in Brazil, where the concept of race is more fluid, would she have been so controversial (Osuji 2019b)? How is one's racial identity determined?

---

[1] The National Association for the Advancement of Colored People was founded in 1909 by a coalition of African Americans and White liberals. The long-standing organization advocates for civil rights, focusing largely, though not exclusively, on African Americans. W. E. B. Du Bois, Ida B. Wells Barnett, and Mary Church Terrell were among its founders.

We learned in chapters 1 and 2 that race is a social construction. This is especially revealed in the fascinating case of someone who seems to be "biologically White" even while claiming to be Black. Is your racial identity simply a matter of your ancestry, or is it something that emerges in the context of your lifetime relationships?

Think about this in another context: Imagine the day a baby is born. Everyone in the child's large, extended family is excited about the new life that has come into the world. Let's suppose the child's mother identifies as Latina, and she has a Latina mother and a Black father. The baby's father is White, raised Jewish. What is the baby? When the hospital staff completes the birth certificate, what would the recorder pick to identify the child's race—Black? Hispanic? White? Other? None of the above?

Taking this one step further, would it matter where the hospital was located? Did you assume this was happening in the United States? What if the birth happened in a Caribbean nation? Canada? Europe? What if you had been born in 1950—in a Southern US hospital? What race you would be? And why does it matter? If you were considered White at birth, might you later change your identity to Black or "multiracial"? Once you grew up to be an adult, what would you put on the census form?

All of these questions are pivotal in a discussion of racial identity—the subject of this chapter. The questions iterate a central point made throughout this book: race is a social construction, as is your racial identity—or, perhaps, identities. This chapter explores the formation and significance of racial identity and the interracial relationships that develop or are impeded in a racially unequal society.

In doing so, we are looking at what sociologists call the *micro level of society*—that is, the part of society that is up close and quite directly observable. You might think of this as the individual level of society—how we see ourselves, how others see us, and how we relate to each other. It is important to see, however, that the micro level of society is shaped by the *macro level* or large-scale social systems and institutions that together constitute society.

In the case of race and ethnic relations, the macro level of racial-ethnic inequality very much shapes who we are as individuals and how we relate to people in different racial-ethnic groups. Even as we go through our daily lives and form highly personal relationships, the macro level of society is ever present. This chapter begins with a discussion of the "closest in" level of society: our racial and ethnic identities.

Who Am I? Racial Identities in a Racialized Society

Framing Question: In what ways does racial inequality in society influence one's identity formation?

Who do you think you are? This simple question packs a lot of meaning and cuts to the heart of the human experience: Humans are not just a bundle of physiological processes. Our capacity for reflection is part of what makes us human. That is, we have a consciousness of ourselves. It is in that consciousness—or self-reflection—that our sense of ourselves as human beings in society is realized. Human consciousness provides the ability to know ourselves and the world around us.

It also provides a way for us to reimagine the possibilities for more equitable intergroup relations.

Individuals in Society: The Formation of Identity

Identity is a person's conception of self. We think of our identity as an individual thing, but identity is very much the result of social relationships and social structures. This does not mean that you are not an individual, but it does means that your identity emerges from your relationships with others and from your specific place in society. Identity is not fixed. Identity is formed over the course of our lifetimes and constantly emerges. Certain experiences, especially during childhood but also in adolescence and adulthood, can be critical moments for identity formation. A particular relationship, a traumatic encounter, a new experience, a life of wealth or extreme poverty, living in racially segregated or integrated environments—these and other social factors all have a lasting impact on our identities.

Several key thinkers are important for understanding the social significance of identity. George Herbert Mead (1863–1931) and Charles Horton Cooley (1864–1929) of the Chicago School of Sociology formulated sociological analyses of identity and the self. Cooley's concept of the *looking-glass self* teaches us that we see ourselves as others see us. The self is the cumulated identity we have that results from the iteration between observation and reflection (Cooley 1902; Erikson 1968). We see how others see us, and we incorporate that awareness into our notion of who we are. Our concept of "self" emerges from this ongoing process. Mead wrote that it is through internalizing how those in our surrounding circles see us that we formulate a sense of self—a process he referred to as *taking the role of the other* (Mead 1934).

Psychologist Erik Erikson (1902–1994) conceptualized identity as a process by which we integrate different experiences and characteristics into a stable definition of self. This process begins at birth and continues through adolescence and adulthood. We do this through our membership in different social groups, including, as we will see, our racial and/or ethnic groups. To Erikson, one's identity is the point of intersection between the individual and community. Although our identity emerges through the specific circumstances of our individual lives, we are located in communities that attach us to particular expectations, values, and worldviews.

George Herbert Mead referred to this as the *generalized other*—the collective expectations that others have of us, especially those who are *significant others*. Mead used the term *significant others* to refer to the most important people in our social circles, a broader usage than how the term is often used today, to refer to one's partner. This formulation of identity means that the social environment is critical to the development of identity, regardless of how personal and individual we think we are. How race is understood in that social environment is then a critical part of the identities we form.

Racial Identity: A Sense of Belonging

Racial identity is the sense one has of oneself as belonging to a racial group. In a nation such as the United States where race is so significant in shaping social institutions, race is a key component of people's identity, as is ethnicity. When you grow up in a society tinged with racism, your racial identity—whatever it is—is bound to be affected, including how ethnicity is linked to social concepts of race. Your racial identity is then a *master status*—that is, it trumps other forms of identity while also intersecting with other master statuses, such as gender, nationality, and age.

Racial-ethnic identities attach us not only to specific racial and ethnic groups but also to particular histories. Your racial-ethnic identity gives you a sense of common belonging, although this varies in the degree to which it is felt. If you are a member of a racial or ethnic minority group, your racial-ethnic identity is likely to be far more salient than it is for those in the dominant group. Note here that in sociological usage, **minority group** refers to any group with less power than a dominant (or majority) group. The term *minority group* has fallen somewhat out of favor only because so-called minorities are becoming a numerical majority of the US population; the point is that the term refers to relationships of power and domination, not numbers.

A racial minority group need not be numerically smaller than the dominant group. In fact, there are many instances in which a minority group, defined in terms of power and subordination, is actually larger than the most powerful or dominating group. South Africa is a case in point. Under apartheid, Whites were a small numerical portion of the population (about 10 percent); Blacks and other persons of color were about 90 percent, and yet Whites exercised total power and control over Blacks and colored people, the racial designations used in South African society.

Racial and ethnic identities are formed as people navigate the various borders that construct race and ethnicity in society and, thus, our own sense of who we are. Sometimes, as is the case for people with a mixed heritage, many feel a sense of belonging to more than one racial or ethnic group, something we explore further later in this chapter.

Feeling a common attachment to others in your racial or ethnic group anchors you to a racial past and present, one that you may not always know but that connects you to a social structure that extends beyond your individual life. Such attachments give you a sense of collective belonging, although strong attachments to particular groups or identities can also be the basis for the exclusion of others. In the United States, the attachment that people of color have with each other provides a strong feeling of collective identity. Whites tend to have more individualistic identities (Ai et al. 2011; Bethel 1999; Triandis 1989).

Racial identity comes with particular expectations about how we behave and what we believe (Schwalbe 2014; Schwalbe et al. 2000). Although people respond to these expectations in different ways, the dominant expectations regarding race both constrain and enable us, depending on our place in the racial hierarchy. As one sociologist has put it, we act in "recognizable patterns and in ways that produce . . . allegiance to racial scripts" (Hughey 2015:148). The White teacher who scolds a young Latino student for "speaking with an accent," the Black teen whose parents instruct him how to behave if stopped by a police officer, the biracial adolescent who switches between thinking of herself as Latina and as Black—these and other scripts about race and ethnicity are played out through routine social interactions. Although we may not always recognize that we are playing out racial scripts, these scripts permeate interactions both within and across racial-ethnic groups. What else would it mean to say that someone is "acting White" (Carbado and Gulati 2013) or is not being "authentically Black"?

Seeing ourselves as others see us is especially complicated in a racially unequal society. Those in racially subordinated groups will see themselves both through the eyes of those in their racial group *and* through the eyes of the dominant group. W. E. B. Du Bois's well-known quotation that opens this chapter speaks to this reality for African American people. Du Bois wrote that African American people develop a unique racial identity in that they must strive to reconcile two selves—that defined by Whites and that derived from their own community. Within this sense of "twoness," African Americans have to find strength to keep "from being torn asunder" (Du Bois [1903] 1996:5). This process is not unique to African Americans. Immigrants who bridge two cultures, even while identifying as American, may also feel that sense of "twoness."

The dilemma that Du Bois so poignantly expressed is today known as an **identity contingency**. Identity contingencies are "the things you have to deal with because you have a given social identity" (Steele 2010:3). If that contingency is racism or ethnic prejudice, your identity will be shaped by these realities. People of color must learn to deal with identity contingencies. African American parents, for example, must teach their children about racism early in life, as will Asian, Native American, and Latino parents. White children, by contrast, may grow up rarely thinking about or talking about race—that is, until confronted with a racial conflict or other awakening experience. Racial identities develop in a social system grounded in the idea that Whites are dominant and all others are subordinate. Navigating this environment thus differs for dominant and subordinate groups.

In overtly racist regimes, a Black person who has the physical characteristics of a White person may try to pass as White to escape racism. Historically, many African Americans engaged in passing, often having to leave behind families and communities, lest their "White" identity be betrayed. By presenting themselves as White (perhaps even for a lifetime), these individuals would have better opportunities and would not be subjected to the ravages of racism (see the "Learning Our Past" section on the next page). The passing person, however, would also experience a great sense of loss, having left the African American community. Even now, some biracial people may "pass" by emphasizing their White identity over their Black identity, perhaps even just in select situations, in order to protect themselves from racial threats (Hobbs 2014; Wilton, Sanchez, and Garcia 2013).

Like other identities, *racial identity is emergent*. Your identity is not fixed at birth. Rather, identities develop over the life course. Your racial-ethnic identity may even change as you encounter new ideas and new life circumstances, which could then lead you to define yourself differently. A White adolescent girl may discover that she has a mixed-race heritage and start hanging out mostly with Black friends, in the process constructing herself to be "Black." Or a second-generation Korean American who was raised to be "American" may leave home for college and begin to explore his Asian heritage. He may take courses in Asian American studies, surround himself with Asian students from many different backgrounds, and start

LEARNING OUR PAST

Can you imagine leaving your family and the community where you grew up to pass as someone from a different racial background than the one into which you were born? That is precisely what some African Americans did during slavery and through the mid-twentieth century. Passing was a way to escape the conditions of racism, but it also involved its own considerable risks. Only some could do it, by virtue of their appearance. They also had to change their clothing, manners of speech, life history, appearance (if possible), and any other markers that would reveal their true identity.

Other people have also used passing as a way of escaping brutal ethnic, sexual, and gender oppression. Jewish people might try to pass to escape anti-Semitism. There are many instances of women who have passed as men for their entire lives (Middlebrook 1998). LGBT people might even liken passing to being "in the closet" to protect themselves from the threat of homophobia. For any individual, no matter the motivation, passing is very risky, given the constant possibility of having one's true identity revealed.

Historian Allyson Hobbs, who has studied African American passing, argues that "the core issue of passing is not becoming what you pass for but losing what you pass away from" (2014:18). Although passing by African Americans is now (and always has been) relatively rare, it reveals the lengths to which people will go in pursuit of freedom and fair treatment.

defining himself as "Asian American." In each of these examples and others, you can see that racial-ethnic identity is emergent and fluid at the same time that it can be quite stable.

The work of developing racial identity addresses a question that White people often ask when they see a group of people of color clustered together in a predominantly White environment—a question explored in *Why Are All the Black Kids Sitting Together in the Cafeteria?*, an examination of racial identity by psychologist and former college president Beverly Tatum (1997). Are Black students sitting together in a predominantly White environment "self-segregating"? Tatum's answer is no. She explains that subordinated groups develop a strong racial identity even when faced with racial and ethnic stereotypes and negative racial encounters.

Tatum's work teaches us that if you are a minority group member, immersing yourself in the culture of your affinity group is an important part of the process of identity formation. Joining a Muslim student organization or participating in the Asian American student union provides a safe space where people of color can explore and then internalize a positive racial or ethnic identity. This is especially relevant during adolescence and early adulthood, when one's identity is being so significantly shaped. If located in a mostly White environment, people of color may surround themselves with symbols and relationships that affirm, rather than deny, their racial identity. Immersion in one's own group as a minority person is thus a necessary route, according to Tatum, for developing a strong and stable racial identity (Tatum 1997). *Identity safety* is achieved when "people believe their social identity is an asset rather than a barrier . . . and that they are welcomed, supported, and valued whatever their background" (Steele and Cohn-Vargas 2013:5).

Several points summarize this discussion of racial identity:

* *Racial identity emerges in particular social and historical contexts.* C. Wright Mills (1959), in founding one of sociology's central concepts, identifies the central task of sociology as understanding the link between people's lives and the historical and social context in which they live. The *sociological imagination* reveals this link between biography and history—that is, understanding the patterns and social processes that shape individual lives. In the case of racial identities, dominant groups "set the parameters within which the subordinates operate" (Tatum 1997:23). As a result, people of color have to pay attention to those who control their outcomes. They will be highly attuned to the dynamics of race, while those in the dominant group will take their racial identity for granted—a point we return to below, in a discussion of Whiteness.

* *Racial identity is linked to other significant identities.* Gender, age, social class, sexuality, and nationality, among other factors, are also integral parts of our identity. Although one factor may be more salient at a given moment than another, these identities intersect and overlap, together constituting who we are. A Native American woman does not think of herself as Native at one moment and a woman at another. But if someone makes a disparaging remark about Native people in front of her, her identity as Native may at that moment seem particularly sharp, just as a sexist comment might heighten her gender identity. In a society structured around inequalities of race, class, gender, and sexuality, each of these social facts intersects with the others in forming our identities and our **identity matrix** (Rockquemore 2002; Thomas, Hacker, and Hoxha 2011). Put another way, the matrix is the configuration of social factors that, taken together, constitute one's definition of self.

* *Racial identity is consequential.* Identity not only is who we think we are but also has outcomes for our well-being—sometimes for the better, sometimes not. People who grow up in a context of being consistently told by powerful people that they are worthless or incompetent may develop a low sense of self-worth. This is a particular risk to members of a racial-ethnic minority group unless there are countervailing forces within the person's family, community, or peer group. Research finds that, although there are psychological risks for people of color growing up in a racist society, developing a strong racial identity is nonetheless beneficial. Numerous studies find that even though society writ large may devalue people of color, having a strong collective attachment as a racial minority can reduce stress, allow a more positive sense of well-being, and help in contending with prevailing racial and ethnic stereotypes (Way et al. 2013).

To sum up, racial identity is multidimensional (Sellers et al. 1998) and linked to the social structure of society. How we see ourselves and how others see us develops as we experience how race is constructed in society. Because the social construction of race is such a complex phenomenon, the social construction of racial identities is too. This is particularly revealed when thinking about multiracial identity.

Borders and Binaries: The Complexities of Multiracial Identity

Framing Question: How is identity forged when people come from more than one racial group?

The number of people who define themselves as being of more than one race is increasing, although the number is still relatively small. Although official census counts are not a perfect indication of how people define themselves, the number of people who have reported in the census that they are of more than one race doubled between 2000 and 2010 (from 2.4 to 4.5 percent of the US population; see figure 4.1). The number who identify as being more than one race is expected to increase again in the 2020 census. The US Census Bureau predicts that the multiracial population will grow to 276 million people (6.2 percent of the population) by 2060 (US Census Bureau 2014).

The 2000 US Census was the first in which people could indicate membership in more than one racial and/or ethnic group. By now, a large proportion of people in the United States likely has a relative or knows someone of mixed background (Masuoka 2017). As you can see in figure 4.2, the geographic distribution of people identifying as being of more than one race is more concentrated in the West and Southwest and in Eastern coastal areas.

Giving people the option to identify as multiracial in the census resulted from the mobilization of multiracial groups who lobbied hard for greater recognition. Politics around how the US Census Bureau defines race, debates about race and

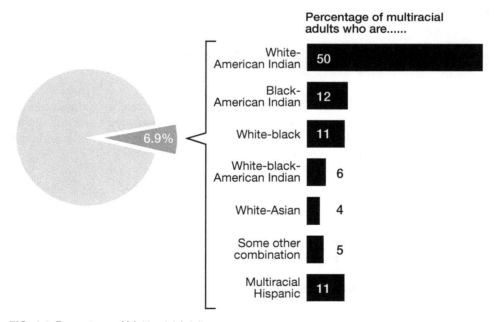

FIG. 4.1 Percentage of Multiracial Adults

Source: Parker et al. 2015:10.

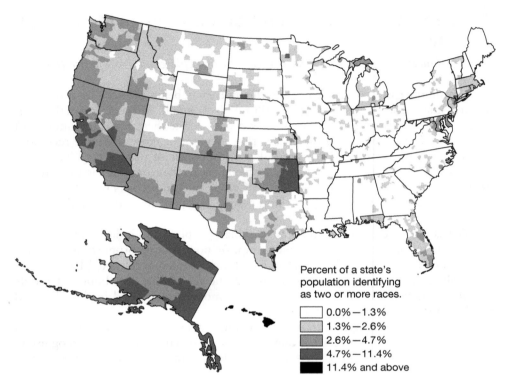

FIG. 4.2 Mapping Multiracial Identification

Note: This map shows the regional distribution of those who define themselves as being of more than one race. What factors do you think influence this distribution? This map was drawn from 2000 US census data; what would you expect to see when the data are available from the 2020 census?

Source: Social Science Data Analysis Network n.d.

adoption, the growth of scholarly research on multiracialism, and the increased visibility of people with multiracial and multiethnic backgrounds—including former president Barack Obama—represent a cultural shift whereby some people can choose their racial identity, even while it is still imposed for many.

Navigating Racial and Ethnic Borders

People with multiracial identities have had to navigate a Black/White binary that has long defined race relations in the United States. Studies of multiracialism now challenge the binary thinking that earlier defined people as either White or Black. Living on the margins of two or more groups means forming a "merged identity" (Root 1992 and 1996). For example, how does a woman born to a Black father and a Latina mother define herself? Maybe Latina? Maybe Black? Maybe both? Either way, forming an identity is more complex for those with multiracial identities (Khanna 2013).

Identity work is the process by which people construct and maintain positive identities distinct from the negative ones applied to them by others (Goffman 1963; Snow and Anderson 1987). Identity work for multiracial people might involve

Just as you cannot judge a book by its cover, you should not judge race by how people look.

Source: Getty Images / eli_asenova.

displaying certain racial or ethnic symbols, making verbal claims to identity, and perhaps even making physical changes, such to hair color, style of dress, or even skin color. In this way, identity work involves aligning ourselves with the norms of the group with which we most identify. For example, Black-White multiracial people report acting differently when in predominantly White settings versus in predominantly Black settings. Sociologist Chandra Waring refers to this as **racial capital**—the repertoire of racial resources (such as language, cultural knowledge, and so forth) that biracial individuals use to navigate racial boundaries and racial contexts. As you can see in the "Living with Racism" segment further down, a bi- or multiracial person might associate with particular groups or disclose her identity only in certain contexts (Snow and Anderson 1987; Waring 2017).

Context matters in shaping how biracial and multiracial people identify themselves. Children whose parents include an American Indian and someone of another race are, for example, more likely to adopt an Indian identity if they live on American Indian homelands (Liebler 2010; Liebler and Zacher 2013). A recent study of Latino students on different college campus environments also illustrates how important social context is in the formation of racial and ethnic identity. Sociologist Daisy Reyes (2017) compared identity formation for Latino students in three different campus environments: a small, private liberal arts college, a large public research university, and a large, regional public university. These campus settings vary in both their resources and the types of students they serve. Each campus

LIVING WITH RACISM

Racial identity is a complex and shifting way that people see themselves. How do people of mixed backgrounds understand their racial identity? "I just say I'm brown," McKenzi McPherson, nine, says. "And I think, Why do you want to know?" This has been explored in a *National Geographic* article:

Maximillian Sugiura, twenty-nine, says he responds with whatever ethnicity provides a situational advantage. Loyalties figure in too, especially when one's heritage doesn't show up in phenotypical facial features, hair, or skin. Yudah Holman, twenty-nine, self-identifies as half-Thai and half-Black but marks "Asian" on forms and always puts "Thai" first, "because my mother raised me, so I'm really proud of being Thai."

Sandra Williams, forty-six [in 2012], grew up at a time when the nation still turned on a Black-White axis. The 1960 census depicted a country that was still 99 percent Black or White, and when Williams was born six years later to parents of mixed Black and White ancestry, seventeen states still had laws against interracial marriage. In Williams's western Virginia hometown, there was only one Asian child in her school. To link her own fair skin and hair to her White ancestry, Williams says, would have been seen by Blacks as a rejection. And so, though she views race as a social construction, she checks "Black" on the census. "It's what my parents checked," she says.

People with complex cultural and racial origins become more fluid and playful with what they call themselves. On playgrounds and college campuses, you'll find such homespun terms as Blackanese, Filatino, Chicanese, and Korgentinian. When Joshua Ahsoak, thirty-four, attended college, his heritage of Inupiat (Eskimo) and Midwestern Jewish earned him the moniker Juskimo, a term he still uses to describe himself (a practicing Jew who breaks kosher dietary laws not for bacon but for walrus and seal meat). Tracey Williams Bautista says her seven-year-old son, Yoel Chac Bautista, identifies himself as Black when he's with her, his African-American parent. When he's with his father, he'll say Mexican. "We call him a Blaxican," she jokes, and says she and her husband are raising him in a home where Martin Luther King Jr. is displayed next to Frida Kahlo. Black relatives warn Williams about the persistence of the one-drop rule, the long-standing practice of seeing anyone with a trace of Black "blood" as Black. "They say, 'He may be half, but he's still the N-word.'"

Source: Funderburg 2013.

has a distinct environment that, in turn, shapes how students define themselves and draw racial-ethnic boundaries between themselves and others. In the small and more elite private university where Latinos are a numerical minority, there is more cooperation and solidarity among Latino students. In this context, students typically experience culture shock, microaggressions, and a lot of tokenism. Latino student marginalization in this context, then, promotes stronger Latino identity.

In the large research university Reyes studied, there are more Latino student organizations, fostering competition among Latino students. As a consequence, students in this context tend to question whether some Latino students are "authenticity Latino." But in this predominantly White setting, Latino students, like other students of color in similar environments, become hyperaware of their racial and ethnic identity.

In the regional public campus Reyes studied, the campus mirrored the community where it was situated—that is, it was largely Latino. In this context, students are less questioning of their Latino identity. Students are also less likely here to adopt

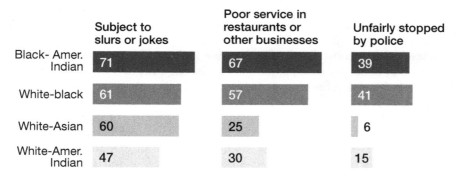

Percentage saying they have ever experienced each of these because of their racial background

	Subject to slurs or jokes	Poor service in restaurants or other businesses	Unfairly stopped by police
Black- Amer. Indian	71	67	39
White-black	61	57	41
White-Asian	60	25	6
White-Amer. Indian	47	30	15

FIG. 4.3 Multiracial Adults and Perceived Discrimination

Source: Parker et al. 2015:8.

identities as "Latino" or "Hispanic," instead adopting such specific regional identities as "Mexican," "Salvadoran," "Guatemalan," and so forth. Reyes's research is a strong reminder of how important social context is in patterning individual racial and ethnic identities. You might use her research to learn about the campus environment where you are situated and how that context affects the identities of students of color on your campus as well as White students.

Research on multiracial identity has also examined such things as outcomes for biracial people and whether being biracial influences political and social attitudes. The findings are mixed. In general, multiracial people tend to have political attitudes that resemble the attitudes of those with a singular racial identity, but there are exceptions. People with some Asian identification, for example, have political attitudes closely aligned with those of White people (Masuoka 2017). Asian-White biracial people also describe discrimination against them as less burdensome than Black-White and Latino-White people report (see figure 4.3). Asian-White biracial people are also more likely to identify as "White" than are Black-White biracial people—who also express more solidarity with Black Americans than do other biracial people (Lee and Bean 2012; Strmic-Pawl 2016). You can see there is a powerful "racial logic" operating as people navigate the terrain of racial inequality.

With cross-race unions more common and more people defining themselves in more than one ethnic or racial category, what will the future of racial inequality look like? Only time will tell. Racial inequality is stubborn. Despite some blurring of racial boundaries, many think the growing presence of biracial and multiracial people does not necessarily challenge the racial hierarchy (Masuoka 2017). Some suggest that the United States will become a tripartite society composed of Whites, Blacks, and Latinos (Bonilla-Silva 2004; also see chapter 12), but others think the Black/White binary will persist, with some groups becoming perceived as "White" while others are "Blackened."

Some people argue that the focus on generating new categories of racial membership only reinforces the idea of race as an immutable characteristic even while the concept of race is unraveling (Brunsma 2006). And, as many point out, the very nature of African American identity is multiracial, given the millions of African American people who have been conceived through multiracial unions. Some say, then, that developing a new category of race to acknowledge multiracial identity only reproduces (even if implicitly) the old one-drop rule, thereby defining race and "Blackness" as somehow fixed or immutable (Spencer 2006). Some also fear that the separation of multiracial people into a distinct category could dilute the civil rights agenda by undercounting those traditionally thought to be African American (Thompson 2007).

Multiracialism underscores the fluidity in the definition of race and reminds us how cultural, social, and political forces shape the very meaning of race in society (Brunsma 2006; Golash-Boza 2016; Rockquemore, Brunsma, and Delgado 2009). Racial boundaries that have been established through law and social practices are actually permeable, even though they are presented to us by the dominant culture as immutable. The complexities of racial identity make this apparent as people try to situate themselves within a racial order that extends far beyond their personal lives. Racial identity, like race, is experienced at the individual (or micro) level, but it is constructed at the societal (or macro) level.

Out of Many, One: Panethnic Identities

The diversity of racial and ethnic groups in US society has also led to a new form of racial-ethnic identity referred to as *panethnicity*. **Panethnicity** is the collective identity formed when multiple ethnic groups forge a sense of shared belonging and then create a new name for their group (Espiritu 1992; Okamoto 2014; Okamoto and Mora 2014:220). As different ethnic, tribal, religious, or national groups come to think of themselves as having a common history or sharing political, cultural, or social interests, they may form a panethnic identity. Activists, for example, may use slogans such as "brown power" or "yellow power" to bring together diverse ethnic groups, organized under a single label to wield more collective power (Okamoto and Mora 2014).

There are numerous examples of panethnic identities. Native American is a panethnic identity in that it consolidates the many and very different indigenous American nations into a forged sense of being "one." Likewise, Latino, Asian American, "people of color," and, for that matter, African American are also panethnic identities in that they link people together under a single name even when there is great diversity of ethnic, regional, and/or national origin under this umbrella (Ocampo 2014).

Panethnicity is often self-generated, but it can be imposed when a dominant group forces consolidation onto diverse ethnic or tribal groups, usually to delineate group rights. When the British colonized Malaysia, for example, they created the category "Malay" to lump together different ethnic groups and distinguish them from the Chinese. These divisions then determined various group rights—or lack thereof. The former Soviet Union also created "Russian" people even when people from the various nations that made up the former Soviet Union would have defined themselves as Ukrainian, Armenian, or other nationalities from within the federated states of the former Soviet Union. These examples show how panethnicity can be the result of government actions that consolidate the power of a dominant group (Okamoto and Mora 2014). This is also why panethnicity can become the basis for intense political mobilization.

A panethnic label, especially when self-generated, is strongly associated with a sense of a common history and a linked fate, including the idea that the fate of others in the group affects you and your group (Okamoto and Mora 2014:223; Wong et al. 2011). When panethnicity is imposed, not self-generated, people are more likely to hold on to their original identity. Panethnicity allows groups to present a united front, especially when they see themselves as mistreated by more powerful groups. In other words, they develop an identity as "insiders" even while being perceived as "outsiders" by the dominant culture.

Panethnic identity can also emerge in response to racial discrimination. People who migrate from Latin America, for example, may not initially think of themselves as Hispanic or Latino. If they encounter discrimination once they enter the United States, however, they are more likely to develop a Hispanic/Latino identity (Golash-Boza and Darity 2008). In her seminal study of panethnicity, Yen Le Espiritu describes Asian American panethnicity as "the development of bridging organizations and solidarities among several ethnic and immigrant groups of Asian ancestry" (1992:14). Her work presents panethnicity as a response to widespread anti-Asian violence and discrimination. Panethnicity among Asian Americans provides a consciousness of collective social standing, even though diverse Asian people may have previously thought of themselves as Korean, Chinese, Japanese, or some other more specific Asian origin. With too many subgroups to be effective, people sometimes organize under a panethnic label to unite against a common oppressor.

Within the United States, panethnic identity has grown in recent years as diverse groups have mobilized to grow and protect their civil rights. Two-thirds of Asian Americans now use the term *panethnic* as part of their identification (Lien, Conway, and Wong 2003). In the early 1990s, only 40 percent of Mexican Americans, Puerto Ricans, and Cuban Americans identified with panethnic labels; by 2008, the percentage had doubled to over 80 percent (Fraga 2012; Jones-Correa and Leal 1996; Tienda and Ortiz 1986).

The extent to which people embrace panethnic identity differs within particular groups. Among immigrants, younger generations may be more likely to adopt a panethnic identity as parents try to hold on to their national identity. Among Latinos, those in the second generation and those with higher levels of education and income are more likely to identify as Latino or Hispanic (de la Garza 1992; Jones-Correa and Leal 1996; Portes and MacLeod 1996). An increasing number of first-generation Latino immigrants now identifies as panethnic. Cuban Americans, though, are less likely than Mexican Americans and Puerto Ricans to identify as Hispanic or Latino (Fraga 2012; Fraga et al. 2010). Among Asian Americans, class and educational differences correlate with panethnic identity (Kibria 2003; Lee 2004; Lien, Conway, and Wong 2003; Masuoka 2006). Among Asian Americans, Koreans are the most likely to identify with panethnicity; Japanese, the least likely (Wong et al. 2011).

Sometimes members of a group will adopt a panethnic identity to assert what they are not. For example, a study of Arab Americans in Detroit found that Arab Americans have adopted a panethnic identity because they do not want to be thought of as "White" (Ajrouch and Jamal 2007). A recent study of students from Arab ancestries has also found that increased Islamophobia has enhanced the feeling of panethnicity that Arab students find, especially when on predominantly White campuses (Jones 2017).

Single-ethnic and panethnic identities can also exist side by side, being separately exercised at different times and in different situations. A specific encounter or context may make a person feel more affiliated with their subgroup identity, whereas in other contexts, they might embrace a more collective identity. These different identities are then interlocking and simultaneous (Espiritu 1992; Nakano 2013; Vo 2004).

Panethnic labels can be quite controversial. Many Chicanos, for example, vehemently object to being called Latino, wanting instead to hold on to their specific group history and identity. Some Chicano activist groups in the US Southwest have viewed the "Hispanic" and "Latino" labels as a threat to their nationalist projects (Oboler 1995). *Latinx* is also a panethnic term—interestingly, one to which the vast majority of "Latin" people object. Only 3 percent of Hispanic/Latino people say they use the term; two-thirds of Latinos say the term should not be used to describe the Hispanic/Latino population. The term is, however, more popular among younger Latinos, 7 percent of whom say they have used "Latinx" to describe themselves—still, quite a small number. Young Latinas (women), though, are more likely than young Latinos (men) to say they use it to describe themselves—14 versus 1 percent (Noe-Bustamante, Mora, and Lopez 2020).

Panethnic terms are clearly tangled up with social and political identities. In another example, some Cubans also object to being called Hispanic, as seen on the bumper stickers that have appeared throughout Miami declaring, "Don't call me Hispanic, I'm Cuban" (Okamoto and Mora 2014:223). Studies of American Indians also confirm the importance of "home" identity. In other words, the pride a person feels in being a part of a particular ethnic group can override any political interest in becoming part of a panethnic collectivity.

Some groups may also fear that adopting a panethnic label will lead to their group being racialized. Some West Indians, for example, do not want to be considered "Black" because of the racism associated with that group status. Panethnicity is usually self-created, but racialization is something that happens to you through the action of others. Rejecting panethnicity can be a way of protecting yourself and your group against the ravages of racism (Itzigsohn 2004; Itzigsohn and Dore-Cabral 2000). Indeed, panethnicity and the racialization process go hand in hand because, without the backdrop of a society marked by race and racism, panethnicity would not likely emerge (Brown and Jones 2015).

Research on panethnicity, like that on multiracial identity, underscores how fluid racial identities can be. Because identity emerges through group interaction and one's social, historical, and political context, racial identity for some can change over time. Fundamentally, understanding panethnicity underscores the point that racial identities are constructed via group interrelationships and boundaries (Okamoto and Mora 2014).

Who's White, and Why Does It Matter? Whiteness and White Privilege

Framing Question: What is White privilege, and what are its consequences?

If you are White, do you think of yourself as having a race? Perhaps you do, although it is not likely to be something that you think about very often. People of color certainly think of you as White. Your being White is very likely one of the first things people of color take note of when meeting you, given the decades of distrust that have marked relations between White people and everyone else. Unlike for people of color, race for White people is typically not a salient identity. That is, White people are usually not very conscious of their racial status because they can take it for granted in a society where Whiteness brings certain privileges and advantages. This is true regardless of whether one thinks about it (Wise 2011).

You can see this based on a simple test that has been used for decades. In this experiment, research subjects are asked to list twenty responses to the simple question, "Who am I?" How would you answer? This is known as the Twenty Statements Test. The TST, first developed in the 1950s, has been used to study people's most salient identities. Theoretically the more important a particular identity is, the more likely someone is to list it. How close a particular identity is to the top of the list also reveals the salience of that given identity.

Over the years, researchers have found that people in racial or ethnic minority groups almost always mention that aspect of their identity and mention it near the top of their list. White people rarely do either (Tatum 1997). More specifically, half of Whites never mention their race, whereas hardly any Black Americans (only 12 percent) say race never crosses their mind (Forman 2004; Forman and Lewis 2006). Simply put, racial identity is far more salient for members of minority groups than it is for White people, even though the salience of racial identity varies for different people and at different points in time (Steck, Heckert, and Heckert 2003).

White identity has been called "transparent" (Doane and Bonilla-Silva 2003; Flagg 1997). Whiteness establishes an invisible norm, meaning that it usually goes unexamined.[2] Whiteness bestows specific and unquestioned privileges and expectations, even though people assume Whiteness to be "raceless." The reality is, though, that race is operative even when only White people are present (Andersen 2003). Here's a somewhat trivial, yet telling, example: If you perform a generic search on Google for an image, searching by terms such as "hand," "finger," or "woman," the images returned are mostly of White people.

White Privilege and the Invisible Backpack

Although many White people do not see their race as salient, it certainly is. Even when White people do not take note of their race, people of color will see it as salient, just as men do not typically see their gender status but women do. As we will see next, White people benefit from their racial status even when they are not conscious of their **White privilege,** the social, cultural, and economic benefits that White people accrue relative to others in a society marked by racial hierarchy.

---

[2] By now you will have noticed that White is capitalized when used as a proper noun. See the "Note on Language" in the preface for a discussion as to why.

WHITE PRIVILEGE

The Invisible Backpack

Peggy McIntosh's influential work on White privilege includes a list of some of the ways that White privilege is manifested in everyday life; examples are shown below. If you were making such a list, what would you add?

- I can go shopping pretty sure that I will not be followed or harassed.
- In the media, I can see people like me well represented.
- I can dress in used clothes or sloppy outfits without people attributing my look to my bad morals.
- I can remain oblivious to the heritage of people of color.
- I can be pretty sure that if I speak to "the person in charge," I will be facing a person of my race.
- If I am stopped for speeding, I will not feel like I have been singled out because of my race.
- I can easily buy greeting cards, books, toys, and so forth that represent people like me.
- I can take a job without someone saying I got the position because of my race.
- I can be fairly sure that if I need medical or legal help, my race will not work against me.

Sources: Adapted from McIntosh 1988, as reprinted in McIntosh 2020.

You can witness this for yourself if you do the exercise at the end of this chapter on the **racial tax**—the extra burden that people of color experience by living with racism. The few White people who understand this are more likely to support policies designed to alleviate racial inequality (Bunyasi 2015).

Peggy McIntosh (2020) has called White privilege the "invisible backpack," something White people carry around with them but do not see. McIntosh has listed the many ways—large and small—that Whiteness confers privilege. For example, when a White person does something wrong, it will not be attributed to their race. See additional examples in "White Privilege: The Invisible Backpack," above.

How did the idea of Whiteness come to exist? People have long had so-called white skin, but the idea of people being White is a relatively recent notion. It originated in the eighteenth century, when notions of race were first developed (see chapter 1; also see Painter 2010). Like other meanings of race, "White" is an idea and an identity invented in the context of racial inequality and perceived difference. Prior to the invention of "White," people in Western Europe were known by their tribe or ethnicity: Celts, Gauls, Phoenicians, Greeks, Romans, and so forth (Painter 2010). With the development of slavery in the New World, "White" developed as a way of distinguishing categories of laborers; White people were free or indentured, but Black slaves were not. In other words, Whiteness has been defined in relationship to "Blackness," with Blackness perceived to be of inferior status and Whiteness of dominant status.

Who gets defined as White and, thus, benefits from the privilege of being White? As we have seen, the meaning of racial categories shifts over time. Some groups now perceived as White were once considered otherwise. Like other racial and ethnic groups, "White" is not a monolithic category, and not all White people benefit equally from White privilege. Also, although some groups may not define themselves as White, if successful, they may be treated as such. In this regard, the "borders of Whiteness are expanding" (Gallagher 2004:60), meaning that some groups, such as middle-class Asian Americans, are increasingly perceived as like Whites because of their economic and social successes. In this sense, "White" has more to do with privilege than skin color per se (Zhou 2004). But just as the borders of Whiteness can expand, can they also contract, "blackening" those who are unable to make their way?

In a related vein, some people may define themselves as White but not be seen by others as such. A telling example comes from a study by scholar Nicholas Vargas. Vargas asked a national sample of Latinos how they identified themselves and how they perceived others as defining them. Vargas found that 40 percent of Latinos identified as White, but only 6 percent said that others saw them as White. In other words, although a significant number of Latinos self-identify as White, others usually defined them as Hispanic. There was a much greater likelihood of Latinos being perceived by others as White if they had lighter skin and a higher socioeconomic status (Vargas 2015). Vargas's research findings are similar to those found for other groups. Dominicans in the United States, for example, are likely to define themselves as Hispan/o or India/o, but others simply perceive them as Black (Itzigsohn, Gorguli, and Vazquez 2005).

White Fragility: A Response to Racism

Surely some White people are not privileged—in the sense that they have lower socioeconomic status than some people of color. Identifying White privilege does not mean that all White people have the same socioeconomic status. But being White does bring certain advantages, not the least of which includes never having to suffer the indignities of racism.

Antiracist activist Robin DiAngelo (2016) has introduced the concept of **White fragility** to describe the unease White people feel when challenged to see their connection to a system of racial inequality. White people can quickly become defensive when challenged to acknowledge racism. They might say, "I don't see race; I only see people." "Don't blame me; slavery was bad, but I didn't have anything to do with it." Or "I'm not racist; I have Black friends." Each of these statements denies, often inadvertently, the continuing reality of racism in America. White fragility is meant to identify what happens when White people deny, argue over, withdraw from, or simply remain silent about racism. Although this behavior might not be intentional, DiAngelo sees White fragility as how White people maintain control, protecting their own power and advantage relative to others.

White people can become allies with those working toward a more racially just society. Being an ally means having to first recognize the existence of White privilege and institutional racism. Becoming a White ally means taking some risks—including the risk that White people feel it is to merely talk about race. Too often Whites remain silent about race, afraid they will say the wrong thing or be called a racist. Ignoring race and racism, however, just reaffirms its presence. For White people to become racial allies means taking several steps: recognizing the invisibility of their own racial identity, acknowledging the privilege that comes with being White, identifying learned racism, and taking responsibility for social change (Ford and Orlandella 2015; Kendi 2019; Saad 2020).

The Consequences of Color: Colorism

The study of Whiteness teaches us that having light skin matters to the formulation of a person's identity and experiences. As we saw in chapter 1, people in various racial and ethnic groups are judged and treated differently within their own groups based on the tone of their skin. The phenomenon is called **colorism**, "the discriminatory treatment of individuals falling within the same 'racial group' on the basis of skin color" (Herring 2004:3).

Colorism is based on the higher value placed on so-called European, or White, features. Although colorism is an issue that people within racial-ethnic communities may not want to acknowledge (at least not outside of their own group), it is a phenomenon with notable consequences, including how people's appearance is judged. Lighter-skinned people tend to reach higher income and educational levels than do those with darker skin (Herring, Keith, and Horton 2004; Hochschild and Weaver 2007).

Colorism does not just occur within the United States. In Latin American societies, skin color is a factor of the stratification system, with those of darker color holding lower status. In India, darker-skinned Hindus have experienced particularly strong prejudice and discrimination (Hall 1995; Herring, Keith, and Horton 2004).

The origins of colorism lie in the history of European colonialism throughout the Western world and in the development of slavery in North America. These patterns of conquest and enslavement, as we know, were based on a system of White supremacy. That would make it seem particularly capricious for people of color to judge others in their group by the shade of their skin, but there is little doubt that this happens. To some degree, being light- rather than dark-skinned has historically provided higher status for African Americans *within* the African American community.

In Latin America and Mexico, colorism began with the Spanish conquest of indigenous people. Spanish colonialists justified their domination through an ideology that portrayed native, darker-skinned people as savage and heathen (Chavez-Duenas, Adames, and Organista 2014; Hunter 2004 and 2007). In the United States, White slave owners assigned labor according to relative color. They might also have extended some privileges to mixed-race children whom they had fathered (Billingsley 1968; Hunter 2004).

The complexity of color stratification is especially apparent in Brazil, where color and class have become intermixed. As the result of this complex system of stratification, a person considered Black in the United States might not be considered so in Brazil. Being "Black" in Brazil is a much fuzzier category. In Brazil, people are more likely to use the term "color" than to think of color as race. Nonetheless, as with race in the United States, color in Brazil has particular consequences for a person's social status and relative privilege or advantage. Color differences in Brazil are also used to refer to the entire population, whereas, in the United States, shades of color are only thought of within minority racial or ethnic groups (Hordge-Freeman

2015; Osuji 2019a; Telles 2009). In the United States, for example, White people do not differentiate among themselves in terms of skin tone.

Differences in how color is considered in Brazil and the United States are the result of specific histories in both places, emphasizing again how racial identity is dependent on specific social contexts. In the American Southwest in the mid-nineteenth century, Anglos (White people of non-Hispanic descent) were more willing to grant citizenship to lighter-skinned Mexicans than to darker-skinned Mexican laborers (Hunter 2004). To this day, Mexican Americans and Asians—particularly darker men—report lower earnings and more experiences of discrimination (Edwards, Carter-Tellison, and Herring 2004; Ortiz and Telles 2008).

Now as in the past, skin tone is also connected to standards of beauty (Craig 2002; Thompson and Keith 2001). Successful women of color have to appear "more White." Popular stars Jennifer Lopez, Beyoncé, and Christina Aguilera, for example, have become more blonde and thin as they have become more successful (Vargas 2010). The growing use of skin-lightening products is also evidence of the perceived importance of light skin among women of color (Glenn 2008; Hill 2000 and 2002).

Colorism and racism are clearly interrelated, because colorism stems from a system of racial inequality. They are not, however, the same thing. Racism is an institutionalized system of exploitation. Although colorism differentiates people based on skin tone, colorism has not structured social institutions, nor has it denied people rights based solely on their membership in particular groups. Certainly colorism involves judgments about people, but it is a manifestation of racism, not an institutionalized system of inequality.

With an increase in the number of multiracial people, will colorism persist? Perhaps not, if there is greater acceptance of multiracial people, but judgments about people based on skin color have been obstinate. If nothing else, this discussion of color emphasizes once again how race is constructed through specific social and historical behaviors.

It's the Little Things that Count: Racial Microaggressions

Framing Question: How do microaggressions illustrate the penetration of racial inequality into everyday life?

The patterns of race in society are everywhere around you—in your head, your self-concept, and the interactions you have with others. Common and repetitive behaviors that minimize, ignore, or insult people of color, are *everyday racism* (adapted from Essed 1991:52). Everyday racism happens in encounters between dominant and subordinate groups. These behaviors happen at the individual or micro level, but they take place in the context of a power structure.

It is usually harder for dominant groups to see how racism is played out in everyday life. The invisibility of racism to dominant groups has been compared to the presence of spikes in some parking lots: the spikes are hardly apparent as long as you go in the right direction, but they will shred your tires if you drive over them backward (Wah 1994). Like the tire spikes, everyday racism can go unnoticed by

White people who easily "flow" with the system. For people of color, everyday racism is a constant reminder of their status as the "other."

The behaviors of everyday racism are what are now called **microaggressions**, "brief and commonplace daily verbal, behavioral, or environmental indignities, whether intentional or unintentional, that communicate hostile, derogatory, or negative racial slights and insults toward people of color" (Sue 2010; Sue et al. 2007:271). These can be momentary and subtle exchanges, possibly not even recognized by the offender. Although often unintentional, microaggressions reflect how stereotypes are activated in the minds and, thus, in the behaviors of dominant groups. Something as seemingly innocuous as a nonverbal exchange—such as the White woman who clutches her bag tightly as a Black man approaches—is an ongoing reminder of racial status.

There are countless examples of microaggression. Ignoring what a Black woman says in a meeting, assuming a Latina to be the maid or a Black man to be a servant at a party, a store clerk following a Black woman but not a White woman around a shop—all of these and many more encounters that people of color experience on a routine basis are examples of microaggression. They may seem minor to some, but they add up. In the context of racial inequality, the seemingly simplest things take on greater meaning. Also, what may seem perfectly acceptable and normal to people of the same social status may be insulting and offensive when the very same behavior occurs between people of unequal status. An example is calling a woman a "girl"—highly demeaning when a White person refers to a Black woman this way but probably only a term of endearment or kidding around between friends of equal status.

Microaggressions have to be understood in the context of power relationships. For example, everyone has probably at some point had the experience of getting slow service in a restaurant, but people of color may experience this on a routine basis. Any one instance of such slow service can trigger a reminder of one's status in society (Allen 2013; Gutiérrez y Muhs et al. 2012). If the person of color so offended mentions this to a White person, the White person may say, "It is no big deal" or "You're wearing race on your sleeve," thus diminishing the person of color's experience—which may consist of much more negativity than this one single instance. Moreover, the minimization itself is yet another microaggression!

Derand Wing Sue and his colleagues, who have extensively studied microaggressions, describe them as occurring in three ways: micro insults, micro assaults, and micro invalidations. *Micro insults* are interactions that convey stereotypes and biased messages. In a cross-race interaction, this could be a situation in which a dominant group member treats the other as second class, unimportant, stupid, incompetent, or perhaps even criminal. A White student, for example, who disregards the authority of a Black professor or who presumes that the Latina professor is somehow less competent than the White man is engaging in a micro insult. In a work environment, the absence of symbols that depict people like you can also be a micro insult.

The second type of microaggression is a *micro assault*. These are explicit remarks or behaviors that disparage and insult people. Using racial epithets, serving White people before people of color, and name-calling are examples. Asking students in a classroom to "speak for their race" is another example (McCabe 2009).

Such micro assaults are very similar to old styles of racism in that they tend to be more deliberate and conscious than other forms of microaggression.

Finally, Sue and his colleagues discuss *micro invalidations*. These are comments and behavior that negate the experience of a person of color. An example might be a comment such as "I never see a person's color" or "Gee, you speak good English." Such comments invalidate the person of color's experience even while heightening their "different" identity.

Microaggressions can be directed against various groups, including women, gays and lesbians, and disabled people. Although these everyday expressions of racism are more subtly expressed than overt racism, they have serious consequences for the people targeted by them—in the form of stress, anger, or simply the avoidance of others. Researchers conclude that microaggressions are cumulative, weighing on people of color, becoming a never-ending burden. Microaggression can also affect how people of color act in mixed-race settings. It can also affect people's performance, such as on examinations or in workplaces (Basford, Offermann, and Behrend 2014). One example comes from research on Asian American undergraduates in elite universities. Asian students in "White institutional space" typically encounter racism but seldom challenge it. Especially for Asian American women, the mix of racism and sexism in such environments is demeaning at the least and can be highly traumatic (Chou, Lee, and Ho 2015).

The stress of dealing with microaggression even has physiological consequences. Studies find that Black people's levels of stress increase (measured in biometric ways) when they interact with White people. Interracial tensions also have physiological consequences for White people: when interacting with Black people, White people's heart rates increase (Blascovich et al. 2001; Markus and Conner 2013). Clearly we would all be better off if we could understand and stop the everyday actions that reproduce racism.

Who Do You Know? Interracial Relationships

Framing Question: How does race shape interpersonal relationships, and what can be done to overcome these social boundaries?

When you make a friend, you are probably not thinking about the social forces that make that friendship possible or that influence whether it will last. Even though you may be unaware of them, the social forces of racism are present. Whether you even have friends from a different racial or ethnic background is influenced by race.

Imagine a wedding party. Your wedding is about as personal an occasion as it gets. You are probably going to invite your best friends to be your bridesmaids or groomsmen. Will they be the same race as you? A clever study of more than one thousand published wedding photographs found in a random online search reveals the paucity of interracial friendships, at least as indicated by the racial makeup of each bridal party. Only 3.7 percent of White brides, but 22 percent of Black brides, had a friend from another race who was close enough to be in their wedding party. Whites are only half as likely to have Black friends among their guests as Blacks are to include White friends. Blacks are also more likely to invite Asians than Whites into their wedding party, but Asians are only one-fifth as likely to invite Blacks

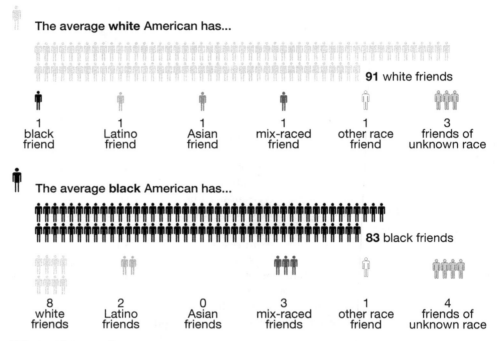

FIG. 4.4 Multiracial Friendships

Source: Ingraham 2014.

(Berry 2011). While such a study, based as it is on photographs, can only determine race based on appearance, it is an interesting indication of the influence of race on close friendship patterns.

Similarly, researchers have calculated the likelihood that people will have friends from racial and ethnic groups other than their own. Researchers asked people to name up to seven people with whom they regularly discuss important matters. They then calculated the typical numbers of friends for Black and White respondents. You can see the results in figure 4.4, above.

Generally speaking, among college students, White students have fewer inter-racial friendships than do students from every other racial-ethnic group. And although Black students tend to have more interracial friendships before college than do White students, they are the only group for whom interracial friendships decline while in college. Social science research can teach us about the conditions under which cross-race relationships are most likely to be made. In college, for example, having interracial roommates, having more interracial contact within residence halls, and participating in extracurricular activities are more likely to produce interracial friendships (Stearns, Buchmann, and Bonneau 2009).

One of the most important factors predicting cross-race friendships is residential and educational segregation (Kim and White 2010). Studies have found that among elementary school children interracial friendships become more common as the student body approaches an equal mix (Briggs 2007; Mouw and Entwisle 2006; Quillian and Campbell 2003). People who have experienced interracial contact in schools and neighborhoods are also more likely as adults to have racially diverse friendship circles, although this pattern does not hold for Asian Americans (Emerson, Kimbro, and Yancey 2002). Within schools, educational tracking also results in a lower probability of students forming interracial friendships, because tracking tends to separate racial groups (Stearns et al. 2009).

Segregated patterns of friendship can, however, be changed by engaging students in programs and activities that bring different groups together. Researchers have found that extracurricular activities that engage people of different backgrounds in common activities build more interracial ties. Socializing with coworkers, engaging in diverse civic activities, and attending multiracial religious services are also linked to more cross-race friendships (Tavares 2011). In college, students who matriculate having already had interracial connections through participation in sports, the arts, and political activities are more likely than other students to build cross-race friendships while in school (Benediktsson 2012).

Research finds that integrated wedding parties are quite unusual, an unobtrusive measure of the degree to which close, interracial friendships are formed.

Source: Getty Images / Digital Vision.

Interaction between people of different racial-ethnic backgrounds can be challenging. Anxiety about interacting with people from different backgrounds, as well as the fear of rejection, can create obstacles to people establishing cross-race friends. These obstacles to friendship can be overcome, however, as demonstrated by a very interesting study of friendship building. In a clever experiment, social psychologists put Latino and White college students (otherwise unknown to each other) in a laboratory setting where the students engaged in closeness-building tasks over a period of three weeks. Prior to the shared activity, the investigators had measured the students' level of implicit prejudice, background characteristics, and levels of anxiety (measured by physiological indicators). Following the three weeks of friendship-building activities, the students kept a ten-day diary, recording their interactions with people outside of the laboratory. Interestingly, it was students who were the most prejudiced at the beginning of the study who reported seeking out more cross-group interactions in the weeks following the initial experiment. Their anxiety levels were also significantly reduced (Page-Gould, Mendoza-Denton, and Tropp 2008).

Such a study shows that people can learn to cross the boundaries of race. Other studies also find that once students have acquired more cross-group friends in their first two years of college, they experience far less anxiety and are more likely to interact with people from a different race by the end of their four years in college (Levin, van Laar, and Sidanius 2003). Studies also find that, although attitudes have an impact on the formation of interracial friendships, campus diversity is important in predicting friendship patterns. Having a cross-race roommate, experiencing more interracial contact in residence halls, and participating in various interracial extracurricular activities are strongly related to the formation of interracial friendships (Stearns et al. 2009). Students of color on campus have more diversity in their friendships than do White students, but this usual difference nearly disappears when schools are more diverse (Fischer 2008).

Research has found that having interracial friendships early in life influences the likelihood of interracial intimacy later on (Shiao 2018). Friendship patterns also differ for African American, Latino, and Asian American adolescents. Latino and Black adolescents tend to establish and maintain friendships for a longer time than do Asian adolescents. Among people of color, Asian American adolescents are also least likely to form close friendships, especially if they are discouraged by their parents from spending time with friends outside of school (Way et al. 2005).

Multiracial youth have unique challenges in establishing friends. If they are rejected by their single-race peers, they will have smaller friendship networks. But multiracial adolescents also form more racially diverse friendship networks than do single-race adolescents and are more likely to bridge or socially connect with diverse friendship networks. Biracial adolescents with Black ancestry also have an especially high rate of friendship, forming bridges between Black persons and people in other racial groups (Quillian and Redd 2009).

Some evidence suggests that interracial relationships are difficult to maintain. In general, interracial friends report engaging in fewer shared activities than do intraracial friends (Kao and Joyner 2004). Interracial friendships are less likely to be reciprocal—that is, characterized by both people reporting the other as a friend (Rude 2010; Vaquera and Kao 2008).

Despite the interpersonal challenges that racism presents in the making of cross-race friendships, these connections are good for us. Interracial contact in the form of friendship brings more interracial closeness. For people of color interracial contact can diminish the effects of perceived discrimination (Tropp 2007). For Whites, interracial friendship is also related to a whole host of transforming attitudes about racial issues, such as acceptance of interracial marriage, a topic examined in chapter 8 (Jacobson and Johnson 2006). All told, interracial friendship is one path to eliminating the fears, misunderstanding, and mistrust that racism produces.

Conclusion

As you have seen, race and racial identity are changing in US society. A Black-White model of race relations no longer makes sense of the complex and shifting forms that racial identities and interactions are taking. Throughout this chapter, you have seen that racial identities develop—and potentially shift—in a context where the social meaning of race per se is also evolving. Attention to racial identity thus necessarily hinges on the particular constellation of racial meanings that exist at any given time in society.

Even in this kaleidoscope of racial meanings, the one thing that persists is that, as one sociologist has put it, "race is both deeply personal and strongly political" (Dalmage 2000:5). The meanings of race and, therefore, the meaning of racial identities are complex and sometimes blurry as new groups enter society, intermarry, and change how they think about race. We simply cannot understand racial identity without understanding the structural and material realities of race (Lewis 2004). The next section of this book moves from examining race on micro levels to examining the structural and institutional systems of race in America.

Key Terms

colorism 96

identity 80

identity contingency 82

identity matrix 84

identity work 86

microaggressions 98

minority group 81

panethnicity 90

racial capital 87

racial identity 80

racial tax 94

White fragility 95

White privilege 93

Critical-Thinking Questions

1. Do you think the increasing numbers of people with multiracial identities will reduce racism in the United States? Why or why not?
2. Does creating new categories to count "race" reify the idea that race is "real" and not a social construction? How can we recognize racial differences without stumbling into racism?

3. Are there some groups in contemporary society who seem to have the privileges of "Whiteness" even if they are not "officially" White? What does this teach you about the social construction of Whiteness?

Student Exercises

4.1. Ask a mixed-race group of individuals to try the Twenty Statements Test. Simply ask them to write down everything they think of in answer to the question, "Who am I?" Once they have finished, ask them to note their race and gender at the bottom of the page. Then compare the responses of people in different groups, analyzing whether they listed their racial and/or ethnic identities. For those who named them, how near the top of the answers given were racial and ethnic identities? Do you see any (other) patterns? How do you explain your findings?

4.2. Using the concept of the "invisible backpack" of White privilege, make your own list of White privileges in everyday life. If you can, compare your list to those made by people from a different racial group. How can such an exercise help us reduce the effects of racism? You can also expand this exercise to develop lists of other forms of privilege, thus developing an *intersectional analysis* of privilege.

4.3. If you can, do this next exercise in a group including both White people and people of color. As you name off each privilege specified in the list below, each person gets one point every time they can answer "true." Once completed, you will very likely find that the number of points White people get far exceeds the number of points people of color get. These differences in the everyday experiences of Whites and people of color are a good illustration of how systemic racism is played out in the everyday experiences of people *even when they have every intention of not being racist*. White privilege prevails for some, while others pay a racial tax.

1. I can take a job in an organization with an affirmative action policy without people thinking I got my job because of my race.
2. I can look at the mainstream media and see people who look like me represented in a wide variety of roles.
3. I can go shopping most of the time pretty well assured that I will not be followed or harassed.
4. If my car breaks down on a deserted stretch of road, I can trust that the law enforcement officer who shows up will be helpful.
5. I have a wide choice of grooming products that I can buy in places convenient to campus and/or near where I live as a student.
6. I never think twice about calling the police when trouble occurs.
7. The schools I have attended teach about my race and heritage and present them in positive, affirming ways.
8. I can be pretty sure that if I go into a business or other organization (such as the university) to speak with the "person in charge," I will be facing a person of my race.
9. I rarely feel that I am being singled out because of my racial-ethnic identity.

10. When I graduate from college, employers will evaluate me based on my skills and accomplishments.

4.4. Do you have a friend (or more than one) from a different racial background than your own? If so, how did you meet? What were the social conditions that enabled this friendship to be formed? If you do not have such friends, what conditions have prevented such a friendship?

Challenging Questions/Open to Debate

Census counts are important for purposes of representation and apportionment of seats in Congress. Some argue that creating new census categories to count multi-racial people weakens the representation of others, especially African Americans. Others think, to the contrary, that multiracial people need to be recognized on their own terms. If you were the director of the census, what would you do and why?

TAKING ACTION AGAINST RACISM

Break Your Bubble

Everyday interactions reproduce racism in countless ways. Likewise, there are many ways you can intervene by interrupting some of the microaggressions that people of color experience. Form relationships with people different from you; when people of color are ignored in group meetings or class discussions, make affirmative statements about what a person of color has contributed to the conversation. Microaffirmations can counter the impact of microaggressions.

Resource: https://www.brown.edu/sheridan/microaggressions-and-micro-affirmations-0

MARCHERS IN NEW YORK CITY -- Marchers in the Harlem section of New York City carry signs denouncing recent racial violence in Alabama.   (65-1093)

CHAPTER 5

Diverse Histories/Common Threads

Race and Ethnicity Build a Nation

As Americans, we originally came from many different shores, and our diversity has been at the center of the making of America.
—Ronald Takaki (1993:428)

OBJECTIVES

- Understand the significance of property, labor, and social control in the history of diverse racial-ethnic groups in American society
- Identify some of the key historical events that have shaped the experiences of diverse groups in the United States
- Relate the patterns of migration and settlement that have characterized the movement of different groups in US society
- Explain how social policies have regulated the inclusion and exclusion of diverse groups in the United States
- Contrast the experience of White ethnic groups with the experiences of people of color
- Identify the current social issues surrounding immigration

What would it take for you to uproot yourself, perhaps leave your family behind, and travel across an ocean or a desert to settle in a new place? Can you imagine being seized by an agent of a shipping company, forced to walk hundreds of miles, and then put into the cargo hold of a ship, crammed together with hundreds of others, and taken thousands of miles away to work for nothing—that is, if you survived the horrific journey at all? In another scenario, what if your land were seized, your home declared part of another nation, and you were then stripped all of your rights?

Each scenario describes the experiences by which some groups became a part of the United States. The scenarios describe the cruel realities of parts of our nation's history. The diverse racial and ethnic groups who today make up this nation have different origins and different histories that are tales of exploitation, forced labor, seizure of lands, and, in many cases, death and extermination. At the same time, US history is also a tale of opportunity seeking, community building, and achievement against the odds. Some of our nation's most horrid historic episodes are behind us, but we cannot understand the present realities of race and ethnicity without knowing something about the histories of our diverse population.

Different racial and ethnic groups have unique experiences in the United States. It is impossible to provide even a brief historical account of all of them in a single chapter of a single book, but certain aspects are common to all. One aspect is *labor*. How people worked and what various groups provided to build this nation are a critical part of the history of race and ethnicity—indeed, the nation's history. Slavery, indentured servitude, contract labor, and being niched into particular forms of work are how racial and ethnic groups have become part of this society.

A second aspect in this mosaic of history is *property*. Whether losing property, being treated as property, or trying to hold or gain property, different groups have specific relationships to patterns of ownership. Property might be in the form of land, but it is also found in the form of money and other financial resources. In the case of slavery, property for some was other human beings. Our racial-ethnic history has created vast property for some, stolen property from others, and provided little, if any, to others. As you will see, the accumulation of property by some at the expense of others has been one of the driving forces of US history.

A third aspect in the history of different groups is *social control*. Whether through armed conflict, violence, the use of law, or the propagation of controlling belief systems, powerful groups have used their resources to control the lives of others. Indeed, labor, property, and social control are part of the fabric of US history. One group might work the land for a more powerful group, resulting in the accumulation of property for those who use their power to create laws and social practices that control the labor and lives of others. As you read through the brief histories of diverse people in the United States, think about how these three factors—labor, property, and social control—have been part of the apparatus of building racial and ethnic inequality in the United States. Further, think about how these three processes reverberate in the dynamics of racial inequality now.

Land of the Free, Home of Native Americans

Framing Question: How have labor, property, and social control marked the different periods of Native American experience?

Of all the racial-ethnic groups in the United States, American Indians and, as you will see, some Mexican Americans are the only people who are indigenous—that is, native—to the mainland United States. Indigenous people also include native groups from Hawaii and Alaska, further complicating the diversity of "American" history. Estimates of the number of indigenous people living in the mainland United States in the earliest years of the country are impossible to know but are guessed to be anywhere from one to ten million people. Some Indian societies were nomadic, moving (perhaps seasonally) for food and water and because of climate. Others built great nations with vast amounts of land and natural resources. Given the great diversity of indigenous societies, how communities were organized and governed varied, depending on the different conditions that groups faced (Takaki 1993).

When Europeans first came to the Americas, indigenous people were widely scattered, both in what is now the mainland United States and throughout Latin America and the Caribbean. In Latin America, Indians were more numerous and organized in larger communities. With the migration of Europeans to the Americas, conquest and the clash of cultures became the dominant pattern. Over time, the population of American Indians was decimated by disease, war, and removal from their homelands. In fact, the history of Native American and European relations generally can be mostly described as one of conquest, famine, and genocide. Native Americans' traditional ways of life were brutally crushed.

Sociologist Matt Snipp (1996) outlines five periods that frame and help us understand American Indian history: *removal*, *assimilation*, *the Indian New Deal*, *termination/relocation*, and *self-determination*. When the first US colonies settled in what are now Virginia and Massachusetts, there was a period of relative harmony between the new colonists and the Indian groups (Philbrick 2006). Any semblance of harmony soon dissipated, however, with the expansion of the European population, the federal government's increased political and military capability, and colonist's desire for more territory.

During the period of *removal*, the US federal government negotiated various treaties, forcing native groups to relinquish their lands and pushing those in the east to the west. As much as Indian nations fought for their survival, with the expansion of the United States to the western frontier, removal became an even more explicit policy of the federal government. During the Andrew Jackson presidency, in 1830, the US Congress passed the **Indian Removal Act**, mandating the removal of all Indian groups to the area identified as Indian Territory (an area eventually reduced to what is now the state of Oklahoma). As part of the now-infamous Trail of Tears, in 1838, thousands of Cherokees, forced to leave their homes and march to Indian Territory, died from cold, disease, and starvation. Those who survived witnessed the devastation of long-standing community structures by the federal removal policy, which left former societies of Indian people profoundly disrupted.

As the result of federal policies, by the nineteenth century American Indians were near extinction. Those who remained were isolated on Indian reservations, where their lives were bleak. White reformers actually argued that the government should "humanely ease American Indians into extinction" (Snipp 1996:392), thus ushering in the period of *assimilation*. The federal government wanted American Indians to adopt the dominant culture and relinquish their traditions and ways of life. The government created the Bureau of Indian Affairs to "civilize" Indians—forcing them into Christianity, educating them in adopting so-called American values, and trying to inculcate the value of private property (Snipp 1996). Indian boarding schools were created to indoctrinate Indian children, who were, as a result, removed from their parents' homes and educated to think that European cultural values were superior to those of tribal nations.

In 1887, Congress passed the General Allotment Act, otherwise known as the Dawes Act. The stated purpose of this law was to integrate Indians into the mainstream, but it did so by forcing them to relinquish communal property. The government seized over ninety million acres of Indian land (two-thirds of all Indian land at the time), thus further isolating American Indian groups who were then scattered across remote reservations (Snipp 1996).

In the 1930s, the *Indian New Deal* reversed the allotment process and acknowledged the value of traditional tribal cultures. A component of President Franklin D. Roosevelt's New Deal, the Indian New Deal briefly brought some relief to American Indians, including support for various infrastructure improvements. Federal programs such as the Civilian Conservation Corps and the Works Progress Administration that benefited countless numbers of other Americans also benefited Indians, but only for a short period of time. In 1934, passage of the *Indian Reorganization Act* allowed tribal governments to self-govern. The act was not without controversy, because some Indians thought that it imposed on reservations an "alien form of government—representative democracy" (Snipp 1996:393).

Following World War II, Congress tried to terminate all special relationships with Indian tribes, including all reservations. American Indians vigorously opposed such changes; only two reservations were actually abolished. Still, the federal government pursued policies that encouraged Indians to move to urban areas. Those policies, coupled with the dire need to find jobs, meant that many Indians left reservations only to encounter urban poverty. The results of this period of *termination/relocation* can still be seen in the fact that the vast majority of American Indians live outside designated Indian areas, according to the US Census Bureau (Norris, Vines, and Hoeffel 2012). Although many have moved to urban areas in search of work, the period of termination and relocation has shaped contemporary residential patterns. We will know more about this distribution when the results of the 2020 census are distributed.

The final period Snipp identifies is *self-determination*. American Indians have a long tradition of resisting the policies and incursions of the federal government. Inspired by the civil rights movement of the 1960s, American Indian activism became even more pronounced. In 1969, several hundred American Indian activists and their supporters occupied Alcatraz Island in San Francisco Bay. They demanded to control the island and demanded a cultural center there controlled by Indians that would be a college, museum, training school, center of ecology, and spiritual center. The occupation lasted for nineteen months until the US government forcibly removed the protesters, many of whom remained even after the government shut down power and telephone service to the island. The Alcatraz occupation, though failing in its objectives, called public attention to the plight of Native peoples and heralded a new direction in Native American activism. The Indian Self-Determination and Education Assistance Act, passed in 1975, authorized specific American Indian tribes to oversee the affairs of their own communities, giving tribal governments a much greater role in reservation affairs.

Today there are about 2.7 million American Indians and Alaska Natives (the category now used by the US Census Bureau to enumerate Alaskan native people). The population of American Indians and Alaska Natives is also growing at a rate faster than the rest of the US population. A small proportion (20 percent) live on reservations, although this arrangement is more common for those who identify as "American Indian alone"—that is, not in combination with other racial or ethnic identities (Norris et al. 2012). Native Americans have a higher poverty rate than the nation as a whole (25 percent of families in 2017, compared to 13 percent of the national population at that time; Wilson 2017).

Although the poverty rate among American Indians is high, a new stereotype of Indians has emerged that depicts them as growing fabulously wealthy through profits made from casino gambling. Is this idea true? The *Indian Gaming Regulatory Act* of 1988 allowed tribal nations to conduct gaming activities, including casino gambling. Because tribes are recognized as sovereign entities, states cannot prohibit Indian gaming. Casino gambling has generated revenue for many groups and is a major means of economic development for Indian communities. As a result of this law, more than two hundred tribes now distribute resources from gaming to tribal members. Indian gaming is not, however, as lucrative as popularly believed, nor is its impact uniform across all tribes. The benefit tends to be greater for tribes operating casinos in more populous states, where incomes are higher and where Indians are not competing with other casinos (Conner and Taggart 2013). To summarize, the overall impact of allowing Indian gaming has been generally positive in terms of more employment, better health, and overall economic development, but not in every case (Gonzales, Lyson, and Mauer 2007; Wolfe et al. 2012).

Stereotypes of American Indians as poor, uneducated, and drunk have obscured the reality of their lives, as have other stereotypes of Indians as exotic and romantic figures who live in an idealized state, somehow closer to nature. Most indigenous people have been highly vulnerable to the social and economic stresses that many other groups have also faced, such as a lack of job opportunities and poor education. A combination of these and other factors such as stolen lands and various federal policies to control and remove their numbers has had a particularly deleterious effect on this group.

The Peculiar Institution: Slavery and Its Aftermath

Framing Question: What is the lingering impact of slavery in US life?

As you think about the different histories of racial and ethnic groups in the United States, you have to imagine simultaneous trails of events. Each trail is a separate line of history, but all of these trails are linked in the nation's development. As the nation was pushing Indians away, it was also developing an economic system dependent on the slave labor of Black people. While American Indians were being forcibly removed to the west, Black Americans were laboring in slavery, and the conflicts that ultimately led to the Civil War were simmering.

Other societies have had slaves, but only in the Americas did slavery develop into a full-blown social and economic institution. Precolonial African nations, for example, depended on slave labor (Fredrickson 2002), but in African societies slaves could marry free people, and their children would be free as well. What distinguishes slavery in the Americas from other forms of slavery is that slavery became the "bedrock of the economy and of the social order" (Kolchin 1993:29). Central to slavery in the New World was the principle of slaves as **chattel**—that is, human beings and their offspring were the property of others for a lifetime.

The first Africans to land in what became the United States arrived at Jamestown, Virginia, in 1619. Historical data are sketchy, but it seems the first Black people on US soil were indentured servants, not slaves. Many of the earliest White settlers were also indentured servants, bound for a period of time to their employers. For example, in the early days of the Virginia colony, most of the workers were White indentured servants. In fact, 75 percent of those arriving in the seventeenth century were indentured servants. As outcasts from England, Germany, and Ireland, many Whites arrived involuntarily at the hands of unscrupulous recruiters. Neither Whites nor Blacks in the early colonies were truly free, and Black and White workers shared class exploitation. Records show that sometimes Black and White workers were partners in running away, but they could also be publicly whipped for having sex.

As the colonies developed over the course of the seventeenth century, slavery emerged as a full-blown economic institution. By the middle of the seventeenth century, courts started to recognize the status of Black people as distinct from that of White servants. Over time, Black servants saw their conditions worsen, culminating in what became the institution of slavery (Takaki 1993).

It is impossible to know how many slaves were transported from western Africa to the New World. The best estimates are between ten and twelve million people, the vast majority of whom were imported to Brazil and the Caribbean. The United States received relatively few in comparison—about 6 percent of the total number of imported people, which comes to between 600,000 and 650,000 people (Genovese 1972; Kolchin 1993).

The forced migration of African people constituted one of the most brutal episodes of world history. During the excruciating *Middle Passage*—the transatlantic transport of slaves from Africa to the Americas—men and women were usually

It is believed that many of the millions of African people who were sold into slavery in the Americas left Africa through the Door of No Return in Senegal, which now stands as a haunting reminder of this horrid period in world history.

Source: Dereje Belachew / Alamy Stock Photo.

chained and packed tightly together so that slave traders could import as many people as possible and increase their profits. Thousands of women and men died from disease during passage, their bodies dumped into the sea. Some simply jumped overboard, preferring death to the horror of living. Historians estimate that between 5 and 20 percent of all transported men and women died during the Middle Passage (Kolchin 1993; Meier and Rudwick 1970).

In the American colonies, slavery first developed around Maryland and Tidewater, Virginia—the area surrounding the Chesapeake Bay. The major crops in the Tidewater area were tobacco and wheat, cultivated for transport to Europe. Although most people today associate slavery in the United States with the Deep South, up until 1790 two-thirds of the slave population resided in the area surrounding the Chesapeake (Fogel and Engermann 1974).

Slavery provided an ideal labor solution for the expanding capitalist economy of the developing nation. Slaves provided the free labor that built the profits both for the plantation class and for Northern industrialists who benefited from sales of tobacco, wheat, rice, indigo, and—later—cotton. Indentured servants had provided sufficient labor through most of the seventeenth century, but as the colonies' economy grew, there was a greater need for workers. Unable to enslave American Indians because of their familiarity with their "home turf," colonists turned to the slave trade for their labor force (Kolchin 1993). By the time George Washington was entering his first term as president of the new United States of America, the slave population was 700,000, in 1790. It quickly grew to 3.2 million by 1850 and was 4 million by 1860.

At the very time that the nation was being founded allegedly on the principles of freedom, independence, and the "natural rights of man," Black men and women were being forced into slave labor. How could the dominant class reconcile this fundamental contradiction between practice and belief? The answer is racism—that is, the idea that Blacks were somehow different and not fully human. Reconciling this inhumane treatment of people with the ideals of the new nation was epitomized in the compromise that defined the original American political system. To settle conflicting state interests between the North and South, for purposes of political representation each Black slave was counted as three-fifths of a person, with none of the rights or privileges given to White men (Meier and Rudwick 1970).

Several features differentiate US slavery from slavery in the Caribbean and Latin America. In the United States, as opposed to the Caribbean, White people were still a significant proportion of the working population; thus it was necessary to develop an ideology that differentiated slave and free labor. Again racism filled this void. Also in the United States, as opposed to the Caribbean and Latin America, the slave population soon reproduced itself, including through forced sexual relations between owners and slaves. This development reduced the need to import slaves via the slave trade. Historians have yet to understand why there were higher birth rates and lower death rates in the United States compared to nations farther south. Perhaps the climate or the harsh conditions in the sugar industry suppressed the rate of population growth in the Caribbean and Latin America. Whatever the explanation, when Britain outlawed the Atlantic slave trade in 1807, the United States still had a growing labor force but no need to continue importing slaves (Kolchin 1993).

The slavery that most people probably imagine now is *antebellum slavery*—the slavery that developed through the growth of the cotton industry, beginning around 1800 and existing until the end of the Civil War. The period of antebellum slavery actually filled a relatively short period in American history. Most slaves prior to 1790 were in the Tidewater region, but by 1820 two-thirds of the slave population had been relocated to the Deep South, where cotton predominated (Fogel and Engermann 1974). Being sold south evoked deep fear among slaves in the more northern regions of slavery—fear of family separation, even worse treatment, and less likelihood of being able to flee.

There is plenty of evidence that slaves resisted slavery in any way they possibly could (Kolchin 1993): running away, holding work stoppages, feigning illness, and organizing outright rebellions. Enslaved people did all they could to preserve their sense of dignity and humanity. While slaves might have pretended to be docile as a means of avoiding worse treatment, despite White stereotypes of slaves as a "happy" people, slaves did all they could to maintain a sense of self-worth in miserable conditions.

Slavery lingered until the end of the Civil War, in 1865, even though the Emancipation Proclamation, freeing most slaves, had been passed in 1863. Slavery was finally outlawed by the Thirteenth Amendment to the US Constitution in 1865. Although only a small number (about one-quarter in 1860) of White Southern families actually owned slaves, the slave-owning class wielded enormous power, concentrating power in the South in the hands of a White aristocracy. White workers had little power in this system, but racist ideology prevented them from seeing that they had any common interests with Black labor (Wilson 1978).

Following the abolition of US slavery at the end of the American Civil War, the period of *Reconstruction* brought new freedoms and new hopes to Black Americans. During Reconstruction, Black Americans had an unprecedented role in public life. Yet the period was also marked by racial violence and attempts to reestablish a Black labor force to redevelop the Southern economy. *Black Codes* were enacted to give newly freed Blacks the right to own property, to marry, and to make contracts, but the codes also kept Black labor virtually enslaved, even if under new rules and regulations, as White Southerners worked to reestablish the system of labor that had been destroyed by the Civil War.

Reconstruction temporarily transformed the racial order by enfranchising Black men and creating a belief in the possibility for freedom (Foner 1988; Hobbs 2014). These newly awarded Black rights were ended, however, as a result of a negotiated agreement between Northern and Southern politicians. The results of the 1876 presidential election were disputed because of questionable ballot returns from three Southern states (Florida, Louisiana, and South Carolina—the only states with Republican governments at the time). Democrats agreed to allow Rutherford Hayes, the Republican candidate, to become president if Republicans withdrew federal troops, who had overseen Reconstruction, from the South. The *Compromise of 1877* thus ushered Hayes into the US presidency. Black Americans, although technically "free," were pawns in a political compromise between conflicting White interests.

Following Reconstruction, "home rule" was returned to the South, and virulent racism reigned. The post-Reconstruction period was a time of intense repression of and violence toward Black Americans and the dismissal of whatever rights they had achieved during Reconstruction. The period's oppression culminated in 1896 when the US Supreme Court ruled in *Plessy v. Ferguson* that the principle of "separate but equal" was constitutional and ushered in the systematic and legal segregation known as *Jim Crow*. The grip of Jim Crow segregation strictly controlled Black-White interactions in the South until the principle of "separate but equal" was overturned and ruled unconstitutional by the Supreme Court's *Brown v. Board of Education* decision in 1954 (see chapter 9).

Upon the emergence of the twentieth century, many Black Americans remained in the South, laboring in agriculture, manufacturing, and, for women, domestic work. Thousands, however, left as they could to seek new forms of work in the expanding industrial economy of Northern and Midwestern cities. With the possibility of employment in an expanding industrial economy and the desire to be free of the grip of Jim Crow racism in the South, approximately one million African American people participated in the Great Migration, between approximately 1915 and 1970. They headed North in one of the greatest population shifts in US history, only to encounter new forms of racism in the Northern and Midwestern cities where they went (Marks 1989; Wilkerson 2010). During this **Great Migration,** many African Americans made a new way for themselves in cities where Jim Crow was not the prevalent social order, although racism was surely present. As we will see below, urbanization and industrialization transformed race relations in the United States. A population that had been mostly enslaved became ready for the dawn of the civil rights movement (see chapter 12).

Today African Americans constitute 13.4 percent of the US population. They now include many who do not date their ancestry from slavery. More recent immigrants come from such diverse places as Nigeria, Ethiopia, the Dominican Republic, and Haiti, among many others. Poverty afflicts many Black Americans, but there is also a significant Black middle class. Many African Americans have risen to the top echelons of American power and are now found in positions of economic, military, and political leadership—including the forty-fourth president of the United States, Barack Obama, and now Vice President Kamala Harris. Still, the inequality between Black and White Americans has been somewhat intractable—that is, characterized by progress for many but stagnation for others, as we will see in later chapters.

Annexing the Southwest: The Mexican American Experience

Framing Question: How has colonization affected the experience of Mexican Americans?

Latinos are a highly diverse population comprised of many different groups. Like other labels used to describe racial and ethnic groups, *Latino* is an umbrella term used to convey common interests shared by diverse people of Spanish descent in the United States. Latinos have, however, unique pasts and different present circumstances but now constitute 18.3 percent of the US population. Mexican Americans make up the largest Latino group, representing 63 percent of the current Latino population in the United States. Indigenous Mexican Americans (called *Chicanas/os*)[1] were the first Latinos to be in what is now the United States. It is that history to which we now turn, with more information on other Latino groups later in this chapter.

Over the course of the sixteenth and seventeenth centuries, Spanish explorers made several expeditions to the California coast as they sought to expand world trade. Organized Spanish colonization of the area now encompassing California began in the mid-eighteenth century when Father Junípero Serra founded the first Franciscan mission, San Diego de Alcalá. Junípero Serra is infamous for his brutal treatment of native Indians, whom he and other Spanish colonizers sought to colonize and convert to Catholicism. The Spanish established twenty-one missions, stretching over five hundred miles through California, from San Diego to Sonoma (Gómez 2018; Takaki 1993).

Other than native Indians, the original settlers in California were Mexicans, whose social order was marked by an elaborate stratification system. At the top of the hierarchy were the landed elite and prosperous officials. Some were Spanish,

---

[1] *Chicana/o* refers to a Mexican person who has become incorporated into the United States as the result of a war treaty. Some Mexican Americans born in the United States prefer to be called Chicana/Chicano because of its association with pride. There is debate within the Mexican American community over what people want to be called. The terms *Chicana/Chicano* emerged in the 1960s as part of a movement for recognition and rights. Some claim that, despite this affirming terminology, the term *Chicano* had been used earlier as an insult. Activists often reclaim such negative terms, however, during social movements to affirm a positive and collective identity (see chapter 4). For more discussion of the politics of language, see the preface to this book.

but most were *mestizo* (mixed). In the middle were small-scale ranchers and farmers. At the bottom were laborers, artisans, and other skilled workers; many were Indians, although their numbers were diminishing (Camarillo 1979). In the early nineteenth century, the Mexican government offered land grants to Mexicans in what is now California on the condition that they convert to Catholicism, and some did so. But by the 1840s, attracted to California's natural resources, more and more Anglos moved west. Once the US federal government clearly articulated its objective to annex California (Takaki 1993), a period of conflict over property between the United States and Mexico commenced.

In 1830, the Mexican government outlawed slavery, but cotton planters in the Southern United States were anxious to expand into the Mexican territory that would become Texas. In 1836, armed Anglo Americans in Texas began an insurrection against Mexican authority in the now infamous Battle of the Alamo. A brutal military campaign followed, eventually leading to the Mexican-American War (1846–1848). Outgunned, the Mexican government lost the war and signed the *Treaty of Guadalupe Hidalgo* (Acuña 2014).

With this treaty, Mexico ceded over one million square miles to the United States, extending the southern US border to the Rio Grande. The land that now includes the states of Texas, California, New Mexico, and Nevada, and parts of Colorado, Arizona, and Utah became US territory, an area of land that was roughly half of what had been Mexico. Overnight the fifty thousand or so Mexicans living in these areas were declared to be US citizens and were given full citizenship rights—in principle but not in practice (De Genova and Ramos-Zayas 2001; Takaki 1993). Once a majority in their own lands, Mexican Americans soon became a minority in the sociological sense of that word (Massey 2008; also see the preface of this volume). As many say today, "We didn't cross the border; the border crossed us."

The quarter century following the Mexican-American War continues to shape the experiences of many Chicanas/os in the United States today. As California and the Southwest changed from a primarily pastoral economy to an industrial one, Mexican workers in the United States increasingly were incorporated into the needs of capitalism. Those who had been landed often became landless. Many who had held large tracts of land as ranchers moved from "riches to rags" (Camarillo 1979:67) as Anglos increasingly took control of the new economic system.

Although in 1848, at the conclusion of the Mexican-American War, Mexicans had outnumbered Anglos by ten to one, the discovery of gold that same year changed everything. People throughout the United States headed West, thinking they would become wealthy as prospectors. Soon the Anglo population overwhelmed the Mexican American population, and Mexican Americans found themselves thoroughly subjected to Anglo domination. Laws and other ordinances were put in place that restricted Mexican American rights. Lands were stolen, and Mexican Americans were targeted for all manner of abuses. The growing hatred and stereotyping of Mexicans is well illustrated by an antivagrancy act passed in California in 1865 that was actually called the "Greaser Act," *greaser* being a highly derogatory term (Feagin and Cobas 2014; Takaki 1993).

With virtually no immigration laws, Mexicans and others found it relatively easy to migrate to the land that had just become the United States. As the economic base of the nation was expanding, there was an increasing need for labor—especially cheap labor that could enrich the profits of business owners. Ranching, agriculture, and mining drew many Mexicans to the Southwest. Growers and industrialists recruited people from far and wide, spending thousands to enlist and transport Mexicans to where they were needed to work, including such places as Colorado, Wyoming, Iowa, Nebraska, and the city of Chicago, Illinois. The rate of immigration of Mexican laborers to the United States became particularly high after the United States restricted Asian immigration in the late nineteenth and early twentieth centuries. As employers actively recruited Mexican workers, the number of Mexican immigrants jumped from about 17,000 per year in 1910 to about 50,000 per year in the 1920s and 740,000 by 1930 (Massey 2008).

As the Mexican population in the United States grew, White opposition intensified. By the late 1920s, when the Great Depression took hold, Mexicans became scapegoats for the failing US economy, and a period of intense anti-Mexican sentiment ensued. During massive deportation from 1929 to 1934, authorities rounded up Mexicans through raids in neighborhoods, factories, and fields, often without a chance for people to gather their belongings. Steeped in anti-Mexican stereotypes, officials often did not attempt to distinguish Mexican immigrants from Mexican American citizens. Thousands of children, including many born in the United States and thus US citizens, were also deported regardless of their citizenship status. This massive deportation cut the population of Mexicans in the United States in half (Olivas 2010; Romo 1996).

By the time the United States entered World War II, the need for labor returned, and the country once again opened its doors to Mexican immigrants. In 1942, the United States and Mexico created the **bracero program**[2]—a formal agreement that permitted Mexican citizens to work in the United States for temporary, renewable periods. The agreement also prohibited discrimination, which was largely ignored by both US growers and the federal government (Massey 2008; Rodríguez, Sáenz, and Menjívar 2008).

Over a half million braceros worked under this arrangement. Mexicans in the bracero program endured poor food, excessive charges for rent, discrimination, and exposure to pesticides, but the program provided growers with a significant source of cheap labor. Even after World War II, when US soldiers returned home wanting jobs, the program was kept alive because of the interests of agribusiness. The bracero program brought nearly five million Mexicans to the United States between 1942 and 1964. It was finally ended over protests about horrific working conditions. Many Mexican Americans today can still trace their roots to this program and can vividly recall horrible memories of it (Olivas 2010).

The Mexican Americans who had fought in World War II were able to take advantage of GI benefits and seek higher education. But others, viewed as disposable labor, worked in low-wage jobs, were segregated in barrios, and attended segregated schools (Perea 2004; Smith 2008). Mexican Americans were subjected to some of the same indignities that afflicted Black Americans under Jim Crow. In the period following World War II, Mexican Americans organized extensively for protection of their civil rights, orchestrating the now-well-known Delano grape strike, led by Cesar Chavez and others. The grape boycott, a protest against working conditions

---

[2] *Bracero* means "laborer" in Spanish.

for many migrant workers, lasted from 1965 to 1970 and resulted in unionization for grape workers for the first time, which set an important precedent for other agricultural laborers (Ferriss and Sandoval 1997; Romo 1996).

Mexican American history teaches us a lot about how racial-ethnic groups have been drawn in as cheap sources of labor while being denied basic rights of citizenship. But Mexican Americans today are just one group of various Latino peoples with different histories and traditions.

Puerto Ricans came to the US mainland beginning in the early twentieth century, continuing through the post–World War II period. Puerto Rican migration is somewhat different from that of other groups, primarily because Puerto Ricans are US citizens and, thus, not immigrants. Puerto Rico became a colony of the United States in 1898 following the Spanish-American War. Puerto Ricans were then granted citizenship under the *Jones-Shafroth Act of 1917*, usually referred to as the Jones Act. Puerto Ricans began to travel back and forth between the island and the US mainland in significant numbers after World War II.

Puerto Ricans were drawn to the jobs that the post–World War II economy provided. By 1950 there were three hundred thousand Puerto Ricans on the mainland, most of them in New York City. By 1970, there were 1.5 million Puerto Ricans on the mainland, a number that has grown to more than 4.9 million in the early twenty-first century. Often employed in low-wage, seasonal jobs, Puerto Ricans have provided much of the work that sustains others, even while their back-and-forth migration patterns have disrupted many Puerto Rican families (Brown and Patten 2013; Carrasquillo and Sánchez-Korrol 1996).

Today Latinos are now the most rapidly growing "minority" population in the United States, including Chicanos, newly arrived Mexican Americans, Puerto Ricans, Cubans, and immigrants from South and Central America. By 2017, people self-identifying as Hispanic were 18 percent of the US population, and that percentage is expected to grow to 28 percent by 2060. Latinos now are widely dispersed across the country, although more concentrated in certain areas. Three-quarters of the Hispanic population live in the West or the South and two-thirds in California, Texas, Florida, or New York (Colby and Ortman 2015; Vespa, Medina, and Armstrong 2020).

Poverty among Latinos is high (15.7 percent in 2018), nearly matching that of African Americans, who had a poverty rate of 18.8 percent in 2018 (Semega et al. 2019). As with African Americans, there is also a significant middle class. Class status likewise varies among the different groups that make up the Latino population. Like African Americans, Latinos have a visible presence in some of the most powerful positions in the land, and they are a population that is increasingly important in shaping national politics. You will learn more about Latinos in the chapters to follow.

Opening the Nation's Doors—and Slamming Them Closed

Framing Question: How have patterns of inclusion and exclusion marked the history of Asian Americans in the United States?

Asian Americans also come from very diverse backgrounds, but the early history of Asian migration centers on Chinese and Japanese movement into the United States. Their histories, like those of other groups, involve the expansion and contraction of the need for labor. Both groups were also subjected to the vagaries of lawmakers who used their power to restrict Chinese and Japanese rights of citizenship.

Chinese Americans

California's annexation by the United States in the Treaty of Guadalupe Hidalgo in the mid-nineteenth century opened a new door for the country to expand into Asia and for Asians to enter the United States (Takaki 1993). Many Chinese people came to the United States to escape harsh conditions in China. They saw the United States as a place where they could have plenty to eat, have opportunities to work, and establish homes. Men arrived with the intention of becoming established and then moving their families. Most came through a "credit-ticket" system in which a broker would lend them the money for passage, and they would repay the broker, with interest, from their earnings in the United States (Takaki 1993).

Between 1850 and 1882, over three hundred thousand Chinese people left southern China to work in America. Many were imported to work as strikebreakers, and they were also relegated to the most dangerous and difficult work available. By 1870, there were sixty-three thousand Chinese people in the United States, three-quarters of whom lived in California (Takaki 1993).

Labor recruiters preferred to recruit young, able-bodied men from China; this and other factors allowed for very few Chinese women to come to the United States. Women's traditional roles in China, the cost of travel, and Chinese women's fears of physical and sexual assault in the United States created a huge imbalance in the ratio of men to women among the Chinese in America (Chow 1996). As an example, of the 11,787 Chinese who came to the United States in 1852, only seven were women. Some Chinese women managed to enter as indentured servants. The extreme sex imbalance created bachelor communities and a lucrative market for prostitution, especially since California law prevented Chinese people from marrying Whites. In the census of 1870, 61 percent of Chinese women living in California listed their occupation as "prostitute" (Takaki 1993).

At first Chinese laborers worked mostly in the mining industry, but the decline of mining, the resistance of White labor, and the building of the transcontinental railroad changed the course of Chinese immigration. Thousands of Chinese workers labored to build the Central Pacific railroad between 1864 and 1869. Railroad work was extremely dangerous, especially as the track was laid to pass through the Sierra Nevada mountains and then beyond into the rugged Western landscape. White workers considered the work too dangerous and demanded better pay and working conditions. Paid less than White workers, Chinese railroad workers were widely recruited by railroad owners, who reaped the profits of this extraordinary labor. Employing Chinese workers saved railroad owners one-third of their costs. Chinese workers fought to improve work conditions, organizing a massive strike in 1867, but the railroad owners cut off their food supply and forced them back to work without any change in their status. Violence and intimidation marked much of the workers' experience (Chang 2019; Takaki 1993).

Once the railroad was completed in 1869, most of the Chinese workers returned to San Francisco, Sacramento, and other places, mostly in California, where new Chinese communities were being formed. San Francisco was also becoming a focal point of industry, and by 1870 half of the city's labor force was Chinese. Chinese people were concentrated in low-wage work and/or were paid less than Whites when they did the same work. Some turned to farming, helping to develop the fruit industry and teaching growers how to construct irrigation systems. Others, shut out of work opportunities, moved into service work, such as laundering (Takaki 1989 and 1993).

By the 1880s, the need for Chinese workers had dissipated. Throughout the course of their labor history in America, Chinese people had been defined as ideal workers, but they were now perceived as a "yellow peril"—a menace to White society. In 1882, the US Congress passed the **Chinese Exclusion Act**, denying the entry of additional Chinese laborers into the country. The door of opportunity that had been briefly opened was now slammed shut. The only Chinese allowed entry to the United States were those who were merchants, teachers, diplomats, students, and tourists (see "Learning Our Past," below, for a brief discussion of Chinese detention on Angel Island in California). Women could only enter if they were married to a merchant. Only because of a natural disaster in 1906 were some Chinese able to re-form families. The San Francisco earthquake of 1906 and a subsequent fire destroyed local official records that provided proof of family relations, prompting many Chinese to claim they had been born in San Francisco. They would then travel back to China and return with those they claimed as "sons"—so-called **paper sons** (Dill 1988). The Chinese Exclusion Act was not rescinded until 1943, when China and the United States became allies in World War II (Chow 1996).

Japanese Americans

Japanese immigration to the United States primarily occurred between 1890 and 1924. Most of the first Japanese immigrants were men, but, unlike among Chinese immigrants, Japanese women were far more likely to emigrate. The strong central Japanese government wanted Japan to appear "noble" to others and thus strictly regulated emigration, requiring those who left to be healthy and literate. The Japanese government thus allowed Japanese women to emigrate as family members (Dill 1988; Takaki 1989). In Japan in the late nineteenth century, poor farming conditions meant that many farmers lost their land and crops. Like the Chinese, many Japanese people thought that coming to the United States would mean high wages and a more successful life.

With some need for labor and the Chinese now excluded, the United States and Hawaii initially welcomed Japanese workers. Between 1885 and 1924, 200,000 Japanese people emigrated to Hawaii and another 180,000 to the US mainland, where they were a smaller proportion of the population. In Hawaii, the government also stipulated that a certain percentage of workers had to be women. Once there, women were assigned to work in the fields. On the mainland, women assisted husbands as unpaid workers in shops and as farmers.

Organized White US workers scorned and attacked Japanese workers and also denied them access to industrial employment, where they might have found better

LEARNING OUR PAST

Remembering Angel Island

When people think of the historic points of entry for immigrants into the United States, most probably think of Ellis Island, the entry point in New York City for thousands of Europeans. However, there is an additional story. Between 1910 and 1940, customs agents separated immigrants arriving in San Francisco from the Pacific by nationality. Coming mostly from Asia, but also from Mexico and Russia, they were ferried to Angel Island, where they were held in quarantine. Chinese people in particular were detained on Angel Island, sometimes for weeks, months, and even years, interrogated about their backgrounds, and often sent back. A fire badly damaged the poorly kept facility in 1940, and only recently were poems discovered that detainees had carved into the walls, expressing their hopes, fears, and yearnings.

If you are ever in San Francisco, a visit to the museum at Angel Island, now a state park, is a very moving and educational experience. The island is now beautiful, with flowers and biking and walking trails, but once you learn about the history of people who were held there, you will feel some of the ghosts of the past.

You can read some of the narratives that detainees at Angel Island wrote, as well as view photographs that have been preserved, at the following sites:

https://www.immigrant-voices.aiisf.org/discover/
http://www.angel-island.com/history.html

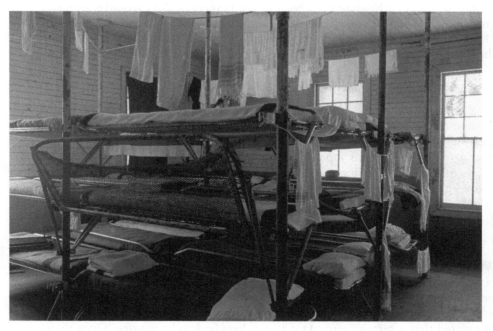

Whereas many White people associate the entry of immigrants with Ellis Island in New York harbor, most Chinese and Japanese immigrants entered through the Angel Island Immigration Station in San Francisco Bay. Often forced to stay for there for months, immigrants experienced inhumane conditions and extreme overcrowding.

Source: Robert Fried / Alamy Stock Photo.

jobs. Instead, the Japanese were relegated to work in farming and, for some, shop-keeping. By 1910, Japanese laborers in California were producing 70 percent of the strawberries, 95 percent of the soybeans, 95 percent of the celery, and huge proportions of the rest of the nation's fruit and vegetable diet (Takaki 1993).

Many Japanese believed their success in agriculture would be the ticket to acceptance, but sadly they were wrong. Anti-immigrant sentiment in the United States began curtailing Japanese immigration. The **Gentlemen's Agreement of 1907**—an agreement between the United States and Japan—barred further entry of Japanese laborers, significantly reducing Japanese immigration. This agreement only allowed women to come as wives of merchants. The result was the system of **picture brides**—marriages arranged by a broker (as was the custom in Japan). A Japanese man in the United States who could not afford to return to Japan selected a wife from picture books provided by brokers. Between 1909 and 1923, 71 percent of the Japanese women arriving in the United States came as picture brides (Glenn 1986; Glenn and Parreñas 1996).

Like the Chinese in America, Japanese people were denied the basic rights of citizenship. This was highlighted in 1922 in a case that ultimately went to the US Supreme Court: *Ozawa v. United States*. Takao Ozawa had emigrated from Japan, graduated from a US high school, and attended the University of California–Berkeley. He moved to Hawaii, where he worked for an American family and raised his own family. But when he applied for naturalization, he was denied. His case ultimately went to the US Supreme Court, where he was denied the right to file for citizenship based on the argument that he was not "Caucasian" (Takaki 1989). The Ozawa case reflects the development of Whiteness as a legal construct.

The first generation of Japanese (*Issei*) in the United States had great hopes that the second generation (*Nisei*) would benefit from their hard work by qualifying for higher education and stronger employment. Issei hopes, however, were dashed in December 1941, when the Japanese bombed the US naval base at Pearl Harbor in Honolulu and sparked nationwide outrage against the Japanese, including those who were American citizens by either birth or naturalization. In 1942, President Franklin D. Roosevelt issued an executive order removing all Japanese people from the American West and ordering them into internment camps throughout the Western states. Japanese Americans were first housed in stockyards and on fairgrounds and racetracks; eventually they were relocated to ten different internment camps. All of their financial assets were frozen, and a massive propaganda campaign targeted them as traitors and "enemy aliens." The US government ultimately paid $16 billion in reparations to detainees and their descendants. For a personal account of the experience of internment, see "Living with Racism," below.

Waves of Whiteness: European Immigration

Framing Question: How has prejudice influenced the history of European immigrants?

White ethnic groups have not been immune to the forces of prejudice and hatred. The earliest immigrants in the seventeenth century were English. Even as late as 1790, when over 80 percent of the US population was White, between 60 and 70 percent of the White population was of English ancestry. The rest were mostly Irish,

LIVING WITH RACISM

The California Alien Land Law and Japanese Americans

Marvin Uratsu was born in Sacramento in 1925. When the Japanese were forcibly removed from the West Coast, he spent his junior year of high school at the Tule Lake internment camp. He was interviewed about his life experience for a student oral history project documenting the lived histories of older Americans of different racial and ethnic backgrounds. Here is an excerpt from Uratsu's experience:

> There was this Alien Land Law that made it impossible for my father to buy land. There was a period before the Alien Land Law that some Japanese American families were able to buy land before the law came into effect. And that was like my wife's family. They were able to buy land before the law went into effect. But in our case, the Uratsu family's case, the law was passed, and they couldn't buy land. That was one of the biggest things. It made it kind of hard for us. We couldn't get citizenship. People from Europe would come over, and after so many years they were able to get their US citizenship, but that wasn't the case for the Japanese, so there were two or three other things that made it difficult to live here and have to work as a day laborer on the farms.

Note: For more histories like Marvin Uratsu's, visit *Telling Their Stories*, online at http://www.tellingstories.org.
Source: Uratsu 2007.

Scottish, and German. By 1920, following extensive European immigration, 90 percent of the US population was White, but less than half (44 percent) of the White population was descended from England (Schneiderman 1996).

Two great waves mark European immigration to the United States. The first wave, roughly from 1815 to 1865, brought primarily German, Irish, and Scandinavian immigrants—that is, mostly Northern and Western Europeans. Jewish immigrants also arrived around 1849, largely from Germany. Later, Jewish immigrants would come from other parts of Eastern Europe, as we will see below.

In the late nineteenth and early twentieth centuries, crop failures and deteriorating economic conditions in Sweden, Norway, and Denmark brought another wave of thousands of people from these countries to US shores. Even while Black Americans were still being held in slavery, the *Homestead Act of 1862* gave free land to those who would farm it for five years. This law attracted Scandinavians especially to the upper Midwest (Hansen 2013).

Between 1820 and 1930, about 4.5 million Irish came to the United States; indeed, by 1840 half of all immigrants were Irish. The potato famine in Ireland in the late 1840s caused the population of the island to decrease by four million. Two million died of starvation. The other two million were people who were able to leave Ireland, and many of them came to the United States. The least expensive route to the United States took the Irish to Boston, one of the major ports of settlement. Given the conditions in Ireland, many arrived dependent on charity. There were few jobs, and the Irish had little to invest in their future. The men took the least-skilled, lowest-paying jobs, digging canals, building bridges, and doing other manual labor, while Irish women worked as domestic servants.

At the time, the Irish were blamed for many of the nation's ills, as are today's immigrants. Stereotyped, ridiculed, and attacked by anti-Irish mobs, Irish immigrants were nonetheless able to gain a foothold in urban politics—for reasons not fully understood. This situation ultimately led to their upward mobility at least into the working class, if not higher. The anti-Irish anger that they encountered also helped them build a strong Irish identity that only further exacerbated hostility toward them (Diner 1996). Arriving in a nation that largely defined itself as Protestant, the Irish were harshly subjected to **nativism** in the form of anti-Catholic hostility. Nativist organizations promoted the idea of the United States as a Protestant country. Such anti-Catholic sentiments surfaced again in 1960 when John Fitzgerald Kennedy, descended from Irish immigrants, was elected the nation's first Catholic US president.

Jewish immigrants to the United States came in their largest numbers between 1880 and 1924. About one-third of all Jewish people in Eastern Europe, numbering about two million, migrated to the United States within that time frame to escape anti-Semitism. By the beginning of World War I alone, one-third of all Jews in Russia and Eastern Europe—mostly Poland, Austria, Hungary, and Romania—had emigrated. By 1920, 1.6 million Jewish people were in New York City, accounting for 43 percent of the city's population (Foner 2005; Takaki 1993). Their arrival was facilitated by the German Jews, who had started arriving in the 1840s and settled in urban areas to work as bankers and merchants. Many had settled on the Lower East Side of Manhattan, where slum conditions in housing tenements were the norm.

Jewish people in the United States have faced exclusion and discrimination, but they have generally been more successful than many other White immigrant groups. Although this has led to numerous false stereotypes of Jewish people, the fact is that they arrived more skilled, better educated, and more accustomed to urban life, factors that facilitated their social and economic mobility (Gold and Phillips 1996).

The second wave of European immigration came roughly between 1880 and 1920, bringing mostly people from Southern Europe, especially Italians. Approximately 2.5 million Italians came to the United States, mostly through Ellis Island. By 1920, there were over eight hundred thousand Italians living in New York City alone (Foner 2005). Spurred to emigrate because their way of life in Southern Italy had been disrupted by negative developments in their agrarian lifestyle, most Italians were dislocated peasants. Arriving in an expanding urban-industrial economy with limited skills, they formed "urban villages" in the major cities of the East Coast and worked mostly in factories and in the construction, sanitation, and food industries.

As opposed to other immigrants, many Italians thought of their move as temporary and held out hope of returning to Italy. They maintained a close connection to their homeland; many did, in fact, repatriate. But they were slow to develop an "Italian" identity; more often than not, "homeland" for an Italian was a region of Italy, such as Sicily or Calabria. Italians became another despised immigrant group in the United States; they were perceived as "swarthy" and associated with criminal tendencies in general and the Mafia in particular. Second- and third-generation Italian Americans, however, became assimilated into the American mainstream (Alba 1996).

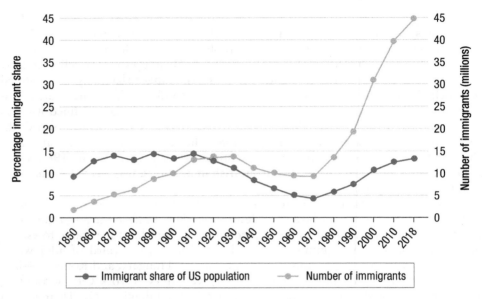

FIG. 5.1 Foreign-Born Population in the United States, 1850–2018

Source: Batalova, Blizzard, and Bolter 2020.

As immigrants became an increasingly large share of the US population in the early twentieth century (see figure 5.1), nativist sentiments surged. White workers perceived immigrant workers as a threat. Hostility and claims that America was a "White" nation were rampant. White supremacists claimed that the surge of immigrants would "dilute the moral fiber of the nation" (Portes and Rumbaut 2014:9), a sentiment that has echoed in current times as right-wing movements have declared that immigrants are degrading the moral fabric of American life.

During earlier periods of immigration, once business no longer needed the cheap source of labor that so many immigrants had provided, the United States had changed its laws to shut down immigration. The **National Origins Act** (also called the *Johnson-Reed Act*), passed by Congress in 1924, put a virtual halt to immigration by establishing a quota system that restricted the entry of new immigrants to 2 percent of the total number of people of each nationality that had been in the United States in 1890. An exception to this quota system, which favored immigrants from Western Europe, explicitly excluded immigration from Asia. Between the Great Depression and World War II, immigration to the United States plummeted, especially by those from Southern Europe, particularly Italy. The law favored immigrants from Northern Europe, especially Germany, Britain, and Ireland (Pedraza 1996). Opportunities for immigrants, once believed to be the path to success, were no longer available.

The National Origins Act reduced immigration to a trickle until 1965, when legislation eliminating the national origins quota was passed. Knowing this earlier history provides a context for understanding some of the resurgent social forces shaping debates about immigration today.

Immigration Now: Changing the Face of the Nation

Framing Question: In what ways is contemporary immigration different from earlier European immigration?

The period from the Great Depression until the mid-1960s in the United States was a period of retrenchment from immigration. Mexicans who had been working under the bracero program, Black Southern migrants, and Puerto Ricans began replacing the need for immigrant labor (Portes and Rumbaut 2014). Through the 1930s, there was little work and, therefore, little incentive for people to migrate. World War II, however, provided a big boost to the economy and increased the need for workers. The stage was set for the pattern of immigration that marks the contemporary period.

With a surging economy and postwar affluence, the United States was poised for a change in its immigration laws. In 1965, Congress passed the *Immigration and Nationality Act of 1965*, usually referred to as the **Hart-Celler Act**. This law has changed the face of the United States, eliminating the national origins quota created by the National Origins Act of 1924. Today, Hart-Celler gives priority to family reunification, replacing occupational skill as the preferred reason for entry. You can see in figure 5.2 that the vast majority of immigrants come for reasons of family unity.

Hart-Celler has had a number of unintended consequences. Recall that one year before the passage of the 1965 law, Congress had ended the bracero program. With the elimination of this program, employers (mostly ranchers and farmers) continued to turn to the same group of laborers, who would now work under clandestine arrangements. Soon these laborers would be labeled "illegal immigrants."

The Hart-Celler law also opened the door to highly skilled immigrants, drawing in well-educated people who were ready to assume professional positions. The result has been a bifurcated immigrant labor market, consisting of highly skilled, often science- and technology-based immigrant workers at the high end, and millions of other, both legal and illegal, immigrants working in low-wage and service work (Portes and Rumbaut 2014; also see chapter 7 of this volume).

As the result of the 1965 law, immigration to the United States dramatically increased, almost reaching the same proportions as during the waves of European immigration from 1880 to 1920. Between 1980 and 2018, the proportion of foreign-born people in the United States rapidly increased from 6.2 percent of the population to 13.5 percent. Experts also predict that immigration will continue to be the largest driver of population growth until midcentury (Batalova and Alperin 2018).

Currently, immigrants are most likely to be coming from Asia, and they are typically better educated than previous generations of immigrants (see figure 5.3). Indeed, as you can see in figure 5.4, immigrants now tend to be better educated than the existing US public, despite stereotypes about immigrants. The Mexican immigrant population has also declined since 2010, largely as the result of changes in the labor market but also as a result of restrictive implementation of immigration law at the Southern US border. No longer does the United States hold the record for resettling world refugees; Canada has surpassed the United States for that distinction (Batalova, Blizzard, and Bolter 2020).

Among the new immigrants to the United States today are those who are undocumented—that is, those who have entered the country illegally. As of 2018 there

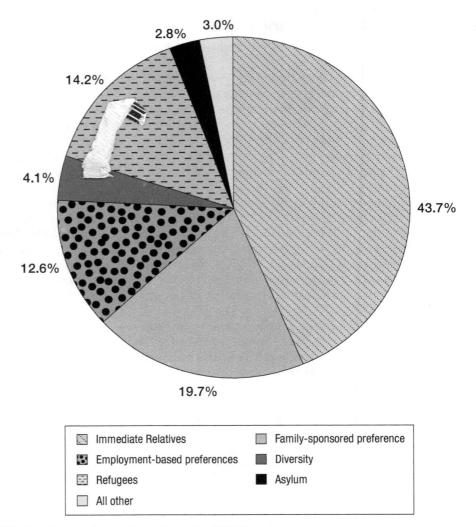

FIG. 5.2 Reasons for Immigrant Admission (2018)

Source: US Department of Homeland Security 2020a.

were estimated to be about 11.3 million undocumented immigrants in the United States. About half of the undocumented are from Mexico; the other half come from diverse countries, including El Salvador, Guatemala, and China. A substantial proportion of the undocumented (two-thirds) have lived in the United States for more than ten years, one-quarter for more than twenty years (Gelatt and Zong 2018).

Undocumented immigration fuels current debates about immigration policy—debates that are often clouded by myths about who these people are and what they do. While many Americans imagine most undocumented immigrants to be Mexican, in reality Mexicans only make up about one-half of those who are undocumented. Others come from different Central and South American nations. Unauthorized immigrants make up about 5 percent of the US workforce, and, despite social

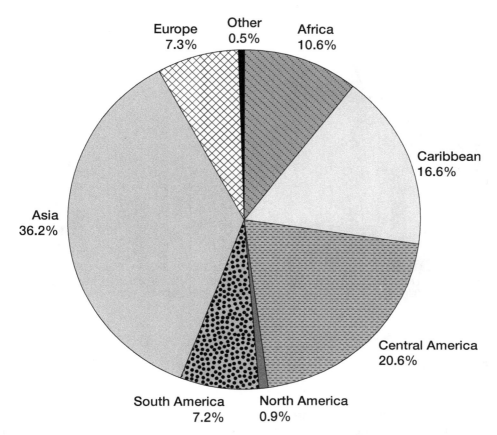

FIG. 5.3 Source of US Immigrants (2018)

Source: US Department of Homeland Security 2020b.

myths, two-thirds of these workers pay state and federal taxes and Social Security (Krogstad, Passel, and Cohn 2019; Massey 2005).

Unless the government passes new immigration law, as of 2020 the Hart-Celler Act stands as federal immigration policy. Still, how policy is implemented depends on presidential and congressional leadership. This fact was vividly evident when, despite laws governing family unification, children were caged and families separated who were seeking refugee status—a heartbreaking chapter in contemporary US history.

As a result of the Hart-Celler law, post-1965 immigration differs from earlier European immigration in a number of ways:

1. Current immigrant populations are coming from different parts of the world, including Southeast Asia, Central and South America, Africa, the Middle East, and the Caribbean (see figure 5.3, above). With the exception of those from China and Japan, earlier immigrants to the United States came largely from the western hemisphere—namely, the westernmost European nations and Mexico. Now immigrants mostly enter the United States from places that differ more in

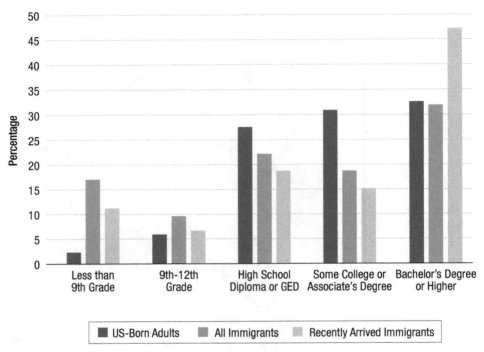

FIG. 5.4 Educational Attainment of Immigrants (2018)

Source: Batalova, Blizzard, and Bolter 2020.

terms of culture, and they are more likely to be perceived as racially different from White Americans (Alba and Nee 2003).

2. New immigrants are more geographically dispersed throughout the nation than was true when earlier immigration waves settled primarily in the nation's cities (Hirschman and Massey 2008).

3. Today's immigrants to the United States are more diverse in their educational and occupational backgrounds (Kibria, Bowman, and O'Leary 2014). Although immigrants are stereotyped as poor and uneducated, seldom do the poorest in any nation immigrate. Immigration takes resources in terms of both financial and social networks.

4. Whereas many earlier immigrants, especially those originating from European nations, experienced upward social mobility over time, post-1965 immigrants are more likely to experience downward mobility. Those who were physicians in their country of origin might become medical technicians, professors, or teachers. College-educated women may immigrate into domestic work (Gans 1992 and 2009; Hondagneu-Sotelo 2007).

The experience of coming to the United States varies. For some, entrance means new opportunities and, perhaps, mobility into a new social status. For others, it means menial labor, poverty, and perhaps disappointment, dashed hopes for a new life. The ugly side of the immigrant experience is that those who arrive with darker skin may find themselves racialized, even though they likely came from a culture where race has little or no meaning (see chapter 2). The wish of many Americans to see the United States as a White society means that the reception for some is colored by racial ideology (L. Chavez 2013).

Even though strong anti-immigrant sentiments have been expressed in recent times, most Americans think that immigrants strengthen the nation through their hard work and talents. A large majority (79 percent) are sympathetic to undocumented immigrants. A majority (58 percent) also oppose building a wall along the US-Mexican border, although there are clear partisan differences about immigration policies. For example, Republicans are less sympathetic toward undocumented immigrants (49 percent) compared to Democrats, only 13 percent of whom say they are not sympathetic toward undocumented immigrants. A large majority of Republicans (82 percent) are also in favor of substantially expanding the border wall, compared to a mere 6 percent of Democrats (Pew Research Center 2019; Suls 2017). The country is clearly divided over exactly how to handle immigration reform. Immigration remains as one of the most contentious issues of our day. As one commentator has said, "Immigration is the civil rights struggle of our times" (Rodriguez 2014).

Ebbs and flows in the demand for labor track alongside the ebbs and flows of populations of different racial-ethnic groups in the United States (Alba 2012; Alba and Foner 2015). Especially at times when native White workers find themselves economically and socially displaced, immigrants become scapegoats for woes that actually have their origins in other economic and social changes. This has been especially evident recently with calls to "build a wall" and to halt immigration across the Southern border. White, working-class men especially may feel intense anger about their own loss of status, and they sometimes displace that anger onto immigrants, who become objectified as the "other." The rise of nativist and populist sentiment that has produced antagonism toward immigrants, especially those from Central America, stems from a perception that somehow White people are losing out because of the success of others.

What structural changes have produced this phenomenon? Urbanization and industrialization have vastly expanded, beginning in the mid-twentieth century and continuing now. The nature of work has also changed, as we will see further in the following chapter. Opportunities for advancement through an industrialized labor force have vanished, and whole sections of the country have witnessed the loss of decent jobs—jobs that were once readily available even to those who did not have an advanced education. These conditions are ripe for the kind of resentment and hostility toward immigrants that has marked the current period of US history.

At the same time, immigration brings cultural changes welcomed by many who see immigrants as enriching the American mosaic. Others think these changes threaten the national identity (Katznelson 2014). Differences in how people see immigration are fueling the national debate about immigration policy. Should the United States focus primarily on securing its borders? Should we deport undocumented immigrants, even if they have children who have been born here? Should people who are undocumented but who have been working, paying taxes, and contributing to the national economy be given a path to citizenship? Are we really a melting pot or simply a simmering stew about to boil over?

As debates about immigration intensify, we are reminded that immigration policies have long disrupted families whose members are otherwise only trying to improve their lives.

Source: Sipa via AP Images.

These questions are not easily answered, and they spark intense debate. As we will see in the chapters to follow, immigrants are a part of every major social institution in the United States. As this chapter has briefly detailed, all of the groups that now make up US society have followed their respective, unique routes to their current status. Linking these group experiences together has been the chain of history.

Conclusion

This chapter opened by identifying three elements central to the history of racial-ethnic groups in the United States: *property*, *labor*, and *social control*. You now see how each played out in the development of the nation's resources. Property was taken from some and acquired by others, even as some people were defined as the property of others. Patterns of immigration or exclusion have tracked alongside the need for cheap sources of labor during periods of economic growth or contraction. In each of the histories told here, social control has been exercised—sometimes through the rule of law but other times through violence or the imposition of belief systems.

Why have some made it and others not? This chapter has provided some of the background needed to begin answering that question. The following chapter details an analytical framework that can further help you to understand the status of different racial-ethnic groups in society.

Key Terms

bracero program 118

chattel 112

Chinese Exclusion Act (1882) 121

Gentlemen's Agreement of 1907 123

Great Migration 115

Hart-Celler Act (1965) 127

Indian Removal Act 110

National Origins Act (1924) 126

nativism 125

paper sons 121

picture brides 123

Critical-Thinking Questions

1. Based on what you have learned in this chapter, what common experiences would you say diverse racial-ethnic groups have had during their incorporation into the United States? Do you see similar patterns as you examine contemporary immigration and race relations?

2. This chapter opened by identifying three themes that organize the racial-ethnic history of the United States: property, labor, and social control. Using your own racial-ethnic group as an example, how do you see these factors reflected in your group's history?

Student Exercises

5.1. Interview someone in your family (immediate or extended) who knows something about your family history. How is your family history similar to or different from any one of the group experiences examined here?

5.2. Analyze the content of one major national news outlet over the course of one week. Identify every mention of contemporary immigration. Then write a brief analysis of how immigration is understood—at least through the perspective of this news outlet. Ask yourself, is it accurate? If so, how? If not, why not?

Challenging Questions/Open to Debate

Few doubt that US immigration policy is in need of reform. The collision of different interests, however, fractures the many constituencies with an interest in immigration policy, including immigrant families and their allies, business interests, state and federal government officials (including police and border patrol agents), and the general public, to name a few. Acknowledging this complexity, determine how you would prioritize the following concerns in framing a new immigration policy: family unification, economic opportunity, labor needs, and national and regional security. You might want to inform your answer by examining public opinion on this issue (see, for example, current polling from the Pew Research Center on immigration policy: http://www.pewresearch.org/topics/immigration/).

TAKING ACTION AGAINST RACISM

Honoring History

Take a course, read, and ask yourself, *Do I know the history of my own racial and/or ethnic group? What do I know about others?* Learn about the history of a group other than your own. How is the history of this group tied to your own history?

Resource: Ronald T. Takaki, *A Different Mirror: A History of Multicultural America* (Boston: Little, Brown, 1993)

CHAPTER 6

Explaining Racial Stratification

Framing the Discussion

If you are neutral in situations of injustice, you have chosen the side of the oppressor. If an elephant has its foot on the tail of a mouse, and you say that you are neutral, the mouse will not appreciate your neutrality.

—Archbishop Desmond Tutu (cited in Brown 1984)

OBJECTIVES

- Identify some of the indicators of racial stratification
- Understand the different dimensions of a structural analysis of racial inequality
- Elaborate the social processes that facilitate ethnic assimilation
- Explain the interconnection between race, class, and gender

- Be able to debate the relative influence of culture and structure in shaping racial inequality
- Analyze the influence of colonialism in shaping global racial inequality

Why does racial inequality exist? If you ask people this question, you might hear some of the following answers: "People just need to change their prejudiced attitudes." Or "Other people have made it. Why can't they? They should just work harder"—this said usually in reference to poor people of color. Or maybe someone will say, "It's not really about race; it's all about class." You have likely heard such explanations, if not from friends and family members, then from public commentators. Such ideas are widely believed, often without a thorough analysis of the assumptions embedded within them or without careful consideration of the facts. That said, none of these explanations for racial inequality can be quickly dismissed; as with most complex topics, there may be a grain of truth in some of them. But that bit of truth dissolves upon closer review of racial inequality in society. That is the purpose of this chapter—to examine the different analytical frameworks that have been developed to explain racial inequality and to use those frameworks throughout the remainder of this book to understand the different institutional dimensions of racial inequality.

People do not usually question the assumptions they make about racial inequality. Ample research exists, though, that lets us examine the common ideas people hold about racism and evaluate the accuracy of these ideas. Sound research reveals facts that can then be interpreted via analytical frameworks guided by theory: Theory in any field provides explanations of observable facts. When a theory no longer suffices to explain a phenomenon that has been carefully observed, the theory must, at the very least, be revised. Theory is not merely an abstract or hypothetical way of thinking. In the social sciences, theory organizes our understanding of parts of the world. In the study of racial inequality, theory tries try to answer certain big questions: Why do some racial and ethnic groups succeed while others fail? Why does racial inequality persist despite changes in people's attitudes and a legal framework of equal opportunity? What social and historical forces have created inequality between racial and ethnic groups? At the heart of such questions is the need to understand racial inequality so we can produce social policies and practices to reduce it. Let's begin by looking at racial stratification.

A Structural Perspective on Racial Inequality

Framing Question: What does it mean to say racism is systemic, and what are the manifestations of systemic racism?

By now you have learned that racism is more than individual attitudes. This book argues that racism is built into the very structure of society. That fact is revealed through looking at the different dimensions of racial stratification. **Racial stratification** refers to the hierarchical arrangement in society by which different racial groups have differential access to economic and social resources, power, and perceived social worth. Certainly individual attitudes are partially to blame for the persistence of inequality, but we are bound to misunderstand even prejudice, much less broader dimensions of racial stratification, if we do not understand the larger context from which racial inequality comes. Sociological analyses of racial inequality ask us to examine the institutionalized practices that have produced and sustained racial inequality.

The various outcomes of racial stratification are examined in subsequent chapters, but a few are highlighted here:

- Hispanic and African American children are about three times as likely to be poor as White children (Semega et al. 2019).
- Even with the expansion of the Black middle class, the gap between Black and White family income today is *the same* as it was in 1967—58 percent (Semega et al. 2019).
- Whether the national unemployment is high or low, unemployment among Black women and men is typically twice the national rate (US Bureau of Labor Statistics 2020a).
- Asian American poverty is higher than poverty among Whites (Semega et al. 2019).

Heavily documented in research, these facts point to the *systemic racism* that characterizes US society. Yet, as we will see in a later section of this chapter, many people find it easier to blame people for their own failures instead of thinking about the institutional structures that oppress them. Why does racial inequality persist? To answer that question, we must look at other features of a structural analysis of racial inequality.

Several key points anchor a structural analysis of racial stratification:

1. Racial inequality is systemic and cannot be understood simply by looking at individual attitudes and actions.
2. Racial stratification distributes resources (both material and sociocultural) unequally and in patterned ways.
3. The past matters in shaping the present.
4. The advantages and disadvantages that accrue to different groups in a system of racial stratification are cumulative.
5. State policies play a role in buttressing racial stratification.
6. Racial inequality is anchored in the macro structures of society but experienced at the micro level of society.
7. Dominant groups have a tendency to blame the victim for racial inequality.
8. Racial stratification overlaps and intersects with other systems of inequality, particularly class and gender.

Let us examine each in more detail, as they form the platform for understanding racial inequality.

Systemic Racism

Racial stratification is a *system* of racial hierarchy, not just a collection of individual attitudes and behaviors. Individual attitudes and actions are no doubt important, but they have developed within institutions that have been founded and maintained to create, enhance, and defend the advantage of some over others. In this sense, racism as an attitude is not just "tacked on" but is endemic to the whole institutional structure of society. Of course, institutions change over time. Some of the most explicit manifestations of racism of the past are no longer prevalent, but, as we will see, racism is still very present . . . at both the individual and the institutional levels. At the institutional level, racism is ever-evolving and changing.

Sociologist Joe Feagin defines institutional patterns of racial inequality as **systemic racism**, a term that has entered common parlance and is now commonly evoked during mass protests against racism. Feagin defined systemic racism as "centrally about the creation, development, and maintenance of White privilege, economic wealth, and sociopolitical power over centuries" (Feagin 2014:14). He continues, "Systemic racism includes the complex array of anti-Black practices, the unjustly gained political-economic power of Whites, the continuing economic and other resource inequalities along racial lines, and the White racist ideologies and attitudes created to maintain and rationalize white privilege and power" (Feagin 2014:6).

The Distribution of Resources

As Feagin argues, systemic racism creates *unjust impoverishment* for people of color and *unjust enrichment* for Whites. This idea may seem inflammatory, as if Whites are somehow undeserving or not working for what they have earned. An individual's work ethic is not really the point. The point is that institutionalized racial inequality is a system that provides advantages and disadvantages that are neither always obvious nor necessarily intentional but that nonetheless benefit White people over others, although to different degrees. We saw this concept earlier in chapter 4 in the discussion of White privilege.

White privilege is often taken for granted because its advantages are not usually recognized by those it benefits. The advantages of White privilege are not equally distributed within the White population, but they are nonetheless real (see "Living with Racism" on the next page). As shown in chapter 4, Peggy McIntosh (1988 and 2020) calls White privilege an "invisible backpack," a bundle of tools, roadmaps, passes, and so forth that help clear the path that White people take when moving through the world.

White people often question the existence of White privilege, a common reaction especially among White people who see themselves as disadvantaged relative to others. White blue-collar workers, for example, may think they have no privilege at all. In fact, they may think that others are gaining advantages *because of* their race or their gender. White privilege is not distributed equally throughout the White population, because the system of racial stratification also intersects with systems of class and gender stratification. Still, although White people may experience inequality and a precarious economic status, they do not experience racism, just as men do not experience the type of sexism that women experience as a result of gender

LIVING WITH RACISM

For me, ignoring race and racism has never been an option. Even when it would have been easier to turn away, there were too many forces and circumstances pulling me back, compelling me to look at the matter square in the face—in *my* face. Although White Americans often think we've had few firsthand experiences with race, because most of us are so isolated from people of color in our day-to-day lives, the reality is that isolation *is* our experience with race. We are all experiencing race, because from the beginning of our lives we have been living in a racialized society, in which the color of our skin means something socially, even while it remains largely a matter of biological and genetic irrelevance. Race may be a scientific fiction—and given the almost complete genetic overlap between persons of the various so-called races, it appears to be just that—but it is a social fact that none of us can escape no matter how much or how little we may speak of it. . . . Race can be a falsehood, even as racism continues to destroy lives and, on the flipside, to advantage those who are rarely its targets.

Source: Wise 2011:1.

inequalities. It is usually easier for White people to think of racism as producing disadvantage for others. Rarely do White people think about the advantages that systemic racism gives them. Not only are White people rarely taught to recognize White privilege, but they also do not typically think about how to change it. As long as White privilege goes unacknowledged, its everyday power persists.

Racial stratification means that economic, cultural, and social resources are distributed unequally by race. You do not have to look very hard to see this effect. A mere glimpse at data on economic levels, educational attainment, health disparities, and other social indicators quickly reveals racial inequality on virtually every measure of socioeconomic well-being (see table 6.1). A persistent income gap, differential unemployment rates, different levels of educational attainment, and higher rates of poverty among African American, Native, and Hispanic Americans are just a few indicators of racial inequality.

TABLE 6.1 Racial Stratification in the United States: Key Indicators, 2018

	White, not Hispanic	African American	Hispanic	Asian American	American Indian
Median income	$70,642	$41,361	$51,450	$87,194	$41,882
Poverty rate	8.1%	20.8%	17.6%	10.1%	20.8%
Unemployment rate	3.5%	7.0%	5.7%	3.0%	5.6%
Bachelor's degree or higher, age 25 and older	35.8%	21.6%	16.0%	53.2%	15.0%

Sources: National Center for Education Statistics 2019; Semega et al. 2019; US Bureau of Labor Statistics 2019a.

Subsequent chapters will examine these indicators in various institutions more thoroughly, but in the United States even such basic facts as how long you live, whether you will be accosted by the police on the streets, or what schools you attend are strongly influenced by race. Moreover, despite the many changes that have come from civil rights protections and the formal elimination of racial segregation, racial disparities have stubbornly persisted. They are indicative of the underlying—indeed, *systemic*—problem of racism in the United States.

The Past Shapes the Present

Past practices and policies reverberate in the inequality that we see today. This is not as simple as thinking that slavery directly caused modern racism or that the annexation of Mexico is the reason for Mexican Americans' current socioeconomic status. These past events matter, but it is the legacy of past practices that has allowed some groups to advance while others have been held back.

For example, how and when a group entered US society really matters. Don't forget that White European groups arrived voluntarily. African Americans arrived in chains; Mexican Americans were annexed as the result of war; Chinese laborers were being forcibly removed from the workplace once their labor was no longer needed. European immigrants arrived in the United States as the industrial economy was expanding, allowing them to get a foothold in various industries. Yet even as they were able to find a place in US society around the turn of the twentieth century, African Americans, though newly freed from slavery, were being subjected to the ravages of Jim Crow racism. In the American South, African Americans were segregated into separate schools, separate housing, and separate public facilities, denied opportunities for economic and social advancement. Even African Americans who moved North to seek better opportunities during the Great Migration found themselves shoved into Black urban ghettoes while also being viciously excluded from labor unions.

Past governmental policies and restrictions on who could acquire housing and where reverberate today in the character of residential neighborhoods and the value of people's property. The federal New Deal, implemented to alleviate the impact of the Great Depression of the late 1920s and 1930s, was a color-blind policy. Yet as part of the New Deal, the Social Security Act of 1935 denied benefits to domestic and agricultural workers—the very occupations that employed the majority of Black men and women at the time. As a result, if you were Black in the 1930s, despite the best intentions of federal policies of assistance, you did not receive the same benefits Whites received (Katznelson 2005). Although you might think this was over one hundred years ago and should not matter now, it made a difference in who could recover from grinding poverty in the American South. Likewise, as we will see in more detail in chapter 9, restrictive housing covenants, redlining of neighborhoods, and bank lending practices of the past have produced vast differences in the value of home properties now, resulting in vast differences in the wealth of White and Black Americans.

In sum, the point of looking to the past to understand racial inequality is not to locate present conditions solely in the past but to see the impact of past decisions and actions on racial inequality in the present. Once we do this, we can understand, as comedian Jon Stewart soberly put it, how the past has "left us with a gaping racial wound that will not heal" (Duchon 2015).

Accumulating Advantage and Disadvantage

People denied opportunities in the past simply start from a different place in the present. Even when obstacles have been removed, such as through the passage of civil rights legislation, past practices mean that groups have a particular challenge just catching up. President Lyndon Johnson captured this well in a famous commencement address delivered at Howard University in 1965. He said, "You do not take a person who, for years, has been hobbled by chains and liberate him, bring him up to the starting line of a race, and then say, 'You are free to compete with all the others' and still justly believe that you have been completely fair" (Johnson 1965).

Johnson's words are reflected in the concept of the **sedimentation of racial inequality,** which refers to the fact that "structural disadvantages have been layered one upon the other to produce Black disadvantage and White privilege" (Oliver and Shapiro 2006:51). Discrimination and racial segregation in the past have prevented people of color from accumulating assets to the same extent as White Americans. How so?

A great example comes from the federal GI Bill, passed in the aftermath of World War II. Historians now claim that the GI Bill was the single most important factor in creating America's middle class. It provided returning veterans access to low-cost home mortgages, business loans, and educational benefits. Specifically, under this bill, if you bought a new house in the newly developing suburbs in the 1950s, you could get a very low-interest loan, perhaps even without making a down payment. This was a huge boon both for the housing market and for those who purchased "starter" homes that appreciated over the years. This benefit gave those who had even modest means some degree of financial equity—an asset that they could then pass on to the next generation or possibly reinvest.

Who benefited? African Americans and other people of color certainly were among those who fought in World War II and were entitled to the benefits of the GI Bill. But systemic racism prevented people of color from being able to access the opportunities that this important legislation provided. One major obstacle was the decision to administer the benefits of the GI Bill in a decentralized way, thus putting its administration in the hands of local officials who in many localities supported segregation and made it difficult, if not impossible, for Black veterans to access the benefits of this legislation.

Racial discrimination in the housing market also prevented veterans of color from acquiring the same benefits that Whites received. Restrictive covenants written into deeds commonly prevented people of color from buying homes in predominantly White neighborhoods. Other discriminatory practices by banks and real estate agents kept people of color out of newly forming suburban neighborhoods in which even buying a small home—a modest financial asset—would pay off over future generations. Denied this possibility, disadvantage accumulated over time for persons of color (Rothstein 2017).

The GI Bill also provided unprecedented access to higher education. Yet when the bill was passed, educational institutions were still highly segregated. In the North, African Americans made up a tiny proportion of students in colleges that were using highly selective criteria for admission. Black veterans in the South were still formally excluded from White institutions of higher education. The GI Bill did provide a boon for enrollment in historically Black colleges, but segregation in education remained a fact of life.

Following World War II, the GI Bill gave returning veterans support for attending college. It is estimated that 48 percent would not have been able to attend without the help of the GI Bill. Yet racial
segregation in the nation's colleges and universities meant that this advantage was not equally
enjoyed by returning Black veterans.

Source: Margaret Bourke-White / Getty Images.

The end result was that a color-blind benefit like the GI bill—in the context
of systemic racism—prevented veterans of color from attaining the same upward
mobility so many White veterans experienced. People of color fell behind the
starting line. Although the GI Bill did foster the growth of a small Black middle
class, the bill's advantages accrued mostly to the White middle class, producing
what Ira Katznelson has called "affirmative action for Whites" (Katznelson 2005).

Generations of White people benefited from this policy, even though the descendants of World War II veterans might not readily recognize the advantage it provided. As sociologists Melvin Oliver and Thomas Shapiro write, "Every circumstance of bias and discrimination against Blacks has produced a circumstance and opportunity of positive gain for Whites" (1995:51). That is how the *sedimentation of racial inequality* works.

State Policies Make a Difference

You can see in the example of the GI Bill that state policies matter in furthering or reducing racial inequality. Note that the GI Bill was a federal program open to all veterans, no matter their race. On the face of it, the program seemed to provide opportunities for Black, Latino, and Native American veterans further their education, find better housing, and perhaps open a small business. Faced with open and legal segregation, though, people of color were excluded by a seemingly color-blind policy that nonetheless left them "cemented to the bottom of society's economic hierarchy" (Oliver and Shapiro 1995:5).

Other state-based policies also contributed to this disadvantage. We do not normally think of the current interstate highway system as racist. Everyone uses it, no one is denied access to it, and it exists due to a huge outlay of federal dollars. We now take for granted that the interstate highway system lets us move relatively easily and quickly from state to state and coast to coast. Begun in the 1950s, the system was designed to reduce city traffic, increase interstate commerce, and facilitate the movement of people, mostly White, from the burgeoning, mostly White suburbs to city jobs. The result was a sharp increase in the number of automobiles, population change with Whites in the suburban ring of cities and people of color in the cities proper, and a shift in the balance of power between cities and suburbs (Sherman 2014).

Whom did the interstate highway system serve best? It strained the transportation budgets of cities and was also built in ways that walled off Black and Latino urban neighborhoods. In many cases, Black and other ethnic neighborhoods were actually destroyed as homes were demolished to make way for highways. Often people of color were cut off from transportation networks that provided access to jobs and the more economically vital parts of the city (Sherman 2014). Once again, policies of the federal government opened doors for some and closed them for others.

Racism at Every Level

A structural perspective locates racial inequality in the macro-structure of society—that is, the roots of racial inequality lie in society's institutions, like the economy, the political system, and so forth. Yet even though it is anchored at the macro level, racial inequality is manifested at different levels of society.

Sociologist Evelyn Glenn delineates this by identifying three levels at which processes of racial inequality appear: *social structure*, *representation*, and *microinteraction*. Social structure refers to the "rules regulating the allocation of power and resources" in society. The representational level refers to the "symbols, language, and images that express and convey racial meanings" (Glenn 2002:12). Microinteraction includes the norms, etiquette, and spatial rules that orchestrate social interaction across racial boundaries. You can also think of these three levels as:

- the institutional level
- the ideological level
- the interaction level

Education provides an example. At the institutional level, a large amount of racial segregation marks the nation's schools and colleges. White men hold the most institutional power by being those most likely to hold positions of leadership, especially in the most prestigious institutions. Racial disparities also persist in educational attainment and in the quality of schools. Being able to attend the very best schools also reproduces racial inequality because those with the most prestigious educational credentials are those most likely to achieve high socioeconomic status.

At the ideological level, the images, ideas, and ideals that are taught in schools implicitly or explicitly promote racial exclusion. For example, how are people of color seen in schoolbooks? Although representations of people of color have improved a lot in recent years, stereotypes continue to disparage people of color, as we saw in chapter 3. What you don't see can be just as damaging as what you do see (Tatum 1997). For example, limited images or histories of people of color in textbooks teach all of us that somehow people of color do not matter much or that they are inferior, marginal, and different—reflections of racial inequality at the level of ideology.

At the level of interaction, race shapes how different groups are treated in schools and how students interact with each other. Latino and Black boys, for example, tend to be labeled early on as "troublemakers." The label alone can be enough to produce behavior that funnels Latino and Black boys into the "school-to-prison pipeline" (Rios 2011).

Racial inequality exists at every level of society, underscoring the importance of change at all levels: how people interact, what they think and believe, and how resources and positions of influence are distributed. You will see in the chapters on social institutions that follow how these different levels of inequality are played out in different spheres, including the professional, the educational, the medical, and the criminal judicial.

Blaming the Victim

Most people, especially those in the dominant group, find it easier to blame people for their own failure than to acknowledge the structural roots of racial inequality. Blaming the victim is a strong narrative in US culture—a narrative that makes individuals responsible for their own outcomes no matter the structural barriers or societal assistance they might face (Ryan 1971).

Individualism is a strong cultural ideal in US society. A culture of individualism gives people unprecedented freedom, but it also obscures the realities of structurally based group inequality. You see evidence of this tendency toward individualism in public opinion: White people are more likely to see a level playing field for all than are people of color. For example, in national polls asking whether discrimination

The invention of the washing machine was accompanied by a campaign to oust Chinese workers from a niche in the labor market that had helped support them. You can see in this 1886 advertisement how racism, nationalism, and xenophobia intersected to exclude Chinese workers.

Source: Library of Congress, Shober & Carqueville Lith Co., c1886.

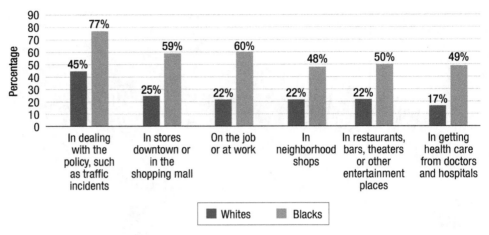

FIG. 6.1 Perceptions of Fair Treatment

Source: Jones 2019.

is to blame for Black Americans' inferior jobs, income, and housing, only 15 percent of Whites said discrimination is mostly to blame. Whites are also far less likely than Black Americans to think Black people are treated less fairly in society (see figure 6.1; Jones 2019). The result is a very strong tendency in this culture to blame people of color for their own plight, such as in thinking that poverty is the result of deficient family values, poor parenting, lack of ambition, or an absence of a solid work ethic. Federal legislation for federal assistance to poor people even reflects this assumption: the Personal Responsibility and Work Opportunity Act—the actual title for federal poverty policy— names "personal responsibility" as the trigger point for poverty (Greenbaum 2015). With such a toehold in the dominant culture, blaming the victim is a deterrent to social policies that would actually alleviate structural inequalities—poverty and racism included.

Intersecting Inequalities: Race, Class, and Gender

Anyone who has experienced the pernicious effects of racial inequality knows how all-consuming racism can be. Race has a social and economic impact all its own, but race also intersects with the influence of other social factors, including social class, gender, age, sexual preference, and nationality, among others.

Intersectional theory examines the intricate connections between different social factors, especially class, race, gender, and sexuality. It is women of color who initiated the substantive analysis of how race, class, gender, and sexuality interrelate (Baca Zinn and Dill 1996). As a second wave of feminism gained momentum in the 1960s and 1970s, women of color criticized the feminist movement for ignoring them. They and their allies developed a new and more complete way of understanding the experiences of diverse groups of women. Now intersectional analyses of race, class, gender, and sexuality have been widely undertaken in most every field of study.

The basic insight of intersectional theory is that race, class, and gender operate simultaneously in shaping the experience of all people (Andersen and Collins

2020; Crenshaw 1989). The point is not to compare and to rank oppressions or to try to discern whether race or class or gender is the most important feature of a person's life. Rather, the point is to understand how race, class, and gender are together embedded in a *matrix of domination* in society (Collins 1990). Race, class, and gender, interwoven into the social structure of society, operate in overlapping and interconnected patterns of power and inequality—together shaping all people's lives.

Of course, at any given moment a given person might feel the influence of one social factor more than another. A Black man stopped by the police in an affluent neighborhood will certainly feel the salience of his race most prominently at that moment. The fact that he is a man, however, is just as important as race in shaping his overall life chances. Likewise, a Latina who is sexually harassed while walking down the street will keenly feel her gender, but her identity as Latina actually merges both her gender and her racial-ethnic identity, likely along with her class and age.

Intersectional theory also teaches us that race, class, and gender are each manifested differently, depending on how these factors interrelate. Masculinity, for example, may be expressed differently in a person who is Latino and poor versus one who is Black and middle class or who is White and poor. Likewise, being a woman is manifested differently depending on her class and race. Intersectionality means that we have to understand the unique and complex ways that people are located in a system of overlapping inequalities. Still, when a Black man of any social class is stopped by the police, the fact that he is Black is what likely matters most at that moment.

By understanding the interconnections of race, class, and gender, we garner a more complete view of how society is organized and how we live our lives, depending on our social location. The social facts of race, class, and gender are not isolated one from the other. Each is manifested differently depending on its configuration with others (Andersen and Collins 2020; Collins 2019). For example, White women are disadvantaged by virtue of their gender but advantaged by virtue of their racial status. In subsequent chapters we'll see in greater detail how intersectionality plays out in the social and economic status of different groups.

The points above lay a foundation for understanding a structural analysis of racial and ethnic inequality. No one analysis can, however, explain the particulars of any given group experience. The sociological frameworks examined in the remainder of this chapter provide particular perspectives that can help explain the ongoing arrangements between race and ethnic groups in the United States.

We Made It . . . Why Can't They? Assimilation and the American Dream

Framing Question: What are the social and historical conditions that enable or block assimilation into US society, and how have different groups experienced assimilation—or not?

Many White, European immigrants have experienced upward mobility over time, which leads many people to think that anyone can make it through hard work and cultural adaptation. Indeed, the ideal of upward mobility is one reason so many immigrants find coming to the United States so appealing. The perception that the

United States is a melting pot[1] of different groups reflects this popular ideal. The relative success of White European immigrants over time has become a standard, however, by which other immigrant groups are judged, even though each immigrant group has faced different historical and contemporary conditions. New immigrants are often scorned for not adopting American culture and instead holding on to their own cultural values, as if changing their cultural frame is all that is needed to succeed. How do groups become integrated into society?

The process by which ethnic groups are incorporated into this single dominant culture is called **assimilation**. Assimilation is typically thought to involve the gradual dissolution of previous ethnic identities as groups take on the cultural and social habits of the new society (Alba and Nee 2003).

For a long time, the **assimilation model** was the standard for how sociologists and others conceptualized the process of immigrant incorporation. Assimilation was thought to progress as immigrant groups came to be more culturally similar to the host society, especially in the second and third generations. Assimilation was also thought to occur through **acculturation**—that is, the adoption by incoming groups of the language, values, and norms of the host society. As the US population has become more ethnically diverse, scholars have revised traditional assimilation theory to recognize the complex and different ways that groups become part of a new society. Older thinking about assimilation now has a somewhat negative connotation for suggesting that new immigrants had to give up their culture if they were to be incorporated into American society.

Several ideas guide new research on the process of assimilation:

1. *Assimilation is not a one-way process.* An ethnic group may lose some of its unique cultural forms over time, but its presence also changes the society it enters (Alba 2012; Alba and Nee 2003). Mexican Americans, as an example, may enter US society and adopt some of its citizens' cultural patterns (language, cultural taste, and so forth), but they will likely also maintain some distinctly Mexican cultural values and behaviors. Furthermore, as groups become incorporated into their new society, the society itself may adopt some of the cultural characteristics of the new group.

2. *Immigrants can maintain an ethnic identity even while assimilating into a new society.* Maintaining ethnic identity for immigrants happens to varying degrees. Immigrant identity involves a complex process of "practices, beliefs, and behaviors that are subject to constant readjustment and reorganization" (Massey and Sánchez 2010:23–24). Immigrant identity remains strongest in the presence of an ongoing flow of immigrants that replenishes strong immigrant identification (Jiménez 2010 and 2017).

3. *Immigrant groups vary in the degree to which they are integrated into society.* The degree of integration depends on the particular social and economic conditions at the time of group entry, as well as the skills and resources that immigrants bring with them (Brown and Bean 2006). Immigrants seldom come

---

[1] The chapter's opening photo shows an event at the Ford English School, which was established in 1914 by Henry Ford to teach immigrant workers American values and language. Pictured are workers in Native dress enter a "melting pot" and emerge "Americanized."

from among the poorest people in the nation of origin, because it takes re-sources to move.

4. *How different groups are welcomed into a host nation is influenced by relation-ships between nations.* That welcome varies along with the economic, politi-cal, and military conditions in the host and sending countries (Rumbaut 1996). The immigration of Cubans into the United States in the 1960s, for example, occurred in the midst of the Cuban Revolution, when the Cuban government nationalized American industries on the island. Most of those who initially fled to the United States during the Cuban Revolution were professionals and other middle-class workers for whom the United States held an open-door policy. An-ticommunist sentiment in the United States kept the door more widely open for Cubans than for other groups; the US government also provided support that enabled many Cubans to do quite well in their new country (Pedraza 1996).

5. *Immigration is shaped by macrostructural conditions but also by the decisions that individuals and families make in the context of their own lives.* Although immigration involves social structural processes, people make decisions about their lives in the context of larger social forces. Political refugees have to make difficult decisions to leave their home nations, often disrupting families and communities. Such is the case when Syrian refugees have had to flee to Europe and the United States as the result of war and violence in their country. In such cases "push" factors are more important than the "pull" that other immi-grants may feel when seeking new opportunities (Massey and Sánchez 2010; Pedraza 1996).

6. *Some groups become racialized through the process of immigration.* Many immigrant groups come from nations where race does not mean what it does in the United States, and they might find themselves subjected to racism once they enter the United States. For example, Latinos from various ethnic back-grounds have not traditionally been considered a "race," but some experience "becoming Brown," especially if they work in low-wage, service-oriented jobs. Groups are more likely to become racialized during periods of intense **nativism** by the dominant group—that is, when dominant groups begin to favor policies that privilege the interests of those already here. Ironically, in the United States strong nativism exists at the same time that the nation extols itself as a nation of immigrants (Kibria, Bowman, and O'Leary 2014).

In sum, assimilation is not a simple linear path that always leads to upward mobility and integration into a new society. Immigrants experience different tra-jectories, including downward, not upward, mobility upon arrival (Gans 1992; Jiménez 2010; Waters 2000). As one example, many Vietnamese, Korean, and West Indian immigrants who were highly educated professionals in their home nations find themselves upon entry into the United States working largely in low-wage service occupations, such as in nail salons and other personal services (Kang 2010).

Segmented assimilation occurs when immigrants may be integrated into some parts of society but not others (Portes and Zhou 1993). Further, the social, eco-nomic, and cultural resources people bring with them influence their chances for assimilation, as does how groups are perceived and received in the host society.

Structural barriers such as poor schools in immigrant neighborhoods or discrimination in the labor market impede immigrant success. Immigrants who become racialized are even less likely to find success. As an expert team of sociologists studying immigration has concluded, "Children of Asian, Black, mulatto, and mestizo immigrants cannot escape their ethnicity and race, as defined by the mainstream. Their enduring physical differences from Whites and the equally persistent strong effects of discrimination based on those differences . . . throw a barrier in the path of occupational mobility and social acceptance" (Portes, Fernández-Kelly, and Haller 2005:1006).

The linkage between race and ethnicity as social constructs reminds us that, like race, ethnicity is a social boundary. The two interweave such that race constructs ethnicity and ethnicity can construct race. The boundaries between the two are fluid and emergent, depending on social and historical conditions (Kibria et al. 2014). Although a Black/White divide has long characterized American society, the increasing presence of new immigrant groups changes the boundaries of what both race and ethnicity mean and how they influence diverse group experiences in an unequal society.

The Race-Class Connection

Framing Question: What does it mean to say that class is shaped by race and vice versa?

People often assert that class, not race, is why so many people of color are of lower socioeconomic status than most Whites. **Class** refers to a system of inequality by which groups have different access to economic, social, and political resources. Certainly class is relevant to a person's economic and social standing, but does class obliterate the influence of race? The fact is that class and race matter together in shaping people's life opportunities, and they combine in particular ways at different times. We can see this by taking a long-range view of how race and class have been conjoined in different periods of US history.

In an important analysis of racial inequality, William Julius Wilson (1978) divides US history into three broad periods that he argues are key to understanding the shifting connection between race and class. Wilson links transformations in the significance of race to key political-economic transitions in US history. Through this long-range lens, Wilson points to large-scale transitions that currently shape the connection between race and class.

The three distinct periods that Wilson identifies have shaped the life chances of African Americans. Each characterizes a different **political economy**, which is the linkage between systems of power and economic systems at given points in time. The periods are

1. the preindustrial economy
2. the industrial economy
3. the postindustrial economy

The preindustrial economy in the United States marked the period of slavery. Although we think of slavery as existing only in the South, the nation's entire economy was dependent on a slave-based system. Under slavery, racial power, especially but not exclusively in the South, was absolute, lying solely in the hands of the White aristocracy. Racial oppression was conscious, deliberate, and explicit—a system of racial power that continued even beyond the end of slavery, especially with the advent of Jim Crow—legally mandated racial segregation. Even though masked by White paternalism, state policies were explicitly racial. During this preindustrial period, there was minimum physical distance between racial groups but maximum social distance.

The industrial period, roughly from the beginning of the twentieth century through World War II, was marked by the growth of industrial labor. Manufacturing, not agriculture, became the economic driver. During this period, race relations were marked by more overt racial and class conflict, especially between White and Black workers, but also between Whites and others. White workers tried to neutralize Black competition in the labor force while managers used race to try to divide the interests of the working class. During this period, Blacks also fled the South as best they could, both to escape the ravages of Jim Crow and to seek new job opportunities. The result was the emergence of an urban, but segregated, Black population.

In the postindustrial period—roughly post–World War II through the present)—the nation's economic base shifted from manufacturing to the service industries. That is, manufacturing jobs declined while those based on service work increased. This transition has been fueled by automation and the use of technology, as well as by the rise of a global economy in which manufacturing jobs have been largely relocated overseas as companies search for cheaper labor.

Wilson argues that this political-economic transformation has had huge and deleterious effect on Black Americans and other people of color. In the postindustrial period, he argues, class has increasing significance in shaping the life chances of people of color, including recent immigrant groups. In an industrial economy people (especially men) could find relatively decent jobs in manufacturing without being highly educated or having advanced technological skills. Without such skills and training in the postindustrial economy, people get stuck in low-wage service work—or they have no work at all. Chronic unemployment and poverty are the result, forming an **urban underclass** consisting of people (mostly of color but also the White working class and poor) at the absolute bottom of the economic system. Those in the urban underclass are largely unable to overcome the barriers posed by structural realignments in the political economy. In this context, class and race intermingle in shaping people's life chances. Furthermore, racial tensions are driven by these social structural transformations. When adding contemporary patterns of immigration to the mix, race and ethnic relations become highly volatile.

In sum, in our postindustrial period, race alone does not determine life chances, as was more likely in earlier periods of time. Yet class and race are still deeply intertwined, meaning neither alone influences people's well-being. Race and class together form a structure of opportunity that has profound effects on the life chances of various groups.

What about Culture? The Culture-Structure Debate

Framing Question: How can we acknowledge the different cultures of racial-ethnic groups without placing the blame for racial inequality on cultural values?

Many popular explanations of racial inequality, especially the persistence of poverty, blame the culture of the disadvantaged for their own lack of success. "If people would only try harder" or "If parents would just raise their children right" are commonly heard refrains routinely leveled at people of color, especially if they are poor.

Does culture have a role in explaining social and economic outcomes? This is a hotly debated question among political commentators, policy makers, and scholars. Understanding this debate requires another look at the concept of culture, as well as at the concept of social structure.

Culture includes many things—both material objects and ideas, such as values, norms, habits, perceptions, attitudes, and so forth. These different ideas are the mental frames that people use to understand and interpret the world they inhabit (Small, Harding, and Lamont 2010). Culture provides a shared outlook for people and frames their understanding of their lived world.

Social structure, however, refers to practices in society, often abstract, that influence people's outcomes in life. Social structure includes behavior, including institutional practices, such as laws, policies, and, perhaps, discrimination. Social structure also comprises the large-scale changes in society—demographic, economic, political, and so forth—that can have adverse effects on different groups (Wilson 2009).

When people point to culture as a cause of racial inequality (or other forms of inequality), they are usually using culture to refer to the attitudes, values, and behaviors of the disadvantaged—as if people's cultural outlook prevents them from succeeding. Despite stereotypes to the contrary, there is considerable evidence that poor people want to work, want to marry, and want to have the resources of a comfortable life. In other words, they hold mainstream values, but their quest to achieve this ideal life is thwarted (Edin and Kefalas 2005; Small et al. 2010). In this sense, it is wrong to see culture as the cause of poverty or other inequalities.

Unique cultural attitudes and behaviors, however, do sometimes emerge among the urban poor, even while they also hold the values of the dominant culture (Venkatesh 2006). People in poor, racially segregated neighborhoods, for example, value "street smarts" and develop other elaborate cultural-meaning systems and behaviors (Anderson 1999). The creation of such cultural adaptations, such as developing a "code of the street," is a reasonable response to a context in which a person has to negotiate their own safety and status. For men, such cultural adaptation might involve displays of hypermasculinity, especially when dominant norms of masculinity (such as being a family provider) are otherwise denied (Majors and Billson 1993). Seen in this way, culture is a creative response for people who develop innovative social and cultural attitudes and behaviors when they are denied the resources of the dominant society. In other words, culture is an *adaptation to social structural conditions*—poverty, segregation, denial of opportunity. Although a distinct culture can exist among disadvantaged people, it is a result of inequality, not a determinant.

Another way of thinking about culture in connection to racial inequality is to look to *dominant culture*, not just the supposed culture of the disadvantaged, to understand the powerful forces that shape social outcomes for different groups

(Wilson 2009). **Cultural capital** refers to the knowledge and resources that advantaged groups get by virtue of their location in society. The best schooling, influential social networks, style of speech, knowledge of elite culture, and other nonmaterial assets form the cultural capital that enable people to succeed and pass their advantages on to later generations. Ignoring the influence of the dominant culture while targeting culture as an explanation for racial inequality misses the elephant in the room—that is, the vast amount of cultural capital that more dominant and privileged groups amass and enjoy, even while they might take such advantages for granted.

The culture-structure debate is usually posited as an either-or proposition, and cultural explanations usually get the most attention from policy makers (Wilson 2009). But culture and structure are two sides of the same coin: Both are connected to racism in society. Although cultural explanations resonate with the value of individualism in US society, asserting culture as the cause of racial inequality obscures the social-structural forces that generate racism and its consequences.

Global Racial Inequality: Colonialism and Postcolonial Theory

Framing Question: How have the specific practices of colonialism shaped US racial inequality, and in what form does colonialism still exist?

Racial inequality takes a particular form in the United States, but racial inequality is also a global phenomenon. Although the meaning of race can vary around the world, patterns of racism, power, and privilege infiltrate the entire world. This is best understood through examining colonialism and postcolonial theory.

Colonialism refers to the process whereby a nation (or, perhaps, a group of nations) assumes control of another country (or people) for purposes of economic exploitation. **Postcolonial theory** is an analytical perspective that emphasizes how the history of colonialism and worldwide empire building has influenced present-day racial stratification (Go 2018). Postcolonial theory interprets colonialism as not over (or "post") but, instead, having an ongoing influence on the status of different racial and ethnic groups who have a history of colonial exploitation. To say *post*colonialism does not mean that colonialism is over, but rather that its effects remain even after a colonial relationship has ended.

Former colonial empires, such as that of Great Britain, as well as other Western nations. have shaped inequality throughout the world. By dominating former colonies, colonial powers have created a racialized system with the Global North (mostly White, Western, and Northern nations in the world) dominating the Global South (nations generally near or below the equator). The Global South is the home of poor people of color, while the dominant group in the Global North is mostly White.

Postcolonial theory emphasizes the legacy of colonialism and empire in structuring racial inequality worldwide. Indigenous groups became racialized through the reach of colonial power, whether they were black Africans imported as slaves to the New World, indigenous Native groups throughout South and Central America, or the colonized people of Southeast Asia.

Postcolonial theory emphasizes the fact that the wealth of Anglo-European nations has been made possible through the expansion of Western power, the

LEARNING OUR PAST

The Bracero Program

The bracero program, also discussed in chapter 5, can be viewed as a form of *internal colonialism*. In this case, the United States did not conquer an external nation, but rather used this program to import workers to serve the needs of business owners at home. The *bracero* ("manual worker") program brought close to five million Mexican workers to the United States starting in 1942 until the program officially ended in the late 1960s. Many Mexican Americans today can trace their origins to this program, as captured in the following narrative of the son of a bracero worker:

> My dad, Celedonio Galaviz, came to the United States of America in 1951. He came to [participate] in the bracero program. He didn't have enough money to make the journey from Jalisco to the [US] border, so my grandmother (on my mom's side) gave them a cow. They looked at it as an investment . . . so they sold the cow for 80 pesos, which was [a lot] of money in that time, and used the money to make the long trip to the [United States]. He had two contracts with the . . . program. The first time he went to Texas, the second time to California. He . . . faced racial discrimination in Texas, like having to use the back entrance at restaurants to eat and drinking out of a water hose. . . . He didn't mind or complain much; he was just glad to be working and making money to help support his family in Mexico. He tells about a time when they were asking all the short men to line up on one side. But they left him out, so [he] step[ped] in line with the short men. Until they noticed him and made him get back in line with the other men. He questioned them, and they said that all the short men were going to pick . . . celery, strawberries . . . and that the taller men were going to pick lemons . . . he was six feet tall. By the time he came to California he was known as a hard worker and was asked to return to work . . . when his contract expired. He was sponsored to come here and work by his boss. He got his green card and later his . . . citizenship. He sent for his family, all seven of us, in 1965. He used to say, "I don't have a lot of money to leave you, but what I do leave you is a land where you can do or be anything you want." We all made good in the United States and are thankful to our mom and dad for bringing us to this land of opportunity.

Source: Galaviz n.d.

domination of indigenous peoples, and the accumulation of wealth by mostly White people at the expense of others (Go 2018). Colonial powers have done this by extracting labor and natural resources from others while also policing and surveilling native populations—either through slavery or via other brutal forms of oppression. We see the impact of colonialism in the fact that the countries most powerful in the world over two hundred years ago remain at the top of the world hierarchy. The wealth of these nations has come at the hands of indigenous people—many (if not all) of whom still struggle for their rights.

From the perspective of postcolonialism theory it is not race per se that has created racial inequality. Rather, postcolonial theory sees the idea of race as having been created for purposes of power and domination. Race was invented for purposes of colonial power (Go 2018). The impact of this creation remains with us today even as racialized concepts of difference evolve and change.

Settler colonialism is a specific form of colonialism referring to the process by which newcomers try to acquire land and property while overpowering indigenous (native) communities. Different from colonialism more generally, settler colonialism does not have to include settlers extracting labor from the conquered group. Settlers do, however, exercise strict social control over the oppressed group, possibly even to the extent of extermination. The history of Native Americans comes to mind. Frequently under settler colonialism, indigenous groups become racialized through an ideological process that is part of the newly imposed social control.

Settler colonialism has marked not only US history but also the global processes of the acquisition of labor and property over the long course of world history. As we have seen, settler colonialism has meant containing and controlling others, erasing their indigenous culture, and, in the extreme, removing people or relocating them to places where their labor is needed (Glenn 2015).

Conclusion

This chapter has laid out a structural perspective on racial inequality, showing that racial inequality can only be understood in the context of specific historical and social conditions. Such a perspective can lead to pessimism about the prospects for social change, because racial inequality seems so entrenched. A structural analysis, though, also provides hope, because inequalities that evolve from structural factors can be changed—that is, if the structures are transformed. Throughout the course of US history, people of color and their allies have organized to resist the structural oppression that racial inequality produces. These actions are examined further in chapter 12.

The important thing to see now is how racial inequality has its roots in institutional practices. The manifestation of racism at the institutional level can be seen in every social institution—work, family, education, health care, and criminal justice, among others—subjects to which we turn next.

Key Terms

acculturation 148	political economy 150
assimilation 148	postcolonial theory 153
assimilation model 148	racial stratification 137
class 150	sedimentation of racial inequality 141
colonialism 153	segmented assimilation 149
cultural capital 153	settler colonialism 155
intersectional theory 146	systemic racism 138
nativism 149	urban underclass 151

Critical-Thinking Questions

1. You are discussing race with a friend who says, "If people would just try harder, they would succeed. That is proven by the experience of immigrant groups." Having read this chapter, what would you now say to your friend?

2. How is blaming the victim consistent with the cultural values of the United States? How is it not? What does your answer suggest for changing this common response to racial inequality?

Student Exercises

6.1 Take one of the groups noted in this chapter and conduct an Internet search of the key events in that group's history in the United States. Then construct a time line of these key moments. What were the particular social and historical contexts at each of these time points? If you can, compare your time line to that of students who selected different groups. What common conditions have the different groups experienced? What is unique to their history, and what do your answers tell you about the perspectives offered in this chapter?

6.2 Talk to someone in your family from an older generation. See whether you can sketch out your family's roots and how your family's own history is linked to the processes described in the chapter. You can find inspiration through watching an episode of Henry Louis Gates's PBS show *Finding Your Roots*.[2] What does your family history say about a structural perspective on racial inequality?

Challenging Questions/Open to Debate

Some argue that class has become more important than race in determining the life chances of people of color. Do you agree or disagree? Does your answer change when considering groups other than African Americans?

TAKING ACTION AGAINST RACISM

Probing Your Perspective

Question commonly repeated ideas about race and racism. Many of these seem to be common sense, but on closer look, they reproduce racist thinking. You can best examine taken-for-granted assumptions by continuing to educate yourself about racism and its impact on diverse groups, including your own.

Resource: Andersen 2020.

[2] For more information on *Finding Your Roots with Henry Louis Gates, Jr.*, visit https://www.pbs.org/weta/finding-your-roots/.

CHAPTER 7

Economic Inequality

Work, Class, and Poverty

As long as poverty, injustice, and gross inequality exist in our world, none of us can truly rest.

—Nelson Mandela (2005)

OBJECTIVES

- Distinguish the importance of income and wealth in shaping racial inequality
- Explain the impact of economic restructuring and growing inequality on people of color
- Analyze the status of people of color in the workforce
- Compare and contrast different explanations of racialized economic inequality
- Discuss how race affects the likelihood of poverty and detail some of the current social policies to that provide support to those in need

Signs of race and economic inequality are all around us. When you pass a highway construction site, who do you see working? Are White men doing the skilled or supervisory labor while people of color, and sometimes women, stand and hold the stop signs? Who do you see begging on the streets or waiting in line at shelters? Who maintains the gardens and lawns in wealthy neighborhoods? For that matter, who works in what jobs on your college campus?

Observations such as these reveal a lot about racial disparities at work and, more generally, in the economic status of different groups. Racial inequity in economic status has been starkly revealed during the global pandemic in 2020. No doubt, many people have suffered, but people of color (namely, Latinos, African Americans, and Native Americans) have paid an especially high price. Early reports indicate that Latinos are the group most likely to say someone in their household had to take a pay cut or lost their job as a result of the virus. The employment of people of color (especially women) in the service sector where essential workers are needed means that many have had to continue working, risking both their own health and that of their family. Obviously millions of people have been harmed by this national disaster, but in the United States, the impact has fallen disproportionately on racial and ethnic minorities (Krogstad, Gonzalez-Barrera, and Noe-Bustamente 2020).

Good economy, bad economy—whichever way it goes, racial inequality lurks not far below the surface and is revealed by such things as income and wealth disparities, employment and unemployment patterns, and the likelihood of being poor. This chapter examines some of the economic realities associated with racial inequality.

Income, Wealth, and Race

Framing Question: What is the difference between income and wealth, and why is this difference significant in describing racial inequality?

In the previous chapter we saw how practices of the past continue to shape race relations in the present. Who gets to work and where and how they are rewarded for their work can carry vestiges of the past, but current realities also shape the different economic statuses of both White people and people of color. We start by examining income inequality.

Income Inequality

Income is the money brought into a household over a given time period from various sources, such as earnings and investment dividends. In 2018 (the most recent year for which national data are available), the **median income** for all households in the United States was $63,179 (Semega et al. 2019). A median is the midpoint: The median income figure means that half of all households have incomes above this level and half below. Of course, what a particular income means depends on such things as family size, region of residence, special needs, state and federal tax obligations, and whether one has any other sources of financial security. The national median income figure does not account for these differences, because it aggregates all households. Still, the figure gives you a picture of how people are faring—and how the nation's economic well-being has changed (or not) over time.

Perhaps an annual income of about $63,000 sounds like a lot to you, but what does it actually provide? Economists estimate that a family living on a median income might own a home but have many years left to pay on the mortgage. The parents probably drive a used car and have older versions of smartphones and other electronics. If the family takes a vacation, they probably stay close to home, possibly staying with relatives or friends. They have no luxuries and only a small savings account, if any. The children are certainly not wearing the most recent fashionable labels (Rose 2014). Is living at the median income a middle-class lifestyle? Certainly not—at least not if middle-class status is judged by what you see in televised sitcoms or dramas, which display images of middle-class comfort that are unattainable on a median income.

Median income for particular groups varies a lot based on a person's race and ethnicity. White non-Hispanic and Asian American median income is higher, on the whole, than is Hispanic and African American median income, as you can see in figure 7.1. Note that we must be careful in what we conclude about the higher median income for Asian Americans, because this broad category includes Asian American groups whose median incomes vary substantially. Further, the income gap between African American and White households has remained unchanged since 1967 (at 59 percent). Nor has the Hispanic-White income gap (at 73 percent) changed much since 1972, the first year that Hispanics were separately enumerated in the federal income data (Semega et al. 2019). Although there has been substantial growth in the African American and Latino middle classes over these years, the persistent income gap tells you that racial inequality is stubborn and substantial.

Factors other than race—such as gender, age, and region of residence—also predict household income, as does the number of earners in a household. Except for Asian Americans, the only households that actually reach the level of national median income are married-couple families with two earners present. Clearly data show the intersection of race, gender, age, and other social factors as predictive of household income. Intersectional analysis also cautions us against making sweeping conclusions without being attentive to some of the additional influences on household well-being. For example, it is commonly said that the income gap between women and men is about 20 percent. That is accurate when looking at *all* women compared to *all* men. Further, this is a substantial change from 1970, when the gender gap in income was 58 percent. But the income gap between women and men changes if we use an intersectional perspective, such as by comparing the income of particular groups of women to White men's income. For example, even when both groups are working year-round and full-time, Hispanic women earn only 54 percent of what White men earn; Black women earn 62 percent, as you can see in figure 7.2. White women working full-time and year-round earn 78 percent of what White men earn.

Income is surely important in determining a person's well-being—and the well-being of that person's family. Volumes of research over the years have shown that income is highly correlated with such things as physical and mental health, victimization by crime, political values, and even how well a person scores on standardized tests. Researchers have also documented that because low-income people

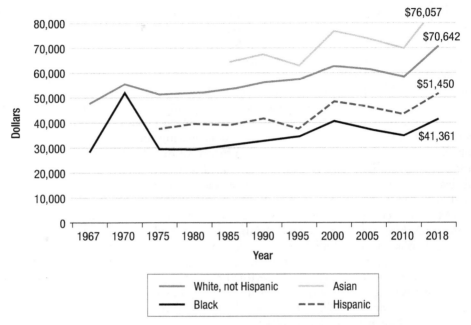

FIG. 7.1 Income Inequality, Median Household Income by Race and Hispanic Origin, 1967–2018

Note: Asians and Hispanics were not enumerated as separate groups until 1987; Hispanics were first enumerated in 1972.

Source: Semega et al. 2019.

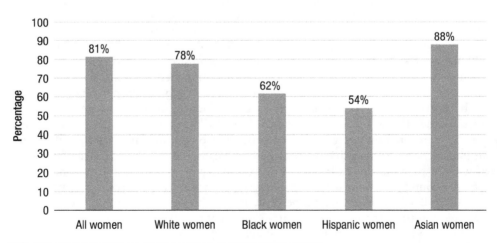

FIG. 7.2 Women's Income as Percentage of White Men's (2018)

Source: US Census Bureau 2020c.

are considerably more likely to suffer from diabetes, obesity, asthma, high blood pressure, and kidney and pulmonary disease, they are at higher risk of severe illness from COVID-19 (Serkez 2020; Shaw et al. 2016). Income is clearly an important predictor of well-being, regardless of racial identity, but the combination of race and low-income status makes a person even more vulnerable to various troubling outcomes. However, as important as income is in predicting overall well-being, wealth—or lack thereof—is even more important.

Race, Wealth, and Debt

To understand how significant wealth is in shaping inequality, imagine the following scenario: Two men work as midlevel managers in a local bank. We will call one John, the other Jordan. They make the same salary and have the same job benefits (health insurance partially supported by the bank, a retirement fund, two weeks of paid vacation, and some sick days allowed each year). Both are married with partners making comparable salaries, so the household income for the two families is the same. Both men consider themselves middle class, and, by most people's understanding of middle class, they are.

John lives in a suburb near his work in a home worth about $300,000. His monthly mortgage payments are affordable because his parents gave the couple a substantial down payment to help them purchase their house. John's parents recently retired and sold the home where John grew up. Because his parents' home had appreciated over time, they were able to pay cash for a small cottage in the retirement community where they now live. John is glad that they are financially comfortable and are able to travel and do other things they enjoy. He is also glad his parents' retirement community provides graduated levels of care should they need it as they grow older. For now John's parents enjoy the many activities the community offers: a pool, a gym, game rooms, and other amenities.

The second man in our hypothetical scenario, Jordan, recently bought a house, but even though he earns the same income that John does, Jordan could not afford to buy in John's neighborhood. In fact, he had to pick up a second part-time job to save enough for a small down payment—a smaller percentage of the purchasing price than what John put down. Jordan's monthly payment is about the same as John's, but his house is only valued at $200,000. Jordan also uses part of his salary to support his aging parents, both of whom have health problems. Jordan is really worried about how he will pay for more health care when his parents need it. He hates the idea of putting them in one of the nearby nursing homes—depressing places where a lot of the residents just sit in the hallways in wheelchairs—but he cannot afford anything better. Unlike John, whose two children will soon be off to college, Jordan has no idea how he will pay tuition at the nearby college for his two children. He is very afraid of increasing his debt. Like John, Jordan considers himself middle class. He was the first in his family to go to college, but, because his parents had a modest income, he left college with a high level of debt.

Two families, both middle class—at least as measured by income, education, occupation, and other job benefits—but two very different life situations. These scenarios could describe any number of families, but in this case John's hypothetical family is White, and Jordan's is Black. Of course, there are Black families with wealth, some even elite, just as there are White families struggling to make ends meet. But given all that you have just heard about John and Jordan, would you say that the two men have similar social class standing? Based on their incomes, occupations, educational level, and job benefits, the answer would be yes, but their overall situations are very different not only because of their parents' differing circumstances but also because of the different appraised values of their homes and their amounts of outstanding debt.

While this scenario is hypothetical, it reveals a fundamental truth about how much wealth matters in determining a person's economic well-being. The economic standing of both men has been shaped by the events that actually preceded their own lives—namely, the resources that John's White family was able to pass on and that put John in a more advantageous position than Jordan, who had to borrow money to go to college. The men's positions now have nothing to do with their individual efforts or levels of achievement. Key to understanding their different life situations is the distinction between *income* and *wealth*—and the importance of debt. Although, as we have seen, differences in income by race are significant, racial differences in wealth are even more substantial, even among people whose economic assets are relatively modest.

Wealth is different from income: **Wealth** is the monetary value of all of one's assets minus outstanding debt. This is also known as a person's *net worth*. For most people, owning a home is their primary asset, but such things as savings, investments, retirement accounts, and other property add to total net worth. The significance of wealth lies not just in the resources it provides but also in the fact that wealth can accumulate over time and can be transmitted to subsequent generations. It works like frequent flier miles: The more you have, the more you can get.

Something as basic as whether a person can retire after a lifetime of work is influenced by their wealth—such as in a retirement account. Now only about half of all workers have an employer-sponsored retirement plan. Having such a plan is more likely among unionized workers or those working for state or federal governments (US Bureau of Labor Statistics 2019b). Current reports also find that a quarter of all Americans have no retirement savings (Federal Reserve Bank 2020). Black and Hispanic workers are almost twice as likely as White workers to not have a retirement account (Federal Reserve Bank 2020). Without such savings, retirees have to rely on Social Security Income, which itself is affected by a person's lifetime earnings, so racial differences in earnings also affect later-life resources. Many find they must continue working well past their retirement age or face the possibility of poverty.

A vast amount of documentation now shows that, while the racial income gap is large and unchanging, the racial gap in wealth is even bigger—astonishingly so. On average, Whites actually have *ten times* the wealth of Black Americans and *ten times* as much as Hispanics. Another way to put this is that for every dollar saved by White Americans, African Americans have ten pennies and Hispanics little more (see figure 7.3).

Just as telling is the fact that one-quarter of Black households in the United States have *no* net worth at all (Thompson 2018). This really matters because having even a small amount of savings can help a person out in a financial emergency. Those without a financial cushion, however small, are more vulnerable in an economic crisis—either personal or societal.

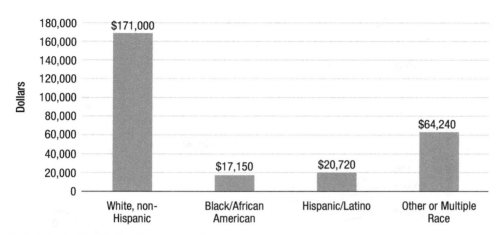

FIG. 7.3 The Wealth Gap (2016)

Source: Board of Governors of the Federal Reserve System 2020.

The wealth gap is partially caused by income inequality. Higher incomes obviously make it possible to save more, and differences in earnings over a lifetime add up. Indeed, the wealth gap between African Americans and Whites grows as the two groups age. Whites accumulate wealth more rapidly than Blacks and Hispanics in early and middle adulthood. The result is that Black Americans and Latinos fall further behind in wealth with every passing year (Killewald and Bryan 2018).

Most people's primary source of wealth, even when modest, is the home they own. Home ownership for Hispanics has improved somewhat in recent years, but for African Americans it has actually worsened. Both Blacks and Hispanics, however, are less likely to own homes than are Whites—even when they are at the same income level. In 2019, three-quarters of White families owned their own home, compared to 45 percent of Hispanics, 44 percent of African Americans, and 58 percent of Asian, Native, Hawaiian, and Pacific Islanders (the latter measured as a single group). Black and Hispanic families are also more vulnerable to losing their homes through foreclosure (US Census Bureau 2020d).

Even prior to the outbreak of the global COVID-19 pandemic, the Great Recession of 2008 hurt Black and Latino homeowners more than other homeowners. Prior to the recession, a large gap in wealth already existed between White families and Black and Hispanic families, but the recession further widened that gap—especially between White middle-class families and Black and Hispanic middle-class families. Economic experts estimate that the recession nearly halved the net worth of Black and Hispanic middle-class households—neither of which have recovered from the recession as well as White middle-class families (Garriga, Ricketts, and Schlagenhauf 2017; Kochhar and Cilluffo 2017; Thomas et al. 2017; US Census Bureau 2020d; and see figure 7.4).

It is simply too soon to know the impact that the COVID-19 pandemic will have on people's wealth. We do know that wealth affects a person's ability to respond to an emergency. Without some level of economic protection from even a modest amount of wealth, any health emergency can plunge a person into financial

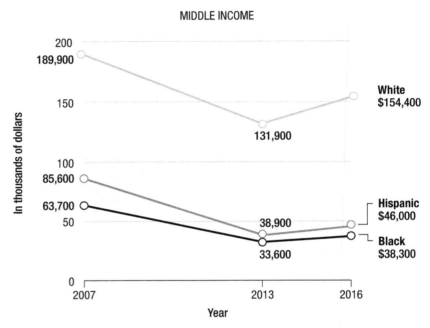

FIG. 7.4 The Impact of the Great Recession on Middle-Class Families, by Race

Source: Kochhar et al. 2017.

crisis. Even their ability to protect themselves through social distancing is a function of how much physical space they have—space being its own consequence of wealth inequality—including such things as whether you can work from home with some degree of privacy or whether you can visit friends in a spacious outdoor yard. Research already shows that the COVID-19 pandemic has widened social and economic inequality in the United States (Institute for Research on Poverty 2020).

The other side of wealth is debt. Because Whites in general have more assets than people of color, they are better positioned to manage whatever debt they have. Studies find that Black and Hispanic households have to spend a higher portion of their monthly income on debt payments (De'Armond and Zhu 2011). Now student loan debt is burying people in debt—making it much more difficult to get established, for example, through buying a home as a young adult. Student loan debt has also been dramatically rising for all groups, but the average debt from student loans is highest among African Americans (Espinosa et al. 2019; Houle and Addo 2018).

Moreover, studies find that White student borrowers are able to pay back student loans sooner than are Black and Hispanic borrowers. A detailed report from the Heller School at Brandeis University finds that after twenty years of repayment, White student borrowers have paid back 94 percent of their student loans; Black borrowers, by contrast, over the same period of time still owe 95 percent of what they borrowed. The amount owed is also compounded by the interest that amasses whenever payments are not able to be made on time, drawing people still further into debt (Sullivan et al. 2019).

Without an understanding of racial differences in wealth (and debt), we cannot fully understand the dynamics of racial inequality in America. Even in the Black and Hispanic middle classes, the wealth gap means there are racial differences in what it means to be middle class. A person may have a good income, own a home, and send their children to college, but substantial racial differences in middle-class lifestyles can still prevail. Wealth matters because its absence makes it more difficult to achieve the dreams that people have for their children (Oliver and Shapiro 2006).

Growing Inequality and Economic Restructuring: Toxic for People of Color

Framing Question: What is economic restructuring, and what is its impact on racial inequality?

Sociologist Thomas Shapiro argues that racial inequality is toxic, especially for people of color. Shapiro uses the term *toxic inequality* to refer to "historic and rising levels of wealth and income inequality in an era of stalled mobility, intersecting with a widening racial wealth gap, all against the backdrop of changing racial and ethnic demographics" (2017:18). He further asserts that toxic inequality is harmful for people of color and many others. The high degree of inequality we are currently experiencing not only stifles the well-being of people of color but also is harmful to other groups, albeit in different ways. By concentrating wealth and power in the hands of a few, high levels of inequality threaten democratic institutions. And great inequality is incompatible with US ideal of opportunity for all for those who try hard enough.

The degree of inequality in society can be assessed by the **Gini coefficient**, a measure of income distribution in a given group or society. Based on a complex calculation of income distribution, the Gini coefficient ranges from zero to one. A zero indicates that there is no inequality; one indicates that one person holds all of the income. Sweden, one of the most equal societies in the world, has a Gini coefficient of .27, while the United States scores .41—the highest among industrialized nations (World Bank 2019).

The Gini coefficient is used to compare the degree of inequality between nations, but it can also be used to measure the degree of inequality *within* particular groups. Current research finds that Whites and Asians—those who on aggregate have the highest incomes—have the highest *within*-group inequality. However, Hispanics, American Indians, and African Americans have *low* within-group inequality (Akee, Jones, and Porter 2019). Income inequality among Whites is also increasing, perhaps explaining some of the anger and frustration of the White working class whose sense of disenfranchisement might be expressed as racism, such as when its members blame people of color rather than understanding how the system of inequality works against many White people too.

The inequality we are witnessing is happening in the midst of massive **economic restructuring**—that is, socioeconomic changes that are fundamentally altering patterns of employment and work. Economic restructuring includes four major components: deindustrialization, the information technology revolution, globalization, and demographic change (Andersen and Taylor 2020). Unknown at this point is what further impact the COVID-19 pandemic will have on economic restructuring—an impact that is likely to be substantial.

Deindustrialization is the shift that began moving the nation away from a manufacturing-based economy to a service-based economy, starting around the end of World War II. When the war ended, about 40 percent of all jobs in the United States were manufacturing jobs. Almost eight decades later, fewer than 20 percent of jobs are now in manufacturing, and the number continues to decline. The loss of manufacturing jobs hits prime-age workers especially hard, particularly if they have only a high school education. Job growth now is also almost entirely in the service sector, especially in health and personal care occupations (Hernandez 2018; US Bureau of Labor Statistics 2020b).

The transition from manufacturing to service changes the work people do and the opportunities work brings. In a manufacturing-based economy, most workers produce goods. In a service-based economy, most jobs involve either direct services (such as medical care, childcare, repair work, and so forth) or the transmission of information (such as lawyers, teachers, and scientists, on the higher-paying end, and insurance processors, fast-food workers, and office clerks, on the lower-paying end).

The shift away from manufacturing is evident in the large numbers of workers who have been displaced from jobs in such areas as steelwork, coal mining, and other industries that have been an economic bedrock for blue-collar workers. Job loss has been especially prominent in so-called Rust Belt states, such as Ohio, Pennsylvania, and West Virginia, among others, where work was traditionally dominated by these blue-collar jobs. Although politicians have made promises to bring back manufacturing jobs, the manufacturing sector continues to decline, with over 5.5 million manufacturing jobs lost since 2000. The loss of manufacturing jobs in the United States does not mean that goods are no longer being produced, but rather that manufacturing is more typically sent abroad, where labor is cheaper. The shift is the result of longtime structural changes, making it unlikely that these jobs will come back in any significant way.

At the same time, the **information technology revolution** has drastically changed the workplace. Information technology now permeates just about every part of the occupational system. At the high end, it means that workers need advanced skills and complex training. At the low end, jobs have become more automated or perhaps have even been turned over completely to robots or other sophisticated information technology. Even traditional manual labor, such as coal mining, is now done utilizing sophisticated technology. Such technological development requires fewer workers, but workers need to have the requisite training. One case in point: No longer are as many miners needed to enter coal shafts. Rather, coal is extracted using electronic instruments that are observed by a few workers who do not actually enter the mine. This is obviously a safer method of extracting coal, but it also employs fewer, though better-educated, workers than was true for blue-collar labor in the past.

In the manufacturing sector, jobs are now more likely to be filled by those with college degrees. In all parts of the labor force people are also now likely to be working with computers: Even if not designing information systems, workers are tapping or clicking on screens to deliver goods, order meals, or transmit information.

Prospective employees without the technological skills or advanced education such jobs require are likely to get stuck in low-wage, low-level service jobs with less steady employment—if they manage to get jobs at all.

Another part of economic restructuring is **globalization**, referring to the increasing economic interdependence between nations around the world. Of course, the economic system has long involved global trade, but globalization has taken on a new form in the context of the decline of the manufacturing sector and the growth of the service sector. Manufacturing production has shifted to parts of the world where labor is cheaper than in the United States. Chances are that the clothes you wear, the goods you own, and even the foods you eat are produced in another part of the world.

At the same time, consumption has expanded in the more affluent nations, producing a desire for more (and cheaper) goods. Manufacturing has not gone away, but it has shifted to other nations, despite calls to bring jobs back to the United States. The provision of services is also being increasingly outsourced to other parts of the world. A transaction initiated from your smartphone might be handled by someone on the other side of the globe. Or the book you read might have been produced in India or another nation where copyeditors and proofreaders are paid less than college-educated US workers.

Globalization also means that money travels around the world more freely. Capital assets made in the United States might be invested abroad when wealthy people find tax havens and other ways to amass even greater wealth. Given the global nature of the world economy, it is simply impossible to be isolated from the reality of a worldwide economic system.

Finally, **demographic change**—that is, change in the characteristics of the population—is also transforming the workplace. Workplaces are now more diverse than ever. One of the biggest changes is the increased presence of women in the labor market and a decrease in the labor force participation rate of men. Among women, African American women have always worked, but the labor force participation of African American, White, Hispanic, and Asian women is now quite similar—at about 55 percent of the civilian, noninstitutionalized population (US Bureau of Labor Statistics 2019a).

Hispanics and Asians are the fastest-growing groups in the workplace. Non-Hispanic Whites, who were 70 percent of the workforce as recently as 2005, are expected to be less than half of the workforce by 2060, while Hispanics are projected to increase to over one-third of the labor force (Toossi 2016).

Altogether, economic restructuring is having a huge effect on all groups, especially on those who have historically relied on manufacturing jobs for decent pay and relatively steady work (Chen 2015; Hochschild 2016). In a manufacturing economy, a person with only a modest amount of education could still get work that might support a family, especially if their job is in a unionized workplace. Now jobs are more likely found in the service sector of the economy. Without advanced education and strong skills, workers are likely to end up in low-wage service jobs—the part of the labor market where people of color predominate.

Moreover, in a service-based economy, technology changes so fast that many skills quickly become obsolete. Workers who are best able to survive in such a market must be nimble—that is, armed with education and the technological skills to survive in a dynamic, competitive workforce.

For people of color, these transformations have resulted in high rates of joblessness and the emergence of an urban underclass (also see chapter 6). The formation of the underclass—composed largely of Black Americans, Latinos, Asian Americans, recent immigrants, and impoverished Whites—has produced an array of social problems that, as we will see, have arisen from the transformation of jobs, including permanent job loss that economic restructuring brings. For many, this can mean permanent, structurally caused joblessness (Wilson 1996).

It is not just the underclass, however, that is affected by these changes. Economic restructuring has also prompted the decline of the traditional working class, leaving many people feeling left behind and no longer attached to the contemporary economy. Without understanding the structural roots of economic restructuring, many White working-class people feel resentment toward racial minorities, as if the success of some people of color is robbing White people of their own opportunities. Racial resentment has certainly driven some of the right-wing political movements of recent years (Hochschild 2016).

Race and the Workplace

Framing Question: What is the social structure of work, and how is it influenced by race and ethnicity?

Every day, millions of Americans get up and go to work. Every day, millions do not. Work ties us to society. Without work, our social bond to society is loosened. We have learned first-hand about the importance of social bonds during the COVID-19 pandemic, when so many people have been cut loose from their usual social bonds—at work, at school, and in their social relationships. A lack of social bonds can cause various forms of distress, such as depression and poor physical health, and can possibly even manifest in crime or violence.

Work is part of a nation's economic institutions—institutions that are based on racial inequality. The consequences of this economic-racial link are all around us: Who works where in your community? Are immigrants clustered in certain occupations? Are young men of color just hanging out on street corners during the hours that other people are spending at work? Who provides the services deemed to be essential: grocery clerks, health and medical care workers, truck and transportation drivers, first responders, and others? How do both race and gender together shape the national workforce? Such observations reveal a lot about the dynamics of racial and ethnic inequality.

These observations reveal the **racial division of labor**—that is, how race shapes who performs the different tasks in a society. The racial division of labor is crosscut by several factors, including gender, age, and immigrant status, among other social variables. As one example, women of color tend to be clustered in occupations where most of the other workers are other women of color. Of course, there are many exceptions to this pattern. In professional jobs, for example, women of color will likely be present but underrepresented. A given woman of color may be one of a few in, for example, an academic department. Race and gender as well as age are intertwined in the division of labor—a salient point in *intersectional theory* (see chapter 6). The entanglement of race and gender inequality also creates quite different outcomes in people's earnings.

Occupational Segregation

The feature that best describes the racial division of labor in society is **occupational segregation**—the pattern by which different groups of people are niched into certain occupations based on characteristics as race, gender, age, and so forth. Data on the distribution of people of color and Whites in the workplace reveal clear patterns of this segregation.

There are significant differences in where different racial-ethnic groups are employed. Whites and Asians are more likely to be in professional and managerial positions than are African Americans and Hispanics (see figure 7.5). African Americans and Hispanics are also more likely to be employed in service occupations than are Whites and Asians. We must take care in interpreting these data, however, as the categories reported by the US Department of Labor, like the US Census Bureau's data, are quite broad and include a range of jobs. Black Americans, Asians, and Hispanics constitute, for example, about 10 percent of all professional workers, but there are vast differences in the jobs that fall within this broad category in terms of pay, prestige, and influence. As you can see in figure 7.6, among health care professions people of color are more likely to be employed in lower-status professional jobs.

Moreover, in other occupational categories, such as "natural resources, construction, and maintenance," people of color are overrepresented. To cite a few examples, Hispanics comprise 47 percent of construction workers, 63 percent of drywall installers, and 53 percent of painters. Similarly, Asians comprise 62 percent of "miscellaneous appearance workers"—most likely nail technicians. African Americans are most overrepresented in such occupations as postal workers, barbers, crossing guards, and home health aides (US Bureau of Labor Statistics 2019a).

Gender and race together shape occupational segregation. As one example, women are 94 percent of all childcare workers; 41 percent of these workers are women of color. Childcare and other occupations where women of color are overrepresented are among the lowest-paid jobs (US Bureau of Labor Statistics 2019a).

Since the passage of the Civil Rights Act of 1964, efforts to desegregate the workforce have been somewhat successful. At the time this bill was passed by Congress, White men had a near total hold on the nation's best jobs. Black and Latino professional workers, for example, historically only served their own communities, as doctors, teachers, undertakers, and so forth. Since the 1960s, desegregation efforts have made some difference, but studies show that desegregation only occurs when there is organized pressure for change, such as from social movements, union activism, judicial rulings, and federal and state governments. Without that push for change, progress stalls (Stainback and Tomaskovic-Devey 2012).

Unemployment and Joblessness

Employment patterns also reveal the persistence of racial discrimination and inequality in the workplace. The **unemployment rate** is calculated as the percentage of people in a given population who are "officially" out of work. Note that the

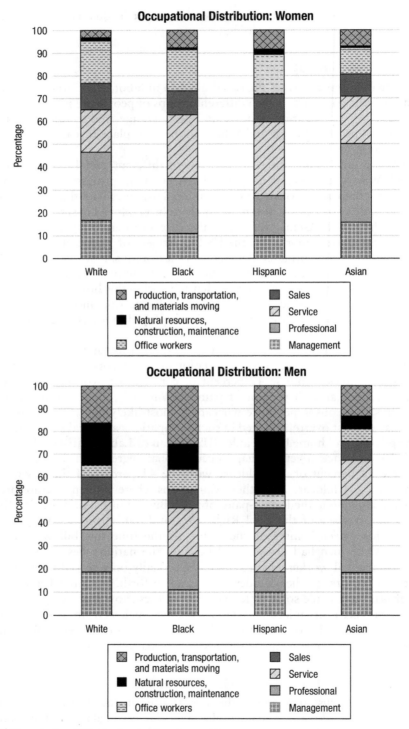

FIG. 7.5 Occupational Distribution by Gender and Race

Source: US Bureau of Labor Statistics 2019a.

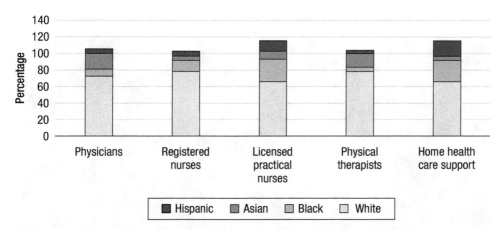

FIG. 7.6 Percent of Employed in Select Health Care Professions by Race (2018)

Note: Totals to more than 100 percent because people may be of more than one race.

Source: US Bureau of Labor Statistics 2019a.

unemployment rate undercounts the actual number of people truly out of work. To be included in the official unemployment rate, a person must have been actively looking for work in the period measured (usually the last four weeks), be available for work, and have no other employment during the period measured. During the global COVID-19 pandemic, this usual definition of unemployment has been loosened somewhat, as unemployment was counted as the number of people filing unemployment claims. Either way, the official unemployment rate excludes discouraged workers or those who, for any reason, are not known by local officials.

The unemployment rate counts numbers of individual persons who are unemployed. **Structural unemployment** is different: It refers to the job losses resulting from an entire industry shutting down. In this case, some jobs permanently disappear. The closing of a steel plant produces structural unemployment, as does the automation of certain kinds of jobs. Whole communities can be decimated by structural unemployment, and affected workers can have even longer periods of unemployment than others, as their skills may be outmoded. When people are reemployed following the elimination of a local factory or other industry, they are typically reemployed at a lesser status, for more poorly paid work. You could see evidence of structural unemployment during the pandemic as industries such as travel and hospitality were so very hard hit, as were workers within these sectors.

Joblessness, then, can actually exceed the official unemployment rate. People who work "under the table" are not included in the unemployment rate, and neither are those who are *underemployed*—that is, those working in jobs for which they are overqualified, such as the barista in a local coffee shop who holds a master's degree or the Uber driver who holds a college degree. With the exception made during the COVID-19 pandemic, typically so-called gig workers and independent contractors are not eligible for unemployment benefits, and neither are part-time or private household workers. Even with its limitations, however, the unemployment rate gives us a good picture of how the economy is working for people.

Whether in good economic times or bad, we can quite accurately predict the Black unemployment rate from the national unemployment rate. Even in a so-called

Whenever the national unemployment rate is announced, we can predict with great certainty that African American employment will be at least double the national rate.

Source: Jim West / Alamy Stock Photo.

good economy, the Black unemployment rate is typically twice that of White workers—and at a level that would be declared a national crisis were it the rate for everyone else. Figure 7.7 compares the unemployment rates for Black, Hispanic, Asian, and White American women and men. Note that these annual figures are based on 2019 annual rates—before the COVID-19 pandemic struck. During the 2020 economic year, as the pandemic raged, unemployment reached levels for all workers that compared to the unemployment seen during the Great Depression of the 1930s. For Black and Latino workers, unemployment during the pandemic soared to close to 20 percent (Krogstad, Gonzalez-Barrera, and Noe-Bustamente 2020).

Especially startling is the high rate of unemployment among minority teens (counted by the US Department of Labor as those between sixteen and nineteen years of age; see figure 7.7). Unemployment among young people is especially problematic because young people are likely to be entering the labor force for the first time. If they are unable to find work, they may become discouraged and alienated from the labor market—a phenomenon that can lead to illegal activity.

The Immigrant Labor Force

Historically immigration flows have been tied to the needs of labor. Laws, policies, and practices have been routinely used throughout history to bring in immigrants when there was a need for more workers (see "Learning Our Past," further down in the chapter). When immigrant labor was no longer needed, restrictive policies pushed them out of the labor force and, often, out of the country altogether.

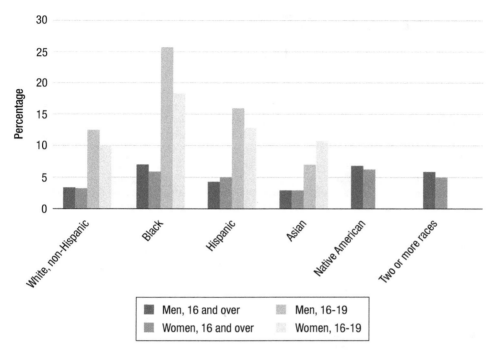

FIG. 7.7 Unemployment by Race, Gender, and Age

Source: US Bureau of Labor Statistics 2019a.

Despite exclusionary policies and the hostilities that so many immigrant groups have faced over time, immigrants remain a vital part of the US labor force. Currently there are twenty-eight million foreign-born workers in the United States—17 percent of the total US workforce, plus about eleven million undocumented workers who do not show up in official data but provide essential labor supporting much of the nation's agricultural, industrial, and service output (US Bureau of Labor Statistics 2019a; and see "Living with Racism," below). Among foreign-born workers are some of the lowest-paid workers but also some of the most highly educated and professional workers. In recent years, foreign-born workers have also been more dispersed geographically than would have been true in the past, when immigrants were mostly located in the largest urban areas.

Currently, men who are foreign-born are more likely to be employed than their native-born counterparts. However, foreign-born women are less likely than native-born women to work, especially if they have young children (US Bureau of Labor Statistics 2019c). Where foreign-born people work, though, reflects clear patterns of ethnic segregation. Foreign-born men are more likely than native-born men to be employed in natural resources, construction, and maintenance, as well as production, transportation, and material moving. Compared to native-born women, foreign-born women are less likely to be in professional occupations, sales, and office work but are more likely to be in natural resources, construction, maintenance, production, and transportation work and material-moving work.

LIVING WITH RACISM

An Undocumented Farm Worker

I'm Odilia Chavez, a forty-year-old migrant farmworker based in Madera, California, the heart of the fertile Central Valley. I'm also a single mother of three: My twenty-year-old eldest son came and joined me in 2004, crossing with a coyote [a smuggler of immigrants into the United States]. My son is now at the university, studying political science. The younger two were born here—American citizens.

I grew up in Santiago Yosondúa, Oaxaca, in southern Mexico. I went to school through third grade, my dad was killed when I was eleven, and we didn't even have enough food to eat. So I went off to work at twelve in Mexico City as a live-in maid for a Spanish family. I'd go back each year to Oaxaca to visit my mom, and the migrants who'd come back from the United States would buy fancy cars and nice houses, while my mom still slept on a mat on the floor in our hut. A coyote told me he could take me to the United States for $1,800. So I went north in 1999, leaving my four-year-old son behind with my mother. I was twenty-six.

We crossed through the desert into Arizona, hiding from the border patrol. I finally arrived in Madera in March of 1999, and I moved into a boarding house for migrant farmworkers. I'd never worked in a field. It was really hard at first—working outdoors with the heat, the daily routine. But I've certainly learned. In a typical year, I prune grapevines starting in April and pick cherries around Madera in May. I travel to Oregon in June to pick strawberries, blueberries, and blackberries on a farm owned by Russians. I take my fourteen-year-old daughter and eight-year-old son with me while they're on their summer break. They play with the other kids and bring me water and food in the field. We'll live in a boarding house with twenty-five rooms for some one hundred people, and everyone lines up to use the bathrooms. My kids and I share a room for $270 a month.

On all the harvests, men and women work side-by-side, doing the same job, and women work just as fast as the men. I've been harassed one time: when a boss who drove us out to the field every day wanted to hug me and said he wouldn't charge me the $8 a day for the ride if I'd go out with him. (Most of us don't have driver's licenses, so the contractors organize rides to work.) I left the job. In California, especially in Fresno and Madera counties, there's an abundance of farm jobs. So you don't have to do one you don't like. . . .

I've seen on the news that some Congress members or American citizens say undocumented workers are taking their jobs. We're not taking their jobs. In the fourteen years I've been here, I've never seen an American working in the fields.

Source: O. Chavez 2013.

Immigrants enter a structure of inequality in the United States in which their participation in the workforce is shaped by several factors, including their own level of education, the composition of their families, employers' practices, and the political-economic relationship between their home nation and the United States (Kibria, Bowman, and O'Leary 2014; also see chapter 6).

Immigrants use various strategies to situate themselves in the labor market. Some form **ethnic enclaves**—that is, niches where there is a clustering of particular immigrant groups in a given occupation or industry (Kibria et al. 2014:62; Wilson and Portes 1980). Nail salons, ethnic food restaurants, and small grocery stores, among other establishments, are evidence of the presence of ethnic enclaves throughout the United States. Ethnic enclaves help immigrants cope with the discrimination they face in the general population, and they also add to the rich diversity of the US public.

Despite immigrants' contributions to the US economy and the nation's dependence on immigrant labor, numerous myths drive how immigrant workers are perceived (see "Myths about Immigration," further down). The fact is that if immigrants, including those who are undocumented, were to leave the United States, the entire US economy would suffer, and so would all of the people who depend on immigrants' services. Yet US immigration policy remains in a quagmire, caught between the interests of employers, reluctance and disagreement among politicians, and strong divisions in public opinion about how policy should be formulated.

Debates about and perceptions of immigration are strongly linked to understandings of race. The **race-immigration nexus** refers specifically to the linkage between race and immigration, including how social institutions, ideology, and social practices frame immigration and end up reinforcing racial ideas (Kibria et al. 2014). Immigration policies that define some immigrants as "good" and others as "bad" reinforce ideas about other racial minorities. For example, stereotyping Asian Americans as a "model minority" supports implicitly (and sometimes explicitly) a stereotype of Black Americans as unwilling to work. In this way, beliefs about immigrants, though often racist in and of themselves, also reproduce racial thinking about other groups.

Explaining Racial Economic Inequality

Framing Question: What are the major reasons for the US labor market's continuing racial inequality?

Data on economic inequality clearly reveal huge differences among racial-ethnic groups. The question remains, why? Several different approaches provide answers, including overt discrimination, differences in human capital, and the split labor market.

Overt Discrimination

Although racial discrimination is now against the law, it continues, both overtly and covertly, to be a significant factor in the life chances of people of color. That discrimination still exists can be documented via **audit studies**, experiments that use actors or other simulations to reveal when discrimination occurs and with what frequency (Feagin 2014; Gaddis 2019). For example, researchers might send two applicants—different in race or ethnicity but identical in terms of prior experience, educational level, and grooming—to a job interview. The goal of such a project is to document the extent to which discrimination occurs when race or ethnicity is the only distinguishing factor between two people. Although audit studies are an excellent tool for documenting the existence of discrimination, they do not explain why such discrimination continues to occur. Audit studies can also be applied to gender discrimination and, potentially, other forms of discrimination.

In one widely cited example of an audit study, researchers generated four identical job résumés that differed only in the names of the applicants. They then sent the four résumés to 1,300 online job advertisements. Two résumés used names

Ethnic enclaves are common in many urban areas. They provide an economic niche in which immigrants can enhance their social and economic capital.

Source: iStockphoto LP / Angelo Cavalli.

MYTHS ABOUT IMMIGRATION

Myth: *Most immigrants are poor.*
Fact: Immigrants are a mix of professional workers, academics, and those who fill low-wage service jobs. Typically the poorest members of the population in a sending nation cannot afford to migrate (US Bureau of Labor Statistics 2019b).

Myth: *Immigrants take jobs away from Americans.*
Fact: Immigrants make many contributions to the US economy, and there is no correlation between immigration and unemployment rates. Immigrant entrepreneurs also create jobs for Americans (Ewing 2016).

Myth: *Immigrants increase the crime rate.*
Fact: Foreign-born people have a much lower crime rate than do native-born people. Stereotypes in the media of immigrants engaged in criminal activity target immigrants for abuse in the criminal justice system (Ewing, Martínez, and Rumbaut 2015).

Myth: *Immigrants don't pay taxes but take advantage of US benefits.*
Fact: Immigrants, including undocumented workers, pay the same taxes and Social Security as US citizens. Immigrants are not eligible for welfare or food stamps unless they have been permanent legal residents for five years. Fewer than 5 percent of all immigrants receive welfare, food stamps, or unemployment benefits (National Immigration Forum 2018).

---

that "sounded White"—Emily and Greg. The other two used names that "sounded Black"—Lakisha and Jamal. The researchers found that "Greg" and "Emily" were far more likely to receive callbacks for an interview than were "Lakisha" and "Jamal," despite all of the applicants' identical backgrounds. Applicants who were "White" had to send ten résumés to get one callback, whereas "Black" applicants had to send fifteen résumés to get one callback—a 50 percent racial gap (Bertrand and Mullainathan 2004).

In another important audit study, the researchers submitted 9,400 randomly generated résumés to online job advertisements. They submitted identical résumés to each advertisement but used names that were distinctively female and male and, presumably, "White" and "Black." In the "female" category were presumably White "Clare" and "May" and presumably Black "Ebony" and "Aaliyah." Similarly, there were two presumably White males, "Cody" and "Jake," and two presumably Black males, "DeShawn" and "DeAndre." In all other characteristics, including college education, the "applicants" were identical. The researchers found greater evidence of racial discrimination in those jobs that involved customer interaction. In general, Black applicants got 14 percent fewer callbacks, but when customer interaction was involved in the job, Black applicants were 28 percent less likely to get a callback. Furthermore, the researchers found that discrimination *increased* when applicants were matched on the highest qualifications (Nunley et al. 2015; Vedantam 2015).

LEARNING OUR PAST

Black Steel Workers

What was work like for Black men working in the steel mills during the post–World War II boom? Their experiences have been chronicled in the documentary *Struggles in Steel: A Story of African-American Steelworkers* (Henderson and Buba 1996).

James Langley worked for thirty-four years at the Bethlehem Steel mill in Sparrows Point, in Baltimore. "You weren't going anywhere but laborer when I was there," he says. "First job that they had for me was laborer. Everybody started as laborer. Us anyway." What did "laborer" mean? "Shovel!" says Earl Fields. "Pick and shovel." These were men who had served for four years in the military during World War II, training to be craftsmen. But, as Francis Brown says, "When we went to Sparrows Point to get jobs, they didn't look anything like that, and you better not ask for anything like that." Fields had been a combat engineer during the war, operating cranes and bulldozers.

In one scene in the documentary, one of the men is moved to tears describing his attempts to become a crane operator. "By me eating, sleeping, praying, I became as good as anybody," he says. "I was determined, and I did it." But Black job seekers had to downgrade their skills and education levels so they would get hired. "If you went down to Bethlehem Steel for a job and you're a smarty or an educated person [a Black person], they didn't want you." Whites, however, inflated their skills and got better jobs.

Jobs in the steel mills are now gone for most workers, but the experience of these Black workers is a stark reminder of how the discrimination they faced in the past contributes to the struggle for advancement that so many Black workers have faced and that, to this day, depresses the resources they could have invested in future generations.

Source: Schoettler 1998.

These studies reveal a fact that many White people continue to deny: Racial discrimination is alive and well in the US job market today. You can sometimes infer discrimination by observing only outcomes, such as differences in income, but courts in recent years have been reluctant to use measured outcomes as proof of discrimination. Often courts want to see *intent* to discriminate, something much harder to prove. Also, people may not directly intend to discriminate but hold implicit biases that have shaped their decisions about hiring and promotion. Audit studies allow researchers to show the presence and frequency of discrimination.

Despite the fact that racial discrimination is now illegal, research still finds an enormous amount of discrimination in the workplace. At every level—hiring, advancement, pay, and access to networks—discrimination is pervasive. While it might not always be overt, the impact discrimination has is the same: it disadvantages people of color in the workplace. Discrimination can be subtle; other times, it may be overt, but it exists, including in the additional work that people of color are called on to do to produce equity in the workplace. This results in what sociologist Adia Harvey Wingfield has called "flatlining"—that is, suppressing the advancement of people of color and shaping the satisfaction that people of color feel at work (Wingfield 2019; Wingfield and Chavez 2020).

Human Capital

Human capital refers to the individual characteristics of workers. Such things as level of education, skills, prior experience, and individual factors like age, marital status, and parenthood are called human capital variables because they can and do influence labor market outcomes. For example, simply having a degree from a more selective university—a human capital variable—influences employment outcomes. Research shows, however, that Black graduates of the most selective institutions only do as well as White candidates from less selective universities, suggesting that even with the best credentials, people of color find it harder to advance (Gaddis 2015).

Still, human capital matters because it influences people's success in the labor market, but it cannot explain the full degree of racial inequality. Researchers have found that Black and Hispanic workers tend to have fewer opportunities to build skills, reducing the value of their human capital. Careful studies also show that, even when human capital characteristics are similar across racial-ethnic groups, some outcomes are not explainable by human capital differences. This points to the ongoing significance of racial discrimination (Pena 2018).

No doubt, getting a good education, acquiring job skills and training, and developing a good work record are important, but other factors are also at play. Having networks that lead to a job, for example, really matters, as demonstrated by research. Sociologist Deirdre Royster studied Black and White working-class men who were equally matched, particularly in having a high school education and a stable residence. Even with these comparable human capital variables, the White men in her sample were better able to find working-class jobs because of the "invisible hand" of referrals from those already in White job networks (Royster 2003). Further research has also found that both Black and White job applicants use networks at similar rates but that networks are less likely to lead to job offers for African Americans (Pedulla and Pager 2019).

A Split Labor Market

Split labor market theory analyzes the workforce as divided into two primary sectors: the *primary labor market* and the *secondary labor market*. There is also an informal underground economy where earnings are illegal or "under the table" (Venkatesh 2006).

The primary labor market has relatively high wages, job benefits, opportunities for advancement and, generally, rules of due process that regulate how employees are treated. Although economic restructuring is also affecting the primary labor market, these remain the best jobs. Even in the primary labor market, however, changes mean that few people can count on staying in the same job or with the same employer over a lifetime.

The secondary labor market, by contrast, has low wages, little opportunity for advancement, few (if any) job benefits, and little formal protection for workers. Fast-food workers, cleaners, some health care workers, and various other service jobs are typical of the secondary labor market. Students often hold such jobs, but rarely do such jobs become lifetime employment for students. Yet vast swaths of workers in the US labor market are in the secondary labor market, especially

Because of the low minimum wage in the United States—$7.25 per hour in 2020—large numbers of employed people still find themselves living perilously close to or in poverty.

Source: Stacy Walsh-Rosenstock / Alamy Stock Photo.

women and people of color. Here workers have little say in how they do their work and may be subjected to the whims of employers.

Each of these explanations of inequality at work provides some perspective on racial inequality in the labor market. At the heart of each explanation are connections between racial inequality and other forms of inequality, such as gender, ethnicity, immigration status, and age. Although no one explanation of economic inequality is complete, together they provide compelling reasons, especially in the context of structural transformations of the workplace, for why so many people lack the resources to live the American Dream they hold dear.

Poverty: America's Basement

Framing Question: How is poverty defined in the United States, and what explains the continuing connection between race and poverty?

Considering it is one of the most affluent nations in the world, the United States has a shockingly high degree of poverty. As shown in figure 7.8, the high rate of poverty among Hispanic, Native American, and African American people is a national disgrace—even at a time when poverty has generally been declining. In 1944, while studying US race relations, Swedish economist Gunnar Myrdal identified the poverty-stricken underclass as "America's basement" (1944:49). Since then, poverty has declined somewhat (from 19 to 11.8 percent among all people), but not as much as we might hope in an otherwise prosperous nation.

Living in poverty is experienced in different ways. It might mean depending on a food bank for meals or living on the street or in a homeless shelter. It might mean skipping meals to be able to pay for a child's school supplies or depending on public

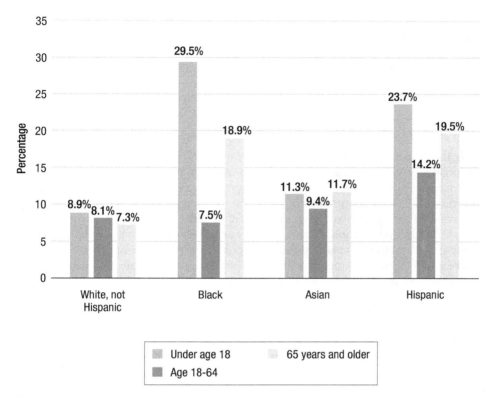

FIG. 7.8 People in Poverty (2018)

Source: Semega et al. 2019.

assistance for infant formula. It probably also means being judged by others as a failure because our nation generally views poor people with great disdain.

Measuring Poverty

However poverty is experienced, there is an official way of measuring it. The federal government calculates the **poverty line** based on a formula established in the 1930s by the US Department of Agriculture. The USDA took the price of a low-cost food budget and multiplied it by three, assuming that food was one-third of a family's budget. That amount, adjusted each year for the cost of living, defines the official poverty line: $25,465 for a family of four, including two children, in 2018 (Semega et al. 2019).

Can you see some problems with this measurement? Unlike in the 1930s, when the measure was established, housing now consumes a much larger proportion of the typical family budget. The official poverty line also does not account for regional differences in the cost of living, nor does it include any accounting for necessary out-of-pocket expenses, such as childcare, medical expenses, work-related expenses (such as transportation and uniforms), and so forth. Moreover, anyone whose income is just a dollar or so above the official poverty line is excluded from the official poverty rate.

Because of these problems with tallying poverty, many researchers have suggested new ways of measuring poverty, including methods that would account for various noncash benefits, such as food stamps, tax credits, and subsidized housing. To date, however, the federal government has not changed the official measure of poverty, possibly because by doing so, as experts estimate, the reported rate of poverty would likely increase (Mattingly and Varner 2015).

Who Are the Poor?

Using the current method of calculating poverty, in 2018 there were thirty-eight million people officially living in poverty in the United States—a full 12 percent of the total national population. (Note that these annual data, the most recent coming available mid-2020, were reported prior to the devastating impact of the 2020 COVID-19 pandemic.) The majority of the poor are White, because they are the largest proportion of the total population. White poverty, nonetheless, is often overlooked because of popular social stereotypes that associate poverty with people of color. Still, African Americans, Hispanics, American Indians, and Asian Americans experience distressingly high and disproportionate rates of poverty. Children of color are especially at risk: A shocking 29.5 percent of African American and 23.7 percent of Hispanic children now live in poverty. This is compared to 8.9 percent of White, non-Hispanic children and 11.3 percent of Asian American children (Semega et al. 2019).

Women and children are the most likely to be poor, as can be vividly seen when you look at poverty rates in different family structures. Regardless of race, female-headed households (that is, households with children and no husband present) have the highest rates of poverty (see figure 7.9). Among Black and Hispanic households, poverty rates for female-headed households are especially high.

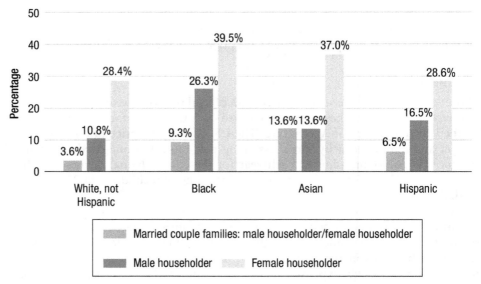

FIG. 7.9 Poverty by Family Structure (in Families with Children Under Age 18)

Source: US Census Bureau 2019c.

Too many people in the United States live in **deep poverty,** formally defined as living below half the official poverty line. As with all poverty, the majority of those in deep poverty are White, but Hispanics and Black Americans are disproportionately living in deep poverty (6.9 percent of Hispanics, 9.4 percent of Blacks, 5.2 percent of Asians, and 3.9 percent of Whites; Semega et al. 2019). People living in such deep poverty include those who are unemployable, the long-term unemployed or underemployed, those who are severely underpaid, and people who are "casualties of poverty"—that is, people overcome by the accumulation of catastrophes that poverty can bring. A serious illness or accident, for example, may mean having to leave the workforce. Without health insurance, bills can pile up, possibly even leading to eviction and, eventually, homelessness. Especially for those with limited financial means, problems can cascade, resulting in deep, perhaps permanent, poverty (Desmond 2016; Gans 2014).

Poverty is problematic enough when it affects a particular family or household, but it is even more problematic when it becomes **concentrated poverty,** involving entire neighborhoods. Concentrated poverty occurs when 40 percent or more of those in a given census area live below the federal poverty line. Concentrated poverty has become especially pronounced since 2000 and has more than doubled for non-Hispanic Whites, although Hispanics and Black Americans are still the most likely to reside in areas of concentrated poverty (Jargowsky 2015; Kneebone 2014). For anyone living in such conditions, concentrated poverty has terrible effects for the whole neighborhood: higher crime rates, more violence, less family stability, and greater likelihood of other social problems.

Why Does Poverty Occur?

If we are to reduce poverty, we have to understand why it occurs. The causes and consequences of poverty are many but can be summed up in two frameworks: social structural explanations and cultural explanations. As we saw in the previous chapter, there is an ongoing debate, both in the public and in scholarly research, about the relative influence of each.

1. *Social structural explanations.* All of the social structural trends we have been examining—economic restructuring, joblessness, and structural unemployment—contribute to high rates of poverty among particular groups. High rates of unemployment for minority men are surely a major cause of poverty. For women, unemployment is important, but employment can also cause poverty for women, given their low wages.

   Low-wage work simply does not lift a person out of poverty. Simple arithmetic bears this out: If you are employed full-time (forty hours per week, fifty-two weeks of the year) at the federal minimum wage (currently $7.25), you will not earn enough to rise above the federal poverty line. In fact, this income barely brings you to 50 percent of the poverty line. Some states and municipalities, sensitive to this concern, have raised the minimum wage, but even with a raise to fifteen dollars per hour, proposed by many, earnings would still leave you living on half the national median income (about $31,000 per year; Semega et al. 2019).

Structural causes of poverty can be direct, as in the case of unemployment. But they can also be indirect (Wilson 2010). Economic and political policies that appear to be race-blind have strong, adverse effects on the most vulnerable groups. Economic restructuring to a high-tech, global economy, for example, benefits highly skilled workers who are less subject to job displacement than are less skilled workers. Racial discrimination of the past means that less skilled workers are more likely to be people of color, although White working-class people are also vulnerable to the same changes. The bifurcation of the labor force that is resulting from economic restructuring is one of the most significant, even though indirect, causes of poverty among the "truly disadvantaged" (Wilson 1987).

Structural explanations of poverty also connect to *intersectional theory*. The simple fact that women of color and their children are the most likely to be poor reveals that gender inequality *in combination with race* is a significant cause of poverty. Low wages, lack of affordable childcare, and welfare policies put women of color in some of society's most impoverished situations. What we know about poverty is that much of the time it is generated because of an emergency—job loss, health care crisis, accident, or other unexpected trauma. And a person already disadvantaged because of race and class and gender has a harder time recovering from such an emergency, which is then likely to cascade. Social structural perspectives on poverty understand the unique vulnerabilities people face because of their position in society, not just their values or attitudes.

2. *Cultural explanations—blaming the victim.* If social structural causes are so critical to understanding poverty, does culture matter? A national culture of judging the poor as somehow undeserving permeates public understanding of the causes of poverty. Such assertions are common but typified by Jared Kushner, former presidential advisor and son-in-law of Donald Trump, who suggested that Black Americans can't get ahead in the United States if they don't want it enough. Referring to whether Black people would vote for Trump, Kushner said, "He can't want them to be successful more than they want to be successful" (Karni 2020). Kushner's view is a common one, despite much sociological evidence to the contrary.

Rather than the absence of a culture of work, a *culture of judgment* is a defining feature of our time (Chen 2015). Such a judgmental attitude blames the poor for their own plight, as if they enjoy being dependent on so-called government handouts—handouts that are actually far less generous than people assume.

Stereotypes about "welfare queens" are rampant in American culture, as is the assumption that the family structures of poor minority people are to blame for poverty. Many people routinely and vigorously assert that people of color are poor because of their presumed reliance on public assistance, the absence of fathers in the family, and poor parenting. People often make these assertions with absolutely no knowledge of or experience with people of color who actually live in poverty. The belief is strong enough that, even with evidence to the contrary and a massive reduction in so-called welfare programs, people continue to insist that poverty stems from bad values or poor personal choices. These unfounded claims are even built into policies that promote marriage as the best solution to women's poverty—policies that completely overlook the risks that marriage can bring, including domestic violence.

Research evidence has consistently disproven the connection between culture and poverty. On the contrary, the data show that the poor want to work, share the same values as the middle class, and do not condone such things as teen pregnancy, father absence, and welfare dependency (Edin and Kefalas 2005; Greenbaum 2015; Kaplan 1996). Yet even in the face of this evidence, the tendency to blame the poor is vivid in the public imagination, leaving little political will to establish social policies that could actually alleviate poverty.

The Safety Net . . . Full of Holes

The idea that poor people do not want to work is now embedded in federal programs to assist those in need. The movement for "welfare reform" culminated in the Personal Responsibility and Work Opportunity Reconciliation Act (PRWORA) passed by Congress in 1996. The very title of the law presumes that a lack of "personal responsibility" is the basis for need. The law requires that recipients of the very limited aid that is available must work.

The PRWORA abolished the original welfare program—Aid to Families with Dependent Children (AFDC), which had been established in 1935. The initial beneficiaries of AFDC in the 1930s were mostly White women and their children. The program grew and by the 1960s had become largely identified with Black women. The public withdrew its support and became downright hostile as people leveled accusations of "welfare dependency" and made presumptions about the promiscuity of Black women (Quadagno 1996). These attitudes culminated in the passage of welfare reform in 1996.

The new welfare law created the current welfare program known as Temporary Assistance for Needy Families (TANF, pronounced "TAN-if"). There are several provisions under TANF:

- Adults receiving TANF are required to work for two years after they start receiving aid. If they are not working, they must participate in community service. The rules about work are complex and vary from state to state, but those receiving TANF must do either paid or unpaid work.
- Opportunities to seek further education or job training are strictly limited.
- There is a two-year limit on the receipt of welfare assistance at any one time and a lifetime limit of five years. States can exempt people from the five-year time limit, but exemptions cannot exceed 20 percent of the total caseload. Some states have made this even more restrictive, such as in Arizona, which has a one-year lifetime limit.
- Unmarried teen parents must stay in school and live at home or in an adult-supervised setting; pregnant women must identify the biological father of the child through a paternity test.
- Anyone ever convicted of a drug felony is banned for life from TANF (and food stamps).
- Specific requirements vary from state to state but can (and usually do) include "family caps"; that is, there is no additional funding available to a recipient who subsequently has another child.

The various provisions of TANF contest the beliefs that poor women only have children to get bigger welfare checks, that the poor enjoy being dependent, and that their need is caused by irresponsibility and a refusal to work. Funding for TANF comes from block grants given to individual states based on their level of AFDC spending in 1994. The funds provided are capped to certain maximums, limiting federal funding for spending on welfare and pushing welfare expenditures to state budgets—budgets already strained for other reasons. As noted in chapter 3, payments under this program are quite small and have shrunk by about 20 percent in recent years. Research has found that not all the block money that goes to states is actually spent on assistance for those in need. Only about one quarter of the funds provide direct cash assistance; another quarter supports childcare and work supplements. But states have had to use block money to fill other budget needs, reducing the impact of the federal changes on support for the poor (Safawi and Floyd 2020).

What has been in the impact of changes in welfare law? Politicians tout the success of welfare reform because the welfare rolls have shrunk since the passage of the PRWORA. What else might be expected, though, with such a restrictive program? The biggest change has been what scholars call a "profound shift from a need-based to a work-based safety net" (Tach and Edin 2017:542). Although it is difficult to assess the overall impact—in part because individual states have a lot of latitude in designing their safety net programs—research finds that the number of nonworking poor mothers has actually increased since passage of new welfare legislation. Cash support to the neediest—that is, those who are not working—has actually declined, and the majority of benefits (such as from the Earned Income Tax Credit) go to working people. Another result is that many of those who have left welfare often just disappear from the system. For many, consistent work is extremely difficult because of many factors, including poor health, decent transportation, and childcare, among other concerns (Powers, Livermore, and Davis 2013; Silva 2013).

Despite its intent to help people become self-sufficient, a decline in TANF support is not associated with an increase in self-sufficiency (Aratani, Lu, and Aber 2014; Katz 2012). In fact, restrictive limits on financial assets that determine eligibility actually discourage TANF participants from building their own financial safety nets (Hamilton, Wingrove, and Woodford 2019).

Stereotypes about welfare abuse still dominate the public discourse. In any population, of course, there will always be a few who take advantage of the system, but the wholesale blame of poor, typically minority, people for their circumstances has torn holes in an already fragile safety net. Consequently, the United States is one of the least generous of the Western industrialized nations in its support for those in need.

Conclusion

It is impossible to overstate the importance of racial differences in economic well-being. Surely money is not everything, but the lack of money lies at the heart of many other problems. In the chapters to follow, we will see a significant relationship between economic well-being and other measures of well-being, such as health, educational attainment, criminal activity, and so forth. Were the nation to make a commitment to lessening the economic inequality between racial-ethnic groups, we could also go a long way toward reducing racial-ethnic tensions.

Key Terms

audit studies 175

concentrated poverty 183

deep poverty 182

deindustrialization 166

demographic change 167

economic restructuring 165

ethnic enclaves 174

Gini coefficient 165

globalization 167

human capital 179

income 158

information technology revolution 166

median income 158

occupational segregation 169

poverty line 181

race-immigration nexus 175

racial division of labor 168

split labor market 179

structural unemployment 171

unemployment rate 169

wealth 162

Critical-Thinking Questions

1. In what ways is economic restructuring, coupled with growing income and wealth inequality, affecting you and your family? Be as specific as possible in your answer.
2. Using the federal poverty line for a family of four ($25,465 in 2018), develop a monthly budget based on expenses for everything you think you would need to support yourself and your family of four (two adults, two children). Use the actual cost of housing, food, and so forth in your locale. What can you afford and not afford? How would you make ends meet on a poverty-level income?
3. How has your economic status (or that of your family) been affected by the 2020 COVID-19 pandemic? How do you think your circumstances compare with those of people of a different racial, class, and gender background from your own? What does this tell you about the influence of intersectional theory in describing the impact of the pandemic?

Student Exercises

7.1. Identify a job you have had. What was the racial and gender composition of the job? What were the wages? Were there job benefits? Was there a formal career ladder or opportunity for advancement? What protections did workers have? Would you describe it as being in the *primary* or the *secondary labor market*? Why? Is this a job you can imagine having for your entire life?

7.2. Look around your community and identify an *ethnic enclave* that you might see. Who lives or works there? Take some time to interview one of the workers there. What is the person's background (education, national origin, time in the United States, skills)? How long has the person been working in this place? Has he or she had other opportunities? What does your interview tell you about immigrant experiences and ethnic enclaves?

Challenging Questions/Open to Debate

An employee of a business organization sends an e-mail to a friend in which the employee makes racially offensive remarks. The employee accidentally sends the e-mail to a colleague who happens to be Latina and who is deeply hurt by what is said. She complains to the head of human resources. Should the employee who sent the remarks (who is otherwise a highly performing member of the organization) be fired? Why or why not?

TAKING ACTION AGAINST RACISM

Opening Opportunities

Exclusion lies at the heart of many practices that produce and reproduce racial inequality. Either at school or in the workplace, go beyond your usual networks to find people who can work toward common goals with you (a study group, a work team, or any such project). Commit yourself to opening opportunities for people of color whose talents and skills are too often overlooked.

Resource: Pedrelli 2014.

Source: iStockphoto LP / _jure

CHAPTER 8

Bringing It Home

Families and Communities

If you're tired of hearing about racism, just imagine living with it.
—Jon Stewart (2014)

OBJECTIVES

- Describe racial-ethnic diversity among contemporary families
- Identify how racism shapes myths about racial-ethnic families
- Understand how the historical treatment of racial-ethnic groups has shaped family structures
- Explain the contributions of structural diversity theory regarding racial-ethnic families

- Describe the connection between racial inequality and care work
- Identify key trends that are shaping racial-ethnic families, especially interracial marriage and immigration
- Analyze current social policies about family and the impact of these policies on racial-ethnic groups

Families are often described as the bedrock of society. Families are supposed to be "havens in a heartless world" (Lasch 1977), in which children are nurtured, adults find solace and comfort, and people care for their elders. The family is idealized as a *private sphere*—that is, a site in society where love and intimacy are the norm and people are shielded from the harsher realities of the *public world*. Some families achieve this ideal; many do not. Either way, the family ideal obscures the social forces that pummel families, often making family life anything but ideal.

All families are influenced by social, historical, and cultural changes, but there are particular effects of such realities for racial-ethnic minority families. Simply trying to raise children in a world where the family needs to buffer children against the harms of racism provides a unique challenge for parents—a fact clearly witnessed by the family grief at funerals for those young Black people killed by the police. On a daily basis, the economic status of too many people of color, including high rates of poverty and being in low-wage work, makes providing basic care even more challenging. Furthermore, the separation of family members because of immigration or high rates of incarceration means that many racial-ethnic families have to cope with unique separations and losses.

All the while, people of color have to endure the punitive social judgments that routinely disparage, misunderstand, and misjudge their families. Much maligned, racial-ethnic minority families have borne the brunt of blame for social problems in the United States. Nonetheless, families for people of color have also been a source of strength and resilience, including, or perhaps especially, during times of great turmoil and trouble. Understanding racial-ethnic families is thus central to understanding the social dynamics of race and racism.

What Do Families Look Like? Diverse Family Forms

Framing Question: What different factors shape family structures, and how does family structure relate to family resources?

Social scientists rely on the US Census Bureau and other national databases for comprehensive information about the current characteristics of our nation's families. The US Census Bureau uses specific terms to count and describe family structures in the United States. The census starts by counting everyone living in a unit as a **household**; the person who owns or rents the unit is termed the **householder**. Within the broad category of household are family households and nonfamily households. **Family households** are those with at least two members who are related by birth, marriage, or adoption. **Nonfamily households** are those in which persons are living alone or in which nonrelatives share the household, such as roommates.

Given this terminology, we can use the census data to describe the different living arrangements of families in the United States. We can also compare families according to race and ethnicity and other social characteristics (such as age, income, and region of residence). The census also uses particular terminology to describe different racial and ethnic groups, as we will see in information reported here.

Figure 8.1 shows the significant diversity in family structures among different racial-ethnic groups. Black families are the most likely to be have a female householder; married couple families are more likely for White and Asian families. The point is not to make moral judgments about different household structures but to

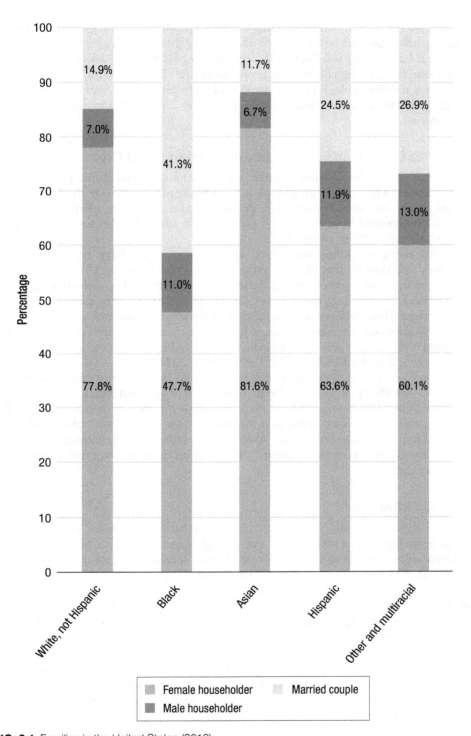

FIG. 8.1 Families in the United States (2019)

Source: US Census Bureau 2019a.

understand the social conditions that influence each. In all racial-ethnic groups, female-headed families are far more likely to be poor; this is especially true for Black and Latino families. Even aside from the impact of the 2020 COVID-19 pandemic, one-third of female-headed households are "food insecure," meaning they lack access to affordable, nutritious food (Coleman-Jensen et al. 2019; Creamer and Mohanty 2019). Clearly different family structures are significantly related to what resources a family has.

Ties that Bind, Bonds that Break: Marriage and Divorce

Figure 8.2 shows the different marital statuses among racial-ethnic groups in the United States. Marriage in all groups is a fragile relationship, one that can be disrupted by any number of issues both personal and societal. The likelihood of marriage is conditioned by a number of factors, including attitudes toward marriage, but also the availability of partners.

With rising economic inequality, young people may have limited financial resources and thus be less likely to enter marriage (Furstenberg 2014). Many low-income women also place motherhood before marriage because they may see motherhood as providing them a more secure identity than they would get from a male partner. Researchers have found that, contrary to much public opinion, low-income women of color place the same high value on marriage that others have, but they find it difficult to achieve the financial security that people usually want before they marry (Edin and Kefalas 2005; Kefalas et al. 2011).

Divorce, too, is influenced by a person's social location in society. Asians and Hispanics are the least likely to be divorced, and White and Black Americans are the most likely. The many causes of divorce include differences in cultural attitudes. Shared cultural attitudes, then, may be one reason for the low rates of divorce among Hispanic households and Asian households. The prevalence of divorce among low-income couples, however, shows the strain that economic struggle can place on families.

How Children Live

Data on different family experiences are especially striking when we look at the living arrangements of children in the United States. Forty-five percent of Black children under the age of eighteen live with their mother only, an increase from 20 percent in 1960 and compared to 25 percent of Hispanic children and 17 percent of White children (US Census Bureau 2019b). Note, though, that the percentage of children living with their mother has increased in all racial-ethnic groups since 1960, although it has declined somewhat in recent years, as shown in figure 8.3.

Divorce, separation, and spousal absence (such as imprisonment) are some reasons for mother-only families, but the biggest factor is the decline in marriages for women who have children. Although popular ideas hold that too many young women have babies, the fact is that the birth rate has fallen for all racial-ethnic groups, including among teenagers. The birth rate for all *unmarried* teens has also fallen, including for Black and Hispanic unmarried teens (Martin et al. 2019). By far the biggest problem for teen mothers is not pregnancy per se but the high rate

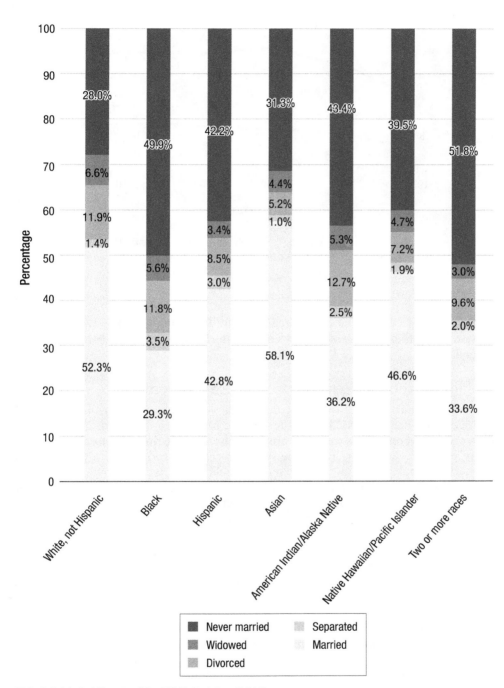

FIG. 8.2 Marital Status of the US Population (2018)

Source: US Census Bureau 2018.

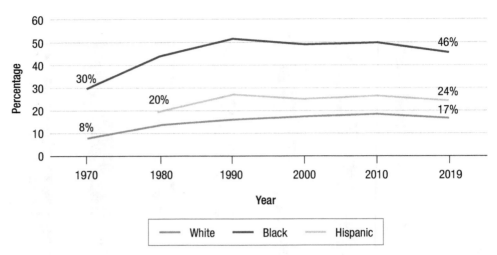

FIG. 8.3 Children Living with Mother Only

Source: US Census Bureau 2019b.

of poverty that accompanies teen pregnancy. Still, it is important to point out that most teen mothers who are poor were already living in poverty before they got pregnant.

Multigenerational Households and Grandparents

Two other changes noticeably affecting families are an increase in the number of multigenerational households and the number of grandmothers raising grandchildren. *Multigenerational households* are those that include three or more generations living together. According to the most recent census information, a full one-fifth of the US population now lives in such households—a trend growing among all racial groups. Multigenerational households are less common among Whites, but 16 percent of White households include at least two adult generations and children. Multigenerational households are most common now among Black Americans, Asian Americans, and Latinos, where close to 30 percent of households are multigenerational (Cohn and Passel 2018).

There is nothing inherently wrong with multigenerational arrangements. People often develop flexible kinship ties to provide additional support for families. But, as with female-headed households, multigenerational households are more likely than others to live in poverty. There is nothing new about having grandparents help raise children, but the number of children living in grandparents' homes has doubled since 1970. While grandparent-maintained households are still a small proportion of the family population, they are most common among African American, American Indian, Asian, and Native Hawaiian families. Sometimes a parent is present but most often not. For example, in 44 percent of the cases where Black children live with a grandparent, no parent is present. High rates of imprisonment explain some of this reality, but recent research also finds a connection between the opioid crises and the number of grandparents raising children (Anderson 2019; Ellis and Simmons 2014).

Multigenerational households have become more common, especially among people of color and, most particularly, for new immigrant groups.

Source: Getty Images / Drazen.

Race and Same-Sex Couples

Only since 1990 have data on what were then called "unmarried partners" been included in national data sets on families and households. Not until 2020 were same-sex couples, both married and unmarried, included in the national census. This has made it hard to show trends among this population over time.

There is not much difference by race in the proportion of same-sex households. What is different is that same-sex racial-ethnic minorities, African American couples especially, are more likely than other same-sex couples to be raising children. In general, same-sex couples also have somewhat higher median incomes than their different-sex counterparts. It would be wrong, though, to conclude that most same-sex couples are higher income earners. One of the myths about same-sex couples, especially men, is that they are all rich. Consistent with other income comparisons, African American, American Indian, and Alaska Native same-sex couples earn only about 63 percent of what Asian and White same-sex couples earn (Kastanis and Wilson 2014; US Census Bureau 2020b).

These facts about American families are quite different from what many people believe to be true. Various myths cloud our understanding of contemporary families, particularly myths about racial and ethnic families. Images of "tiger moms," Black matriarchs, overbearing Latina mothers, and absent fathers abound in popular culture and, as we will see, generate misleading ideas that too often also frame social policies otherwise meant to help families in need.

Social stereotypes imagine gay and lesbian families to be largely rich White couples, but the truth is that there is more racial diversity among LGBT families than among heterosexual married families.

Source: Blend Images / Alamy Stock Photo.

Mythologizing Families: Racial Beliefs about Families

Framing Question: How has racism influenced social myths about families?

Despite the diversity in family forms, there is a persistent idea that a two-parent, married, heterosexual couple with a male breadwinner and a stay-at-home mother is best for all concerned (Baca Zinn, Eitzen, and Wells 2015). Although few households match this model, the *family ideal* has a firm grip on cultural beliefs about families.

The persistence of the family ideal means that families that deviate from this presumed norm are imagined as somehow dysfunctional and unstable, as if they condone teen pregnancy, do not value marriage, and are misguided in how they raise their children. Racial and ethnic stereotypes infiltrate this ideal as the families of people of color (along with the White poor) get blamed for numerous social problems in society (Baca Zinn et al. 2015). As with other stereotypes, the truth about family life is obscured by misleading and false assumptions.

One example is the *tiger mom myth* about Asian families. The tiger mom stereotype portrays Asian American families—particularly mothers—as overly strict in their childrearing with an unrelenting emphasis on academic achievement (Chua 2010). While it is true that Asian culture has traditionally emphasized children's obedience to their elders and strict discipline (Lee and Zhou 2004), the "tiger mom" label is a sweeping overgeneralization—that is, a stereotype—about all Asian mothers. In reality, Asian American women are more complex than the stereotype suggests. Studies also show that young Asian Americans are highly aware of the stereotypes targeting them. They report feeling pressure to do well in school, especially in science. In general, young Asian students attain higher educational achievement than other groups, but high-pressure parenting also has negative consequences for them, such as when parents perceive time with friends as having an adverse effect on grades and then discourage their children from socializing (Hanson and Gilbert 2012; Yi 2013).

Stereotypes depict Latino families, to cite another example, as strongly family centered and rooted in machismo. There is, however, more variation among Latino families than the stereotype suggests. *Machismo* is often misunderstood as a simplistic expression of male dominance and authoritarianism. In reality, machismo is anchored in traditional concepts of honor among Latino men, not just domination (Baca Zinn 1982; Mirandé 1997). A more nuanced understanding of machismo reveals how masculine norms among Latinos have been shaped and constrained by the subordinate position that Latino men have within society (Zambrana 2011).

The idea of **familism** within the Latino community refers to the strong attachment to family that has been a traditional part of Latino culture. Within Latino culture, family attachment is thought to be more important than individual identity. As with machismo, however, overgeneralizing about familism among Latinos oversimplifies the diversity and complexity of Latino families. Latinos tend to have more frequent family interaction and a strong sense of attachment to family, but traditions also change with economic and social transitions in society and within Latino communities. Among Chicanos, for example, research finds there is some decline in close-knit kinship as new generations encounter different social conditions. Familism also tends to decline as socioeconomic status rises, as measured by such things as proximity to family members, coresidence, and financial support (Baca Zinn and Zambrana 2019; Zambrana 2011).

It is difficult for any family to remain stable among societal change, but kinship ties are a considerable source of support when families are stressed. Not only is such support critical for racial-ethnic minority families, but strong family networks are also important in fostering educational and economic success in all families.

African American families are also subjected to numerous social myths, a primary one being the myth of Black **matriarchy**. A matriarchy is a society in which women hold the power. The myth of Black matriarchy typifies Black women as holding power within Black families. This stereotype is also used to explain various social problems in Black communities, as if Black women emasculate their men and keep them from forming strong family attachments (Moynihan 1965). There is no doubt that African American women have had to be strong and assertive to survive in a racist world, and many are the sole earners within their families. Yet translating this fact into the idea of powerful Black women who emasculate Black men is a gross racial stereotype and one that completely distorts the relative powerlessness of Black families—and Black women in particular.

Stereotypes of Native American families are also rooted in misconceptions about Native cultures. Traditional family forms among Native Americans are as diverse as the many tribal nations that make up the Native population (Glick and Han 2015; Walls and Whitbeck 2012). Romanticized ideas of Native American families as living a peaceful, bucolic existence belie the reality that many Native families face intense social pressures, not the least of which is a history of isolation, exclusion, and invisibility. Add to that the poverty that so many Native families experience and we see how distorted dominant concepts of Native families can be (Erhart and Hall 2019).

In sum, beliefs about racial-ethnic families, at least as held by outsiders, rarely reflect the realities of family life within these different communities and groups. Families are never as simple as common stereotypes suggest. Yet stereotypes, as we have seen throughout this book, have a hold on how people tend to think about other groups. In the absence of other information, stereotypes easily take root and blossom, often to the detriment of actually meeting family needs.

Families in the Making: Diverse Histories of Family Formation

Framing Question: How have past practices influenced contemporary racial-ethnic families?

People experience their families as a network of personal relationships, but those relationships are shaped by larger histories that extend beyond individual lives. As argued before in this book, the past shapes the present. This is as true for family structures as for other social institutions.

Family experiences for all groups in the United States have been dramatically transformed by the history of industrialization and, more recently, changes in the economic structure of society. Coercive labor and the disruptions incurred by economic displacement have especially influenced the families of people of color (Glenn 2002). Whether the families of Japanese agricultural workers, Chinese railroad workers, Black slaves, or Mexican miners, people of color have faced an onslaught of experiences that have separated their families, robbed them of resources, and deprived them of the rights enjoyed by other families. In the face of racial and ethnic oppression, families have typically had to be resilient and build their own support systems.

The process of industrialization in Western society has profoundly influenced family formation among diverse racial and ethnic groups. Prior to industrialization, households were the primary site for economic production. Work was performed largely in households where women's labor was vital to the economy (Dill 1988).

For Black families in slavery, women's labor was central. Under slavery, African American families had no rights—including the right to marry and form families. Slaves could not marry, nor were their children their own. Rather, slave children were the property of slave owners and could be given as property to others, as frequently happened. One such example is Ona Judge Staines, a slave of George and Martha Washington. When threatened with being given away to Martha Washington's granddaughter, Ona Judge Staines ran away and lived to the age of seventy-five as a fugitive (Dunbar 2017).

During the age of chattel slavery in the United States, Black families were separated according to the needs of the slave-owning class. There is a belief that slavery weakened family ties, but slaves constructed kinship ties however they could and maintained a belief in marriage as a long-term commitment. Children born outside of marriage were accepted as family. Even though not formally recognized in law, marriage ceremonies between slaves were frequent. Furthermore, kinship networks functioned as a source of resistance to oppression, making family a vital part of the path toward African American freedom (Dill 1988; Genovese 1972; Gutman 1976).

Like Black slaves, Chinese Americans earlier in US history were denied the right to form families. Except under a few special circumstances, Chinese women were denied entry to the United States, even while their spouses worked to build the nation's infrastructure. Chinese immigrant men would use what they earned in the United States to support families in China, but the only Chinese women who were allowed to enter the United States in the early twentieth century were merchants' wives. Split households became the most common family form for Chinese Americans. Not until 1965, when the Immigration and Nationality Act lifted immigration quotas (see chapter 5), were Chinese families able to reunite in the United States (Dill 1988).

In the American Southwest, the US conquest of Mexican lands uprooted families and forced many Mexican men into labor camps. Sometimes women and children could accompany men to the labor camps, but not always. When men had to leave families to find work, they would leave behind female-headed households, a form of family that prevailed in Chicano communities in the mid-nineteenth century. Much of the history of Chicano families and, now, Latino immigrant families is marked by constant disruption as people migrate to find work (Baca Zinn et al. 2015; Dill 1988).

Industrialization and the emergence of factories has also shaped the history of diverse families in the United States. With industrialization, the production of goods moved outside of the household. Industrial labor created a wage-based economy that devalued women's unpaid labor in the home. Home became idealized as a refuge from work—at least for those in the more privileged classes. During this transition, White women had few legal rights, but they were glorified as having their proper place within the family. Women of color were given none of this honor, although their labor has been critical to economic production.

These brief histories show the influence of larger structural forces on family experiences. Similar patterns affect other groups as well—groups whose family histories are shaped by economic dislocation, exclusionary social policies, and widespread social changes. The next section details the components of a structural analysis of family experiences.

Structuring Families: Structural Diversity Theory

Framing Question: How does structural diversity theory help us explain contemporary life for different racial-ethnic groups?

Structural diversity theory identifies the societal forces that shape families, both historically and in the present day (Baca Zinn 2010; Baca Zinn et al. 2015). There are five major points made by this theoretical perspective on families.

1. *Racial patterns in family formation are rooted in the inequality of work and labor.* Families are hardly immune to the patterns of labor that have marked

the experiences of racial-ethnic groups throughout US history. The unequal opportunities people encounter strongly influence the structure and well-being of families. Something as basic as whether men can find work will determine whether they are even perceived as "marriageable" (Wilson 1978 and 1996). Unemployment or persistent low wages can plague families, making it difficult to hold them together. This is certainly true for all families, but, given the economic inequalities for racial-ethnic groups, it is especially true for racial-ethnic minority families.

The economic interests of employers also shape family life. For example, having strong families may threaten employers who want workers to be most loyal to their jobs, not their families (Dill 1988). Whether families are able to hold together can, for example, be influenced by whether family members can find work—and where. Most work organizations treat people first as workers, not as family members. Now global capitalism is also producing a new family form: **transnational families**, in which family members are dispersed across not just regional but also national borders.

2. *Race intersects with class and gender in shaping diverse family structures.* Intersectional theory asserts that race, class, and gender together shape different family experiences. Even within the same racial-ethnic group, family experiences will differ depending on social class. As we saw in the previous chapter, female-headed households are far more likely to be poor than other households, a fact that is true in all racial-ethnic groups but is especially pronounced for African American and Latina households. This is a vivid illustration of the intersection of gender, race, and class in shaping family life.

Likewise, the intersection of race, class, and gender means that women's and men's experiences in the family are different depending on their race, gender, and class status. Thus there are significant differences among men in their ability to support families. Gender roles within families are also manifested differently depending on a person's race and class.

3. *Families are formed through social structure as well as human agency.* Clearly social structures and processes, both historical and contemporary, shape family experiences. This book has emphasized the importance of social structures in all matters pertinent to race relations. Still, social structures do not exist without the specific actions of people—that is, *human agency*. Both dominant and subordinate groups take actions that affect family life. The actions of dominant groups have tremendous power to influence families, such as through the creation of policies that deny federal funding to poor women seeking abortions.

Subordinated groups also engage in behaviors that help them adapt to family stresses, such as sending one's children to other caretakers when work obligations demand it. There are countless examples of coping behaviors—many of them positive but others not—whereby family members adapt to their situation. Simply put, we cannot fully understand families without acknowledging the influence of both social structure and human agency.

4. *Each of the social myths about racial-ethnic families that we have examined above is an ideological construction.* Ideologies are systems of beliefs that attempt to justify the existing status quo. The representation of racial-ethnic minority families as somehow dysfunctional is an example. For instance, the belief

that the families of people of color are pathological can thwart attempts to make effective change by blaming families for their own plight. In this way, existing racial inequalities are maintained. Such beliefs are too often embedded in social policies that have a deleterious effect on racial-ethnic minorities.

5. *Families can be sites of resistance against racism and other forms of oppression.* Most typically the families of people of color are depicted in terms of social problems. What gets overlooked from this stereotype is how families nurture and sustain people even in the face of racial oppression. Teaching children how to cope with racism and ethnic prejudice is one way that families prepare their members to resist the assaults of racial inequality (Elliott and Aseltine 2013). As sites of resistance, families also provide a counterbalance to the dominant narrative that describes people of color as a social problem or as culturally deviant.

In sum, structural diversity theory emphasizes that family structures and processes are part of the overall racial structure of society. Within their families, people of color have rarely been given the same degree of legal or social protection that other families have. Indeed, families of people of color are far more likely to be scrutinized by the state—by police, social welfare agencies, school systems, and the like. The watching eyes of so many state agencies can make it seem that social problems, such as violence and substance abuse, are more common among the families of people or color. These problems, however, may not be as visible in White, middle-class, and elite families. No doubt the pressures that family members experience because of racial inequality can lead many to problematic behaviors, but family social problems can usually be traced to social causes, not just individual motivations.

Caring across the Life Course

Framing Question: How is care work distributed across the intersecting social structures of race, class, and gender?

Care work is a relatively new term used to describe the labor that people do to sustain life, including such things as childcare, cleaning, and cooking. Care work is also known as **reproductive labor,** a concept originally developed by Friedrich Engels ([1884] 1972), a colleague of Karl Marx, to analyze the work people do to maintain and reproduce the labor force. *Care work* or *reproductive labor* is indispensable to the economy, both historically and now.

Care work has traditionally been unpaid and most commonly done by women in the privacy of the home in the form of housework and childcare. Now, however, more care work is paid labor, although it is still somewhat invisible and often taken for granted. All women do a lot of care work, but women of color are those most often found in "back rooms" of care work—cleaning, cooking, and throwing out the trash. Care work also includes work done by social workers, therapists, salon workers, and so forth. Especially as White women have increasingly moved into paid labor, women of color have provided a large share of care work, working as nannies, cleaners, and personal care aides (Glenn 1992). Their care work is done both in public sites and in private homes. Because of the hidden nature of so much care work, it is hard to estimate who does it, how much they do, and how much they earn. Estimates say there are more than twenty million nannies, housecleaners, daycare workers, home care aides, and social workers, among other care workers in the United States (Duffy 2011; Hodges 2020). The essential nature of this work has been vividly exposed during the 2020 COVID-19 pandemic when so much care work—both in the home and in workplaces—was shouldered by women—and especially women of color.

A gender and race division of labor positions women of color and recent immigrant women in low-wage care work. In fact, the presence of care work at the bottom of the labor market is a large contributing factor to race, gender, and class inequality in the United States. As we saw in the previous chapter, various forms of care work are among the lowest paid and least regarded occupations. It is women of color who are the most likely to do the most devalued forms of care work, especially private domestic work and childcare. Care work done in private homes is also often "under the table," meaning that employers often do not pay taxes and Social Security or other job benefits, such as health insurance, sick leave, or vacation. The privately negotiated nature of such work puts tremendous discretion in the hands of employers, often women themselves. And studies show that private employers in the home often treat care workers as if they are invisible and have no lives of their own (Hodges 2020; Rollins 1985; Romero 2002 and 2012).

Racial attitudes shape different conceptions of care work, depending on who performs it. Done by White, bourgeois women, care work is typically glorified as "women's special role," as if the work is some sort of spiritual calling. When associated with women of color, care work tends to be perceived as menial labor requiring little skill or job training (Roberts 1997b). This racialized perception is apparent in class and race-based depictions of stay-at-home moms: Middle-class, White, stay-at-home moms are praised; poor women of color who stay home to care for their children are stigmatized as lazy welfare cheats.

Conceptions of care work are thus entangled with the racialization of occupations. Parenting is a deeply social activity, one that has specific racialized and gendered meanings. When you hear the phrase "to mother someone," what comes to mind? Most likely you associate mothering with nurturing care. However, when you hear "to father," do you only imagine the biological act of conceiving a child? Most likely. Motherhood and fatherhood are deeply social concepts and, as such, carry the gender and racial baggage that burdens a racially unequal society.

Racially Controlling Images of Motherhood

Feminist author Adrienne Rich (1976) posits that motherhood is an institution—meaning motherhood is a complex system of social behaviors organized into a social structure. For women of color, motherhood is a racialized and gendered institution because it is entangled with these forms of inequality. Mothering practices are shaped by both race and gender, as are how people perceive mothers and how mothers perceive themselves, as described earlier in the discussion of the tiger mom stereotype for Asian American mothers. All mothers use various strategies to keep their children safe (Ridolfo, Chepp, and Milkie 2013), but women of color also have to "socialize children for survival" (Collins 1990). Regardless of class or race, all mothers feel they have to shield their sons and daughters from harm, but gender, class, and race shape mothers' perceptions of the harms their children face and the strategies they use to try to protect them. Numerous researchers have shown that African American mothers encourage a stronger sense of independence in their daughters than do White mothers (Elliott and Aseltine 2013).

Concepts of motherhood are deeply influenced by racial beliefs. Motherhood is glorified in White middle-class families but deeply stereotyped for the families of people of color. Black motherhood is typified by various controlling images, including that of the "mammy" (Collins 2000). Women of color are well aware of these controlling images and have to negotiate a path through stereotypes of themselves as welfare dependent, on the one hand, and "strong Black women," on the other (Dow 2015). Latina mothers are stereotyped as all-caring and consumed by the mothering role, Jewish mothers as guilt-inducing. All such stereotypes derive from simplistic concepts of women's more complex mothering identities.

When women of color define their own notions of motherhood, themes of resilience and sharing emerge. Sharing mothering is a long-standing practice within Black communities, noted in the concept of **othermothers** (Collins 2000), the term for those who raise children other than their own. Economic necessity and other realities of Black women's participation in the labor force mean that someone other than the biological parent may have to care for children. Marian Robinson, the mother of former first lady Michelle Obama, performed this role in the White House for Malia and Sasha Obama, for example.

Mothers now have to navigate new conceptions of motherhood, because a culture of intensive parenting has taken hold. Scholars have found two trends most influencing contemporary parenting: rising economic insecurity and the spread of an ideal of "intensive parenting" (Nomaguchi and Milkie 2020). *Intensive parenting* is the idea and practice of super-engagement with one's children—an ideal that adversely affects all parents but puts particular stresses on women of color (Elliott, Powell, and Brenton 2015; Slaughter 2015). Studies find that parenting stress is significantly lower among Whites and American Indians than among Black and Hispanic parents (Nam, Wikoff, and Sherraden 2015).

The Myth of the Absent Black Father

Fatherhood also carries racial meanings, meanings that are entangled with gender and class. Black fathers, in particular, are routinely stereotyped as absent from their families, as if they do not care about their children. It is true that significant numbers of children live with only one parent (about half). About 10 percent of those children live with their father only (US Census Bureau 2019b). This fact is often overlooked by those who cling to common stereotypes of father absence.

It is true that Black American households are more likely than those in any other group to have female heads of households, as we have seen. The term *absent*, however, has taken on a pejorative meaning, especially for Black families, as if men are not present at all in the life of the family. This pejorative idea assumes a particular standard of family by which all other families are judged, even when we know that family forms vary across racial-ethnic groups. Research finds that when fathers are separated from their children, they experience a great sense of loss (Coles and Green 2010).

Studies of Black, low-income fathers show the difficulties they face in trying to support children. Some walk away or do not admit to being a father, but research finds that more fathers than the stereotype suggests are engaged with their children and do the best they can to support them (Johnson and Young 2016; Posey-Maddox 2017). Many are determined to be involved in their children's lives, and they provide intermittent support when they can, but fatherhood often comes after a brief relationship with, and involving little commitment to, the mother. The odds of sustaining a relationship are weakened when there is not a strong attachment to the mother (Edin and Nelson 2013).

Stereotypes of low-income fathers blame their cultural values for any absence from their children's lives, but the disconnection of fathers is as much the result of economic and class-based factors as of cultural values per se. In fact, social class erases many of the differences that exist between Black and Latino fathers and others (Newman and Messengill 2006).

Eldercare

You can tell a lot about a society by how it treats its elders. By that standard, the United States is not doing very well. The aging population is a growing share of the total US population and is expected to continue growing as the baby boomer generation ages. Although racial-ethnic diversity is most pronounced in the younger generation, the share of older people (those more than sixty-five years old) who are racial-ethnic minorities is also expected to increase. Life expectancy is also predicted to increase, especially among men, although women will continue to outlive men. All racial-ethnic groups are expected to experience an increase in life expectancy, especially Black, non-Hispanic men and American Indians and Alaska Natives (Frey 2015; Medina, Sabo, and Vespa 2020).

Who cares for the elderly? In the United States, typically individual families are on their own to figure out how to care for elder parents. High-quality institutional care is expensive. Even middle-income families are likely to find that high-quality care is out of reach of their budgets. As a consequence, individual family members, usually women, provide most eldercare in the United States.

There are, however, significant racial differences in how eldercare is provided. Studies find that older White people are the most likely to be isolated in old age—that is, living alone, without children nearby, and with limited contact with religious organizations (Taylor, Chatters, and Taylor 2019). Generally Whites are also more likely than racial-ethnic minorities to reside in nursing homes. Hispanic use of nursing homes is generally low, although African Americans, Hispanics, and Asian Americans are now a growing percentage of nursing home residents.

As in US society as a whole, segregation, not integration, is the norm in nursing homes. Racial segregation is particularly a problem because nursing homes with the greatest concentration of racial and ethnic minorities have more limited financial resources and are more likely to be deficient in clinical treatment, personal care, and safety. Although researchers note some general improvements in the quality of nursing home care, racial disparities in the quality of care remain (Akamigbo and Wolinsky 2007; Howard et al. 2002; Konetzka and Werner 2009; Li et al. 2015; Smith et al. 2007).

For all racial groups, however, the predominant form of eldercare is home-based. Traditionally Latinos and Black Americans have given family caregiving, and thus eldercare, an especially strong value. Different cultural beliefs continue to shape people's experiences with home-based eldercare. Black Americans and Mexican Americans report stronger obligations to support aging parents than do White Americans (Evans, Coon, and Belyea 2014; Fingerman and Birditt 2011).

Ironically, Black families have fewer resources to provide care for aging parents because of the economic differentials that exist across racial groups, even though the Black elderly generally have greater care needs than do Whites. African Americans are also significantly less likely to use hospice care than are Whites (Kwak, Haley, and Chiriboga 2008).

Changing Trends for Racial-Ethnic Families

Framing Question: How have some of the social changes in society particularly affected different racial-ethnic families?

Families are not immune from social changes in the society at large. Population changes alone are changing America's families and will be creating new challenges for meeting the needs of both the nation's older population and the growing number of young people. At the same time, increased racial and ethnic diversity, changes in the number of interracial marriages, and the influence of immigration patterns will likely affect family experiences in the years ahead.

One of the biggest changes facing the United States is population change. The nation's youth will increasingly be composed of people of color, particularly Asian and Hispanic youth. Demographers predict that the number of White youth will continue to decline for years to come (Frey 2015). At the other end of the population distribution, White people will remain the largest share of the aging population. As they die, the nation's population will tilt toward being populated by more people of color.

Still, in the immediate future the number of White seniors will increase substantially, largely because of longer life expectancy. Moreover, the senior population is predicted to increase much more than will the number of people in the labor force—that is, those who generally provide the support for both the young and the old. The older group, mostly White, will then be competing for social and economic resources with the younger group, mostly people of color. This could produce a strong generational divide between what one commentator has called "the gray and the brown" (Brownstein 2010, cited in Frey 2015:35). How families will adapt to these changes remains to be seen.

Loving across Racial Lines: Interracial Dating and Marriage

Another change affecting families and race relations is the increasing number of interracial marriages. At one time, interracial marriage was completely illegal, both between Whites and Blacks and between Whites and other groups (see "Learning Our Past," below). In the mid-nineteenth century, for example, fearing a threat to "racial purity," California outlawed marriage between White and Chinese people

LEARNING OUR PAST

Laws against Interracial Marriage

Beginning in the 1600s, various American colonies and later states passed laws that prevented freed Black slaves from marrying Whites. Having such a relationship—or even the suggestion of one—could, until very recently, get you murdered. Until the Supreme Court ruled such bans against interracial marriage unconstitutional, a lot of effort went into preventing both sexual and marital unions, not only between Whites and Blacks but also between Whites and other groups. Early in Maryland's history, for example, a White woman who married a Black man would then be considered a slave.

Prior to *Loving v. Virginia,* thirty-nine states had enacted antimiscegenation laws—that is, laws preventing interracial marriage. The specifics of such laws varied state to state; some prohibited marriage not only between Whites and Blacks but also between Whites and "Indians," referring to Native Americans; "Hindus" (South Asians); "Mongolians" (a racist term that lumped together Chinese, Japanese, and Koreans); and "Malays" (Filipinos).

Section 20-54 of the Virginia Code stated, "It shall hereafter be unlawful for any white person in this State to marry any save a white person, or a person with no other admixture of blood than white and American Indian. For the purpose of this act, the term 'white person' shall apply only to the person who has no trace whatever of any blood other than Caucasian; but persons who have one-sixteenth or less of the blood of the American Indian and have no other non-Caucasic blood shall be deemed to be white persons."

Source: Volpp 2000.

and between Whites and so-called Malays, a term referring to Filipinos (Takaki 1989).

Only relatively recently in US history did the Supreme Court rule on bans against interracial marriage. The deciding case involved a couple, Mildred Delores Jeter Loving (a Black woman also descended from Rappahannock American Indians) and Richard Loving (a White man). The Lovings were married in 1958 in Washington, DC. When they returned to Virginia, the police raided their home in the middle of the night and charged the couple with violating the Virginia law that prohibited interracial relationships. Nine years later, the Supreme Court ruled that laws prohibiting interracial marriage were unconstitutional (*Loving v. Virginia,* 388 U.S. 1 [1967]).

Today interracial marriages are a small but growing percentage of all marriages in the United States. In 1970, less than 1 percent of marriages was interracial. Even more telling was that at that time only one-quarter of Americans approved of interracial relationships (Lee 2015). Today 10 percent of marriages in the United States are interracial, and one in six newly married people marry someone of a different race or ethnicity. Over one-third of Americans (39 percent) say different races marrying each other is a good thing for society (see figure 8.4; Livingston and Brown 2017; Rico, Kreider, and Anderson 2018).

Despite these changes, crossing interracial boundaries can still be difficult because doing so "involves steep asymmetries of power and resources" (Alba and

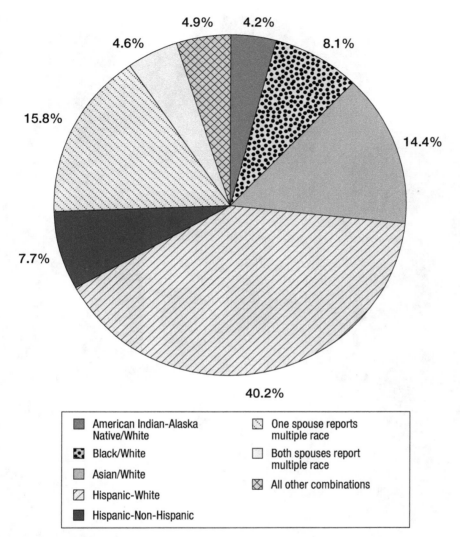

FIG. 8.4 Percentage of Interracial/Interethnic Couples (2012–2016)

Source: Rico et al. 2018.

Foner 2015:38). Even now, with changing attitudes about interracial relationships, interracial couples still encounter significant opposition from family and friends, even though discomfort with interracial relationships can be expressed in subtle ways (Childs 2005; Dalmage 2000; Osuji 2019a).

Studies of online dating sites illustrate how constricting racial boundaries can be. People seem to generally choose Internet dates based on appearance. Researchers who have analyzed online dating sites have observed that Whites are especially likely to choose those who appear to be White and that Blacks select dates mostly with people who appear Black. Latinos who themselves look "White" also select other Latinos who look "White." Race and gender combinations likewise influence choices

Interracial marriage, though still somewhat rare in the United States, is increasing in frequency and has long been thought to be an important part of reducing racial and ethnic prejudice in society.

Source: age fotostock / Alamy Stock Photo.

made on online dating sites. White men are more likely than other men to select Asian women, but they generally exclude Black women as potential dating partners. White women, however, tend not to select Asian men (Feliciano and Robnett 2014; Feliciano, Robnett, and Komaie 2009).

Patterns of race and gender are also apparent in who marries whom. Perceptions of marriageability are shaped by both race and gender. Latinos are twice as likely to intermarry as are Black Americans. Asian females are more likely to intermarry than are Asian men. Black men are more likely to intermarry than are Black women (Lee 2015). Almost two-thirds of all interracial marriages are White-Black marriages, over two-thirds of which are Black husbands with White wives. Latino intermarriage has been increasing, most frequently among non-Hispanic Whites.

Among immigrants, foreign-born people are less likely to intermarry than are native-born people. Still, one in six of all marriages now involves immigrants; half of these, in turn, involve immigrants marrying native-born partners. Again, racial boundaries are significant. Immigrants considered White are more likely to marry native-born partners, while Black immigrants are far less likely to cross this color line (Lichter, Qian, and Tumin 2015). It appears that the social construction of race penetrates even our most intimate decisions.

Certain social structural conditions also influence the likelihood of intermarriage. Increased migration, the ease of global transportation and communication, and, of course, changed attitudes all produce more exposure between groups and the possibility for romantic attachments to develop. The likelihood of interracial marriage is also shaped by cultural preferences and various constraints, such as marriage laws or social controls imposed by families. In other words, proximity makes intermarriage more likely (Qian and Lichter 2011; Rodríguez-Garcia 2015). In cultures where there is a tradition of arranged marriages, parents are likely to exert pressure on their children to not marry outside the ethnic group, believing it will bring great dishonor on the family and weaken the maintenance of ethnic identities and culture (Kasinitz et al. 2008; Pyke 2014).

Many believe that as more people date, fall in love, and marry across racial-ethnic lines, the barriers between race and ethnic groups will disappear. Interracial marriage has long been seen as the ultimate measure of racial integration (Gordon 1964). Despite this belief, intermarriage does not necessarily reduce racial and ethnic prejudice. Indeed, Whites may find themselves "colorized" by an interracial marriage. Children of mixed-race marriages involving a White and a Black parent also tend to be defined as Black even if that is not how they self-identify (Rodríguez-Garcia 2015). Interracial dating and marriage do, however, bring about an understanding among White people of the salience of race, making them more aware of and attentive to racism (Vasquez 2014).

Families and Immigration

As we have seen, immigration is transforming the racial and ethnic makeup of the US population. Immigration also brings new cultural forms, including changes in family structures and values. Even while families are changed by the immigration experience, they are critical to the immigration process, as they provide networks and support systems for new arrivals.

Over time, US immigration policy has constructed how families develop. Family reunification has been a central theme of immigration policy, albeit in restricted ways. Depending on the economic interests of dominant groups, only certain family members have been allowed admission. Thus, while immigration policy has altered the racial-ethnic composition of the United States, it has also restricted what counts as a legitimate family (Lee 2013). Families themselves often use more expansive concepts of family to include **fictive kin** (Nelson 2020; Stack 1974)—that is, those individuals who are part of an extended family network but are not biological kin.

Currently, two-thirds of immigrants enter the United States through family reunification policies. This means that prospective immigrants who are immediate relatives must be

* spouses of US citizens
* unmarried minor children of US citizens, under twenty-one years of age
* parents of US citizens and at least twenty-one years old as petitioners for a parent (US Citizenship and Immigration Services 2018)

A limited number of visas are awarded each year for other family members to enter the United States, but the number issued is small. The United States is unique in this way because in other industrialized nations migration is mostly driven by employment needs, not family concerns. Of course, employment figures in US immigration patterns, but the focus on families is a much stronger feature of US immigration policy (American Immigration Council 2019).

The family-based immigration system was upended in 2018 when the Trump administration started separating families seeking refugee status at the southern border. Presented as an attempt to deter unlawful immigration, the policy took children from their parents, placed them in detention cages, and treated most inhumanely. There was such a public outcry that the administration was forced to change course and a federal court ordered the government to reunify families. It is unknown exactly how many children were actually reunited with their parents, but large numbers are still separated (Sacchetti 2019).

Immigrants use family networks as a way to settle in and to seek work, but in doing so they also reconstitute family structures and roles. Immigration, for example, can change existing gender roles in families. Men who migrate without their wives may take on more household work and childcare. Both men and women rely on extended family networks for care (Hondagneu-Sotelo 2007). In other words, family structures have to be adaptable to new situations. This is true when migration crosses national borders, but it can also be true during internal movement as family members seek work where they can find it.

Within immigrant families, children are particularly vulnerable, especially when immigration is illegal (Bean, Brown, and Bachmeier 2015; Dreby 2010). Undocumented families and their children live with the constant threat of deportation and separation from family members. Even when born in the United States, children in undocumented families fare worse in educational achievement (Pyke 2014). Young people's inability to get green cards also hampers access to good jobs. Their educational and employment disadvantages, however, disappear when the parents are able to obtain legal status.

Race is central to family experiences as immigrants encounter a new culture. New racial identities may be imposed on immigrants even though they may never have been considered a "race" in their homeland. Just as race shapes immigrants' experiences, however, so do immigrants shape the concept of race (Pyke 2014).

Immigrants are shifting the color line in the United States, moving the nation away from a traditional Black-White divide to a far more complex racial structure, one that deeply affects families. Who people marry, how they define themselves, how others see them, and what resources a given family may have are all shaped by the shifting conceptions of race in the United States. For immigrants, as well as others, race shapes every dimension of family life, including "immigrant identities, family structures and living arrangements, who marries whom and who is likely not to marry at all, where families reside and children go to school, levels of educational attainment, marital and nonmarital fertility, the kind of jobs people do and how much they earn, exposure to crime, access to healthcare, and how long people live" (Pyke 2014:194). In short, families are on the front lines of the nation's racial challenges.

Families and Social Policy

Framing Question: How have social policies to assist families embedded pejorative assumptions about race and poverty?

The preservation of "family values" has been a recent rallying cry for fixing social problems in the United States. The assumption seems to be that if people would only embrace "traditional family values," our nation's problems would be solved. This is reflected in often-heard statements that if people would just raise their children right, or if men would assume their responsibilities as fathers, then families would not be "broken" and people would not fall into a cycle of poverty, substance abuse, and crime. Fixing the family and not the society, according to this logic, is the solution to our nation's troubles.

Such arguments have framed many of the social policies designed to help families, especially poor, minority families. Federal assistance to those in need embeds this assumption in the very title of the TANF program, focusing on "personal responsibility." The federal government has spent billions of dollars on marriage promotion campaigns. Marriage promotion campaigns provide support groups and workshops mostly to low-income couples to help them improve their relationships. Although marriage counseling can be helpful to some couples, it hardly addresses what causes so many low-income minority couples to break up: economic stress (Greenbaum 2015).

Some of our family policies even punish people rather than help them when they are unable to support their children. Putting fathers in jail for not paying child support, for example, does little to help men find decent jobs so they can support their children. (Of course, there are those who are irresponsible, who walk away from family responsibilities, and who spend money frivolously rather than paying child support.)

Are we, though, really doing enough to help families whether or not they would benefit from a marriage promotion campaign—that is, whether they fit the traditional family ideal? Obviously families are better off where there are two incomes, but is it a given that a parent and children are necessarily better off with the other parent in the home as well?

Current cultural and policy assumptions about the need for male breadwinners can be traced back to the influence of the infamous Moynihan Report. Issued in 1965 under the Johnson administration, the Moynihan Report still reverberates today in national family policies. In perhaps its most widely quoted passage, the report states, "At the heart of the deterioration of the fabric of Negro [*sic*] society is the deterioration of the Negro [*sic*] family" (Moynihan 1965:5). Then–assistant secretary of labor Daniel Patrick Moynihan singled out female-headed families as producing a "tangle of pathology," arguing that the reversal of men's and women's roles in the family was a root cause of poverty in the Black community.

We have seen that Black and Hispanic poverty and unemployment are higher than among other groups. Black children are also more likely than others to live in single-parent families. But it was Moynihan's conclusion that poverty was caused by the structure of Black families, and not by economic inequalities, that set off a firestorm of criticism. Moynihan placed the blame for racial inequality *within* Black families, specifically those headed by Black women. He assumed that the solution to Black American inequality was to reinstate men as heads of household.

Moynihan ignored a great deal of social science research on the resilience of minority families as well as the fact that single-parent families typically emerge in societies where men are absent because of war or incarceration (Gans 2011). Moynihan also ignored US policies over the years that had separated and torn apart families. Arguing that people of color should strive to be in traditional families was particularly ironic given that national policies had specifically denied this family form to so many racial-ethnic minorities over the years. Laws against intermarriage, barring family members from entering the country, disregarding citizenship rights for children born in the United States, and other policies have denied and continue to deny certain groups ideal conditions in which to form strong families. That people have done so despite these structural barriers is a sign of family strength, not pathology.

Conclusion

What all families need are economic policies that lift families out of poverty and provide jobs that pay a living wage—to women as well as men. Simply paying the nation's care workers wages that reflect the value of this essential work would go a long way toward assisting American families (Slaughter 2015).

Also needed are more generous family-leave policies, more and higher quality childcare, and less racially unequal institutional care. Compared to other industrialized nations, the United States is quite stingy when it comes to family support policies. Paid maternity leaves, more vacation time, and strong social assistance programs all tend to be more generous in other nations. At the core of family social policies should be recognition of the diverse forms of contemporary families, including the nation's racial-ethnic minority families. Family policies that rely on old notions of a family ideal simply cannot meet the different needs of today's men and women and their children.

Key Terms

care work 201

familism 197

family household 190

fictive kin 210

household 190

householder 190

matriarchy 197

nonfamily household 190

othermothers 203

reproductive labor 201

structural diversity theory 199

transnational families 200

A Critical-Thinking Question

Female-headed households are the most likely households in the United States to be poor. Were you advising Congress on such policies to alleviate this connection, what would you recommend, and what research would you use to support your argument?

Student Exercises

8.1. Using the website of the National WIC Association (https://www.nwica.org/wic -basics), look up the provisions in your state for poor women and their children under the Special Supplemental Nutrition Program for Women, Infants and Children (known as WIC; pronounced "wick"). What percent of children in the state you selected are "food insecure"? What is the average food benefit under the WIC program? How would you determine whether this is adequate to meet children's needs?

8.2. Oral history is a method often used to recover the experiences of family members. Older family members are especially invaluable for recalling the historic and family events that have shaped the family in the present. Conduct an oral history with one of the older members of your family. What specific historical events are most important in this family? Was race or ethnicity important in this family's background? What kind of work did members of different generations do, and who took care of the family? If possible, in a multiracial/multiethnic class, compare and contrast the oral histories that you collect, and discuss the influence of race and ethnicity on the experiences of diverse families.

Challenging Questions/Open to Debate

Compared to other Western, industrialized nations, the United States has some of the least generous benefits for family care, including child- and eldercare, as well as care for those with special needs. Should the federal government use tax dollars to provide paid leave for those who need it? What impact would such a policy have on particular racial groups?

TAKING ACTION AGAINST RACISM

Create Community

Learn from antiracist educators, and support the teachers and community leaders who are working against racism. If you are in school, make a point of taking classes from teachers who are known for their work against racism. Understand that changing racial inequality will not happen quickly. Continue educating yourself about race and racism as a lifelong commitment.

Resource: Saad 2020.

Source: Ethel Wolvovitz / Alamy Stock Photo

CHAPTER 9

Race and Place

Residential and Educational Segregation

A child miseducated is a child lost.
—attributed to President John F. Kennedy

OBJECTIVES

- Describe patterns of racial segregation in housing
- Discuss changing patterns of racial segregation in schools
- Explain the causes and consequences of the racial gap in educational achievement
- Explain how people can challenge the deficit model of education

Imagine a young girl—we'll call her Marsha—who lives in a middle-class neighborhood outside of a major US city. Both of her parents work full-time, usually commuting into the city to work. Marsha attends public schools and earns good grades. Her parents expect Marsha to go to college. They have saved as much money as they can to pay the tuition, room, and board. If they need to, they can borrow money at a reasonable interest rate, based on the equity they have built up in the house they bought many years ago. They live in a neighborhood where the value of their home is now more than what they initially paid.

Another young girl, Cassandra, also earns good grades. She and her mother, a single parent, live inside the central city. Cassandra's mother works in a local nursing home. She often has to pick up extra shifts to make ends meet. When she does, Cassandra stays with her aunt, but she has to take a bus after school to her aunt's neighborhood. If her mother works late, Cassandra spends the night with her aunt and takes the bus back to school the next morning. Cassandra's mother, like Marsha's parents, dreams of sending Cassandra to college, but she has no idea how she will pay for it. She has a very small savings account, but most of her income goes to meeting basic expenses. Now she has a substantial outstanding balance on her credit card after she had to charge needed medical supplies not covered by her health insurance when Cassandra's grandmother became ill.

Here are two families, each with their own challenges, and two young girls, each working hard in school and dreaming of a good life ahead. Most likely you imagined Marsha as White and Cassandra as Latina or African American. Each scenario could describe people from different racial backgrounds. Certainly there are Latino and African American families with the same resources as Marsha's White family, but there are more White families in Marsha's family's situation, while more Black and Latino families face Cassandra's situation. Taken together, these cases reveal some of the dynamics of racial inequality in US housing and education.

Sociologist George Lipsitz has written, "Relations between races are relations between places" (2011:6). Two of those places are where people live and where they go to school. Housing and education, the subjects of this chapter, are key components of racial inequality in the United States. They are the places where people live day to day, but they are also places that are highly segregated by race.

Think about this: Do you live in a place with open space, nice views, good transportation, easily accessible shopping, and good schools nearby? During the 2020 COVID-19 pandemic, have you had access to safe outdoor places where you could see your friends? Is your neighborhood crime-free? Who lives near you? As a high school student, were you challenged in school? Were the school facilities well equipped with current books, science labs, computer equipment, and other resources? What racial-ethnic groups were in your classes?

Answers to these questions will tell you a lot about racial segregation in the United States, especially if you compare your answers to those of someone from a different racial-ethnic background. If you are Black or Latino and not living in a high-income family, chances are that you went to a school that was predominantly populated by students of color. If you are Asian American, you likely went to a more integrated school. If you are White, you might have gone to a racially integrated school, but the odds are that you had a better school than most schools with a predominantly minority enrollment.

Housing and education have been on the front lines of the movement for civil rights, and with good reason. Some of the key victories of the civil rights movement have involved policies intended to address racial segregation in housing and in schools. Indeed, many of the legal cases that now define racial equality under the law have come about because of housing and education.

The **Fair Housing Act of 1968** prohibits discrimination in housing. Prior to that, the landmark Supreme Court case ***Brown v. Board of Education*** (1954) ruled school segregation unconstitutional. Yet now, almost seven decades later, residential and educational segregation by race remain a stubborn reality of American life. The vast majority of Black, Latino, and Asian students attend schools that are intensely segregated. At the same time, White students have very little exposure to students of color. As experts conclude, such high degrees of segregation "place the promise of *Brown* at grave risk" (Frankenberg et al. 2019:4). We start by looking at residential segregation.

Living in Separated Spaces: Housing and Residential Segregation

Framing Question: How is racial segregation measured, and what are some of its consequences?

Residential segregation is the pattern by which different racial and ethnic groups live apart from one another. Residential segregation is significant not because there

The start of this community garden in the Lower Ninth Ward of New Orleans is typical of how community effort brings people together to create nurturing spaces even in the poorest neighborhoods.

Source: Jim West / Alamy Stock Photo.

is anything necessarily wrong with people living near people like themselves but because racial segregation is highly correlated with people's social and economic resources. Residential segregation is related to the quality and value of housing, the likelihood of exposure to crime and violence, access to transportation, the quality of schools, and countless other measures of well-being.

Even a person's physical health is impacted by residential segregation (also see chapter 10). We've seen this during the COVID-19 pandemic wherein African American and Latino people have born a disproportionate burden of illness and death from the virus. Why? There are many reasons, but residential segregation is among them. People of color are more likely to live in densely populated areas, making it more difficult to practice the social measures of distancing that have been found to protect people from this illness. People of color are also more likely to live in multigenerational households, making it more difficult to isolate when someone gets sick. Further, jails and prisons—which are "home" for too many people of color—are known to have put people at very high risk for contracting COVID-19. All told, racial residential segregation contributes to the likelihood of adverse health (Centers for Disease Control and Prevention 2020).

People living in racially segregated, low-income, disadvantaged neighborhoods also typically have less access to the healthiest and freshest food. In such neighborhoods, there are fewer supermarkets than in better-off places. Small neighborhood stores where food is more expensive are more likely to be found in racially segregated, low-income neighborhoods. Neighborhoods populated mostly by people of color, especially if they are poor, are twice as likely to have fast-food chains, food sources known to be linked to poorer health (Block, Scribner, and DeSalvo 2004; Cannuscio et al. 2014; Walker, Keane, and Burke 2010). Various alternative food practices, such as community-supported agriculture programs, farmer's markets, and food banks, promise to alleviate some of this disparity, but too often these services are too expensive for lower-income people to access. Further, studies have found that providers of such programs often hold racial attitudes that impede the participation of people of color (Galt et al. 2017; Larimore 2018).

Racially segregated neighborhoods exacerbate existing economic disadvantages. Low-income, minority neighborhoods are dotted with payday lenders, pawnshops, and other places that charge exorbitant fees, leaving people with the fewest resources actually paying more for what they need. As if that were not enough, the dominant society heaps negative social judgments on people living in such neighborhoods. Residents there are less valued by the dominant society, no matter the residents' actual character, values, and ideals.

Simply put, place matters, and race shapes place. As an example, Black families, even when they earn five times more than low-income White families, are more likely to live in neighborhoods where many people are poor. Few middle-class White families face such conditions. Racial segregation is also particularly hard on children. Racial minority families with children are actually even more segregated than families without children (Massey 2020). Has the nation made progress in reducing racial segregation? In some ways, yes, but in other ways, no—as we will see in the next section.

Chocolate Cities, Vanilla Suburbs?[1] Changing Patterns of Residential Segregation

Measuring segregation is not an easy matter, but even a glimpse at where people live reveals that the United States is quite segregated. Many of the nation's largest cities are now "majority-minority"—that is, most of their population is Black, Latino, and Asian—with a large part of the White population living in the suburbs and outer fringes of the city. At the same time, downtown areas are becoming quite racially and ethnically diverse. Some White people, especially younger ones, are now moving into cities, attracted by walkable neighborhoods, cultural resources, and some decline in the crime rate (Semuels 2015). Although cities are becoming diverse, how integrated or segregated are they?

This is a complex question. By some measures, residential segregation has declined across the nation since the 1960s, especially segregation between Black and White American households. However, the complexity of residential patterns arises from the influx of immigrants, the increasing diversity of the population, and the growing inequality that has concentrated affluence in certain neighborhoods and poverty in others. Segregation patterns also vary significantly in different regions and between different groups. Among people of color, African Americans remain the most segregated, followed by Latinos and then Asian Americans (Massey 2020).

How much segregation is detected depends to some extent on how it is measured. Some measures account for the *distribution* of populations. Other measures calculate the *isolation* of groups (or lack of exposure) from each other. These are not necessarily the same thing.

The extent to which two groups are *distributed* across a given place—a city or a school system, for example—is represented by the **index of dissimilarity**. This index, which can range from zero to one hundred (or sometimes zero to one), shows how many people of a given group would have to move in order to reach an even distribution of groups in the area being examined.

It takes quite sophisticated quantitative analyses to calculate the index of dissimilarity for various cities and regions. Generally speaking, however, analysts agree that an index of sixty or greater is indicative of a high degree of racial segregation (Rugh and Massey 2014). Figure 9.1 shows the index of dissimilarity for the ten largest cities in the United States. As you can tell, by this measure our cities remain highly racially segregated.

The index of dissimilarity only measures the *distribution* of groups in a given area. For example, if a given city is 70 percent Black and Latino and all of its neighborhoods are 70 percent Black and Latino, then the index of dissimilarity would not reveal segregation, because each neighborhood reflects the racial composition of the city. What if, however, most of the White population in this city lived in its suburbs? Common sense would tell you that this is a very segregated city. Social scientists then use additional measures to assess the degree of *isolation* or *exposure* that groups have to each other.

[1] The term *chocolate city* was first coined by the punk band Parliament in their song about Washington, DC, which they described as a "chocolate city" (Parliament 1975). The phrase "chocolate cities/vanilla suburbs" was then adapted by sociologists to describe racial segregation in the nation's cities (Farley et al. 1978).

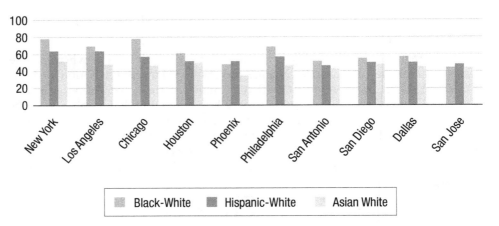

FIG. 9.1 Index of Dissimilarity, Ten Largest US Cities

Source: Frey, Brookings Institution, and University of Michigan Social Science Data Analysis Network n.d.

Measures of isolation find that the segregation between Latinos and Whites and between Asians and Whites in recent years has actually *increased* even while the index of dissimilarity between these groups has been relatively steady. The isolation of Blacks has actually declined in recent years, but only because of their greater exposure to other people of color. The exposure of Blacks to Whites has hardly changed over the past two decades. American Indians tend to be less segregated than other groups; however, segregation for American Indians is greater in cities where they are a higher proportion of the population (Byerly 2019).

How much racial segregation we see depends on where and how we look. Since 1990, the racial segregation of neighborhoods has declined, but when we look at whole metropolitan areas, segregation has increased significantly, especially between Black and White Americans. Suburbs have become more diverse, but many Whites keep moving farther out of cities. Many metropolitan areas, such as Chicago, Detroit, and Milwaukee, continue to have very high degrees of racial segregation.

In many places, segregation is so extreme that scholars refer to it as **hypersegregation,** a phenomenon that occurs when nearly all of the residents of a given area are of the same group (Massey and Denton 1998). Researchers find that the number of hypersegregated metropolitan areas has decreased since 1970 but that there has been little change in since the degree of hypersegregation. By 2010, one-third of Black metropolitan residents and one-quarter of Latinos lived in hypersegregated areas (Massey 2020; Massey and Tannen 2015).

Hypersegregated areas are typically characterized by *concentrated poverty*, as described in chapter 7. Concentrated poverty occurs when 40 percent or more of the population in a given area is poor. This means that even people who are not poor but live in such areas are surrounded by poverty. Concentrated poverty declined in the 1990s when the economy was booming and social policies countered some of the trends toward segregation. But since then, concentrated poverty has more than doubled (Jargowsky 2015). Figure 9.2 shows the percentage of people in different racial-ethnic groups who live in neighborhoods where there is concentrated poverty.

You can see that Blacks and Hispanics, even when they are not poor, are the groups most likely to live in areas with concentrated poverty.

Concentrated poverty in the United States is particularly acute in the Midwest and Northeast, areas that have been particularly hard hit by the decline in manufacturing jobs. In Syracuse, New York, for example, two-thirds of the city's poor Black and Latino people live in areas of concentrated poverty. Other areas of the nation are not immune, however. Half of the Black poor in Fresno, California, live in neighborhoods of concentrated poverty, as do half of the Latino poor in the McAllen-Edinburg metropolitan area of Texas. In such neighborhoods, police-community tensions are high, unemployment is rampant, and schools are often failing (Jargowsky 2015).

Quantitative measures of segregation are telling, but they cannot account for the actual degree of interaction that groups might have with each other even in integrated spaces. A given neighborhood, for example, might be well integrated but Black, Latino, and White neighbors rarely visit each other's homes, do things together, or share personal details about their lives. One illustration of this phenomenon is found in the history of the American South, where little physical distance existed between Black and White people but maximum social distance was the norm (Grigoryeva and Ruef 2015). Even in racially integrated neighborhoods in the early twenty-first century, residents' perceptions of how integrated a neighborhood is varies by race. White people perceive more integration than people of color do. Whites, African Americans, and Latinos all say that they value integrated neighborhoods, but White Americans only think such neighborhoods are desirable when Whites remain as a significant portion of the population (Krysan, Carter, and van Londen 2017). Within integrated neighborhoods, there is also typically segregation block by block (Rich 2008 and 2009).

With the expansion of the Black and Latino middle class, many African Americans and Latinos have moved into suburban areas (Lacy 2007; Pattillo 2007

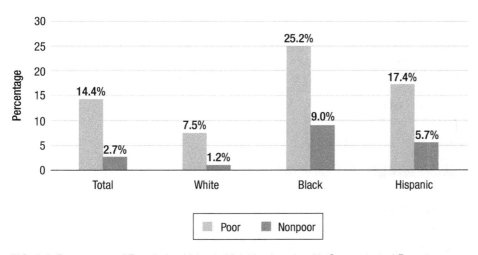

FIG. 9.2 Percentage of Population Living in Neighborhoods with Concentrated Poverty

Source: Orfield and Frankenberg 2014.

and 2013). Still, middle-class Black Americans, on average, live in poorer neighborhoods than Whites (Pattillo 2005).

When people of color move into predominantly White areas, they encounter what sociologist Elijah Anderson has termed **White space**—that is, areas in which Black people perceive themselves to be "typically absent, not expected, or marginalized when present" (2015:10). White space can be anywhere—a neighborhood, school, workplace, or anywhere White people are the dominant group. When people of color enter White space, they likely feel uncomfortable, as if the place is "off limits." White people, however, rarely perceive the same thing, instead imagining White space to be neutral or simply unremarkable. This concept underscores the fact that racial segregation and integration are not simply about numbers. *Segregation and integration are fundamentally social constructs* that involve not just who is present and who is not but also how people relate to and perceive one another. See the "Living with Racism" segment below for an illustration.

LIVING WITH RACISM

Black People in "White Spaces"

Elijah Anderson is a distinguished sociologist on faculty at Yale University. Author of many books and widely cited for his scholarship on race and ethnicity, Anderson, as a Black man, nonetheless experiences racial harassment upon entering what he calls "White space." He writes,

> Several years ago, I vacationed in Wellfleet, Massachusetts, a pleasant Cape Cod town full of upper-middle-class White vacationers, tourists, and working-class White residents. During the two weeks that my family and I spent there, I encountered very few other Black people. We had rented a beautiful cottage about a mile from the town center, which consisted of a library and a few restaurants and stores catering to tourists. Early one weekday morning, I jogged down the road from our cottage through the town center and made my way to Route 6, which runs the length of the Cape from the Sagamore Bridge to Provincetown. It was a beautiful morning, about 75 degrees, with low humidity and clear blue skies. I had jogged here many times before. At 6 a.m., the road was deserted, with only an occasional passing car. I was enjoying my run that morning, listening to the nature sounds and feeling a sense of serenity. It seemed I had this world all to myself. Suddenly a red pickup truck appeared and stopped dead in the middle of the road. I looked over at the driver, a middle-aged White man, who was obviously trying to communicate something to me. He was waving his hands and gesticulating, and I immediately thought he might be in distress or in need of help, but I could not make out what he was saying. I stopped, cupped my hand to my ear to hear him better, and yelled back, "What did you say?" It was then that he made himself very clear. "Go home! Go home!" he yelled, dragging out the words to make sure I understood. I felt provoked, but I waved him off and continued on my way.

Source: Anderson 2015:14–15.

How Does Segregation Happen?

How have we become such a segregated nation? There is no single reason. Many White people think that racial segregation is a choice that people of color make.

Strangely, no one ever accuses White people of choosing to live in segregated neighborhoods. Individual choice matters to some extent, as people clearly make decisions about where to live, but social-structural factors—both past and present—cause racial segregation and the racial disparities found in housing today.

Discrimination is certainly one cause of residential segregation. *Audit studies* (see chapter 7), for example, find that about 20 percent of the time White home seekers are favored over others, by being shown homes in mostly White neighborhoods and getting more favorable terms for home financing. Real estate agents have been known to employ **steering**—that is, directing potential Black and Latino homebuyers away from neighborhoods that are predominantly White. Agents may do so unintentionally or simply by thinking that this would be the buyer's choice. Nonetheless, steering has been shown to be a common practice that reflects *implicit bias* (Eberhardt 2019; Kwate et al. 2013; Turner and Ross 2005).

Discrimination can also occur even when the practices that produce it are seemingly color-blind. For example, a person might behave in ways they believe will help protect the value of their property, such as objecting to the placement of low-income or affordable housing in their neighborhood. Or communities might pass zoning ordinances that bar the construction of multiple-unit dwellings. These and other apparently well-intended actions have discriminatory outcomes, even if there is no explicit racial bias. Yet there are consequences for people of color.

In other words, discrimination is not always intentional, nor is it readily detected. Fair housing laws prohibit discrimination, but proving that discrimination has occurred is not easy. Antidiscrimination laws put the burden of proof on individual victims who may not even be aware of it while it is happening. Also, victims of discrimination have to know their rights and have the resources and willingness to pursue a claim of discrimination. Consequently, even with antidiscrimination laws and policies in place, discrimination can continue unabated.

Another phenomenon that shapes racial disparities in housing is the dynamic of neighborhoods "turning" when people of color move in. It is well documented that property values are lower in areas where there are high proportions of people of color (Anacker 2010; Pattillo 2013). If a neighborhood starts to change from mostly White to the inclusion of more people of color, its residents often see their property values start to fall. This initial decline can start a vicious cycle as more White people move out, thus causing further deterioration in the value of homes. Those who stay will find their assets dwindling. Studies show that, controlling for the characteristics of the housing units and the education, occupation, income, and marital status of residents, housing appreciates more slowly in predominantly Black and Latino neighborhoods compared to White neighborhoods (Denton 2001; Flippen 2004; Kim 2000).

Practices of lending institutions are also a major reason for racial disparities in housing. Analysts have concluded that an "unequal system of housing finance (among other racial and class discriminatory practices) has indelibly shaped the geography and demography of metropolitan areas, creating clear patterns of uneven development marked by disinvestment that has disadvantaged central cities and advantaged suburbs" (Pattillo 2013:513).

One way this has happened is through **redlining,** a practice from the 1930s that rated different residential areas in terms of their worthiness for mortgage lending. Areas that were heavily minority were typically redlined, making it nearly impossible for people to get mortgages in these areas. The practice was deemed illegal under the Federal Housing Act of 1968, but there is ample evidence that, although overtly denying housing to people of color has diminished, significant discrimination remains in loan denials and mortgage costs (Quillian, Lee, and Brandon 2020). Such practices make it less likely and more expensive for minority borrowers to finance a home.

Another practice that has contributed to racial disparities in housing is **predatory lending,** which became especially apparent in the Great Recession between 2007 and 2009 and the resulting housing foreclosure crises. Predatory lending refers to the practice of financing very high-risk loans and doling out **subprime mortgages** with little review of the borrower's ability to pay. The practice was the main reason for the Great Recession. Although the recession affected most Americans, African Americans were much more likely than other groups to be prey to such practices (Thomas et al. 2017).

Approving a subprime mortgage—a housing loan that has higher interest rates than the prime lending rate—is almost the reverse of redlining: instead of denying people loans, granting subprime mortgages makes it much more expensive to borrow money, which also increases the risk of default. Numerous studies show that Latinos and African Americans have been far more likely to receive higher-cost and higher-risk loans, thus lowering their disposable income and putting them at greater risk of foreclosure (Rugh, Albright, and Massey 2015).

Most Americans' single most important financial asset is their home. Any threat of losing one's home has drastic consequences. The foreclosure crisis that accompanied the Great Recession had strong racial dimensions, and these continue to resonate today in the status of people of color. Even after controlling for income, borrowers' creditworthiness, and home values, researchers have concluded that racial segregation was a major predictor of the foreclosure crisis. Many Americans were hurt by this crisis, but the cost to Black Americans was especially substantial. Specifically, research has found that Black Americans have paid an additional 5 to 11 percent in monthly mortgage payments, collectively losing millions in home equity (Rugh and Massey 2010; Rugh et al. 2015). How much different groups lose in their home value as a result of the COVID-19 pandemic in 2020 remains to be seen, but if the past is predictive, it is likely that the hardest hit will the lowest income groups, where African Americans, Latinos, and Native Americans are overrepresented. Already research has found that Black Americans, Latinos, and low-income people have been more likely to miss rent and mortgage payments during the COVID-19 pandemic (Greene and McCargo 2020).

The Consequences of Residential Segregation

The impact of racial segregation obviously has substantial consequences. Lipsitz summarizes the impact this way: "Relegating people of different races to different spaces produces grossly unequal access to education, employment, transportation, and shelter. It exposes communities of color disproportionately to environmental hazards and social nuisances while offering Whites privileged access to economic opportunities, social amenities, and valuable personal networks" (Lipsitz 2011:6).

Indeed, the impact of racial disparities in housing is hard to underestimate. At the individual level, people separated from each other are less likely to develop friendships or know each other well enough to refute racial stereotypes. Even in racially integrated neighborhoods, racial norms and patterns of interaction may prevent people from knowing each other. As seen earlier, social distance may be greater than physical distance. White residents might also dictate the norms of the neighborhood by, for example, controlling homeowner associations or intervening in residents' daily practices, such as pet care, lawn care, style of decor, and so forth (Mayorga-Gallo 2014).

For people of color, the disadvantages that come from housing inequality also disrupt lives. Among renters, eviction disproportionately affects African Americans and, to a lesser extent, Latinos. Black women actually experience the highest incidence of eviction (Desmond 2016; Pattillo 2013). Frequent moving also disrupts children's education, although, on the positive side, children who move from poor areas to higher-income areas end up with better educational achievement than do those who remain in poor areas (Orfield 2013).

Residential segregation also has a huge impact on the education of the nation's children. Racial segregation means that Black and Latino students are more likely to attend schools where large proportions of the children are poor (Fahle et al. 2020). Having poor schools in a neighborhood can discourage people from moving there even if they desire an integrated neighborhood. Thus, poor schools help produce residential segregation, and residential segregation produces poor schools. Either way, given its connection to educational segregation, residential segregation stifles the achievement of students of color. We thus turn to the topic of race and education.

Learning in Unequal Places: Schooling in a Racially Unequal Society

Framing Question: How has racial segregation affected access to high-quality education?

Perhaps we would not care quite so much about residential segregation if it were not so closely tied to educational outcomes. The fact is that the vast majority of schools that serve children of color, especially low-income children of color, are inferior to those schools serving Whites. Poorer facilities, lower test scores, higher dropout rates, and fewer college-preparatory courses all mark schools in segregated Black and Latino areas (Darling-Hammond 2004 and 2010).

Segregation and Resegregation: The Aftermath of *Brown*

Frederick Douglass wrote, "Once you learn to read, you will be forever free." Having been born a slave, Douglass knew the cost of not having an education. Slaves were seldom allowed to learn to read. Many did so nonetheless, knowing that literacy was a way to gain freedom. Yet throughout US history, racial inequality in education has prevailed (see "Learning Our Past," below).

Interview with Teacher and Civil Rights Activist Julia Matilda Burns, 2013

The US Library of Congress holds a number of oral histories that were taken as part of its Civil Rights History Project. In this interview, Julia Matilda Burns describes her experiences as a young girl growing up in the 1950s, attending all-Black schools. Mrs. Burns went on to become a schoolteacher as well as a civil rights activist in Holmes County, Mississippi. At the time of the interview, Mrs. Burns was seventy-six years old, and she reflected on the encouragement teachers had given her when she was a young student in the segregated schools of Mississippi.

> My major influence that I can recall was my tenth grade English teacher. Very smart lady, very smart, and she just had a liking for people who wanted to do something. And I guess she could see in me what I could not see in myself, and she suggested to me that I should go to college and major in English. And that's what I did. And I think about her continuously now . . . what an impact that was on my life. . . . You know, tenth grade children, they don't think about their future. . . . they're just having a good time. . . .
>
> During that time, teachers took an interest in children's well-being and their future. All the way through high school, there was some teacher telling you what you ought to do or what you should do. And those teachers even visited the families in the community and told the parents, "Your child did this, your child did that." And believe it or not, you know, if it's good, the parent will work with it. If not, the parent would try to correct it.

Source: Civil Rights History Project 2013.

Until 1900, more than half of all Black adults in the United States were unable to read or write (Snyder 1993). Literacy rates among Black Americans improved over the twentieth century as young children were able to get at least a basic education, even if in segregated schools. American Indian children in the late nineteenth and early twentieth centuries were forced into so-called Indian schools—forced to give up their own cultural ways and become acculturated into the dominant culture, as required by the US government. In the Western United States, Chinese students were denied entry into public schools until 1905, when the Supreme Court required the state of California to extend public education to the children of Chinese immigrants, few as they were because of the Chinese Exclusion Act of 1882.

Segregated schools were deemed lawful by the US Supreme Court in the 1896 *Plessy v. Ferguson* decision, which enshrined the principle of "separate but equal" into US constitutional law. Homer Plessy was a mixed-race man, a Creole, from Louisiana who had been arrested in 1892 for sitting in the "White" section of a railroad car, thus violating the Separate Car Act that had been passed in Louisiana in 1890. A coalition of civil rights organizations challenged his arrest, ultimately taking his case to the US Supreme Court. But in 1896 the Supreme Court ruled that maintaining "separate but equal" public facilities was constitutional, schools included. *Plessy v. Ferguson* ushered in the infamous period of Jim Crow segregation, legitimating racial segregation in virtually every area of life and including the now-infamous separate bathrooms for "White" and "colored," separate water fountains, separate seating areas on public buses, and, most especially, separation of children in public schools.

Activism by people of color continued to challenge legally authorized racial segregation throughout the twentieth century, culminating in the landmark *Brown v. Board of Education* decision in 1954. Seven years prior to the *Brown* decision, a federal court of appeals in California had ruled in *Mendez v. Westminster* that separate schools for Mexican Americans in California were unconstitutional, striking down segregation for children of Mexican, Asian, and Indian descent (Foley 2005). Thurgood Marshall, the African American attorney who argued the *Brown* case before the Supreme Court and later became the first African American Supreme Court justice, participated in the *Mendez* case, which no doubt influenced his argument in the *Brown* decision (Blanco 2010).

Brown v. Board of Education combined four cases involving segregated schools in Kansas, South Carolina, Virginia, and Delaware. In Virginia, a sixteen-year-old student initiated the case when she organized a school walkout to protest segregation. In the state courts, only the judge in Delaware ruled segregation to be illegal. Presenting the case to the Supreme Court, Thurgood Marshall, supported by the National Association for the Advancement of Colored People (NAACP), argued that segregation harmed Black children. Looking back on it now, the argument could have been more broadly framed, showing the harm done by segregation to all of society. At the time, however, research focused on the damage to Black children

The effort to desegregate Little Rock Central High School in 1957 required military escorts to protect the nine young Black children who enrolled in the school. Resistance from White citizens was so severe that Arkansas governor Orval Faubus closed all of the Little Rock high schools for the entire 1958–1959 school year to avoid integrating the schools.

Source: Everett Collection Historical / Alamy Stock Photo.

that racial inequality produced. It was the first time social science evidence was used to support an argument before the Supreme Court.

In its unanimous decision, the Supreme Court ruled that separate schools were a violation of the rights of equal protection guaranteed to all citizens under the Fourteenth Amendment of the US Constitution, which promises equal protection under the law. Asserting that education is the most important function of local and state governments, the Court concluded that "the doctrine of 'separate but equal' has no place . . . in the field of public education" and that "separate educational facilities are inherently unequal" (US Supreme Court 1954).

Despite such a strong Supreme Court ruling, the *Brown* decision did not change things overnight. Following *Brown*, many Whites fiercely resisted desegregation. School boards, especially in the South, did all they could to skirt desegregation. In Arkansas, the governor simply closed the schools altogether to avoid desegregation. In Virginia, the governor and the legislature created policies they actually had the nerve to title "Massive Resistance." Such policies made it nearly impossible for Black students to enroll in White schools and allowed schools to close if ordered to desegregate (Daugherity 2014; Vecchione 1987).

White parents also pulled their children from public schools, especially in the South. New private schools were created for Whites—schools that came to be known as "segregation academies." Although the Supreme Court had ordered schools to desegregate "with all deliberate speed," it took years before school districts actually complied with court-ordered desegregation—and then only following continued pressure from civil rights organizations and, eventually, the federal

Intense policing in schools, especially those populated largely by Hispanic and Black schools, has become so pronounced that some schools resemble prisons rather than learning environments.

Source: Bob Daemmerich / Alamy Stock Photo.

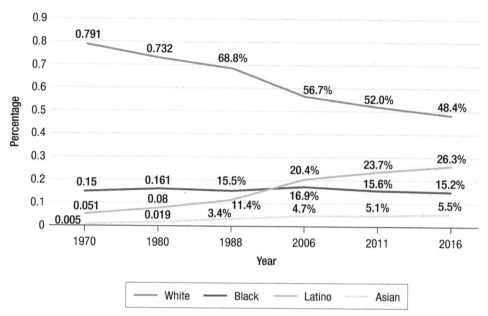

FIG. 9.3 Percentage of Student Population in Public Schools

Source: Frankenberg et al. 2019:16.

government (Clotfelter 1976; Moye 2005; Reece and O'Connell 2016).[2] Further, as figure 9.3 shows, Whites have become a much smaller percentage of students in the public schools, both as the population of Latinos and Asians has grown and as many White families have withdrawn from public schools by placing their children in private schools. White parents who do so may not see themselves as racist, but they think private schools provide a better education (Hagerman 2018). Whether racist or not, their actions reproduce racial inequality in education.

Schools finally opened completely to students of color between the 1960s and the mid-1970s. But even as late as 1968—fourteen years after the *Brown* decision—81 percent of Black students in the South still attended majority Black schools; two-thirds were in schools that were 90 to 100 percent Black (Frankenberg et al. 2019; Orfield 2001). Civil rights groups persistently mobilized throughout the South to bring pressure on Southern school districts and colleges to desegregate. Only after great reluctance to do so did the federal government ultimately step in. By the mid-1960s, the walls of segregation started to crumble, and by the mid-1970s numerous court-ordered desegregation plans were implemented, despite ongoing protests by many White communities in the North as well as the South. There was, though, significant progress during this time period, as hundreds of schools throughout the nation desegregated (Massey 2020; Reardon and Owens 2014).

---

[2] As just one example, I, a White woman, was a student in Georgia public schools in the 1960s. Not until my senior year of high school in 1966 did my school admit any Black students. Even then, only four Black students were admitted to a senior class (and no other classes) of about 130. This token desegregation came solely as the result of court orders, following insistence by activist Black citizens.

Our Resegregated Schools

Experts do not agree on exactly how much segregation has changed in US schools, but one thing is clear: the isolation of students of color—Black Americans and Latinos, in particular—has increased significantly since the late 1980s (see table 9.1; Frankenberg et al. 2019). Segregation differs, however, by region, in different kinds of institutions, and for different racial-ethnic groups. Asians, for example, are generally less segregated than Latinos and African Americans. In addition, as with residential segregation, how much segregation is found depends on how it is measured. Like residential segregation, educational segregation is also detected in terms of either *dissimilarity* (distribution across an area) or *isolation* (separation of groups from one another). Black school students are the most segregated in the Northeast, Latinos in the Northeast and South.

The concentration of people of color within cities, coupled with White flight to the suburbs, means that even when the distribution of students of color in a particular school district matches their representation in the city population, they can still be isolated from White students. Isolation indexes show that students have very little exposure to other racial-ethnic groups when Whites leave the city proper in substantial numbers. This is precisely what has happened.

Even with some studies showing a decline in segregation, as measured by the index of dissimilarity, Black and Latino students are, in general, much more isolated from White students than they were in 1980. Since that time, the proportion of Black students attending majority Black schools has also risen dramatically. And, as you can see in table 9.1, large numbers of Black and Latino students attend so-called majority-minority schools that are 90 percent or more Black and Latino. Nationwide, the typical Latino student attends a school that is 57 percent Latino. Latinos are also now more segregated in schools than are Black students (Orfield and Frankenberg 2014). With the number of Latino students growing, their segregation is predicted to increase unless there is a major shift in educational policies.

These patterns of segregation are evident in typical classroom experiences. Figure 9.4 shows the exposure different students have to students of different racial and ethnic backgrounds. The figure shows that the typical White student attends school where 70 percent of the other students are White, 8 percent are Black, 14 percent are Latino, and only 4 percent are Asian. Black, Latino, and Asian students experience more diversity in their schools, but Black and Latino students are likely to be in schools with large proportions of Black and Latino students, while Asian students seem to be in the most diverse school environments. Of course, data like

TABLE 9.1 **Percentage of Students in 90 to 100 Percent of Non-White Schools, 1968–2016**

	1968	1988	2001	2006	2011	2016
Black	64.3%	32.1%	37.4%	38.5%	38.8%	40.1%
Latino	23.1%	33.1%	37.4%	40.0%	41.1%	41.6%

Source: Frankenberg et al. 2019:29.

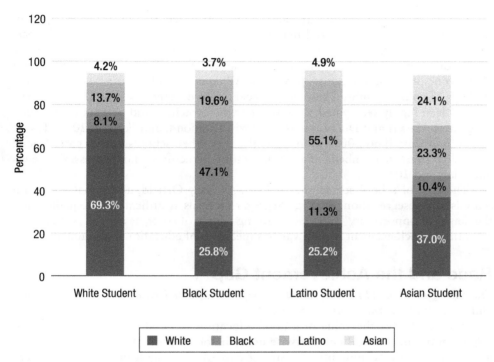

FIG. 9.4 Racial Composition of Schools Attended by Typical Student of Each Race (2016–2017)

Source: Frankenberg et al. 2019:23.

these only show school enrollment; they do not account for the actual interaction students have within the schools, where they may even be more segregated from each other through practices like classroom placement, academic tracks, friendship circles, and so forth (Frankenberg et al. 2019).

Since 1980, the walls of segregation have been reconstructed. By the mid-1970s, massive desegregation had taken place in the South, primarily because of strong oversight by the federal courts. Now, however, Black students in the South are even more segregated that they were in the 1980s, although not as strictly segregated as they had been prior to *Brown*, when racial segregation was absolute. Efforts to desegregate have completely stalled. Several court decisions have also supported the termination of many of the desegregation plans of earlier years. The result is that most of the gains of the post-*Brown* era have been lost as schools are now resegregating (Frankenberg et al. 2019).

Students are segregated not only by race and ethnicity but also by social class. Rising inequality has shaped how neighborhoods are populated, thus affecting the composition of schools. Poverty is also clearly linked to school segregation. Nationwide, in schools with a majority of minorities, most of the students—two-thirds by most estimates—are poor. In predominantly White schools, by contrast, typically only about one-third of students are poor. Moreover, segregation by socioeconomic class has notably increased since the 1970s (Massey 2020; Reardon and Owens 2014).

Finally, even when schools are statistically integrated, there is often segregation within. In other words, a school may be numerically balanced in terms of the percentages of different racial-ethnic groups, but internal segregation means that they follow different paths—both educationally and socially. White students are more likely to be placed in college-prep courses, AP courses, and honors curricula, while students of color are more likely to be tracked into different classes. These patterns can result in highly segregated schools even when teachers and parents value racial integration (Lewis and Diamond 2015; Lewis, Diamond, and Forman 2015; Tyson, Darity, and Castellino 2005). Consequently, even when schools desegregate, "racial inequality [remains] embedded in organization structures and processes" (Lewis and Diamond 2015:86).

The cost of school segregation is high. As Gary Orfield, a national expert on schools and resegregation, puts it, "Segregation feeds stratification, inequality, and the denial of opportunity" (2013:44). Young people of color, as a result, suffer from a continuing achievement gap on various measures of educational attainment.

Race and the Achievement Gap

Framing Question: How has racial segregation affected educational achievement, and what explains the achievement gap?

No one doubts the value of a good education. A good education can lead to opportunities that would be otherwise unattainable. Indeed, the belief in education as a path to upward mobility is a strong part of the American Dream. Yet every day we see evidence of failure in US schools. News of failing students, discontented teachers, dilapidated facilities, and inadequate educational resources frequent the headlines. At the heart of these concerns are huge racial disparities—disparities so stark that commentator Jonathan Kozol calls them the "shame of the nation." Kozol even goes so far as to say that the nation operates *apartheid schools*—a reference to the different education children of color receive relative to White children (Kozol 2006 and 2012). The result is the racial *achievement gap*.

Race and Educational Outcomes

The **achievement gap** refers to racial differences in educational opportunity, learning, and achievement. The achievement gap is extensively documented and indicated by various measures. The gap matters for individual students, because having a good education is increasingly important for success in the current economic structure; that is, the best jobs demand the skills a well-educated person is expected to be able to develop. Education also matters for society as a whole, because the nation needs not just the scientific skills but also the critical thinking and social intelligence that education promises to deliver. Without a well-educated citizenry, the nation simply cannot compete efficiently in the increasingly global and technological economy.

In fact, the United States is losing ground in educational stature relative to other nations. Compared to other economically developed nations—Asia and various European nations—the United States ranks poorly on standardized international math and science tests, known as PISA (Programme for International Student Assessment) tests (see figure 9.5). Furthermore, the poor US performance is largely

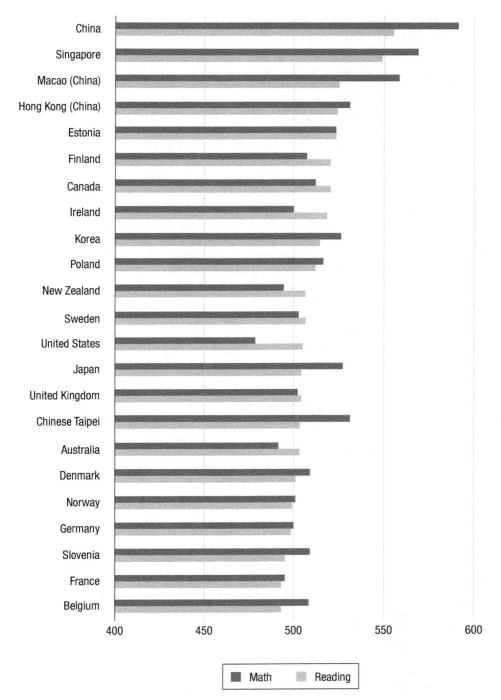

FIG. 9.5 Mean International Scores on PISA Tests

Source: Schleicher 2019.

explained by the gap in White and Asian versus Black and Latino test scores (Darling-Hammond 2010). In other words, were the nation to close the racial achievement gap, not only would students of color benefit, but the nation's educational standing would also improve relative to the rest of the world. As Linda Darling-Hammond, renowned education scholar, puts it, "It is our continuing comfort with profound inequality that is the Achilles heel of American education" (2010:8).

Differences in educational achievement are the subject of much highly detailed and telling research. On numerous measures, Black and Latino students lag behind White and Asian American students. Some progress has been made, however, and many students of color have been successful in the nation's schools. Progress is unsteady, however. The racial gap in achievement also closed substantially from the 1960s into the 1980s as schools desegregated (Orfield 2013).

More recently, the gap between Black and White and between Hispanic and White students has narrowed, explained by the fact that Black and Hispanic scores on achievement tests have been rising faster than those of White students. Achievement gaps also vary considerably from state to state. States where the disparities in educational achievement are greatest are those where there are also the largest racial gaps in income, poverty, and unemployment, suggesting that addressing the nation's growing inequality would go a long way toward reducing the disparities in student achievement (Educational Opportunity Monitoring Project 2020).

Underachievement in school is the result of a complex and prolonged series of steps in which students of color are underresourced, poorly taught, overly punished, and, as a result, more likely to fail or drop out. Underachievement accounts for the large difference in educational attainment that is still present across racial and ethnic groups (see figure 9.6). What is more, the differences found in earlier education carry over into differences in student achievement in college (Byrd, Brunn-Bevel, and Sexton 2014). Black and Latino college students, for example, are overrepresented in the least selective colleges and underrepresented in the nation's more selective colleges and universities (Supiano 2015).

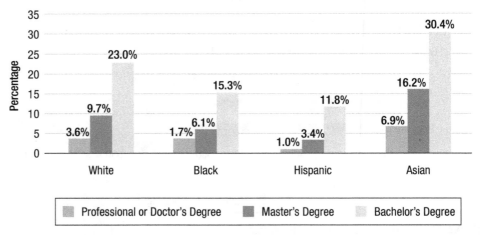

FIG. 9.6 Higher Educational Attainment by Race, 2018 (Persons 18 Years and Older)

Source: National Center for Education Statistics 2019.

Measures of educational achievement are typically based on nationally standardized exams, but other measures also show the seriousness of this problem. School dropout rates show that Native American, Black, and Latino students graduate from high school less frequently than Whites. Students of color are, in fact, overrepresented in every category that measures the achievement gap—dropout and graduation rates, school suspensions, college attendance, and others (National Center for Education Statistics 2012; Noguera 2008). The result for Latino and African American students is *subtractive schooling*—that is, an educational process that "divests youth of important social and cultural resources, leaving them progressively vulnerable to academic failure" (Valenzuela 1999:3).

Explaining the Achievement Gap

Scholars document the many ways in which students of color are vulnerable to poor educational outcomes. The big question is why these students are so vulnerable.

Black and Latino parents are often blamed for their children's level of achievement because of a misconception that Black and Latino parents do not value education. Research, though, finds that the average Black parent actually values education more and has higher expectations for their child than does the average White parent. Black parents are also just as involved in their children's education as are White parents. National data also show that Black high school students are more likely than White students to discuss grades and school issues with their parents and friends (Blau 2003; Harris 2011; Lewis and Diamond 2015). Blaming parents for the racial achievement gap simply does not hold up through research.

Others claim that students of color are influenced by an *oppositional culture*. The argument is that students underachieve because they think of school success as "acting White." Researchers have failed to find strong support for this idea, although some suggest that if this influence exists, it is more likely among Black students who are attending predominantly White high schools. Studies find overall, however, that Black students are actually very much like White students in their attitudes about grades, college attendance, and other measures of achievement (Lewis and Diamond 2015; Tyson 2011).

In general, Black students seem to have more proschool attitudes than do White students. Furthermore, high-achieving Black students tend to be the most popular among their peers. In short, there is little consistent support for the idea that students of color disdain academic success. Certainly school peer cultures stratify social groups—geeks, jocks, stoners, and so forth—and all students, regardless of race, have to navigate this tricky terrain of social hierarchies and social judgments. Students of color have the additional burden of having to navigate the terrain of racism, and they are very much aware of having to do so (Carter 2007; Harris 2011; Lewis and Diamond 2015).

Many people typically blame parents and young people of color for educational failure, but the main reason for the achievement gap is inequality in schools. On virtually every measure of school quality—test scores, class size, teacher qualifications and turnover, facilities and district spending, and the presence of a college-preparatory curriculum—schools with large majorities of Black and Latino students fall below predominantly White schools (Darling-Hammond 2010; Ladson-Billings 2006; Noguera 2008).

While it is too soon to know the long-term impact that the COVID-19 pandemic will have on the educational achievement gap, there is no doubt that the effect will be strong. When schools shut down in 2020, virtually all students in the United States missed face-to-face instruction. In many cases, when they could, parents had to take on some degree of home schooling. But the pandemic further exposed and likely will further exacerbate racial and social class differences in educational achievement. We already know that the closure of schools even during a normal summer results in a significant loss in learning. Students who entered the pandemic with an existing deficit in learning are less likely to make up that deficit upon the reopening of schools. Also, the quality of education that students have received in a virtual format during the pandemic has been affected by such things as access to the Internet and whether parents were working in or out of the home and able to home school their children. Children living in less safe neighborhoods—or violent families—might also have found school to be a safer place than home, thus affecting learning. Any way we look at it, we are likely to find that the pandemic will have worsened, not lessened, preexisting gaps in educational achievement (Rothstein 2020; Slay 2020; Soland et al. 2020).

Inequality in schools means there are different educational opportunities for students. Teachers with strong academic backgrounds and certification produce students who achieve more. On every measure of teacher quality (certification, subject matter training, pedagogical training, experience, and college attended), schools that serve large numbers of minority students have generally less qualified teachers. In addition, even when teachers are strong, teacher turnover in such schools is very high (Darling-Hammond 2010).

Curriculum differences in schools that serve predominantly minority students also put those students at an educational disadvantage. Students simply learn more when they have a high-quality curriculum that prepares them for college-level work, ample and current textbooks, and modern laboratory facilities and libraries. The absence of such high-quality curricula and learning environments in predominantly minority schools reverberates in the educational achievement of the students who attend these schools.

Within the same schools, **tracking**—separating students according to presumed ability—puts many students of color at a disadvantage. Much research shows that racial-ethnic minority and lower-income students are overrepresented in lower tracks within schools. At the same time, they are underrepresented in tracks that provide honors experiences, advanced placement courses, and other programs for gifted students (Oakes 2005; Tyson 2011). That a student of color is in a lower track can also reinforce teachers' lower expectations that the student will learn.

A final explanation for the achievement gap is the impact of school discipline. Increased policing, cameras in schools, and zero-tolerance policies have contributed to a disciplinary regime in schools that tends to criminalize any student who violates school rules (Kupchik 2010). This burden has fallen especially hard on Latino and African American students. Studies find that many teachers tend to perceive Black and Latino youth as dangerous and threatening, thus subjecting them to more surveillance and discipline. Subjective judgments, for example, about Latino and Black youth who display a "street" style in their dress and demeanor can cast them in a negative light. Once a student is labeled a deviant, the label sticks, and punishment might come more often, in a process that has been called the "school to prison pipeline" (Ferguson 2000; Shedd 2015).

In schools, Black and Latino students are more likely to be put in detention, suspended, or expelled. In fact, Black students are seven times more likely to be punished than are White students and Latinos twice as likely. Asian American students, however, may be viewed through the "model minority" stereotype that protects them from disciplinary action (Ferguson 2000; Morris and Perry 2016). You might conclude that differing punishments occur because Black and Latino students misbehave more. Studies show, however, that Black and Latino students are punished more *even when there is no difference in how students actually behave*. Even when Black and Latino students engage in the same behaviors as White students, Black and Latino students are more likely to be punished. Boys, especially, engage in a broad range of disruptive behaviors at school, but African American boys are far more often referred to disciplinary authorities. The behavior of students of color is more frequently responded to with disciplinary action based strictly on subjective judgments by those in authority (Morris 2005; Rios 2011; Skiba et al. 2002).

How much of the achievement gap can be explained by the fact that students of color are also more likely to be poor? No doubt, poverty is a large part of the problem in education. When large numbers of disadvantaged students are concentrated in a school, educational achievement drops. Moreover, the concentration of low-income minority students in schools has been increasing nationwide, a function of the increase in concentrated poverty (Rothstein 2013).

With more than 20 percent of the nation's children living below the poverty line and even larger percentages of Black and Hispanic children among the poor, US schools are not immune from poverty's grip. In schools with large numbers of poor children, all students—both the poor and the nonpoor—do worse. Moreover, low-income students in high-poverty schools do worse than poor students who attend more affluent schools (Darling-Hammond 2010).

Poverty alone, however, cannot account for the entire gap in educational achievement. Race and poverty are so entangled that it is often difficult to tease out the influence of one or the other. Still, race also matters in and of itself, as demonstrated through the volumes of research showing the impact of race on educational experiences. Denying that race matters in shaping educational experiences is a sure way to miss much of what happens as students progress through their education. Social class, including poverty, surely shapes the experiences of different groups of students, but if we do not include race as part of the picture, we will not fully understand the challenges students of color face—at all levels of education.

Failing schools rob children of the social and cultural capital that enables success. **Social capital** refers to the access people have to networks and relationships that bolster their progress in life. *Cultural capital* refers to the noneconomic assets that a person holds, often by virtue of education. Cultural capital includes not only a person's knowledge but also what is referred to as soft skills: speech patterns, general demeanor, social networks, and etiquette, to name a few. Just like money, cultural capital is an asset in that it provides people with a form of power and access to the dominant culture. Without it, a person remains an outsider.

Social and cultural types of capital are both enhanced by a high-quality education. Each provides a tool kit that helps people navigate their way through society. Education, of course, imparts skills—reading, critical thinking, calculating skills, and so forth—but social and cultural capital are just as valuable, albeit more subjective. When functioning well, schools impart social and cultural capital as well as knowledge, but schools tend to reward students who already bring certain kinds of cultural capital into the schools with them (Lewis and Diamond 2015). Such factors as educated parents, early reading, and exposure to the arts all can give students a leg up even before they enter school. Although we think of schools as great equalizers, they in fact tend to reproduce any inequalities that existed before students began their formal education.

The reasons for the racial achievement gap are many, and they overlap, making policy solutions particularly complex. Explanations of the achievement gap include many levels of analysis—the social structures of schools, patterns of social interaction, and the beliefs and perceptions that teachers and students have of racial-ethnic groups. These parts of the achievement gap, as educational specialists conclude, "mutually reinforce each other and collectively generate different educational trajectories" (Lewis and Diamond 2015:167).

Succeeding against the Odds: Race and School Success

Framing Question: What factors affect the possibility of achievement in education even in the context of racial inequality?

Studying the racial achievement gap reveals the enormous social forces that are impeding educational attainment for students of color. The harm done to the nation's children is great in terms of lost potential, both to individual children and to society as a whole. No doubt the forces of racial inequality in the schools contribute to the stubborn persistence of an underclass and to the nation's ability to compete in the new global economy. But what if we think about education in a different way and ask not just what impedes the education of minority youth but also how students of color succeed?

Shaun Harper, an education professor, has done just that. Harper conducted a national study of African American college men, interviewing them on forty-two different college campuses around the United States. His focus on Black men is especially important because they make up one of the most disadvantaged groups in terms of high school completion, college attendance, and college graduation. By focusing on successful men, Harper challenged what he calls a *deficit perspective*; he developed a framework that identifies how students of color find their way to success even in the context of a racially unequal landscape (Harper 2012 and 2015).

Harper found that achieving Black men had parents who consistently held high expectations for their sons' education, even if the parents were not themselves college-educated. Parental influence alone was not enough, however. Influential teachers, beginning in early schooling, also ensured that the young men had the information, resources, and support needed to succeed in school. These three things—*information*, *resources*, and *support*—were critical throughout students' educational paths (Harper 2015).

Information can be as basic as understanding what courses are needed in high school (or earlier) to be competitive in college admissions. It can also mean understanding the college admissions process and potential funding sources. Resources include financial support but also such things as the availability of books, test preparation, and other crucial educational materials. Support could also refer to financial support, but, critically, it also means the support of peers, teachers, and community leaders. Finally, the students in Harper's research had to be able to respond to the racism they encountered in college (or school) through engaging in productive social networks, not just getting angry (Harper 2015).

Harper's research is consistent with what many other scholars have found about student success. Support from family, peers, and teachers is critical, but individual resources are not enough. Research on Latinas, for example, finds that being successful in school means carving paths that provide mentoring support and information while also maintaining a positive Latina identity and forming group ties that affirm Latina identity (Barajas and Pierce 2001). Such identity work can be especially critical when students of color enter educational institutions that are culturally structured as middle-class White environments. Learning how to navigate such environments is a key part of student success (Stephens et al. 2012). Teachers and others can help by creating classroom experiences that promote what scholars call *identity safety*—that is, classroom environments that empower students of color by acknowledging racial realities and using student diversity as a teaching resource, not a handicap (Steele and Cohn-Vargas 2013).

Ensuring the educational success of students of color is not simply a matter of individual identities or individual relationships. Schools have to structure resources to help students of color succeed. Such practices can cultivate success for students of color and, in so doing, will likely enhance educational paths for all students.

Conclusion

Since the days of Jim Crow segregation, there has been much progress in reducing residential and educational segregation, even if major problems remain. Progress is being challenged, though, by retrenchment in the courts, weak enforcement of existing policies, and the attitude that we no longer need racially based interventions.

Key decisions by the US Supreme Court have limited possible remedies for school desegregation. For example, in *Milliken v. Bradley* (1974) the Supreme Court ruled that school systems were not responsible for desegregation across district lines unless they had intentionally discriminated. Discrimination is now rarely so explicit. A series of such cases has meant that court-ordered desegregation efforts have declined, evidenced by the resegregation of schools.

National educational policy has also tended to make individual schools or school districts responsible for change. Teachers often shoulder the blame. How schools are funded also robs poorer districts of the resources to create better schools. In other nations, education is usually funded centrally. In the United States schools rely on local taxes, meaning that low-income areas simply have fewer resources to build better schools. Although there is not a perfect correlation between funding and school quality, there is a strong association (Darling-Hammond 2010).

There is clearly a strong link between educational and residential segregation, and reducing either will require attention to both. With regard to housing, fair housing policy includes a wide range of programs designed to eliminate discrimination and reduce segregation. These include targeting predatory lending practices, reporting landlord abuses, and monitoring cases of discrimination. Federal housing policy has shifted from densely packed, large public housing units to voucher programs designed to disperse people rather than concentrate them into dense high-crime areas. In principle, housing voucher programs reduce concentrated poverty, but the concentration of poor people in inner cities has meant that these programs have had a negligible impact (DeLuca, Garboden, and Rosenblatt 2013). Also, better-off communities, when faced with the possibility of affordable housing coming into their area, often organize to prevent it, arguing that it will affect their own property values (Semuels 2015).

Public attitudes also shape the nation's response to segregation. A large majority of the American public says they would prefer to live in a community made up of a mix of different races (Pew Research Center 2008), but few actually live in such communities. Further, more than three-quarters of White Americans say that Black children have as good a chance as White children to get a good education (Gallup editors 2014). Inconsistency in the beliefs and actions of so many White Americans confirms Malcolm X's famous observation that "America preaches integration and practices segregation" (in Haley 1963). The strong assumption that change should be color-blind and not race-specific when race still matters thwarts attempts to continue the nation's work toward desegregating neighborhoods and schools (Darby and Saatcioglu 2014).

"Social distance can breed contempt," says Bryan Stevenson, founder and director of the Equal Justice Initiative (Stevenson 2015b). His statement reminds us that racial segregation breeds misunderstanding, stereotypes, and accusations of blame leveled against society's most vulnerable. Without a renewed societal commitment to ending the segregation that divides us, we fail a significant portion of the national citizenry, including failing a commitment to the nation's children. A renewed value placed on integration, not individualism, would go a long way toward ending the segregation that the civil rights movement fought so hard to overcome.

Key Terms

achievement gap 232

Brown v. Board of Education (1954) 217

Fair Housing Act of 1968 217

hypersegregation 220

index of dissimilarity 219

Plessy v. Ferguson (1896) 226

predatory lending 224

redlining 224

residential segregation 217

social capital 237

steering 223

subprime mortgages 224

tracking 236

White space 222

Critical-Thinking Questions

1. Review the two opening scenarios in this chapter. Given what you have learned in this chapter, what would you predict about the educational path of the two young girls? What would help them both achieve their educational dreams?
2. What does it mean to say that education reproduces the inequality already found in society at large?

Student Exercises

9.1. Go to CensusScope (https://www.censusscope.org) and click on the *Segregation* tab. Navigating the information on this website, report on the segregation indexes for an area of your choosing. Does segregation in this area vary for different racial-ethnic groups? Given what you might know about this particular area, what do you think explains the segregation patterns? Put together a report on which groups are the most segregated in the city you have chosen.

9.2. Using figure 9.4 as an example, construct a figure (or table) that gives an approximation of the racial composition in your high school. Would you describe your high school as integrated, segregated, or hypersegregated? What factors in your community explain this?

Challenging Questions/Open to Debate

Many of the gains made in closing the achievement gap from the 1960s into the 1980s came as a result of race-conscious desegregation efforts. Since then, schools have resegregated, and courts and school districts have largely lost what gains were made. Should *race-conscious* efforts to desegregate the schools be reimplemented, or should the nation allow *race-blind* policies to govern education?

TAKING ACTION AGAINST RACISM

Integrate with Intent

Identify an organization of which you are a part (a school, church, workplace, and so forth). Find out how well represented different racial-ethnic groups are in this location. Is your organization racially segregated or integrated? In what specific ways? What organizations in this place are promoting racial integration and how? Identify a project you could be part of that would promote racial integration.

Resource: Teaching Tolerance: https://www.tolerance.org

Source: AP Photo / L. M. Otero

CHAPTER 10

It Gets to You

Health Care and the Environment

*All communities and persons across this nation [should] live
in a safe and healthful environment.*
—President William Jefferson Clinton (1994)

OBJECTIVES

- Detail some of the indicators of health disparities by race and ethnicity
- Explain the reasons for persistent health disparities

- Identify different dimensions of institutional racism in the health care system
- Analyze the link between racism and reproductive health
- Define and explain environmental racism

The COVID-19 global pandemic that ravaged the world beginning in 2020 was a massive, worldwide disaster—the consequences of which are still unfolding. As the pandemic began to spread, people sometimes said that the virus knew no bounds and that anyone could get it. Viruses do not discriminate. Or do they?

Certainly during the pandemic everyone has been affected one way or another. In the United States alone, the death rate skyrocketed; schools closed; businesses shuttered; unemployment reached unprecedented levels; people were ordered to stay home. Everyone felt at risk—at least those who were listening to the warnings of scientists. And yet we know that in the United States there is a racial dimension to everything. The COVID-19 pandemic is no exception, as we will see in this chapter.

It is too soon to know the many ways that racism shaped the pandemic, although the influence of race—and class and gender and sexual orientation—will be studied for years to come. We will need more information and detailed research to uncover all of the implications of this national—indeed, international—disaster in economic, social, political, cultural, and medical terms. We will not know the full impact of this horrid pandemic on our lives and on our different social institutions for years. But there are some things we know already:

- As the disaster unfolded, then-president Donald Trump insisted on calling COVID-19 the "Chinese virus." Hate crimes against Asian Americans spiked. In the latter half of March 2020 alone, there were over one thousand reports to an antihate website from Asian Americans who had experienced physical assaults, verbal abuse, or other forms of discrimination. The FBI, which monitors hate crime in the United States, warned that such crimes were likely to surge (Margolin 2020).
- Anyone with a preexisting health condition was more susceptible to the lethal effects of the coronavirus. African Americans are known to have higher rates of asthma, diabetes, and hypertension—all underlying conditions that made racial disparities a likely correlate to the rate of infection and the likelihood of death from COVID-19 (Centers for Disease Control and Prevention 2020).
- Being in densely populated areas creates a greater risk of infection. Because people of color are more likely to live in overcrowded areas, they were more vulnerable to the disease. Multigenerational households, more common among Latinos and African Americans, posed another risk of contracting the virus (Centers for Disease Control and Prevention 2020).
- In the places where illness and death rates were reported by race, we could see that African Americans and Latinos were more likely to be ill or die than would have been expected, given their share of the population. Nationally, African American deaths are twice as high as their proportion in the population. Latinos also make up a greater share of confirmed cases than would be predicted from their size in the population; in some places Latino deaths were four times the proportional rate. As one example, in Wisconsin, African Americans were 27 percent of deaths from COVID-19, although they are only 6 percent of the population. And in Virginia, where Latinos are 10 percent off the population, by mid-2020 they accounted for nearly half of all cases (Centers for Disease Control and Prevention 2020; Godoy 2020; Johnson and Buford 2020; Kendi 2020; Neavling 2020).

- High rates of unemployment were unprecedented for all groups, but Latino and African American unemployment was higher than for White workers, and more Latinos than other groups said someone in their household had taken a pay cut or lost a job as a direct result of the pandemic (Allard and Brundage 2019; Krogstad, Gonzalez-Barrera, and Noe-Bustamante 2020; US Bureau of Labor Statistics 2020a).
- Latino, African American, and Asian American workers are overrepresented in low-wage service work—occupations that made heroes of many but also put these essential workers at risk of contracting the disease (US Bureau of Labor Statistics 2019a).
- American Indians, Native Alaskans, Hispanics, and African Americans are the groups least likely to have health insurance (see figure 10.4, later in this chapter). They are thus less likely to have access to the best health care.
- The digital divide means that people of color and low-income groups are less likely to have access to the Internet, which was crucial during the pandemic for such things as delivery services, information, and contact via social media. People with less access to the Internet might also be less well informed about the disease and more socially isolated.
- Income disparities mean that better off people would likely be better able to stock up on food and needed medical supplies.
- People with more limited cell phone plans, by virtue of rural isolation or low income, would have had less data on their plans, thus making them less able to connect continuously to family and friends during lockdowns.

Well into the future we will learn of the many dimensions of this disaster—a disaster that in some ways knew no bounds but in other ways had a different impact on the nation's most vulnerable populations. As important as the medical response is to such a virus, social factors—including the social behavior of racism—is just as significant in the spread and treatment of this health crisis.

It Makes You Sick: Race and Health Disparities

Framing Question: In what ways does racism shape differences in people's patterns of health?

There are many indicators of racial and ethnic differences in health and wellness. On virtually every measure, racial-ethnic minorities in the United States have poorer health than Whites. As we will see below, racial disparities are found in higher rates of mortality, early onset of disease, and greater severity and consequences of disease. Furthermore, health disparities for people of color have persisted over time and at all levels of income and education (Williams and Mohammed 2013).

This is made clear to some extent when answering a simple question: Did you get a good night's sleep last night? Being short on sleep is highly associated with an increased risk of early mortality, but how well you sleep is also associated with your racial, ethnicity, gender, and occupational status. If you are Black, you are quite likely to be short on sleep compared to Whites and Latinos. Among both Blacks and Latinos, being short on sleep increases with higher professional status. For Whites, the reverse is true: Whites are shorter on sleep when in lower-status roles. Black women professional workers have the least sleep of all. White women professionals are the least likely to be short on sleep (Jackson et al. 2014). These facts may surprise you, but they point to the significance of race and social class in predicting an important measure of good health.

You would expect, with some improvement in the socioeconomic status of racial minorities, that health disparities would be declining. In a few instances they are, but with some health conditions the disparities have actually increased. As an example, in 1950 Black and White Americans had comparable death rates from heart disease and cancer. Now African Americans have higher death rates from these two diseases than do Whites (National Center for Health Statistics 2019). Black women are also still more likely to get breast cancer at an early age and are diagnosed at later disease stages (Dean at al. 2014). The sections below examine some of the evidence of health care disparities, including a discussion of the reasons for such inequalities.

Race: A Matter of Life and Death

Starting with the simple reality of a person's **life expectancy**—the average number of years a person born in a particular year can expect to live—race and ethnicity matter. Life expectancy in the United States has increased for all groups over time, but significant differences remain based on both race and gender. Women in every racial-ethnic group live longer than their male counterparts, but African American men have the shortest life expectancy of all (National Center for Health Statistics 2019; see figure 10.1).

Hispanics actually have longer life expectancy than do White non-Hispanics—a phenomenon referred to as the *Hispanic paradox* (Markides and Eschbach 2011). You would think that Hispanic life expectancy would be more comparable to that of African Americans, given the similarity in their socioeconomic status. It appears that one reason for the longer life expectancy of Hispanics is their lower rate of smoking (Lariscy et al. 2016), but experts do not yet have a complete understanding of this paradox, nor whether it will hold up during the pandemic.

The timing and cause of death is also somewhat predictable based on race. **Death rate** (also called the *mortality rate*) is calculated by measuring the number of deaths in a given population, relative to the population size, in a given period of time. Death rates are often adjusted by age to account for the different age distribution within racial-ethnic populations. To provide an example, the age-adjusted death rate for all diseases in 2018 for non-Hispanic Whites was 734.5 per 100,000 in the population but higher for African Americans at 854.1 per 100,000. For other groups, the death rate was lower: Native Americans/Alaska Natives, 587.5; Hispanics/Latinos, 524.7; and Asian and Pacific Islanders, 393.6 (National Center for Health Statistics 2019). Again, the impact of COVID-19 remains unknown.

In addition to the overall death rate, the major causes of death for different populations are also shaped by race and ethnicity. African Americans have higher rates of death than do Whites for all of the leading causes of death (heart disease, cancer, stroke, diabetes, and homicide; National Center for Health Statistics 2019). In fact, experts have estimated that about one hundred thousand Black people die prematurely each year. Were there no racial disparities in health, Black people would not die so young (Kung et al. 2008; Williams and Mohammed 2009 and 2013).

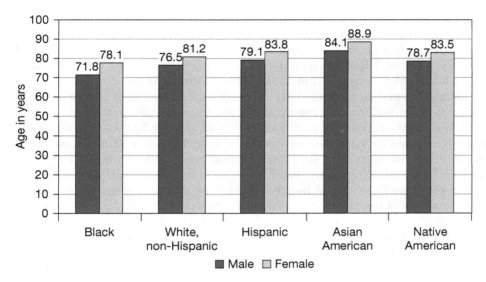

FIG. 10.1 Life Expectancy in the United States by Racial Group (2014)

Source: Arias 2016.

Patterns of death vary for different diseases but are strongly based on a person's social status. Native Americans, for example, have lower death rates from heart disease and cancer compared to Whites and African Americans but are more likely to die from motor vehicle accidents. Latinos also have lower death rates from heart disease and cancer than do Whites but have higher death rates from influenza. Asian Americans have the best health of all. You must be careful interpreting this statistic, however, because the category "Asian American" includes many different groups, as is also true for Latinos, and there can be great divergence in health within these groups.

For all groups, health also varies with a person's gender and social class status. As a result, a complex intersectional analysis is critical for understanding detailed patterns of health in the United States. One illustration of this concept is in how the combined influence of race and gender predicts death rates by various causes. Homicide is the fifth leading cause of death for African American men, the only group for whom this cause of death is among the top ten causes of death. Death from HIV/AIDS is also shockingly high among African American men, who are eight times as likely to die from HIV as are Whites. Hispanics are twice as likely as Whites to die from HIV (National Center for Health Statistics 2019). Health, no doubt, is a physiological reality, but understanding that reality requires a social, not just physiological, analysis. Race, given its centrality to social context, must be part of our understanding of health.

Another important indicator of the health status of different populations is **infant mortality**, measured as the number of infant deaths—counting those under one year of age—in a given year per one thousand births. In fact, infant mortality is commonly used as an indicator of a nation's well-being as a whole.

Infant mortality is quite low in the United States compared to that of other nations of the world (5.7 per one thousand births in 2018), but infant mortality among African Americans and Native Americans gives a more disturbing picture of the nation's health. Infant mortality for African Americans was 10.8; for American Indians and Alaska Natives, 8.2 in 2018 (Ely and Driscoll 2020).

Among Latinos in the United States, overall infant mortality is actually quite low, but varies in different Latino populations. Puerto Ricans in the United States have a higher infant mortality rate than do Whites (5.6 per 1,000 births for Puerto Ricans, compared to 4.6 for non-Hispanic Whites), but other Latinos have lower rates of infant mortality than do Whites. Latinos born outside of the United States also have lower infant mortality than have those born within the United States. No one has yet figured out why, although experts think that having strong community ties may be part of the explanation (Viruell-Fuentes et al. 2013).

No doubt poverty also plays a role in determining a group's infant mortality rate. The good news is that, for all groups, infant mortality rates have declined significantly since the 1980s and continue to do so (Ely and Driscoll 2020). This is an indication that the nation can do more to reduce infant mortality.

Feeling the Burden: Stress and Hypertension

Everybody knows what stress is. Whether because of studying for exams, working long hours, or just feeling frazzled by too much to do, everyone feels stress at one time or another. Chronic stress, though, can produce **hypertension**, a condition of elevated blood pressure. Elevated blood pressure is physiological, but physicians know that blood pressure varies depending on social and environmental conditions. You might have, at one time or another, experienced *white coat syndrome*, the elevation in blood pressure that commonly occurs simply by going to the doctor's office. Such an elevation in blood pressure, though, is typically fleeting. Hypertension based on racial inequality can be life changing.

African American men and now Mexican-origin men are the two groups in the United States most likely to live with uncontrolled hypertension. Even while they are sleeping, African Americans maintain higher levels of blood pressure than Whites (National Center for Health Statistics 2019). Why?

One answer is that racism itself is a source of stress. Constantly being on the alert for potential insults or other microaggressions wears a person down. Medical researchers have concluded that racial differences in stress not only exist but also are the key factor linking racial status to poor health.

Simply put, cumulative exposure to stress from racism is detrimental to health. In studies of exposure to stress, researchers consistently find that African Americans—men especially—have a higher prevalence of stress and more accumulation of different stresses than do Whites. Latinos born in the United States also have prevalence rates and patterns of stress similar to African Americans. Foreign-born Hispanics are more similar to White Americans in their stress profiles. Financial and relationship problems are the most prevalent causes of stress in the US population. There is little doubt that experiencing multiple sources of stress is correlated with poor physical and mental health (Sternthal, Slopen, and Williams 2011).

Race and Risk: Alcohol and Substance Abuse

Behaviors such as smoking, drinking, and drug abuse are all known health risks, and they have a racial dimension. Without actual data, racial stereotypes prevent some people from knowing who engages in various risky behaviors. Contrary to stereotypes, for example, American Indians are *less likely* to be heavy alcohol users than are Whites. Whites are actually the group most likely to report current use of alcohol. And on college campuses, African American, Latino, and Asian students are much less likely to be binge drinkers compared to White students (National Center for Health Statistics 2019; Substance Abuse and Mental Health Services Administration 2014).

Patterns of illegal drug use also vary by race and ethnicity. The use of illegal drugs is highest among American Indian, Alaska Natives, Native Hawaiians, Pacific Islanders, and those identified as two or more races. Illicit drug use is lowest among Asian Americans. Usage varies, however, depending on the substance. Marijuana and the misuse of prescription drugs are the most common forms of substance abuse among all people in the United States, but Asian Americans are the least likely to have used marijuana in the past year (Substance Abuse and Mental Health Services Administration 2019).

Public concern about substance abuse of late has focused on the misuse of opioids—a class of drugs that includes heroin and various synthetic painkillers. For many years, opioids in the form of heroin were identified as primarily a problem involving poor, urban people of color. But heroin use has changed and now involves mostly White men and women in their late twenties and who live outside urban areas. Estimates are that as many as 90 percent of those misusing prescription opioids are White (Cicero et al. 2014; Om 2018).

Nonetheless, racial bias continues to play a role in the response to the opioid crises. Drug sentences remain much higher for Black users than for Whites. How opioid abuse has been depicted in the media also has a strong racial dimension. Detailed content analyses of the popular press over ten years (2001 to 2011) show that Black and Latino heroin users are typically criminalized, whereas White, suburban users (mostly women) are portrayed sympathetically (Netherland 2016).

It is easy to attribute risky behaviors such as substance abuse to individual factors, but individual behaviors have a social context. For example, there is some evidence that young people of color are less likely to drink because they perceive (and rightly so) a greater risk if they are seen as being out of control. Among African Americans and Latinos, having a strong religious faith also seems to deter drinking. The use of illicit drugs also depends on the drugs' availability and expense (Holt et al. 2015; Keyes et al. 2015; Wade and Peralta 2017). With regard to opioid misuse, researchers find that physicians' racial bias leads them to prescribe painkillers less often to people of color. Some also argue that factors such as a strong feeling of belonging in a racial or ethnic community lessens the abuse of illegal substances. This does not mean that substance abuse is not a problem among minority populations. It is only to say that social context is an important part of explaining differences in risk-taking behavior.

Race Weighs In: Obesity and Eating Disorders

The impact of racism in the United States is lived in our bodies. Even such basic facts of health as a person's weight are patterned by racial inequality and, therefore, risks to health. Only 30 percent of the US population lives with what the National Institutes of Health defines as a *healthy body weight*—a measure of a person's weight relative to their height. As with other health measures, there are substantial differences in body weight because of race, ethnicity, and gender, as you can see in figure 10.2. Black women and Mexican-origin men are the least likely to have a healthy body weight. Black and White women, along with White, non-Hispanic men, are most likely to be overweight or obese. Poverty also influences weight: people living below the poverty line are less likely to be a healthy weight (National Center for Health Statistics 2019).

Being overweight is only one part of the problem. Eating disorders such as anorexia and bulimia are also associated with racial-ethnic identities. The beauty ideal for women in American culture is of a thin—often *extremely* thin—body. Women who internalize the extreme as an ideal are those most likely to develop eating disorders as they strive to attain this unhealthy look. For women of color, though, different cultural ideals that value larger women may mediate against disordered eating. White women are more likely to become anorexic and/or engage in extreme weight loss (National Center for Health Statistics 2019).

Now, however, more women of color are developing eating disorders in the form of anorexia and bulimia. Why? Studies find that eating disorders are more likely among women of color who identify with the dominant White cultural ideal. In other words, women are more at risk for eating disorders when they overly identify with a "culture of thinness." Women of color, however, are more likely to be at risk for eating disorders when they have low levels of ethnic identity—that is, when they adopt the White ideal of beauty, not the ideals traditionally specific to their own group (Opara and Santos 2019).

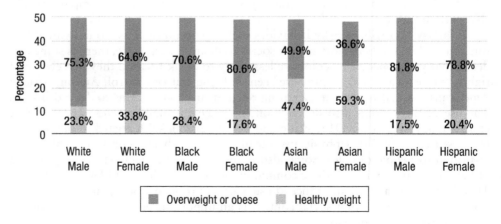

FIG. 10.2 Healthy Body Weight and Overweight/Obese in the United States

Source: National Center for Health Statistics 2019.

Immigrant Health

Given the high rate of immigration in the United States, health researchers are increasingly interested in immigrant health. In the United States, 60 percent of Asians and about one-third of Latinos are foreign-born (Flores 2017; López, Ruiz, and Patten 2017). Foreign-born people generally have better health outcomes than do their counterparts in the United States. Yet the longer an immigrant remains in the United States, the worse their health becomes. Why? Experts explain this as the result of geographic isolation, residential segregation, and the decline in socioeconomic status that tends to follow immigration. Researchers have also found that Latino immigrant neighborhoods have less access to green space, as their neighborhoods tend to have limited park availability (Garcia, Gee, and Jones 2016). This can affect a person's overall health.

To date, most studies of immigrant health have focused on Latinos. Research shows that Latinos born outside the United States, in general, have less heart disease, cancer, and other illnesses than do US–born Latinos. This may be in part because those in the best health are those most likely to make the migration journey, but it is also partially explained by the fact that Latinos are a younger population than other groups. Still, compared with US–born Latinos, foreign-born Latinos generally have fewer health problems (Centers for Disease Control and Prevention 2020; Consuelo Nacional de Población 2008).

Despite public myths that immigrants abuse the US health care system, the fact is that immigrants underutilize health care services. Per capita health care expenses are far less for Latino immigrants than for US–born Latinos. Latino immigrants have lower expenditures for emergency room visits, hospitalizations, and prescription drugs, with one exception: children. Expenses for emergency room visits by Latino immigrant children are higher than for US–born Mexican children, even though immigrant children use the emergency room less often. This is explained by the fact that Mexican immigrants wait longer to seek treatment and thus are sicker once they go to an emergency room (Mohanty 2006).

The greatest problem by far, however, for Mexican immigrants in the United States is their lack of health insurance. Estimates are that half of the Mexican immigrant population in the United States has no insurance coverage. Without insurance, a person is especially vulnerable when they get sick or injured (see figure 10.3).

Why Do Racial Health Disparities Persist?

Framing Question: How can we explain the persistence of racial disparities in health?

Documenting health care disparities is one matter and explaining them quite another. There are several reasons for racial health disparities, but two primary explanations are: (1) the connection between race and class; and, (2) the persistence of racial residential segregation.

The Race-Class Connection

One of the most important questions about health disparities in the United States is the relationship between race and social class. Are the disparities that we see primarily the result of the lower socioeconomic status of racial-ethnic populations? To some extent—perhaps a large extent—yes, but race and class both have effects of their own. Class and race are, in fact, so entangled that it can be difficult to parse out the influence of each.

In general, people in poor households, regardless of race, have poorer health and less access to high-quality health care. Various indicators of health are certainly tied to social class status. National surveys, for example, examine a broad range of health care quality measures, including access to preventive care, treatment for acute illnesses, chronic disease management, and the quality of health care settings, such as doctors' offices, emergency rooms, dialysis centers, nursing homes, hospices, home health care services, and so forth. No matter what measure of health we use, poverty matters.

Poverty is without question very hard on a person's health. Poverty brings higher rates of teenage pregnancy, higher levels of stress, higher infant mortality rates, lower birth weight for babies, and greater risk of crime and violence—all indicators of health. Concentrated poverty brings even greater exposure to environmental hazards, which then produce poor health outcomes. And during the COVID-19 pandemic, low-income status has surely been a factor in a person's risk of disease.

Because concentrated poverty is more common among African Americans and Latinos, poverty, race, and class intermingle in producing health outcomes. Even with the interaction of class and race, each has an independent effect on health (Barr 2014; LaVeist 2005; LaVeist and Isaac 2012). As one example, among African American women with college degrees, infant mortality rates are still higher than among White, Latina, and Asian women who have not completed high school (Green and Hamilton 2019).

Perhaps even more poignant is a study of military veterans finding that Black, Hispanic, and multiple-race veterans have poorer health and higher levels of activity limitations once they return home from military service. Why? Class status explains some of this pattern, but so do military experiences. Black, Latino, and multiple-race soldiers, even accounting for social class, are exposed to greater harms during military service (Sheehan et al. 2015).

No doubt, social class is a significant correlate of whether a person has good health or bad, but race matters in and of itself. One way to see this is through the impact of racial segregation on health outcomes.

Racial Segregation and Its Connection to Health

Racial segregation also has serious consequences for a person's health, a fact that has become painfully obvious during the COVID-19 pandemic. Indeed, racial segregation is one of the major reasons for racial health disparities in the United States. Residential segregation is strongly associated with various measures of health. The social isolation that results from segregation, for example, is known to affect the health of African Americans. Studies of Latinos also show that those in the most highly segregated Latino neighborhoods have relatively little access to medical specialists and, thus, poorer health outcomes (Anderson 2017).

In general, people living in racially segregated neighborhoods also have less access to facilities that promote good health. This includes quality health care services and the presence of nearby stores that sell healthy food. Such stores are rarer in segregated minority neighborhoods (Larimore 2018).

Many studies have documented that residential segregation is related to a variety of negative health outcomes: preterm births, stress, and the likelihood of specific diseases. The linkage of residential segregation to crime also creates health risks because of the greater likelihood of violence, including the threat of violence by the police (Kwate and Threadcraft 2017).

Highly segregated cities are also bad for White people's health, although not to the same extent as for Black and Latino residents. Segregated cities also harm White people's health because such cities tend to have characteristics that harm everyone. Exposure to pathogens, congestion, and higher crime rates, to name a few such features, mean that everyone's well-being is compromised. Specialists have concluded that were living conditions more equal, racial health disparities would likely diminish (Collins and Williams 1999; LaVeist et al. 2011).

Institutional Racism and the Health Care System

Framing Question: How does institutional racism shape the health care system?

People of color's reduced access to quality health care and treatment in the health care system in general is a major reason for their poor health outcomes. As one example, see "Living with Racism," below. Large disparities with regard to care for people of color have been well documented. As just one example, as you can see in figure 10.3, people of color have fewer paid sick days at work than other groups. There have been recent improvements recently in general access to decent health care in the United States, most notably in greater health insurance coverage since the passage of the Affordable Care Act in 2010 (addressed in more detail below). Whether these improvements will persist with changes in this federal law remain to be seen. On various other measures, however, disparities of care remain, especially for African Americans and other people of color (National Center for Health Statistics 2019).

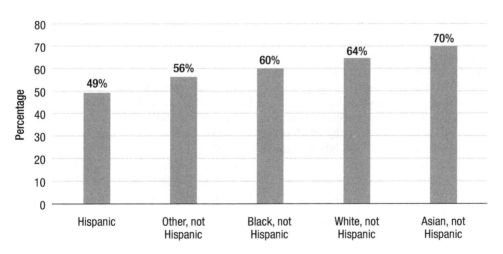

FIG. 10.3 Who Has Access to Paid Sick Days?

Note: Percentages are calculated for employees eighteen years and older. "Other, not Hispanic" includes American Indians, Alaska Natives, and those reporting multiple race identities. They are grouped together to protect anonymity because they were small populations in the national sample.

Source: Institute for Women's Policy Research 2016.

The Immortal Life of Henrietta Lacks

At a once-unmarked grave in rural Virginia now stands a memorial to a largely unknown Black woman whose death has since saved countless numbers of lives. Henrietta Lacks was a tobacco farmer in rural Virginia, part of an extended family descended from slaves. In 1951, Henrietta Lacks went to Johns Hopkins Hospital in Baltimore for what she felt as a knot in her abdomen. Hopkins was the closest hospital to her that would treat Black patients. She was diagnosed with cervical cancer and died a few months later at the age of thirty-one after experiencing terrible pain as the cancer metastasized throughout her body.

Unbeknownst to Lacks's family, doctors cultured some of her cancer cells when she died. For reasons still unknown, other people's cancer cells lived only for a few days, which prevented their use in biomedical research, whereas Henrietta Lacks's cells lived on, allowing scientists to put the cells into mass production. The *HeLa cells*, named in her honor, have become the basis for groundbreaking research of cancer and countless cancer treatments over the years.

Henrietta Lacks's story has been largely unknown; until the early twenty-first century her family knew nothing about how her cells had influenced the development of biomedical research. Author and journalist Rebecca Skloot, sharing the proceeds of her best-selling book, *The Immortal Life of Henrietta Lacks*, created the Henrietta Lacks Foundation, which provides financial support to people in need, including members of Lacks's family, because they have contributed to so much scientific research even without their knowledge or consent.

Sources: Skloot 2010; also visit the Henrietta Lacks Foundation, online at http://henriettalacksfoundation.org.

Institutional racism in the health care system is clearly part of the reason so many people of color in the United States suffer worse health outcomes. Institutional racism shows up in the inadequate delivery of health care to people of color as well as in the biases that health care providers are likely to hold. Overall people of color, especially if poor, receive less costly and less intensive medical care. For example, Black and White women are the most likely to get mammograms and American Indians and Alaska Native the least (National Center for Health Statistics 2019). Racial-ethnic minorities underutilize health care services in general, a pattern partially explained by socioeconomic status but also by the fact that people of color are less likely than Whites to have a regular source of care. Numerous studies have found that health care providers also treat people of color differently. For example, racial-ethnic patients are subjected to longer waiting times in emergency rooms because of the stereotypes held by emergency room staff, who too often, as one study showed, hesitate to treat Black people whom they perceive to be criminals (Lara-Millan 2014).

Studies have also documented that Black, Hispanic, and Asian patients, especially children, are less likely to be given pain medications for things like broken bones. One such study showed that Black children being treated for appendicitis in hospital emergency rooms are far less likely than White children to be given pain medication (Goyal et al. 2015). Another study of emergency rooms finds that Black patients are 60 percent less likely than other groups to get pain medications even for the same reported levels of pain (Fleegler and Schechter 2015). Researchers explain these differences as resulting from bias on the part of health care providers—bias that may be unintentional but exists nonetheless.

We've Got You Covered: Health Insurance

One piece of good news about race and health is the increase in the number of people covered by health insurance since the passage in 2010 of the **Affordable Care Act (ACA)**, informally referred to as Obamacare. Prior to the ACA's passage, fifty million Americans (18 percent of the population) had no health insurance. Twenty percent of African Americans and one-third of Hispanics had no coverage (DeNavas-Walt, Proctor, and Smith 2010). By 2019, the number of uninsured Americans dropped to 8 percent of the population, with the gaps in coverage among Whites, Blacks, Asians, and Latinos closing (Keisler-Starkey and Bunch 2020). Whether these trends will continue, however, is questionable given the repeated threats to repeal this major law.

Even with the passage of the ACA, people of color are still less likely to be covered by health insurance (either private or public) than are White American (see figure 10.4, below) Much of this gap is explained by the fact that White Americans are more likely to have coverage through employers, whereas people of color are more likely to need federal and state-based health coverage, including Medicaid. Adults are generally less likely to be covered than are children, mostly because of low-income children's Medicaid eligibility (Tolbert, Orgera, Singer and Damico 2019).

Poverty and immigration status explain much of the gap in insurance coverage, but significant shares of the uninsured are also among those who have recently immigrated to the United States. Undocumented workers are excluded from

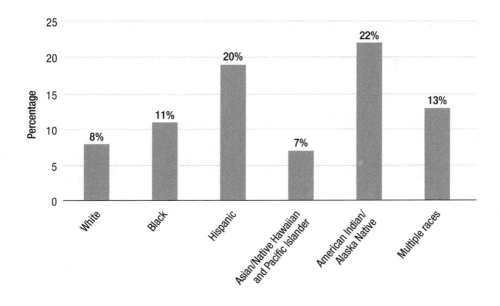

FIG. 10.4 Uninsured Percentage by Race/Ethnicity (2019)

Source: Kaiser Family Foundation 2019.

Medicaid coverage, and there is a five-year waiting period for Medicaid enrollment even for those who have entered the country legally (HealthCare.gov 2020).

Health Care Workers

One of the problems complicating the treatment of racial-ethnic minorities in the US health care system is the status of people of color as workers in this system. You can see in table 10.1 that, relative to their proportion in the overall population, Black Americans and Latinos are highly underrepresented in higher-status jobs in health care (for example, as physicians and surgeons, physician's assistants, and dentists) but are overrepresented in the lowest-status and most poorly paid health care jobs (such as work-at-home health aides and personal care workers).

Why does this matter? It matters because the more prestigious health care occupations provide more income, job security, and opportunities for advancement. Just as in the labor force more generally (see chapter 7), there is a dual labor market within health care with people of color overrepresented in the secondary labor market where jobs are less well remunerated and where there are fewer opportunities for upward mobility. Also, as we have seen during the COVID-19 pandemic, the overrepresentation of people of color in service work within the health care industry, as with all health care workers, increases this group's risk of contracting coronavirus.

Research finds that the more minority providers there are, the better the care patients receive. African Americans and Latinos are less likely than Whites to think their physicians care about them (Sewell 2015). People are also more likely to

TABLE 10.1 Representation of People of Color in Select Health Care Occupations

	Black	Hispanic/Latino	Asian American
Physicians and surgeons	8.2%	6.8%	18.1%
Physicians' assistants	4.7%	5.1%	7.9%
Dentists	3.7%	4.7%	13.5%
Physical therapists	5.3%	5.0%	14.7%
Registered nurses	12.3%	6.9%	8.7%
Nurse practitioners	10.6%	3.4%	4.0%
Clinical laboratory technicians	17.1%	11.0%	9.4%
Dental hygienists	7.0%	11.9%	2.4%
Emergency medical technicians and paramedics	9.7%	8.4%	3.1%
Licensed practical nurses	28.4%	12.4%	5.4%
Medical records technicians	13.2%	9.8%	6.9%
Home health aides	33.9%	5.6%	16.7%
Personal care aides	11.4%	3.5%	9.6%

Source: US Bureau of Labor Statistics 2019a.

Members of the National Nurses United stand in protest among empty shoes representing nurses whom they say have died from COVID-19. The union, whose protest was staged on May 7, 2020, in Lafayette Park, across from the White House, in Washington, DC, during Nurses' Week, demanded that their employers and the federal government "provide safe workplaces by providing optimal personal protective equipment (PPE), safe staffing, presumptive eligibility for workers' compensation benefits, and more" during the novel coronavirus pandemic.

Source: Chip Somodevilla / Getty Images.

utilize health care services when their physician is of the same race. Whites and Asian Americans are far more likely than African Americans, Blacks, and Native Americans to be treated by physicians of their same race. Having a matched-race physician also reduces the bias that people of color experience (Sacks 2013).

Care and Cultural Competence

Evidence such as that above shows that good health is not solely about access but also about what happens once a person enters a health care facility. Stereotypes, attitudes, and *implicit biases* (also see chapter 2) can all affect a person's health. For example, people of color are more likely than Whites to receive discourteous care, which can then affect health outcomes (Kwate and Meyer 2011; LaVeist, Nuru-Jeter, and Jones 2003).

Much empirical evidence shows that White medical care workers tend to hold negative implicit racial biases and explicit racial stereotypes. These implicit biases can persist even when a person's explicit racial attitudes are color-blind. In the end, institutional racism can operate even without people consciously intending to discriminate. As people have become more aware of the power of implicit bias and health disparities, there has been a movement to educate health care workers to both recognize and understand cultural differences that can exist between care workers and their patients. **Cultural competence,** as it is called, involves care workers becoming aware of their own cultural particularities as well as having the capacity to recognize, value, and work with cultural differences (White 2011).

With an increasingly racially diverse and multicultural society in the United States, cultural competence has become increasingly important in the training of those who will be working in health care settings. Cultural competence does not come easily and, in most cases, has to be learned, because people have a tendency to assume a more ethnocentric point of view. Yet cultural competence is crucial to patients' well-being and recovery from illness. A health care provider's ability to communicate, to empathize, and to explain treatment across cultural differences can mean the difference between life and death.

Cultural competence acknowledges that a patient's beliefs about health and decisions about treatment may be based upon the patient's cultural background. It is increasingly important in our multicultural society for medical and health care staff to be alert to cultural factors, especially when working with underserved populations. Indeed, it is also critical when working on global health care.

Up Close and Personal: Race and Reproductive Politics

Framing Question: How does racism affect reproductive health?

Reproductive politics refers to the linkage between systems of power and a person's most intimate medical matters, such as birth control, abortion, and pregnancy. Race pervasively intrudes into every facet of life in the United States, and matters of personal health are no exception. Throughout its history in the United States, racism has robbed people of color of reproductive rights. Social attitudes and explicit social policies have determined whether, how, and when people of color are able to reproduce. Although some of the extreme abuses of the past have ended, they still resonate in contemporary reproductive politics.

Eugenics

Eugenics refers to practices that purport to improve the human race by controlling the reproduction of people deemed to be "inferior" or somehow genetically compromised. Historically, eugenics movements have stemmed from notions of racial superiority and inferiority and have kindled some of the most horrendous acts of violence in human history. Eugenics formed the ideological backbone that resulted in the annihilation of Jewish people during the Nazi Holocaust, because Nazis believed Jews to be unfit and biologically inferior to the so-called Aryan race (see chapter 1). Throughout US history, practices like forced sterilization, medical experimentation, and outright annihilation have also marked the history of Native Americans, Latinos, and African Americans.

Eugenics movements typically claim that inferiority is rooted in the biological character of the targeted group. Such claims are based on *pseudoscience*—that is, ideas that claim to have scientific grounding when in fact they do not. Over time, however, a great deal of effort has been put into pseudoscientific practices, such as measuring the skulls of Black criminals to try to explain crime as a function of brain size. True science, however, has often been developed using people of color as research subjects, often without consent or with incomplete information. The "Learning Our Past" segment, below, provides one such case study. Strictly with regard to reproductive politics, however, is the development of the birth control pill that, in the late 1950s, was tested on Puerto Rican women in Puerto Rico (Briggs 2002).

LEARNING OUR PAST

The Infamous Tuskegee Syphilis Study

The Tuskegee syphilis experiment is a notorious case of medical abuse. Starting in the 1930s and continuing into the 1970s, the US Public Health Service deliberately withheld medical treatment from four hundred Black men who had been recruited as research subjects in a study of the advanced stages of syphilis.

All of the study participants, mostly sharecroppers from around Tuskegee, Alabama, were told they were getting free government health care. They were never told that they had syphilis and were given no treatment at all. Instead, the men were carefully observed so that physicians could see how the late stages of syphilis progressed in the human body.

Some of the men received occasional aspirin for headaches, but not one was given penicillin, a drug that physicians knew could have saved the men's lives. Doctors watched as many of the men died from the untreated disease, which at the time participants were told was "bad blood," a common umbrella term of the time that comprised various ailments such as exhaustion and anemia.

Not until 1972 was this horrendous experiment revealed to the public, when whistleblowers leaked details to the press. At that time only a few of the participants were still living. The Tuskegee experiment then became the impetus for federal regulations that now require informed consent and voluntary participation in all research—medical or other. In 1997, President Clinton issued a formal apology to the African American community for this horrendous abuse of federal power and unethical medical practice.

How could such a thing happen? The Tuskegee experiment can only now be understood in the context of the extreme racism and stereotyping of Black men and sexuality that was rampant at the time. The disregard by the federal government for Black lives also reverberates in much of the distrust that many African American citizens still feel toward federal health programs today.

Sources: Jones 1993; Reverby 2009.

Reproductive Control and Forced Sterilization

Regulating the reproduction of people of color has been a central theme in the history of racial oppression in the United States (Garcia 2012; Roberts 1997a). At times regulation has meant encouraging reproduction—such as during slavery, when slave owners encouraged the breeding of slaves to increase the unpaid labor force. At other times women of color have been denied the right to bear children, such as through forced sterilizations and other birth control policies that discouraged reproduction.

For example, during the 1950s and 1960s, backed by US interests in economic development, various programs promoted contraception for Puerto Rican women (Briggs 2002). In addition, Puerto Rican women on the island were routinely coerced into sterilization, a procedure that became so common that it was referred to as *la operación*. Women were often not informed that the procedure was irreversible, and, as a result, by the late 1960s a full one-third of Puerto Rican women of childbearing age had been sterilized (Gutiérrez 2008; Roberts 1997a).

Sterilization abuse has been part of Native American history too. In the early 1970s a government investigation found that physicians at the Indian Health Service had sterilized large numbers of Native American women without their consent. Native women were threatened with losing their health care access if they did not consent to the procedure. In many cases a doctor would perform a sterilization procedure without a woman's consent while she was having, for example, a needed appendectomy. For their part, physicians working for the Indian Health Service were exempt from the usual medical practice of required consent. From 1960 to 1980, when these practices were rampant, there was, not surprisingly, a steep decline in the Native American birth rate (Lawrence 2000).

To this day Black and Hispanic women in the United States are still more likely to be sterilized than are White women (see figure 10.5). For some women, this has

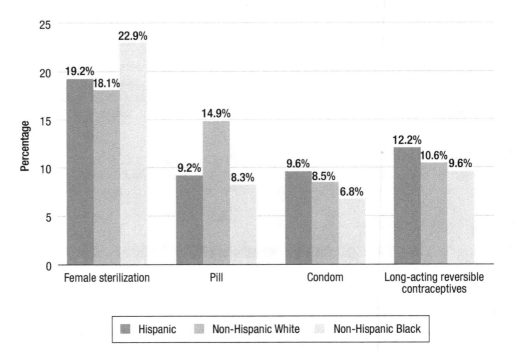

FIG. 10.5 Contraceptive Use by Race

Source: Daniels and Abma 2018.

been a choice, but in the context of past abuses it is easy to wonder under what circumstances women face this decision and how well informed they are about its consequences.

Policies regarding federal funding for reproductive health are also telling. Federal policy prohibits the use of public funds for abortion, except in a few states where state funds, not federal funds, can be used. This law, passed by Congress in 1976 and known as the Hyde Amendment, primarily affects Medicaid recipients and thus is particularly restrictive for women who rely on government assistance for their reproductive health. Sterilization, by contrast, is fully covered by Medicaid, although there is a thirty-day waiting period between giving consent and having the procedure. This rule is intended to protect women on public assistance from the past abuses of forced sterilization; more advantaged women, however, are not usually subjected to the same notification requirement.

Race Beliefs and Contemporary Reproductive Politics

Although eugenics is now highly discredited, its impact can still be seen in some of the contemporary politics in the United States concerning contraception and birth control. Past practices have made some radical Black activists suspicious of any form of birth control promoted by federal or state agencies, believing it to constitute a form of genocide. On the other side, some White supremacist groups fear that Whites will be outnumbered by people of color even though differences in birth rates between racial-ethnic groups are relatively small in the United States.

Reproductive politics continue to be influenced by racial beliefs. Black and Latina women are stereotyped in the dominant culture as "breeders"—an attitude reflected in the assumption that poor women of color have children only to increase their welfare payments. This attitude, though never based in fact, has been encoded into law, such as in federal "family cap" policies that deny federal aid to recipients if they have another child (also see chapter 7). The revised federal welfare policy of 1996 also provided a cash reward to some states that successfully limited out-of-wedlock births to women receiving Temporary Assistance for Needy Families (Gutiérrez 2010).

Such policies reveal the extent to which racial stereotypes about reproduction continue to frame national policy and debates about reproductive rights. Anti-immigrant sentiment is also part of contemporary reproductive politics. Immigrant women and men face a number of challenges in seeking any form of health care. Even for legal immigrants, constantly shifting policies and programs deter access to health care—reproductive and otherwise. Undocumented workers may avoid seeking care out of fear of repercussions for them or their family. Lack of insurance, limited information, and laws that have limited health care for undocumented workers all contribute to a poor climate of health, reproductive or otherwise, for immigrants (Gutiérrez 2010).

Contemporary reproductive politics are a dense tangle of competing social movements and racial and gender ideologies. Usually lost amid competing arguments and passionately felt political opinions about reproduction is the actual reproductive health of women of color. They—especially the poor among them—are subjected to inadequate information, inadequate resources, and lack of access to high-quality reproductive health. Yet they have been consistently manipulated by policies that allow them neither the freedom to have children nor the freedom to decide not to. Only in this context can we begin to understand what reproductive freedom would really mean for people of color (Joffe and Parker 2012; Roberts 1997a).

Racism in the Air We Breathe: Environmental Racism

Framing Question: What impact does racism have on people's environment, and what is the environmental justice movement?

In January 2016, a federal emergency was declared in Flint, Michigan, because the city's water was contaminated with lead. City residents were warned not to drink the water. By then, however, local officials already knew about the water's lead contamination, and city residents had been drinking it for more than a year without knowing it was contaminated. Large numbers of the city's children were found to have suffered high levels of lead exposure, a condition very damaging to their long-term physical health and social development. Adults exposed to lead also may develop various illnesses such as kidney ailments, abdominal pain, and decline in mental functioning. According to engineering experts, not one neighborhood in the city of Flint had safe drinking water (Hanna-Attisha 2018).

Angry residents demanded the resignation of the state's governor and the city leadership because of their disregard for the health and safety of Flint's residents.

When it was revealed in 2015 that the drinking water in Flint, Michigan, was contaminated, residents demanded the resignation and arrest of Governor Rick Snyder for knowingly allowing the city's residents to drink dangerously polluted water.

Source: Jake May / Associated Press.

About two years before, the city's manager, in a cost-cutting measure, had switched the water source from clean water supplied by Lake Huron to the polluted Flint River. Residents immediately started complaining about the color, smell, and taste of the water, but no change was made—other than raising the price for water. City officials also found unacceptable levels of coliform bacteria in Flint's water, and so they pumped extra chloride into the system. The water then became so highly corrosive that it caused lead to leach from the supply pipes into home plumbing, basically poisoning city residents.

At the time, Flint had a population near one hundred thousand people, 55 percent of them African American and another 9 percent other people of color. Prior to the water crisis, Flint had already been devastated by the closure of several major automobile plants. Unemployment in Flint is twice that of the rest of the nation. Forty-two percent of the population in Flint lives below the poverty line—more than 2.5 times the poverty rate in Michigan and almost 3 times that of the nation as a whole (US Census Bureau 2020a).

The poisoning of the water in Flint, Michigan, called public attention to the strong connection between racial inequality and environmental pollution. Many asked, had the population of Flint been White and more economically advantaged, would the city water have ever been allowed be so poisoned? The pattern reflected by the situation is known as **environmental racism**, by which racial-ethnic minorities are disproportionately exposed to environmental wastes and other hazards (Brulle and Pellow 2006). This means that toxic waste facilities and other pollutants are more likely to be located in neighborhoods that are largely populated by people of color. Even something as basic to a person's health as having adequate plumbing facilities is known to be associated with racial inequality. American Indians and Alaska Natives, for example, are less likely to have basic plumbing facilities than are other groups (Gasteyer et al. 2016).

Environmental racism has a class dimension to it as well. Exposure to pollution and toxic waste occurs in poor and working-class White neighborhoods, but people of color are disproportionately affected by environmental hazards. Alarming disparities in such things as exposure to lead and access to plumbing and other forms of sanitation are affected by the proportion of people of color in given neighborhoods. Blacks and Latinos are more likely to be exposed to higher levels of various toxic substances (Kravitz-Wirtz et al. 2016). Also, census tracts with higher proportions of people of color are more exposed to various toxic substances (Gasteyer et al. 2016; Kravitz-Wirtz et al. 2016; Sampson and Winter 2016; Schulz et al. 2016). Native American areas are particularly susceptible to environmental racism, with many having to travel long distances simply to get water (Chappell 2020).

Environmental racism includes a policy dimension as well; there is less enforcement of environmental regulations in areas populated by people of color. Additionally, people of color are underrepresented in leadership positions in environmental organizations, even though people of color have taken an active role in organizing movements against environmental racism. In sum, environmental racism is "any policy, practice, or directive that differentially affects or disadvantages (whether intentional or unintended) individuals, groups, or communities based on race or color" (Dr. Benjamin Chavis, cited in Bullard 1994:497).

Siting Waste

The evidence of environmental racism is substantial. Most studies that document this pattern tend, however, to be based on local studies. National studies are more difficult to undertake because of the complexity of mapping such a large area and correlating sites with population data. The most comprehensive national study to date has found that African Americans and Hispanics disproportionately live within one mile of toxic waste facilities (Mohai and Saha 2007). Comprehensive assessments of risk at a national level also show that Blacks and Latinos are more likely than Whites to be exposed to higher levels of nitrogen dioxide gas and other toxic substances. Further, these racial differences persist, even controlling for various social and economic characteristics of individuals and households (Kravitz-Wirtz et al. 2016).

Various other local studies have also shown that large percentages of people of color live in areas where there are higher levels of toxic waste and releases. The NAACP has found, for example, that a huge proportion of African Americans (80 percent) live within thirty miles of a coal-powered plant, a fact that may explain the much higher rates of asthma found among African American children (Brulle and Pellow 2006).

A number of facts have become clear from studies of environmental racism:

- Areas with a large percentage of non-White residents have higher levels of toxic release in the air (Arora and Cason 1998; Bullard 2008; Kim, Campbell, and Eckerd 2014).
- Compared to White Americans, African Americans are more likely to live near landfills, airports, and oil refineries (Centers for Disease Control and Prevention 2013).
- Immigrants to the United States are more likely than nonimmigrant residents to live in places with high levels of pollution (Mohai and Saha 2006; Pellow and Brehm 2013).
- Hispanics have a greater likelihood of working in occupations where rates of injury or death are highest (Byler 2013).
- Latinos are more likely to be exposed to pesticide poisoning because of their work as farm and garden laborers (US Bureau of Labor Statistics 2019a).
- More than 70 percent of African Americans compared to 58 percent of Whites live in counties that are in violation of federal clean air laws and standards (Payne-Sturges and Gee 2006; Russell 2011).

Intent or Innocence?

The facts above show the vast disparities in the United States in exposure to toxic environmental hazards. Researchers studying environmental risks conclude that exposure to toxic substances is "a pathway through which racial inequality literally gets into the body" (Sampson and Winter 2016:279). Why does environmental racism occur? Is it because polluters deliberately discriminate against people of color and poor people? Does class explain toxic waste dumping more than race? Is dumping just a matter of market forces because it is cheaper for companies to situate landfills, toxic waste dumps, and other pollutants in less economically valuable neighborhoods? Do polluters avoid neighborhoods where people have more resources to resist environmental degradation? All of these questions drive different explanations of environmental inequity.

Here's what we know: Both race and class are significant in explaining patterns of pollution, but class alone is not a sufficient explanation. Race and class are entangled, but race also has effects of its own. Research on toxic waste dumping has concluded that factors uniquely associated with race explain much of the location of hazardous waste facilities (Mohai and Saha 2007). Housing discrimination, racial steering, and the factors associated with racial residential segregation all contribute to environmental racism.

There is also a bit of the "chicken and the egg" conundrum in considering environmental racism. Do disadvantaged groups move to areas where properties are already cheaper because of environmental conditions, or do property values decline once a neighborhood becomes predominantly populated by people of color? Both are probably true, but the end result is that racial disparities exist (Sze and London 2008). Market forces also operate in this dynamic. Companies that produce toxic products select places where land and labor are cheaper. The fact is that such places, regardless of the actual intent of corporate leaders, tend to be the places where racial-ethnic minorities live. These populations also are less likely than others to have the resources to leave (Been and Gupta 1997). Even if companies intentionally engage in such behavior, it is very difficult to prove intent to discriminate in the courts if people sue polluters.

Finally, the NIMBY ("not in my backyard") phenomenon comes into play: Financially better-off communities have more resources to resist pollutants in their neighborhoods than do others. Even with the mobilization of people of color and others through the environmental justice movement, seldom do less advantaged communities have the political power to fight corporate power.

The Environmental Justice Movement

Environmental justice is "the principle that all people and communities are entitled to equal protection of environmental and public health laws and regulations" (Bullard 1994:495). The environmental justice movement took shape in the 1970s and 1980s when residents in different communities organized against risks they identified in their communities. Typically environmental justice initiatives are locally focused, organized by residents, and often led by women. Environmental justice includes people from communities of color, indigenous people, and working-class people organizing to combat the disproportionate burden of harm faced by these communities. A very large body of evidence shows how environmental risks are also strongly associated with various social, educational, developmental, psychological, and health outcomes (Brulle and Pellow 2006; Pellow 2007 and 2016; Takeuchi et al. 2016).

Although many environmental justice organizations are locally based, they generally share the common outlook that individuals have the right to be protected from environmental degradation. Native people, for example, have a long history of resistance to environmental injustice, as they have had to fight for food and water security and for the protection of their land, including the protection of sacred sites.

Advocates for environmental justice have been an important voice in pointing out the dumping of toxic waste and the presence of pollution in predominantly low-income and racial-ethnically diverse residential communities.

Source: Jim West / Alamy Stock Photo.

Native women have been especially significant as leaders in these movements (Gilio-Whitaker 2019).

The environmental justice movement typically targets actions that address the disproportionate risks people of color and the poor face from environmental hazards. Leaders in the movement have also argued that the burden for proving harm done should be shouldered by those who produce the harm, including large corporations. Because it is so difficult to prove intentional discrimination by polluters, movement leaders have also argued that the standard of proof should be the differential impact of dumping, not intent per se (Pellow and Brulle 2007).

The deterioration of the Earth's resources is cause for worry for all people of the world. The risks are clear, and the fate of the world depends on how well we address this critical issue. Even though environmental degradation and climate change affect us all, part of the solution has to be recognizing and addressing the specific effects on people of color—both in the United States and around the globe.

Climate Change: Are We All in It Together?

A final dimension of environmental racism is the differential impact climate change has on people of color—both nationally and abroad. Two points are clear: (1) even though climate change threatens life for us all, people of color suffer differential risks, and, (2) people of color contribute less to climate change (Roberts and Parks 2007; Takeuchi et al. 2016).

To the first point, the effects of climate change and natural disasters are not equally experienced. Although the consequences of such things as hurricanes, tornadoes, floods, and now climate change can devastate entire communities, people of color are disproportionately vulnerable (Fox Gotham, Lauve-Moon, and Powers 2017; Klinenberg 2002; Tierney 2007). The impact of Hurricane Katrina on the Gulf Coast in 2005 is one telling example. Although Katrina's devastating impact was felt by many groups of people, low-income African Americans were far more likely to die or, if they survived, to be displaced from their homes (Weber and Peak 2012).

Experts point out that people of color are typically the first to feel the long-term effects of air pollution, extreme heat, drought, food and water shortages, storms, and floods. Furthermore, when disasters occur, people of color and the poor in general have the fewest resources to deal with such crises. In the aftermath of a disaster, such things as an increase in energy costs will also have a disproportionate burden on those who are already struggling.

To the second point, ironically those most affected by climate change are also those least likely to contribute to it. The most disadvantaged and marginalized populations generally use less carbon-based fuel, thus contributing less to the development of climate change than other groups. In one specific example, Native Americans whose lands have been deforested have not been those whose practices contribute to climate change. They have seen much in the way of natural resources extracted from their lands—leaving the land barren—and little remuneration (Harlan, Pellow, and Roberts 2015).

Conclusion

As the nation clearly witnessed during the COVID-19 pandemic, racial disparities in health outcomes are stark and persistent. But they can be changed. We tend to think that improved medical treatment and new technologies of care are the best conduits to better health. No doubt, medical advances matter, but a unique experiment also shows the importance of addressing the broader social context if we are to improve the health of people of color.

One clever experiment makes this clear: medical researcher Stephen Woolf and his colleagues compared the number of lives saved by medical advances compared to those saved by equalizing Black and White mortality rates through such causes of poor health as environment and lack of access to medical care. The researchers found that for every life saved by biomedical advances, five would be saved by eliminating the discrepancy in health care treatment between African Americans and Whites. They concluded, "Achieving equity may do more for health than perfecting the technology of care" (Woolf et al. 2008:S26).

This one experiment shows that with attention to the significance of race, we can make advancements in reducing health disparities. Reducing economic inequality writ large will also have to be part of this equation, as will reducing residential segregation, which we have seen to be so important in reproducing various aspects of racial inequality. You have seen by now how racism affects every social institution in the United States, health care included. In the next chapter we turn to another of the most important institutions where racism has so harmed human lives: criminal justice.

Key Terms

Affordable Care Act (ACA) 255
cultural competence 258
death rate 246
environmental justice 265
environmental racism 263

eugenics 258
hypertension 248
infant mortality 247
life expectancy 246
reproductive politics 258

Critical-Thinking Questions

1. Why is residential segregation such a strong predictor of racial health disparities?
2. What evidence do you see of the connection between race and reproductive politics? Use a current news report as evidence of your claims.

Student Exercises

10.1. Pay a visit to your local emergency room, and make a count, as best you can, of the number of people waiting there and their racial-ethnic composition. Then look up the percentage of people of color in the population of your city, county, or state. Is the proportion of the population of people of color in the ER waiting room representative of the population of the area? Why or why not?

10.2. Examine the data in figure 10.5. What differences do you see in contraceptive use, comparing women of different racial-ethnic backgrounds? How do you explain what you see?

Challenging Questions/Open to Debate

Imagine you are the owner of a company that generates toxic waste from your production process. You are under pressure by your Board of Directors to cut costs, so you look for and find a run-down area of a nearby community where you can dispose of the toxic material. As it turns out, the nearby residents are about 85 percent African American and Latino. If you dispose of the waste there, does this make you a racist?

TAKING ACTION AGAINST RACISM

Healing the Environment

If you are planning a career in health care, familiarize yourself with the movement for cultural competence—that is, developing practices that enable you to work effectively with people from diverse backgrounds.

At the same time, the COVID-19 pandemic has taught us how quickly a national disaster of any kind can devastate the nation, with a disparate impact on people of color. Climate change, for example, can affect large swaths of the US public but is predicted to have a particularly dire effect on communities of color.

Locate organizations in your community that are addressing the threat of climate change, and learn whether they are specifically investigating the impact of environmental threats on communities of color.

Resources:

National Prevention Information Network, "Cultural Competence in Health and Human Services," Centers for Disease Control and Prevention (website), August 17, 2020, https://npin.cdc.gov/pages/cultural-competence.

Sarah Kaplan, "Climate Change Is Also a Racial Justice Problem," *Washington Post*, June 29, 2020, https://www.washingtonpost.com/climate-solutions/2020/06/29/climate-change-racism/.

Source: ZUMA Press, Inc. / Alamy Stock Photo

CHAPTER 11

Justice and Injustice

Race, Crime, and the Criminal Justice System

Where justice is denied, where poverty is enforced, where ignorance prevails, and where any one class is made to feel that society is an organized conspiracy to oppress, rob, and degrade them, neither persons nor property will be safe.
—Frederick Douglass (1886)

OBJECTIVES

- Report the difference in perceptions and facts about race and crime
- Explain how crime statistics are influenced by the social construction of race
- Understand who is most likely to be victimized by crime
- Describe the history of hate crime in the United States, and relate current

- data on the incidence of such crimes
- Detail the facts about immigration and crime
- Evaluate the impact of institutional racism within different elements of the criminal justice system
- Explain the social structural components that connect race and crime

In the wake of so many widely publicized police shootings of Black men and women in the United States and the racist taunts about Latino immigrants as "murderers and rapists," sober analyses of the role of racism in the criminal justice system is sorely needed. There are laws in place in US society that give equal protection under the law to all people regardless of the color of their skin. The overwhelming majority of people from all racial groups are also law-abiding citizens. All people want to live in communities that are safe, that are free from violence, and where they need not worry whether their children will be shot by the police, especially if the child is doing nothing wrong. Black and Latino families know that a little swagger or an edgy attitude toward the police can get a young Black or Latino person shot. As a result, a large majority (84 percent) of African Americans believe they are treated less fairly than Whites by the police and by the criminal justice system as a whole (Horowitz et al. 2019). There is much evidence that they are right.

Vigilante justice—that is, in the context we are discussing here, violent acts committed by White people against Black Americans, Mexican Americans, Asian Americans, and indigenous people—has also been a perennial theme throughout US history. Violence against people of color is not new, nor is this the first time in our nation's history when racial violence has rocked our cities. Whether current calls for police reform and greater justice in the administration of law will actually be instituted remains to be seen. Racism in the criminal justice system is widespread, multifaceted, and long-standing. Changing this will require more than a little reform, because race influences so much in both the criminal justice system and the conditions that put people into this obstinate system of punishment and social control.

The connection between race and crime is a heated subject in US society, the stuff of TV dramas, political campaigns, and daily conversation. The subject polarizes people, with one side crying that the police are racist, the other side decrying "Black criminality" (Bobo 2015). Add to that the stereotypes of Latino immigrants as criminally inclined, and you have a potent mix of racism in the administration of justice.

As the protests against police brutality against people of color have so vividly exposed, nearly every aspect of crime and justice in the United States involves race. Black Lives Matter—a movement that began in 2013 after George Zimmerman was acquitted after he shot and killed a young Black man, Trayvon Martin, in 2012—has sparked a cry for reform in police and the administration of justice. This movement has also exposed the long history of violence against Black people by vigilantes and the police.

In the heat of public discussions about race and criminal justice, it can be is difficult to discern the facts about race, crime, and justice in the United States, but here is an initial glimpse:

- African American men are seven times more likely to be imprisoned than are White men, and Hispanic men three times as likely (Bronson and Carson 2019).
- Black Americans are more than twice as likely as White Americans to be shot and killed by the police; Latinos are also disproportionately shot by police relative to their size in the US population (Tate, Jenkins, and Rich 2020).
- Seventy percent of those who have been found wrongfully convicted, based on DNA evidence, are people of color—mostly African Americans but also Hispanics and Asian Americans (Innocence Project 2020; Stevenson 2015a).
- Native American women are twice as likely as Black and White women to be victims of rape; Hispanic and Asian women are the least likely to be rape victims (Planty et al. 2016).
- Seventy-seven percent of Americans do *not* blame immigrants for crime, although 20 percent of the US public think immigrants are more to blame for crime than other groups. In fact, immigrants are actually less likely than native-born Americans to commit a crime (Ewing, Martínez, and Rumbaut 2015; Gonzalez-Barrera and Connor 2019).

This chapter examines how the US criminal justice system is influenced by institutional racism, now also called *systemic racism*. This exploration includes identifying who is most likely to be victimized by crime, who commits crime, and who is most likely to be punished. Throughout the chapter you should ask yourself how racism influences how justice is delivered—or not.

We begin by examining public perceptions of crime and their basis in fact.

Race and Crime: Myths and Realities

Framing Question: How does the media depict the connection between race and crime, and how does this distort the reality of crime in the United States?

Tune in to the local evening news on any given night in just about any city, and you will very likely see images of violent crime—perhaps murder, arson, armed robbery, or assault. More often than not, the perpetrator will be a person of color, probably African American or Latino. If you were to base your understanding of crime on what you see in the local news, you would think the United States is a crime-ridden society. You would probably also conclude that Black Americans and Latinos are more prone to committing crime than are other groups. You would also probably think that crime is increasing in America.

In truth, violent crime has been on the decline in recent years (see figure 11.1), although the frequent reportage of the high murder rate in some cities leads people to think that violent crime is on the rise everywhere. In those neighborhoods where crime has increased in recent years, careful studies conclude that racial disadvantage is the primary cause (Krivo et al. 2018). Although Black Americans and Latinos are

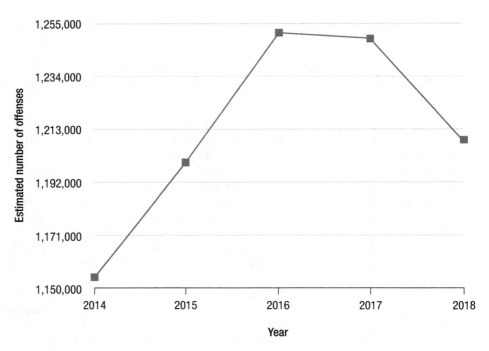

FIG. 11.1 Violent Crime in the United States (2014–2018)

Source: Federal Bureau of Investigation 2018b.

more likely to be arrested for crime than are White Americans, questions remain about whether this is because African Americans actually commit more crime or are just policed more. Further, despite crude stereotypes about immigrants as criminals, the truth is that immigrants are actually less likely to commit crime than are native-born citizens. African Americans are also more likely to be crime victims than are White Americans (Morgan and Oudekerk 2019).

Even in the face of this information, research studies show that racial-ethnic minorities are more likely to be shown in the media as crime suspects than they are to be shown as victims. Except for while the COVID-19 pandemic has captured the nation's attention and during weather emergencies, crime gets more attention than any other subject in local news reporting. Ordinarily, though, African Americans are much more likely to be shown in the media as linked to violence than are White people, even though the majority of violent crime is actually committed by Whites. Muslims are also quite likely to be stereotyped in the media as criminal terrorists (Rivera 2014).

Media images of crime may provide dramatic entertainment, but when those images are racialized, as they typically are, they reinforce controlling images of people of color. Such images also depict the justice system in a distorted manner. Crime dramas, for example, show clients being well represented by attorneys who are locked in battle against each other. In fact, most criminal cases are settled quickly through plea bargaining. Attorneys may barely know their clients as they rush to get cases through the court docket (Barak, Leighton, and Cotton 2015). Yet manufactured media images lead viewers to believe that the US system of justice is neutral and fair, making it then easy to conclude that anyone prosecuted by this system must have done something wrong.

Research also shows that racial bias—both implicit and explicit—is linked to how people perceive crime. Those holding the highest degree of racial bias are more likely to see crime as increasing. They are also more likely to explain crime in individualistic terms—that is, by understanding crime solely as a consequence of individual behavior without comprehending the societal context in which crime occurs and is punished (Callanan 2012; Drakulich 2015).

Public perceptions of the connection between race and crime are seldom based in fact but result instead from how they are constructed via the mass media. Just imagine how people might think differently about crime if the media narrative were to shift from associating people of color with criminality to focusing on the victimization of people of color by the history of racism.

Counting Crime: The Social Construction of Racial Categories

Framing Question: How is crime measured, and does race influence the reporting of such data?

National data on crime come from two primary sources: the FBI's Uniform Crime Reports and the Department of Justice's National Crime Victimization Surveys. **Uniform Crime Reports** (UCR) provide data on crimes reported, crimes cleared, and persons arrested. Police departments collect these data and forward the information to state and federal authorities. Seven types of offenses committed are then used to create the **crime index**: murder/nonnegligent manslaughter, rape, robbery, aggravated assault (with a weapon), burglary, larceny/theft, and motor vehicle theft. Only murder, rape, robbery, and aggravated assault are included in the *violent crime rate*.

Supplementary UCR information addresses murder victims, offenders, and incident characteristics. Keep in mind that UCR data include only those crimes that come to the attention of police agencies. People who can hide their crimes are excluded from the crime statistics. Also, police departments vary in how and whether they report victims' and perpetrators' race, ethnicity, and other characteristics.

The **National Crime Victimization Survey** (NCVS) is conducted annually, based on a representative national sample of US households. These data are the primary source of information about nonfatal violent and property crimes, based on victims' self-reports. The survey results are then reported by the US Bureau of Justice Statistics—part of the US Department of Justice—and made available online to the public, as are data from the Uniform Crime Reports. The NCVS includes data on various crimes, but, unlike the Uniform Crime Reports, it also collects information on domestic and intimate partner violence.

Both the UCR and the NCVS provide invaluable information about crime and its victims, but there are limitations to both sources of data. For example, the Uniform Crime Reports only include those crimes where an arrest has taken place. Unreported crime goes undetected, as do crimes reported to the police but dropped, such as if the police do not believe a report or if police use their own bias to determine whether a crime is found. Victimization surveys are based on self-reports by crime victims and thus can also be unreliable. Victims may only report certain crimes, and racial bias can affect such reports, as could perhaps the wish to not disclose certain perpetrators. Victims of domestic violence, for example, are notoriously reluctant to report such acts of violence both because they may fear the violence will escalate after a report and because they may fear the loss of household income should the perpetrator go to jail.

Neither the UCR nor the NCVS includes corporate crime, except for individual acts of fraud or embezzlement. Crimes committed as a result of institutional practices are not reflected in the official crime statistics. As a consequence, it might be easy to conclude that corporate crime is not as harmful as other crimes. But in truth, the impact of corporate crime on people's lives can be enormous—even greater than the impact of street crimes in terms of the magnitude of the cost and how many people are affected.

Even more problematic is how race and ethnicity are defined and categorized in official crime statistics. Starting in 1933, the Uniform Crime Reports included three categories for race: White, Black, and "other." Today there are five categories for "race" in UCR data: White, Black, American Indian and Alaska Native, Asian, and Native Hawaiian or other Pacific Islander. Why don't these categories match those provided by the US Census Bureau?

Where are the Latinos, you might ask? "Mexican" was added as a category in the Uniform Crime Reports in 1934 but then dropped in 1941. Between 1980 and 1985, a separate category for Hispanics was created, but the designation was then dropped. Beginning in 2013, the Uniform Crime Reports started to again include Hispanic/Latino arrests in a separate category (Gabbidon and Greene 2018; Walker, Spohn, and Delone 2012). In other words, UCR data treat race and ethnicity as distinct categories.

The data in table 11.1 are gathered from the Uniform Crime Reports, and they make clear that ethnicity is reported apart from race, making comparisons with Latinos/Hispanics and other groups difficult, to say the least. Some local agencies do not even collect information on ethnicity, so you can see that the number of total arrests is not the same for "racial" groups and for "ethnic" groups. Moreover, fluctuations in how Latinos have been categorized over time make it virtually impossible to study long-term trends—that is, *longitudinal analyses* (Gabbidon and Greene 2016; Walker et al. 2012).

Data on Native Americans in the Uniform Crime Reports are also obscured by the fact that Native Americans fall under a complex array of jurisdictional legal entities. Not all tribal police agencies send arrest data to UCR, so Native American arrests may be undercounted. In the current NCVS, Native Americans are counted as "other" along with Alaska Natives; Asians, Native Hawaiians, and other Pacific Islanders; and persons of two or more races. This is hardly a reasonable way to understand crime for such diverse groups.

The NCVS is also problematic in how race and ethnicity are counted. The NCVS has included racial categories since 1973. Originally the categories were White, Black, and other (Asian/Pacific Islanders, American Indians, and Aleuts and Eskimos). Hispanics were not included as a separate category until 1977. Now the NCVS reports data for Whites, Blacks, Hispanics, and others, depending on how respondents self-identify.

TABLE 11.1 Arrests for All Crimes in Crime Index, by Race and Ethnicity, 2015

	Total arrests	White	Black or African American	American Indian or Alaska Native	Asian	Native Hawaiian or other Pacific Islander
Number	5,583,383	3,734,292	1,633,054	131,935	70.285	13,817
Percent distribution	100	66.9	29.2	2.4	1.3	0.2

		Not Hispanic	Hispanic
Number	4,767,763	3,738,422	938,341
Percent distribution		79.9	20.1

Note: Individual percentage distribution figures do not total 100 due to rounding.
Source: Federal Bureau of Investigation 2016.

In sum, how agencies categorize race and crime is fraught with problems. Consequently we must use caution when interpreting the broad categories of "race" and "ethnicity" in official data. Among other things, when the category of "other" appears in such statistics, it usually includes groups with very different experiences (Asians, Native Americans, Alaska Natives, Pacific Islanders, and people identifying as mixed race). The category "Hispanic" includes Cubans, Puerto Ricans, Mexicans, and many other groups, all varying in their social and economic circumstances.

Racial and ethnic categories are also inconsistent over time and from agency to agency. As a result, measuring the association between race and crime is flawed— but as this information is disseminated, it nonetheless shapes people's thinking about the connection between race and crime.

The racial and ethnic categories in these reports also reify race and ethnicity as if they were fixed categories. In fact, as we have learned, race and ethnicity are social constructions. Racial and ethnicity identity in victimization data is based on self-reports but forced into the categories given in the surveys. Arrest data from the Uniform Crime Reports might just as easily be based on how a police officer checks a box as on how a person self-identifies.

One consequence of the complexity of how crime is tabulated and recorded is an overwhelming emphasis on African American crime. As you review the data included here on crime and crime victimization, keep the imperfections in the official statistics in mind while noting that these sources remain the best available national information on crime. Scholars often collect their own data, adding to the richness of what we know, but the official data remain the only source for general patterns in crime commission and victimization. At the heart of these crime statistics lurks the issue of race as a social construction.

Race, Violence, and Victimization

Framing Question: How do race, gender, and class influence patterns of victimization by crime?

The problematic nature of crime statistics notwithstanding, African Americans are the most likely to be victimized by serious violent crime—that is, rape, sexual assault, robbery, and aggravated assault (see figure 11.2). At the same time, however, victimization by crime for all groups, including people of color, has actually declined in recent years, with the exception of rape and serious intimate partner violence. Early reports show that domestic violence has likely increased during the coronavirus pandemic as people have been ordered to stay in their homes. Not just in the United States but also all around the world, calls to domestic abuse hotlines have surged as the triggers for domestic violence—stress, unemployment, and other personal crises—escalated during the pandemic (Taub 2020).

Age also has a great deal to do with the likelihood of crime victimization. People under twenty-four years of age are the most likely to be victimized by crime. Household income is another factor in predicting crime victimization. Generally speaking, people in the lowest income brackets are most likely to be victimized by crime. Poverty is a clear correlate of the likelihood of victimization by crime, especially among younger people (Lauritsen, Heimer, and Lang 2018).

Research on victimization by crime has tended to focus on crimes such as homicide, rape, and armed robbery. But what if we were to change our concept

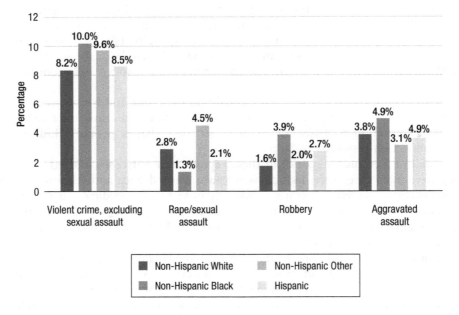

FIG. 11.2 Victimization Rates by Race/Ethnicity

Source: US Bureau of Justice Statistics 2019.

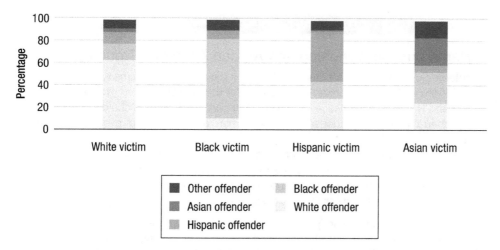

FIG. 11.3 Percentage of Violent Crimes by Victim and Offender's Race and Ethnicity

Source: Morgan and Oudekerk 2019.

of victimization? Official statistics on crime victimization overlook certain actions that could well be construed as crime. One example is the theft of Native American land by White settlers. Another is the manipulation of the housing market by Wall Street investors, which victimized millions of people during the Great Recession and caused countless economic losses. Such information is not found in official crime statistics (Barak et al. 2015). While official crime statistics can reproduce racial narratives that blame people of color for the vast majority of crime, other forms of crime are overlooked.

Crime victimization data also teach us that crime victims and perpetrators tend to be of the same race and ethnicity. White-on-White crime, for example, is far more common than Black-on-White crime or Hispanic-on-White crime (see figure 11.3; Morgan and Oedekerk 2019). The vast majority of violent crimes against Black Americans are by committed Black offenders, and similarly for Hispanics. The one example of crime that is most likely committed by one racial-ethnic group against another is hate crime.

Hate Crime

The United States has a long and gruesome history of **hate crime,** most notably in the history of lynching (see "Learning Our Past," below). Beginning in 1990, the federal government started collecting data on hate crime, now included in the FBI's Uniform Crime Reports. Hate crime is formally defined as crime that includes evidence of prejudice based on race, religion, sexual orientation, ethnicity, disability, gender, or gender identity. Hate crime can be directed against individuals, but it also includes crimes against property, such as the desecration of mosques, temples, and churches.

LEARNING OUR PAST

Vigilante Justice: Lynching and African American Trauma

In the face of contemporary concerns about race and crime, it may be easy for some to forget the vigilante justice that terrorized African American communities for much of US history. Through much of the late nineteenth and twentieth centuries, even the smallest perceived violation could result in death as White mobs lynched and murdered thousands of Black men, mostly—but not exclusively—in the American South.

The Delta Oral History Project conducted interviews from 1995 to 1996 with African Americans in the Delta region of Mississippi. Many of their narratives recall the fear, trauma, and terror that were constant under this form of vigilante justice. The following is an excerpt of such a narrative, by Dr. L. C. Dorsey, who grew up in Sunflower County, Mississippi:

> There was a tremendous amount of fear in the community and in almost every house of this faceless group of people who arrived at your home at night, on horses and in cars, to drag you out and kill you for any little infraction of rules you didn't always know about. People worried tremendously about their sons and the menfolk in their families. People worried that if a White man looked at a Black girl, and they tried to keep them in the background because they couldn't protect them. They couldn't protect their wives and stuff. What you remember about it was the fear, that there was no way to be protected. . . . It was all this fear that these people had of White folk, that they would come and get you in the middle of the night and kill you. I understood the fear so strongly that it wouldn't even let them [the adults] talk out loud.

Source: Interview of L. C. Dorsey by Owen Brooks and Kim Lacy Rogers, Jackson, Mississippi, June 21, 1996, pp. 119–20 in Rogers 1999.

One of the most horrid forms of hate crime in the United States is the historic lynching of Black Americans, acts of terror that spanned the period from the end of Reconstruction until well into the twentieth century. Most lynchings were neither recorded nor prosecuted, but scholars estimate that at least 3,500 Black people were lynched over this time period. Less well known is that Mexican Americans were also victims of widespread lynching, particularly in the period following the Mexican-American War. From roughly 1848 until 1928, scholars estimate there to have been approximately six hundred lynchings of people of Mexican origin in the United States (Carrigan and Webb 2003).

The lynching of Latinos and Black Americans was mostly done with the collusion of law enforcement and with little or no prosecution of the violent offenders. As an early form of domestic terrorism, lynching was how Whites asserted social control over the Black and Mexican population (Carrigan and Webb 2003; Mirandé 2019; Pérez 2020). Current forms of hate crime include the mass shootings of people of color that have become all too common—in churches, nightclubs, on the street, and other places where shooters (typically young, White men) express their rage through mass slaughter. Hate crime statistics vastly underestimate the extent of hate crime because the only hate crimes that appear in official data on crime are those reported to the police, classified as such, and then passed on to the FBI. The data we do have, however, provide significant information about these patterns of violent victimization.

TABLE 11.2 **Hate Crime in the United States, 2018**

Based on	Number of reported incidents	Number of victims
Race/ethnicity/ancestry	4047	5155
Religion	1419	1550
Sexual orientation	1196	1445
Disability	159	179
Gender	47	61
Gender identity	168	189

Source: Federal Bureau of Investigation 2018a.

Racially motivated behavior is the most common form of hate crime (see table 11.2). African Americans are the most likely targets of hate crimes, victimized grossly disproportionately to their representation in the overall population (1,943 of the 7,120 reported incidents, over one-quarter of all reported hate crimes in 2018). Anti-Jewish hate crime and hate crimes directed against gay men are the next most common forms (Federal Bureau of Investigation 2018a). Hate crimes against Muslims have also become more frequent, especially as Donald Trump's presidential campaign in 2015 and 2016 ignited a surge in anti-Muslim violence (Potok 2016). More recently Asian Americans have also been subjected to increased hate crime as public sentiment against Asians was inflamed by the labeling of the COVID-19 pandemic a "Chinese virus."

The FBI does not categorize hate crime data according to victims' immigrant status. Even if they did, undocumented immigrants would likely be reluctant to report crimes against them for fear of detention or deportation. Experts note, however, that hate crimes against Hispanic-identified people have increased in recent years, especially as anti-immigrant hate crimes have become more frequent (Federal Bureau of Investigation 2018a; Mosley 2019).

Often hate crimes are committed not just by individuals but also by organized movements, such as White supremacist groups (Levin and Nolan 2016). Such movements emerge under particular social and historical conditions, particularly when dominant groups perceive a racial threat to their status in society. White people who try to defend their place in society may come to think that gains for racial-ethnic groups are coming at the expense of White people. The surge in hate crimes and the increased activity of White supremacist groups during the Trump presidency are evidence of this phenomenon. Movements based on hatred threaten the safety and well-being of targeted groups.

Immigration and Crime: Rhetoric and Fact

Framing Question: Do immigrants commit more crimes than native-born US residents?

Immigrants have a long history of being demonized as criminals: At the beginning of the twentieth century, Irish immigrants were stereotyped as prone to gang violence. Italians have been depicted as mobsters, as if all were part of the Mafia. Mexican and South and Central American immigrants, especially men, are stereotyped as violent "macho" men. Despite the rhetoric, the fact is that crime is lower among immigrants than among other populations (Ewing et al. 2015).

Although the majority of Americans think immigrants make the country stronger, one-quarter believe that immigrants are more likely than US citizens to commit serious crimes. Half of Americans also think immigrants are making crime worse (Pew Research Center 2018). There is, however, little connection between perceptions of immigrant crime and reality.

Numerous studies have found that *crime is committed less frequently by immigrants*—of all ethnicities—than by native-born people, including crimes committed against those in the same ethnic group. It is true that the longer immigrants remain in the country, the more likely it is that they will be involved with crime. First-generation Americans—that is, immigrants—are 45 percent less likely to commit violent crimes than are second- and third-generation Americans of the same ethnicity. Furthermore, this pattern holds for Hispanic, White, and Black immigrants. Contrary to popular belief, a higher concentration of immigrants within a neighborhood is also associated with lower rates of violent crime (Krivo et al. 2018; Xie and Baumer 2019). And, as immigration has increased in recent years, violent crime has actually decreased (Ousey and Kubrin 2014). The fact is that immigrants are far more likely to be victims of crime than to be offenders (Martinez 2014; Martinez and Valenzuela 2006).

Claims that immigrants are criminals are false. The fact is that recent immigrants are less likely to commit crime than other groups.

Source: AP Photo / Craig Ruttle.

A better predictor of crime than immigration per se is social disorganization within communities (e.g., an absence of community organizations, churches, and watch groups). Immigrant communities tend to produce strong social bonds; thus crime rates in such communities tend to be lower (Emerick et al. 2013; Martinez 2014).

Criminal Injustice: Race and the Administration of Justice

Framing Question: How does racism influence the administration of justice in the United States?

Until recently African Americans were the largest minority group in the United States, but they have now been surpassed by Latinos. As 13 percent of the US population, African Americans are overrepresented in virtually every indicator of criminal justice—in victimization by crime, in the likelihood of arrest, and as prisoners in local jails and in state and federal prisons. Increasingly Latinos are also overrepresented in the criminal justice system, increasing as a proportion of the nation's incarcerated citizens (Bronson and Carson 2019).

At every stage of criminal justice—or "criminal injustice," as many call it—people of color are routinely overpoliced and disproportionately arrested and convicted. When convicted, African Americans are likely to receive longer sentences than others, often even for the same crimes others commit. They are also far more likely to be given the death penalty and make up almost half of all death row inmates (Snell 2019). Despite a constitutional guarantee of equal protection under the law, racism is deeply embedded in our nation's police forces and criminal courts and deeply embedded in the administration of justice. Scholars have demonstrated that even without the presence of overt prejudice, racism in our nation's courts is systemic and institutionalized (Rios, Carney, and Kelekay 2017; Van Cleve 2016).

Although closely matched in socioeconomic status to African Americans, Hispanic men are imprisoned at about half the rate that are African American men but at over three times that of White men (Bronson and Carson 2019). Still, a routine traffic stop is a risky encounter for Latinos, as it is for African Americans. Research shows that Latinos have a disproportionate risk of arrest and citation from traffic stops, and unauthorized immigrants may be subject to deportation. Because the police are likely to racialize them, Latinos face some of the same risks that African Americans face (Armenta 2016). Researchers have also found that, even when they have legal immigration status, Latinos are reluctant to contact the police after being victimized by a crime because they fear the police will deport them (Menjívar et al. 2018).

There are many widely held misperceptions about race and crime, but there is substantial evidence that race plays a significant role in the execution of justice. In the midst of widespread public fears about race and crime, it is easy to overlook the fact that 70 percent of all arrests are of White people. Whites are also arrested for two-thirds of all rapes, and they commit most of the White-collar crime, such as embezzlement and fraud, in the United States (Federal Bureau of Investigation 2016). Still, relative to their size in the population, African Americans and Latinos are a disproportionate number of those caught in the criminal justice system. Why?

Do African Americans and Latinos commit more crime, or are they just targeted more by the criminal justice system? We address this question in the last section

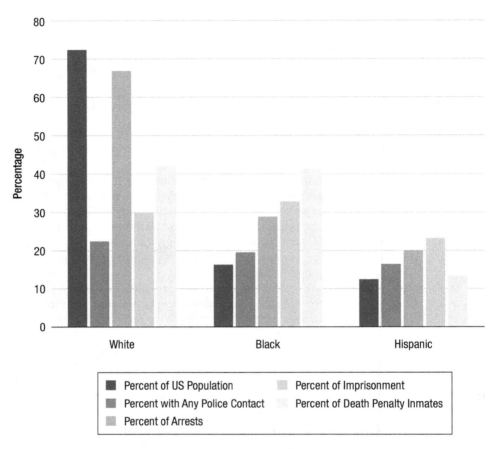

FIG. 11.4 Race and Ethnicity in the Criminal Justice System

Sources: Bronson and Carson 2019; Davis, Whyde, and Langton 2018; Federal Bureau of Investigation 2018a; NAACP Legal Defense and Educational Fund, Inc., 2020.

of this chapter but must first examine the different steps in the administration of justice. Racial discrimination persists in the United States through every step of the criminal justice system, starting with the likelihood of arrest (see figure 11.4) and continuing all the way through the administration of the death penalty. Although racial discrimination is not as overt as it was years ago—when, among other things, African Americans were formally excluded from serving on juries and could be lynched for the mere hint of violating a social norm—extensive evidence of institutional racism remains in the US system of justice.

Policing and Social Control

Racial stereotypes portray young Black and Latino men as suspicious and potentially dangerous. As a consequence and starting at an early age, Black and Latino young men and boys are targeted for enhanced scrutiny from various authorities. Ample research finds that Black and Latino boys are more likely to be suspended,

LIVING WITH RACISM

The Routinization of Police Harassment: A Young Boy's Story

Dr. Victor Rios is a distinguished sociologist who studies race, crime, and juvenile justice. In *Punished: Policing the Lives of Young Black and Latino Boys* (2011), he examines the criminalization of minority youth in their routine encounters with police and state agencies. Rios knows his subject well—not only as a scholar but also as someone who was routinely hassled by the police as a young boy. His account of those times is a classic example of the policing of minority youth:

> Growing up I experienced constant police harassment and brutality, making me normalize police violence in my community. I personally had my face stomped to the cement by the police at age fifteen. My younger brother had been dragged out of a car through the window and beaten at age fourteen by a gang of notorious police officers who called themselves "the Riders." When we filed complaints with the Oakland Police Department or talked to lawyers for help, we were ignored. It seemed that there was nothing we could do about unsanctioned police violence, that no one cared, and that there were no avenues for getting the word out.

Source: Rios 2015:59.

put in detention, or expelled from school, even as early as middle school. Being labeled early as a troublemaker has long-term consequences (Ferguson 2000; Rios 2011 and 2015).

According to sociologist Victor Rios, what happens to Black and Latino males is **social death**—a process by which they lose their humanity. Rios writes that male Latino and Black youths experience social death by being "rendered as criminal suspects not just by police but by schools, community centers, social workers, merchants, community members, and even family members. By the time that these young men become young adults, their lives have been policed, punished, and dehumanized by various institutions" (Rios 2015:60). Rios, now a highly successful academic scholar, describes his own early experience with police in his community in "Living with Racism," above.

The result of such intensive policing is that by age eighteen about one-third of Black men have experienced at least one arrest, compared to 22 percent of White men. As young people enter their twenties, the racial gap in arrest rates grows: nearly half (49 percent) of Black men have been arrested at least once by age twenty-three, compared to 38 percent of White men (Brame et al. 2014).

The routine suspicion with which Black and Latino men are viewed is also familiar to them. Black and Latino men can report many personal experiences of being stopped for questioning for "driving while Black" or "driving while Brown." With some frequency Black and Latino men, regardless of social class, are stopped by police for "being in the wrong neighborhood," even if the neighborhood is in fact their own.

This is an example of **racial profiling**—that is, the practice of using race—and race alone—as a criterion for stopping or detaining a person on suspicion of their having committed a crime. Racial profiling is a well-known and highly common phenomenon, evidenced in one way by studies that have examined the frequency of motorists being stopped, ticketed, and searched. Black Americans are pulled over for traffic stops by police more often than are Whites. Although there are only small differences between whether Black and Latino drivers are ticketed once stopped, Blacks and Hispanics are three times more likely to be searched compared to Whites (Langton and Durose 2013). Studies have also shown that Black Americans are four times more likely than Whites to experience the use of force during encounters with the police; Hispanics, twice as likely (Hyland, Langton, and Davis 2015). Traffic stops are annoying to anyone but can be especially frightening if you are a person of color. For Black and Latino citizens, any police encounter can be deadly. The public has now witnessed this all too often. Breonna Taylor, Philando Castile, Eric Garner, Sandra Bland, Michael Brown, Freddie Gray, and others: These became household names to many for the first time when the public viewed the brutal death of George Floyd at the hands of police in May 2020. Tragically there are likely to be others added to this list by the time you read this book.

Research on police shootings has been limited because police departments alone keep such records, if they are kept at all. What we know from some studies is that young Black men are one-quarter of those shot and killed by police and Hispanics 19 percent—both overrepresented relative to their proportion in the population (Fox et al. 2019; Tate et al. 2020). Less well known is the fact that Native Americans are the group most likely to be killed by law enforcement officers (Hansen 2017).

Protests against the all-too-common police shootings of Black and Hispanic people have sparked greater awareness of racial profiling in the United States in recent years.

Source: David Grossman / Alamy Stock Photo.

The victims of police shootings have almost always been young, are usually but not always men, and are commonly shot while fleeing or resisting arrest or perhaps just showing some "attitude." The shooters are mostly White officers, but officers of color have killed too.

Racial bias has much to do with the likelihood that a police officer will shoot a person. Various controlled experiments have shown that *implicit racial bias* increases the likelihood that someone will shoot even an unarmed target when that target is African American. Scientifically tested in laboratory settings, these findings have serious implications for actual police behavior. A police officer may have to make a quick decision to shoot or not shoot a suspect. Implicit bias that the officer may not even be aware of can trigger their response (Eberhardt 2019). Such findings are now being used in training programs for police officers in an effort to reduce unwarranted police shootings.

Clearly the issue of police brutality is a serious concern for the US public. Eighty-four percent of African Americans say Blacks are treated less fairly than Whites by the police; 63 percent of Whites believe this (Gramlich 2019). What remains to be seen is whether bias training will be enough: probably not, because, as the Black Lives Matter movement shows, racism in police departments is *systemic*. That is, it goes beyond the misdeeds of a few "bad apples" or changing some bad attitudes. Changing police behavior is a matter of both individual and institutional change. Whether the nation has the political will to tackle the institutional issues is yet to be seen.

Getting Tough on Crime: Racial Disparities in Sentencing

Under the Reagan administration in the 1980s, the United States undertook a crusade to "get tough on crime." The result, as we will see, was a dramatic increase in imprisonment. Sentencing policies were also changed. Prior to the "get tough" movement, judicial officials had more discretion than they do now in sentencing decisions. The new, more punitive approach—based on explicit social policies such as mandatory sentencing for drug offenses and the infamous "three strikes, you're out" policy—reduced judicial discretion. The result was a swelling of the nation's incarcerated (Gabbidon and Greene 2016).

Even with some relaxing of these policies, patterns of racial disparities in sentencing continue to be seen. Research shows that Black and Hispanic offenders are more likely than Whites to be incarcerated after arrest. Discrimination in sentencing means that Black and Latino offenders often receive longer sentences for the same crime when compared to their White counterparts. Factors such as severity of the crime, the offender's employment status, a prior record, and even the region of the country in which they are tried have a role in sentencing, too, but an offender's race matters in and of itself (Spohn 2015).

Racial minorities are also given longer sentences for minor crimes such as drug offenses. Some research shows than Hispanics receive even harsher sentences than do African Americans—at least in regions where they are the majority population (Ulmer and Johnson 2004). People of color who victimize Whites are also sentenced more harshly than when the victim is of the same race. As concluded by a national review of current research on sentencing, "There is compelling evidence that those who murder Whites, and particularly Blacks who murder Whites, are sentenced to death and executed at disproportionately high rates" (Spohn 2015:56).

The research on racial disparities in sentencing is complex and often highly nuanced, but the end result is that Black and Latino men convicted of crime serve more time than do White, non-Hispanic men (Bradley and Engen 2016). Black and Latino offenders also received harsher punishments when tried in courts with lower minority representation, in jurisdictions in the American South, and when the offender is young. Moreover racial disparities in sentencing are *more pronounced* for less severe offenses. Native Americans face even greater odds of incarceration than do Latinos and Africans Americans, whereas Asian American receive sentences and conviction rates comparable to White Americans (Franklin 2018; Franklin and Henry 2020).

Given these facts, it is little wonder than that nation's jails and prisons are bulging. As legal scholar Michelle Alexander has noted, "The fact that more than half of the young Black men in any large American city are currently under the control of the criminal justice system (or saddled with criminal records) is not—as many argue—just a symptom of poverty or poor choices but rather evidence of a new racial caste system at work" (Alexander 2010:16).

Mass Incarceration

The most obvious indication of this new racial caste system is the US prison system. The emergence of more punitive criminal justice policies has created a new social

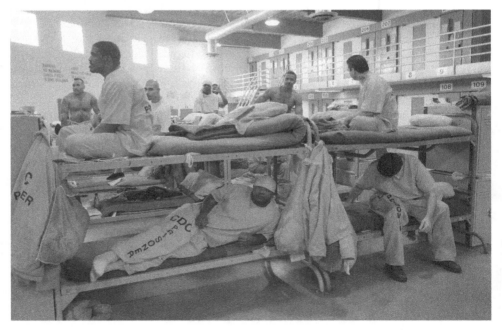

Mass incarceration of Hispanic and Black people has been called "the new Jim Crow."

Source: AP Photo / Spencer Weiner.

problem: the **mass incarceration** of people of color. Some argue that the problem of mass incarceration is now greater than the problem of crime per se (Coates 2015). The impact of mass incarceration falls not just on incarcerated individuals but also on families, communities, and society as a whole. Among other threats created by mass incarceration, it establishes a large class of citizens (ex-felons) who are forever disenfranchised from voting, thus imperiling democracy. The shifts in population apportionment brought by mass incarceration also shift the balance of power from urban centers to suburban and rural areas, because as more people from urban areas are incarcerated, they are disenfranchised, thus giving more voting clout to suburban and rural areas (Haynie 2019; Remster and Kramer 2018).

The United States now has the highest imprisonment rate of any nation in the world, holding one-quarter of the world's prisoners while having only 5 percent of the world's population. The increase in imprisonment in the United States has been dramatic since the mid-1970s, when a "war on drugs" was launched by the Nixon administration. From the mid-1970s to the mid-1980s, the US incarceration rate doubled and then doubled again over the next ten years. By 2017, the nation's imprisonment rate had reached 440 per 100,000 people (Bronson and Carson 2019), although imprisonment rates have fallen somewhat in very recent years.

People of color are a hugely disproportionate number of those in prison: 60 percent of the imprisoned are members of only 30 percent of the US population (see figure 11.5). Race and ethnicity are the most important factors in explaining these high rates of incarceration, even at a time when the actual crime rate has declined (Bronson and Carson 2019).

The mass incarceration of African Americans has been unprecedented in US history. In 1980, for example, 5.5 percent of Blacks had a history of felony conviction, compared to 2.1 percent of the adult population overall. By 2010, the US felony

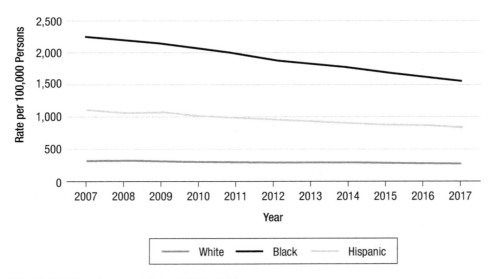

FIG. 11.5 US Imprisonment Rates (2007–2017)

Source: Bronson and Carson 2019.

conviction rate for Blacks had risen to 18.3 percent, with rates over 20 percent in many states, compared to 6.4 percent for the overall adult population (Uggen 2016).

It may seem that the increase in imprisonment accounts for the recorded drop in the US crime rate, but the relationship between crime rates and incarceration is not as clear as you might think. Most experts attribute the increase in imprisonment to social policies that stemmed from the war on drugs. Increases in imprisonment occur largely because of drug arrests and not more serious crimes. Though no more likely to sell illegal drugs than are Whites, people of color have the highest arrest rates for drug offenses. What was to have been a war on drugs has turned into a war on young Black and Hispanic men.

John Ehrlichman, former chief domestic advisor for the Nixon administration, reported that the war on drugs was a specific policy of the Nixon administration (under which mass incarceration started to expand) designed to neutralize the anti-war left and Black people, who had grown increasingly radical in the 1970s (see chapter 12). In Ehrlichman's words, "We knew we couldn't make it illegal to be either against the war or Black, but by getting the public to associate the hippies with marijuana and Blacks with heroin, and then criminalizing both heavily, we could disrupt those communities" (Ehrlichman, cited in Baum 2016).

What has evolved from the war on drugs was the creation of a **carceral state**, defined as a society in which concerns about security are widespread and prisons become a mechanism for social control of a population. Increased surveillance of public places, high rates of imprisonment, and fear of crime also permeate such a society. It is clear that in the United States the consequences of a carceral state are worst for poor and minority men (Western 2007 and 2018).

The Spillover Effect: Social Consequences of Mass Incarceration

Imprisonment leaves a permanent mark. Postrelease, those who have served time find themselves deprived many of the basic rights of US citizenship. The consequences of the carceral state for both individuals and whole communities can be devastating. Analyst Christopher Uggen (2016) calls this the **spillover effect**, the consequences of imprisonment that profoundly affect the lives of former prisoners and the people around them. Even with a clean record, a former prisoner will find it very difficult to find work. In most states, felons lose the right to vote, and in many places they cannot receive public assistance.

The likelihood of employment after prison falls especially hard on Black men, as shown by sociologist Devah Pager in her widely cited studies of employment, race, and former prisoners. Pager developed a clever research design utilizing role players who posed as ex-convicts looking for work. Her fake job seekers included both Black and White men, some with a criminal record, others without. They all used the exact same script while looking for work. The results of her study reveal the great extent to which both race and ex-con status influence the likelihood of employment. All of the ex-cons in her study, Black and White, received fewer callbacks for interviews than did those with no record. But most interesting was her finding that Black men who were *not* ex-cons were less likely to be invited back for job interviews than were Whites who were ex-cons. In other words, the effect of race alone actually exceeds the effect of incarceration (Pager 2007; Pager and Pedulla 2015; Phelps and Pager 2016).

Once released from prison, former prisoners (who may be in their prime working years) face severe material hardship. A comprehensive study of former prisoners finds that more than half are unemployed, two-thirds receive public assistance, and many have to rely on women relatives for financial support and housing. Their disadvantage leaves former prisoners among the least socially integrated in society. "Material insecurity combined with the adjustment to social life outside prison creates a stress of transition that burdens social relationships in high-incarceration communities" (Western et al. 2015:1512).

The spillover effect also impacts families and communities. For children alone, the consequences of having a parent in prison are tremendous. One million Black children now have a father in jail. More than half of the Black fathers in prison report being the family breadwinner. Sixty-two percent of Black children have a parent who has gone to prison, compared to 17 percent of Hispanic children and 15 percent of White children (Coates 2015).

Communities are affected by the spillover as well. Having large numbers of ex-offenders in a given place has negative effects for the whole community; for one thing, it raises the unemployment rate of the area. High rates of incarceration also lessen the availability of marriageable men. Fewer marriageable men means more female-headed households and, thus, higher rates of poverty. A cycle of poverty is generated—not because of people's values but because of unemployment and a family's reliance on a woman's lower wages.

The National Research Council has also concluded that the costs of mass incarceration to the nation are so significant as to outweigh the benefits of a "get tough on crime" approach (Travis, Western, and Redburn 2014). It is true that some White, rural communities have lobbied for and benefited from having prisons located in their communities as a boost to employment. But more generally the expansion of prisons, costing over $80 billion per year, consumes funds that could otherwise be spent on education and social services to help poor, minority communities. The cost of mass incarceration to the nation's people of color cannot be overestimated.

Death Row and Wrongful Conviction

Debates about capital punishment in the United States have long included discussions of the impact of racial discrimination. The United States is the only Western democracy that still utilizes the death penalty. The constitutionality of the death penalty has been challenged repeatedly over the years in a complex series of cases before the US Supreme Court. In 1972, the Supreme Court ruled in *Furman v. Georgia* that the death penalty was unconstitutional. The decision rested on the lack of uniformity from state to state in determining whether a penalty of death was warranted. Only four years later, in *Gregg v. Georgia* (1976), the Court reversed itself, with a slight majority of the justices ruling that state statutes had eliminated the procedural disparities found earlier in the determination of death penalty judgments. Legal scholars and some Supreme Court justices nonetheless argued that the administration of the death penalty carried with it great race and class bias (Walker et al. 2012).

In 1987, the death penalty was constitutionally tested again when Warren McCleskey, a Black man in Georgia, was sentenced to death for shooting and killing a White police officer. In his petition to the Court, attorneys for McCleskey argued that there was racial discrimination in death penalty cases and based McCleskey's appeal on research finding that murder defendants were more likely to receive the death penalty when the victim was White. In the highly controversial *McCleskey v. Kemp* decision, the Supreme Court ruled that no racial bias was specifically found in the McCleskey case. Warren McCleskey was executed in the electric chair in 1991.

Current constitutional law allows capital punishment, although it is questionable whether the Supreme Court will eventually determine that capital punishment constitutes cruel and unusual punishment. People debate the death penalty on various grounds, especially moral ones. Public opinion about the death penalty is divided along racial lines. Nearly two-thirds (59 percent) of White Americans favor the death penalty and half of Hispanics (47 percent) support it, but only one-third (36 percent) of African Americans do (Masci 2018). Several states have now repealed the death penalty based on various concerns, citing racial discrimination among them.

Although race per se has not been the main argument in recent challenges to the death penalty, descriptive data certainly suggest that racial discrimination is still a factor in rulings for the death penalty. Almost three thousand prisoners are on death row in the United States, 42 percent of whom are Black, far out of proportion to the numbers of Black people in the general US population. Both the number and proportion of death row prisoners who are Black has been fairly constant since 2000. California, Texas, and Florida account for almost half of those on death row, even though those three states combined only contain between one-quarter and one-third of the US population (Snell 2019).

Research on racial discrimination in death penalty cases shows that "race continues to be a significant factor in the administration of capital punishment" (Poveda 2009:566). Racial disparities in judgments for the death penalty seem to be higher in cases where the evidence is less clear. In other words, there is less racial difference in death penalty decisions in the most aggravated and clear-cut cases. In cases that are not so clear-cut, racial disparities are higher (professor of law David C. Baldus, cited in Barak et al. 2015:278). Various factors other than race are related to death penalty decisions, including whether the defendant has adequate legal counsel, the race of the victim, and the accused's prior record. Scholars debate the extent to which race itself plays a role when there is a death-eligible trial, but the large percentage of people of color on death row certainly suggests that race matters.

Equally disturbing are cases of wrongful conviction. Sixty percent of the exonerations that have occurred as a result of exculpatory DNA evidence are of people of color, most of them African American (Gross, Possley, and Stephens 2017; Stevenson 2015a and 2015b). One of the main reasons for wrongful conviction is eyewitness testimony, notoriously unreliable as evidence and certainly influenced by racial bias. A troublingly large portion of the cases of Black prisoners being exonerated after serving a prison sentence are those in which White eyewitnesses identified a Black person as the culprit.

Even though the number of cases where wrongful conviction has been proven is small, research indicates that the combination of race of the defendant and race of the victim is a significant factor in wrongful convictions (Harmon 2004). Death penalty cases and wrongful convictions are two more ways that racial injustice pervades the criminal justice system. As sociologists have concluded, how Whites racially frame Black men in criminalized terms is central to how much discrimination is weighed against Black men (Feagin 2013; Free and Ruesink 2012).

Explaining the Race-Crime Connection

Framing Question: What factors influence the connection between race and crime?

This chapter has shown the extent to which racial inequality seeps into the system of justice. What remains is explaining why crime is higher among some groups and how racial inequality is central to that pattern. Are people of color, particularly African Americans, more likely to commit crime? If so, why? Or are people of color just more likely to be identified by the criminal justice system, labeled early as delinquent, and then trapped in an unjust system?

These may seem like simple questions, but they are not. We have already seen how official statistics distort how race and crime are reported. Throughout this chapter we have also seen how race influences the administration of justice. Even considering these facts, though, crime rates are still higher among some groups than others. The question is why. There are plenty of people in every race and ethnic group who engage in criminal behavior. Understanding criminal behavior—and then developing policies to reduce it—requires as a basis an understanding of the conditions and contexts in which crime is most likely to occur.

Criminologists debate various theories about crime, the particulars of which are too nuanced to report here. But one thing is certainly true: "Crime and crime control are inseparable from the changing reality of inequality, hierarchy, and power" (Barak et al. 2015:2). Based on criminological theory, several points can be made to frame a theoretical and social structural analysis of the connection between race and crime:

1. *Crime has both objective and subjective dimensions.* The subjective dimensions of crime include the perceptions and fears that people hold, many of which are generated by media narratives that distort the actual truth about crime. Subjective beliefs also shape what is considered crime and what is not. In addition, dominant beliefs about crime reinforce racial inequality by labeling people of color as criminals, potentially increasing the surveillance and social control over minority populations.

   According to **labeling theory**, once a person or group is identified as "criminal," the label sticks, and it is then difficult for the person to shed it. Dominant groups also have greater power than others to apply labels, especially on the most disadvantaged. Labeling theory helps explain the cycle that emerges when people of color are identified early on as troublemakers, are punished, and are potentially pushed into more misbehavior. Once identified as deviant or criminal, the person so labeled finds it difficult to escape the system of social control. Victor Rios calls this cycle **hypercriminalization**, "a process by which an individual's nondeviant behavior and everyday interaction become treated as risk, threat, or crime and, in turn, have an impact on his or her perceptions, worldview, and life outcome" (Rios 2015:63). Hypercriminalizing young people of color then produces what Rios calls a system of constant *punitive social control.*

2. *Criminal behavior is shaped by the actions and decisions of individual actors, but those actors operate within a social environment.* Understanding the social context of crime does not ignore or excuse the criminal behavior of individuals, but it locates the cause of such behavior in social factors, not in individual attitudes or beliefs. Environmental factors such as family instability, overcrowding, concentrated poverty, and residential segregation shape the behaviors of people living in such contexts. While it is easy to simply blame a person for bad behavior, that behavior can often be understood in the context of social disorganization. For example, when social bonds are loosened (such as from chronic unemployment), crime and other forms of antisocial behavior can result from strong feelings of alienation from the dominant society (Emerick et al. 2014).

3. *Human beings develop cultures in response to social conditions, but cultures alone do not explain criminal behavior.* Some attribute high levels of crime by people of color, men especially, to a subculture of violence, as if people's values and cultural norms were the basis for criminal behavior. Such a view is common especially among White Americans, much less so among Black Americans. When whole communities are segregated from mainstream institutions and deprived of the resources needed for success, subcultures can develop, particularly as forms of resistance. Sociologists have long argued that when people are unable to achieve the goals established by the dominant society, they may find illegitimate means to achieve success (Merton 1938).

Urban ethnographer Elijah Anderson (1999) has studied the culture of poor inner-city communities and what he calls the *code of the street*—a set of behaviors and attitudes that develop in poor, inner-city, Black neighborhoods. The code is a survival strategy that provides people with respect in a context where they are otherwise devalued. The code is also a means of protection against potentially aggressive and violent behavior. Seen in this way, being "cool," "tough," and "streetwise" is a mode of self-defense. But these behaviors and attitudes are often interpreted by outsiders (including, possibly, the police) as threatening and disrespectful.

Acknowledging that particular cultural forms may develop in underprivileged communities does not, however, provide an adequate understanding of criminal action. Cultures emerge in the context of social structures as people adapt to the conditions they face. As with individualistic explanations, explanations that rely solely on culture overlook the social structures that deprive people of sound economic, political, and social opportunities.

4. *The economic system blocks opportunity for some while providing greater advantage for others, producing conditions ripe for criminal behavior.* In chapter 7, we saw the problems associated with the very high rates of unemployment among minority young people. Structural unemployment, little opportunity for economic advancement, and the isolation of young people of color in residentially segregated and poor neighborhoods produce the urban underclass

(Wilson 1987). Individuals' minds and cultural values are not the source of this problem.

Much, though not all, of the urban underclass is comprised of young people of color, the group most likely to be apprehended and held in the criminal justice system. Black male joblessness in particular is, then, one of the prime reasons for high rates of crime. As put by sociologists Robert Sampson and William Julius Wilson, who have extensively studied such neighborhoods, "Patterns of residential inequality give rise to the social isolation and ecological concentration of the truly disadvantaged, which in turn leads to structural barriers and cultural adaptations that undermine social organization and hence the control of crime" (Sampson and Wilson 1995:38; see also Krivo et al. 2018, and see Sampson, Wilson, and Katz 2018). Although Sampson and Wilson note the role of culture in urban crime, they argue that it is the social structure of blocked opportunity that produces much criminal behavior.

5. *Systemic racial inequality pervades the administration of justice* (Barak et al. 2015). Patterns of inequality not only produce criminal behavior but also shape how the system of justice operates. This chapter has shown how each step of the criminal justice process engages racial inequality. Racial discrimination within the criminal justice system is usually not overt, but it is nonetheless systematic. Factors such as the ability of people to pay for sound representation, to post bond, or to return to good jobs following incarceration are all conditioned on a person's available resources.

Despite the idea that justice is said to be blind, systematic racial discrimination "occurs at all stages of the criminal justice system, in all places, and at all times. That is to say, there is discrimination in arrest, prosecution, and sentencing (stages); in all parts of the country (places); and without any significant variation over time" (Walker et al. 2012:29, parentheticals original). Race must be central to the understanding of crime and criminal justice (Peterson et al. 2018).

Conclusion

At the turn of the nineteenth century, based on his detailed study of the city of Philadelphia, the great sociologist W. E. B. Du Bois wrote, "Crime is a phenomenon of organized social life and is the open rebellion of an individual against his social environment" (Du Bois 1899:235). Du Bois might be surprised to see how much crime still plagues many of the most disadvantaged communities in our nation. For many people of color, new economic and social opportunities are unprecedented, and we should remember those successes while also looking at the disruptive and criminal behavior of others.

The harms done to people from crime are real and cannot be denied. Yet even while acknowledging the human suffering that stems from crime, it is important to see the structural injustices that produce criminal behavior. People are quick to blame individual misbehavior for crime, but a more accurate, though, and complex analysis of crime shows the societal factors involved. Understanding the social structure of crime will more likely lead to social policies that reduce both crime and the racial disparities that pervade the criminal justice system.

Key Terms

carceral state 290

crime index 275

hate crime 279

hypercriminalization 293

labeling theory 293

mass incarceration 289

National Crime Victimization Survey 275

racial profiling 285

social death 285

spillover effect 290

Uniform Crime Reports 275

Critical-Thinking Questions

1. What evidence do you see in your community of a *carceral state*?
2. Using arrest rates, sentencing, or incarceration as your example, describe how *institutional racism* operates in the criminal justice system.

Student Exercises

11.1. Using the tool provided by the US Bureau of Justice Statistics' NCVS Victimization Analysis Tool (http://www.bjs.gov/index.cfm?ty=nvat), build a table involving personal victimization by crime. You will need to select a year (or range of years) as well as a victimization type. Select race/ethnicity as your first variable and then a second variable of your choice. What does your table reveal, and how would you explain what you observe?

11.2. Go to the Web page of the Innocence Project (https://www.innocenceproject .org), and review the profiles provided of prisoners who have now been exonerated based on exculpatory DNA evidence. Of the cases included, how many of the exonerated appear to be people of color? Make a list of all the contributing causes of conviction. What patterns do you see?

Challenging Questions/Open to Debate

Some argue that policing has assumed too broad a role in responding to emergencies that other responders (such as social workers, substance abuse counselors, and other crisis intervention workers) are better able to handle without escalating the situation at hand. Advocates of this position argue that shifting funding and responsibility for noncriminal situations to the police criminalizes behaviors that could be handled otherwise and risks escalation into violent encounters. Think of a situation where police have routinely been called (public drunkenness, suicide threat, mental health emergency, and so forth). Should such a situation require police action, or should public resources be diverted to other emergency responders?

TAKING ACTION AGAINST RACISM

Interrogating Injustice

Many organizations are fighting to challenge racism in the criminal justice system, Black Lives Matter among them. There are many issues to address, including redistributing funds from policing to social services, eliminating cash bail requirements, addressing mass incarceration, developing plans for the reentry of former prisoners back into their communities, and others. You can get involved by supporting organizations addressing these issues.

Resources:

Equal Justice Initiative, https://eji.org

Black Lives Matter, https://blacklivesmatter.com

The initiative to end cash bail, at the Center for American Progress, https://www.americanprogress.org/issues/criminal-justice/reports/2020/03/16/481543/ending-cash-bail/

Source: iStockphoto LP / Boarding1Now

CHAPTER 12

The Long Search for Racial Justice
Learning from the Past and Moving Forward

In order to get beyond racism, we must first take account of race. There is no other way. And in order to treat some persons equally, we must treat them differently.
—Supreme Court Justice Harry Blackmun (*University of California Regents v. Bakke* 1978:407)

Reverend Martin Luther King Jr.'s call (1963) to create a society in which people will "one day live in a nation where they will not be judged by the color of their skin but by the content of their character" inspires the ideal of color blindness. King's ideal guides much of our nation's approach to racial justice. A legal framework of equal rights is in place and undergirded by the constitutional principle of *equal protection*, established by the Fourteenth Amendment to the US Constitution, in 1868. King's exhortation, given at a time of racial crisis in US history, appealed to the American conscience to live up to a color-blind ideal as the path toward racial justice.

History has shown, however, that color-blind initiatives do not necessarily dismantle the entrenched system of racial inequality in the United States, as we have seen throughout this book. Despite the appeal of King's call, a fundamental question arises: How can we dismantle the *systemic racism* that permeates our society?

Given that racism is systemic—that is, built into the institutional structure of society—what strategies can best produce change? Should we use *color-blind* approaches to achieve racial equality, or do we need *race-conscious* actions? These questions guide the content of this chapter.

The color-blind ideal is consistent with the American belief in individualism and personal merit—that is, the idea that people should be judged and treated based on their actions and not on their personal characteristics, such as race, class, gender, or any number of other categorizations. This is an ideal many embrace, and it guides much of the legislation that protects civil rights for various groups. The color-blind ideal has also been the hallmark of various movements for social justice, including the civil rights movement.

But is this ideal enough? We have seen that even with laws in place that guarantee equal rights, racial inequality persists and is deeply embedded in US institutions. The Black Lives Matter movement as well as the long history of antiracist protest have shown us that even with color-blind approaches in place, some people are still treated as if their lives do not matter. Over time, race-specific changes have also been needed in order to open doors for previously excluded groups. Desegregating education, for example, sometimes required giving explicit consideration of race to build more diverse college admissions. The Black Lives Matter movement has asked the nation to consider what we must do to stop the racist treatment of Black men and women. And with that question now before us, what must we do to see not only that Black lives matter but also that the lives of Latinos, indigenous people, and Asian Americans matter, as do the lives of all people who have been robbed of human dignity and opportunity because of racism?

What strategies for change will enable us to move forward, and how should we think about antiracist change now? These questions are especially pressing as the United States has recently been rocked by mass racial protests, especially in the aftermath of the police murder of George Floyd. But this is not the only outrage that has demanded our attention. It is now a well-known fact that African Americans, Latinos, and members of the Navaho Nation have been far more likely to contract COVID-19 and die from it; this sobering fact puts racial disparities in US health care in stark relief. During the pandemic, Latinos have also been the hardest hit in terms of job loss (Krogstad et al. 2020). Even aside from these startling and troubling developments, incidents of racial hatred and acts of violence have risen in recent years, often fueled by statements from national leaders that vilified immigrants and antiracist protestors.

As the United States becomes more multiracial, thinking about race and antiracist change becomes evermore critical and complicated. Reducing racism and transforming racist institutions is not a simple task, nor is it likely to be accomplished quickly, as the nation's long-standing struggle for racial justice shows. Change is needed at every level of US culture and institutions—in individual awareness and education; within work, health, and criminal justice organizations; and in state and federal policy. Making change, though, requires that we have some understanding of different philosophies of change along with an awareness of the struggles and accomplishments of the past. It is to past forms of protest that we now turn.

The Early Road to Civil Rights

Framing Question: What are some of the earliest ways that people resisted racial and ethnic oppression?

Resistance to oppression can take many forms and is shaped by forces both internal and external to particular groups. Since before the founding of the United States, indigenous people fought hard for the preservation of their lands and lives. At varying points in US history, African Americans, Chicanos, Asian Americans, and other people of color have also had to fight for their rights and protect themselves from the harms of racial oppression. Sometimes the struggle for justice has meant outright revolt, and other times more subtle forms of resistance. During the days of slavery, for example, African Americans challenged the authority of White supremacy through whatever means possible, sometimes by slave revolts, sometimes by running away. Everyday actions of resistance under slavery could also have been as subtle as spitting in an owner's meal, feigning illness to slow work, or sabotaging a slave owner's property. The enslaved person's ultimate form of resistance lay in not allowing their mind to be controlled by a slave owner's beliefs.

Following the abolition of slavery in the United States in 1865, newly freed Black people were emboldened by the unprecedented freedoms found during the period of post–Civil War Reconstruction. This freedom was soon followed by massive repression, including changes to law as well as organized opposition by vigilante groups. By the end of the 1870s, a massive wave of retaliation had risen, beginning, some would say, with the formation of the Ku Klux Klan in 1865 and the gradual appearance of other White supremacist groups that terrorized Black communities. As we saw in the previous chapter, scholars estimate that, at least counting those we know about, close to five thousand people were lynched between 1882 and 1968. Most, but not all, were African American. Lynching of Black and Mexican Americans was often a public spectacle, conducted with the collusion of local law authorities acting in accordance with the wishes of the Anglo community (Acuña 2005; Carrigan and Webb 2003; Delgado 2009).

Even under these harsh conditions, people resisted in any way they could (Carson et al. 1987). Ida B. Wells's antilynching crusade is just one example (Giddings 2009). Resistance leaders were common in communities of color, which historian Elsa Barkley Brown calls "communities of struggle" (Brown 1995). We may not now know the names of all those Black, Latino, Asian, and Native American community leaders, but their struggles poured the foundation for those who followed. As historian Clayborne Carson and colleagues conclude, "A complex, powerful, and explosive cluster of human intentions was at the heart of almost all the struggles for justice, survival, defense, and transformation which were carried on by Black people" (Carson et al. 1987:5). You could say the same about other communities of color too.

Early on, especially following the Anglo annexation of the North American Southwest, Mexican Americans resisted their oppression in a variety of ways. Especially on the US borderlands of Arizona, New Mexico, Texas, and California, Mexican Americans fought for the rights of citizenship even while functioning as an internal colony within the United States, following the Mexican-American War that had ended in 1848. As a result of the Treaty of Guadalupe Hidalgo signed that year, Mexican Americans lost their homeland rights. In response, they fiercely resisted their oppression, sometimes through armed resistance but also through nonviolent protest and litigation, especially as Anglos used legal chicanery to rob Mexican Americans of their rights. Anglos seized land and robbed Mexican Americans of various rights even though many had been settled in the Southwest since the seventeenth century (M. Rodríquez 2014).

One of the most important developments during the early twentieth century for African American people was the widespread creation of Black institutions: universities, newspapers, mutual aid societies, women's organizations, banks, funeral homes, fraternal or sororal organizations, and others (Giddings 2007; Hughey and Parks 2011). During this time, Black communities "established their own network of medical, nursing, legal training institutions, and normal schools" (Hine 2004:1065), resulting in a professional class that was later critical to the evolution of Black activism. Urban Blacks, especially in the North, developed a tradition of business ownership and professional work in Black community (Williams 1998). These entities formed a system of parallel institutions to White society, providing safe spaces and communication networks that paved the way for what became the civil rights movement (Hine 2004).

The leadership that emerged from early Black and Mexican American civil rights work is impressive yet not as well known as it should be. The dogged work of African Americans, Asian Americans, Latinos, and Native Americans over the years laid some of the groundwork for civil rights organizing later in the twentieth century. There are numerous examples of such pathbreaking work, some of which is only now being discovered. Well known now is W. E. B. Du Bois, who cofounded the National Association for the Advancement of Colored People in 1909. The NAACP remains one of the most influential civil rights organizations in the United States. A. Philip Randolph organized the Brotherhood of Sleeping Car Porters in 1925, the first labor union that gave Black Americans the right to organize and be recognized as part of the American Federation of Labor. Countless African American women leaders—Mary Church Terrell, Ida B. Wells, Mary McLeod Bethune, and others—were likewise critical to the success of this historic struggle. Many of those who provided visionary leadership worked behind the scenes and, thus, are often less remembered and, in some cases, are only being recognized and celebrated today. Latinos founded the League of United Latin American Citizens in 1929 to fight discrimination and provide more education for their communities. In 1929, Japanese Americans founded the Japanese American Citizenship League, based on having earlier formed various civic clubs that had supported second-generation Japanese Americans (Takaki 1989). Under the leadership of Cesar Chavez, the United Farm Workers led a massive strike against the nation's grape industry, protesting working conditions for Chicano and Filipino grape pickers—a strike that began in 1965, lasted five years, and brought national attention to the exploitation of agricultural laborers (Ferriss and Sandoval 1997). These and other protest actions tell a long tale of people of color acting as agents of their own history, individually as well as collectively (see "Living with Racism," below).

LIVING WITH RACISM

A Professor, Not a Porter: Lawrence Matsuda

Social justice is rooted firmly in my life experiences and relationships. Being a minority in a White society is an issue I cannot escape. Recently I rented a luggage cart at Sea-Tac Airport in Seattle to pick up my wife's luggage at the United Airlines' carousel. While I was looking, a tall middle-aged White male approached me and pointed to his luggage on the carousel. He said, "My bag is over there." Showing no emotion, I turned and responded, "I am a professor, not a porter. I am afraid you'll have to pick up your own baggage."

Regardless of my professional accomplishments, training, or status, being an Asian American in a White society has meant being mistaken for: a waiter instead of a customer in a Chinese restaurant, a porter at the airport, a shoeshine person at a hotel, a foreigner from Japan, a Korean immigrant, and countless others. It makes me angry to deal with racial stereotypes that are insensitive, personally annoying, and insulting. Although I handle each situation differently, I found any response, no response, any exchange, or any reply makes me feel debased as a human being. I wonder, "Why even bother?"

I have experienced almost all the Asian racist remarks, ethnic slurs, insults, or well-meaning comments that effectively separate me from the larger White society in the United States. My blood pressure rises, triggering the adrenaline rush, especially when the offender feels he or she has delivered an insult so creative that surely I must have never heard it before. Nevertheless, my personal racial issues are: How can I channel my anger to creative endeavors that are positive, and how can that anger and energy be used for the betterment of the human family at large? I feel strongly that how one handles the anger in response to racism is the key to having a healthy life and being a productive citizen. From the point of view of my career, these feelings generate the following questions: How have these experiences shaped my identity? My teaching style? My perceived purpose in life and my career in education? Some of these questions will be answered, but most will raise more fundamental questions like: What do you believe? What do you value most? What can you do? *What do you believe?*

Source: Matsuda 2005:51–52.

Sociologist Aldon Morris (1986) argues that early organizing by Black people provided the intellectual, financial, organizational, and informational resources that were crucial in the mobilization of the civil rights movement. The internal strengths of the Black community provided the vision, energy, and skills that spawned civil rights organizing in the 1950s and 1960s (Carson et al. 1987). Even with internal resources of strength and resilience, there were limits in the early years to how much people could resist. Historian Darlene Clark Hine puts it succinctly with regard to Black communities in the first half of the twentieth century. "Fettered by inadequate economic resources, and dogged by the ever-present specter of white violence and terror," she writes, ". . . the marginal and precarious status of most African Americans severely restricted the space in which they could fashion resistance" (Hine 2004:1066).

External events—namely, the two world wars—helped forge the path toward protest. Black American, Mexican American, Native American, and Asian American men and women fought in both wars. When President Woodrow Wilson declared that the entry of the United States into World War I was to "make the world safe for democracy" (1917), people noticed that soldiers were fighting for democracy abroad while Black, Mexican, and other troops were not enjoying democracy back at home. Seeing this contradiction, A. Philip Randolph pressured the federal government to integrate the heavily segregated armed forces. Thus in 1941 President Franklin D. Roosevelt signed an order forbidding racial discrimination in federal agencies and companies engaged in war-related work. Then, in 1948, President Harry S. Truman signed Executive Order 9981, compelling the armed forces to desegregate at every level: "There shall be equality of treatment and opportunity for all persons in the armed forces," the order read, "without regard to race, color, religion, or national origin" (Truman 1948).

That same year Dr. Hector Garcia established the American GI Forum to advocate for the rights of Hispanic veterans who had returned from service during World War II. Today the American GI Forum still works to protect veterans' rights. These and other efforts gave hope to those longing to have their human rights affirmed.

The Civil Rights Movement

Framing Question: What are some of the landmark events of the civil rights movement, and how have they influenced the US laws and practices today?

One of the most profoundly influential developments of modern history—the civil rights movement—transformed the lives of African American people in the United States and also changed the legal and social framework that has given rights to many others, including Latinos, Asian Americans, women, LGBTQ people, and people with disabilities (Andersen 2004). As one example, when in 2020 the US Supreme Court ruled in *Bostock v. Clayton County* that federal employment law protects LGBTQ workers, the decision rested on the inclusion of the word "sex" in the Civil Rights Act of 1964. One of the ironies in American history is that the word "sex" had been added as an amendment to the bill's language by segregationist Howard Smith (House representative from Virginia), who thought that exploiting sex as a way of asserting women's rights was such a joke that the legislation would never pass. As a result of this language, perhaps even an ironic mistake, many people who have benefited from this landmark civil rights legislation are linked in history to the civil rights struggle.

A Movement Unfolds

The civil rights movement was inspired by Mohandas Gandhi's leadership of the Indian independence movement against British control. His movement spawned liberation movements around the world as people of color organized to throw off colonial rule and sought self-determination. The wide reach of the civil rights movement makes it one of the most transformative moments in world history and, no less, US history.

Victory over years of Jim Crow segregation came in 1954 with the Supreme Court's decision in *Brown v. Board of Education*, a major triumph for the NAACP, whose attorneys, most especially Thurgood Marshall, championed the case. In 1967, Marshall became the first African American appointed to the US Supreme Court. Recall that seven years before the *Brown* decision Marshall had represented Sylvia Mendez, a young girl at the time, who had been barred from attending California public schools. Argued before the California federal court, *Mendez v. Westminster* found the separate schools California was maintaining for Mexican, Asian, and Indian children to be unconstitutional (Foley 2005). Sylvia Mendez was awarded the Presidential Medal of Freedom in 2011, based on the precedent her case had established.

When *Brown* was decided in 1954, it provided a "detonating spark" (Bennett 1964:17) to the long-smoldering desire of Black people to enjoy full rights in the United States. As we have seen, the Black community had, prior to the 1950s, fought for their rights in many ways (Marks 1990). "Years of legal work, various court challenges, community organizing, and wrangling with school officials preceded this momentous decision. After all, it was not *Brown* per se that overthrew the social order of Jim Crow segregation but the mass mobilization of Black people and their White allies" (Andersen 2004:1079). So important were the precursors to the 1950s movement that historians conclude the *Brown* decision was actually the culmination, not the impetus, of the Black freedom struggle (Hine 2004).

Just fourteen days before the *Brown* decision, another Supreme Court decision had signaled that the nation was moving toward protecting greater civil rights. In *Hernandez v. Texas* the Court considered the petition of Peter Hernandez, a Mexican American man who had been tried for murder before an all-White jury. Hernandez's legal team included all Mexican American lawyers—the first Mexican American lawyers to argue before the US Supreme Court. They maintained that, even though Mexican Americans were defined as "White," they were treated as a separate class, such as by being excluded from juries and in other ways being overtly discriminated against. Therefore Mexican Americans should be protected, as were Black Americans, by the Fourteenth Amendment. The Supreme Court ruled unanimously in Hernandez's favor, giving Mexican Americans equal protection under the law and thereby extending the protections of the Fourteenth Amendment to other groups based on nationality and ethnicity. With the *Menendez* decision in place and *Brown* having struck down the "separate but equal" legal doctrine, there was new hope that Jim Crow segregation could be dismantled once and for all.

The Montgomery Bus Boycott

By 1955 Black people had already long been organizing to eradicate Jim Crow, and that summer a murder crystalized the movement. Emmett Till, a fourteen-year-old from Chicago, had been visiting family in rural Mississippi when he allegedly flirted with a White woman shopkeeper. Infuriated, the woman's husband and his half-brother, White men, abducted Emmett from his bed in the middle of the night, tortured him, and then finally killed him, dumping his body into the Tallahatchie River. When Emmett's mangled body was sent to his mother, Mamie, in Chicago, she insisted that the casket remain open for the funeral viewing so that the world could see how brutally her son had been killed. Tens of thousands of mourners filed past his casket, and images of his mutilated body were published in newspapers and magazines across the nation, infuriating Black Americans and stirring the conscience of many White Americans, who could vividly see the effects of racism. Till's murder galvanized the Black community. It was only ninety-five days after Till's murder that on December 1, 1955, in Montgomery, Alabama, Rosa Parks was arrested when she refused to give up her seat to a White passenger on a segregated bus.

Later it was often recounted that Parks, exhausted after a long day of work, had simply been too tired to move when the White bus driver had ordered her to change her seat, but this telling evokes the stereotype of the old, passive Black woman. In truth, Rosa Parks had long been engaged in activism prior to the events of that fateful day. She was the secretary for the local chapter of the NAACP, a position she had held since 1943. Nor was this the first time she had refused to obey the segregation rules on a city bus. Parks once reflected, "My resistance to being mistreated on the buses and anywhere else was just a regular thing with me and not just that day" (Carson et al. 1987:38). Through Rosa Parks's arrest, the NAACP found the opportunity they had been looking for to challenge segregation in Montgomery.

In Montgomery, Alabama, as in many Southern cities of the day, Jim Crow segregation was the rule. Black and White children could not attend the same schools. Black citizens could not be buried in White cemeteries. Black Americans could not vote. Not only were basic rights of citizenship denied to Black people, but everyday actions were also governed by Jim Crow's subtle norms (so-called rules of *racial etiquette*) and by explicit social policies. A Black person and a White person could not ride a taxi together (Branch 1988), nor could such a pair play checkers on public property. In retrospect, these regulations seem ridiculous, and yet they operated to maintain as complete a system of White supremacy as possible.

Buses in Montgomery were even more segregated than elsewhere. Some cities had a "floating line," whereby White passengers would fill in from the front and Blacks from the back. In Montgomery, however, Black passengers had to enter the bus through the front door, pay their fare, exit the bus, walk back, and reenter through the back door so as not to pass through the "White section" and run the risk of a passing Black man's leg touching a White woman's knees (Branch 1988). Within a federal military base in Montgomery, buses were integrated, but soldiers had to rearrange themselves into segregated seating patterns when the bus reentered municipal property.

Following Parks's arrest, Black leaders in Montgomery called for a total boycott of the bus line; it was neither the first time nor last that a boycott would be used to push back against the constraints imposed by racism. Black citizens in Baton Rouge, Louisiana, for example, had organized a bus boycott in 1953 to protest segregated seating there. In Baton Rouge, in Montgomery, and in most other cities in the South, Black riders made up the majority of bus passengers; hence boycotting the buses had the potential to economically cripple the bus company.

The Montgomery bus boycott lasted for an entire year. During this time, Black people in Montgomery organized their own extensive transportation network, relying on volunteer drivers who had their own cars as well as soliciting contributions to support taxi rides. Many walked long distances to work, sacrificing time and energy for the civil rights cause. Boycott organizers demanded three things from the bus company: (1) that bus drivers treat Black riders with courtesy, (2) that the bus company employ Black drivers on mostly Black routes, and (3) that seating be first come, first served (Branch 1988; Robinson 1987).

The boycott ended only when the US Supreme Court affirmed in 1956 that segregation on the buses was unconstitutional. As news of the decision spread, one Black person declared, "God Almighty has spoken from Washington, D.C.!" (Branch 1988:193). The Montgomery movement renewed feelings that change was possible if only the federal government would enforce the nation's existing laws. The boycott was also significant because it resulted in the rise of Black leadership, most notably that of Martin Luther King Jr. but also that of less visible ordinary citizens, particularly women from the local Black colleges who mobilized to challenge segregation (Robinson 1987). As the movement unfolded, this kind of grassroots leadership became essential.

Confronting Evil: Nonviolent Civil Disobedience

Following Montgomery, a full decade of extraordinary and visible activism fueled the civil rights movement. Protests were locally organized, often supported by national organizations such as the Congress of Racial Equality and the Southern Christian Leadership Conference, among others, but the movement developed from the grassroots.

Although many of the civil rights movement's most iconic leaders were men, women's leadership was critical to the historic movement's success.

Source: Everett Collection Inc. / Alamy Stock Photo.

It may be hard for people who did not live through this period of US history to imagine what it was like to witness these unfolding events. At the time, there were only three major television networks, which most Americans used to get the national news. In the decade spanning 1955 and 1965 the American public saw reportage of fire bombings of Black churches, demonstrators pummeled by fire hoses, Southern sheriffs refusing to allow Black people to vote, and the assassination of movement leaders, all of which brought the civil rights movement to the nation's living rooms. The violence directed against peaceful Black protesters particularly shocked many Americans, thus creating support among some White allies.

As its primary strategy, the civil rights movement used **nonviolent civil disobedience**. The objective was to disrupt the everyday workings of segregation by refusing to obey segregation-related laws, customs, and norms. Demonstrators were specifically trained in passive resistance, such as going limp when police tried to arrest them—which makes the arrest much more difficult—or not fighting back when they were being beaten by police or angry White mobs—which arouses the moral outrage of many onlookers. Nonviolent civil disobedience was also intended to deflect accusations that Black people were inciting violence and instead highlight the rampant and horrific violence of White racism.

The philosophy of the civil rights movement rested on an appeal to Christian values and a call for peace and understanding. Churches provided many of the organizing spaces as well as the values that guided the movement. Accordingly, resisting segregation was seen as confronting evil. The hope was to win White people's support through appeals to "brotherhood." As we will see, this philosophy of change is in distinct contrast to the more radical movement that eventually developed in the struggle for civil rights. The idea was that the "hearts and minds" of White Americans would change through appeals to conscience, and nonviolent action was central to that plan. The demands of the civil rights movement were essentially three:

1. access to public facilities and services
2. desegregation of education
3. the right to vote

One of the early struggles over the desegregation of schools came in 1957 in Little Rock, Arkansas. Local leaders, along with the NAACP, tried to enroll nine Black students in Little Rock High School. So strong was Governor Orval Faubus's resistance to integration that he called out the State National Guard to block the students' entry. Ultimately President Eisenhower had to call in one thousand soldiers from the 101st Airborne of the US Army to restore order and protect the young Black students. Rather than comply with federal orders, Governor Faubus resisted further by closing all four public high schools in Little Rock for a full school year. He was not alone in doing so. Virginia senator Harry Byrd organized other politicians to close an entire school system and many other public schools from 1958 to 1959, also in an attempt to stall desegregation (Branch 1988; Carson et al. 1987).

Even when facing such staunch opposition, the movement to desegregate pushed on. Protests were organized in many places—far too many to detail here. In Greensboro, North Carolina, four first-year students from historically Black college North Carolina A & T organized a sit-in at the local Woolworth's lunch counter in the winter of 1960. Sit-ins had been held before in other places, but the one in Greensboro captured national attention because it was the first to be nationally televised. Many students and community members joined in, and images of their protest were beamed across the nation by the news media. Sit-ins then spread to at least five other states (Branch 1988; Carson 1981).

That same year, the NAACP sued to have James Meredith, a Black man, enrolled at the University of Mississippi. The university registrar had refused to admit him to the segregated school, setting off a major crisis in the city of Oxford. It took twenty-three thousand soldiers (including the US Army, Marines, and Air Force) and many casualties to stop the rioting ignited by White students and others in objection to Meredith's enrollment. Under intense pressure from Black leaders and with a total lack of cooperation from the state's governor, President Kennedy finally federalized the Mississippi National Guard to escort Meredith safely to campus in the fall of 1962 (Branch 1988; Carson et al. 1987).

The press against segregation was relentless. In Albany, Georgia, hundreds of protesters, including Martin Luther King Jr., were arrested during a months-long campaign to desegregate buses and register Black voters. Freedom Rides began in 1961, in which Black and White riders deliberately traveled together from Northern states into the South to challenge segregated seating on the buses. During Freedom Summer, in 1964, hundreds of volunteers, including White and Black students from the North, streamed into the South to work on voter registration campaigns

(McAdam 1990 and 1999). Each of these and many other events kept the pressure on local municipalities and the federal government to enforce existing civil rights laws. Quite a few of the young people who participated and led this movement later became senior statespeople, including Representative John Lewis of Georgia, who in 1965 had been severely beaten on the Edmund Pettus Bridge in Selma, Alabama, when Alabama state troopers charged the crowd demonstrating for voting rights. "Bloody Sunday," as it became known, because of the violence done to peaceful protesters, became critical to the passage of the Voting Rights Act of 1965.

Many who lived through or are just learning about the civil rights movement find it hard to fathom the extreme violence that arose in opposition to civil rights. A bomb blast killed four young Black girls in Birmingham in 1963 while they were attending Sunday school. During Freedom Summer, the Ku Klux Klan brutally murdered three civil rights volunteers—James Cheney, a Black man; Michael Schwerner, a White man; and Andrew Goodman, also White—who had been investigating another church bombing in Mississippi. The following year, in 1965, the Klan murdered Viola Liuzzo, another White ally, when she was shuttling fellow civil rights activists to the airport. She had just participated in the famous march for voting rights from Selma to Montgomery that had been undertaken in response to Bloody Sunday. Countless lives were lost—children's as well as adults'—in the fight to win basic rights of citizenship for Americans of all colors.

Achievements of the Civil Rights Movement

The sacrifices of people's lives are a deep stain on the nation, but they seemed to not be in vain when President Lyndon Johnson signed the **Civil Rights Act of 1964.** The law was enacted to "enforce the constitutional right to vote, to confer jurisdiction upon the district courts of the United States to provide injunctive relief against discrimination in public accommodations, to authorize the Attorney General to institute suits to protect constitutional rights in public facilities and public education, to extend the Commission on Civil Rights, to prevent discrimination in federally assisted programs, to establish a Commission on Equal Employment Opportunity, and for other purposes" (Civil Rights Act 1964).

Even with the passage of the Civil Rights Act, voting registrars in many parts of the United States continued to use any number of techniques to disqualify Black voters, such as literacy tests that were virtually impossible to pass. It took a second law, the **Voting Rights Act of 1965,** to prohibit such evasions. The law states that "No voting qualification or prerequisite to voting, or standard, practice, or procedure shall be imposed or applied by any State or political subdivision to deny or abridge the right of any citizen of the United States to vote on account of race or color" (Voting Rights Act 1965).

The major accomplishments of the civil rights movement were the dismantling of Jim Crow segregation and the assembly of an equal rights framework in the law. Just as important, however, was change in the national consciousness. The civil rights movement ushered in a national push for color blindness, but this was clearly not enough to combat the vast racial inequality that remained in the United States. Despite the progress the civil rights movement made, many of the major needs of the Black community remained unmet. Poverty was widespread in Black communities: In 1965, 42 percent of Black people were still poor, compared to over half in 1955. Activists argued that civil rights gave people the right to sit in restaurants where they couldn't afford to eat. Nor was poverty limited to the South, where the focus of the civil rights movement had been trained. In other parts of the country, people of color were still suffering the indignities of racism, as was soon to be revealed when many of the nation's cities outside the South erupted in riots.

Power to the People: The Movement's Radical Turn

Framing Question: What were some of the more radical tactics and philosophies used by the Black protest movement as it unfolded?

People of color have never been monolithic in their political views, nor are they now (Hine 2004). From the very beginning, divergent philosophies have driven Black protest against oppression in the United States. So, too, with the varied underpinnings of the Chicano movement (which will be explored later in this chapter). By the mid-1960s, many Black activists were frustrated by the lackluster response of the federal government to civil rights demands and the gradualism of change. There was also a growing awareness of inadequate attention to racism outside of the South. Even as the original civil rights movement continued into the mid-1960s, a more radical approach to change was building.

The Student Nonviolent Coordinating Committee (SNCC, pronounced "snick") was one of the early organizations to question the civil rights approach, even while SNCC workers were deeply engaged within the movement. Founded by John Lewis, later to become a much-admired US senator, SNCC began informally when Black students organized the Greensboro sit-ins. As their work unfolded, SNCC activists worked in parts of the South usually considered by other civil rights organizers to be too dangerous or too hard to organize. But SNCC held to a philosophy of grassroots leadership: They would not impose the will of senior civil rights leaders on local residents but would instead let leadership emerge from within local struggles. This way people from the community would be able to sustain the movement when national organizations left (Carson 1981). This nonhierarchical style of organization later influenced other movements by other people of color as well as parts of the early women's movement, as we will see.

SNCC had initially adopted the nonviolent approach of other civil rights organizations, but during voter registration drives in the South, SNCC leaders became increasingly frustrated with the US government's failure to more fully embrace and enforce civil rights goals. Some SNCC leaders thought that Martin Luther King Jr. was too willing to compromise with the White establishment. They also became suspicious of White liberals and raised questions about whether integration should be the major goal.

Over time, SNCC's leaders became more radical, demanding a more confrontational approach to change, and fractures developed within the civil rights movement. Some, such as Stokely Carmichael (who in 1969 changed his name to Kwame Ture), declared the movement a revolution (Carson 1981), focusing less on civil rights and more on Black power. Even Martin Luther King Jr., who is mostly remembered for his strategy of nonviolent civil disobedience, was becoming more radical prior to his assassination in 1968. He was vocally critical of the US role in the Vietnam War and began focusing his actions on the economics of poverty (Branch 1988, 1998, and 2006).

The civil rights movement, challenging racial segregation and White Southern racists, shifted from a focus on converting the attitudes of White people to criticizing the White power structure. SNCC also began to see the importance of organizing the poor, not just working for voting rights.[1] A new tone and direction for Black protest was emerging with a new target for change: institutional racism (Carmichael and Hamilton 1967).

At the time, society was changing faster than Black Americans were progressing. Even with civil rights protections increasingly in place, many Black people, both rural and urban, were living in poverty. Fighting segregation in the South no longer seemed to be the only problem. Although the Black middle class was beginning to find a stronger foothold in US institutions, many were unable to take advantage of the new civil rights protections to move themselves forward, impeded by poverty and lingering racist attitudes.

The more radical approach that was brewing within the movement came to a head in the summer of 1965 when riots broke out in the Watts neighborhood of Los Angeles. Precipitated by a traffic stop of a Black motorist by a White police officer, tensions between the city's police and Black neighborhood residents erupted into a six-day civil uprising, resulting in thirty-five deaths, more than four thousand arrests, and millions of dollars of destroyed property.

Watts was the first of many riots in US cities throughout the mid-1960s, highlighting the fact that racism is not merely a matter of individual conscience or prejudiced attitudes but an entire system of racial injustice. "The system," as it was referred to, became identified as the problem. Changing the system was the solution. In 1967, the Kerner Commission, established by President Lyndon B. Johnson to examine the causes of the urban riots, concluded, "What white Americans have never fully understood, but what the Negro [*sic*] can never forget, is that white society is deeply implicated in the ghetto. White institutions created it, white institutions maintain it, and white society condones it" (the Kerner Commission, in Kerner 1968:1).

Striking Back: Black Power and Black Pride

This new thinking—moving from a focus on individual prejudicial attitudes to identifying injustices embedded within the system—turned a page in the history of Black protest and stirred political organizing within other communities of color. Whereas the civil rights movement had sought equal treatment within society's institutions, the Black power movement criticized those same institutions, calling for a complete overthrow of the existing power structure. Racial solidarity, not integration, was the rallying cry. The influence of Black power is still evident today in the widespread use of the term *systemic racism*—a direct descendent of the idea of institutional racism.

---

[1] SNCC members wore blue denim coveralls to symbolize solidarity with the working class. Jeans have long since been co-opted by the fashion industry (and can be quite expensive!), and few know that they were initially inspired by SNCC's politics, as Tanisha Ford points out (2013).

The civil rights movement had taught that racial injustice stemmed from White people's moral failures. The Black power movement, however, targeted systematic and institutional racism, not just attitudinal change. Black power leaders took their inspiration from Malcolm X, who had himself been influenced by the teachings of Elijah Muhammad and the Nation of Islam.

Malcolm X believed that Black people should throw off the chains of racism "by any means necessary," including violence if need be. His penetrating ideas spoke to the anger and frustration of Black people, especially those in poor urban areas. At times Malcolm X argued that Black people should separate themselves from Whites so that they could be self-governing. Early on he referred to Whites as "devils," but later in his life, after traveling to Africa, he argued that Whites could become allies to Black people in their struggle for freedom.

Malcolm X was one of the first leaders to articulate a link between the struggles of African Americans and African nations. His ideas transformed the Black protest movement even while his radicalism was met by numerous threats on his life. He was assassinated in 1965, but his speeches and his writing, already widely influential, became even more so after his death. His autobiography, published posthumously in 1965, remains a classic, one of the most influential American autobiographies and required reading for many students.

The Black power movement inspired a very different racial consciousness from anything that had come before. New meanings of "Blackness" developed that were anchored in Black pride. The slogan "Black is beautiful" inspired the recognition and celebration of Black people's African roots. Growing one's hair naturally, celebrating African arts and culture, and changing to an African-inspired mode of dress became strong symbols of racial pride. Black people even changed how they referred to themselves in the context of the Black pride movement. No longer "Negroes" but African Americans, Black people embraced "Blackness" as a positive identity—one that was self-generated and not imposed by White society. Black Americans also began to see themselves as part of a **diaspora**—that is, the connection that Black people have across the globe because of the interconnectedness of their experiences.

The Black Panther Party

One of the most radical of the groups to emerge from the Black power movement was the Black Panther Party, a militant group that urged Black people to strike back at the White establishment. The Black Panther Party's tactics were much more confrontational than those of most other protest organizations. The Panthers thought that the nonviolence of the civil rights movement had not served Black people well. Instead, they argued that Black people should arm themselves as protection against White brutality, especially police brutality, and urged Black people to create and abide by self-governed institutions. The Black Panther Party's Ten-Point Program called for full employment, education, housing, an end to police brutality, and the freeing of all incarcerated Black men, among other demands.

As this more radical movement evolved, the political framework of antiracism changed, and so did the response. The revolutionary approach of the Black Panther Party was a much more aggressive and a potentially violent assault on dominant White institutions and was perceived by dominant groups as far more dangerous than previous movements had been. As racial protest gave way to Black power, White people's support dissipated. Even more significantly, the federal government instigated a massive wave of repression against radical Black activists and the Black Panther Party in particular. An FBI counterintelligence program called COINTELPRO infiltrated the Black Panther Party and other radical groups. Ultimately the Black Panther Party disintegrated after the imprisonment and murder of many of its leaders (Nelson 2015).

Although short-lived and too radical for many, the Black Panther Party has had a lasting impact on how people think about racism and how other groups have formed protest movements. Not everyone supported the revolutionary zeal or actions of the Black Panther Party; yet its influence and that of other parts of the Black power movement are still with us today. The Black power framework produced the concept of *institutional racism* that undergirds much of the study of racism today and can be traced to thinkers like Malcolm X, whose work shaped the philosophy of Black power.

One of the greatest contributions of the Black Panther Party and the Black power movement more generally is the articulation of an understanding of the structural roots of racism. Just as significantly, the Black power movement changed people's consciousness. Black people and other people of color created a strong sense of racial solidarity that continues to influence how people self-identify, as we will see in greater detail below. In addition, the Black power movement's analysis of power has led White people to have to confront the privilege that they hold by virtue of the racial power structure. Although the revolution that the Black power movement advocated has certainly not occurred, the mindset that the movement created still informs thinking today.

The Many Faces of Racial Liberation

Framing Question: What other movements did the civil rights and Black power movements inspire?

The civil rights and Black power movements uniquely influenced other people of color, who have organized around their own histories, identities, and socioeconomic locations in the United States. All racial-ethnic groups have had a long history of resisting their own oppression, but the Black power movement gave new direction to resistance and "molded the consciousness" of people of color (Omatsu 2016:60).

Among others, Chicanos were stirred by the awakening of racial consciousness. Like the early activism of Black civil rights, Mexican American people had a long history of resistance. From the mid-nineteenth century and into the twentieth, the Mexican American civil rights movement had sought to end discrimination, including fighting for rights to education, work, and full citizenship, both formal and informal. Inspired by the Black power movement, though, Mexican American activists began to see the work of mainstream civil rights organizations as too gradual, too moderate, and too willing to accommodate Anglos. Inspired by the Black power and Black Pride movements, Mexican American activists, many of them young students, forged a new movement, one more akin to the radical politics of Black power (García 2014; M. Rodríguez 2014).

Many identify the Chicano movement's beginning in 1970, when Mexican Americans in East Los Angeles mounted the largest demonstration ever held to protest the disproportionately high number of Mexican Americans being killed in the Vietnam War. The new Chicano movement affirmed the ties of Mexican American people to their Mexican heritage, emphasizing their collective roots. A new identity as "Chicana/o" was forged, based on the idea that Chicanos are an indigenous people with mixed Indian and Spanish heritages and who shared a homeland, "Aztlan" (referring to Aztec civilization). This new identity recognized and reclaimed the historical, revolutionary, and anticolonial struggles of Mexican people as they struggled against the Yankee annexation of their homeland.

Although *Chicano* had once been used as a derogatory term against Mexican people, the new Chicana/o movement reclaimed the term as an affirmation of cultural pride and heritage. *Chicanismo* became a new identity that tied people together in common cause across class, region, and different Mexican ethnicities. Community-oriented newspapers provided the communication system that linked different geographies where Chicanos lived—California, Texas, New Mexico, Arizona, all places where Mexican American people engaged in "collective reimagining" (Blackwell 2011) of their heritage and their new politics.

Like the Black power movement, the new Chicano movement tended to be locally focused, with no central national leadership per se (M. Rodríguez 2014). It was also largely youth driven. Chicanas/os challenged the understanding of race in "Black" and "White" terms, instead claiming a unique and proud identity as *mestizaje*. Previously known as "Spanish Americans," Chicanas/os embraced their mixed racial heritage, forging a new and now lasting new identity. The establishment of a new proud Chicana/o identity drew connections between gender, race, and sexuality, heralding the later development of intersectionality, as Chicanas saw themselves as allied with Black women and other women of color (Blackwell 2011).

Chicana/o political activists engaged in boycotts, walkouts, and, strikes, such as the student strike at San Francisco State College in 1968—a signal event that demonstrated the new consciousness of people of color unified by linked interests. A coalition of African American, Chicano, Asian American, and American Indian students organized the strike, which lasted almost five months. The striking students demanded a new curriculum that would include study of the history and works of people of color. They also demanded the creation of a Black student union, as well as more recruitment of faculty of color and more admission of students of color. Throughout college campuses in the 1960s and 1970s, students and faculty demanded more African American, Asian American, Chicana/o, and Native American studies—curricular changes in higher education that benefit students today in the form of ethnic and racial studies programs.

The period of the late 1960s and 1970s was a time of vast social activism as millions of people across the United States were inspired by the movements of people of color, the anti–Vietnam War movement, student movements on college campuses, and the budding feminist movement. Various groups developed analyses of their own relationships to systems of oppression, many of which were directly inspired by the analysis of institutionalized oppression. For example, the Gray Panthers, who obviously patterned their organization's name on the Black Panthers', developed an analysis of institutional ageism in terms similar to the analysis of institutional racism that marked movements for racial justice.

Native Americans, African Americans, Puerto Ricans, and Mexican Americans all argued that they suffered from institutional oppression. Even though each group faced unique conditions and grievances, each was inspired by the radical analysis of institutional oppression. More people of color rejected what they saw as the assimilationist goals of the civil rights movement and forged a new identity and a political stance that emphasized collective empowerment.

The Native American assertion of Red power is one example. Reflecting the political influence of the Black power movement, in the late 1960s Native Americans asserted that the takeover of their native lands by White colonizers and the genocide of their people linked all Native groups into a single political force. When Native Americans seized and occupied Alcatraz Island in 1969 (see chapter 5), they used arguments similar to those of the Black power movement, insisting that the land they occupied was theirs to reclaim.

LEARNING OUR PAST

Emilio Aguayo

Emilio Aguayo is a Chicano muralist in Washington State whose parents immigrated to the United States from Mexico in the 1920s. His narrative, collected as part of an oral history project at the University of Washington, details his family's experiences and also relates a classic example of immigrants' ambitions, hard work, and hopes for their children.

We're immigrants from Mexico . . . Dad crossed after working in the foundries in the railroads of northern Mexico and journeyed north. . . . He crossed into Colorado to work . . . with his uncles. Mother followed in a different way. She was separated at the death of her parents to go to live with her aunt and her family who had moved up to Colorado. My father [met my mother in Sedgwick]. . . . They were married for fifty years and eight days. . . . My father went to the eighth grade in Mexico, my mother to the fourth grade. They never had a chance for education.

Their story is the classic immigrant story, which was to go north to America where life would be better for the family. They wanted a better life and opportunity for education, which they stressed throughout their lives. . . . They always said that they would open the door to opportunity, which is education, and it was our job to push the door open and make the most of what we had.

We did farmwork to augment the family income after my dad settled down and became a regular track hand for the Union Pacific in that area—a job in which he suffered discrimination because, first of all, the White section foreman told him that as long as he was foreman, he [my dad] would never be made permanent full-time as an employee, but when the man was on vacation, my dad made it. But he was still discriminated on because the man hated that he had to have him as a worker. My dad never made more than $400 a month on his salary as a track hand, but we had a large garden and cattle and pigs and chickens that augmented our semisubsistence way of living, and with that he also helped the older kids begin to go to college.

All six of us went to college, living up to my folks' American Dream that, even though they would never have an education, someday their kids would have a college education. . . .

The Chicano movement for civil rights protested discrimination against Americans of Mexican descent—that is, *Chicanos*. Depicted here is the end of a six hundred–mile march from Calexico, California, to the state capitol in 1971.

Source: Bettman / Getty Images.

My family was not farmworkers full-time. . . . We did a lot of thinning, lot of row crop work. We did a lot of potato picking and things like that. And I remember those conditions . . . that are often romanticized as "Oh, what a beautiful sunset" . . . sunrise or sunset. It's not so beautiful, it's not so romanticized when you have to go out there and do the hard, butt-busting work of picking mile-long rows of white Idaho and red russet and red Pontiac potatoes that we had to do to make extra money to make ends meet for the family. My mother also cleaned ducks and cleaned fish and took in laundry, and we did odd jobs. . . . When we wanted spending money, we mowed lawns and took care of people's lawns when they were on vacation and spaded gardens and collected hubcaps from cars off the side of the highway and empty beer bottles to sell for spending money, or sold fish. We hunted and fished in the river. And all those early beginnings bear witness to those teachings and those hard-work, working-class ethics that my parents had. Work hard and always do your best in school and get an education. Your school comes first.

Source: University of Washington n.d.

Likewise, Asian Americans developed a new political consciousness in the 1960s and 1970s, redefining what it meant to be Asian. A new *panethnic identity* linked the experiences of diverse Asian groups, including Japanese Americans, Chinese Americans, Korean Americans, and others (see chapter 4; Espiritu 1992). Asian Americans united around analyses of institutional oppression that paralleled the one generated by the Black power leaders—Malcolm X and others—who had inspired them (Louie and Omatsu 2001; Omatsu 2016).

In each of these examples, increased racial consciousness and racial solidarity highlighted the connection between different experiences of racism and institutional power—a framework that is now found in cries against systemic racism. Throughout the late 1960s and 1970s, people of color questioned how their experiences were linked, and people of color began defining themselves as a political whole, even with their unique histories and identities. The phrase *people of color* emerged to emphasize groups' common experiences of institutional oppression (Omatsu 2016). The phrase itself is derived from the collective work of women of color, who first coined the term "women of color" to emphasize the commonality among Black, Native, Latina, and Asian women. The new identity as "people of color" means that racial and ethnic minorities within the United States see their experiences as related but also as tied to the status of people of color across the globe.

The histories of these different movements show us that change takes many forms and is led by many different groups. Importantly, the most significant changes in race relations have occurred because of the mobilization of people of color. Will current social movements generate further social change? Will contemporary movements work within existing institutions or against them—or both? Do we need movements that are race-specific or more universal in their approach? These are the questions now before us.

Contemporary Movements for Racial Justice

Framing Question: What direction is the movement for racial justice taking now?

Contemporary movements for racial justice can learn lessons from movements of earlier years, but they also emerge from and respond to contemporary conditions. Contemporary social movements may differ from movements of the past, although there may be similarities. But the circumstances have changed, and people working for change have to do so within the current context and with whatever resources they have. Sometimes those resources are local; other times they are more national. Contemporary racial justice movements also benefit from being able to organize using social media—a tool that allows people to connect even across vast distances. Still, the politics of change tap into people's responses to conditions of racial inequity, and, like the civil rights, Black power, and Chicano movements, the responses can involve tremendous creativity in confronting unjust conditions.

Black Lives Matter

The Black Lives Matter movement was founded by Alicia Garza, a community activist in Oakland, California, following the 2013 acquittal of George Zimmerman in the death of Trayvon Martin, a seventeen-year-old Black boy. After the acquittal, Garza posted what she called a "love letter to Black people" on Facebook. Distressed over the disregard for and dehumanization of Trayvon Martin's life and Black people's lives in general, Garza said that she wanted to give her young son a less bleak view of Black people than what was found in the mainstream media. She also wanted to give her son a sense of the possibilities that organizing Black people in a dignified way could bring (Cobb 2016). Garza was joined by her friends

Across the United States, numerous groups have staged "die-ins" to protest mass incarceration and police shootings of Black and Hispanic people. Here activists from Artists for Justice stage such a demonstration in Times Square.

Source: Pacific Press Media Production Corp. / Alamy Stock Photo.

Patrisse Cullors and Opal Tometi. In response to Garza's post, Cullors tweeted "#BlackLivesMatter," and the movement was thus named.

In the beginning, Black Lives Matter spread through spontaneous actions throughout the United States—usually in specific communities, often on college campuses. Now the movement has grown into one of the major contemporary voices for antiracist action. Black Lives Matter is organized through an informally structured national network of chapters. The movement relies on grassroots organizing and resists hierarchical leadership, though it has become a major national organization. Black Lives Matter uses similar tactics to the civil rights movement sit-ins, staging "die-ins" and mass protests against police brutality and the murder of Black people. In its cries against systemic racism, Black Lives Matter uses a structural framework akin to the Black power movement's, calling for transformative institutional change, specifically in policing but more broadly to protect the lives of all Black people.

Early on in its inception, and similar to the strategy of the Black Panther Party, Black Lives Matter adopted a ten-point program called "Campaign Zero" that called for the end of both police brutality and the militarization of the police. Although the influence of previous movements on the Black Lives Matter movement are evident, the differences are notable. Like earlier movements, Black Lives Matter asserts that anti-Black racism permeates US society, and BLM affirms the value and dignity of Black people's lives. Going beyond earlier movements, however, BLM is specifically intersectional, embracing queer, transgender, disabled, undocumented, and *all* Black people (Black Lives Matter n.d.). This inclusive perspective is not intended to divide attention paid to the value of Black people's lives. Rather, it is a very inclusive call for liberation.

As the Black Lives Matter movement has captured national attention, some have responded that "All lives matter." Although this expression may seem well intended, movement activists argue that refusing to acknowledge the specific plight of Black people diminishes the specific value of Black lives, thus reinforcing color-blind racism. As one commentator has asked, "Whose color gets erased when we go blind?" (Cauce 2016). The point of Black Lives Matter is to strongly and intentionally value the lives of all Black people. While the intent is not to diminish or devalue the lives of others, Black Lives Matter asserts the importance of explicitly and consciously valuing Black people—in all their diversity.

Organizing for Change

When recognizing the injustice of racial inequality, people often ask what they can do to create change. There is no single or simple answer. Sometimes making change means first changing ourselves—our attitudes, our knowledge, our awareness of inequality. This can be the very first step, and it means making a commitment to educating yourself about the injustice you see. You cannot be an effective agent for change without some degree of education (formal and informal) about what you are trying to change.

Change can also mean forming alliances with people who have a common interest in making change. This, too, is not easy, because people will come to coalitions with their own agendas, their own perspectives, and their own opinions about how to make change. Throughout this book you have seen (in the "Taking Action against Racism" features) many examples of how people have organized to make change. People sometimes organize locally, such as by creating or supporting a food bank or organizing a community garden in a racially segregated neighborhood. Coalitions are important in racial justice movements, but they can be fragile—especially across racial and ethnic lines. There has, for example, often been an uneasy alliance between people of color and White people (Carson et al. 1987), but White allies are needed if the struggle for racial justice is to succeed.

Some movements for racial justice approach change through existing institutions, such as the NAACP or the Mexican American Legal Defense and Educational Fund. Others work to produce alternative institutional structures, such as the Black Panther Party did with the Free Breakfast for School Children Program. The fight for racial justice sometimes means working within existing institutions to effect change. Other times demonstrations and protests that are critical of dominant institutions are needed—direct actions like the sit-ins of the civil rights movement, BLM's "die-ins," and the marches against racism and in support of Black Lives Matter that are happening now.

Some activists work for change through legislation and social policy, such as lobbying to support "Dreamers"—the young immigrants who were brought to the United States as children but who are subject to deportation. There are countless examples of people working for change through legislative channels or through work with nonprofit organizations.

Communication networks are also critical to the success of social protests, but they often come through outlets alternative to the mainstream media. Historically, for example, the African American press played a significant role in civil rights organizing. Now social media are an effective tool for organizing, as we have seen with mass movements like the worldwide Women's March, first held in 2017 on the day following Donald Trump's presidential inauguration, and like the March for Our Lives, organized by students following the 2018 mass shooting at Marjorie Stoneman Douglas High School in Parkland, Florida. Increasingly social media platforms like Twitter, TikTok, Instagram, and Facebook have become effective organizing tools (Jackson et al. 2020).

The goals of racial justice movements are many and cannot be reached through single or unidimensional solutions. Different times also call for different actions. The historical record teaches us that the struggle for racial justice involves multiple groups taking different approaches to effect change. Sometimes change comes in local settings; other times it plays out on the national stage. People sometimes organize for change under some of the worst conditions imaginable. But even then, they use whatever resources they can to advocate for their rights.

A fundamental question remains in contemporary programs for change: Is color blindness the best path to racial justice, or are race-specific plans needed? The section below examines some of the major paths to change being pursued now, some of which are color-blind approaches and others of which are race-specific. As you read about these different strategies, you might ask yourself what approach would best address the particular issues you are confronting.

Color-Blind or Color-Conscious? Frameworks for Change

Framing Question: How do color-blind and race-conscious programs for change differ, and how effective are each?

We can draw many lessons from the racial protest movements of earlier years and those forming now. First is simply an understanding of what *activism* means. Many people tend to think that a single leader or single type of action is what guides social change. **Activism**, though, takes many forms and is defined by the "multiple ideas, concepts, strategies, and ideologies that [people use] to guide, organize, and direct civil rights and social justice struggles" (Behnken 2016:3). It is impossible to detail all the approaches that have been taken to address the racial inequalities permeating the United States, but four basic frameworks of change are highlighted below.

Civil Rights and the Law

As a result of the activism of many people working for racial justice, a legal framework is now in place in the United States that, at least in principle, provides equality under the law. This framework was founded on the **Fourteenth Amendment to the US Constitution**, passed in 1868, granting *equal protection* under the law. Specifically, the Fourteenth Amendment states: "No state shall make or enforce any law which shall abridge the privileges or immunities of citizens of the United States; nor shall any state deprive any person of life, liberty, or property, without due process of law, nor deny to any person within its jurisdiction the equal protection of the laws" (US Constitution 1868, sec. 1). The Civil Rights Act of 1964 further cemented these rights by outlawing discrimination based on race, color, religion, sex, or national origin.

Many groups can thank the Black protest movement for the activism that ultimately resulted in the civil rights bill. Since its passage, this law has been interpreted as also protecting the rights of the aged and people who have disabilities. It has also been interpreted as protecting the rights of pregnant women, who, for example, cannot be terminated from employment simply because of pregnancy—a practice that was common before passage of this law. LGBTQ rights have also been extended based on the meaning of the Fourteenth Amendment and the Civil Rights Act of 1964, as have the rights of religious minorities. The Civil Rights Act created the Equal Employment Opportunity Commission, which enforces federal laws that outlaw employment discrimination and protects claimants against employer retaliation.

Civil rights laws are founded in *color-blind* values, which are now widely shared within the US public. Indeed, today it is so socially unacceptable in most places to identify as a racist that large numbers of White Americans claim that they "do not see race" (Wingfield 2015). This does not mean that racism, even overtly expressed, has disappeared. Quite the contrary, as witnessed in the rise of White supremacist groups and hate crimes, especially against American Muslims following Donald Trump's 2016 election to the presidency.

Nonetheless, civil rights are the bedrock of US cultural values and social policy. But are these protections enough? In principle, the concept of civil rights means that people have equal access to society's benefits—access to jobs, education, and the right to vote, but we know this is not yet the case. Having civil rights laws on the books is one thing. Realizing their promise is quite another.

What is more, civil rights protections require constant vigilance. In recent years, many of the rights won as the result of the civil rights movement have been chipped away. The Voting Rights Act, for example, lost much of its power when the Supreme Court invalidated some of its major provisions in 2013. New voter identification laws, changes in voting procedures, and various redistricting plans enacted by states across the Union are disenfranchising many American citizens—especially African Americans and Latinos.

In sum, the civil rights framework is foundational to realizing racial justice in the United States, but it is not enough. Civil rights laws protect individual rights but do not necessarily transform the social and economic standing of racial and ethnic groups. Guaranteeing equal rights also does little, if anything, to reduce the poverty rampant among the nation's people of color. Civil rights laws do not change the underlying social structural practices and patterns that continue to exclude people of color from jobs, education, good health care, and other rights. The color-blind framework of civil rights may be embraced by most, but it is not changing the status of many.

Affirmative Action

Affirmative action is the practice of remedying past discrimination by using race-conscious measures to recruit and admit racial-ethnic minorities to positions in employment and education. Affirmative action is a strategy for change that has been very effective at enhancing access to jobs and education for underrepresented groups. Because affirmative action is a *race-conscious* method of addressing racial inequality, it has been both controversial and misunderstood. Many myths also surround affirmative action policies and practices, so it is important that we understand the background of this strategy for change.

Affirmative action can be dated as far back as 1965, when President Lyndon B. Johnson required all federal contractors to file plans for hiring minority employees. This plan was enhanced in 1969 by President Richard Nixon, who added the requirement that federal employers file goals and timetables for hiring minority employees. Nixon also added women as a protected class to be included in affirmative action plans. As a result, not only have many African American, Latino, Asian American, and Native American people benefited from affirmative action, but White women have as well, as have their families.

As it currently stands, affirmative action requires employers and institutions of higher education to make extra effort to recruit and hire women and people of color or, in the case of colleges, to admit more students of color. Employers must demonstrate the efforts they take to ensure fairness and to target minority applicants for jobs. Prior to the rollout of affirmative action policies, it was perfectly legal to hire people without any advertisement or outreach to previously excluded groups. In higher education, federally supported institutions also have to file plans for diversifying their student bodies.

The first major legal challenge to affirmative action came in 1978 in *Regents of the University of California v. Bakke* (pronounced "BOCK-ee"). Allan Bakke was a White male who was denied admission to the medical school at the University of California–Davis. At the time, the medical school had a "set aside" program, under which they reserved sixteen of their one hundred admission slots for minority applicants. Bakke sued and took his case all the way to the Supreme Court. In 1978, using the equal protection clause of the Fourteenth Amendment, the Supreme Court ruled that the campus *could not* use quotas when admitting students to medical school but *could* take race into account when reviewing medical applicants. In other words, race could be considered as part of an applicant's file, but quotas were unconstitutional. As of 2020 the *Bakke* decision remains the law of the land. It has been challenged a number of times but has been upheld to date.

The *Bakke* decision was also upheld in a second important case involving affirmative action, *Grutter v. Bollinger*, decided in 2003. Barbara Grutter, a White woman, sued the University of Michigan Law School for not admitting her. This is a complex case, but ultimately the Supreme Court upheld the *Bakke* decision, stating that diversity in education was a *compelling state interest*. The Court ruling was based in part on social science data showing that all students actually learn more when they are being educated in more diverse settings. As in the *Bakke* decision, in *Grutter* the Supreme Court ruled that universities could take race in account along with other factors when making admissions decisions.

Despite the controversies surrounding affirmative action, a majority of the US public supports it, although they are somewhat more likely to do so when it is applied to women rather than to race: 67 percent of the public support affirmative action programs for women and 58 percent for racial minorities (Riffkin 2015).

Affirmative action programs have benefited both White women and people of color. These benefits, however, only accrue to those who are already well positioned to take advantage of employment and educational opportunities. Despite myths that unqualified minorities take jobs from White men under affirmative-action initiatives, the fact is that, under affirmative action, people must be qualified for the positions they seek. In this regard, affirmative action programs have been most effective in opening access to educated and well-trained people but do little to alleviate poverty and other forms of inequality that are part of the system of racial stratification. Other programs are needed to accomplish that.

Antipoverty Programs

Neither civil rights nor affirmative action programs provide a solution to the poverty that permeates US society; hence the need for a third approach: antipoverty policy. Job training and job creation programs that can address the massive unemployment that has produced such a large underclass are also needed.

Consider plans to raise the minimum wage as an example. People working at the lowest minimum wage standards cannot get out of poverty even by working full-time and year-round (see chapter 7). Raising the minimum wage helps, but even more than doubling the minimum wage to fifteen dollars per hour would barely move people above the poverty line without a second income or a second job.

Living wage campaigns have called attention to this problem, and some progress is being made, but there is a long way to go. Besides, raising the minimum wage only helps those who are already working. Job training and job creation programs are critically needed to give people the credentials they need to compete in an increasingly technology-based economy.

Antipoverty and job creation policies have been increasingly difficult to sustain, however, as so much of the general public is quite hostile to so-called entitlement programs. Relative to other industrialized Western nations, the United States is quite meager in its social support programs, reflecting the cultural belief that success ought to be based on individual merit. As we have seen throughout this book, social structures of racial inequality impede a person's ability to get ahead. Without programs to lift people out of poverty, the nation will continue to face all of the problems that poverty creates. Some suggest that, if the United States were to develop universalistic antipoverty and job creation programs instead of race-specific programs, political support would be more likely (Wilson 1987).

The Diversity Agenda

A fourth approach to activism—one that has grown in its influence in recent years— is the diversity agenda, referring to the variety of programs and plans intended to make organizations (such as workplaces and schools) more inclusive and welcoming of various groups of people. Diversity is an all-inclusive concept, referring to racial and ethnic diversity but also including, for example, women, LGBTQ individuals, people with disabilities, and religious minorities. As the United States becomes more diverse, more people (including leaders of organizations) are recognizing how much the nation is changing, and they are developing diversity plans within their own organizations to address the change.

Research shows that embracing diversity has positive outcomes for the goals of a given group. As indicated in the *Grutter* case, research has shown that students learn more in more diverse settings. This means that not only does diversity improve learning outcomes for people of color, but White students also learn more when their schools and curricula include diverse people with different experiences and perspectives (Gurin, Dey, and Hurtado 2002). In the business world, companies with more diverse working groups has been shown to increase market size, sales, and company profits (Herring 2009). Increased diversity in groups tends to stimulate innovation and prevent people from falling into a singular or preestablished mindset (Page 2007).

The diversity agenda prompts organizations to require training and educational seminars to reduce the *implicit biases* that we know people hold (see chapter 2). Those biases can be based on race, ethnicity, or any number of other social characteristics. Diversity workshops then attempt to reduce such bias, noting that because racism is learned it can be "unlearned." Such work points to the importance of education in changing the information that people have about each other.

The limitation of the diversity framework is that it does not change the fundamental institutional structures that generate bias and inequality to begin with. As such, it can become what sociologists Joyce Bell and Douglas Hartmann (2007) call "happy talk"—which celebrates and recognizes difference but does little to challenge the systemic inequality of White privilege (Andersen 1999 and 2003).

You can see the challenge of diversity work in figure 12.1. Most Black and Hispanic Americans think more needs to be done to achieve racial equality for Black and White people, but far fewer White people think so. Moreover, a significant number of White Americans (20 percent) think we have gone too far.

Most people have faith that young people will improve the nation's race relations. But here the evidence for change is mixed. Among White people aged eighteen to twenty-nine years, about half think the country has not done enough to achieve Black-White equality; about 40 percent think the effort has been about right (Horowitz et al. 2019). Will this translate into action?

Each year the Higher Education Research Institute at the University of California–Los Angeles administers a survey to all incoming first-year college students in the nation. The results gauge how attitudes change over time. Figure 12.2 shows whether the entering class of 2018 strongly agreed or agreed somewhat that racial discrimination is no longer a problem in America. As you can see, men are more likely to think discrimination is a nonissue than are women, and significant differences exist across different racial and ethnic groups. Fewer than half (48.6 percent) of all entering first-year students said that it was essential or very important to them personally to better promote racial understanding (Stolzenberg et al. 2019).

Change cannot be solely attitudinal. Changing our attitudes and educating ourselves and others is certainly necessary if we are to understand and transform the racial inequality that besets us. But as we have seen throughout this book, attitudinal change is not enough; institutional change is essential if we want to achieve true equality in the United States.

In many ways people of color have much better opportunities now than before, but much more still needs to be done. No single framework detailed above guides actions for social change (see table 12.1). Do we need *color-blind* or *race-conscious* strategies for change? The successes of the past tell us that both are needed. The problems associated with racism are many, and no single approach for social change is adequate in and of itself. All of them are necessary.

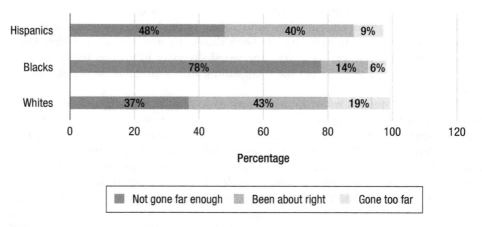

FIG. 12.1 Attitudes toward Racial Change

Source: Horowitz et al. 2019.

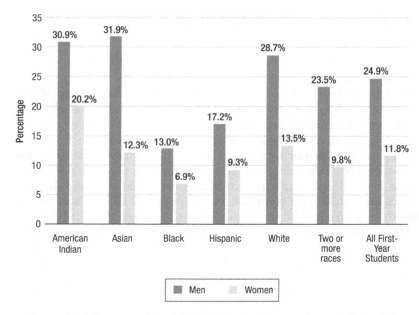

Question Asked: Do you agree that racial discrimination is *no longer* a major problem in America?

FIG. 12.2 Views on Racial Discrimination: First-Year College Students (2018)

Source: Stolzenberg et al. 2019.

TABLE 12.1 Race and Social Change: Frameworks for Change

	Civil Rights	Affirmative Action	Employment/ Antipoverty Policy	Antiracism; Awareness; Diversity
Focus:	Equal rights; antidiscrimination	Improvement of opportunity structures	Job creation; raising minimum wage; public assistance	Attitudinal change; education
Implementation:	Law and social policy	Employment and educational policy	Social policy; antipoverty measures; living wage campaigns	Diversity training; unlearning racism; reducing implicit bias
Who benefits:	People of color; white women; LGBTQ people; disabled people; age groups; religious minorities	Middle-class and elite people of color; White women	Poor and working-class people of color; White poor and working class	Corporations; educational institutions; non-profit organizations; individual minds
Limitations/ criticisms:	De facto segregation persists; does not address economic inequality	Does not address poverty; generates backlash	Does not address noneconomic forms of racism	Change is attitudinal, not institutional

The New Multicultural/Multiracial Society: Where Are We Going?

Framing Question: What impact is the increased diversity of the US population likely to have on racial inequality?

As the United States becomes more diverse in its racial-ethnic composition, new questions about the future of race and ethnicity emerge—and will continue to evolve. With a more diverse population and more people identifying as multiracial, will the meaning of race change? Given that race is a social construction, most likely. If so, will racism diminish or simply take new forms? These questions guide some of the discussion about the future of race and ethnicity in the United States.

The color line in the United States has historically been drawn around the division between Black and White. That color line, though, was delineated when African Americans were the nation's largest racial minority group. Now Latinos have surpassed Black Americans as a proportion of the population (Latinos constitute 17 percent and Black Americans 13 percent of the US population). Latinos and Asians are also expected to continue growing—with both the Latino population expected to double and the Asian population to increase by 79 percent by 2050. The White American population is expected to decline by about 6 percent by 2050 (Ortman and Guarneri 2009).

The color line is also being blurred by immigration, higher rates of racial-ethnic intermarriage, and an increase in the number of those who identify as multiracial, especially among young people (Bean et al. 2009; Bean and Lee 2009; Lee and Bean 2007 and 2012). The old Black-White binary that has historically defined race in the United States is no longer as sharp as it once was.

How will these major changes affect our ideas about race? Will they eradicate or blur racial boundaries? Who will be assimilated into the privileges of society? Who will be at the top and the bottom, and what will the "middle" look like?

Sociologist Eduardo Bonilla-Silva has suggested that the United States may evolve into a **tripartite society**—that is, a society that still divides people into Black and White categories but where there is a middle category that he calls "honorary Whites" (2004). This would be a system of racial stratification more similar to that of Latin American and certain Caribbean nations. How does he explain this?

Bonilla-Silva argues that those on the non-White side of the color line have shared experiences of oppression and exploitation. They have also been racialized as "Black" or, in some cases, "Brown." The post–civil rights era, though, has brought changes to the system of racial and ethnic inequality. Bonilla-Silva, therefore, classifies the Black/Brown category as "collective Black."

The White category includes non-Hispanic White people but also new White immigrants, totally assimilated White Latinos, and light-skinned multiracial people. The intermediate group of "honorary Whites" would include light-skinned Latinos, such as Cubans and some segments of Mexican and Puerto Rican communities, plus various Asian American groups (e.g., Chinese Americans, Korean Americans, Japanese Americans, Filipino Americans), most multiracial people, and Middle Easterners. At the bottom of this stratified system will be the "collective Black," including Vietnamese, Hmong, and other Southeast Asian American groups who have low social and economic status, dark-skinned Latinos, Black Americans, new

West Indian and African immigrants, and those he calls "reservation-bound" Native Americans (Bonilla-Silva 2004; Bonilla-Silva and Glover 2004).

At the core of this triracial system remains White supremacy. Groups who would fall into the White or honorary White categories do so mainly based on social class but also partly on skin tone. Bonilla-Silva argues that because of the dominance of color-blind racism, a tripartite system of racial inequality appears to be "kinder and gentler" but is nonetheless still anchored in the dominance of White people. Only time will tell whether Bonilla-Silva's projections come to be, but evidence of this system of racial inequality is emerging now. Many Asian Americans have equaled or surpassed White, non-Hispanic Americans in socioeconomic status. Certainly some middle-class and elite people of color have been highly successful, in some cases even surpassing working-class and poor Whites, who see themselves as increasingly left behind. Some Latinos, depending on their national origin and social class, already define themselves as White (Forman, Goar, and Lewis 2004).

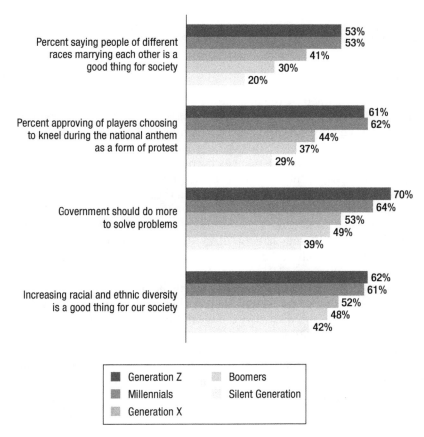

FIG. 12.3 Generation Z and the Millennials: Political Views

Note: As defined in this research, Generation Z includes those born after 1996, millennials 1981–1996, Generation X 1965–1980, boomers 1946–1964, and the Silent Generation 1928–1945.

Source: Parker, Graf, and Igielnik 2019.

Many put their hopes in the changing perspectives and experiences of the millennial generation (those born from 1981 to about the mid-1990s, people in their twenties and thirties as of 2020) and now Generation Z (those born from about the mid-1990s to the early 2010s). Both generations are the most diverse to date on a number of characteristics, and they are thought to be more tolerant and less racist than previous generations. Is this true? Members of Gen Z and millennials, as you can see in figure 12.3, are similar in their political views and more progressive on racial issues than earlier generations. Still, like all generations, there is diversity within these groups, and it is far too early to say how generational views will change with time (Clement 2015; Parker, Graf, and Igielnik 2019).

Even with a more complex system of racial hierarchy, race still matters. As Jennifer Lee and Frank Bean conclude, based on the demographic and socioeconomic status of diverse groups in the United States, "Despite the increased diversity, race is not declining in significance, nor is the color line disappearing" (2012:433). Group boundaries may not be as sharp as they once were, but racism endures. What race and ethnicity become in the future remains to be seen, but the past shows us how, even with evolving constructions of race, race still matters—and matters a lot—in US society (West 1994).

Conclusion

It is easy to become overwhelmed by the magnitude of our nation's racial problems. It would be naive not to take a fairly dim, perhaps pessimistic, view of the possibilities for change, but it is equally important to maintain hope. Change has occurred, and more is possible (Killian 1971). As this chapter has shown, over the course of history the long march toward racial justice has been led by ordinary people, some of whom rose to prominence. Others worked more quietly, but diligently, on the ground, organizing what has in fact been a revolution in the nature of racial inequality—but an incomplete one (Killian 1968).

More than one-third of Americans now say they are worried about race relations in the United States, including half of Black Americans and one-quarter of Whites. (This survey did not include Latinos or Asian Americans.) This is a large increase even since 2014, when only 19 percent of Whites said they were concerned about US race relations (Norman 2016). No doubt, media attention to shootings, threats to deport vast numbers of undocumented workers, calls to require Muslim Americans to register in a national database, the Black Lives Matter movement, and the rise in White supremacist hate crimes have shown that racism persists in the United States and is perhaps not even as subtle as people were starting to believe.

Furthermore, many of the conditions that ignited earlier protests still remain. High rates of poverty still exist—and not just among Black Americans but also among Latinos, Puerto Ricans, Native Americans, some Asian Americans, and many Whites, who are, after all, the majority of the poor. High rates of unemployment, urban blight, and police brutality against people of color are all too common. While much has changed since the early days of the civil rights movement, much remains to be done.

Some things are fairly certain: The US population will continue to become more diverse. The public will continue to debate policies to alleviate race and ethnic inequality, including immigration policy, health care, educational access, income inequality, environmental degradation, and crime control, among others. If we fail to understand how each is connected to racial inequality, change will not be effective.

Will the nation move toward a more racially just union, or will we reverse the course to greater inclusion? Strong political divisions in the United States seem to rest on how determined people are to make this a more racially inclusive and just society. Despite the challenge of bringing the country together, the history of racial protest in the United States shows us that change does not come from above. Change comes from the efforts of people who challenge existing practices and social institutions and who use education and changes in consciousness to achieve their goals. It also comes from alliances, no matter how fragile, between White people and people of color, when White people are equipped to develop both the knowledge and the empathy to be good allies.

Among many pockets of the US population is a clear desire to do something about racial inequality. That sentiment also may be growing, but people don't always know how to get started. Ignoring race is clearly not the answer. This chapter's opening epigraph presents a challenge from Supreme Court Justice Harry Blackmun to a public that wants a color-blind society but does not know how to get there. Blackmun wrote in his dissent in the *Bakke* case that, "In order to get beyond racism, we must first take account of race. There is no other way. And in order to treat some persons equally, we must treat them differently."

Key Terms

activism 322

affirmative action 323

Civil Rights Act (1964) 310

diaspora 313

Fourteenth Amendment to the US Constitution (1868) 322

Grutter v. Bollinger (2003) 324

nonviolent civil disobedience 308

Regents of the University of California v. Bakke (1978) 324

tripartite society 328

Voting Rights Act (1965) 310

Critical-Thinking Questions

1. How would you compare the nonviolent civil disobedience tactic of the civil rights movement to the contemporary Black Lives Matter movement? Note the ways these movements are both similar and different.

2. If you could do just one thing to reduce racial inequality in the United States, what would you do, and why?

Student Exercises

12.1. Identify someone (other than yourself) who has been active to some degree in antiracist protests. What has moved them to participate? What do they think are the best strategies for change? How do you think their race, social class, level of education, age, and region of residence influence their commitment to this movement?

12.2. Watch one of the twelve episodes of *Eyes on the Prize* (available via streaming and possibly in your school library). Afterward, write a short essay detailing what you learned from this period of history. How have things changed since?

12.3. Identify a social movement in your community (or a national one). What strategy does this group use to effect change? Would you call it a color-blind approach or a race-specific approach? Why is this approach the most effective for this particular change objective—or would you suggest a different tack?

Challenging Question/Open to Debate

With increased racial and ethnic diversity in the US population, will we create a society that is more racially tolerant and inclusive or less so?

TAKING ACTION AGAINST RACISM

Support Antiracist Organizations

Support organizations that challenge racial injustice. There are many that do so. You can help by familiarizing yourself with the agendas and strategies of different organizations (see some selected websites below), showing up for meetings, listening to people of color as leaders, volunteering, providing financial support to the extent you are able, and so forth.

Resources: Following are a few of the many important organizations working for racial justice, on both the national and local levels:

Color of Change, https://colorofchange.org

Advancement Project, https://advancementproject.org/about-advancement-project/

NAACP, https://naacp.org

Dream Defenders, https://dreamdefenders.org/our-story/

Glossary

acculturation   the process by which immigrant groups adopt the language, dress, values, and norms of the host society

achievement gap   the racial differences in educational opportunity, learning, and achievement

activism   the ideas, concepts, and strategies that intentionally guide social change

affirmative action   the practice of remedying past discrimination using race-conscious measures

Affordable Care Act (ACA)   formally known as the Patient Protection and Affordable Care Act, a federal law passed in 2010 that provides a system of health insurance exchanges and that brings health insurance to more people in the United States than ever before

anti-Semitism   the hatred and disparagement of Jewish people

assimilation   the process by which ethnic groups are incorporated into the dominant culture

assimilation model   a theoretical perspective analyzing the process by which immigrant groups become integrated into host society

audit studies   experiments using actors and/or other simulations to reveal when discrimination occurs

authoritarian personality   characterized by having little tolerance for difference, being rigid in judgments of others, and being highly obedient to authority

aversive racism   subtle form of prejudice guided by unconscious beliefs about the inferiority of racial-ethnic groups

bracero program   a formal agreement initiated in 1942 between the United States and Mexico that permitted Mexican citizens to work in the United States for temporary, renewable periods

***Brown v. Board of Education* (1954)**   the US Supreme Court decision that ruled school segregation in public facilities, including schools, unconstitutional

capitalism   an economic system based on the pursuit of profit and private ownership

carceral state   a society wherein security spreads everywhere as a mechanism for social control of the population

care work   life-sustaining labor, such as childcare, cleaning, and cooking

chattel   the state of being a piece of property or slave for life

Chinese Exclusion Act (1882)   a law denying the entry of Chinese laborers to the United States

Civil Rights Act (1964)   the US law banning discrimination in employment and creating the Equal Employment Opportunity Commission

class   a system of inequality by which groups have different access to economic, social, and political resources

colonialism   the process whereby a nation (or, perhaps, a group of nations) assumes control of another country (or people) for purposes of economic exploitation

color-blind racism   the idea that it is best to just ignore race and to look at people as if they are all alike

colorism   prejudice and discrimination directed against darker-skin-toned individuals or groups

concentrated poverty   the occurrence wherein 40 percent or more residents of a given census area fall below the federal poverty line

content analysis   a method of research that systematically documents the images in various cultural artifacts

controlling image   an image that restricts ideas about people, particularly people of color

crime index   the measure of crimes that includes murder/nonnegligent manslaughter, rape, robbery, aggravated assault, burglary, larceny/theft, and motor vehicle theft

critical race theory   the viewpoint that the media and popular culture reflect and re-create hierarchical systems of race, class, and gender in society

cultural appropriation   the process by which privileged groups consume and "claim" the culture of an oppressed or colonized group

cultural capital   (see also *social capital*) the non-economic assets—knowledge and resources—that advantaged groups get by virtue of their location in society

cultural competence   the ability to both recognize and understand cultural differences

cultural hegemony   the pervasive and excessive influence of one culture throughout society

cultural production   the process by which cultural images and ideas are made

cultural racism   the images and ideas that presume the superiority of Whites and the inferiority of people of color

culture   the beliefs and practices that orient people to their society

culture of affirmation   the beliefs that provide groups with a positive identity

culture of resistance   the beliefs that people create explicitly to challenge controlling images in the dominant culture

death rate   a calculation of the number of deaths in a given population, relative to the population size, in a given period of time

deep poverty   living below half the official federal poverty line

deindustrialization   the shift away from a manufacturing-based economy to a service-based economy

demographic change   population change, including change in the characteristics of a given population

diaspora   the connection that a given people has across the globe because of the interconnectedness of their experiences

discrimination   behavior that treats groups differently because of a presumed characteristic

dominant culture   the culture associated with the most powerful group in society

economic restructuring   socioeconomic changes that alter patterns of employment, including deindustrialization, technological change, globalization, and demographic change

environmental justice   the principle that all people and communities are entitled to equal protection of the environment and in public health

environmental racism   the pattern by which racial-ethnic minorities are disproportionately exposed to environmental hazards

ethnic enclaves   clusters of particular immigrant groups in a given occupation or industry

ethnic group   identifiable group of people who share a common culture, language, regional origin, and/or religion

ethnocentrism   the belief that one's group is superior to all other groups

eugenics   practices that purport to improve the human race by controlling the reproduction of people deemed to be "inferior" or genetically compromised

Fair Housing Act (1968)   the US federal law prohibiting discrimination in housing

familism   a pattern among Latinos of a very strong attachment to family

family household   a census unit that includes at least two members related by birth, marriage, or adoption

fictive kin   those who are part of an extended family network, even if not biologically related

Fourteenth Amendment to the US Constitution (1868)   the constitutional decision granting equal protection under the law

genocide   an international crime that destroys, in whole or part, a national, ethnic, racial, or religious group

genotype   full set of genes found in a given organism

Gentlemen's Agreement of 1907   an agreement between the United States and Japan that barred further entry of Japanese laborers

Gini coefficient   the measure of income distribution in a given group or society, ranging from zero to one

globalization   the increasing economic linkage between different nations

Great Migration   the movement of large numbers of African Americans to Northern and Midwestern cities beginning in the early twentieth century and lasting for almost six decades

Grutter v. Bollinger (2003)   the US Supreme Court decision upholding the right of universities to consider race along with other factors in admissions decisions

Hart-Celler Act (1965)   the US federal immigration law eliminating the national origins quota created by the Immigration Law of 1924 and giving priority to family reunification and occupational skill as criteria for entry to the United States

hate crime   a criminal action characterized by evidence of prejudice based on race, religion, sexual orientation, ethnicity, disability, gender, or gender identity

household   everyone living in a residential unit

householder a person who owns or rents a residential unit

human capital the individual characteristics of workers, such as education, skills, prior experience, age, and marital status

hypercriminalization the process by which an individual's behaviors become treated as a high risk, threat, or crime

hypersegregation the occurrence of nearly all of the residents of a given area being of the same group

hypertension the condition of elevated blood pressure

hypodescent *see* one-drop rule

identity a person's self-conception

identity contingency something to be dealt with that derives from one's identity

identity matrix the configuration of social factors that constitute one's definition of self

identity work the process by which people construct and maintain positive identities

ideology a constellation of beliefs purporting to justify and defend the status quo

implicit bias the unconscious, negative associations held against particular groups

income the money brought into a household over a given period of time from various sources, such as earnings

index of dissimilarity the measure of the extent to which two groups are distributed across a given place

Indian Removal Act (1830) a US federal law mandating the removal of all Indian groups to the area identified as Indian Territory

infant mortality the number of infant deaths in a given year per one thousand births

information technology revolution the process by which information technology permeates society

institutional racism the seemingly sanctioned pattern of racial advantage and disadvantage

intersectional theory a perspective underscoring that race, class, gender, sexuality, and other social factors intertwine to produce the particular experiences of all people in society

labeling theory the analysis suggesting that once a person or group is identified a particular way, the label sticks

laissez-faire racism the tendency for White people to minimize the effects of racism and do nothing about it

life expectancy the average number of years a person born in a particular year can expect to live

mass incarceration the pattern by which inordinately large numbers of people of color are imprisoned

mass media the channels of communication that transmit information to a wide segment of the population

matriarchy a society in which women hold the power

median income the income level at which half the population has higher income and half lower income

meritocracy a system whereby people are hierarchically arranged solely based on their achievements

microaggressions commonplace verbal or behavioral instances that communicate insults toward people of color

minority group a group with less power than a dominant group

National Crime Victimization Survey an annual survey of the United States that provides information about violent (nonfatal) and property crimes

National Origins Act (1924) also known as the Immigration Act of 1924, a US federal law that restricted the entry of new immigrants to 2 percent of the total number of people of each nationality that had been in the United States in 1890

nativism an ideology promoting the interests of people already living within a given nation

nonfamily household a census unit wherein persons are living alone or wherein nonrelatives share a residential unit

nonviolent civil disobedience the philosophy and practice of disrupting patterns of legal or cultural oppression by refusing to obey laws, customs, and norms

objectification the process of treating a human being as an object or thing

occupational segregation the pattern by which different groups of people are niched into certain occupations based on characteristics such as race, gender, or age

one-drop rule the practice wherein a certain amount of presumed "Black blood" legally defined someone as Black

othermothers women who raise children other than their own

panethnicity the collective identity formed when multiple ethnic groups forge a sense of shared belonging

paper sons the many Chinese men who were claimed as sons when California's official records of familial relationship had been destroyed by fire

phenotype the sum total of observable physical characteristics, including those influenced by environmental factors

picture brides Asian women in marriages arranged by a broker

Plessy v. Ferguson (1896) the US Supreme Court decision that allowed the practice of "separate but equal"

political economy the linkage between power and economic systems

popular culture the beliefs, ideas, images, and objects that are part of everyday life

postcolonial theory an analytical perspective emphasizing how the history of colonialism and empire building around the world has influenced present-day racial stratification

poverty line the official measure of poverty based on a 1930s calculation of the cost of a basic food budget, multiplied by three and adjusted for the cost of living

predatory lending the practice of financing very high-risk loans with little review of the borrower's ability to pay

prejudice a negative attitude toward a person or group based on their presumed characteristics

race a group treated as distinct in society based on presumed characteristics that have been interpreted as signifying inferiority or superiority

race-immigration nexus the linkage between immigration and race, specifically how social institutions, ideology, and social practices regarding immigration reinforce racial ideas

racial capital the repertoire of racial resources—such as language, cultural knowledge, and so forth—that biracial individuals use to navigate racial boundaries and racial contexts

racial division of labor the organization of different tasks as based on race

racial formation the process by which racial categories are created, inhabited, transformed, and/or destroyed

racial frames racial constructs that mediate how we see ourselves and others

racial identity the sense one has of oneself as belonging to a racial group

racialization the social process by which a group comes to be defined as a race

racial profiling the practice of using race as *the* criterion for detaining someone on suspicion of having committed a crime

racial resentment the belief among White people that White people are the aggrieved group and that people of color are somehow getting something for nothing or receiving special benefits based on race

racial stratification the hierarchical arrangement in society by which different racial groups have different access to economic and social resources, power, and perceived social worth

racial tax the extra burden that people of color experience by living with racism

racism the belief system that purports to justify racial inequality

redlining the practice of rating different residential areas in terms of their worthiness for mortgage lending based on race

Regents of the University of California v. Bakke (1978) the US Supreme Court decision that colleges cannot use quotas in college admissions but can take race into account

reproductive labor the work done to maintain and reproduce the labor force

reproductive politics the linkage between systems of power and intimate medical matters such as birth control, abortion, and pregnancy

residential segregation the pattern by which different racial and ethnic groups live apart from one another

sedimentation of racial inequality the structural disadvantages that have historically emerged to produce racial disadvantage

segmented assimilation the process that differentiates various dimensions of integration for immigrant groups

settler colonialism a specific form of colonialism referring to the process by which newcomers try to acquire land and property while overpowering indigenous (native) communities

social capital   (see also *cultural capital*) the access people have to networks and relationships that further their success

social death   the process by which a person loses their humanity

spillover effect   the consequences of imprisonment, experienced after release, that make it difficult for former prisoners to succeed

split labor market   a theory analyzing the workforce as divided into two sectors—the primary labor market and the secondary labor market

steering   the practice whereby real estate agents direct people of color away from neighborhoods that are predominantly White

stereotype   an oversimplified set of beliefs about the members of a societal group

stereotype threat   a pattern whereby a group's performance is affected by the invocation of a group stereotype

structural diversity theory   a theory that identifies the social forces that shape families, both historically and currently

structural unemployment   a pattern of massive job loss caused by the closing of particular industries

subprime mortgages   housing loans with a higher interest rate than the prime lending rate

symbolic annihilation   the under- and misrepresentation of certain groups of people in the media

symbolic ethnicity   allegiance to an ethnic group that is felt without having to incorporate ethnicity into one's daily behavior

systemic racism   a complex array of racial practices that divide social, economic, and political resources along racial lines

tracking   the pattern of schooling that separates students into groups according to presumed ability

transnational families   families wherein members are dispersed across national borders

tripartite society   a society wherein people are divided into three racial categories—Black, White, and honorary White

unemployment rate   the percentage of people in a given population who are out of work based on official calculations

Uniform Crime Reports   the FBI's annual reports of crime rates based on numbers of crimes reported, crimes cleared, and persons arrested

urban underclass   those who are largely permanently unemployed and stuck at the absolute bottom of the economic system

Voting Rights Act (1965)   the US federal law prohibiting discriminatory practices in voting

wealth   the monetary value of all of a person's assets minus their outstanding debt, also called *net worth*

White fragility   the unease White people feel when challenged to see their connection to a system of racial inequality

White privilege   the social, cultural, and economic benefits that White people accrue in a society marked by racial hierarchy

White space   the places in which Black people feel marginalized when present

White supremacy   the systemized consideration of White people as superior to people of color

xenophobia   fear of foreigners

References

ABC News. 2015. "Oklahoma of Sigma Alpha Epsilon Blames Racist Video on 'Horrible Cancer': Board Apologized for Video Showing Members Reciting Racist Chant." March 11. Retrieved October 14, 2020 (https://abcnews.go.com/US/oklahoma-chapter-sigma-alpha-epsilon-blames-racist-video/story?id=29570686).

Acuña, Rodolfo. 2005. "Crocodile Tears: Lynching of Mexicans." *HispanicVista.com*, July 20.

———. 2014. *Occupied America: A History of Chicanos*. 8th ed. Upper Saddle River, NJ: Pearson.

Adelman, Larry, exec. prod. 2003. *Race: The Power of an Illusion*. Directed by Christine Herbes-Sommers, Tracy Heather Strain, and Llewellyn Smith, coproduced by Jean Cheng. Television series. San Francisco: California Newsreel.

Adorno, Theodor Wiesengrund, Else Frenkel-Brunswik, Daniel J. Levinson, and R. Nevitt Sanford. 1950. *The Authoritarian Personality*. New York: Harper and Row.

Agency for Healthcare Research and Quality. 2015. *2014 National Healthcare Quality and Disparities Report*. Rockville, MD: Agency for Healthcare Research and Quality. Retrieved October 2, 2020 (https://archive.ahrq.gov/research/findings/nhqrdr/nhqdr14/2014nhqdr.pdf).

Ai, Amy L., Carol Plummer, Grace Heo, Catherine M. Lemieux, Cassandra E. Simon, Patricia Taylor, and Valire Carr Copeland. 2011. "Racial Identity–Related Differential Attributions of Inadequate Responses to Hurricane Katrina: A Social Identity Perspective." *Race and Social Problems* 3(1):13–24.

Ajrouch, Kristine J., and Amaney Jamal. 2007. "Assimilating to a White Identity: The Case of Arab Americans." *International Migration Review* 41(4):860–79.

Akamigbo, Adaeze B., and Frederic D. Wolinsky. 2007. "New Evidence of Racial Differences in Access and Their Effects on the Use of Nursing Homes among Older Adults." *Medical Care* 45(7):672–79.

Akee, Randall, Maggie R. Jones, and Sonya R. Porter. 2019. "Race Matters: Income Shares, Income Inequality, and Income Mobility for all U.S. Races." *Demography* 56(3):999–1021.

Alba, Richard D. 1996. "Italian Americans: A Century of Ethnic Change." Pp. 172–81 in *Origins and Destinies: Immigration, Race, and Ethnicity in America*, edited by Silvia Pedraza and Rubén G. Rumbaut. Belmont, CA: Wadsworth.

———. 2012. *Blurring the Color Line: The New Chance for a More Integrated America*. Cambridge, MA: Harvard University Press.

Alba, Richard D., and Nancy Foner. 2015. *Strangers No More: Immigration and the Challenges for Integration in North America and Western Europe*. Princeton, NJ: Princeton University Press.

Alba, Richard D., and Victor Nee. 2003. *Remaking the American Mainstream: Assimilation and Contemporary America*. Cambridge, MA: Harvard University Press.

Alexander, Michelle. 2010. *The New Jim Crow: Mass Incarceration in the Age of Colorblindness*. New York: The New Press.

Allard, Mary Dorinda, and Vernon Brundage Jr. 2019. "American Indians and Alaska Natives in the U.S. Labor Force." *Monthly Labor Review* (November). US Bureau of Labor Statistics. Retrieved October 2, 2020 (https://www.bls.gov/opub/mlr/2019/article/american-indians-and-alaska-natives-in-the-u-s-labor-force.htm).

Allen, Quaylan. 2013. "'They Think Minority Means Lesser Than': Black Middle-Class Sons and Fathers Resisting Microaggressions in the School." *Urban Education* 48(2):171–97.

Allport, Gordon W. 1954. *The Nature of Prejudice*. Cambridge, MA: Addison-Wesley.

Alsultany, Evelyn. 2012. *Arabs and Muslims in the Media: Race and Representation after 9/11*. New York: New York University Press.

American Bar Association. 2000. "Hate Speech and the First Amendment: Debating the 'Mighty Constitutional Opposites.'" Archived text retrieved October 14, 2020 (https://docplayer.net/83821072-Hate-speech-and-the-first-amendment-debating-the-mighty-constitutional-opposites.html).

American Immigration Council. 2019. "How the United States Immigration System Works." Washington, DC: American Immigration

Council. Retrieved October 2, 2020 (https://www.americanimmigrationcouncil.org/sites/default/files/research/how_the_united_states_immigration_system_works.pdf).

Anacker, Katrin B. 2010. "Still Paying the Race Tax? Analyzing Property Values in Homogeneous and Mixed-Race Suburbs." *Journal of Urban Affairs* 32(1):55–77.

Andersen, Margaret L. 1999. "The Fiction of Diversity without Oppression: Race, Ethnicity, Identity, and Power." Pp. 5–20 in *Critical Ethnicity: Countering the Waves of Identity Politics*, edited by Robert Tai and Mary Kenyatta. Boulder, CO: Rowman & Littlefield.

———. 2003. "Whitewashing Race: A Critical Review." Pp. 21–34 in *Whiteout: The Continuing Significance of Race*, edited by Eduardo Bonilla-Silva and Woody Doane. New York: Routledge.

———. 2004. "From *Brown* to *Grutter*: The Diverse Beneficiaries of *Brown v. Board of Education*." *University of Illinois Law Review* 2004(5):1073–98.

———. 2020 *Getting Smart about Race: An American Conversation*. Lanham, MD: Rowman & Littlefield.

Andersen, Margaret L., and Patricia Hill Collins. 2020. *Race, Class, and Gender: An Anthology*. 10th ed. San Francisco: Cengage.

Andersen, Margaret L., and Howard F. Taylor. 2020. *Sociology: The Essentials*. 10th ed. Boston: Cengage.

Anderson, Carol. 2016. *White Rage: The Unspoken Truth of Our Racial Divide*. New York: Bloomsbury.

Anderson, Elijah. 1999. *Code of the Street: Decency, Violence, and the Moral Life of the Inner City*. New York: W. W. Norton.

———. 2015. "The White Space." *Sociology of Race & Ethnicity* 1(1):10–21.

Anderson, Kathryn F. 2017. "Racial Residential Segregation and the Distribution of Health-Related Organizations in Urban Neighborhoods." *Social Problems* 64(2):256–76.

Anderson, Lydia. 2019. "States with High Opioid Prescribing Rates Have Higher Rates of Grandparents Responsible for Grandchildren." The Opioid Crisis and Grandparents Raising Children, last revised April 22. Washington, DC: US Census Bureau. Retrieved October 2, 2020 (https://www.census.gov/library/stories/2019/04/opioid-crisis-grandparents-raising-grandchildren.html).

Anderson, Margaret. 1988. *The American Census*. New Haven, CT: Yale University Press.

Aratani, Yumiko, Hsien-Hen Lu, and J. Lawrence Aber. 2014. "Shrinking the Public Safety Net or Helping the Poor Play by the Rules? The Changes in the State-Level Policies that Affected Low-Income Families with Children in the Welfare Reform Era: 1994–2002." *American Journal of Evaluation* 35(2):189–213.

Araujo, Keka. 2019. "Rep. Ocasio-Cortez Explains Her Race and Ethnicity." *DiversityInc*, February 15. Retrieved October 2, 2020 (https://www.diversityinc.com/alexandria-ocasio-cortez-black-ancestry-doesnt-mean-black/).

Archambault, Mark E., James A. Van Rhee, Gail S. Marion, and Sonia J. Crandall. 2008. "Utilizing Implicit Association Testing to Promote Awareness of Biases regarding Age and Disability." *Journal of Physician Assistant Education* 19(4):20–26.

Arias, Elizabeth. 2016. "Changes in Life Expectancy by Race and Hispanic Origin in the United States, 2013–2014." NCHS Data Brief, no. 244 (April), Figure 3 and Figure 4. Hyattsville, MD: National Center for Health Statistics. Retrieved October 2, 2020 (https://www.cdc.gov/nchs/data/databriefs/db244.pdf).

Armenta, Amada. 2016. "Racializing Crimmigration." *Sociology of Race & Ethnicity* 3(1): 82–95.

Arora, Seema, and Timothy N. Cason. 1998. "Do Community Characteristics Influence Environmental Outcomes? Evidence from the Toxics Release Inventory." *Journal of Applied Economics* 1(2):413–53. Retrieved October 2, 2020 (https://www.tandfonline.com/doi/pdf/10.1080/15140326.1998.12040529).

Arth, Zachary William, and Andrew C. Billings. 2019. "Touching Racialized Bases: Ethnicity in Major League Baseball Broadcasts at the Local and National Levels." *The Howard Journal of Communications* 30(3):230–48.

Asakawa, Gil. 2011. "Being Stereotyped Out of Ignorance Isn't as Bad as Flat-Out Racism, But . . ." *Nikkei View: The Asian American Blog*, August 30. Retrieved October 2, 2020 (http://nikkeiview.com/blog//?s=ignorance).

Associated Press. 2004. "A Sleeping Four-Month-Old . . ." AP image no. 040825027895, taken in Madera, California, September 19. Retrieved

October 21, 2020 (http://www.apimages.com/metadata/Index/Associated-Press-Domestic-News-California-Unite-/d26afe53a8e4da11af9f0014c2589dfb/1/0).

Baca Zinn, Maxine. 1982. "Chicano Men and Masculinity." *Journal of Ethnic Studies* 10(2):29–44.

———. 2010. "The Family as a Race Institution." Pp. 357–82 in *The Sage Handbook of Race and Ethnic Studies*, edited by Patricia Hill Collins and John Solomos. Thousand Oaks, CA: Sage Publications.

Baca Zinn, Maxine, and Bonnie Thornton Dill. 1996. "Theorizing Difference from Multiracial Feminism." *Feminist Studies* 22(2):321–31.

Baca Zinn, Maxine, D. Stanley Eitzen, and Barbara Wells. 2015. *Diversity in Families.* 10th ed. Upper Saddle River, NJ: Pearson.

Baca Zinn, Maxine, and Ruth Zambrana. 2019. "Chicanas/Latinas Advance Intersectional Thought and Practice." *Gender & Society* 33(5):677–701.

Barajas, Heidi L., and Jennifer L. Pierce. 2001. "The Significance of Race and Gender in School Success among Latinas and Latinos in College." *Gender & Society* 15(6):859–78.

Barak, Gregg, Paul Leighton, and Allison Cotton. 2015. *Class, Race, Gender, and Crime: The Social Realities of Justice in America.* 4th ed. Lanham, MD: Rowman & Littlefield.

Barr, Donald A. 2014. *Health Disparities in the United States: Social Class, Race, Ethnicity, and Health.* 2nd ed. Baltimore: Johns Hopkins University Press.

Basford, Tessa E., Lynn R. Offermann, and Tara S. Behrend. 2014. "Do You See What I See? Perceptions of Gender Microaggressions in the Workplace." *Psychology of Women Quarterly* 38(3):340–49.

[Basset, Delfin Carbonell]. 2013. "Speedy Gonzales' Relationship with the Hispanic Community." *Huffington Post*, October 3. Originally published on *Voxxi* as "Speedy Gonzales: An Icon and Symbol for Hispanics." Retrieved October 2, 2020 (http://www.huffingtonpost.com/2013/10/03/speedy-gonzales-hispanic_n_4039787.html).

Batalova, Jeanne, Brittany Blizzard, and Jessica Bolter. 2020. "Frequently Requested Statistics on Immigrants and Immigration in the United States." *Migration Information Source*, February 14. Migration Policy Institute. Retrieved October 2, 2020 (https://www.migrationpolicy.org/article/frequently-requested-statistics-immigrants-and-immigration-united-states).

Batalova, Jeanne, and Elijah Alperin. 2018. "Immigrants in the U.S. States with the Fastest-Growing Foreign-Born Populations." *Migration Information Source*, July 20. Migration Policy Institute. Retrieved October 2, 2020 (https://www.migrationpolicy.org/article/immigrants-us-states-fastest-growing-foreign-born-populations).

Baum, Dan. 2016. "Legalize It All: How to Win the War on Drugs." *Harper's Magazine*, March 27. Retrieved October 2, 2020 (http://harpers.org/archive/2016/04/legalize-it-all/).

Bean, Frank D., Susan K. Brown, and James D. Bachmeier. 2015. *Parents without Papers: The Progress and Pitfalls of Mexican American Integration.* New York: Russell Sage.

Bean, Frank D., Cynthia Feliciano, Jennifer Lee, and Jennifer Van Hook. 2009. "The New U.S. Immigrants: How Do They Affect Our Understanding of the African American Experience?" *The Annals of the American Academy of Political and Social Science* 621:202–20.

Bean, Frank D., and Jennifer Lee. 2009. "Plus ça Change . . . ? Multiraciality and the Dynamics of Race Relations in the United States." *Journal of Social Issues* 65(1):205–19.

Been, Vicki, and Francis Gupta. 1997. "Coming to the Nuisance or Going to the Barrios: A Longitudinal Analysis of Environmental Justice Claims." *Ecology Law Quarterly* 24(1):1–56.

Behm-Morawitz, Elizabeth, and David Ta. 2014. "Cultivating Virtual Stereotypes? The Impact of Video Game Play on Racial/Ethnic Stereotypes." *The Howard Journal of Communications* 25(1):1–15.

Behnken, Brian D., ed. 2016. *Civil Rights and Beyond: African American and Latino/a Activism in the Twentieth Century United States.* Athens: University of Georgia Press.

Bell, Joyce M., and Douglas Hartmann. 2007. "Diversity in Everyday Discourse: The Cultural Ambiguities and Consequences of 'Happy Talk.'" *American Sociological Review* 72(6):895–914.

Benediktsson, Mike O. 2012. "Bridging and Bonding in the Academic Melting Pot: Cultural Resources and Network Diversity." *Sociological Forum* 27(1):46–69.

Bennett, Claudette. 2000. "Racial Categories Used in the Decennial Censuses, 1790 to the Present." *Government Information Quarterly* 17(2):161–80.

Bennett, Lerone, Jr. 1964. *The Negro Mood*. New York: Johnson Publishing.

Berry, Brent. 2011. "Friends for Better or for Worse: Interracial Friendship in the United States as Seen through Wedding Party Photos." *Demography* 43(3):491–510.

Bertrand, Marianne, and Sendhil Mullainathan. 2004. "Are Emily and Greg More Employable than Lakisha and Jamal? A Field Experiment on Labor Market Discrimination." *American Economic Review* 94(4):991–1013.

Bethel, Elizabeth Rauh. 1999. *The Roots of African American Identity: Memory and History in Free Antebellum Communities*. London: Macmillan.

Bethencourt, Francisco. 2014. *Racisms: From the Crusades to the Twentieth Century*. Princeton, NJ: Princeton University Press.

Billingsley, Andrew. 1968. *Black Families in White America*. Englewood Cliffs, NJ: Prentice-Hall.

Black Lives Matter. N.d. "About." Retrieved October 22, 2020 (https://blacklivesmatter.com/about/).

Blackwell, Maylei. 2011. *Chicana Power! Contested Histories of Feminism in the Chicano Movement*. Austin: University of Texas Press.

Blanco, Maria. 2010. "Before *Brown*, There Was *Mendez*: The Lasting Impact of *Mendez v. Westminster* in the Struggle for Desegregation." *Perspectives*, March. Washington, DC: Immigration Policy Center, American Immigration Council. Retrieved October 2, 2020 (https://www.americanimmigrationcouncil.org/sites/default/files/research/Mendez_v._Westminster_032410.pdf),

Blascovich, Jim, Wendy Berry Mendes, Sarah B. Hunter, Brian Lickel, and Neneh Kowai-Bell. 2001. "Perceiver Threat in Social Interactions with Stigmatized Others." *Journal of Personality and Social Psychology* 80(2):253–67.

Blau, Judith R. 2003. *Race in the Schools: Perpetuating White Dominance?* Boulder, CO: Lynne Rienner.

Blinder, Scot, and Lydia Lundgren. 2019. "Roots of Group Threat: Anti-prejudice Motivations and Implicit Bias in Perceptions of Immigrants as Threats." *Ethnic and Racial Studies* 42(12): 1971–89.

Block, Jason P., Richard A. Scribner, and Karen B. DeSalvo. 2004. "Fast Food, Race/Ethnicity, and Income: A Geographic Analysis." *American Journal of Preventive Medicine* 27(3):211–17.

Blumer, Herbert. 1958. "Race Prejudice as a Sense of Group Position." *Pacific Sociological Review* 1(1):3–7.

Board of Governors of the Federal Reserve System. 2020. "2016 Survey of Consumer Finances." Federal Reserve System, last updated September 28. Retrieved October 19, 2020 (https://www.federalreserve.gov/econres/scf_2016.htm).

Bobo, Lawrence D. 1999. "Prejudice as Group Position: Microfoundations of a Sociological Approach to Racism and Race Relations." *Journal of Social Issues* 55(3):445–72.

———. 2004. "Inequalities that Endure? Racial Ideology, American Politics, and the Peculiar Role of the Social Sciences." Pp. 13–42 in *The Changing Terrain of Race and Ethnicity*, edited by Maria Krysan and Amanda E. Lewis. New York: Russell Sage Foundation.

———. 2006. *Prejudice in Politics: Group Position, Public Opinion, and the Wisconsin Treaty Rights Dispute*. Cambridge, MA: Harvard University Press.

———. 2015. "Foreword: The Racial Double Homicide of Trayvon Martin." Pp. xi–xv in *Deadly Justice: Trayvon Martin, Race, and the Criminal Justice System*, edited by Devon Johnson, Patricia Y. Warren, and Amy Farrell. New York: New York University Press.

———. 2018. "Understanding 'No Special Favors': A Quantitative and Qualitative Mapping of the Meaning of Responses to the Racial Resentment Scale." *Du Bois Review: Social Science Research on Race* 15(2):323–52.

Boguhn, Alexandrea. 2015. "White Men Will Now Host CNN and All Broadcast Sunday Morning Political Talk Shows." *Media Matters Blog*, April 24. Retrieved October 2, 2020 (https://mediamatters.org/blog/2015/04/24/white-men-will-now-host-cnn-and-all-broadcast-s/203407).

Bonilla-Silva, Eduardo. 2004. "From Bi-racial to Tri-racial: Towards a New System of Racial Stratification in the USA." *Ethnic and Racial Studies* 27(6):931–50.

———. 2017. *Racism without Racists: Color-Blind Racism and the Persistence of Racial Inequality in the United States*. 5th ed. Lanham, MD: Rowman & Littlefield.

Bonilla-Silva, Eduardo, and Karen S. Glover. 2004. "'We Are All Americans!': The Latin Americanization of Race Relations in the United States." Pp. 149–83 in *The Changing Terrain of Race and Ethnicity*, edited by Maria Krysan and Amanda E. Lewis. New York: Russell Sage.

Bradley, Mindy S., and Rodney L. Engen. 2016. "Leaving Prison: A Multilevel Investigation of Racial, Ethnic, and Gender Disproportionality in Correctional Release." *Crime and Delinquency* 62(2):253–79.

Brame, Robert, Shawn D. Bushway, Ray Paternoster, and Michael G. Turner. 2014. "Demographic Patterns of Cumulative Arrest Prevalence by Ages 18 and 23." *Crime & Delinquency* 60(3):471–86.

Branch, Taylor. 1988. *Parting the Waters: America in the King Years, 1954–1963.* New York: Simon and Schuster.

———. 1998. *Pillar of Fire: America in the King Years, 1963–1965.* New York: Simon and Schuster.

———. 2006. *At Canaan's Edge: America in the King Years, 1965–1968.* New York: Simon and Schuster.

Brandt, Mark J., and Christine Reyna. 2014. "To Love or Hate Thy Neighbor: The Role of Authoritarianism and Traditionalism in Explaining the Link between Fundamentalism and Racial Prejudice." *Political Psychology* 35(2):207–23.

Brenan, Megan. 2020. "Optimism about Black Americans' Opportunities in U.S. Falls." Gallup Organization, September 16. Retrieved November 5, 2020 (https://news.gallup.com/poll/320114/optimism-black-americans-opportunities-falls.aspx).

Briggs, Laura. 2002. *Reproducing Empire: Race, Sex, Science, and U.S. Imperialism in Puerto Rico.* Berkeley: University of California Press.

Briggs, Xavier de Souza. 2007. "'Some of My Best Friends Are . . .': Interracial Friendships, Class, and Segregation in America." *City & Community* 6(4):263–90.

Bronson, Jennifer, and E. Ann Carson. 2019. *Prisoners in 2017.* Prisoners Series, April 24. NCJ 252156. Washington, DC: US Bureau of Justice Statistics. Retrieved October 2, 2020 (https://www.bjs.gov/content/pub/pdf/p17.pdf).

Brooks, Dwight E., and Lisa P. Hébert. 2006. "Gender, Race, and Media Representation." Pp. 297–317 in *The SAGE Handbook of Gender and Communication*, edited by Bonnie J. Dow and Julia T. Wood. Thousand Oaks, CA: Sage Publications.

Brooks, Jamie D., and Meredith Ledford King. 2008. *Geneticizing Disease: Implications for Racial Health Disparities.* Washington, DC: Center for American Progress. Retrieved October 2, 2020 (https://cdn.americanprogress.org/wp-content/uploads/issues/2008/01/pdf/geneticizing_disease.pdf).

Brown, Anna, and Eileen Patten. 2013. "Hispanics of Puerto Rican Origin in the United States, 2011." Hispanic Trends, Pew Research Center, June 19. Retrieved October 2, 2020 (http://www.pewhispanic.org/2013/06/19/hispanics-of-puerto-rican-origin-in-the-united-states-2011/).

Brown, Elsa Barkley. 1995. "Imaging Lynching: African American Women, Communities of Struggle, and Collective Memory." Pp. 100–124 in *African American Women Speak Out on Anita Hill–Clarence Thomas*, edited by Geneva Smitherman. Detroit: Wayne State University Press.

Brown, Hana, and Jennifer A. Jones. 2015. "Rethinking Panethnicity and the Race-Immigration Divide: An Ethnoracialization Model of Group Formation." *Sociology of Race & Ethnicity* 1(1):181–91.

Brown, Robert McAfee. 1984. *Unexpected News: Reading the Bible with Third World Eyes.* Louisville, KY: Westminster John Knox Press.

Brown, Susan K., and Frank D. Bean. 2006. "Assimilation Models, Old and New: Explaining a Long-Term Process." *Migration Information Source*, October 1. Washington, DC: Migration Policy Institute. Retrieved October 2, 2020 (http://www.migrationpolicy.org/article/assimilation-models-old-and-new-explaining-long-term-process).

Brownstein, Ronald. 2010. "The Gray and the Brown: The Generational Mismatch." *National Journal*, July 24, pp. 14–22.

Brulle, Robert J., and David N. Pellow. 2006. "Environmental Justice: Human Health and Environmental Inequalities." *Annual Review of Public Health* 27:103–24. Retrieved October 2, 2020 (https://www.annualreviews.org/doi/pdf/10.1146/annurev.publhealth.27.021405.102124).

Brunsma, David L., ed. 2006. *Mixed Messages: Multiracial Identities in the "Color-Blind" Era.* Boulder, CO: Lynne Rienner.

Bullard, Robert D., ed. 1994. *Unequal Protection: Environmental Justice and Communities of Color.* New York: Random House.

———. 1996. "Symposium: The Legacy of American Apartheid and Environmental Racism." *St. John's Journal of Legal Commentary* 9:445–74.

———. 2008. *Dumping in Dixie: Race, Class, and Environmental Quality.* Boulder, CO: Westview Press.

Bunyasi, Tehama Lopez. 2015. "Color-Cognizance and Color-Blindness in White America: Perceptions of Whiteness and Their Potential to Predict Racial Policy Attitudes at the Dawn of the Twenty-First Century." *Sociology of Race & Ethnicity* 1(2):209–24.

Burke, Meghan A. 2019. *Colorblind Racism.* Medford, MA: Polity Press.

Burke, Sara E., John F. Dovidio, Sylvia P. Perry, Diana J. Burgess, Rachel R. Hardeman, Sean M. Phelan, Brooke A. Cunningham, Mark W. Yeazel, Julia M. Przedworski, and Michelle van Ryn. 2017. "Informal Training Experiences and Explicit Bias against African Americans among Medical Students." *Social Psychology Quarterly* 80(1):65–84.

Butler, Anthea. 2015. "Shooters of Color Are Called 'Terrorists' and 'Thugs.' Why Are White Shooters Called 'Mentally Ill'?" *Washington Post*, June 18. Retrieved Octobr 29, 2020 (https://www.washingtonpost.com/posteverything/wp/2015/06/18/call-the-charleston-church-shooting-what-it-is-terrorism/).

Byerly, Jack. 2019. "The Residential Segregation of the American Indian and Alaska Native Population in US Metropolitan and Micropolitan Areas, 2010." *Demographic Research*, April 16, 40(article 33):963–74. Retrieved October 2, 2020 (https://www.demographic-research.org/volumes/vol40/33/40-33.pdf).

Byler, Christen G. 2013. "Hispanic/Latino Fatal Occupational Injury Rates." *Monthly Labor Review* 136(2):14–23.

Byrd, W. Carson, Rachelle J. Brunn-Bevel, and Parker R. Sexton. 2014. "'We Don't All Look Alike': The Academic Performance of Black Student Populations at Elite Colleges." *Du Bois Review: Social Science Research on Race* 11(2):353–85.

Cabrera, Nolan León. 2014. "Exposing Whiteness in Higher Education: White Male College Students Minimizing Racism, Claiming Victimization, and Recreating White Supremacy." *Race, Ethnicity, and Education* 17(1):30–55.

Callanan, Valerie J. 2012. "Media Consumption, Perceptions of Crime Risk and Fear of Crime: Examining Race/Ethnic Differences." *Sociological Perspectives* 55(1):93–116.

Camarillo, Albert. 1979. *Chicanos in a Changing Society.* Dallas: Southern Methodist University Press.

Cannuscio, Carolyn C., Amy Hillier, Allison Karpyn, and Karen Glanz. 2014. "The Social Dynamics of Healthy Food Shopping and Store Choice in an Urban Environment." *Social Science & Medicine* 122(December):13–20.

Carbado, Devon W., and Mitu Gulati. 2013. *Acting White: Rethinking Race in Post-racial America.* New York: Oxford University Press.

Carmichael, Stokely, and Charles V. Hamilton. 1967. *Black Power: The Politics of Liberation.* New York: Vintage Books.

Carrasquillo, Héctor A., and Virginia Sánchez-Korrol. 1996. "Migration, Community, and Culture: The United States–Puerto Rican Experience." Pp. 98–109 in *Origins and Destinies: Immigration, Race, and Ethnicity in America*, edited by Silvia Pedraza and Rubén G. Rumbaut. Belmont, CA: Wadsworth.

Carrigan, William D., and Clive Webb. 2003. "The Lynching of Persons of Mexican Origin or Descent in the United States, 1848 to 1928." *Journal of Social History* 37(2):411–38.

Carson, Clayborne. 1981. *In Struggle: SNCC and the Black Awakening of the 1960s.* Cambridge, MA: Harvard University Press.

Carson, Clayborne, David J. Garrow, Vincent Harding, and Darlene Clark Hine, eds. 1987. *Eyes on the Prize: America's Civil Rights Years; A Reader and Guide.* New York: Penguin.

Carter, Prudence L. 2007. *Keepin' It Real: School Success Beyond Black and White.* New York: Oxford University Press.

Casad, Bettina J., Zachary W. Petzel, and Emily A. Ingalls. 2019. "A Model of Threatening Academic Environments Predicts Women STEM Majors' Self-Esteem and Engagement in STEM." *Sex Roles* 80(7–8):469–88.

Cauce, Ana Mari. 2016. Distinguished Lecture on Diversity in Higher Education (text). Delivered at the Center for the Study of Diversity, University of Delaware, Newark, Delaware, April 22. Retrieved October 2, 2020 (https://www.washington.edu/president/2016/04/22/distinguished-lecture-on-diversity-in-higher-education-at-university-of-delawares-center-for-the-study-of-diversity/).

Centers for Disease Control and Prevention. 2013. *CDC Health Disparities and Inequality Report: United States, 2013*. Supplement to *Morbidity and Mortality Weekly Report* 62(3), November 22. Retrieved October 2, 2020 (http://www.cdc.gov/mmwr/pdf/other/su6203.pdf).

———. 2019. "Infant Mortality." Reproductive Health, *CDC.org*, last reviewed September 10. Retrieved November 10, 2020 (https://www.cdc.gov/reproductivehealth/maternalinfanthealth/infantmortality.htm).

———. 2020. "Health Equity Considerations and Racial and Ethnic Minority Groups." CDC.gov, updated July 24. Retrieved October 2, 2020 (https://www.cdc.gov/coronavirus/2019-ncov/community/health-equity/race-ethnicity.html?CDC_AA_refVal=https%3A%2F%2Fwww.cdc.gov%2Fcoronavirus%2F2019-ncov%2Fneed-extra-precautions%2Fracial-ethnic-minorities.html).

Cervantes, Andrea Gomez, Daniel Alvord, and Cecilia Menjívar. 2018. "'Bad Hombres': The Effects of Criminalizing Latino Immigrants through Law and Media in the Rural Midwest." *Migration Letters* 15(2):182–96.

Chang, Gordon H. 2010. "Eternally Foreign: Asian Americans, History, and Race." Pp. 216–33 in *Doing Race: 21 Essays for the Twenty-First Century*, edited by Hazel Rose Markus and Paula M. L. Moya. New York: W. W. Norton.

———. 2019. *Ghosts of Gold Mountain: The Epic Story of the Chinese Who Built the Transcontinental Railroad*. Boston: Houghton Mifflin Harcourt.

Chappell, Bill. 2020. "Coronavirus Cases Spike in Navajo Nation, Where Water Service is Often Scarce." *National Public Radio*, March 26. Retrieved October 2, 2020 (https://www.npr.org/sections/coronavirus-live-updates/2020/03/26/822037719/coronavirus-cases-spike-in-navajo-nation-where-water-service-is-often-scarce).

Chavez, Leo R. 2013. *The Latino Threat: Constructing Immigrants, Citizens, and the Nation*. 2nd ed. Stanford, CA: Stanford University Press.

Chavez, Odilia. 2013. "Farm Confessional: I'm an Undocumented Farm Worker." *Modern Farmer*, November 6. Written and translated from the original Spanish by Lauren Smiley. Retrieved October 2, 2020 (http://modernfarmer.com/2013/11/farmworker-confessional/).

Chavez-Duenas, Nayeli, Hector Y. Adames, and Kurt C. Organista. 2014. "Skin-Color Prejudice and Within-Group Racial Discrimination: Historical and Current Impact on Latino/a Populations." *Hispanic Journal of Behavioral Sciences* 36(1):3–26.

Chen, Victor Tan. 2015. *Cut Loose: Jobless and Hopeless in an Unfair Economy*. Berkeley: University of California Press.

Childs, Erica Chito. 2005. *Navigating Interracial Borders: Black-White Couples and Their Social World*. New Brunswick, NJ: Rutgers University Press.

Chou, Rosalind, Kristen Lee, and Simon Ho. 2015. "Love Is (Color)Blind: Asian Americans and White Institutional Space at the Elite University." *Sociology of Race & Ethnicity* 1(2):302–16.

Chow, Esther Ngan-Ling. 1996. "Family, Economy, and the State: A Legacy of Struggle for Chinese American Women." Pp. 110–24 in *Origins and Destinies: Immigration, Race, and Ethnicity in America*, edited by Silvia Pedraza and Rubén G. Rumbaut. Belmont, CA: Wadsworth.

Chua, Amy. 2010. *Battle Hymn of the Tiger Mother*. New York: Penguin.

Churchill, Ward. 1993. "Crimes against Humanity." *Z Magazine* 6(March):43–47.

Cicero, Theodore J., Matthew S. Ellis, Hilary Laura Surratt, and Steven P. Kurtz. 2014. "The Changing Face of Heroin Use in the United States: A Retrospective Analysis of the Past 50 Years." *JAMA Psychiatry* 71(7):821–26. Retrieved October 2, 2020 (https://jamanetwork.com/journals/jamapsychiatry/fullarticle/1874575).

Cisneros, J. David. 2008. "Contaminated Communities: The Metaphor of 'Immigrant as Pollutant' on Media Representations of Immigration." *Rhetoric and Public Affairs* 11(4):569–602.

Civil Rights Act of 1964. Pub.L. 88-352, 78 Stat. 241 (1964). Text retrieved October 21, 2020 (https://www.govinfo.gov/content/pkg/STATUTE-78/pdf/STATUTE-78-Pg241.pdf).

Civil Rights History Project. 2013. *Julia Matilda Burns Oral History Interview Conducted by John Dittmer in Tchula, Mississippi, 2013 March 13.* Video. Library of Congress. Retrieved October 2, 2020 (https://www.loc.gov/item/afc2 010039_crhp0073/).

Clement, Scott. 2015. "Millennials Are Just as Racist as Their Parents." *Washington Post*, June 23. Retrieved October 2, 2020 (https://www.wa shingtonpost.com/news/wonk/wp/2015/06/23/ millennials-are-just-as-racist-as-their-parents/).

Clinton, William Jefferson. 1994. "Memorandum on Environmental Justice." To heads of all departments and agencies in the US federal government upon issuance of Executive Order 12898, "Federal Actions to Address Environmental Justice in Minority Populations and Low-Income Populations," Washington, DC, February 11. Text retrieved October 21, 2020 (page 280 of https://www.govinfo.gov/ content/pkg/WCPD-1994-02-14/pdf/WCPD -1994-02-14-Pg279.pdf).

Clotfelter, Charles T. 1976. "School Desegregation, 'Tipping,' and Private School Enrollment." *Journal of Human Resources* 11(1):13–20.

Coates, Ta-Nehisi. 2015. "The Black Family in the Age of Mass Incarceration." *The Atlantic* (October):60–84. Retrieved October 2, 2020 (https://www.theatlantic.com/magazine/archive /2015/10/the-black-family-in-the-age-of-mass- incarceration/403246/).

Cobb, Jelani. 2016. "The Matter of Black Lives." *New Yorker*, March 16, pp. 34–40. Retrieved October 2, 2020 (https://www.newyorker.com /magazine/2016/03/14/where-is-black-lives-ma tter-headed).

Cohn, D'Vera, and Jeffrey S. Passel. 2018. "A Record 64 Million Americans Live in Multigenerational Households." Fact Tank, Pew Research Center, April 5. Retrieved October 2, 2020 (https://www.pewresearch.org/fact-tank/2 018/04/05/a-record-64-million-americans-live- in-multigenerational-households/).

Colby, Sandra L., and Jennifer M. Ortman. 2015. *Projections of the Size and Composition of the U.S. Population, 2014–2060.* Washington, DC: US Census Bureau.

Coleman-Jensen, Alisha, Matthew P. Rabbitt, Christian A. Gregory, and Anita Singh. 2019. *Household Food Security in the United States in 2018, ERR-270.* Economic Research Service, US Department of Agriculture. Retrieved October

2, 2020 (https://www.ers.usda.gov/webdocs/p ublications/94849/err-270.pdf).

Coles, Roberta L., and Charles Green. 2010. *The Myth of the Missing Black Father.* New York: Columbia University Press.

Collins, Chiquita A., and David R. Williams. 1999. "Segregation and Mortality: The Deadly Effects of Racism?" *Sociological Forum* 14(3):495–523.

Collins, Patricia Hill. 1990. *Black Feminist Thought: Knowledge, Consciousness, and the Politics of Empowerment.* Boston: Unwin and Hyman.

———. 2019. *Intersectionality as Critical Social Theory.* Durham, NC: Duke University Press.

Conner, Thaddieus W., and William A. Taggart. 2013. "Assessing the Impact of Indian Gaming on American Indian Nations: Is the House Winning?" *Social Science Quarterly* 94(4):1016–44.

Consuelo Nacional de Población. 2008. *Migration and Health: Latinos in the United States.* Berkeley: University of California Center for Health Policy Research.

Cooley, Charles Horton. 1902. *Human Nature and Social Order.* New York: Scribner's.

Cottom, Tressie McMillan. 2019. *Thick.* New York: The Free Press.

Craig, Maxine Leeds. 2002. *Ain't I a Beauty Queen? Black Women, Beauty, and the Politics of Race.* New York: Oxford University Press.

Creamer, John, and Abinash Mohanty. 2019. "Poverty Rate for People in Female- Householder Families Lowest on Record." BCTV, October 24. Retrieved October 2, 2020 (https://www.bctv.org/2019/10/24/poverty-rate -for-people-in-female-householder-families-lo west-on-record/).

Crenshaw, Kimberlé. 1989. "Demarginalizing the Intersection of Race and Sexuality: A Black Feminist Critique of Antidiscrimination Doctrine, Feminist Theory, and Anti-racist Politics." *University of Chicago Legal Forum* 140:139–67.

Crockett, Stephen A., Jr. 2015. "SAE Frat Member Apologizes for Singing Racist Song." *The Root*, March 26. Retrieved October 2, 2020 (https:// www.theroot.com/sae-frat-member-apologizes -for-singing-racist-song-1790859235).

Cumminos, Peter. 1963. "Race, Marriage, and Law." *The Harvard Crimson*, December 17. Retrieved October 2, 2020 (https://www.th ecrimson.com/article/1963/12/17/race-marriage -and-law-pamerican-racism/).

Dalmage, Heather. 2000. *Tripping on the Color Line: Black-White Multiracial Families in a Racially Divided World*. New Brunswick, NJ: Rutgers University Press.

Daniels, Jessie. 2013. "Race and Racism in Internet Studies: A Review and Critique." *New Media & Society* 15(5):695–719.

Daniels, Kimberly, and Joyce Abma. 2018. "Current Contraceptive Status among Women Aged 15–49: United States, 2015–2017." *NCHS Data Brief* (327, December). National Center for Health Statistics, Centers for Disease Control and Prevention. Retrieved October 21, 2020 (https://www.cdc.gov/nchs/data/databriefs/db327-h.pdf).

Darby, Derrick, and Argun Saatcioglu. 2014. "Race, Justice, and Desegregation." *Du Bois Review: Social Science Research on Race* 11(1):87–108.

Darling-Hammond, Linda. 2004. "The Color Line in American Education: Race, Resources, and Student Achievement." *Du Bois Review: Social Science Research on Race* 1(2):213–46.

———. 2010. *The Flat World and Education: How America's Commitment to Equity Will Determine Our Future*. New York: Teachers College Press.

Daugherity, Brian J. 2014. "Desegregation in Public Schools." *Encyclopedia Virginia*, last modified May 30. Retrieved October 2, 2020 (http://www.encyclopediavirginia.org/Desegregation_in_Public_Schools).

Davis, Elizabeth, Anthony Whyde, and Lynn Langton. 2018. Contacts Between Police and the Public, 2015. Special Report, October, US Bureau of Justice Statistics, US Department of Justice. Retrieved October 21, 2020 (https://www.bjs.gov/content/pub/pdf/cpp15.pdf).

De'Armond, De'Arno, and Dandan Zhu. 2011. "Determinants of Consumer Debt: An Examination of Individual Credit Management Variables." *Journal of Finance and Accountancy* 7(1):1–17.

Dean, Lorraine, S. V. Subramanian, David R. Williams, Katrina Armstrong, Camille Z. Charles, and Ichiro Kawachi. 2014. "The Role of Social Capital in African-American Women's Use of Mammography." *Social Science & Medicine* 104(March):148–56.

De Genova, Nicholas, and Ana Y. Ramos-Zayas. 2003. *Latino Crossings: Mexicans, Puerto Ricans, and the Politics of Race and Citizenship*. New York: Routledge.

de la Garza, Rodolfo O. 1992. "From Rhetoric to Reality: Latinos and the 1988 Election in Review." Pp. 171–81 in *From Rhetoric to Reality: Latino Politics in the 1988 Elections*, edited by Rodolfo O. de la Garza and Louis DeSipio. Boulder, CO: Westview Press.

Delgado, Richard. 2009. "Law of the Noose: A History of Latino Lynching." *Harvard Civil Rights-Civil Liberties Law Review* 44:297–312.

DeLuca, Stefanie, Philip M. E. Garboden, and Peter Rosenblatt. 2013. "Segregating Shelter: How Housing Policies Shape the Residential Locations of Low-Income Minority Families." *Annals of the American Academy of Political and Social Science* 647(1):268–99.

DeNavas-Walt, Carmen, Bernadette D. Proctor, and Jessica C. Smith. 2010. *Income, Poverty, and Health Insurance Coverage in the United States: 2009*. Last revised June 25, 2020. Washington, DC: US Census Bureau. Retrieved October 2, 2020 (https://www.census.gov/data/tables/2010/demo/income-poverty/p60-238.html).

Denton, Nancy. 2001. "Housing as a Means of Asset Accumulation: A Good Strategy for the Poor?" Pp. 232–66 in *Assets for the Poor: The Benefits of Spreading Asset Ownership*, edited by Thomas M. Shapiro and Edward N. Wolff. New York: Russell Sage Foundation.

Desmond, Matthew. 2016. *Evicted: Poverty and Profit in the American City*. New York: Crown Publishers.

DiAngelo, Robin. 2016. *White Fragility: Why It's So Hard for White People to Talk about Racism*. Boston: Beacon Press.

Dill, Bonnie Thornton. 1988. "'Our Mothers' Grief': Racial-Ethnic Women and the Maintenance of Families." *Journal of Family History* 13(1):415–31.

Diner, Hasia. 1996. "Erin's Children in America: Three Centuries of Irish Immigration to the United States." Pp. 161–71 in *Origins and Destinies: Immigration, Race, and Ethnicity in America*, edited by Silvia Pedraza and Rubén G. Rumbaut. Belmont, CA: Wadsworth.

Dines, Gail, and Jean McMahon Humez, eds. 2014. *Gender, Race, and Class in the Media: A Critical Reader*. 4th ed. Thousand Oaks, CA: Sage Publications.

Dirks, Danielle, and Jennifer C. Mueller. 2010. "Racism and Popular Culture." Pp. 115–29 in *Handbook of the Sociology of Racial and Ethnic Relations*, edited by Hernán Vera and Joe R. Feagin. New York: Springer.

Doane, Ashley W., and Eduardo Bonilla-Silva, eds. 2003. *White Out: The Continuing Significance of Racism*. New York: Routledge.

Douglass, Frederick. 1886. "Southern Barbarism." Speech given on the occasion of the 24th anniversary of the Emancipation Proclamation, Washington, DC, April 16.

Dow, Dawn M. 2015. "Negotiating 'the Welfare Queen' and 'the Strong Black Woman': African American Middle-Class Mothers' Work and Family Perspectives." *Sociological Perspectives* 58(1):36–55.

Drakulich, Kevin M. 2015. "Explicit and Hidden Racial Bias in the Framing of Social Problems." *Social Problems* 62(3):391–418.

Dreby, Joanna. 2010. *Divided by Borders: Mexican Migrants and Their Children*. Berkeley: University of California Press.

Du Bois, W. E. B. 1899. *The Philadelphia Negro: A Social Study*. Philadelphia: University of Pennsylvania Press.

———. [1903] 1996. *The Souls of Black Folk*. New York: Penguin.

Duchon, Richie. 2015. "Charleston Church Shooting Leaves Jon Stewart Jokeless." *NBC News*, updated June 19. Retrieved October 2, 2020 (http://www.nbcnews.com/storyline/charleston-church-shooting/charleston-church-shooting-leaves-jon-stewart-jokeless-n378236).

Duffy, Mignon. 2011. *Making Care Count: A Century of Gender, Race, and Paid Care Work*. New Brunswick, NJ: Rutgers University Press.

Dunbar, Erica Armstrong. 2017. *Never Caught: Ona Judge Staines, the President's Runaway Slave Woman*. New Haven, CT: Yale University Press.

Durkheim, Émile. [1895] 1964. *The Division of Labor in Society*. New York: Free Press.

Eastman, Susan T., and Andrew C. Billings. 2001. "Biased Voices of Sports: Racial and Gender Stereotyping in College Basketball Announcing." *The Howard Journal of Communications* 12(4):183–201.

Eberhardt, Jennifer L. 2019. *Biased: Uncovering the Hidden Prejudice that Shapes What We See, Think, and Do*. New York: Penguin/Random House.

Edin, Kathryn, and Maria Kefalas. 2005. *Promises I Can Keep: Why Poor Women Put Marriage before Motherhood*. Berkeley: University of California Press.

Edin, Kathryn, and Timothy J. Nelson. 2013. *Doing the Best I Can: Fatherhood in the Inner City*. Berkeley: University of California Press.

Educational Opportunity Monitoring Project. 2020. "Racial and Ethnic Achievement Gaps." Stanford Center for Education Policy Analysis, Stanford University. Retrieved October 2, 2020 (https://cepa.stanford.edu/educational-opportunity-monitoring-project/achievement-gaps/race/).

Edwards, Korie, Katrina Carter-Tellison, and Cedric Herring. 2004. "For Richer, for Poorer, Whether Dark or Light: Skin Tone, Marital Status, and Spouse's Earnings." Pp. 65–91 in *Skin Deep: How Race and Complexion Matter in the "Color Blind" Era*, edited by Cedric Herring, Verna M. Keith, and Hayward Derrick Horton. Urbana: University of Illinois Press.

Elliott, Sinikka, and Elyshia Aseltine. 2013. "Raising Teenagers in Hostile Environments: How Race, Class, and Gender Matter for Mothers' Protective Carework." *Journal of Family Issues* 34(6):719–44.

Elliott, Sinikka, Rachel Powell, and Joslyn Brenton. 2015. "Being a Good Mom: Low-Income, Black Single Mothers Negotiate Intensive Mothering." *Journal of Family Issues* 36(3):351–70.

Ellis, Renee R., and Tavia Simmons. 2014. *Coresident Grandparents and Their Grandchildren: 2012*. Washington, DC: US Census Bureau. Retrieved October 5, 2020 (https://www.census.gov/content/dam/Census/library/publications/2014/demo/p20-576.pdf).

Ely, Danielle M., and Anne K.Driscoll. 2020. "Infant Mortality in the United States, 2018: Data from the Period Linked Birth/Infant Death File." *National Vital Statistics Reports* 69(7). Retrieved November 10, 2020 (https://www.cdc.gov/nchs/data/nvsr/nvsr69/NVSR-69-7-508.pdf).

Embrick, David G., J. Talmadge Wright, and András Lukács, eds. 2012. *Social Exclusion, Power, and Video Game Play: New Research in Digital Media and Technology*. New York: Lexington Books.

Emerick, Nicholas A., Theodore R. Curry, Timothy W. Collins, and S. Fernando Rodriguez. 2014.

"Homicide and Social Disorganization on the Border: Implications for Latino and Immigrant Populations." *Social Science Quarterly* 95(2):360–79.

Emerson, Michael O., Rachel T. Kimbro, and George Yancey. 2002. "Contact Theory Extended: The Effects of Prior Racial Contact on Current Social Ties." *Social Science Quarterly* 83(3):745–61.

Engels, Friedrich. [1884] 1972. *The Origin of the Family, Private Property, and the State.* New York: International.

Erba, Joseph. 2018. "Media Representations of Latina/os and Latino Students' Stereotype Threat Behavior." *The Howard Journal of Communications* 28(January/March):83–102.

Erhart, Ryan, and Deborah Hall. 2019. "A Descriptive and Comparative Analysis of the Content of Stereotypes about Native Americans." *Race and Social Problems* 11(September):225–42.

Erikson, Erik. 1968. *Identity, Youth, and Crisis.* New York: Norton.

Espinosa, Lorelle L., Jonathan M. Turk, Morgan Taylor, and Hollie M. Chessman. 2019. *Race and Ethnicity in Higher Education: A Status Report.* Washington, DC: American Council on Education.

Espiritu, Yen Le. 1992. *Asian American Panethnicity: Bridging Institutions and Identities.* Philadelphia: Temple University Press.

Essed, Philomena. 1991. *Understanding Everyday Racism: An Interdisciplinary Theory.* Newbury Park, CA: Sage.

Evans, Bronwynne C., David W. Coon, and Michael J. Belyea. 2014. "Worry among Mexican American Caregivers of Community-Dwelling Elders." *Hispanic Journal of Behavioral Sciences* 36(3):344–65.

Ewing, Walter [A]. 2016. "Immigrant Workers Enhance and Expand the U.S. Economy." American Immigration Council, June 29. Retrieved October 5, 2020 (https://immigration impact.com/2016/06/29/immigrant-workers-enhance-expand-u-s-economy/).

Ewing, Walter A., Daniel E. Martínez, and Rubén G. Rumbaut. 2015. *The Criminalization of Immigration in the United States: July 2015.* Washington, DC: American Immigration Council. Retrieved October 5, 2020 (https://w ww.americanimmigrationcouncil.org/sites/defau lt/files/research/the_criminalization_of_immi gration_in_the_united_states.pdf).

Fahle, Erin M., Sean F. Reardon, Kalogrides Demetra, Ericka S. Weathers, and Jang Heewon. 2020. "Racial Segregation and School Poverty in the United States, 1999–2016." *Race and Social Problems* 12(1):42–56.

Farley, Reynolds, Howard Schuman, Suzanne Bianchi, Diane Colasanto, and Shirley Hatchett. 1978. "'Chocolate City, Vanilla Suburbs': Will the Trend toward Racially Separate Communities Continue?" *Social Science Research* 7(2):319–44.

Feagin, Joe [R]. 2006. *Systemic Racism: A Theory of Oppression.* New York: Routledge.

———. 2010a. *Racist America: Current Realities and Future Reparations.* New York: Routledge.

———. 2010b. *The White Racial Frame: Centuries of Racial Framing and Counter-framing.* New York: Routledge.

———. 2013. "Race and Justice: Wrongful Convictions of African American Men." *Contemporary Sociology* 42(January):81–83.

———. 2014. *Racist America: Roots, Current Realities, and Future Reparations.* 3rd ed. Lanham, MD: Rowman & Littlefield.

Feagin, Joe R., and José A. Cobas. 2014. *Latinos Facing Racism: Discrimination, Resistance, and Endurance.* Boulder, CO: Paradigm.

Federal Bureau of Investigation. 2016. *Crime in the United States, 2015.* Criminal Justice Information Services Division. Retrieved October 5, 2020 (https://ucr.fbi.gov/crime-in-the-u.s/2015/crime-in-the-u.s.-2015).

———. 2018a. *2018 Hate Crime Statistics, Table 1.* Criminal Justice Information Services Division. Retrieved October 5, 2020 (https://u cr.fbi.gov/hate-crime/2018/topic-pages/tables/table-1.xls).

———. 2018b. "Violent Crime Offense Figure: Five-Year Trend, 2014–2018." *Crime in the United States, 2018.* US Department of Justice. Retrieved October 21, 2020 (https://ucr.fbi.gov /crime-in-the-u.s/2018/crime-in-the-u.s.-2018/topic-pages/violent-crime).

Federal Reserve Bank. 2020. *Report on the Economic Well-Being of U.S. Households in 2019–May 2020.* Last updated May 21. Retrieved November 10, 2020 (https://www.federalreserve .gov/publications/2020-economic-well-being-of -us-households-in-2019-retirement.htm).

Feldman, Marcus W. 2010. "The Biology of Ancestry: DNA, Genomic Variation, and Race." Pp. 136–59 in *Doing Race: 21 Essays for the Twenty-First Century*, edited by Hazel Rose Markus and Paula M. L. Moya. New York: W. W. Norton.

Feliciano, Cynthia, and Belinda Robnett. 2014. "How External Racial Classifications Shape Latino Dating Choices." *The DuBois Review: Social Science Research on Race* 11(2):295–328.

Feliciano, Cynthia, Belinda Robnett, and Golnaz Komaie. 2009. "Gendered Racial Exclusion among White Internet Daters." *Social Science Research* 38(1):39–54.

Ferber, Abby. 1998. *White Man Falling: Race, Gender, and White Supremacy*. Lanham, MD: Rowman & Littlefield.

Ferguson, Ann Arnett. 2000. *Bad Boys: Public Schools in the Making of Black Masculinity*. Ann Arbor: University of Michigan Press.

Ferriss, Susan, and Ricardo Sandoval. 1997. *The Fight in the Fields: Cesar Chavez and the Farmworkers Movement*. Edited by Diana Hembree, foreword by Gary Soto. Boston: Houghton Mifflin.

Fingerhut, Adam W. and Cleopatra M. Abdou. 2017. "The Role of Healthcare Stereotype Threat and Social Identity Threat in LGB Health Disparities." *Journal of Social Issues* 73(3):493–507.

Fingerman, Karen L., and Kira S. Birditt. 2011. "Relationships between Adults and Their Aging Parents." Pp. 219–32 in *Handbook of the Psychology of Aging*, 7th ed., edited by K. Warner Schaie and Sherry L. Willis. New York: Elsevier Academic Press.

Fischer, Mary J. 2008. "Does Campus Diversity Promote Friendship Diversity? A Look at Interracial Friendships in College." *Social Science Quarterly* 89(3):631–55.

Flagg, Barbara J. 1997. "'Was Blind but Now I See': White Race Consciousness and the Requirement of Discriminatory Intent." Pp. 629–31 in *Critical White Studies: Looking Behind the Mirror*, edited by Richard Delgado and Jean Stefancic. Philadelphia: Temple University Press.

Fleegler, Eric W., and Neil L. Schechter. 2015. "Pain and Prejudice." *Journal of the American Medical Association Pediatrics* 169(11):991–93.

Flippen, Chenoa. 2004. "Unequal Returns to Housing Investments? A Study of Real Housing Appreciation among Black, White, and Hispanic Households." *Social Forces* 82(4):1523–51.

Flores, Antonio. 2017. "2015, Hispanic Population the United States Statistical Portrait: Age/Gender/Marital Status/Fertility (Table 9)." Hispanic Trends, Pew Research Center, September 18. Retrieved October 5, 2020 (https://www.pewresearch.org/hispanic/2017/09/18/2015-statistical-information-on-hispanics-in-united-states/#current-age).

Fogel, Robert William, and Stanley L. Engermann. 1974. *Time on the Cross: The Economics of American Negro Slavery*. New York: W. W. Norton.

Foley, Neil. 2005. "Over the Rainbow: *Hernandez v. Texas*, *Brown v. Board of Education*, and *Black v. Brown*." *UCLA Chicano-Latina Law Review* 25(Spring):139–52.

Foner, Eric. 1988. *Reconstruction: America's Unfinished Revolution, 1863–1877*. New York: Harper and Row.

Foner, Nancy. 2005. *In a New Land: A Comparative View of Immigration*. New York: New York University Press.

Ford, Kristie A., and Josephine Orlandella. 2015. "The 'Not-So-Final Remark': The Journey to Becoming White Allies." *Sociology of Race & Ethnicity* 1(2):287–301.

Ford, Tanisha C. 2013. "SNCC Women, Denim and the Politics of Dress." *Journal of Southern History* 79(3):625–58.

Forman, Tyrone A. 2004. "Color-Blind Racism and Racial Indifference: The Role of Racial Apathy in Facilitating Enduring Inequalities." Pp. 43–66 in *The Changing Terrain of Race and Ethnicity*, edited by Maria Krysan and Amanda E. Lewis. New York: Russell Sage Foundation.

Forman, Tyrone A., Carla Goar, and Amanda E. Lewis. 2004. "Neither Black nor White? An Empirical Test of the Latinization Thesis." *Race and Society* 5(1):65–84.

Forman, Tyrone A., and Amanda E. Lewis. 2006. "Racial Apathy and Hurricane Katrina: The Social Anatomy of Prejudice in the Post–Civil Rights Era." *Du Bois Review: Social Science Research on Race* 3(1):175–202.

Fox, Joe, Adrian Blanco, Jennifer Jenkins, Julie Tate, and Wesley Lowery. 2019. "What We've Learned about Police Shootings 5 Years after Ferguson." *Washington Post*, August 9. Retrieved October 5, 2020 (https://www.wa

shingtonpost.com/nation/2019/08/09/what-weve-learned-about-police-shootings-years-after-ferguson/?arc404=true).

Fox Gotham, Kevin, Katie Lauve-Moon, and Bradford Powers. 2017. "Risk and Recovery: Understanding Flood Risk Perceptions in a Postdisaster City—The Case of New Orleans." *Sociological Spectrum* 37(6):335–52.

Fraga, Luis Ricardo. 2012. *Latinos in the New Millennium: An Almanac of Opinion, Behavior, and Policy Preferences*. New York: Cambridge University Press.

Fraga, Luis Ricardo, John J. Garcia, Rodney E. Hero, Michael Jones-Correa, Valerie Martinez-Ebers, and Gary Segura, eds. 2010. *Latino Lives in America: Making it Home*. Philadelphia: Temple University Press.

Frankenberg, Erica, Jongyeon Ee, Jennifer B. Ayscue, and Gary Orfield. 2019. *Harming Our Common Future: America's Segregated Schools 65 Years after* Brown. Los Angeles: The Civil Rights Project/Proyecto Derechos Civiles, Center for Education and Civil Rights, University of California, Los Angeles.

Franklin, Benjamin. [1751] 1961. "Observations Concerning the Increase of Mankind, Peopling of Countries, etc." in Papers of Benjamin Franklin, Vol. 4, July 1, 1750–June 30, 1753, edited by Leonard W. Labaree. New Haven, CT: Yale University Press. Text with commentary retrieved October 14, 2020 (https://founders.archives.gov/documents/Franklin/01-04-02-0080).

Franklin, Travis W. 2018. "The State of Race and Punishment in America: Is Justice Really Blind?" *Journal of Criminal Justice* 59:18.

Franklin, Travis W., and Tri Keah S. Henry. 2020. "Racial Disparities in Federal Sentencing Outcomes: Clarifying the Role of Criminal History." *Crime and Delinquency* 66(1):3–32.

Franssen, Vicky, Kristof Dhont, and Alain Van Hiel. 2013. "Age-Related Differences in Ethnic Prejudice: Evidence of the Mediating Effect of Right-Wing Attitudes." *Journal of Community & Applied Social Psychology* 23(3):252–57.

Fredrickson, George M. 2002. *Racism: A Short History*. Princeton, NJ: Princeton University Press.

Free, Marvin D., and Mitch Ruesink. 2012. *Race and Justice: Wrongful Convictions of African American Men*. Boulder, CO: Lynne Rienner.

Frey, William H. 2015. *Diversity Explosion: How New Racial Demographics Are Remaking America*. Washington, DC: The Brookings Institute.

Frey, William H., Brookings Institution, and University of Michigan Social Science Data Analysis Network. N.d. "New Racial Segregation Measures for States and Large Metropolitan Areas: Analysis of the 2005–2009 American Community Survey." Michigan Population Studies Center, Institute for Social Research. Retrieved October 20, 2020 (https://www.psc.isr.umich.edu/dis/census/segregation.html).

Fryberg, Stephanie A., and Alisha Watts. 2010. "We're Honoring You, Dude: Myths, Mascots, and American Indians." Pp. 458–80 in *Doing Race: 21 Essays for the Twenty-First Century*, edited by Hazel Rose Markus and Paula M. L. Moya. New York: W. W. Norton.

Funderburg, Lisa. 2013. "The Changing Face of America." *National Geographic* 224(4):80–91. Retrieved October 15, 2020 (paywall; https://www.nationalgeographic.com/magazine/2013/10/changing-face-america/).

Furstenberg, Frank F. 2014. "Fifty Years of Family Change: From Consensus to Complexity." *Annals of the American Academy of Political and Social Science* 654(1):12–30.

Gabbidon, Shaun L., and Helen Taylor Greene. 2018. *Race and Crime*, 5th ed. Thousand Oaks, CA: Sage Publications.

Gaddis, S. Michael. 2015. "Discrimination in the Credential Society: An Audit Study of Race and College Selectivity in the Labor Market." *Social Forces* 93(4):1451–79.

———. 2019. "Understanding the 'How' and 'Why' Aspects of Racial-Ethnic Discrimination: A Multimethod Approach to Audit Studies." *Sociology of Race & Ethnicity* 5(4):443–55.

Galaviz, Sal. N.d. "The Promised Land." Bracero History Archive, Item #3227. Retrieved October 5, 2020 (http://braceroarchive.org/items/show/3227).

Gallagher, Charles A. 2003. "Color-Blind Privilege: The Social and Political Functions of Erasing the Color Line in America." *Race, Gender & Class* 10:22–37.

———. 2004. "Racial Redistricting: Expanding the Boundaries of Whiteness." Pp. 59–76 in *The Politics of Multiracialism: Challenging Racial Thinking*, edited by Heather M. Dalmage. Albany: State University of New York Press.

Gallagher, Mike, and Cameron McWhirter. 1998. "Chiquita Secrets Revealed." *Cincinnati Enquirer*, May 3.

Gallup editors. 2014. "Gallup Review: Black and White Differences in Views on Race." Gallup Organization, December 12. Retrieved October 5, 2020 (http://www.gallup.com/poll/180107/gallup-review-black-white-differences-views-race.aspx).

Galt, Ryan E., Katharine Bradley, Libby Christensen, Cindy Fake, Kate Munden-Dixon, Natasha Simpson, Rachel Surls, and Julia Van Soelen Kim. 2017. "What Difference Does Income Make for Community Supported Agriculture (CSA) Members in California? Comparing Lower-Income and Higher-Income Households." *Agriculture and Human Values* 34(2):435–52.

Gans, Herbert J. 1979. "Symbolic Ethnicity: The Future of Ethnic Groups and Cultures in America." *Ethnic and Racial Studies* 2(1):1–20.

———. 1992. "Second-Generation Decline: Scenarios for the Economic and Ethnic Futures of the Post-1965 American Immigrants." *Ethnic and Racial Studies* 15(2):173–92.

———. 2009. "First Generation Decline: Downward Mobility among Refugees and Immigrants." *Ethnic and Racial Studies* 32(9):1658–70.

———. 2011. "The Moynihan Report and Its Aftermaths." *Du Bois Review: Social Science Research on Race* 8(2):315–27.

———. 2014. "Studying the Bottom of American Society." *Du Bois Review: Social Science Research on Race* 11(2):195–204.

Garcia, Jennifer J., Gilbert C. Gee, and Malia Jones. 2016. "A Critical Race Theory Analysis of Public Park Features in Latino Immigrant Neighborhoods." *Du Bois Review: Social Science Research on Race* 13(Fall):397–411.

Garcia, Lorena. 2012. *Respect Yourself, Protect Yourself: Latina Girls and Sexual Identity.* New York: New York University Press.

García, Mario T. 2014. *The Chicano Movement: Perspectives from the Twenty-First Century.* New York: Routledge.

Garriga, Carlos, Lowell R. Ricketts, and Don E. Schlagenhauf. 2017. "The Homeownershp Experience of Minorities during the Great Recession." *Federal Reserve Bank of St. Louis Review* 99(1):139–67.

Gasteyer, Stephen P., Jennifer Lai, Brittany Tucker, Jennifer Carrera, and Julius Moss. 2016. "Basics Inequality: Race and Access to Complete Plumbing Facilities in the United States." *Du Bois Review: Social Science Research on Race* 13(2):305–26.

Gelatt, Julia, and Jie Zong. 2018. *Settling In: A Profile of the Unauthorized Immigrant Population in the United States.* Fact Sheets, Migration Policy Institute, November. Retrieved November 10, 2020 (https://www.migrationpolicy.org/research/profile-unauthorized-immigrant-population-united-states).

Genovese, Eugene. 1972. *Roll, Jordan, Roll: The World the Slaves Made.* New York: Pantheon.

Georgevich, Mary. 2007. "Theme Party Provokes Outrage." *Santa Clara*, February 14. Retrieved October 5, 2020 (https://www.thesantaclara.org/blog/theme-party-provokes-outrage).

Gerbner, George. 1972. "Violence in Television Drama: Trends and Symbolic Functions." Pp. 28–187 in *Television and Social Behavior*, vol. 1, edited by G. A. Comstock and E. Rubenstein. Washington, DC: US Government Printing Office.

Giddings, Paula J. 2007. *In Search of Sisterhood: Delta Sigma Theta and the Challenge of the Black Sorority Movement.* New York: William Morrow.

———. 2009. *Ida: A Sword among Lions: Ida B. Wells and the Campaign against Lynching.* New York: Harper.

Gilio-Whitaker, Dina. 2019. *As Long as Grass Grows: The Indigenous Fight for Environmental Justice; From Colonization to Standing Rock.* Boston: Beacon Press.

Gimlin, Debra L. 2002. *Body Work: Beauty and Self-Image in American Culture.* New York: Routledge.

Glaubke, Christina R., Patti Miller, McCrae A. Parker, and Eileen Espejo. 2001. *Fair Play: Violence, Gender, and Race in Video Games.* Oakland, CA: Children Now.

Glenn, Evelyn Nakano. 1986. *Issei, Nisei, War Bride: Three Generations of Japanese American Women in Domestic Service.* Philadelphia: Temple University Press.

———. 1992. "From Servitude to Service Work: Historical Continuities in the Racial Division of Paid Reproductive Labor." *Signs* 18(1):1–43.

———. 2002. *Unequal Freedom: How Race and Gender Shaped American Citizenship and*

Labor. Cambridge, MA: Harvard University Press.

———. 2008. "Yearning for Lightness: Transnational Circuits in the Marketing and Consumption of Skin Lighteners." *Gender & Society* 22(3):281–302.

———. 2015. "Settler Colonialism as Structure: A Framework for Comparative Studies of U.S. Race and Gender Formation." *Sociology of Race & Ethnicity* 1(1): 52–72.

Glenn, Evelyn Nakano, and Rhacel Salazar Parreñas. 1996. "The Other Issei: Japanese Immigrant Women in the Pre–World War II Period." Pp. 125–40 in *Origins and Destinies: Immigration, Race, and Ethnicity in America*, edited by Silvia Pedraza and Rubén G. Rumbaut. Belmont, CA: Wadsworth.

Glick, Jennifer E., and Seung Y. Han. 2015. "Socioeconomic Stratification from Within: Changes within American Indian Cohorts in the United States, 1990–2010." *Population Research and Policy Review* 34(1):77–112.

Go, Julian. 2018. "Postcolonial Possibilities for the Sociology of Race." *Sociology of Race & Ethnicity* 4(4): 439–51.

Godoy, Maria. 2020. "What Do Coronavirus Racial Disparities Look like State by State?" National Public Radio, May 30. Retrieved October 5, 2020 (https://www.npr.org/sections/health-shots/2020/05/30/865413079/what-do-coronavirus-racial-disparities-look-like-state-by-state).

Goff, Phillip A., Matthew C. Jackson, Brooke Di Leone, Allison Lewis, Carmen M. Culotta, and Natalie A. DiTomasso. 2014. "The Essence of Innocence: Consequences of Dehumanizing Black Children." *Journal of Personality and Social Psychology* 106(4):526–45.

Goffman, Erving. 1963. *Stigma: Notes on the Management of Spoiled Identity.* Englewood Cliffs, NJ: Prentice-Hall.

Goings, Kenneth W. 1994. *Mammy and Uncle Mose: Black Collectibles and American Stereotyping.* Bloomington: Indiana University Press.

Golash-Boza, Tanya. 2016. "A Critical and Comprehensive Theory of Race and Racism." *Sociology of Race & Ethnicity* 2(2):129–41.

Golash-Boza, Tanya, and William Darity Jr. 2008. "Latino Racial Choices: The Effects of Skin Colour and Discrimination on Latinos' and Latinas' Racial Self-Identifications." *Ethnic and Racial Studies* 31(5):899–934.

Gold, Steven J., and Bruce Phillips.1996. "Mobility and Continuity among Eastern European Jews." Pp. 182–94 in *Origins and Destinies: Immigration, Race, and Ethnicity in America*, edited by Silvia Pedraza and Rubén G. Rumbaut. Belmont, CA: Wadsworth.

Gómez, Laura E. 2018. *Manifest Destinies: The Making of the Mexican American Race.* 2nd ed. New York: NYU Press.

Gonzales, Angela A., Thomas A. Lyson, and K. W. Mauer. 2007. "What Does a Casino Mean to a Tribe? Assessing the Impact of Casino Development on Indian Reservations in Arizona and New Mexico." *Social Science Journal* 44(3):405–19.

Gonzalez-Barrera, Ana, and Phillip Connor. 2019. "Around the World, More Say Immigrants Are a Strength than a Burden." Global Attitudes and Trends, Pew Research Center, March 14. Retrieved October 5, 2020 (https://www.pewresearch.org/global/2019/03/14/around-the-world-more-say-immigrants-are-a-strength-than-a-burden/).

Gordon, Milton M. 1964. *Assimilation in American Life.* New York: Oxford University Press.

Goyal, Monika K., Nathan Kuppermann, Sean D. Cleary, Stephen J. Teach, and James M. Chamberlain. 2015. "Racial Disparities in Pain Management of Children with Appendicitis in Emergency Departments." *Journal of the American Medical Association Pediatrics* 169(11):996–1002.

Gramlich, John. 2019. "From Police to Parole, Black and White Americans Differ Widely in Their Views of Criminal Justice System." Fact Tank, Pew Research Center, May 21. Retrieved October 5, 2020 (https://www.pewresearch.org/fact-tank/2019/05/21/from-police-to-parole-black-and-white-americans-differ-widely-in-their-views-of-criminal-justice-system/).

Graves, Joseph L. 2001. *The Emperor's New Clothes: Biological Theories of Race at the New Millennium.* New Brunswick, NJ: Rutgers University Press.

———. 2004. *The Race Myth: Why We Pretend Race Exists in America.* New York: Dutton.

Green, Tiffany, and Tod G. Hamilton. 2019. "Maternal Educational Attainment and Infant Mortality in the United States: Does the

Gradient Vary by Race/Ethnicity and Nativity?" *Demographic Research* 41:713–52.

Greenbaum, Susan D. 2015. *Blaming the Poor: The Long Shadow of the Moynihan Report on Cruel Images about Poverty*. New Brunswick, NJ: Rutgers University Press.

Greene, Solomon, and Allana McCargo. 2020. "New Data Suggests COVID-19 Is Widening Housing Disparities by Race and Income." *Urban Wire* (blog), May 29. Urban Institute. Retrieved November 5, 2020. https://www .urban.org/urban-wire/new-data-suggest-covid -19-widening-housing-disparities-race-and-inc ome.

Greenhouse, Steven. 2004. "Abercrombie & Fitch Bias Case Is Settled." *New York Times*, November 17. Retrieved October 15, 2020 (https://www.nytimes.com/2004/11/17/us/a bercrombie-fitch-bias-case-is-settled.html).

Greenwald, Anthony G., Debbie E. McGhee, and Jordan L. K. Schwartz. 1998. "Measuring Individual Differences in Implicit Cognition: The Implicit Association Test." *Journal of Personality and Social Psychology* 74(6):1464–80.

Grigoryeva, Angelina, and Martin Ruef. 2015. "The Historical Demography of Racial Segregation." *American Sociological Review* 80(4):814–42.

Gross, Samuel R., Maurice Possley, and Klara Stephens. 2017. "Race and Wrongful Convictions in the United States." National Registry of Exonerations, March 7. Irvine: National Registry of Exonerations, Newkirk Center for Science and Society, and the University of California–Irvine. Retrieved October 5, 2020 (http://www.law.umich.edu /special/exoneration/Documents/Race_and_ Wrongful_Convictions.pdf).

Grzanka, Patrick R. 2014. "Media as Sites/Sights of Justice." Pp. 131–37 in *Intersectionality: A Foundations and Frontiers Reader*, edited by Patrick R. Grzanka. Boulder, CO: Westview Press.

Guarneri, Christine E., and Christopher Dick. 2012. "Methods of Assigning Race and Hispanic Origin to Births from Vital Statistics Data." Paper prepared for the Federal Committee on Statistical Methodology Annual Meeting, Washington, DC, January 12, 2012. Retrieved October 5, 2020 (https://nces.ed.gov/FCSM/pdf/ Guarneri_2012FCSM_X-B.pdf).

Gurin, Patricia, E. L. Dey, and Sylvia Hurtado. 2002. "Diversity and Higher Education: Theory and Impact on Educational Outcomes." *Harvard Educational Review* 72(3):330–66.

Gutiérrez, Elena R. 2008. *Fertile Matters: The Politics of Mexican-Origin Women's Reproduction*. Austin: University of Texas Press.

———. 2010. "Latina/o Sex Policy." Pp. 90–102 in *Latina/o Sexualities: Probing Powers, Passions, Practices, and Politics*, edited by Marysol Asencio. New Brunswick, NJ: Rutgers University Press.

Gutiérrez y Muhs, Gabriella, Yolanda Flores Niemann, Carmen G. González, and Angela P. Harris. 2012. *Presumed Incompetent: The Intersections of Race and Class for Women in Academia*. Boulder: University Press of Colorado.

Gutman, Herbert. 1976. *The Black Family in Slavery and Freedom*. New York: Vintage.

Guyll, Max, Stephanie Madon, Loreto Prieto, and Kyle C. Scherr. 2010. "The Potential Roles of Self-Fulfilling Prophecies, Stigma Consciousness, and Stereotype Threat in Linking Latino-a Ethnicity and Educational Outcomes." *Journal of Social Issues* 66(1):113–30.

Hagerman, Margaret A. 2018. *White Kids: Growing Up with Privilege in a Racially Divided America*. New York: New York University Press.

Haley, Alex. 1963. "A Candid Conversation with the Militant Major-Domo of the Black Muslims." Alex Haley Interviews Malcolm X. *Playboy* 10(5). Text retrieved October 20, 2020 (https://alexhaley.com/2020/07/24/alex-haley-interviews-malcolm-x/).

Hall, Ronald. 1995. "The Bleaching Syndrome: African Americans' Response to Cultural Domination vis-à-vis Skin Color." *Journal of Black Studies* 26(2):172–84.

Hall, Stuart. 1997. "Introduction." Pp. 1–2 in *Representation: Cultural Representations and Signifying Practices*, edited by Stuart Hall. London: Sage Publications.

Hamilton, Leah, Twila Wingrove, and Kati Woodford. 2019. "Does Generous Welfare Policy Encourage Dependence? TANF Asset Limits and Duration of Program Participation." *Journal of Children & Poverty* 25(2):101–13.

Hanna-Attisha, Mona. 2018. *What the Eyes Don't See: A Story of Crisis, Resistance, and Hope in an American City*. New York: One World.

Hansen, Elise. 2017. "The Forgotten Minority in Police Shootings." CNN, updated November 13. Retrieved October 5, 2020 (https://www.cnn.com/2017/11/10/us/native-lives-matter/index.html).

Hansen, Karen V. 2013. *Encounter on the Great Plains: Scandinavian Settlers and the Dispossession of Dakota Indians, 1890–1930*. New York: Oxford University Press.

Hanson, Sandra L., and Emily Gilbert. 2012. "Family, Gender and Science Experiences: The Perspective of Young Asian Americans." *Race, Gender & Class* 19(3–4):326–47.

Harder, Jenna A., Victor N. Keller, and William J. Chopik. 2019. "Demographic, Experiential, and Temporal Variation in Ableism." *Journal of Social Issues* 75(3):683–706.

Harlan, Sharon L., David N. Pellow, and J. Timmons Roberts. 2015. "Climate Justice and Inequality." Pp. 127–63 in *Climate Change and Society: Sociological Perspectives*, edited by Riley E. Dunlap and Robert J. Brulle. New York: Oxford University Press.

Harmon, Talia Roitberg. 2004. "Race for Your Life: An Analysis of the Role of Race in Erroneous Capital Convictions." *Criminal Justice Review* 29(1):76–96.

Harper, Shaun R. 2012. *Black Male Student Success in Higher Education: A Report from the National Black Male College Achievement Study*. Philadelphia: University of Pennsylvania, Center for the Study of Race and Equity in Education.

———. 2015. "Black Male College Achievers and Resistant Responses to Racist Stereotypes at Predominantly White Colleges and Universities." *Harvard Educational Review* 8 (Winter):646–75.

Harris, Angel. 2011. *Kids Don't Want to Fail: Oppositional Culture and the Black-White Achievement Gap*. Cambridge, MA: Harvard University Press.

Havrilla, Katrina. 2010. "A Sociological Influence in *Dora the Explorer*." *Footnotes* 38(2):10.

Haynie, Kerry L. 2019. "Containing the Rainbow Coalition: Political Consequences of Mass Racialized Incarceration." *Du Bois Review: Social Science Research on Race* 16(1):243–51.

HealthCare.gov. 2020. "Immigrants: Coverage for Lawfully Present Immigrants." US Centers for Medicare & Medicaid Services. Retrieved October 5, 2020 (https://www.healthcare.gov/immigrants/lawfully-present-immigrants/).

Henderson, Ray, and Tony Buba. 1996. *Struggles in Steel: A Story of African-American Steelworkers*. Documentary. Book by Dennis C. Dickerson. Distributed by California Newsreel.

Hernandez, Richard. 2018. "The Fall of Employment in the Manufacturing Sector." *Monthly Labor Review*, US Bureau of Labor Statistics, August. Retrieved October 5, 2020 (https://www.bls.gov/opub/mlr/2018/beyond-bls/the-fall-of-employment-in-the-manufacturing-sector.htm).

Herring, Cedric. 2004. "Skin Deep: Race and Complexion in the 'Color Blind' Era." Pp. 1–21 in *Skin Deep: How Race and Complexion Matter in the "Color Blind" Era*, edited by Cedric Herring, Verna M. Keith, and Hayward Derrick Horton. Urbana: University of Illinois Press.

———. 2009. "Does Diversity Pay? Race, Gender, and the Business Case for Diversity." *American Sociological Review* 74(2):208–24.

Herring, Cedric, Verna M. Keith, and Hayward Derrick Horton, eds. 2004. *Skin Deep: How Race and Complexion Matter in the "Color Blind" Era*. Urbana: University of Illinois Press.

Higginbotham, Elizabeth, and Margaret L. Andersen, eds. 2016. *Race and Ethnicity in Society: The Changing Landscape*. 4th ed. Belmont, CA: Wadsworth/Cengage.

Hill, Mark E. 2000. "Color Differences in the Socioeconomic Status of African American Men: Results of a Longitudinal Study." *Social Forces* 78(4):1437–60.

———. 2002. "Skin Color and the Perception of Attractiveness among African Americans: Does Gender Make a Difference?" *Social Psychology Quarterly* 65(1):77–91.

Hine, Darlene Clark, ed. 1993. *Black Women in America: An Historical Encyclopedia*, vols. 1 and 2. Brooklyn: Carlson Publishing Inc.

———. 2004. "The *Briggs v. Elliott* Legacy: Black Culture, Consciousness, and Community before *Brown*, 1930–1954." *University of Illinois Law Review* 2004(5):1059–72. Retrieved October 5, 2020 (https://illinoislawreview.org/wp-content/ilr-content/articles/2004/5/Hine.pdf).

Hirschman, Charles, and Douglas S. Massey. 2008. "Places and Peoples: The New American Mosaic." Pp. 1–21 in *New Faces in New Places: The Changing Geography of American Immigration*, edited by Douglas S. Massey. New York: Russell Sage Foundation.

Hobbs, Allyson. 2014. *A Chosen Exile: A History of Racial Passing in American Life*. Cambridge, MA: Harvard University Press.

Hochschild, Arlie Russell. 2016. *Strangers in Their Own Land: Anger and Mourning on the American Right*. New York: The New Press.

Hochschild, Jennifer L., and Vesla Weaver. 2007. "The Skin Color Paradox and the American Racial Order." *Social Forces* 86(2):9643–70.

Hodges, Melissa J. 2020. "Intersections on the Class Escalator: Gender, Race, and Occupational Segregation in Paid Care Work." *Sociological Forum* 35(1):24–49.

Holt, Cheryl L., David L. Roth, Jin Huang, and Eddie M. Clark. 2015. "Gender Differences in the Roles of Religion and Locus of Control on Alcohol Use and Smoking among African Americans." *Journal of Studies on Alcohol and Drugs* 76(3):482–92.

Hondagneu-Sotelo, Pierrette. 2007. *Doméstica: Immigrant Workers Cleaning and Caring in the Shadows of Affluence*. Berkeley: University of California Press.

hooks, bell. 1992. *Black Looks: Race and Representation*. Boston: South End Press.

Hordge-Freeman, Elizabeth. 2015. *The Color of Love: Racial Features, Stigma, and Socialization in Black Brazilian Families*. Austin: University of Texas Press.

Horowitz, Juliana Menasce, Anna Brown, and Kiana Cox. 2019. "Race in America 2019." Social and Demographic Trends, Pew Research Center, April 9. Retrieved October 5, 2020 (https://www.pewsocialtrends.org/2019/04/09/race-in-america-2019/).

Houle, Jason N., and Fenaba R. Addo. 2018. "Racial Disparities in Student Debt and the Reproduction of the Fragile Middle Class." *Sociology of Race & Ethnicity* 5(4):562–77.

Howard, Daniel L, Philip D. Sloane, Sheryl Zimmerman, J. Kevin Eckert, Joan F. Walsh, Verita C. Buie, Persephone J. Taylor, and Gary G. Koch. 2002. "Distribution of African Americans in Residential Care/Assisted Living and Nursing Homes: More Evidence of Racial Disparity?" *American Journal of Public Health* 92(8):1272–77. Retrieved October 5, 2020 (https://www.ncbi.nlm.nih.gov/pmc/articles/PMC1447229/).

Huggins, Nathan. 2007. *Harlem Renaissance*. New York: Oxford University Press.

Hughey, Matthew W. 2014. *The White Savior Film: Content, Critics, and Consumption*. Philadelphia: Temple University Press.

———. 2015. "We've Been Framed! A Focus on Identity and Interaction for a Better Vision of Racialized Social Movements." *Sociology of Race & Ethnicity* 1(1):137–52.

Hughey, Matthew W., and Gregory S. Parks, eds. 2011. *Black Greek-Letter Organizations 2.0: New Directions in the Study of African American Fraternities and Sororities*. Foreword by Theda Skocpol. Jackson: University Press of Mississippi.

Hunt, Darnell, and Ana-Christina Ramón. 2020. *Hollywood Diversity Report 2020: A Tale of Two Hollywoods*. UCLA College Social Sciences, Institute for Research on Labor and Employment. Retrieved October 14, 2020 (https://socialsciences.ucla.edu/wp-content/uploads/2020/02/UCLA-Hollywood-Diversity-Report-2020-Film-2-6-2020.pdf).

Hunt, Darnell, Ana-Christina Ramón, Michael Tran. 2019. "Hollywood Diversity Report 2019: Old Story, New Beginning." UCLA College Social Sciences, Institute for Research on Labor and Employment. Retrieved October 14, 2020 (https://socialsciences.ucla.edu/wp-content/uploads/2019/02/UCLA-Hollywood-Diversity-Report-2019-2-21-2019.pdf).

Hunter, Margaret. 2004. "Light, Bright, and Almost White: The Advantages and Disadvantages of Light Skin." Pp. 22–44 in *Skin Deep: How Race and Complexion Matter in the "Color Blind" Era*, edited by Cedric Herring, Verna M. Keith, and Hayward Derrick Horton. Urbana: University of Illinois Press.

———. 2007. "The Persistent Problem of Colorism: Skin Tone, Status, and Inequality." *Sociology Compass* 1(1):237–54.

Hyland, Shelley, Lynn Langton, and Elizabeth Davis. 2015. "Police Use of Nonfatal Force, 2002–2011." Special report, US Bureau of Justice Statistics, US Department of Justice, November. Retrieved October 5, 2020 (https://www.bjs.gov/content/pub/pdf/punf0211.pdf).

Ingraham, Christopher. 2014. "Three-Quarters of Whites Don't Have Any Non-White Friends." Economic Policy, *Washington Post*, August 25. Retrieved October 15, 2020 (https://www.washingtonpost.com/news/wonk/wp/2014/08/25/three-quarters-of-whites-dont-have-any-non-white-friends/).

Innocence Project. 2020. "DNA Exonerations in the United States." Retrieved October 5, 2020 (https://www.innocenceproject.org/dna-exonerations-in-the-united-states/?gclid=EAIaIQobChMIlOGx0vHi6AIVBD0MCh1l5wtlEAAYASAAEgIz9fD_BwE).

Institute for Research on Poverty. 2020. "COVID-19 and Poverty." *Focus* 36(3). Retrieved November 10, 2020 (https://www.irp.wisc.edu/wp/wp-content/uploads/2020/10/Focus-36-3a.pdf).

Institute for Women's Policy Research. 2016. "Paid Sick Days Access and Usage Rates Vary by Race/Ethnicity, Occupation, and Earnings." Briefing Paper #B356, February. Retrieved November 10, 2020 (https://iwpr.org/wp-content/uploads/2020/08/B356-paid-sick-days.pdf).

Irizarry, Yasmiyn. 2013. "Is Measuring Interracial Contact Enough? Racial Concentration, Racial Balance, and Perceptions of Prejudice among Black Americans." *Social Science Quarterly* 94(3):591–615.

Itzigsohn, Jose. 2004. "The Formation of Latino and Latina Panethnic Identities." Pp. 197–216 in *Not Just Black and White: Historical and Contemporary Perspectives on Immigration, Race, and Ethnicity in the United States*, edited by Nancy Foner and George M. Fredrickson. New York: Russell Sage.

Itzigsohn, Jose, and Carlos Dore-Cabral. 2000. "Competing Identities: Race, Ethnicity and Panethnicity among Dominicans in the United States." *Sociological Forum* 15(June):225–47.

Itzigsohn, Jose, Silvia Gorguli, and Obed Vazquez. 2005. "Immigrant Incorporation and Racial Identity: Racial Self-Identification among Dominican Immigrants." *Ethnic and Racial Studies* 28(1):50–78.

Iyengar, Shanto. 2010. "Race in the News: Stereotypes, Political Campaigns, and Market-Based Journalism." Pp. 251–73 in *Doing Race: 21 Essays for the Twenty-First Century*, edited by Hazel Rose Markus and Paula M. L. Moya. New York: W. W. Norton.

Jackson, Chandra L., Frank B. Hu, Susan Redline, David R. Williams, Josiemer Mattei, and Ichiro Kawachi. 2014. "Racial/Ethnic Disparities in Short Sleep Duration by Occupation: The Contribution of Immigrant Status." *Social Science & Medicine* 118(October):71–79.

Jackson, Sarah J., Moya Bailey, and Brooke Foucault Welles. 2020. *#Hashtag Activism: Networks of Race and Gender Justice*. Foreword by Genie Lauren. Cambridge, MA: MIT Press.

Jacobson, Cardell K., and Bryan R. Johnson. 2006. "Interracial Friendship and African American Attitudes about Interracial Marriage." *Journal of Black Studies* 36(4):570–84.

Jargowsky, Paul A. 2013. "Concentration of Poverty in the New Millennium: Changes in Prevalence, Composition, and Location of High Poverty Neighborhoods." Century Foundation and Rutgers Center for Urban Research and Education.

———. 2015. "Architecture of Segregation: Civil Unrest, the Concentration of Poverty, and Public Policy." Issue brief, the Century Foundation, Rutgers University, August 9. Retrieved October 5, 2020 (https://community-wealth.org/sites/clone.community-wealth.org/files/downloads/report-jargowsky.pdf).

Jayadev, Arjun, and Robert Johnson. 2017. "Tides and Prejudice: Racial Attitudes during Downturns in the United States, 1979–2014." *Review of Black Political Economy* 44(3–4):379–92.

Jaynes, Gregory. 1982. "Suit on Race Recalls Lines Drawn under Slavery." *New York Times*, September 30, section Bm page 16. Retrieved October 12, 2020 (https://www.nytimes.com/1982/09/30/us/suit-on-race-recalls-lines-drawn-under-slavery.html).

Jiménez, Tomás Roberto. 2010. *Replenished Ethnicity: Mexican Americans, Immigration, and Identity*. Berkeley: University of California Press.

———. 2017. *The Other Side of Assimilation: How Immigrants Are Changing American Life*. Oakland: University of California Press.

Joffe, Carole, and Willie J. Parker. 2012. "Race, Reproductive Politics, and Reproductive Health Care in the United States." *Contraception* 86(1):1–3.

Johnson, Akilah, and Talia Buford. 2020. "Early Data Shows African Americans Have

Contracted and Died of Coronavirus at an Alarming Rate." ProPublica, April 3. Retrieved October 5, 2020 (https://www.propublica.org/article/early-data-shows-african-americans-have-contracted-and-died-of-coronavirus-at-an-alarming-rate).

Johnson, Lyndon B. 1965. Commencement address given at Howard University, Washington, DC, June 4. Video and transcript retrieved October 5, 2020 (https://www.americanrhetoric.com/speeches/lbjhowarduniversitycommencement.htm).

Johnson, Maria S., and Alford A. Young. 2016. "Diversity and Meaning in the Study of Black Fatherhood: Toward a New Paradigm." *Du Bois Review: Social Science Research on Race* 13(Spring):5–23.

Jones, Jacqueline. 2013. *A Dreadful Deceit: The Myth of Race from the Colonial Era to Obama's America*. New York: Basic Books.

Jones, James H. 1993. *Bad Blood: The Tuskegee Syphilis Experiment*. New York: Free Press.

Jones, James M., John F. Dovidio, and Deborah L. Vietze. 2014. *The Psychology of Diversity: Beyond Prejudice and Racism*. Malden, MA: Wiley Blackwell.

Jones, Jeffrey M. 2019. "Americans Less Satisfied with Treatment of Minority Groups." Gallup, February 20. Retrieved October 16, 2020 (https://news.gallup.com/poll/246866/americans-less-satisfied-treatment-minority-groups.aspx).

Jones, Veronica. 2017. "The Racialization of Arab Panethnic Identity: Exploring Students' Ingroup and Outgroup Social Positionings." *Race, Ethnicity and Education* 20(6):811–28.

Jones-Correa, Michael, and David L. Leal. 1996. "Becoming 'Hispanic': Secondary Panethnic Identification among Latin American–Origin Populations in the United States." *Hispanic Journal of Behavioral Sciences* 18(2):214–54.

Jordan, Winthrop D. 1968. *White Over Black: American Attitudes toward the Negro, 1550–1812*. Chapel Hill: University of North Carolina Press.

Kaiser Family Foundation. 2019. "Uninsured Rates for the Nonelderly by Race/Ethnicity." State Health Facts. Retrieved November 10, 2020 (https://www.kff.org/uninsured/state-indicator/nonelderly-uninsured-rate-by-raceethnicity/?currentTimeframe=0&sortModel=%7B%22colId%22:%22Location%22,%22sort%22:%22asc%22%7D).

Kang, Miliann. 2010. *The Managed Hand: Race, Gender, and the Body in Beauty Service Work*. Berkeley: University of California Press.

Kao, Grace, and Kara Joyner. 2004. "Do Race and Ethnicity Matter among Friends? Activities among Interracial, Interethnic, and Intraethnic Adolescent Friends." *Sociological Quarterly* 45(3):557–73.

Kaplan, Elaine Bell. 1996. *Not Our Kind of Girl: Unraveling the Myths of Black Teenage Motherhood*. Berkeley: University of California Press.

Kaplan, Sarah. 2020. "Climate Change Is Also a Racial Justice Problem." *Washington Post*, June 29. Retrieved October 21, 2020 (https://www.washingtonpost.com/climate-solutions/2020/06/29/climate-change-racism/).

Karni, Annie. 2020. "Kushner, Employing Racist Stereotype, Questions if Black Americans 'Want to Be Successful.'" *New York Times*, October 26. Retrieved November 10, 2020 (https://www.nytimes.com/2020/10/26/us/politics/kushner-black-racist-stereotype.html).

Kasinitz, Philip, John H. Mollenkopf, Mary C. Waters, and Jennifer Holdaway. 2008. *Inheriting the City: The Children of Immigrants Come of Age*. New York: Russell Sage Foundation.

Kastanis, Angeliki, and Bianca Wilson. 2014. "Race/Ethnicity, Gender and Socioeconomic Wellbeing of Individuals in Same-Sex Couples." Williams Institute, UCLA. Retrieved October 5, 2020 (https://escholarship.org/uc/item/71j7n35t).

Katz, Sheila. 2012. "TANF's 15th Anniversary and the Great Recession: Are Low-Income Mothers Celebrating Upward Economic Mobility?" *Sociology Compass* 6(8):657–70.

Katznelson, Ira. 2005. *When Affirmative Action Was White: An Untold History of Racial Inequality in Twentieth-Century America*. New York: Norton.

———. 2014. Plenary Session at the 109th Annual Meeting of the American Sociological Association, San Francisco, California, August 16–19.

Kaufman, Sarah Beth. 2019. "The Criminalization of Muslims in the United States, 2016." *Qualitative Sociology* 42(4):521–42.

Kefalas, Maria J., Frank F. Furstenberg, Patrick J. Carr, and Laura Napolitano. 2011. "'Marriage Is More Than Being Together': The Meaning of

Marriage for Young Adults." *Journal of Family Issues* 32(7):845–75.

Keisler-Starkey, Katherine, and Lisa N. Bunch. 2020. "Health Insurance Coverage in the United States: 2019." Current Population Reports, US Bureau of the Census, September. Retrieved November 10, 2020 (https://www.census.gov/content/dam/Census/library/publications/2020/demo/p60-271.pdf).

Kendi, Ibram X. 2019. *How to Be an Antiracist.* New York: One World.

———. 2020. "Why Don't We Know Who the Coronavirus Victims Are?" Ideas, *The Atlantic,* April 1. Retrieved October 5, 2020 (https://www.theatlantic.com/ideas/archive/2020/04/stop-looking-away-race-covid-19-victims/609250/).

Kennedy, Merrit. 2020. "U.S. Charges Suspect in El Paso Walmart Shootings with Hate Crimes." *NPR,* February 6. Retrieved October 14, 2020 (https://www.npr.org/2020/02/06/803503292/u-s-charges-walmart-gunman-in-el-paso-with-hate-crimes).

Kerner, Otto, chairman [Kerner Commission]. 1968. *Report of the National Advisory Commission on Civil Disorders.* Washington, DC: US Government Printing Office. Copy of text retrieved October 5, 2020 (https://babel.hathitrust.org/cgi/pt?id=mdp.39015000225410&view=1up&seq=19).

Keyes, Katherine M., Thomas Vo, Melanie M. Wall, Raul Caetano, Shakira F. Suglia, Silvia S. Martins, Sandro Galea, and Deborah Hasin. 2015. "Racial/Ethnic Differences in Use of Alcohol, Tobacco, and Marijuana: Is There a Cross-over from Adolescence to Adulthood?" *Social Science & Medicine* 124(January):132–41.

Khanna, Nikki. 2013. *Biracial in America: Forming and Performing Racial Identity.* Lanham, MD: Lexington Books.

Kibria, Nazli. 2003. *Becoming Asian American: Second Generation Chinese and Korean American Identities.* Baltimore: Johns Hopkins University Press.

Kibria, Nazli, Cara Bowman, and Megan O'Leary. 2014. *Race and Immigration.* Malden, MA: Polity.

Killewald, Alexandra, and Brielle Bryan. 2018. "Falling Behind: The Role of Inter- and Intragenerational Processes in Widening Racial and Ethnic Wealth Gaps through

Early and Middle Adulthood." *Social Forces* 2(December):705–40.

Killian, Lewis M. 1968. *The Impossible Revolution? Black Power and the American Dream.* New York: Random House.

———. 1971. "Optimism and Pessimism in Sociological Analysis." *The American Sociologist* 6(4):281–86.

Kim, Ann H., and Michael J. White. 2010. "Panethnicity, Ethnic Diversity, and Residential Segregation." *American Journal of Sociology* 115(5):1558–96.

Kim, Sunwoong. 2000. "Race and Home Price Appreciation in Urban Neighborhoods: Evidence from Milwaukee, Wisconsin." *The Review of Black Political Economy* 28(2):26–28.

Kim, Yushim, Heather Campbell, and Adam Eckerd. 2014. "Residential Choice Constraints and Environmental Justice." *Social Science Quarterly* 95(1):40–56.

King, Martin Luther, Jr. 1963. "I Have a Dream." Address made at the Lincoln Memorial during the March On Washington for Jobs and Freedom, Washington, DC. Speech text and audio accessed October 12, 2020 (https://www.npr.org/2010/01/18/122701268/i-have-a-dream-speech-in-its-entirety).

Klinenberg, Eric. 2002. *Heat Wave: A Social Autopsy of Disaster in Chicago.* Chicago: University of Chicago Press.

Kneebone, Elizabeth. 2014. "The Growth and Spread of Concentrated Poverty, 2000 to 2008–2012." Metropolitan Opportunity Series, Brookings Institution, July 31. Retrieved October 5, 2020 (http://www.brookings.edu/research/interactives/2014/concentrated-poverty).

Kochhar, Rakesh, and Anthony Cilluffo. 2017. "How Wealth Inequality Has Changed in the U.S. since the Great Recession, by Race, Ethnicity and Income." Fact Tank, Pew Research Center, November 1. Retrieved October 5, 2020 (https://www.pewresearch.org/fact-tank/2017/11/01/how-wealth-inequality-has-changed-in-the-u-s-since-the-great-recession-by-race-ethnicity-and-income/).

Kolchin, Peter. 1993. *American Slavery, 1619–1877.* New York: Hill and Wang.

Konetzka, R. Tamara, and Rachel M. Werner. 2009. "Disparities in Long-Term Care: Building Equity into Market-Based Reforms." *Medical Care Research and Review* 66(October):491–521.

Kozol, Jonathan. 2006. *The Shame of the Nation: The Restoration of Apartheid Schooling in America*. New York: Broadway Books.

———. 2012. *Savage Inequalities: Children in America's Schools*. New York: Broadway Books.

Kravitz-Wirtz, Nicole, Kyle Crowder, Anjum Hajat, and Victoria Sass. 2016. "The Long-Term Dynamics of Racial/Ethnic Inequality in Neighborhood Air Pollution Exposure, 1990–2009." *Du Bois Review: Social Science Research on Race* 13(2):237–60.

Krivo, Lauren J., María B. Vélez, Christopher J. Lyons, Jason B. Phillips, and Elizabeth Sabbat. 2018. "Race, Crime and the Changing Fortunes of Urban Neighborhoods, 1999–2013." *Du Bois Review: Social Science Research on Race* 15(1):47–68.

Krogstad, Jens Manuel, Ana Gonzalez-Barrera, and Luis Noe-Bustamente. 2020. "U.S. Latinos among Hardest Hit by Pay Cuts, Job Losses Due to Coronavirus." Fact Tank, Pew Research Center, April 3. Retrieved October 5, 2020 (https://www.pewresearch.org/fact-tank/2020/04/03/u-s-latinos-among-hardest-hit-by-pay-cuts-job-losses-due-to-coronavirus/).

Krogstad, Jens Manuel, Jeffrey S. Passel, and D'Vera Cohn. 2019. "5 Facts about Illegal Immigration in the U.S." Fact Tank, Pew Research Center, June 12. Retrieved October 5, 2020 (https://www.pewresearch.org/fact-tank/2019/06/12/5-facts-about-illegal-immigration-in-the-u-s/).

Krysan, Maria, Courtney Carter, and Marieke van Londen. 2017. "The Diversity of Integration in a Multiethnic Metropollis: Exploring What Whites, African Americans, and Latinos Imagine." *Du Bois Review: Social Science Research on Race* 14(1):35–71.

Kung, Hsiang-Ching, Donna L. Hoyert, Jiaquan Xu, and Sherry L. Murphy. 2008. "Deaths: Final Data for 2005." *National Vital Statistics Reports* 56(10):1–124. Retrieved October 5, 2020 (https://www.cdc.gov/nchs/data/nvsr/nvsr56/nvsr56_10.pdf).

Kupchik, Aaron. 2010. *Homeroom Security: School Discipline in an Age of Fear*. New York: New York University Press.

Kuppens, Toon, and Russell Spears. 2014. "You Don't Have to Be Well-Educated to Be an Aversive Racist, but It Helps." *Social Science Research* 45:211–23.

Kwak, Jung, William E. Haley, and David A. Chiriboga. 2008. "Racial Differences in Hospice Use and in-Hospital Death among Medicare and Medicaid Dual-Eligible Nursing Home Residents." *The Gerontologist* 48(1):32–41.

Kwate, Naa O. A., Melody S. Goodman, Jerrold Jackson, and Julen Harris. 2013. "Spatial and Racial Patterning of Real Estate Broker Listings in New York City." *The Review of Black Political Economy* 40(4):401–24.

Kwate, Naa O. A., and Han H. Meyer. 2011. "On Sticks and Stones and Broken Bones: Stereotypes and African American Health." *Du Bois Review: Social Science Research on Race* 8(1):191–98.

Kwate, Naa O. A., and Shatema Threadcraft. 2017. "Dying Fast and Dying Slow in Black Space: Stop and Frisk's Public Health Threat and a Comprehensive Necropolitics." *Du Bois Review: Social Science Research on Race* 14(2):535–56.

Lacy, Karen R. 2007. *Blue-Chip Black: Race, Class, and Status in the New Black Middle Class*. Berkeley: University of California Press.

Ladson-Billings, Gloria. 2006. "From the Achievement Gap to the Education Debt." *Educational Researcher* 36(October):3–12.

Langton, Lynn, and Matthew Durose. 2013. "Police Behavior during Traffic and Street Stops, 2011." Special report, US Bureau of Justice Statistics, US Department of Justice, revised October 17, originally published September 2013. Retrieved October 5, 2020 (http://www.bjs.gov/content/pub/pdf/pbtss11.pdf).

Lara-Millán, Armando. 2014. "Public Emergency Room Overcrowding in the Era of Mass Imprisonment." *American Sociological Review* 79(5):866–87.

Larimore, Savannah. 2018. "Cultural Boundaries to Access in Farmers Markets Accepting Supplemental Nutrition Assistance Program (SNAP)." *Qualitative Sociology* 41(1):63–87.

Lariscy, Joseph T., Claudia Nau, Glenn Firebaugh, and Robert A. Hummer. 2016. "Hispanic-White Differences in Lifespan Variability in the United States." *Demography* 53(1):215–39.

Lasch, Christopher. 1977. *Haven in a Heartless World: The Family Besieged*. New York: Basic Books.

Lauritsen, Janet L., Karen Heimer, and Joseph B. Lang. 2018. "The Enduring Significance of Racial and Ethnic Disparities in Male Violent Victimization, 1973–2010." *Du Bois Review: Social Science Research on Race* 15(1):69–87.

LaVeist, Thomas A. 2005. "Disentangling Race and Socioeconomic Status: A Key to Understanding Health Inequalities." *Journal of Urban Health* 82(2 Suppl 3): iii26–iii34.

LaVeist, Thomas A., and Lydia A. Isaac, eds. 2012. *Race, Ethnicity and Health: A Public Health Reader*. 2nd ed. Hoboken, NJ: Jossey-Bass.

LaVeist, Thomas A., Amani Nuru-Jeter, and Kiesha E. Jones. 2003. "The Association of Doctor-Patient Race Concordance with Health Services Utilization." *Journal of Public Health Policy* 24(3–4):312–23.

LaVeist, Thomas [A.], Keshia Pollack, Roland Thorpe, Ruth Fesahazion, and Darrell Gaskin. 2011. "Place, Not Race: Disparities Dissipate in Southwest Baltimore When Blacks and Whites Live under Similar Conditions." *Health Affairs* 30(10):1880–87. Retrieved October 5, 2020 (https://www.healthaffairs.org/doi/full/10.1377/hlthaff.2011.0640).

Lawrence, Jane. 2000. "The Indian Health Service and the Sterilization of Native American Women." *American Indian Quarterly* 24(3):400–419.

Leavitt, Peter A., Rebecca Covarrubias, Yvonne A. Perez, and Stephanie A. Fryberg. 2015. "'Frozen in Time': The Impact of Native American Media Representations on Identity and Self-Understanding." *Journal of Social Issues* 71(1):39–53.

Lee, Catherine. 2013. *Fictive Kinship: Family Reunification and the Meaning of Race and Nation in American Immigration*. New York: Russell Sage.

Lee, Jennifer. 2015. "From Undesirable to Marriageable: Hyper-selectivity and the Racial Mobility of Asian Americans." *Annals of the American Academy of Political and Social Science* 662(1):79–93.

Lee, Jennifer, and Frank D. Bean. 2007. "Reinventing the Color Line: Immigration and America's New Racial/Ethnic Divide." *Social Forces* 86(2):561–86.

———. 2012. "A Postracial Society or a Diversity Paradox?" *Du Bois Review: Social Science Research on Race* 9(2):419–37.

Lee, Jennifer, and Min Zhou. 2004. *Asian American Youth: Culture, Identity and Ethnicity*. New York: Routledge.

Lee, Sara S. 2004 "Marriage Dilemmas: Partner Choices and Constraints for Korean Americans in New York City." Pp. 285–98 in *Asian American Youth: Culture, Identity and Ethnicity*, edited by Jennifer Lee and Min Zhou. New York: Routledge.

Lee, Sharon M. 1993. "Racial Classification in the U.S. Census, 1890–1900." *Ethnic and Racial Studies* 16(1):75–94.

Levin, Jack, and Jim Nolan. 2016. *The Violence of Hate: Understanding Harmful Forms of Bias and Bigotry*. 4th ed. Lanham, MD: Rowman & Littlefield.

Levin, Shana, Colette van Laar, and Jim Sidanius. 2003. "The Effects of Ingroup and Outgroup Friendships on Ethnic Attitudes in College: A Longitudinal Study." *Group Processes and Intergroup Relations* 6(1):76–92.

Levy, Aharon, Eran Halperin, Martijn van Zomeren, and Tamar Saguy. 2019. "Inter-racial Gateways: The Potential of Biracials to Reduce Threat and Prejudice in Inter-racial Dynamics." *Race and Social Problems* 11(2): 119–32.

Lewis, Amanda E. 2004. "'What Group?' Studying Whites and Whiteness in the Era of 'Color-Blindness.'" *Sociological Theory* 22(4):623–46.

Lewis, Amanda E., and John B. Diamond. 2015. *Despite the Best Intentions: How Racial Inequality Thrives in Good Schools*. New York: Oxford University Press.

Lewis, Amanda E., John B. Diamond, and Tyrone A. Forman. 2015. "Conundrums of Integration: Desegregation in the Context of Racialized Hierarchy." *Sociology of Race & Ethnicity* 1(1):22–36.

Lewis, David Levering. 1981. *When Harlem Was in Vogue*. New York: Knopf.

Li, Yue, Charlene Harrington, Helena Temkin-Greener, Kai You, Xueya Cai, Xi Cen, and Dana B. Mukamel. 2015. "Deficiencies in Care at Nursing Homes and Racial-Ethnic Disparities across Homes Fell, 2006–11." *Health Affairs* 34(7):1139–46.

Lichter, Daniel T., Zhenchao Qian, and Dmitry Tumin. 2015. "Whom Do Immigrants Marry? Emerging Patterns of Intermarriage and Integration in the United States." *Annals of* the American Academy of Political and Social Science 662(1):57–78.

Liebler, Carolyn A. 2010. "Homelands and Indigenous Identities in a Multiracial Era." Social Science Research 39(4):596–609.

Liebler, Carolyn A., and Meghan Zacher. 2013. "American Indians without Tribes in the Twenty-First Century." Ethnic and Racial Studies 36(11):1910–34.

Lien, Pei-te, M. Margaret Conway, and Janelle Wong. 2003. "The Contours and Sources of Ethnic Identity Choices among Asian Americans." Social Science Quarterly 84(2):461–81.

Lincoln, Abraham. [1858] 1907. Joint Debate with Stephen A. Douglas for US Senate, Charleston, Illinois, September 18. Reproduced text retrieved October 14, 2020 (https://www.nps.gov/liho/learn/historyculture/debate4.htm).

Linshi, Jack. 2015. "Student in Racist Frat Video Sorry for 'Horrible Mistake.'" Time, March 10. Retrieved October 14, 2020 (https://time.com/3740006/oklahoma-sae-racist-chant-parker-rice/).

Lipsitz, George. 2011. How Racism Takes Place. Philadelphia: Temple University Press.

Livingston, Gretchen, and Anna Brown. 2017. "Intermarriage in the U.S. 50 Years after Loving v. Virginia." Social and Demographic Trends, Pew Research Center, May 18. Retrieved October 5, 2020 (https://www.pewsocialtrends.org/2017/05/18/intermarriage-in-the-u-s-50-years-after-loving-v-virginia/).

López, Gustavo, Neil G. Ruiz, and Eileen Patten. 2017. "Key Facts about Asian Americans, A Diverse and Growing Population." Fact Tank, Pew Research Center, September 8. Retrieved October 5, 2020 (https://www.pewresearch.org/fact-tank/2017/09/08/key-facts-about-asian-americans/).

Louie, Steve, and Glenn Omatsu. 2001. Asian Americans: The Movement and the Moment. Los Angeles: UCLA Asian American Studies Center Press.

Majors, Richard, and Janet Mancini Billson. 1993. Cool Pose: The Dilemmas of Black Manhood in America. New York: Touchstone.

Malcolm X. 1965. The Autobiography of Malcolm X. With Alex Haley. New York: Grove Press.

Mandela, Nelson. 2005. Address for the Make Poverty History Campaign, London, England, February 3. Text retrieved October 19, 2020 (http://www.mandela.gov.za/mandela_speeches/2005/050203_poverty.htm).

Manning, Maurice M. 1998. Slave in a Box: The Strange Career of Aunt Jemima. Charlottesville: University of Virginia Press.

Margolin, Josh. 2020. "FBI Warns of Potential Surge in Hate Crimes against Asian Americans amid Coronavirus." ABC News, March 27. Retrieved October 5, 2020 (https://abcnews.go.com/US/fbi-warns-potential-surge-hate-crimes-asian-americans/story?id=69831920).

Markides, Kyriakos S., and Karl Eschbach. 2011. "Hispanic Paradox in Adult Mortality in the United States." Pp. 227–40 in International Handbook of Adult Mortality, International Handbooks of Population 2, edited by Richard G. Rogers and Eileen M. Crimmins. Dordrecht, The Netherlands: Springer.

Marks, Carole [C]. 1989. Farewell, We're Good and Gone: The Great Black Migration. Bloomington: Indiana University Press.

———. 1990. "The Civil Rights Movement." Lecture notes, University of Delaware.

———. 1999. The Power of Pride: Stylemakers and Rulebreakers of the Harlem Renaissance. New York: Crown.

Markus, Hazel Rose, and Alana Conner. 2013. Clash! 8 Cultural Conflicts that Made Us Who We Are. New York: Hudson Street Press.

Markus, Hazel Rose, and Paula M. L. Moya. 2010. "Doing Race: An Introduction." Pp. 1–102 in Doing Race: 21 Essays for the Twenty-First Century, edited by Hazel Rose Markus and Paula M. L. Moya. New York: W. W. Norton.

Martin, Joyce A., Brady E. Hamilton, Michelle J. K. Osterman, and Anne K. Driscoll. 2019. "Births: Final Data for 2018." National Vital Statistics Reports 68(13):1–47. Retrieved October 5, 2020 (https://www.cdc.gov/nchs/data/nvsr/nvsr68/nvsr68_13-508.pdf).

Martinez, Ramiro, Jr. 2014. Latino Homicide: Immigration, Violence, and Community. 2nd ed. New York: Routledge.

Martinez, Ramiro, Jr., and Abel Valenzuela Jr., eds. 2006. Immigration and Crime: Race, Ethnicity, and Violence. New York: New York University Press.

Masci, David. 2018. "5 Facts about the Death Penalty." Fact Tank, Pew Research Center, August 2. Retrieved October 5, 2020 (https://

www.pewresearch.org/fact-tank/2018/08/02/5
-facts-about-the-death-penalty/).

Mason, Lisa Reyes, Yunju Nam, and Youngmi
Kim. 2014. "Validity of Infant Race/Ethnicity
from Birth Certificates in the Context of
U.S. Demographic Change." *Health Services
Research* 49(1):249–67. Retrieved October 5,
2020 (https://www.ncbi.nlm.nih.gov/pmc/articl
es/PMC3922476/).

Massey, Douglas S. 2005. "Five Myths about
Immigration: Common Misconceptions about
U.S. Border-Enforcement Policy." *Immigration
Policy in Focus* 4(6):1–11. Retrieved November
10, 2020 (https://www.americanimmigrati
oncouncil.org/sites/default/files/research/IPC
%20five%20myths.pdf).

———. 2008. "Foreword." Pp. xi–xiii in *Latinas/
os in the United States: Changing the Face
of America*, edited by Havidan Rodríquez,
Rogelio Sáenz, and Cecilia Menjívar. New York:
Springer.

———. 2020. "Still the Linchpin: Segregation and
Stratification in the USA." *Race and Social
Problems* 12(1):1–12.

Massey, Douglas S., and Nancy Denton. 1998.
*American Apartheid: Segregation and the
Making of the Underclass*. Cambridge, MA:
Harvard University Press.

Massey, Douglas S., and Magaly R. Sánchez. 2010.
*Brokered Boundaries: Creating Immigrant
Identities in Anti-immigrant Times*. New York:
Russell Sage Foundation.

Massey, Douglas S., and Jonathan Tannen.
2015. "A Research Note on Trends in
Black Hypersegregation." *Demography*
52(3):1025–34.

Mastro, Dana. 2008. "Effects of Racial and
Ethnic Stereotyping." Pp. 325–42 in *Media
Effects: Advances in Theory and Research*, 3rd
ed., edited by Jennings Bryant and Mary Beth
Oliver. New York: Taylor & Francis.

———. 2015. "Why the Media's Role in Issues of
Race and Ethnicity Should Be in the Spotlight."
Journal of Social Issues 71(1):1–16.

Masuoka, Natalie. 2006. "Together They Become
One: Examining the Predictors of Panethnic
Group Consciousness among Asian Americans
and Latinos." *Social Science Quarterly*
87(5):993–1011.

———. 2017. *Multiracial Identity and Racial
Politics in the United States*. New York: Oxford
University Press.

Matsuda, Lawrence Y. 2005. "A Professor, Not a
Porter." *Community and Difference: Teaching,
Pluralism, and Social Justice* 261:51–75.

Mattingly, Marybeth, and Charles Varner. 2015.
"Poverty." *Pathways, Special Issue: State of the
States: The Poverty and Inequality Report*. Palo
Alto, CA: The Stanford Center on Poverty and
Inequality.

Maunder, Rachel D., Sinead C. Day, and Fiona
A. White. 2020. "The Benefit of Contact for
Prejudice-Prone Individuals: The Type of
Stigmatized Outgroup Matters." *Journal of
Social Psychology* 160(1):92–104.

Mayorga-Gallo, Sarah. 2014. *Behind the
White Picket Fence: Power and Privilege in
a Multiethnic Neighborhood*. Chapel Hill:
University of North Carolina Press.

Mazzocco, Philip J., Timothy C. Brock, Gregory
J. Brock, Kristina R. Olson, and Mahzarin R.
Banaji. 2006. "The Cost of Being Black: White
Americans' Perceptions and the Question of
Reparations." *Du Bois Review: Social Science
Research on Race* 3(2):261–97.

McAdam, Doug. 1990. *Freedom Summer*. New
York: Oxford University Press.

———. 1999. *Political Process and the
Development of Black Insurgency, 1930–1970*.
2nd ed. Chicago: University of Chicago Press.

McCabe, Janice. 2009. "Racial and Gender
Microaggressions on a Predominantly White
Campus: Experiences of Black, Latina/o and
White Undergraduates." *Race, Gender & Class*
16(1–2):133–51.

McCarthy, Justin. 2019a. "52% Describe Problem
of Crime in the U.S. as Serious." Politics, the
Gallup Organization, November 13. Retrieved
October 15, 2020 (https://news.gallup.com/
poll/268283/describe-problem-crime-serious.as
px).

———. 2019b. "Most Americans Say Segregation
in Schools a Serious Problem." Education, the
Gallup Organization, September 17. Retrieved
October 5, 2020 (https://news.gallup.com/poll/
266756/americans-say-segregation-schools-seri
ous-problem.aspx).

McDowell, Amy D. 2017. "'This Is for the Brown
Kids!' Racialization and the Formation of
'Muslim' Punk Rock." *Sociology of Race &
Ethnicity* 3(2):159–71.

McIntosh, Peggy. 1988. "White Privilege and Male
Privilege: A Personal Account of Coming to See
Correspondences through Work in Women's

Studies." Working paper 189. Wellesley, MA: Wellesley Centers for Women. Retrieved October 15, 2020 (https://nationalseedproject .org/images/documents/White_Privilege_and_ Male_Privilege_Personal_Account-Peggy_Mc Intosh.pdf).

———. 2020. *On Privilege, Fraudulence, and Teaching as Learning: Selected Essays, 1981– 2019.* New York: Routledge.

McKay, James, and Helen Johnson. 2008. "Pornographic Eroticism and Sexual Grotesquerie in Representations of African American Sportswomen." *Social Identities* 14(4):491–504.

McNary, Dave. 2018. "Latinos Still Have Highest Moviegoing Rate in U.S., but Asians Are Close Behind." *Variety*, April 4. Retrieved October 15, 3030 (https://variety.com/2018/film/news/latino -asian-moviegoers-mpaa-study-1202743713/).

Mead, George Herbert. 1934. *Mind, Self, and Society.* Chicago: University of Chicago Press.

Medina, Lauren, Shannon Sabo, and Jonathan Vespa. 2020. "Living Longer: Historical and Projected Life Expectancy in the United States, 1960–2020." *Current Population Reports*, February. US Census Bureau. Retrieved November 10, 2020 (https://www.census.gov/c ontent/dam/Census/library/publications/2020/d emo/p25-1145.pdf).

Meier, August, and Elliott Rudwick. 1970. *From Plantation to Ghetto.* Rev. ed. New York: Hill and Wang.

Melamed, David, Christopher W. Munn, Leanne Barry, Bradley Montgomery, and Oneya F. Okuwobi. 2019. "Status Characteristics, Implicit Bias, and the Production of Racial Inequality." *American Sociological Review* 84(6):1013–36.

Menjívar, C., William Paul Simmons, Daniel Alvord, and Elizabeth Salerno Valdez. 2018. "Immigration Enforcement, the Racialization of Legal Status, and Perceptions of the Police: Latinos in Chicago, Los Angeles, Houston, and Phoenix in Comparative Perspective." *Du Bois Review: Social Science Research on Race* 15(1):107–28.

Merton, Robert K. 1938. "Social Structure and Anomie." *American Sociological Review* 3:672–82.

———. 1949. "Discrimination and the American Creed." Pp. 99–126 in *Discrimination and the National Welfare*, edited by Robert W. MacIver. New York: Harper and Brothers.

Middlebrook, Diane Wood. 1998. *Suits Me: The Double Life of Billy Tipton.* New York: Houghton-Mifflin.

Mills, C. Wright. 1959. *The Sociological Imagination.* New York: Oxford University Press.

Mirandé, Alfredo. 1997. *Hombres y Machos: Masculinity and Latino Culture.* Boulder, CO: Westview Press.

———. 2019. *Gringo Injustice: Insider Perspectives on Police, Gangs, and Law.* New York: Routledge.

Mohai, Paul, and Robin Saha. 2006. "Reassessing Racial and Socioeconomic Disparities in Environmental Justice Research." *Demography* 43(2):383–99.

———. 2007. "Racial Inequality in the Distribution of Hazardous Waste: A National-Level Reassessment." *Social Problems* 54(3):343–70.

Mohanty, Sarita A. 2006. "Unequal Access: Immigrants and U.S. Health Care." Special report, American Immigration Council, July 1. Retrieved October 5, 2020 (https://www.am ericanimmigrationcouncil.org/sites/default/files/ research/Unequal%20Access.pdf).

Morgan, Marcyliena, and Dawn-Elissa Fischer. 2010. "Hiphop and Race: Blackness, Language, and Creativity." Pp. 509–27 in *Doing Race: 21 Essays for the Twenty-First Century*, edited by Hazel Rose Markus and Paula M. L. Moya. New York: W. W. Norton.

Morgan, Rachel E., and Barbara A. Oudekerk. 2019. "Criminal Victimization, 2018." Bulletin, US Bureau of Justice Statistics, US Department of Justice, September. Retrieved October 5, 2020 (https://www.bjs.gov/content/pub/pdf/cv18.pdf).

Morning, Ann. 2011. *The Nature of Race: How Scientists Think and Teach about Human Difference.* Berkeley: University of California Press.

Morris, Aldon D. 1986. *The Origins of the Civil Rights Movement: Black Communities Organizing for Change.* New York: Free Press.

Morris, Edward W. 2005. "'Tuck in That Shirt!' Race, Class, Gender, and Discipline in an Urban School." *Sociological Perspectives* 48(1):25–48.

Morris, Edward W., and Brea L. Perry. 2016. "The Punishment Gap: School Segregation and Racial Disparities in Achievement." *Social Problems* 63(1):68–86.

Mosley, Tonya. 2019. "The 'Forgotten' History of Anti-Latino Violence in the U.S." *Here & Now*, WBUR, November 25. Retrieved November 10, 2020 (https://www.wbur.org/hereandnow/2019/11/25/history-violence-against-latinos).

Mouw, Ted, and Barbara Entwisle. 2006. "Residential Segregation and Interracial Friendship in Schools." *American Journal of Sociology* 112(2):394–441.

Moye, J. Todd. 2005. *Let the People Decide: Black Freedom and White Resistance Movements in Sunflower County, Mississippi, 1945–1986*. Chapel Hill: University of North Carolina Press.

Moynihan, Daniel Patrick. 1965. *The Negro Family: The Case for National Action*. Washington, DC: US Department of Labor, Office of Policy Planning and Research. Revised text retrieved October 5, 2020 (https://www.dol.gov/general/aboutdol/history/webid-moynihan).

Mueller, Jennifer C., Danielle Dirks, and Leslie Houts Picca. 2007. "Unmasking Racism: Costuming and Engagement of the Racial Order." *Qualitative Sociology* 30:315–55.

Mueller, Jennifer C., Apryl Williams, and Danielle Dirks. 2018. "Racism and Popular Culture: Representation, Resistance, and White Racial Fantasies." Pp. 69–89 in *Handbook of the Sociology of Racial and Ethnic Minorities*, edited by Joe Feagin and P. Batur. New York: Springer.

Mukherjee, Siddhartha. 2017. *The Gene: An Intimate History*. New York: Scribner.

Murray, Pauli. 1997. *States' Laws on Race and Color*. Athens: University of Georgia Press.

Myrdal, [Karl] Gunnar. 1944. *An American Dilemma: The Negro Problem and American Democracy*. New York: Harper & Brothers.

NAACP Legal Defense and Educational Fund, Inc. 2020. "Death Row USA, Winter 2020." Quarterly report, January 1. Retrieved October 5, 2020 (https://www.naacpldf.org/wp-content/uploads/DRUSAWinter2020.pdf).

Nakano, Dana Y. 2013. "An Interlocking Panethnicity: The Negotiation of Multiple Identities among Asian American Social Movement Leaders." *Sociological Perspectives* 56(4):569–95.

Nam, Yunju, Nora Wikoff, and Michael Sherraden. 2015. "Racial and Ethnic Differences in Parenting Stress: Evidence from a Statewide Sample of New Mothers." *Journal of Child and Family Studies* 24(2):278–88.

National Center for Education Statistics. 2012. "Table 219.50. Number and Percentage of 9th- to 12th-Graders Who Dropped Out of Public Schools, by Race/Ethnicity, Grade, and State or Jurisdiction: 2009–10." *Digest of Education Statistics, 2013*. Washington, DC: US Department of Education. Retrieved October 5, 2020 (https://nces.ed.gov/programs/digest/d13/tables/dt13_219.50.asp).

———. 2019. "List of Reference Tables." *Digest of Education Statistics, 2018*. US Department of Education. Tabular data linked to this page. Retrieved November 10, 2020 (https://nces.ed.gov/programs/digest/d18/tables_1.asp).

National Center for Health Statistics. 2019. *Health, United States, 2018*. Hyattsville, MD: US Department of Health and Human Services, Centers for Disease Control and Prevention, and National Center for Health Statistics. Retrieved October 5, 2020 (https://www.cdc.gov/nchs/data/hus/hus18.pdf).

National Immigration Forum. 2018. "Fact Sheet: Immigrants and Public Benefits." August 21. Retrieved October 5, 2020 (https://immigrationforum.org/article/fact-sheet-immigrants-and-public-benefits/).

National Prevention Information Network. 2020. "Cultural Competence in Health and Human Services." Centers for Disease Control and Prevention (website), August 17. Retrieved October 21, 2020 (https://npin.cdc.gov/pages/cultural-competence).

Neavling, Steve. 2020. "Black People Make Up 12% of Michigan's Population—and at Least 40% of Its Coronavirus Deaths." News Hits, *Detroit Metro Times*, April 2. Retrieved October 5, 2020 (https://www.metrotimes.com/news-hits/archives/2020/04/02/black-people-make-up-12-of-michigans-population-and-at-least-40-of-its-coronavirus-deaths).

Negrón-Muntaner, Frances. 2015. *The Latino Media Gap*. New York: Columbia University, Center for the Study of Ethnicity and Race.

Nelson, Margaret K. 2020. *Like Family: Narratives of Fictive Kinship*. New York: Routledge.

Nelson, Stanley, writter, prod., dir.. 2015. *The Black Panthers: Vanguard of the Revolution*. Film. Firelight Films, Inc., and the Independent Television Service (ITVS).

Netherland, Julie. 2016. "The War on Drugs that Wasn't: 'Wasted Whiteness,' 'Dirty Doctors,' and

Race in Media Coverage of Prescription Opioid Misuse." *Culture, Medicine, and Psychiatry* 40(December):664–86.

Newman, Katherine S., and Rebekah Peeples Messengill. 2006. "The Texture of Hardship: Qualitative Sociology of Poverty, 1995–2005." *American Review of Sociology* 32:423–46.

New York Times editorial board. 2016. "The Corrosive Politics that Threaten L.G.B.T.Q. Americans." Opinion. *New York Times*, June 15. Retrieved October 12, 2020 (https://www.nytimes.com/2016/06/15/opinion/the-corrosive-politics-that-threaten-lgbt-americans.html).

Noe-Bustamante, Luis, Lauren Mora, and Mark Hugo Lopez. 2020. "About One-in-Four U.S. Hispanics Have Heard of Latinx, but Just 3% Use It." Hispanic Trends, Pew Research Center, August 11. Retrieved November 5, 2020 (https://www.pewresearch.org/hispanic/2020/08/11/about-one-in-four-u-s-hispanics-have-heard-of-latinx-but-just-3-use-it/).

Noguera, Pedro A. 2008. *The Trouble with Black Boys . . . and Other Reflections on Race, Equity, and the Future of Public Education.* San Francisco: Jossey-Bass.

Nomaguchi, Kei, and Melissa Milkie. 2020. "Parenthood and Well-Being: A Decade in Review." *Journal of Marriage and Family* 82(February):198–223.

Norman, Jim. 2016. "U.S. Worries about Race Relations Reach a New High." Social Policy and Issues, the Gallup Organization, April 11. Retrieved October 5, 2020 (https://news.gallup.com/poll/190574/worries-race-relations-reach-new-high.aspx).

Norris, Tina, Paula L. Vines, and Elizabeth M. Hoeffel. 2012. "The American Indian and Alaska Native Population: 2010." *2010 Census Briefs*, US Census Bureau, January. Retrieved October 5, 2020 (http://www.census.gov/prod/cen2010/briefs/c2010br-10.pdf).

Nunley, John M., Adam Pugh, Nicholas Romero, and R. Alan Seals. 2015. "Racial Discrimination in the Labor Market for Recent College Graduates: Evidence from a Field Experiment." *The B.E. Journal of Economic Analysis & Policy* 15(3):1093–125. Retrieved October 5, 2020 (https://www.degruyter.com/view/journals/bejeap/15/3/article-p1093.xml?language=en).

Oakes, Jeannie. 2005. *Keeping Track: How Schools Structure Inequality.* New Haven, CT: Yale University Press.

Oboler, Suzanne. 1995. *Ethnic Labels, Latino Lives: Identity and the Politics of (Re) Presentation in the United States.* Minneapolis: University of Minnesota Press.

Ocampo, Anthony C. 2014. "Are Second-Generation Filipinos 'Becoming' Asian American or Latino? Historical Colonialism, Culture and Panethnicity." *Ethnic and Racial Studies* 37(3):425–45.

Okamoto, Dina. 2014. *Redefining Race: Asian American Panethnicity and Shifting Ethnic Boundaries.* New York: Russell Sage.

Okamoto, Dina, and G. C. Mora. 2014. "Panethnicity." *Annual Review of Sociology* 40:219–39.

Olivas, Michael A. 2010. "My Grandfather's Stories and Immigration Law." Pp. 223–28 in *The Latino Condition*, 2nd ed., edited by Richard Delgado and Jean Stefanic. New York: New York University Press.

Oliver, Mary Beth, Keunyeong Kim, Jennifer Hoewe, Mun-Young Chung, Erin Ash, Julia K. Woolley, and Drew D. Shade. 2015. "Media-Induced Elevation as a Means of Enhancing Feelings of Intergroup Connectedness." *Journal of Social Issues* 71(1):106–22.

Oliver, Melvin L., and Thomas M. Shapiro. 2006. *Black Wealth/White Wealth: A New Perspective on Racial Inequality.* 2nd ed. New York: Routledge.

Om, Anjali. 2018. "The Opioid Crisis in Black and White: The Role of Race in our Nation's Recent Drug Epidemic." *Journal of Public Health* 40(4):e614–15.

Omatsu, Glenn. 2016. "The 'Four Prisons' and the Movements of Liberation: Asian American Activism from the 1960s to the 1990s." Pp. 60–100 in *Contemporary Asian America*, 3rd ed., edited by Min Zhou and Anthony C. Ocampo. New York: New York University Press.

Omi, Michael, and Howard Winant. 1986. *Racial Formation in the United States: From the 1960s to the 1980s.* New York: Routledge.

———. 2015. *Racial Formation in the United States: From the 1960s to the 1980s.* Rev. ed. New York: Routledge.

Opara, Ijeoma, and Noemy Santos. 2019. "A Conceptual Framework Exploring Social Media, Eating Disorders, and Body Dissatisfaction among Latina Adolescents." *Hispanic Journal of Behavioral Sciences* 41(3):363–77.

Opel, Richard A., Jr., and Kim Barker. 2020. "New Transcripts Detail Last Moments for George Floyd." *New York Times*, updated August 11. Retrieved October 15, 2020 (https://www.ny times.com/2020/07/08/us/george-floyd-body -camera-transcripts.html).

Orfield, Gary. 2001. *Schools More Separate: Consequences of a Decade of Resegregation*. Cambridge, MA: Civil Rights Project, Harvard University.

———. 2013. "Housing Segregation Produces Unequal Schools: Causes and Solutions." Pp. 40–60 in *Closing the Opportunity Gap: What America Must Do to Give Every Child an Even Chance*, edited by Prudence L. Carter and Kevin G. Welner. New York: Oxford University Press.

Orfield, Gary, and Erica Frankenberg. 2014. *"Brown" at 60: Great Progress, a Long Retreat, and an Uncertain Future*. Los Angeles: Civil Rights Project/Proyecto Derechos Civiles, University of California–Los Angeles.

Orta, Irem M. 2013. "The Impact of Cross-Group Romantic Relationships on Intergroup Prejudice." *Social Behavior and Personality* 41(1):1–6.

Ortiz, Vilma, and Edward Telles. 2008. *Generations of Exclusion: Mexican Americans, Assimilation, and Race*. New York: Russell Sage.

Ortman, Jennifer, M., and Christine E. Guarneri. 2009. "United States Population Projections: 2000 to 2050." US Census Bureau. Retrieved October 5, 2020 (https://www.census.gov/c ontent/dam/Census/library/working-papers /2009/demo/us-pop-proj-2000-2050/analytical -document09.pdf).

Osuji, Chinyere K. 2019a. *Boundaries of Love: Interracial Marriage and the Meaning of Race*. New York: New York University Press.

———. 2019b. "Freedom and Frustration: Rachel Dolezal and the Meaning of Race." *Contexts* 18(3):36–41.

Ousey, Graham C., and Charis E. Kubrin. 2014. "Immigration and the Changing Nature of Homicide in US Cities, 1980–2010." *Journal of Quantitative Criminology* 30(3):453–83.

Page, Scott E. 2007. *The Difference: How the Power of Diversity Creates Better Groups, Firms, Schools, and Societies*. Princeton, NJ: Princeton University Press.

Page-Gould, Elizabeth, Rodolfo Mendoza-Denton, and Linda R. Tropp. 2008. "With a Little Help from My Cross-Group Friend: Reducing Anxiety in Intergroup Contexts through Cross-Group Friendship." *Journal of Personality and Social Psychology* 95(5):1080–94.

Pager, Devah. 2007. *Marked: Race, Crime, and Finding Work in an Era of Mass Incarceration*. Chicago: University of Chicago Press.

Pager, Devah, and David S. Pedulla. 2015. "Race, Self-Selection, and the Job Search Process." *American Journal of Sociology* 120(4):1005–54.

Painter, Nell Irvin. 2010. *The History of White People*. New York: Oxford University Press.

Parker, Kim, Nikki Graf, and Ruth Igielnik. 2019. "Generation Z Looks a Lot like Millennials on Key Social and Political Issues." Social and Demographic Trends, Pew Research Center, January 17. Retrieved October 5, 2020 (https:/ /www.pewsocialtrends.org/2019/01/17/genera tion-z-looks-a-lot-like-millennials-on-key-so cial-and-political-issues/).

Parker, Kim, Juliana Menasce Horowitz, Rich Morin, and Mark Hugo Lopez. 2015. "Multiracial in America: Proud, Diverse and Growing in Numbers." Social and Demographic Trends, Pew Research Center, June 11. Retrieved October 15, 2020 (https://www.pewsocialtrends .org/2015/06/11/multiracial-in-america/).

Parliament. 1975. *Chocolate City*. Casablanca 831, May. NBLP 7014. Published by Malbiz, Ricks Music. Full album playlist retrieved October 5, 2020 (https://www.youtube.com/watch?v=DG sb5DADbKU&list=PL3HYPdxEFT2KMFqoD-O95_HHusczT8tQ4).

Pattillo, Mary. 2005. "Black Middle-Class Neighborhoods." *Annual Review of Sociology* 31:305–29.

———. 2007. *Black on the Block: The Politics of Race and Class in the City*. Chicago: University of Chicago Press.

———. 2013. "Housing: Commodity Versus Right." *Annual Review of Sociology* 39:509–31.

Payne-Sturges, Devon, and Gilbert C. Gee. 2006. "National Environmental Health Measures for Minority and Low-Income Populations: Tracking Social Disparities in Environmental Health." *Environmental Research* 102:154–71.

Pedraza, Silvia. 1996. "Origins and Destinies: Immigration, Race, and Ethnicity in American History." Pp. 1–20 in *Origins and Destinies: Immigration, Race, and Ethnicity in America*, edited by Silvia Pedraza and Rubén G. Rumbaut. Belmont, CA: Wadsworth.

Pedrelli, Robin. 2014. "Ten Ways Employees Can Support Diversity and Inclusion." *Profiles in Diversity Journal*, September 8. Retrieved October 19, 2020 (https://diversityjournal.com/14154-10-ways-employees-can-support-diversity-inclusion/#:~:text=1%20Know%20the%20diversity%20goals%20and%20vision%20of,effort.%204%20Become%20culturally%20competent.%20More%20items...%20).

Pedulla, David S., and Devan Pager. 2019. "Race and Networks in the Job Search Process." *American Sociological Review* 84(December):983–1012.

Pellow, David N. 2007. *Resisting Global Toxics: Transnational Movements for Environmental Justice.* Cambridge, MA: MIT Press.

———. 2016. "Toward a Critical Environmental Justice Studies: Black Lives Matter as an Environmental Justice Challenge." *Du Bois Review: Social Science Research on Race* 13(2):221–36.

Pellow, David N., and Hollie Nyseth Brehm. 2013. "An Environmental Sociology for the Twenty-First Century." *Annual Review of Sociology* 39(July):229–50.

Pellow, David N., and Robert J. Brulle. 2007. "Poisoning the Planet: The Struggle for Environmental Justice." *Contexts* 6(1):37–41.

Pena, Anita Alves. 2018. "Skills and Economic Inequality Across Race and Ethnicity in the United States: New Evidence on Wage Discrimination Using PIAAC." *Review of Black Political Economy* 45(1):40–68.

Penner, Andrew [M.], and Aliya Saperstein. 2008. "How Social Status Shapes Race." *Proceedings of the National Academy of Sciences of the United States of America* 105(50):19628–30. Retrieved October 5, 2020 (https://www.pnas.org/content/105/50/19628).

———. 2013. "Engendering Racial Perceptions: An Intersectional Analysis of How Social Status Shapes Race." *Gender & Society* 27(3):319–44.

Perea, Juan F. 2004. "Buscando America: Why Integration and Equal Protection Fail to Protect Latinos." *Harvard Law Review* 117(5):1420–69.

Pérez, Maritz. 2020. "A History of Anti-Latino State-Sanctioned Violence: Executions, Lynchings, and Hate Crimes." Pp. 25–43 in *Gringo Injustice: Insider Perspectives on Police, Gangs, and Law*, edited by Alfredo Mirandé. New York: Routledge.

Peterson, Ruth D., Lauren J. Krivo, and Katheryn Russell-Brown. 2018. "Color Matters: Race, Ethnicity, Crime, and Justice in Uncertain Times." *Du Bois Review: Social Science Research on Race* 15(1):1–11.

Pettigrew, Thomas F. 2009. "Post-racism?" *Du Bois Review: Social Science Research on Race* 6(2):279–92.

Pettigrew, Thomas F., Linda R. Tropp, Ulrich Wagner, and Oliver Christ. 2011. "Recent Advances in Intergroup Contact Theory." *International Journal of Intercultural Relations* 35(3):271–80.

Pew Research Center. 2008. "Americans Say They Like Diverse Communities; Election, Census Trends Suggest Otherwise." Social and Demographic Trends, December 2. Retrieved October 5, 2020 (http://www.pewsocialtrends.org/2008/12/02/americans-say-they-like-diverse-communities-election-census-trends-suggest-otherwise/).

———. 2018. "Shifting Public Views on Legal Immigration into the U.S." US Politics and Policy, June 28. Retrieved October 5, 2020 (https://www.people-press.org/2018/06/28/shifting-public-views-on-legal-immigration-into-the-u-s/).

———. 2019. "Most Border Wall Opponents, Supporters Say Shutdown Concessions Are Unacceptable." Pew Research Center, January 16. Retrieved November 10, 2020 (https://www.pewresearch.org/politics/2019/01/16/most-border-wall-opponents-supporters-say-shutdown-concessions-are-unacceptable/).

Phelps, Michelle S., and Devah Pager. 2016. "Inequality and Punishment: A Turning Point for Mass Incarceration?" *Annals of the American Academy of Political and Social Science* 663:185–203.

Philbrick, Nathaniel. 2006. *Mayflower: A Tale of Community, Courage, and War.* New York: Viking.

Phillip, Abby. 2014. "Emoji's Race Problem May Finally Be Going Away." *Washington Post*, November 4. Retrieved October 5, 2020 (https://www.washingtonpost.com/news/the-intersect/wp/2014/11/04/emojis-race-problem-may-finally-be-going-away/).

Picca, Leslie, and Joe Feagin. 2007. *Two-Faced Racism: Whites in the Backstage and Frontstage.* New York: Routledge.

Pitcher, Ben. 2014. *Consuming Race*. New York: Routledge.

Planty, Michael, Lynn Langton, Christopher Krebs, Marcus Berzofsky, and Hope Smiley-McDonald. 2016. "Female Victims of Sexual Violence, 1994–2010." Special report, US Bureau of Justice Statistics, US Department of Justice, revised May 31, originally published March 2013. Retrieved October 5, 2020 (https://www.bjs.gov/content/pub/pdf/fvsv9410.pdf).

Portes, Alejandro, Patricia Fernández-Kelly, and William Haller. 2005. "Segmented Assimilation on the Ground: The New Second Generation in Early Adulthood." *Ethnic and Racial Studies* 28(6):1000–1040.

Portes, Alejandro, and Dag MacLeod. 1996. "What Shall I Call Myself? Hispanic Identity Formation in the Second Generation." *Ethnic and Racial Studies* 19(3):523–47.

Portes, Alejandro, and Rubén G. Rumbaut, eds. 2014. *Immigrant America: A Portrait*. 4th ed. Berkeley: University of California Press.

Portes, Alejandro, and Min Zhou. 1993. "The New Second Generation: Segmented Assimilation and Its Variants." *Annals of the American Academy of Political and Social Science* 530(1):74–96.

Posey-Maddox, Linn. 2017. "Schooling in Suburbia: The Intersections of Race, Class, Gender, and Place in Black Fathers' Engagement and Family-School Relationships." *Gender and Education* 29(5):577–93.

Potok, Mark. 2016. "Anti-Muslim Hate Crimes Surged Last Year, Fueled by Hateful Campaign." Southern Poverty Law Center, November 14. Retrieved October 5, 2020 (https://www.splcenter.org/hatewatch/2016/11/14/anti-muslim-hate-crimes-surged-last-year-fueled-by-hateful-campaign).

Poveda, Tony G. 2009. "The Death Penalty in the Post-*Furman* Era: A Review of the Issues and the Debate." *Sociology Compass* 3(4):559–74.

Powers, Rebecca S., Michelle M. Livermore, and Belinda C. Davis. 2013. "The Complex Lives of Disconnected Welfare Leavers: Examining Employment Barriers, Social Support and Informal Employment." *Journal of Poverty* 17(4):394–413.

Punyanunt-Carter, Narissra M. 2008. "The Perceived Realism of African American Portrayals: Effects of Racial and Ethnic Stereotyping." *The Howard Journal of Communications* 19: 241-257.

Purdie-Vaughns, Valerie, Claude M. Steele, Paul G. Davies, Ruth Ditlmann, and Jennifer Randall Crosby. 2008. "Social Identity Contingencies: How Diversity Cues Signal Threat or Safety for African Americans in Mainstream Institutions." *Journal of Personality and Social Psychology* 94(4):615–30.

Pyke, Karen. 2014. "Immigrant Families and the Shifting Color Line in the United States." Pp. 194–213 in *The Wiley Blackwell Companion to the Sociology of Families*, edited by Judith Treas, Jacqueline Scott, and Martin Richards. Hoboken, NJ: Wiley Blackwell.

Qian, Zhenchao, and Daniel T. Lichter. 2011. "Changing Patterns of Interracial Marriage in a Multiracial Society." *Journal of Marriage and the Family* 73(5):1065–84.

Quadagno, Jill. 1996. *The Color of Welfare: How Racism Undermined the War on Poverty*. New York: Oxford University Press.

Quillian, Lincoln, and Mary E. Campbell. 2003. "Beyond Black and White: The Present and Future of Multiracial Friendship Segregation." *American Sociological Review* 68(4):540–66.

Quillian, Lincoln, John J. Lee, and Honoré Brandon. 2020. "Racial Discrimination in the U.S. Housing and Mortgage Lending Markets: A Quantitative Review of Trends, 1976–2016." *Race and Social Problems* 12(1):13–28

Quillian, Lincoln, and Rozlyn Redd. 2009. "The Friendship Networks of Multiracial Adolescents." *Social Science Research* 38(2):279–95. Retrieved October 15, 2020 (https://www.ncbi.nlm.nih.gov/pmc/articles/PMC6258020/).

Ramasubramanian, Srividya. 2015. "Using Celebrity News Stories to Effectively Reduce Racial/Ethnic Prejudice." *Journal of Social Issues* 71(1):123–38.

Ravichandran, Padma, Brandel France De Bravo, and Rebbecca Beauport. 2016. "Young Children and Screen Time (TV, Computers, etc.)." National Center for Health Research, May 28. Retrieved November 6, 2020 (http://www.center4research.org/young-children-screen-time-tv-computers-etc/).

Reardon, Sean F., and Ann Owens. 2014. "60 Years after *Brown*: Trends and Consequences of School Segregation." *Annual Review of Sociology* 40(July):199–218.

Reece, Robert L., and Heather A. O'Connell. 2016. "How the Legacy of Slavery and Racial Composition Shape Public School Enrollment in the American South." *Sociology of Race & Ethnicity* 2(1):42–57.

Remster, Brianna, and Rory Kramer. 2018. "Shifting Power: The Impact of Incarceration on Political Representation." *Du Bois Review: Social Science Research on Race* 15(2):417–39.

Reverby, Susan M. 2009. *Explaining Tuskegee: The Infamous Syphilis Study and Its Legacy*. Chapel Hill: University of North Carolina Press.

Reyes, Daisy Verduzco. 2017. "Disparate Lessons: Racial Climates and Identity-Formation Processes among Latino Students." *Du Bois Review: Social Science Research on Race* 14(Fall):447–70.

Rich, Adrienne. 1976. *Of Woman Born: Motherhood as Experience and Institution*. New York: W. W. Norton.

Rich, Meghan A. 2008. *Diversity Block by Block: Homeowners' Perceptions of Race, Class, and Neighborhood Change in an Integrated Urban Neighborhood*. PhD dissertation, University of Delaware.

———. 2009. "'It Depends on How You Define Integrated': Neighborhood Boundaries and Racial Integration in a Baltimore Neighborhood." *Sociological Forum* 24(4):828–53.

Rico, Brittany, Rose M. Kreider, and Lydia Anderson. 2018. "Examining Change in the Percent of Married-Couple Households that Are Interracial and Interethnic: 2000 to 2012–2016." Social, Economic, and Housing Statistics Division, US Census Bureau. Retrieved October 20, 2020 (https://www.census.gov/content/dam/Census/library/working-papers/2018/demo/SEHSD-WP2018-11.pdf).

Ridolfo, Heather, Valerie Chepp, and Melissa A. Milkie. 2013. "Race and Girls' Self-Evaluations: How Mothering Matters." *Sex Roles* 68(7–8):496–509.

Riffkin, Rebecca. 2015. "Higher Support for Gender Affirmative Action than Race." Politics, the Gallup Organization, August 26. Retrieved October 5, 2020 (https://news.gallup.com/poll/184772/higher-support-gender-affirmative-action-race.aspx).

Rios, Victor M. 2011. *Punished: Policing the Lives of Black and Latino Boys*. New York: New York University Press.

———. 2015. "Police, Punished, Dehumanized: The Reality for Young Men of Color Living in America." Pp. 59–80 in *Deadly Injustice: Trayvon Martin, Race, and the Criminal Justice System*, edited by Devon Johnson, Patricia Y. Warren, and Amy Farrell. New York: New York University Press.

Rios, Victor M., Nikita Carney, and Jasmine Kelekay. 2017. "Ethnographies of Race, Crime, and Justice: Toward a Sociological Double-Consciousness." *Annual Review of Sociology* 43:493–513.

Rivadeneyra, Rocío, L. Monique Ward, and Maya Gordon. 2007. "Distorted Reflections: Media Use and Latino Adolescents' Conceptions of Self." *Media Psychology* 9(2):261–90.

Rivera, Christopher. 2014. "The Brown Threat: Post-9/11 Conflations of Latina/os and Middle Eastern Muslims in the U.S. American Imagination." *Latino Studies* 12(1):44–65.

Roberts, Diana. 1994. *The Myth of Aunt Jemima: White Women Representing Black Women*. New York: Routledge.

Roberts, Dorothy. 1997a. *Killing the Black Body: Race, Reproduction, and the Meaning of Liberty*. New York: Vintage.

———. 1997b. "Spiritual and Menial Housework." *Yale Journal of Law and Feminism* 9(51):51–80.

———. 2012. *Fatal Invention: How Science, Politics and Big Business Re-create Race in the Twenty-First Century*. New York: The New Press.

Roberts, J. Timmons, and Bradley C. Parks. 2007. *A Climate of Injustice: Global Inequality, North-South Politics, and Climate Policy*. Cambridge, MA: MIT Press.

Robinson, JoAnn. 1987. *The Montgomery Bus Boycott and the Women Who Started It*. Knoxville: University of Tennessee Press.

Rockquemore, Kerry Ann. 2002. "Negotiating the Color Line: The Gendered Process of Racial Identity Construction among Black/White Biracial Women." *Gender & Society* 16(4):485–503.

Rockquemore, Kerry Ann, David L. Brunsma, and Daniel J. Delgado. 2009. "Racing to Theory or Retheorizing Race? Understanding the Struggle to Build a Multiracial Identity Theory." *Journal of Social Issues* 65(1):13–34.

Rodriguez, Christina. 2014. "Comments: Symposium on Race." Presented at the 109th annual meeting of the American Sociological

Association, August 16–19, San Francisco, California.

Rodríguez, Clara E. 2000. *Changing Race: Latinos, the Census, and the History of Ethnicity in the United States*. New York: New York University Press.

Rodríguez, Havidán, Rogelio Sáenz, and Cecilia Menjívar, eds. 2008. *Latinas/os in the United States: Changing the Face of America*. New York: Springer.

Rodríquez, Marc Simon. 2014. *Rethinking the Chicano Movement*. New York: Routledge.

Rodríguez-Garcia, Dan. 2015. "Intermarriage and Integration Revisited: International Experiences and Cross-Disciplinary Approaches." *Annals of the American Academy of Political and Social Science* 662(1):8–36.

Roediger, David R. 2002. *Colored White: Transcending the Racial Past*. Berkeley: University of California Press.

Rogers, Kim Lacy. 1999. "Lynching Stories: Family and Community Memory in the Mississippi Delta." Pp. 113–30 in *Trauma and Life Stories: International Perspectives*, edited by Kim Lacy Rogers, Selma Leydesdorff, and Graham Dawson. New York: Routledge. Retrieved October 2, 2020 (https://www.dickinson.edu/download/downloads/id/134/lynchingstoriesrogers).

Rollins, Judith 1985. *Between Women: Domestics and Their Employers*. Philadelphia: Temple University Press.

Romero, Mary. 2002. *Maid in the U.S.A.* New York: Routledge.

———. 2012. *The Maid's Daughter: Living Inside and Outside the American Dream*. New York: New York University Press.

Romo, Ricardo. 1996. "Mexican Americans: Their Civic and Political Incorporation." Pp. 84–97 in *Origins and Destinies: Immigration, Race, and Ethnicity in America*, edited by Silvia Pedraza and Rubén G. Rumbaut. Belmont, CA: Wadsworth.

Root, Maria P. P., ed. 1992. *Racially Mixed People in America*. Thousand Oaks, CA: Sage.

———, ed. 1996. *The Multiracial Experience: Racial Borders as the New Frontier*. Thousand Oaks, CA: Sage.

Rose, Stephen J. 2014. *Social Stratification in the United States: The American Profile Poster*. New York: The New Press.

Rothstein, Richard. 2013. "Why Children from Lower Socio-economic Class, on Average, Have Lower Academic Achievement than Middle-Class Children." Pp. 61–76 in *Closing the Opportunity Gap: What America Must Do to Give Every Child an Even Chance*, edited by Prudence L. Carter and Kevin G. Welner. New York: Oxford University Press.

———. 2017. *The Color of Law: A Forgotten History of How Our Government Segregated America*. New York: Basic Books.

———. 2020. "The Coronavirus Will Explode Achievement Gaps in Education." Opinion, *Shelterforce*, April 13. Retrieved October 5, 2020 (https://shelterforce.org/2020/04/13/the-coronavirus-will-explode-achievement-gaps-in-education/).

Royster, Deirdre. 2003. *Race and the Invisible Hand: How White Networks Exclude Black Men from Working-Class Jobs*. Berkeley: University of California Press.

Rude, Jesse. 2010. "Best Friends Forever? Race and the Stability of Adolescent Friendships." *Social Forces* 89(2):585–607.

Rugh, Jacob S., Len Albright, and Douglas S. Massey. 2015. "Race, Space, and Cumulative Disadvantage: A Case Study of the Subprime Lending Collapse." *Social Problems* 62(2):186–218.

Rugh, Jacob S., and Douglas S. Massey. 2010. "Racial Segregation and the American Foreclosure Crisis." *American Sociological Review* 75(5):629–51.

———. 2014. "Segregation in Post–Civil Rights America." *Du Bois Review: Social Science Research on Race* 11(2):205–32.

Rumbaut, Rubén G. 1996. "Origins and Destinies: Immigration, Race, and Ethnicity in American History." Pp. 1–20 in *Origins and Destinies: Immigration, Race, and Ethnicity in America*, edited by Silvia Pedraza and Rubén G. Rumbaut. Belmont, CA: Wadsworth.

———. 2009. "Pigments of Our Imagination: On the Racialization and Racial Identities of 'Hispanics' and 'Latinos.'" Pp. 15–36 in *How the U.S. Racializes Latinos: White Hegemony and Its Consequences*, edited by José A. Cobas, Jorge Duany, and Joe R. Feagin. New York: Paradigm.

Russell, Lesley M. 2011. "Reducing Disparities in Life Expectancy: What Factors Matter?" Paper presented at the Workshop on Reducing Disparities in Life Expectancy, as part of the Roundtable on the Promotion of Health Equity and the Elimination of Health Disparities, held by the Institute of Medicine, Washington, DC, February 24.

Ryan, William. 1971. *Blaming the Victim.* New York: Pantheon.

Saad, Layla F. 2020. *Me and White Supremacy: Combat Racism, Change the World, and Become a Good Ancestor.* Naperville, IL: Sourcebooks.

Saad, Lydia. 2019. "Fewer See Equal Opportunity for Blacks in Jobs, Housing." Gallup Organization, January 21. Retrieved November 5, 2020 (https://news.gallup.com/opinion/gallup/246137/fewer-equal-opportunity-blacks-jobs-housing.aspx).

———. 2020. "U.S. Perceptions of White-Black Relations Sink to New Low." Gallup Organization, September 2. Retrieved November 5, 2020 (https://news.gallup.com/poll/318851/perceptions-white-black-relations-sink-new-low.aspx).

Sacchetti, Maria. 2019. "ACLU Says 1,500 More Migrant Children Were Taken from Parents by the Trump Administration." *Washington Post,* October 24. Retrieved November 12, 2020 (https://www.washingtonpost.com/immigration/aclu-says-1500-more-migrant-children-were-taken-from-parents-by-trump-administration/2019/10/24/d014f818-f6aa-11e9-a285-882a8e386a96_story.html).

Sacks, Tina K. 2013. "Race and Gender Concordance: Strategy to Reduce Healthcare Disparities or Red Herring? Evidence from a Qualitative Study." *Race and Social Problems* 5(2):88–99.

Safawi, Ali, and Ife Floyd. 2020. "TANF Benefits Still Too Low to Help Families, Especially Black Families, Avoid Increased Hardship." Center on Budget and Policy Priorities, updated October 8. Retrieved November 6, 2020 (http://www.cbpp.org/research/tanf-cash-benefits-have-fallen-by-more-than-20-percent-in-most-states-and-continue-to-erode).

Sampson, Robert J., and William Julius Wilson. 1995. "Toward a Theory of Race, Crime, and Urban Inequality." Pp. 37–56 in *Crime and Inequality,* edited by John Hagan and Ruth D. Peterson. Stanford, CA: Stanford University Press.

Sampson, Robert J., William Julius Wilson, and Hanna Katz. 2018. "Reassessing 'Toward a Theory of Race, Crime and Urban Inequality': Enduring and New Challenges in 21st Century America." *Du Bois Review: Social Science Research on Race* 15(1):13–34.

Sampson, Robert J., and Alix S. Winter. 2016. "The Racial Ecology of Lead Poisoning: Toxic Inequality in Chicago Neighborhoods, 1995–2013." *Du Bois Review: Social Science Research on Race* 13(2):261–84.

Saperstein, Aliya, and Andrew M. Penner. 2014. "Beyond the Looking Glass: Exploring Fluidity in Racial Self-Identification and Interviewer Classification." *Sociological Perspectives* 57(2):186–207.

Schleicher, Andreas. 2019. "PISA 2018: Insights and Interpretations." Organization for Economic Cooperation and Development. Retrieved October 6, 2020 (https://www.oecd.org/pisa/PISA%202018%20Insights%20and%20Interpretations%20FINAL%20PDF.pdf).

Schmader, Toni, Katharina Block, and Brian Lickel. 2015. "Social Identity Threat in Response to Stereotypic Film Portrayals: Effects on Self-Conscious Emotion and Implicit Ingroup Attitudes." *Journal of Social Issues* 71(1):54–72.

Schneiderman, Howard G. 1996. "The Protestant Establishment: Its History, Its Legacy—Its Future?" Pp. 141–51 in *Origins and Destinies: Immigration, Race, and Ethnicity in America,* edited by Silvia Pedraza and Rubén G. Rumbaut. Belmont, CA: Wadsworth.

Schoettler, Carl. 1998. "For Black Steel Men: The Living Wasn't Easy." *Baltimore Sun,* February 2. Retrieved October 19, 2020 (https://www.baltimoresun.com/news/bs-xpm-1998-02-02-1998033014-story.html).

Schulz, Amy J., Graciela B. Mentz, Natalie Sampson, Melanie Ward, Rhonda Anderson, Ricardo de Majo, Barbara A. Israel, Toby C. Lewis, and Donele Wilkins. 2016. "Race and the Distribution of Social and Physical Environmental Risk: A Case Example from the Detroit Metropolitan Area." *Du Bois Review: Social Science Research on Race* 13(2):285–304.

Schwalbe, Michael. 2014. *Rigging the Game: How Inequality Is Reproduced in Everyday Life.* New York: Oxford University Press.

Schwalbe, Michael, Sandra Godwin, Daphne Holden, Douglas Schrock, Shealy Thompson, and Michele Wolkomir. 2000. "Generic Processes in the Reproduction of Inequality:

An Interactionist Analysis." *Social Forces* 79(2):419–52.

Schwartzman, Luisa F. 2007. "Does Money Whiten? Intergenerational Changes in Racial Classification in Brazil." *American Sociological Review* 72(6):940–63.

Sellers, Robert M., Mia A. Smith, J. N. Shelton, Stephanie A. J. Rowley, and Tabbye M. Chavous. 1998. "Multidimensional Model of Racial Identity: A Reconceptualization of African American Racial Identity." *Personality and Social Psychology Review* 2(1):18–39.

Semega, Jessica, Melissa Kollar, John Creamer, and Abinash Mohanty. 2019. *Income and Poverty in the United States: 2018*. Washington, DC: US Census Bureau.

Semuels, Alana. 2015. "White Flight Never Ended." *The Atlantic*, July 30. Retrieved October 6, 2020 (http://www.theatlantic.com/business/arc hive/2015/07/white-flight-alive-and-well/3999 80/).

Serkez, Yaryna. 2020 "Who Is Most Likely to Die from the Coronavirus?" Opinion, *New York Times*, June 4. Retrieved October 6, 2020 (http s://www.nytimes.com/interactive/2020/06/04/op inion/coronavirus-health-race-inequality.html).

Sewell, Abigail A. 2015. "Disaggregating Ethnoracial Disparities in Physician Trust." *Social Science Research* 54(November):1–20.

Shaheen, Jack G. 2014. *Reel Bad Arabs: How Hollywood Vilifies a People*. Northampton, MA: Olive Branch Press.

Shapiro, Thomas M. 2017. *Toxic Inequality: How America's Wealth Gap Destroys Mobility, Deepens the Racial Divide and Threatens Our Future*. New York: Basic Books.

Shaw, Kate M., Kristina A. Theis, Shannon Self-Brown, Douglas W. Roblin, and Lawrence Barker. 2016. "Chronic Disease Disparities by County Economic Status and Metropolitan Classification, Behavioral Risk Factor Surveillance System, 2013." *Preventing Public Disease* 13(September):160088. Retrieved October 6, 2020 (https://www.cdc.gov/pcd/issue s/2016/16_0088.htm).

Shedd, Carla. 2015. *Unequal City: Race, Schools, and Perceptions of Injustice*. New York: Russell Sage Foundation.

Sheehan, Connor M., Robert A. Hummer, Brenda L. Moore, Kimberly R. Huyser, and John S. Butler. 2015. "Duty, Honor, Country, Disparity: Race/Ethnic Differences in Health and Disability among Male Veterans." *Population Research and Policy Review* 34(6):785–804.

Sherman, Bradford P. 2014. "Racial Bias and Interstate Highway Planning: A Mixed Methods Approach." *CUREJ: College Undergraduate Research Electronic Journal*, January 1. Philadelphia: University of Pennsylvania. Retrieved November 12, 2020 (http://reposit ory.upenn.edu/cgi/viewcontent.cgi?article=1208 &context=curej).

Shiao, Jiannbin Lee. 2018. "It Starts Early: Toward a Longitudinal Analysis of Interracial Intimacy." *Sociology of Race & Ethnicity* 4(4):508–26.

Silva, Jennifer M. 2013. *Coming Up Short: Working-Class Adulthood in an Age of Uncertainty*. New York: Oxford University Press.

Skiba, Russell J., Robert S. Michael, Abra Carroll Nardo, and Reece L. Peterson. 2002. "The Color of Discipline: Sources of Racial and Gender Disproportionality in School Punishment." *Urban Review* 34(4):317–42.

Skloot, Rebecca. 2010. *The Immortal Life of Henrietta Lacks*. New York: Crown Books.

Slaughter, Anne-Marie. 2015. *Unfinished Business: Women, Men, Work, Family*. New York: Random House.

Slay, Bre-Ann. 2020. "COVID-19 Will Intensify Education Inequities for Black Students." *Diverse Issues in Higher Education*, May 2020. Retrieved October 6, 2020 (https://diverseeduc ation.com/article/177796/).

Small, Mario Luis, David L. Harding, and Michéle Lamont. 2010. "Introduction: Reconsidering Culture and Poverty." *Annals of the American Academy of Political and Social Science* 629(1):6–27.

Smith, David Barton, Zhanlian Feng, Mary L. Fennell, Jacqueline S. Zinn, and Vincent Mor. 2007. "Separate and Unequal: Racial Segregation and Disparities in Quality across U.S. Nursing Homes." Datawatch, *Health Affairs* 26(5): 1448–58. Retrieved October 6, 2020 (https://www.healthaffairs.org/doi/full/10 .1377/hlthaff.26.5.1448).

Smith, Robert Courtney. 2008. "Latino Incorporation into the United States: Local and Transnational Perspectives." Pp. 36–53 in *Latinas/os in the United States: Changing the Face of America*, edited by Havidán Rodríguez, Rogelio Sáenz, and Cecilia Menjívar. New York: Springer.

Smith, Stacy L., Marc Choueiti, Katherine Pieper, Kevin Yao, Ariana Case, and Angel Choi. 2019. "Inequality in 1,200 Popular Films: Examining Portrayals of Gender, Race/Ethnicity, LGBT and Disability from 2007 to 2018." Annenberg Foundation and the USC Annenberg Inclusion Initiative, September. Retrieved October 14, 2020 (http://assets.uscannenberg.org/docs/aii -inequality-report-2019-09-03.pdf).

Snell, Tracy L. 2019. "Capital Punishment, 2017: Selected Findings." US Bureau of Justice Statistics, US Department of Justice, July. Retrieved October 6, 2020 (https://www.bjs.gov /content/pub/pdf/cp17sf.pdf).

Snipp, C. Matthew. 1996. "The First Americans: American Indians." Pp. 390–403 in *Origins and Destinies: Immigration, Race, and Ethnicity in America*, edited by Silvia Pedraza and Rubén G. Rumbaut. Belmont, CA: Wadsworth.

———. 2003. "Racial Measurement in the American Census: Past Practice and Implications for the Future." *Annual Review of Sociology* 29:563–88.

———. 2010. "Defining Race and Ethnicity: The Constitution, the Supreme Court, and the Census." Pp. 105–22 in *Doing Race: 21 Essays for the Twenty-First Century*, edited by Hazel Rose Markus and Paula M. L. Moya. New York: W. W. Norton.

Snow, David A., and Leon Anderson. 1987. "Identity Work among the Homeless: The Verbal Construction and Avowal of Personal Identities." *American Journal of Sociology* 92(6):1336–71.

Snyder, Tom, ed. 1993. *120 Years of American Education: A Statistical Portrait*. Washington, DC: National Center for Education Statistics.

Social Science Data Analysis Network. N.d. "United States: Multiracial Profile." Charts and Trends, *CensusScope*. Retrieved October 6, 2020 (http://www.censusscope.org/us/chart_ multi.html).

Sohad, Murrar, and Markus Brauer. 2018. "Entertainment-Education Effectively Reduces Prejudice." *Group Processes and Intergroup Relations* 21(7):1053–77.

Soland, Jim, Megan Kuhfeld, Beth Tarasawa, Angela Johnson, Erik Ruzek, and Jing Liu. 2020. "The Impact of COVID-19 on Student Achievement and What It May Mean for Educators." Brown Center Chalkboard, Brookings Institution, May 27. Retrieved October 6, 2020 (https://www.brookings.edu/ blog/brown-center-chalkboard/2020/05/27/the -impact-of-covid-19-on-student-achievement-an d-what-it-may-mean-for-educators/).

Sotomayor, Sonia. 2013. *My Beloved World*. New York: Knopf.

Spencer, Rainier. 2006. *Challenging Multiracial Identity*. Boulder, CO: Lynne Rienner.

Spohn, Cassia. 2015. "Race, Crime, and Punishment in the Twentieth and Twenty-First Centuries." *Crime and Justice* 44(1):49–97.

Stack, Carol. 1974. *All Our Kin: Strategies for Survival in a Black Community*. New York: Harper.

Stainback, Kevin, and Donald Tomaskovic-Devey. 2012. *Documenting Desegregation: Racial and Gender Segregation in Private Sector Employment since the Civil Rights Act*. New York: Russell Sage.

Stearns, Elizabeth, Claudia Buchmann, and Kara Bonneau. 2009. "Interracial Friendships in the Transition to College: Do Birds of a Feather Flock Together Once They Leave the Nest? A Magazine of Theory and Practice." *Sociology of Education* 82(2):173–95.

Steck, Laura West, Druann Maria Heckert, and D. Alex Heckert, 2003. "The Salience of Racial Identity among African-American and White Students." *Race & Society* 6(1):57–73.

Steele, Claude M. 2010. *Whistling Vivaldi and Other Clues to How Stereotypes Affect Us*. New York: Norton.

Steele, Claude M., and Joshua Aronson. 1995. "Stereotype Threat and the Intellectual Test Performance of African Americans." *Journal of Personality and Social Psychology* 69(5):797–811.

Steele, Dorothy M., and Becki Cohn-Vargas. 2013. *Identity Safe Classrooms: Places to Belong and Learn*. Thousand Oaks, CA: Sage.

Stenberg, Amandla. 2015. "Don't Cash Crop My Cornrows." Tumblr. Video. Retrieved October 15, 2020 (https://amandla.tumblr.com/post/10 7484511963/dont-cash-crop-my-cornrows-a- crash-discourse-on).

Stepanikova, Irena. 2012. "Racial-Ethnic Biases, Time Pressure, and Medical Decisions." *Journal of Health and Social Behavior* 53(3):329–43.

Stephens, Nicole M., Stephanie A. Fryberg, Hazel R. Markus, Camille S. Johnson, and Rebecca Covarrubias. 2012. "Unseen Disadvantage: How American Universities' Focus on

Independence Undermines the Academic Performance of First-Generation College Students." *Journal of Personality and Social Psychology* 102(6):1178–97.

Sternthal, Michelle J., Natalie Slopen, and David R. Williams. 2011. "Racial Disparities in Health." *Du Bois Review: Social Science Research on Race* 8(1):95–113.

Stevenson, Bryan. 2015a. *Just Mercy: A Story of Justice and Redemption.* New York: Spiegel and Grau.

———. 2015b. "Just Mercy: A Story of Redemption." FYE Campus Talk, University of Delaware, Newark, Delaware, October 6.

Stewart, Jon. 2014. "Race/Off." *The Daily Show,* August 28. YouTube video retrieved October 6, 2020 (https://www.youtube.com/watch?v=T_98ojjIZDI).

Stolzenberg, Elena Bara, Kevin Eagan, Edgar Romo, Elaine Jessica Tamargo, Melissa C. Aragon, Madeline Luedke, and Nathaniel Kang, N. 2019. *The American Freshman: National Norms Fall 2018.* Los Angeles: Higher Education Research Institute, UCLA. Retrieved October 6, 2020 (https://www.heri.ucla.edu/monographs/TheAmericanFreshman2018.pdf).

Strmic-Pawl, Hephzibah V. 2016. *Multiracialism and Its Discontents: A Comparative Analysis of Asian-White and Black-White Multiracials.* Lanham, MD: Lexington Books.

Strom, Margot Stern. 2013. *Facing History and Ourselves: Holocaust and Human Behavior, Resource Book.* Brookline, MA: Facing History and Facing Ourselves National Foundation. Book text retrieved October 6, 2020 (https://hs.humboldtunified.com/ourpages/auto/2013/11/12/58027792/Holocaust_Human_Behavior.pdf).

Strother, Logan, Spencer Piston, and Thomas Ogorzalek. 2017. "Pride or Prejudice? Racial Prejudice, Southern Heritage, and White Support for the Confederate Battle Flag." *Du Bois Review: Social Science Research on Race* 14(1):295–323.

Substance Abuse and Mental Health Services Administration. 2014. *Results from the 2013 National Survey on Drug Use and Health: Summary of National Findings.* National Survey on Drug Use and Health Series H-48, US Department of Health and Human Services Publication No. (SMA) 14-4863, September. Rockville, MD: Substance Abuse and Mental Health Services Administration. Site for download retrieved October 6, 2020 (https://store.samhsa.gov/product/Results-from-the-2013-National-Survey-on-Drug-Use-and-Health-Summary-of-National-Findings/sma14-4863).

———. 2019. *Results from the 2018 National Survey on Drug Abuse and Health: Detailed Tables.* June. Rockville, MD: Center for Behavioral Health Statistics and Quality, Substance Abuse and Mental Health Services Administration. Retrieved October 6, 2020 (https://www.samhsa.gov/data/sites/default/files/cbhsq-reports/NSDUHDetailedTabs2018R2/NSDUHDetailedTabs2018.pdf).

Sue, Derand Wing. 2010. *Microaggressions in Everyday Life: Race, Gender, and Sexual Orientation.* Hoboken, NJ: Wiley.

Sue, Derand Wing, Christina M. Capodilupo, Gina C. Torino, Jennifer M. Bucceri, Aisha M. B. Holder, Kevin L. Nadal, and Marta Esquilin. 2007. "Racial Microaggressions in Everyday Life: Implications for Clinical Practice." *American Psychologist* 62(4):271–86.

Suina, Joseph H. 1992. "Preserving Many Worlds: The Cultural Dimension since 1492." Paper presented at the ISAM Annual Conference, 1492–1992 Reconsidered, Dana Hall School, Wellesley, Massachusetts, May 5.

Sullivan, Laura, Totjana Meschede, Thomas Shapiro, and Fernanda Escobar. 2019. *Stalling Dreams: How Student Debt Is Disrupting Life Chances and Widening the Racial Wealth Gap.* Waltham, MA: Institute on Assets and Social Policy, The Heller School, Brandeis University.

Suls, Rob. 2017. "Most Americans Continue to Oppose U.S. Border Wall, Doubt Mexico Would Pay For It." Fact Tank, Pew Research Center, February 24. Retrieved October 5, 2020 (https://www.pewresearch.org/fact-tank/2017/02/24/most-americans-continue-to-oppose-u-s-border-wall-doubt-mexico-would-pay-for-it/).

Summers, Juana. 2020. "Trump Calls Harris a 'Monster,' Reviving Patterns of Attacking Women of Color." *National Public Radio,* October 9. Retrieved November 6, 2020 (https://www.npr.org/2020/10/09/921884531/trump-calls-harris-a-monster-reviving-a-pattern-of-attacking-women-of-color).

Supiano, Beckie. 2015. "Racial Disparities in Higher Education: An Overview." Facts and Figures, *The Chronicle of Higher Education,* November 10. Retrieved October 6, 2020 (http s://www.chronicle.com/article/racial-disparities-in-higher-education-an-overview/).

Sze, Julie, and Jonathan K. London. 2008. "Environmental Justice at the Crossroads." *Sociology Compass* 2(4):1331–54.

Tach, Laura, and Kathryn Edin. 2017. "The Social Safety Net after Welfare Reform: Recent Developments and Consequences for Household Dynamics." *Annual Review of Sociology* 43:541–61.

Takaki, Ronald T. 1989. *Strangers from a Different Shore: A History of Asian Americans*. New York: Penguin.

———. 1993. *A Different Mirror: A History of Multicultural America*. Boston: Little, Brown.

Takeuchi, David T., Lisa Sun-Hee Park, Yonette F. Thomas, and Samantha Teixeira. 2016. "Race and Environmental Equity." *Du Bois Review: Social Science Research on Race* 13(2):215–20.

Tate, Julie, Jennifer Jenkins, and Steven Rich. 2020. "Fatal Force: 1,005 People Have Been Shot and Killed by Police in the Last Year." *Washington Post*, updated October 5, originally published June 19. Retrieved October 6, 2020 (https://www.washingtonpost.com/graphics/investigations/police-shootings-database/).

Tatum, Beverly Daniel. 1997. *Why Are All the Black Kids Sitting Together in the Cafeteria? And Other Conversations about Race*. New York: Basic Books.

Taub, Amanda. 2020. "A New Covid-19 Crisis: Domestic Abuse Rises Worldwide." The Interpreter, *New York Times*, April 6. Retrieved October 6, 2020 (https://www.nytimes.com/2020/04/06/world/coronavirus-domestic-violence.html).

Tavares, Carlos Daniel. 2011. "Why Can't We Be Friends: The Role of Religious Congregation-Based Social Contact for Close Interracial Adolescent Friendships." *Review of Religious Research* 52(4):439–53.

Taylor, Howard F. 2008. "Defining Race." Pp. 7–13 in *Race and Ethnicity in Society: The Changing Landscape*, edited by Elizabeth Higginbotham and Margaret L. Andersen. Belmont, CA: Wadsworth/Cengage.

Taylor, Robert J., Linda M. Chatters, and Harry O. Taylor. 2019. "Race and Objective Social Isolation: Older African Americans, Black Caribbeans, and Non-Hispanic Whites." *The Journals of Gerontology: Series B* 74(November):1429–40.

Telles, Edward. 2009. "The Social Consequences of Skin Color in Brazil." Pp. 9–24 in *Shades of Difference: Why Skin Color Matters*, edited by Evelyn Nakano Glenn. Stanford, CA: Stanford University Press.

Thakore, Bhoomi T. 2014. "'Must See TV: South Asian Characterizations in American Popular Media." *Sociology Compass* 8(2):149–56.

Thomas, Anita J., Jason D. Hacker, and Denada Hoxha. 2011. "Gendered Racial Identity of Black Young Women." *Sex Roles: A Journal of Research* 64(7–8):530–42.

Thomas, Melvin E., Richard Moye, Loren Henderson, and Hayward Derrick Horton. 2017. "Separate and Unequal: The Impact of Socioeconomic Status, Segregation, and the Great Recession on Racial Disparities in Housing Values." *Sociology of Race & Ethnicity* 4(2): 229–44.

Thompson, Brian. 2018. "The Racial Wealth Gap: Addressing America's Most Pressing Epidemic." Personal Finance, *Forbes*, February 18. Retrieved October 6, 2020 (https://www.forbes.com/sites/brianthompson1/2018/02/18/the-racial-wealth-gap-addressing-americas-most-pressing-epidemic/).

Thompson, Maxine S., and Verna M. Keith. 2001. "The Blacker the Berry: Gender, Skin Tone, Self-Esteem, and Self-Efficacy." *Gender & Society* 15(3):336–57.

Thompson, Victor. 2007. "A New Take on an Old Idea: Do We Need Multiracial Studies?" *Du Bois Review: Social Science Research on Race* 3(2):437–47.

Tienda, Marta, and Vilma Ortiz. 1986. "'Hispanicity' and the 1980 Census." *Social Science Quarterly* 67:3–20.

Tierney, Kathleen J. 2007. "From Margins to the Mainstream? Disaster Research at the Crossroads." *Annual Review of Sociology* 33:503–25.

Tolbert, Jennifer, Kendal Orgera, Natalie Singer, and Anthony Damico. 2019. "Key Facts about the Uninsured Population." Issue Brief, Kaiser Family Foundation, December. Retrieved November 10, 2020 (http://files.kff.org/attachment//fact-sheet-key-facts-about-the-uninsured-population).

Toossi, Mitra. 2016. "A Look at the Future of the U.S. Labor Force to 2060." *Spotlight on Statistics*, US Bureau of Labor Statistics, September. Retrieved October 6, 2020 (https://

www.bls.gov/spotlight/2016/a-look-at-the-futur e-of-the-us-labor-force-to-2060/pdf/a-look-at -the-future-of-the-us-labor-force-to-2060.pdf).

Torres, Jessica, and Cristina López G. 2015. "Study: Hispanic Guests and the Sunday Shows; Fewer Appearances on English-Language Programs, Single-Issue Emphasis on Immigration Continues." Media Matters for America, July 20. Retrieved October 15, 2020 (https://www .mediamatters.org/msnbc/study-hispanic-guests -and-sunday-shows-fewer-appearances-english- language-programs-single).

Towbin, Mia Adessa, Shelley A. Haddock, Toni Schindler Zimmerman, Lori K. Lund, and Litsa Renee Tanner. 2004. "Images of Gender, Race, Age, and Sexual Orientation in Disney Feature-Length Animated Films." *Journal of Feminist Family Therapy* 15(4):19–44.

Towler, Lottie. 2018. "TV Binge-Watching Increasingly Pronounced in Mature SVOD Markets." Ampere Analysis, October 17. Retrieved October 15, 2020 (https://www.am pereanalysis.com/insight/tv-binge-watching-in creasingly-pronounced-in-mature-svod-mar ketstowler).

Travis, Jeremy, Bruce Western, and Steve Redburn, eds. 2014. *The Growth of Incarceration in the United States: Exploring Causes and Consequences.* Washington, DC: National Academies Press.

Triandis, Harry C. 1989. "The Self and Social Behavior in Differing Cultural Contexts." *Psychological Review* 96(3):506–20.

Trillin, Calvin. 1986. "Black or White." American Chronicles, *The New Yorker*, April 14, pp. 62–78.

Tropp, Linda R. 2007. "Perceived Discrimination and Interracial Contact: Predicting Interracial Closeness among Black and White Americans." *Social Psychology Quarterly* 70(1):70–81.

Truman, Harry S. 1948. Executive Order 9981, "Establishing the President's Committee on Equality of Treatment and Opportunity in the Armed Services." Washington, DC, July 26. Text retrieved October 22, 2020 (https://www.tr umanlibrary.gov/node/320313).

Turner, Margery Austin, and Stephen L. Ross. 2005. "How Racial Discrimination Affects the Search for Housing." Pp. 81–100 in *The Geography of Opportunity: Race and Housing Choice in Metropolitan America*, edited by Xavier de Souza Briggs. Washington, DC: The Brookings Institution.

Tyson, Karolyn. 2011. *Integration Interrupted: Tracking, Black Students, and Acting White after "Brown".* New York: Oxford University Press.

Tyson, Karolyn, William Darity Jr., and Domini R. Castellino. 2005. "It's Not 'a Black Thing': Understanding the Burden of Acting White and Other Dilemmas of High Achievement." *American Sociological Review* 70(4):582–605.

Uggen, Christopher. 2016. "Crime, Punishment, and American Inequality." *Focus* 32(Fall–Winter):1–7.

Ulmer, Jeffery T., and Brian Johnson. 2004. "Sentencing in Context: A Multilevel Analysis." *Criminology* 42(1):137–78.

United Nations. 1948. General Assembly Resolution 260A (III), Article 2. "The Convention of the Prevention and Punishment of the Crime of Genocide," December 9. Office of the UN Special Adviser on the Prevention of Genocide. Copy of text retrieved October 6, 2020 (http://www.un.org/en/ga/search/view_doc .asp?symbol=A/RES/260(iii)).

University of California Regents v. Bakke. 1978. 438 US 265, pp. 402–408. Retrieved October 22, 2020 (https://tile.loc.gov/storage-services/s ervice/ll/usrep/usrep438/usrep438265/usrep438 265.pdf).

University of Washington. N.d. "Emilio Aguayo: United Farm Workers (UFW); MEChA de UW; Muralist for the Ethnic Cultural Center." Seattle Civil Rights and Labor History Consortium, University of Washington. Retrieved October 5, 2020 (http://depts.washington.edu/civilr/aguayo .htm).

Uratsu, Marvin. 2007. "Marvin Uratsu." Interview by Ashlyn P. and Julianna B., with Sophia S. and Jeff M., with Howard Levin. *Telling Their Stories: Oral History Archives Project*, May 9. Retrieved October 6, 2020 (https://www.te llingstories.org/internment/uratsu_marvin/ind ex.html).

US Bureau of Justice Statistics. 2019. "NCVS Victimization Analysis Tool (NVAT)." Office of Justice Programs, US Department of Justice, updated November. Retrieved November 10, 2020 (https://www.bjs.gov/index.cfm?ty=nvat).

US Bureau of Labor Statistics. 2019a. *2018 Employment and Earnings Online.* Tabular data linked from this page, modified March 9. Retrieved November 10, 2020 (https://www.bls .gov/opub/ee/2018/cps/annual.htm).

———. 2019b. "Union Workers More Likely than Nonunion Workers to Have Retirement Benefits in 2019." *TED: The Economics Daily*, October 25. Retrieved November 10, 2020 (https://www.bls.gov/opub/ted/2019/union-workers-more-likely-than-nonunion-workers-to-have-retirement-benefits-in-2019.htm).

———. 2019c. *Labor Force Characteristics of Foreign-Born Workers Summary*. Economic News Release, US Department of Labor.

———. 2020a. "The Employment Situation— September 2020." News Release, October 2. Retrieved November 10, 2020 (https://www.bls.gov/news.release/archives/empsit_10022020.pdf).

———. 2020b. "Occupations with the Most Job Growth." Employment Projections, last modified September 1. Retrieved November 10, 2020 (https://www.bls.gov/emp/tables/occupations-most-job-growth.htm).

US Census Bureau. 2014. "Table 10. Projections of the Population by Sex, Hispanic Origin, and Race for the United States: 2015 to 2060." NP2014-T10, Population Division, US Department of Commerce, December. Site for download retrieved October 6, 2020 (https:www.census.gov/data/tables/2014/demo/popproj/2014-summary-tables.html).

———. 2018. "Marital Status, Table S1202." Retrieved December 9, 2020 (https://data.census.gov/cedsci/table?q=marital%20status&tid=ACSST1Y2019.S1201&hidePreview=false).

———. 2019a. "America's Families and Living Arrangements: 2019; Table H1. Households by Type and Tenure of Householder for Selected Characteristics: 2019." Last revised October 16. Retrieved October 20, 2020 (https://www.census.gov/data/tables/2019/demo/families/cps-2019.html).

———. 2019b. "Historical Living Arrangements of Children." Tables CH2, CH3, and CH4, November. Retrieved November 4, 2020 (https://www.census.gov/data/tables/time-series/demo/families/children.html).

———. 2019c. "POV-03. People in Primary Families with Related Children Under 18 by Family Structure, Age, and Sex: Below 100 Percent of Poverty." Retrieved October 19, 2020 (https://www.census.gov/data/tables/time-series/demo/income-poverty/cps-pov/pov-03.html#par_textimage_10).

———. 2019d. "Population Estimates, July 1, 2019." *Quick Facts*. Accessed November 4, 2020). Link to various data retrieved November 6, 2020 (https://www.census.gov/programs-surveys/popest/data/tables.html).

———. 2019e. "Race/Ethnicity and the 2020 Census." Census 2020. March 23. Retrieved November 5, 2020 (https://www.census2020now.org/faces-blog/same-sex-households-2020-census-r3976).

———. 2020a. "Quick Facts: Flint City, Michigan; United States." Tabular data searchable from link retrieved November 12, 2020 (https://www.census.gov/quickfacts/fact/table/flintcitymichigan,US/IPE120219).

———. 2020b. "Characteristics of Same-Sex Couple Households: 2005 to Present." US Department of Commerce. Retrieved October 6, 2020 (https://www.census.gov/data/tables/time-series/demo/same-sex-couples/ssc-house-characteristics.html).

———. 2020c. "Historical Income Tables: People; Table P-36. Full-Time, Year-Round Workers by Median Income and Sex." US Department of Commerce, last revised September 15. Retrieved October 19, 2020 (https://www.census.gov/data/tables/time-series/demo/income-poverty/historical-income-people.html).

———. 2020d. "Quarterly Residential Vacancies and Homeownership, Fourth Quarter 2019." Release Number: CB20-05, US Department of Commerce, January 30. Retrieved October 6, 2020 (https://www.census.gov/housing/hvs/files/qtr419/Q419press.pdf).

US Citizenship and Immigration Services. 2018. "Family of U.S. Citizens." Last updated March 23. Retrieved November 10, 2020 (https://www.uscis.gov/family/family-of-us-citizens).

US Congress. 1917. "Public Laws of the United States of America Passed by the Sixty-Fourth Congress, 1915–1917," session II, chap. 145, signed into law March 2, The Jones-Shafroth Act. Pp. 951–68 of *The Statutes at Large of the United States of America, from December 1915, to March 1917: Concurrent Resolutions of the Two Houses of Congress and Recent Treaties, Conventions, and Executive Proclamations*, vol. 39. Washington, DC: US Government Printing Office. Facsimile of text retrieved October 13, 2020 (https://www.loc.gov/law/help/statutes-at-large/64th-congress/c64-incomplete.pdf). See especially section 3.

US Constitution. 1787. Signed and ratified by the delegates in Philadelphia, Pennsylvania, September 17. Text retrieved October 13, 2020 (https://www.archives.gov/founding-docs/constitution-transcript).

———. 1868. Art. 14, ratified by the Senate and House of Representatives of the United States in Washington, DC, July 20. Text retrieved October 22, 2020 (https://memory.loc.gov/cgi-bin/ampage?collId=llsl&fileName=015/llsl015.db&recNum=739).

US Department of Homeland Security. 2020a. "Table 6. Persons Obtaining Lawful Permanent Resident Status by Type and Major Class of Admission: Fiscal Years 2016 to 2018." *2018 Yearbook of Immigration Statistics*, last updated September 29, originally published 2019. Washington, DC: US Department of Homeland Security, Office of Immigration Statistics. Retrieved October 16, 2020 (https://www.dhs.gov/immigration-statistics/yearbook/2018/table6).

———. 2020b. "Table 2. Persons Obtaining Lawful Permanent Resident Status by Region and Selected Country of Last Residence: Fiscal Years 2016 to 2018." *2018 Yearbook of Immigration Statistics*, last published January 6, originally published 2019. Washington, DC: US Department of Homeland Security, Office of Immigration Statistics. Retrieved October 16, 2020 (https://www.dhs.gov/immigration-statistics/yearbook/2018/table2).

US Supreme Court. 1954. *Brown v. Board of Education*, 347 US 483. Text retrieved October 6, 2020 (https://tile.loc.gov/storage-services/service/ll/usrep/usrep347/usrep347483/usrep347483.pdf).

Valenzuela, Angela. 1999. *Subtractive Schooling: U.S.–Mexican Youth and the Politics of Caring*. Albany: State University of New York Press.

Van Ausdale, Debra, and Joe R. Feagin. 2000. *The First R: How Children Learn Race and Racism*. Lanham, MD: Rowman & Littlefield.

Van Cleve, Nicole Gonzalez. 2016. *Crook County: Racism and Injustice in America's Largest Criminal Court*. Stanford, CA: Stanford University Press.

Vandermaas-Peeler, Alex, Daniel Cox, Molly Fisch-Friedman, and Robert P. Jones. 2018. "Diversity, Division, Discrimination: The State of Young America." MTV and PPRI, January 10. Retrieved November 5, 2020 (https://www.prri.org/research/mtv-culture-and-religion/).

Vaquera, Elizabeth, and Grace Kao. 2008. "Socioeconomic Origin: Do You Like Me as Much as I Like You? Friendship Reciprocity and its Effects on School Outcomes among Adolescents." *Social Science Research* 37(1):55–72.

Vargas, Deborah R. 2010. "Representations of Latina/o Sexuality in Popular Culture." Pp. 117–36 in *Latina/o Sexualities: Probing Powers, Passions, Practices, and Policies*, edited by Marysol Asencio. New Brunswick, NJ: Rutgers University Press.

Vargas, Nicholas. 2015. "Latina/o Whitening? Which Latinas/os Self-Classify as White and Report Being Perceived as White by Other Americans?" *Du Bois Review: Social Science Research on Race* 12(1):119–36.

Vasquez, Jessica M. 2014. "Race Cognizance and Colorblindness: Effects of Latino/Non-Hispanic White Intermarriage." *Du Bois Review: Social Science Research on Race* 11(2):273–93.

Vecchione, Judith, dir. 1987. "Fighting Back, 1957–1962." Episode 2, written by Steve Fayer, in *Eyes on the Prize: America's Civil Rights Years, 1954–1965*, created and executive produced by Henry Hampton. Television series. [Boston]: Blackside.

Vedantam, Shankar. 2015. "Despite Improving Job Market, Blacks Still Face Tougher Prospects." *Morning Edition*, National Public Radio, October 1. Retrieved October 6, 2020 (https://www.npr.org/2015/10/01/444912628/despite-improving-job-market-blacks-still-face-tougher-prospects).

Venkatesh, Sudhir A. 2006. *Off the Books: The Underground Economy of the Urban Poor*. Cambridge, MA: Harvard University Press.

Vera, Hernán, and Andrew Gordon. 2003. *Screen Saviors: Hollywood Fictions of Whiteness*. Lanham, MD: Rowman & Littlefield.

Vespa, Jonathan, Lauren Medina, and David M. Armstrong. 2020. *Demographic Turning Points for the United States: Populations Projections for 2020 to 2060*. US Census Bureau, revised February. Retrieved November 10, 2020 (https://www.census.gov/content/dam/Census/library/publications/2020/demo/p25-1144.pdf).

Villarosa, Linda. 2002. "A Conversation with: Joseph Graves; Beyond Black and White in Biology and Medicine." *New York Times*, January 1, section F, page 5. Retrieved October 6, 2020 (https://www.nytimes.com/2002/01/01/heal

th/a-conversation-with-joseph-graves-beyond-b lack-and-white-in-biology-and-medicine.html).

Viruell-Fuentes, Edna, Jeffrey D. Morenoff, David R. Williams, and James S. House. 2013. "Contextualizing Nativity Status, Latino Social Ties, and Ethnic Enclaves: An Examination of the 'Immigrant Social Ties Hypothesis.'" *Ethnicity & Health* 18(6):586–609.

Vo, Linda Trinh. 2004. *Mobilizing an Asian American Community*. Philadelphia: Temple University Press.

Volpp, Leti. 2000. "American Mestizo: Filipinos and Antimiscegenation Laws in California." *U.C. Davis Law Review* 33(4):795–835. Retrieved October 6, 2020 (https://lawreview.l aw.ucdavis.edu/issues/33/4/Constructing/Davis Vol33No4_Volpp.pdf).

Voting Rights Act of 1965. Pub. L. 89-110, 79 Stat. 437 (1965). Text retrieved October 21, 2020 (https://www.govinfo.gov/content/pkg/STA TUTE-79/pdf/STATUTE-79-Pg437.pdf).

Wade, Jeannette, and Robert L. Peralta. 2017. "Perceived Racial Discrimination, Heavy Episodic Drinking, and Alcohol Abstinence among African American and White College Students." *Journal of Ethnicity in Substance Abuse* 16(2):165–80. Retrieved October 6, 2020 (https://www.ncbi.nlm.nih.gov/pmc/articl es/PMC6007018/).

Wah, Lee Mun, prod., dir., and script collab. 1994. *The Color of Fear: A Film*. Coproduced by Monty Hunter, script collaboration with Robert Goss and Richard C. Bock. Stir-Fry Productions, Oakland, California.

Walker, Renee E., Christopher R. Keane, and Jessica G. Burke. 2010. "Disparities and Access to Healthy Food in the United States: A Review of Food Deserts Literature." *Health & Place* 16(5):876–84.

Walker, Samuel, Cassia Spohn, and Miriam Delone. 2012. *The Color of Justice: Race, Ethnicity, and Crime in America*. Belmont, CA: Wadsworth.

Walls, Melissa L., and Les B. Whitbeck. 2012. "The Intergenerational Effects of Relocation Policies on Indigenous Families." *Journal of Family Issues* 33(9):1272–93.

Wambugu, Daniel Maina. 2018. "Which Country Watches the Most TV?" WorldAtlas, October 1. Retrieved November 6, 2020 (https://www.wo rldatlas.com/articles/which-country-watches-the -most-tv.html).

Wang, Grace. 2010. "A Shot at Half-Exposure: Asian Americans in Reality TV Shows." *Television and New Media* 11:404–27.

Waring, Chandra D. L. 2017. "'It's like We Have an "In" Already': The Racial Capital of Black/ White Biracial Americans." *Du Bois Review: Social Science Research on Race* 14(1):145–63.

Waters, Mary C. 2000. *Black Identities: West Indian Immigrant Dreams and American Realities*. Cambridge, MA: Harvard University Press.

Watson, Amy. 2019. "Daily On-Demand TV Viewing Time in Selected Countries Worldwide 2018, by Age Group." Media and Advertising: Radio, TV, and Film, Statista, November 26. Retrieved October 15, 2020 (https://www.statista.com/statistics/276748/a verage-daily-tv-viewing-time-per-person-in-se lected-countries/).

Way, Niobe, Rachel Gingold, Marianna Rotenberg, and Geena Kuriakose. 2005. "Close Friendships among Urban, Ethnic-Minority Adolescents." *New Directions for Child and Adolescent Development* 107(March):41–59.

Way, Niobe, Maria G. Hernandez, Leoandra O. Rogers, and Diane L. Hughes. 2013. "'I'm Not Going to Become No Rapper': Stereotypes as a Context of Ethnic and Racial Identity Development." *Journal of Adolescent Research* 28(4):407–30.

Weber, Lynn, and Lori Peak, eds. 2012. *Displaced: Life in the Katrina Diaspora*. Austin: University of Texas Press.

Wellman, David T. 1977. *Portraits of White Racism*. New York: Cambridge University Press.

West, Cornel. 1982. *Prophesy Deliverance: An Afro-American Revolutionary Christianity*. Philadelphia: Westminster Press.

———. 1994. *Race Matters*. New York: Vintage.

Western, Bruce. 2007. *Punishment and Inequality in America*. New York: Russell Sage Foundation.

———. 2018. *Homeward: Life in the Year after Prison*. New York: Russell Sage Foundation.

Western, Bruce, Anthony A. Braga, Jaclyn Davis, and Catherine Sirois. 2015. "Stress and Hardship after Prison." *American Journal of Sociology* 120(5):1512–47.

White, Augustus A., III. 2011. *Seeing Patients: Unconscious Bias in Health Care*. With David Chanoff. Cambridge, MA: Harvard University Press.

White, Deborah Gray. 1999. *Ar'n't I a Woman? Female Slaves in the Plantation South*. New York: W. W. Norton.

Wilkerson, Isabel. 2010. *The Warmth of Other Suns: The Epic Story of America's Great Migration*. New York: Random House.

Williams, David R., and Selina A. Mohammed. 2009. "Discrimination and Racial Disparities in Health: Evidence and Needed Research." *Journal of Behavioral Medicine* 32(1):20–47.

———. 2013. "Racism and Health II: A Needed Research Agenda for Effective Interventions." *American Behavioral Scientist* 57(8):1200–1226.

Williams, Juan. 1998. *Thurgood Marshall: American Revolutionary*. New York: Three Rivers Press.

Wilson, Kenneth, and Alejandro Portes. 1980. "Immigrant Enclaves: An Analysis of the Labor Market Experiences of Cubans in Miami." *American Journal of Sociology* 86(2):295–319.

Wilson, Valerie. 2017. "Digging Into the 2017 ACS." *Working Economics Blog*, Economic Policy Institute, September 14. Retrieved November 10, 2020 (https://www.epi.org/blog/digging-into-2017-acs-income-native-americans-asians/).

Wilson, William Julius. 1973. *Power, Racism, and Privilege: Race Relations in Theoretical and Sociological Perspectives*. New York: Collier Macmillan.

———. 1978. *The Declining Significance of Race: Blacks and Changing American Institutions*. Chicago: University of Chicago Press.

———. 1987. *The Truly Disadvantaged: The Inner City, the Underclass, and Public Policy*. Chicago: University of Chicago Press.

———. 1996. *When Work Disappears: The World of the New Urban Poor*. New York: Knopf.

———. 2009. "Toward a Framework for Understanding Forces that Contribute to or Reinforce Racial Inequality." *Race and Social Problems* 1(1):3–11.

———. 2010. "Why Both Social Structure and Culture Matter in a Holistic Analysis of Inner-city Poverty." *Annals of the American Academy of Political and Social Science* 629(May):200–219.

Wilson, Woodrow. 1917. Joint address to Congress, leading to a declaration of war against Germany. Pp. 3–8 in 65th Congress, 1st Sess. Senate Doc. No. 5, Serial No. 7264. Washington, DC,

April 2. Text retrieved October 21, 2020 (https://www.ourdocuments.gov/doc.php?flash=false&doc=61).

Wilton, Leigh S., Diana T. Sanchez, and Julie A. Garcia. 2013. "The Stigma of Privilege: Racial Identity and Stigma Consciousness among Biracial Individuals." *Race and Social Problems* 5(1):41–56.

Wingfield, Adia Harvey. 2015. "Color-Blindness Is Counterproductive." Politics, *The Atlantic*, September 13. Retrieved October 6, 2020 (https://www.theatlantic.com/politics/archive/2015/09/color-blindness-is-counterproductive/405037/).

———. 2019. *Flatlining: Race, Work, and Health Care in the New Economy*. Berkeley: University of California Press.

Wingfield, Adia Harvey, and Koji Chavez. 2020. "Getting In, Getting Hired, Getting Sideways Looks: Organizational Hierarchy and Perceptions of Racial Discrimination." *American Sociological Review* 85(1):31–57.

Wingfield, Adia H., and Joe Feagin. 2012. "The Racial Dialectic: President Barack Obama and the White Racial Frame." *Qualitative Sociology* 35(2):143–62.

Winograd, Ken. 2011. "Sports Biographies of African American Football Players: The Racism of Colorblindness in Children's Literature." *Race, Ethnicity and Education* 14(3):331–49.

Wise, Tim J. 2011. *White Like Me: Reflections on Race from a Privileged Son*. 3rd ed. Brooklyn: Soft Skull Press.

Wolfe, Barbara, Jessica Jakubowski, Robert Haveman, and Marissa Courey. 2012. "The Income and Health Effects of Tribal Casino Gaming on American Indians." *Demography* 49(2):499–524.

Women's Media Center. 2019. "The Status of Women in the U.S. Media 2019." Retrieved November 6, 2020 (https://tools.womensmediacenter.com/page/-/WMCStatusofWomeninUSMedia2019.pdf).

Wong, Janelle, S. Karthick Ramakrishnan, Taeku Lee, and Jane Junn. 2011. *Asian American Political Participation: Emerging Constituents and Their Political Identities*. New York: Russell Sage.

Woolf, Stephen, Robert E. Johnson, George E. Fryer, George Rist, and David Satcher. 2008. "The Health Impact of Resolving Racial

Disparities: An Analysis of U.S. Mortality Data." *American Journal of Public Health* 98(September):S26–S28.

World Bank. 2019. "Gini Index (World Bank Estimates)—Country Ranking." Data via *Index Mundi*, last updated December 28. Retrieved October 6, 2020 (https://www.indexmundi.com /facts/indicators/SI.POV.GINI/rankings).

Wright, Lawrence. 1994. "One Drop of Blood." *New Yorker*, July 25, pp. 46–55.

Xie, Min, and Eric C. Baumer. 2019. "Crime Victims' Decisions to Call the Police: Past Research and New Directions." *Annual Review of Criminology* 2(1):217–40.

Yi, Joseph. 2013. "Tiger Moms and Liberal Elephants: Private, Supplemental Education among Korean-Americans." *Society* 50(2):190–95.

Zacks. 2017. "Your Complete Guide to Everything Owned by Viacom." *Nasdaqu.com*, July 10. Retrieved November 6, 2020 (https://www.na sdaq.com/articles/your-complete-guide-everyth ing-owned-viacom-2017-07-10).

Zambrana, Ruth Enid. 2011. *Latinos in American Society: Families and Community in Transition.* Ithaca, NY: Cornell University Press.

Zhou, Min. 2004. "Are Asian Americans Becoming 'White?'" *Contexts* 3(1):29–37. Retrieved October 15, 2020 (https://journals.sagepub .com/doi/pdf/10.1525/ctx.2004.3.1.29).

Zuckerman, Laurence. 1998. "Paper Forced to Apologize for Articles about Chiquita." *New York Times*, June 29. Retrieved November 6, 2020 (https://www.nytimes.com/1998/06/29/us /paper-forced-to-apologize-for-articles-about-c hiquita.html).

Author Index

Subject Index

CPSIA information can be obtained
at www.ICGtesting.com
Printed in the USA
BVHW050615030321
601242BV00003B/3